NICHOLAS OF CUSA'S DIDACTIC SERMONS: A SELECTION

Translated and introduced
by
JASPER HOPKINS

THE ARTHUR J. BANNING PRESS
LOVELAND, COLORADO

See also by the same translator
Nicholas of Cusa's Early Sermons: 1430 –1441.
Banning Press, 2003

Library of Congress Control Number: 2007928577

ISBN 0-938060-53-8

Printed in the United States of America

Copyright © 2008 by The Arthur J. Banning Press, Loveland, Colorado 80538. All rights reserved.

PREFACE

The title of this present volume tends to be misleading. For it suggests that Nicholas's *didactic* sermons are to be distinguished from his *non-didactic* ones—ones that are, say, more inspirational and less philosophical, or more devotional and less theological, or more situationally oriented and less Scripturally focused. Yet, in truth, all 293 of Nicholas's sermons are highly didactic, highly pedagogical, highly exegetical.[1] To be sure, there are inspirational and devotional elements; but they are subordinate to the primary purpose of teaching. Likewise, only occasionally[2] do the sermons show signs of addressing local circumstances that are idiosyncratic to the respective churches in Koblenz, Trier, Mainz, Augsburg, Frankfurt, Brixen, and Rome. Rather, their Scriptural focus more often than not yields up interpretations that are allegorical—or otherwise figurative—in a general way that allows Nicholas to draw inferences about the relationship between the intellect and the senses, about the unity of the virtues, the two natures in Christ, human freedom of will, the gifts of the Holy Spirit, the inter-relationship of faith and reason, the triune nature of God, the role of conscience, the precepts of the natural law, time as the image of eternity, the four stages of a knowledge of God, Christ as Wisdom Incarnate, God as Beauty, the Holy Spirit as Love, … and so on. Each of the sermons contains more than one major theme, so that no sermon dwells at length upon a single topic so as to sound pedantic and inappropriately academic. On the contrary: in a limited measure Nicholas's sermons tend to entice through their extensive display of original metaphor, of striking imagery, of fresh vocabulary, and of erudite knowledge of earlier writers such as Plato, Aristotle, Augustine, Anselm, Albertus Magnus, and Meister Eckhart.

Given the wealth of the overlapping themes that one encounters in the sermons,[3] I found the attempt to group them by topic to be unmanageable. And it seemed of little value to arrange them merely in chronological sequence. Accordingly, both my principle of selection and my principle of arrangement turned out to be purely subjective: I selected the sermons that most appealed to me, and I arranged them according to my own degree of interest in them.

The translations were made from the Latin texts contained in Volumes XVI – XIX of the series *Nicolai de Cusa Opera Omnia* (Hamburg: Meiner Verlag). The printed editions of these texts are

Preface

exemplary when it comes to their identifying Nicholas's sources; and the collations themselves bear the marks of the masterly meticulousness with which their editors worked. My appending, to this present volume, a short list of additions and corrections does not belie the outstanding work of the respective editors. Rather, the list attests to how exceedingly painstaking it is to work with Medieval manuscripts; furthermore, it attests to the fact that even when the most competent scholars do their very best, their accomplishment inevitably falls short of utter perfection—though not of our utter admiration for the very high degree of perfection that has been attained.

I am especially appreciative of the fact that these scholarly editors, who are associated either directly or indirectly with the Institut für Cusanus-Forschung, agreed to let me see pre-publication copies of the most recently published fascicles of the sermons. I cite, in the Bibliography, the names of all the editors of the fascicles that comprise Volumes XVI – XIX, which constitute the complete sermons.

Since I have now reached the age in life where this present set of translations will have to conclude my major scholarly activity, I would like to pay tribute to those German colleagues from whose writings on Cusanus, and from personal contact with whom, I have over the years continually profited. I am thinking of the early director of the Cusanus Institute, Prof. Rudolf Haubst[†]; of the two subsequent co-directors, Profs. Klaus Kremer[†] and Klaus Reinhardt; of the historian Prof. Erich Meuthen; and of Prof. Werner Beierwaltes, Head of the Cusanus-Commission of the Heidelberger Akademie der Wissenschaften. There are, of course, others in whose scholarly debt I stand. Mention of them all by name would, though deserved, be here too lengthy.[4]

The present volume was completed during my sabbatical leave from the College of Liberal Arts at the University of Minnesota. Before the leave even began, I was aided by the University's Alice A. Welch, of the Department of Inter-Library Loans in Wilson Library. She expeditiously obtained for me articles and books that were relevant to the present project. Ingrid Fuhrmann in the Secretariat of the Cusanus Institute was also helpful in expeditious ways, as was also the Institute's Dr. Alfred Kaiser.

                                          Jasper Hopkins, Ph.D.
                                        Professor of Philosophy
                                        University of Minnesota
                                        Minneapolis, Minnesota 55455
                                        http://www.cla.umn.edu/jhopkins/

NOTES TO THE PREFACE

1. In Sermon CCXXXVI Nicholas states that his preaching on this feast-day will be briefer than usual so that those who have come (to Brixen) from a distance may return home to the fields at this time of Harvest. Elsewhere (Sermon CXLVII (**8**)) he admonishes against priests' taking money for hearing confessions. And still elsewhere (Sermon CCLX (**3**)) he upbraids local parishioners who partake of the Eucharist without paying attention to the sermon.

2. Hervé Martin, *Le métier de prédicateur en France septentrionale à la fin du Moyen Âge (1350 – 1520)* [Paris: Cerf, 1988], distinguishes didactic sermons from sermons that teach about a religious subject (pp. 573 f.). However, I am using the term "didactic" in a broader sense—one that includes a reference to teaching, whether teaching about a religious subject or not.

3. See, for example, the many different themes in Sermon CLXXXVII or in Sermon CLXXXIX.

4. I will, however, mention especially also Italy's Prof. Giovanni Santinello,[†] along with Germany's Dr. Hermann Schnarr and Dr. Gerhard G. Senger—all of whom have made invaluable contributions to Cusanus scholarship, as has also Prof. Walter A. Euler, the current director of the Cusanus Institute.

TABLE OF CONTENTS

Introduction	ix
Selected Cusan Sermons	1 – 465
(See itemized listing below)	
Abbreviations and *Praenotanda*	466
Corrigenda for the Latin texts	467
Bibliography	471
Paradigma Filiae Adoptivae Explanatur	1
(The Parable of the Adopted Daughter Is Expounded)	
Tu Es Christus	7
(You Are the Christ)	
Dominabuntur Populis	11
(They Shall Rule over People)	
Multifarie Multisque Modis	20
(On Many Occasions and in Many Ways)	
Puer Crescebat	33
(The Child Grew)	
Loquere et Exhortare	41
(Speak and Exhort)	
Pange, Lingua, Gloriosi Corporis Mysterium	56
(Sing, O Tongue, of the Mystery of the Glorious Body)	
Ostendite Mihi Numisma	60
(Show Me the Coin)	
Qui Me Invenerit	75
(He Who Finds Me)	
Suscepimus, Deus, Misericordiam Tuam	85
(We Have Received Your Mercy, O God)	
Fides autem Catholica	95
(The Catholic Faith)	

Table of Contents

Gaudete et Exsultate   115
(Be Glad and Rejoice)

Trinitatem in Unitate Veneremur   127
(We Worship Trinity in Oneness)

Spiritus autem Paraclitus   132
(But the Spirit, the Paraclete)

Qui Me Invenerit Inveniet Vitam   146
(He Who Finds Me Shall Find Life)

Maria Optimam Partem Elegit   150
(Mary Has Chosen the Best Part)

Tota Pulcra Es, Amica Mea   168
(You Are All-fair, O My Love)

Non Sumus Ancillae Filii   178
(We Are Not Children of the Bondwoman)

Beati Qui Habitant in Domo Tua   189
(Blessed Are They Who Dwell in Your House)

Michael et Angeli Eius   192
(Michael and His Angels)

Nos Revelata Facie   204
(We, with Unveiled Face)

Qui Credit in Filium Dei   211
(He Who Believes in the Son of God)

Non in Solo Pane Vivit Homo   225
(Man Does Not Live by Bread Alone)

Beatus Es, Simon Bar Iona   233
(Blessed Are You, Simon Bar-Jona)

Ecce Ascendimus Hierosolymam   237
(Behold, We Go Up to Jerusalem)

Confide, Fili   243
(Be of Good Cheer, Son)

Ubi Est Qui Natus Est Rex Iudaeorum?   247
(Where Is He Who Is Born King of the Jews?)

Hoc Facite in Meam Commemorationem   262
(This Do in Remembrance of Me)

Qui Manducat Hunc Panem (He Who Eats of This Bread)	272
Erunt Primi Novissimi (The First Shall Be Last)	291
Ubi Venit Plenitudo Temporis (When the Fullness of Time Was Come)	296
In Caritate Radicati et Fundati (Rooted and Grounded in Love)	307
Quaecumque Scripta Sunt (Whatever Things Were Written)	319
Non Diligamus Verbo neque Lingua (Let Us Love Not in Word or with Lip-Service)	332
Suadeo Tibi Emere (I Counsel You To Buy from Me Fire-tried Gold)	342
Respice de Caelo (Look Down from Heaven)	352
Assumptus Est in Caelum (He Was Taken Up into Heaven)	367
Sufficit Tibi Gratia Mea (My Grace Is Sufficient for You)	377
Paraclitus autem (But the Paraclete . . .)	385
Spiritu Ambulate (Walk in the Spirit)	399
Ex Ipso, per Ipsum, et in Ipso Of Him, by Him, and in Him	412
Una Oblatione Consummavit (By One Sacrifice He Has Perfected ...)	423
Una Oblatione (By One Offering)	434
Iam autem Die Festo Mediante (Now, about the Middle of the Feast ...)	442
Repexit Humilitatem (He Has Regarded the Humility ...)	452

INTRODUCTION TO CUSA'S SERMONS

1. *Preliminary Remarks*. Nicholas of Cusa's sermons display a richness of terminology and metaphor, a detailed conversance with Scripture, and a fecund interlacing of themes. The sermons dare not be ignored by anyone who seeks to fathom the mind of this fifteenth-century philosopher and theologian. For in terms of importance they are comparable to Nicholas's other writings. Not only do they embody many of the motifs that are dealt with in the systematic treatises and in the dialogues, but they even enhance these motifs in appreciable ways. One example of an enhancement is seen in Sermon XXIII (**15**), where each of us is asked to imagine that he is Adam and has been placed in the world as was Adam. We are then shown by Nicholas how from the world we could be led, through an observation of the world's natural objects and processes, to a knowledge of God's existence—and even of His triunity. This discussion, through its pithiness and through its very starting point, enhances and redirects and refocuses the approach taken in *De Docta Ignorantia* I and II.

Nicholas wrote down some of his sermons *after* they were preached, others of them *before* they were preached; and several of them were preached without ever being written down. Almost all of the ones written down are sermon-sketches, rather than full-fledged literary accomplishments, although a few of them—e.g., Sermons XXII, XXIV, and XLI—are "small theological masterpieces," to borrow Walter Euler's description.[1] Moreover, all the sermons are written in Latin, except for Sermon XXIV, which was composed by Nicholas in German. In addition, Sermon LXXVI was written down in German by a hearer in Vienna, where Nicholas preached it. In fact, Nicholas preached mainly in German, although we have no actual record of his German wordings other than the words found in the two sermons just indicated. And even those words may not all have been the actual words, or actual sequences of words, as preached. That Nicholas sometimes also preached in Latin—especially to the clergy and especially in Rome—cannot seriously be doubted. Yet, the exact number of occasions on which he so preached remains a matter of surmise. We must avoid assuming that the sermons preached in Latin were the ones that we find written down in better, more stylized, Latin. For it could easily be the case that other sermons—ones not preached in Rome but preached nonetheless before clergy—were preached in Latin, *as the*

Introduction

more simplified Latin could be said to attest!

One manuscript of the sermons, viz., Codex Cusanus 220, contains copies of sermons written in Nicholas's own hand. Two other manuscripts, *Codices Vaticani* 1244 and 1245, though not autographs, were commissioned by Nicholas and were examined and corrected by him. At this juncture, we must avoid making a second dubious assumption—viz., the assumption that just because Nicholas looked over these two manuscripts they contain the more reliable readings whenever they conflict with the readings of the other manuscripts; for such need not be the case. For example, in Sermon CCLX, at **24**:10, the editors of the printed edition of that Latin text opt for the word "contracta" because *Codex Vaticanus* 1245 has this word. However, the correct reading is "incontracta", which both *Codex Magdeburg* 38 (Berlin) and *Codex Ashburnham* 1374 (Florence) have.

2. *Important Minor Themes.* From the sermons we glean many points, some of which are more significant than are others but all of which are of interest. Among the interesting but relatively minor points are such poignant observations as the following ten: (a) The Virgin Mary was indeed very beautiful; yet, her beauty was not a seductive beauty.[2] (b) The Layman (Latin: *Idiota*) whom Nicholas fictionalizes as a discussant in his works *Idiota de Sapientia, Idiota de Mente,* and *Idiota de Staticis Experimentis* is taken by Nicholas to be illiterate[3] but to be capable, nonetheless, of reading the world-book, i.e., the book of nature. (c) Every sin that is contrary to love is a mortal sin.[4] (d) He who seeks God only when it benefits him loves himself more than he loves God.[5] (e) He who loves himself more than he loves God ends up in eternal self-hatred.[6] (f) Christ is *minimus homo* (the smallest human being) because, unlike others, He was a complete human being from the moment of His conception.[7] (g) In this present world there is no such thing as a perfect circle (as even Plato taught).[8] (h) In Deuteronomy 6:5 and Luke 10:27 man is commanded to love God with all his heart, soul, strength, and mind. Although one cannot do so without the assistance of Divine grace, and cannot in this lifetime do so perfectly even with the assistance of grace, one can nevertheless come to love God in such a way that he loves nothing as much as he loves God, i.e., loves nothing more than he loves God.[9] (i) Solomon was first a man and then was wise; Christ was first Wisdom and then was a man.[10] (j) God cannot hate anything that He has created; but He can love one thing more than another.[11]

Introduction

3. *Important Major Themes.* It soon becomes evident that the foregoing sample of themes is not really a sample of *minor* themes—at least, not if the themes are considered in and of themselves. They may be called "relatively minor" only inasmuch as, and insofar as, Nicholas chooses not to develop them either in the written sermons or elsewhere. Yet, certainly, he could easily have expanded upon them had he chosen to; and, for all we know, he did so in his oral delivery from the pulpit. Other of his themes may be called "relatively major" themes in the corresponding sense that they are developed more extensively either within the total corpus of sermons or within his other works. Let us explore but four of these focal areas.

3.1. *Faith and Reason.* The first thing that strikes one regarding Nicholas's treatment—in the sermons—of the relationship between faith and reason is how different the emphasis is from the emphasis in his treatises and dialogues. In particular, the ostensible role of faith is *promoted*, and the ostensible role of reason is *demoted*.

3.1.1. In the sermons Nicholas speaks of faith as overcoming, or vanquishing, reason;[12] and he even speaks of faith as belief that goes against reason.[13] Moreover, this perspective is found not only in the late sermons but even in the early ones. Sermon IV, for example, portrays faith as bridging the gap when reason founders while encountering improbability. In that same sermon God is said to be believed-in not only without proof but also without evidentness.[14] And in Sermon XII (**34**) we are told to elevate ourselves unto God by pure faith rather than by means of signs, examples, empirical evidences. No amount of empirical evidence, for instance, will show that in the Eucharist the bread is transubstantiated into the Body of Christ. Similarly, no amount of empirical evidence that is available to natural reason will suffice to prove that Jesus is the Son of God, that He is God incarnate.[15]

Christ's performing of miracles tends to support the belief that He is the Son of God.[16] And yet, empirical reason can always maintain that these unusual events are not real miracles, for it cannot establish that they are worked *by the power of God*. Moreover, natural reason cannot understand how it is that while Jesus's body lay dead in the tomb, His soul descended unto the lower parts of the earth, as Ephesians 4:9 teaches, or descended unto Hell, as certain of the creeds state. Although the super-wondrous mystery of the union of Christ's divine nature with His human nature is altogether incomprehensible, says Nicholas, it is not unbelievable.[17] Indeed, faith, based on revelation, impels one to believe in spite of one's not understanding.[18]

Moreover, continues Nicholas making use of a metaphor, faith is sterile, is barren: it has no reasons; it begets, produces, educes, adduces no reasons.[19] Indeed, the more reasons it would evince, the less it would be entitled to be called faith.[20] So, whereas the intellect is fertile—ever adducing, formulating, furnishing rational grounds—faith does not rely upon rational grounds. Abraham is regarded by Nicholas as epitomizing the man of faith. Abraham believed that God would help Sarah to conceive, even though she was past the age of childbearing[21] and even though experience taught that such conceiving would be counter to past experience. Yet, Abraham believed that with God all things are possible. Even *that* is possible which, for us, is highly *improbable* and, hence, unreasonable to expect. Yet, Abraham's trust in God and his belief in God's word went still further: for, later still, he believed—against all human experience—that if he obeyed God by sacrificing Isaac, God would resurrect Isaac from the dead.[22] He *believed*—even though natural reason tells us that resurrection from the dead is empirically *impossible*.[23] Abraham's reason must die, says Nicholas, in order that his faith should live.[24]

3.1.2. Surely, the foregoing declarations are extreme; and they have no parallel in Nicholas's systematic works. Yet, in the sermons they are not altogether untempered and unqualified, although their emphasis does prevail. In order to apprehend Nicholas's true perspective, we must approach his topic as he develops it: viz., dialectically.[25] That is, when we ask on his behalf whether faith vanquishes reason, we must recognize that he answers both *Yes* and *No*. And we must discern that in order to apprehend the truth about his position, we are required to bring both of these answers into a unity of consciousness. We have just seen how it is that reason *is* suspended,[26] how reason is said to have to die, to have to be vanquished. And yet, reason *is not* vanquished. For it is needed by faith, since the basis of faith is the fact of God's existence[27] and since the belief that God exists is reasonable. We have already alluded to the early Sermon XXIII, where in section **15** Nicholas sketches a line of reasoning to the effect that if we were to enter the world as did Adam, and if we were alone as was Adam originally, we could be led, reflectively, by our observations of the empirical world, unto a knowledge of God. Nicholas advances a corresponding line of reasoning in his later Sermon CLXXXVII (**2**):

> Since whatever things the perceptible world contains are finite,

> they cannot exist of themselves. For the finite can exist in a way different from the way it does exist; and so, its *being* is not eternity, which cannot exist in a way other than it does. Nor is [the world's *being*] infinity or absolute necessity. And so, if that which is not eternity itself were to exist from itself, it would exist before it existed—[something impossible]. Thus, then, we come, necessarily, to a Beginning of all finite things—[a Beginning] which is infinite ..., etc.

Only a modicum of intelligence is needed, thinks Nicholas, in order to grasp a line of reasoning such as the foregoing one.[28] And such a line of reasoning furnishes a foundation for faith, so that now Nicholas may speak plausibly of "the certitude of faith" (*certitudo fidei*)[29] and of "doubtless faith" (*indubia fides*).[30] Given this foundation and given the belief-in-God that is supported by it, the believer can go on to sense the sustaining presence of God in his life. As the Psalmist counsels: "O taste and see that the Lord is sweet."[31] This experiential knowledge is of more worth, thinks Nicholas, than are the attempts to understand with the intellect just *what* God is.

3.1.3. And now we are back at the *Yes*: faith does vanquish reason when we seek to know what God is. For God is beyond knowability by finite minds. Such minds can only symbolize God, can only select appropriate metaphors by means of which to envision Him. For just as the body's eye cannot look directly at the sun, which is so bright as to be blinding, so too the mind's eye, i.e., the intellect, cannot gaze upon the Infinite Brightness that God is.[32] But in recognizing that God is Something than which nothing better can be thought, the intellect can recognize that God is Goodness itself,[33] is Beauty itself,[34] is Love itself.[35] Thus, at this juncture, the answer again becomes *No*: the intellect is not overwhelmed; rather, it is needed for discerning what the description of God is and for discerning that the Being that answers to this description is Infinite and, thus, beyond all positive human conception.[36] We can conceive of what this Being is not;[37] we can conceive, for instance, that it is not not-Love. But we can have no positive, non-metaphorical conception of what Infinite Divine Love either is or is like, since between the finite and the Infinite there is no proportional relation.[38] But of this very fact—the fact of infinite disproportionality—reason is the one to inform us. Furthermore, through our knowledge of the historical Christ we learn something of what God's Love is like *ad nos* (i.e., in relation to us), though never what it is *in se* (i.e., in and of itself).

3.1.4. So, in the end, Nicholas in and through his sermons never loses sight of the essential role of reason, even though he accentuates the role of faith. Reason sees *that God is* but cannot see, non-symbolically, *what God is* in and of Himself. Reason sees, as Nicholas puts it, that faith's sterility is really a kind of fertility.[39] For faith leads to truth. For not only does believing sometimes lead to understanding,[40] but also one's acting upon the teaching of Christ will oftentimes have the result that one will come to discern that Christ's teachings are true.[41] The intellect discerns, too, even its own weakness[42] and even the fact of its own darkness:[43] "The object of the will is the good. But sin so darkens and depresses the intellect that it makes the good to seem to be the bad." Thus, Nicholas is alert to the phenomenon that theologians refer to as the noetic effect of sin.[44]

As one would expect, Nicholas agrees with Augustine and with Scripture that faith is a gift of God, is a grace.[45] For unaided by God, one does not come to have faith, does not come to say with Job "I know that my Redeemer liveth."[46] For the knowledge referred to by Job is the kind of *certitude* that comes by faith, not the kind of *certainty* that comes from "seeing is believing." Faith's certitude is grounded in religious experience; empirical certainty is grounded in perceptual experience. Faith, says Nicholas, is a *visio invisibilis*, a seeing of the invisible[47]—*toto caelo* different from ordinary perceptual vision. The ability-to-believe is, teaches Nicholas, the highest power of the soul;[48] it excels the intellective power, even as the intellective power excels the perceptual power. Nicholas is also willing to agree with Augustine that, in a more ordinary sense, believing differs from thinking, insofar as to believe is to think *with assent*.[49] Yet, although one's believing that Jesus is the Son of God is his thinking this proposition and assenting to it, nonetheless this kind of believing first becomes religious faith when one obeys Christ; for belief without obedience is not faith of the sort that makes one pleasing to God. And only the latter kind of faith is saving faith. In the sermons Nicholas seems to go beyond Augustine's emphasis on *cum assensione cogitare* when he speaks of our assenting as being our freely bringing our intellect into submission (*servitus*).[50] But this discrepancy is only apparent, for Nicholas is viewing the intellect as at times wayward, because of pride, so that it is in need of the guidance of revelation. And Augustine held this same view.

3.1.5. Let there be no doubt about the fact that Nicholas is not really asking the man of faith to discard reason altogether, not really asking him to let reason die, in an unqualified sense. Rather, he is ask-

Introduction

ing only that reason realize its own limitations and accept the legitimacy of faith. He is clear about his claim that reason can assure us of the existence of God but that reason cannot think God's nature and God's attributes except metaphorically. Thus, when he speaks of knowing that God *exists*, he emphasizes the power of reason and of intellect, whereas when he speaks of knowing God's *nature*, he emphasizes faith and revelation and symbolism. Regarding the *former emphasis*, we must not lose sight of such passages as Sermon XX (**5**:6-11), where we read:

> [We ascend unto God] by way of *perceptible things* qua things caused. According to Augustine, this fact [holds true] for several reasons: either (a) because nothing has brought itself into existence or (b) because from what is changeable we must come [inferentially] to what is Unchangeable, from the imperfect we must come to the Perfect, from what is good we must come to what is Best, etc.

Regarding the *latter emphasis*, we must not lose sight of passages such as Sermon CXXXV (**17**:15-20):

> Note that God is visible not to the outer eyes (which are capable of attaining [only] material and temporal objects) but to the eye of the heart (and this is the intellect). And He is visible to the eye of the intellect only in accordance with the condition of the world, viz., only by means of symbolism.

Sometimes the point about the Divine Nature's being knowable by us only symbolically, and never as it is in and of itself, is expressed by Nicholas paradoxically: God, because of His *infinite knowability*, is *unknowable*.[51] But Nicholas adds: He is unknowable, analogously to the way in which light, visible of itself, may, because of its resplendence, be unseeable by our eyes, which become temporarily blinded.

3.1.6. In the sermons, then, we find that Nicholas, like Augustine, does not lose sight of the importance of reason in rendering belief in God's existence not just plausible but also assured. Yet, reason, unaided by grace, by revelation, by religious experience, cannot arrive at the Christian God—the Incarnate God.[52] Nonetheless, it can arrive at the true belief that God is triune,[53] even if it can never conceive properly of God's *non-numerical* triunity.[54] Accordingly, a balanced interpretation of Nicholas's position requires us to recognize that some of his remarks are rhetorical flourish, are dramatizations, are super-emphases that make their point hyperbolically—as one might expect in a sermon but not in a treatise.

Introduction

In order better to appreciate the rhetorical force of Nicholas's sermons, and so that we may better make allowances for it, we may focus upon a striking instance of it:

> [The following] is a lovely contemplation: [viz.,] how it is that our soul—*by renouncing freedom of choice* (which is the life of the rational spirit) [and] by subjecting itself to the authority of God's word ([an authority] made evident to us through Christ)—dies unto itself and by thus dying enters into life. [The soul dies unto itself] because within it there reigns only the enlivening and nourishing word-of-God—[a state] that comes about through the faith that the word of God has been revealed to us through the Son.[55]

Now, obviously, the soul cannot, in an unqualified sense, renounce its use of free choice. It can do so only in the qualified sense of freely placing itself under the rule and guidance of the word of God as taught by Christ—that is, by choosing to obey God's commands and by continually reaffirming this decision. But such a reaffirmation does not constitute either a suspension of (the use of) free choice or a relegating of free choice from oneself. Indeed, we must not interpret Nicholas's statement radically. Similarly, when Nicholas states that a believer ought to exercise a faith that *overcomes* reason, that *vanquishes* reason, he must be interpreted not radically but in the light of other things that he says in favor of the emergence of confirming grounds—things such as that in the soul the Christian faith is as sight,[56] that Christ is *ratio absoluta*,[57] that *visio intellectualis* results from *fides*, i.e., "that through the certitude of faith one arrives at love for God and that together with love that is rooted in faith there comes an intellectual vision, i.e., knowledge; for by means of love a living faith proceeds continually onwards unto seeing and unto knowledge."[58]

3.2. *Four Levels of a Knowledge of God's Nature.* In further developing his conception of the knowledge of God, Nicholas in Sermon CCLVIII distinguishes four levels of access to God, four levels of God's accessibility. The first level differs considerably from the approach of natural theology, even though Nicholas refers to it as natural knowledge. For it is natural not in the sense that one makes inferences from observations of material objects within the cosmos, or world, but in the sense that one's own natural desires afford some understanding of what God is—insofar as we can form a conception of His perfection.[59]

3.2.1. Man, says Nicholas, is by virtue of his rational nature inclined toward truth, justice, goodness, life, knowledge. And

Introduction

through these things man is naturally inclined toward God, in whom these things are one.[60] For, as Augustine reasoned in *De Libero Arbitrio* II, God is either Truth itself or Something higher than Truth, if there is something higher. A similar point, thinks Nicholas, holds for Justice, Goodness, etc. And so, like Augustine, Nicholas finds it natural to conceive of God—who is envisioned as the object of rational human nature's desires—in terms of the moral and ontological perfections that the mind and the rational will are directed toward. Accordingly, he deems the names of these perfections to be appropriate names for God—appropriate, that is, for purposes of prayer and of worship.

3.2.2. But there is a second, and higher, way of conceiving of God, viz., the negative way, which Nicholas refers to as "*via mystica negationis*."[61] He calls the way of negation *mystical* in the sense that it is a hidden mode of knowledge, for it does not disclose just what God is but signifies only what He is not. And yet, notes Nicholas, negative propositions about God implicitly entail affirmative propositions about Him. Hence, the negation "God is not nameable" implies the affirmation "God exceeds everything nameable." However, this affirmation does not yield a positive notion of the Divine Nature. Accordingly, negations are "truer" statements about God than are affirmations.[62] For it is truer to say, for example, "God is not life" than to say "God is Life." For the former implies that God is more than life, or than Life, whereas the latter does not. Indeed, the *via mystica negationis* likewise implies that God is not not-life, since He is beyond the distinction between life and not-life. So at this second level, the rational human spirit conceives of God as transcending everything that would constitute the unitive perfectibility of the objects of its inclinations.

3.2.3. But the rational human spirit that truly loves God may hope to obtain a third kind of access to God: viz., a face-to-Face seeing of God. This vision is reserved for the next life, although the Apostle Paul[63] obtained a foretaste of it in this lifetime; and others, too, may be graced with such a mystical foretasting. Paul's *praegustatio mystica* differs from the *via mystica negationis* inasmuch as it is an *encountering* and not simply a *conceptualizing*. It is mystical because it takes place not only beyond the five senses and the imagination but also beyond the reason and the intellect, so that it is a non-cognitive encounter in which the soul is aware non-conceptually and non-perceptually—though not non-intuitively—of its unitive encounter with

Divine Goodness and Divine Love. In Sermon CCLVIII Nicholas describes this encounter as a face-to-Face vision in which the Face of God is still somewhat bedarkened, in the sense that no knowledge of His Essence is acquired.

Elsewhere in speaking of mystical encounter, Nicholas uses more radical language—language reminiscent of Meister Eckhart. For, like Eckhart, he speaks of our being transubstantiated into the life of Christ.[64] But when he thus speaks, he is no longer thinking of mystical encounter in the way that, say, Hugh of Balma[65] thinks of it. Rather, he is expressing the fact of each believer's union with Christ—expressing it in a theologically hyper-vivid, hyper-rhetorical way. That is, Nicholas uses the expression "face-to-Face vision of God" in two different senses: (a) face-to-Face$_1$ experience of God—call it mystical experience—occurs in this lifetime and is an experience reserved for but relatively few. By contrast, (b) face-to-Face$_2$ experience of God—call it sonship (*filiatio*)—will be attained, by all believers, in the next lifetime. Unlike mystical experience, sonship does not involve the suspension of the activity of the intellect. Sonship is perfected in the next life, although it begins in this life—begins upon conversion, as Nicholas indicates in Sermon CLXXXVI (**13**:5-7).

So we need to distinguish between (1) Nicholas's claims about mystical experience, (2) his claims about sonship, and (3) his claims about a believer's being incorporated into Christ,[66] his being transformed into Christ,[67] Christ's "digesting" the believer into Himself.[68] The radical-sounding phrases "transformation into," "incorporation into," and "digestion into" belong to the rhetoric of preaching and are meant both to grab attention and to articulate the theological doctrine of the believer's union with God through Christ. Every believer, upon conversion, is translated unto and into eternal life. As Nicholas writes: "By means of Your death we have been translated unto life, even as the priest transubstantiates bread into Your Body on the altar."[69] But when Nicholas speaks more carefully, and less rhetorically, he expresses the same point by implying that the believer becomes transformed into a more and more perfect *image* of Christ, whom he loves.[70] The believer is supposed to seek to become ever more *Christlike*, ever more *Godlike*.[71] And although Nicholas states that believers become deified, he never means that they become God or have their human nature transformed into becoming the Divine Nature. Nor does Nicholas teach, à la Averroës, that after the soul leaves the body, it loses its personal identity and becomes one with the world-soul.

Introduction

So whereas in the treatises and the dialogues Nicholas sticks with the terms "*deiformis*" and "*Christiformis*," he prefers in the sermons the expressions "*in Christum transformari*" and "*in Deum transformari*." But the transformation that is being spoken of is a spiritual transformation, not an ontological transformation. For the Divine Nature and the human nature remain forever distinct, even though through participation in Christ's human nature a believer's human nature obtains its perfection.[72] A striking instance of Nicholas's use of dramatic language is seen in Sermon CCLXXXIV (**7**), where we read: "He who believes in Jesus becomes 'Jesus,' i.e., 'saved'. For Jesus is the Savior." Here Nicholas appeals, dramatically, to the fact that the name "Jesus" means "Savior,"[73] so that, figuratively speaking, in becoming saved from sins one may be said to become 'Jesus'. But just as here Nicholas is making a spiritual point and not a point about ontological identity, so in his stating that a believer becomes transformed into Christ, he is also making only a spiritual point. This fact becomes perfectly patent in Sermon CCLXXII (**13**):

> The inner man ... can be like Christ. I mean "like" not with respect to an exact likeness, which cannot be attained, but with respect to a certain outcome, which in each [inner man] is distinct. By way of illustration: all men partake of the incorruptible specific form of humanity, although one man does so differently from another man. Therefore, that transformation [i.e., transforming likeness] by means of which a man is transformed in spirit (i.e., in the inner man) can occur, other things being equal, all the while that the man remains a man.
>
> For just as the Lord who is the Son of God put on the form of a servant,[74] so the servants who are sons of Adam put on the form of the Lord in baptism, (where they are anointed with lotus oil), so that they may be Christlike.[75]

3.2.4. The fourth level of a knowledge of God is the knowledge that God has of Himself and of His own Quiddity. No finite mind has this knowledge.[76] And since God is the only Infinite Mind, only Infinity itself, viz., God, knows Infinity itself. Even in the next lifetime human minds will have no knowledge of God as He is in and of Himself. Rather, they will have a fuller knowledge of God as He is knowable in and through Christ, with whom each believer's soul will be more perfectly united. In Sermon CCLVIII (**14-15**), which dates from 1456, Nicholas is espousing the same position that he put forth in *De Docta Ignorantia* I, 26 (**88**), completed in 1440. But even earlier—viz., in Sermon XVI (**8**), preached on Christmas Day, 1432, perhaps in Koblenz—Nicholas stated that "the primary object of the Divine Intellect is God Himself." This is a point that harks back not only to Thomas Aquinas but also to Albertus Magnus and to Aristotle, by both of whom Aquinas was influenced.

But unlike Aristotle, and more in line with St. Albert and St. Thomas, Nicholas maintains that God knows not only Himself but also individuals and everything that He has created:

> As Artisan of all things, God knows the species and forms of these things, even as a writer [knows] the letters formed by himself, of which he is the cause.... God knows, in a more perfect way, all that angels or men know or can know. He works all in all. And so, He not only knows generally but also knows each thing individually; for otherwise His knowledge would not be perfect.[77]

But just as God is an Artisan who has intimate knowledge of all that He has made, so too He wills to be known through all that He has made. Thus, the heavens declare the glory of God,[78] and, thus, God created rational beings in order that they might see His glory and display His glory in themselves.[79] But man, in sinning, robbed God of His glory, as it were. For thereby he marred human nature and in that way detracted from God's artisanship, as it were. Here Nicholas follows Anselm's account in the *Cur Deus Homo* and emphasizes with Anselm both God's glory and His honor.[80]

Now, although the magnificence of God's power, wisdom, and craftsmanship are displayed in the universe, Nicholas teaches lucidly that the universe is not 'God in His visible state of Being'. That is, Nicholas distances himself clearly from pantheism. It is therefore ironic that he should at times have been accused of pantheism. This charge was brought, initially, by his contemporary John Wenck, who in *De Ignota Litteratura* ascribed to Nicholas the doctrine that "all things coincide with God," so that "God is the Totality of things."[81] More recently, others, too, have taught that Nicholas's writings display his pantheistic tendencies. Like Wenck, they have viewed Nicholas as teaching that the universe is God in His contracted (i.e., restricted) state of Being. And they go beyond Wenck in wrongly interpreting a passage in Nicholas's *De Possest*: "Quid igitur est mundus nisi invisibilis dei apparitio? Quid deus nisi visibilium invisibilitas ...?"[82] By construing "*apparitio*" as *appearance*, these interpreters take Nicholas to be teaching that the world is God in His visible state, whereas Nicholas means only that the world is the *manifestation* of God, means only that the heavens declare the glory of God: "What, then, is the

Introduction

world except the manifestation of the invisible God? What is God except the invisibility of visible things ...?"

In *De Docta Ignorantia* Nicholas indicates that the universe is not God because God alone is absolute, whereas the universe, along with its parts, is diminished through being contracted.[83] Now, in the later sermons Nicholas reaffirms his opposition to pantheism. In particular, Sermon CCXVI (**23-24**) conveys Nicholas's belief that the world's magnitude is finite; and it indicates that God is prior to and superior to the universe. Unfortunately, in *De Docta Ignorantia* Nicholas did not take pains to dissociate himself from pantheism; indeed, he even used the term "emanation,"[84] which misleadingly suggests that the world, in emanating from God, is of the Divine substance. Yet, *"emanatio"* and *"emanare"* are Nicholas's substitute words for *"creatio"* and *"creare"* when the doctrine of the universe's origin is being discussed endorsingly. Nowhere in the sermons does Nicholas refer to the universe as "the body of God." Rather, echoing the thought of St. Paul in Colossians 2:9, he chooses to say that Christ is the Body of God (CLXXVIII (**7**)).

3.3. *Maria, mater Dei.* Nicholas accepts the orthodox theological doctrine that the Virgin Mary was impregnated by the power of the Holy Spirit and without a male seed. As such, she is θεοτόκος (*theotocos*), the God-bearer, the mother of God. In the sermons she is exalted above all other human beings, having prerogatives that, taken together, no other human being has. In Sermon VIII, which eulogizes Mary, Nicholas identifies some of these prerogatives and privileges. "She was privileged, foremostly, with a prerogative against evil, because *not only did she never sin but she was not even able to sin.*"[85] Moreover, she is the most God-loved of all creatures.[86] She was beautiful with a beauty that excels that of all other mortals.[87] She was ignorant of nothing.[88] Indeed, she has very great achievements of intellect, memory, and will.[89] (Nicholas does not tell us what these achievements were but rather intimates that they were what enabled her to overcome the world, the flesh, and the Devil). She is exalted above all the choirs of angels.[90] She possessed natural virtue, so that she lived in a state of innocence.[91] Because she had love for God and for neighbor, she had all the moral virtues. For "he who has love has all the moral virtues, and he who does not have love has no moral virtue," since love is the bond of perfection, as says the Apostle Paul.[92] Furthermore, in addition to the theological virtue of love, she possessed in a most excellent way the other two theological virtues: viz., faith and hope. Mary was full of all grace[93]—so full that "as purely a creature she was not capable of greater grace."[94] She is so merciful that she is deserving of the name "Queen of Mercy."[95] She will intercede for believers who supplicate her—intercede with her son, who is also the Son of God. By believers she is to be adored with an adoration of hyperdulia,[96] i.e., with the highest kind of adoration that creatures can licitly exhibit toward saints.

The one theological problem that Nicholas unself-consciously encounters in conjunction with his adoration and exaltation of Mary has to do with the prerogative of purity that he ascribes to her in association with her fullness of grace. For it can seem theologically abberant to assert that Mary never sinned and was never able to sin. Traditional orthodox theologians wanted to say that Jesus alone was without sin,[97] so that He alone did not deserve to die, death being the penalty for sin.[98] So if Mary did not sin, why did she die?—unless, that is, she was martyred. Accordingly, Nicholas would be committed both to belief in her martyrdom and to belief that Jesus was not the only sinless mortal—both of which beliefs appear problematical. As if realizing this fact, Nicholas in a later sermon states explicitly that Christ alone is sinless.[99] Now, there are three possible interpretations of Nicholas's statement here in conjunction with his previous statements in Sermons VI and VIII: (a) Nicholas changed his mind during the interval between writing down Sermon VIII and writing down Sermon CCLXXVI; (b) Nicholas unwittingly contradicts himself; (c) Nicholas means that Mary had no *actual sin* and no capability of *actually sinning*; but she had *original sin* and, thus, was not totally free of sin, as was Christ.

If we suppose that the last interpretation is the correct one, we save Nicholas from contradiction—but without saving him from theological abberation. For if Mary was born with original sin, she could not rightly be said to be unable to sin unless not only the guilt of original sin were removed but also the consequences of original sin were removed. And, indeed, if Mary were given every grace and were full of grace, she would, it seems, have been free of the stain of original sin. But, in that case, there would remain a theological difficulty in maintaining that she died a natural death. So Nicholas could preserve the consistency of his ideas by subscribing to the following propositions: (a) Mary was born with a human nature that inherited the guilt of Adam's sin; (b) this guilt was forgiven her because of her belief, at

Introduction

the time of the Annunciation, that her son, Jesus, would through an act of atonement save her and others from their sins;[100] (c) Mary died as a martyr. Alternatively, he could deny that Jesus was the sole human being to live a sinless life and to be born free of the guilt of original sin. He could maintain that Mary, too, was born free of the stain of original sin, as well as maintaining that she remained free of all actual sin, so that she is not included—any more than was Jesus—in the Apostle Paul's verdict that "all have sinned and come short of the glory of God" (Romans 3:23). Nicholas appears to have chosen this alternative; indeed, his ideas clearly aim in the direction of this alternative. Still, it was not until 1854 that the Church officially endorsed the doctrine of Mary's immaculate conception—a doctrine promulgated by Pope Pius IX in his encyclical *Ineffabilis Deus*.

So if Nicholas teaches the doctrine of Mary's immaculate conception, he must explain why Mary was subject to death. Instead of addressing this issue directly, he tells us that her natural death was governed by five special privileges, or prerogatives[101]—a view adopted from Albertus Magnus.[102] First, Mary foreknew the time of her death. Secondly, Christ escorted Mary into Heaven. Thirdly, Mary was free of a painful death. Fourthly, she arose immediately after dying. And, fifthly, she was assumed bodily and alive into Heaven, once having arisen.

3.4. *Love, Will, and Self.* One of Nicholas's most quotable passages is found in Sermon CCLXXVII (**23**): "Because the soul conforms itself to that which it loves: when it loves itself, it conforms itself to itself. And because it does not have from itself the fact of its existing and living, it does not love itself when it loves itself. But if it loves God (from whom it has its existing and being alive [and] in whose image it is) and does not love itself, in order to love God more: then it loves itself...."[103] Nicholas adapts this passage from Augustine's *Commentary on the Gospel of John* 123.5. And he delights in the paradoxical thought that the soul does not love itself when it loves itself. For beneath the surface-paradoxicality lies hidden, as he believes, a profound spiritual truth: the soul that seeks its own good must seek it in Goodness itself; for whoever is alienated from the Good is alienated also from himself qua participant in the Good, qua one who is made in the image of the Good. Thus, just as the soul is *not supposed to love itself* in place of loving God or more than it loves God, so also it *is supposed to love itself* as a participant in God's glory.[104] A sinner is to

Introduction

return to his heart, as the Latin Bible says,[105] so that he may become conscious of the sins that alienate him from God[106] and so that he may repent. For when he repents and enters further into himself, he sees God's light within himself[107] and is enabled to conquer himself[108] by acquiring, with God's help,[109] the moral virtues.

Nicholas never loses sight of the measure of the inalienable free will that human beings have. Indeed, the power of free assent is inherent in human nature.

> Consider carefully the fact that the human soul is constituted from four elements of its own. For the soul is immaterial, [and] its elements are immaterial. For we experience that the human soul is a certain immaterial power that sends forth from itself a fourfold movement: viz., an appetitive movement, a movement of anger, a movement of reason, and a voluntary, or free, movement. Now, because the soul is of an intellectual nature, it endeavors to steer these four movements intellectually by modulating intellectually the impulse of each movement. The modulation of the appetitive movement is called temperance; and the modulation of the movement of anger is called courage; and the modulation of the movement of reason is called prudence; and the modulation of the movement of free will is called justice.[110]

At times, Nicholas says not just that the *will* is free but that the *mind* is free and that free choice is present in the mind:

> The following ought not to be ignored: that freedom of choice is present in the mind, so that the mind has within itself the source of its own acts and so that it controls its own works.... And it has this freedom because it is created in the image of God. And to one who considers carefully, it is evident that the First Cause qua Cause placed His likeness in the mind, so that the mind is a living image, or a caused cause. And it is not possible that the mind's dignity be wrested [from it].[111]

Nicholas's view regarding the human soul's inherent freedom is neither radical nor naive. For Nicholas recognizes that the will is often conflicted, since, as Paul says, there is in the believer "another law ..., fighting against the law of my mind ...,"[112] so that "the good which I will, I do not; but the evil which I will not, that I do."[113] Nonetheless, notes Nicholas, "the will cannot be compelled to give its assent."[114] But it can be tempted and seduced by the Devil, the Serpent, who seduced Eve and Adam. Now, although *sin* mars the soul and detracts from its moral and ontological excellence, nonetheless the *ability to sin* contributes to the soul's nobility[115] by displaying the soul's freedom of choice, i.e., by constituting an aspect—though not an essential aspect—

Introduction

of the soul's freedom of choice. "The soul that sinneth, it shall die" say the Scriptures.[116] But the Scriptures also say that "love covers all sins"[117] and "blessed are they ... whose sins are covered."[118] True love—God's love—covers defilement and deformity so that these blemishes become invisible to all. True love is like a stone that renders a man invisible.[119] God's love not only covers but also transforms: it makes a son of man to be a son of God.[120] Whereas God's forgiving love purifies the soul and blots out the sin,[121] the world's love can do neither. Carnal love that is enthralling blinds the lover, so that in his beloved he does not see the blemishes seen by everyone else.[122] But Divine love covers and transforms, so that the soul's stains will disappear from the sight of every mind's eye.

4. *Conclusion.* Nicholas's sermons command our respect. Some of them are longer; some are shorter. Some are complete sketches; some are incomplete sketches. Some are in better Latin; others are in worse Latin. But all of them are insightful and instructive in important ways. To the extent that the sermonizing is also a philosophizing, the latter feature does not draw us away from Scripture but leads us into its richness. The sermons are, indeed, didactic—aiming to teach believers how to imitate Christ, how rightly to love themselves by loving God, how it is that they ought not to neglect the adoration of Mary, ought not to forget that the sacrament of baptism is regenerative, that in the Eucharist God transubstantiates the bread and the wine. The more philosophical moments either inform or remind that God is *Being* (*esse ipsum*),[123] not *a being* (*ens*), that the human intellect *abstracts* various universal forms from various kinds of sensory images,[124] that there is a *lex naturalis*,[125] that the maximum and the minimum coincide in the infinite,[126] that each thing exists insofar as it is one,[127] that each of the cardinal virtues is present in the other,[128] that there is nothing in the intellect that was not previously in the senses,[129] that nothing unknown is loved,[130] that art imitates nature,[131] that there is no proportion of the finite to the infinite,[132] that God's abode is the Coincidence of coincidences[133]—and so on. In the end, then, the sermons aim to edify through teaching; and they teach through philosophizing and theologizing, though always in combination with interpreting Scripture.

Whether as parish priest or as bishop or as cardinal, Nicholas was true to his clerical calling to preach the Gospel. And in preparation for his preaching he complied with the commandment of Christ: "Search the Scriptures, for you think in them to have life everlasting; and the same are they that give testimony of me."[134]

NOTES TO THE INTRODUCTION

1. Walter A. Euler, "Entwicklungsgeschichtliche Etappen und Schwerpunktmäßige Themenverschiebungen in den Sermones?" *MFCG*, 30 (2005), p. 85: "kleine theologische Meisterwerke". Other sermons may be added to this list of Meisterwerke: e.g. IV and CCXVI and CCXLIII.
2. Sermon VI (**18**).
3. See Sermon CXXV (**4**:7-8).
4. Sermon XXXVII (**19**).
5. Sermon XXXVII (**18**).
6. Sermon CCXLVI (**21**).
7. Sermon XVII (**11**). Nicholas does not believe that every *conceptus* is a human being, consisting already of a rational soul. This view came later in the history of the Church.
8. Sermon CCLXIII (**24**).
9. Sermon VII (**28**).
10. Sermon CCLXXVII (**10**).
11. Sermon CLXXII (**1**).
12. Sermon CCLXVIII (**18-19**).
13. Sermon CCLXXXVI (**3**).
14. Sermon IV (**9**).
15. "There are some things that are set forth by a teacher and [are such that] the students do not believe the teacher unless [those things] are demonstrated to the intellect. For example, when a certain claim is made—say, [the claim] that there is [but] one world—it is not believed unless it is demonstrated by evidential considerations. By means of the evidential considerations the intellect sees that the claim is true, and it believes. However, there are other things that cannot be demonstrated either to the sensory eye or to the intellectual eye—as is the claim that the true man Jesus is the true Son of God." Sermon CLXXXVI (**3**:1-9).
16. Sermon CCLXIII (**5**). See also CCLXV (**9**) and CXXXV (**7**).
17. Sermon XVII (**9-10**).
18. Sermon CXC (**9**).
19. Sermon CCLXXV (**3**).
20. Cf. Sermon CLXXXVI (**3**:18-19), where Nicholas indicates the possibility that faith is diminished where there is evidence that leads to certainty.
21. Sermon CCLXXV (**4**).
22. Hebrews 11:17-19.
23. Sermon CCLXVIII (**18-19**).
24. *Loc. cit.*
25. "… dialectically": i.e., in Kierkegaard's sense, not Hegel's.
26. Cf. Sermon CXC (**9**): "For faith does not guide by means of persuasion and reason; rather, it impels [one]—in spite of his not understanding—to undertake the journey."
27. Sermon IV (**20**).
28. Sermon CLXXXIX (**19**:20-24).
29. Sermon CLXXXVII (**16**). Cf. CLXXXVI (**8**:15-19).

Notes to the Introduction

30. Sermon CCLXXVI (**27**).
31. Psalms 33:9 (34:8).
32. Sermon CLXXXVII (**8-9**).
33. Sermons CCLVIII (**15**) and CCLXIX (**11**).
34. Sermon CCXLIII (**28**).
35. *Loc. cit.*
36. Sermon CCLVIII (**14 & 16**). In other words, our positive conception of God is but a surmise. Sermon CLXXXVII (**5**).
37. Sermon IV (**32**).
38. Sermons III (**11**) and IV (**34**) and VII (**32**) and CLXXII (**1**).
39. Sermon CCLXXV (**3**).
40. Isaias (Isaiah) 7:9 (Old Latin version). See also Sermons XIX (**6**) and CXXXV (**7**).
41. Cf. John 7:17.
42. Sermon CCXXXV (**3**).
43. Sermon CXCIII (**15**:1-3).
44. Sermons CCXXXV (**3**) and CXCIII (**15**:1-3) and CLXXXIX (**3**:1-4).
45. Sermons IV (**16**) and VI (**15**) and CXX (**5**:8) & CXXXV (**6**). CCLXXXIV (**14**). Ephesians 2:8.
46. Job 19:25.
47. Sermon CCLXVIII (**19**). Cf. CLXXXIX (**3**:1): "Fides christiana in anima est sicut visus." Yet, faith can lead to *visio intellectualis* (CLXXXVII (**16**)).
48. Sermon CCLXVIII (**18-19**).
49. Sermon CLXXXIX (**19**). Augustine, *De Praedestinatione Sanctorum*, II, 5 (*PL* 44:963).
50. Sermon CLXXXIX (**19**:5-6). Cf. CXX (**5**:11-12): "Qui credit, redigit intellectum in servitutem et humiliationem. Quod nota!"
51. Sermon CCXLI (**5**).
52. See, *supra*, the section on faith and reason.
53. Concerning reason and God's triunity, see Sermon XXXVIII (**12**).
54. See Jasper Hopkins, "Verständnis und Bedeutung des dreieinen Gottes bei Nikolaus von Kues," *MFCG* 28 (2003), pp. 135-164.
55. Sermon CLXXXVI (**13**:20-27).
56. Sermon CLXXXIX (**3**).
57. CCLXIX (**9**).
58. CLXXXVII (**16**).
59. Regarding inferences to perfections, see Sermon XX (**9**).
60. Sermon CCLVIII (**8**).
61. Sermon CCLVIII (**11**).
62. With Sermon CCLVIII cf. Sermon XX (**10**), as concerns Nicholas's preference for the *via negativa*.
63. II Corinthians 12:2-4.
64. See, *infra*, n. 68.
65. See Jasper Hopkins, *Hugh of Balma on Mystical Theology: A Translation and an Overview of His De Theologia Mystica* (Minneapolis: Banning, 2002).
66. Sermon VI (**9**).
67. Sermon III (**11**). Cf. CLI (**10**:13-20).

Notes to the Introduction

68. Sermon XII (**33**).
69. Sermon III (**11**).
70. Cf. Sermons CLXXII (**3**) and CCLI (**12**:12-17).
71. Sermon XII (**34**). But in XII (**35**) Nicholas again speaks after the fashion of Eckhart.
72. Sermon XXII (**37-41**).
73. Matthew 1:21.
74. Philippians 2:7.
75. Sermon CCLXXII (**13**:3-17).
76. Nicholas makes this point not only in Sermon CCLVIII but also in Sermon XXII (**10**) and elsewhere.
77. Sermon CCLXX (**4**).
78. Psalms 18:2 (19:1).
79. Sermon CCLI (**2**). See also, and especially, CCIV (**6-7**).
80. See Jasper Hopkins, "Nicholas of Cusa's Intellectual Relationship to Anselm of Canterbury," pp. 54–73 in Peter J. Casarella, editor, *Cusanus: The Legacy of Learned Ignorance*. Washington, D. C.: The Catholic University of America Press, 2006.
81. Cusanus, *Apologia Doctae Ignorantiae* 24 in my translation and edition entitled *Nicholas of Cusa's Debate with John Wenck*.
82. Cusanus, *De Possest* **72**:6-7 (in my edition, contained in my *Concise Introduction to the Philosophy of Nicholas of Cusa*).
83. Cusanus, *De Docta Ignorantia* II, 9 (**150**).
84. Cusanus, *De Docta Ignorantia*, II, 4 (**116**).
85. Sermon VIII (**27**). See also VIII (**13**) and VI (**15**).
86. Sermon VIII (**28**).
87. Sermons VIII (**30**) and VI (**16**).
88. Sermon VIII (**27**).
89. Sermon VIII (**28**).
90. Sermon VIII (**31**).
91. Sermon VI (**17**).
92. Colossians 3:14. Sermon VI (**18**).
93. Luke 1:28.
94. Sermon VIII (**28**).
95. Sermon VIII (**27**).
96. Sermon VIII (**31**).
97. Cf. II Corinthians 5:21. Hebrews 4:15. I Peter 2:22. Galatians 3:22. I John 1:8 & 10.
98. Romans 5:12.
99. Sermon CCLXXVI (**30**:14-16): "Unde omnis homo argui potest de peccato, quantum est de natura sua, eo solo excepto, qui sic est Filius hominis, quod et Filius Dei."
100. See Anselm, who in the *Cur Deus Homo* II, 16 holds this view.
101. Sermon VIII (**25**).
102. *Loc. cit.*
103. "Et nota: ex quo anima se conformat illi, quod amat, et dum se amat, se sibi conformat. Et quia a se non habet, ut sit et vivat, non se amat, quando se amat. Sed

Notes to the Introduction

si Deum amat, a quo habet esse et vivere, cuius est imago, et se non amat, ut illum magis amet, tunc se amat ..." CCLXXVII (**23**:1-6). See also Augustine, *In Joannis Evangelium*, CXXIII, 5 (*PL* 35:1968).

104. Sermon XXXVII (**18**:15-16).
105. Isaias (Isaiah) 46:8. Sermon XXXVII (**19**:37-38).
106. Isaias (Isaiah) 59:2.
107. Sermon V (**39**).
108. Sermon CCLIV (**9**:11).
109. "... God's mercy can assist some men to return to their heart ...." Sermon XXXVII (**19**:36-38).
110. Sermon CCXLVIII (**12**:1-16). Temperance, courage, prudence, and justice are the four cardinal virtues of ancient Greece.
111. Sermon CCLI (**15**:2-10).
112. Romans 7:23. Sermon CCII (**6**:1-4).
113. Romans 7:19.
114. Sermon CCII (**6**:1-2).
115. Sermon CLXXXVII (**10**).
116. Ezechiel (Ezekiel) **18**:4 & 20.
117. Proverbs 10:12.
118. Romans 4:7. I Peter 4:8. Psalms 31:1 (32:1).
119. Sermon CCXLI (**12**:1-2 and **12**:15-16).
120. Sermon CCXLI (**13**:4-5). I John 3:2.
121. Isaias (Isaiah) 43:25.
122. Sermon CCXLI (**12**:17-21). This sermon is one of the few places in which Nicholas distinguishes his use of the noun "*caritas*" and his use of the noun "*amor*"; for here "*caritas*" is used to refer to God's love, since *Caritas Deus est*, whereas "*amor*" is used to refer to profane love, to *mundi amor*. See section **14** of the sermon.
123. E.g., Sermon CCXVI (**17-19**).
124. Sermons CLXXII (**3**) and CLXXIV (**2-3**) and CCXLVI (**15**).
125. Sermon CCLXXII (**22-24**).
126. Sermon CCXLIV (**21**).
127. Sermon CCXLVI (**3**).
128. Sermon CLXXVIII (**6**).
129. Sermon CLXXXVII (**8**).
130. Sermon CCXLI (**5**).
131. Sermon CCXVI (**27**).
132. Sermon CLXXII (**1**).
133. Sermon CCLXVIII (**9-10**).
134. John 5:39.

Paradigma Filiae Adoptivae Explanatur*
(The Parable of the Adopted Daughter Is Expounded.)
[March 26, 1445; preached in Koblenz][1]

PART ONE
The Illustration Is Given of the King Who by means of His Son Recovered His Lost Adopted Daughter

[1] In order that the guidance of the people may be clearer, let an illustration be presented.

A king had an adopted daughter, who was led away by a deceiver and conducted to a distant region. And since that deceiver reared her in his ways for many years, she developed a certain love for him. [2] The king, through his only-begotten son, made inquiries after her everywhere. When the son found her in a bleak desert, he disclosed to her (*a*) her origin and (*b*) her adoption as the daughter of the supreme king and (*c*) her being a co-heir and (*d*) the fact that he was sent by his father to bring her back. And although she chose to ask many questions as to the truth of this matter, and although the son answered them, she could not readily be persuaded to believe that there was a better land and that she would become the queen of that land, (even as she was also not able to be persuaded that she had been born naturally of a father and a mother and had spent nine months in a womb, etc.). For it seemed to her that reason did not agree with this and that therefore it ought not to be believed. Hence, for a long time she rejected all these [representations] as false. However, by means of many miracles and signs the son began to get her to believe, to some extent. But the deceiver, as best he could, persuaded her not to believe.

[3] Nevertheless, after hearing the son frequently and after recognizing him to be very lovable, she believed him. And because she ascertained that the son loved her very fervently, she loved him exceedingly in return. But after she saw that from that place and from that association with the deceiver she had contracted many infirmities, and after she saw that the son of the king would know about these deficiencies: she desired to be loved, but she feared that she never could be. Therefore, she grieved and did not cease to groan and wail. And although the son consoled her, she replied that she could not imagine that he could love her, since she had become unseemly and infirm. [4] Now, the son, not wanting her to grieve so much, deliberat-

ed on how he could reassure her. And he found no way to do so except by assuming her deficiencies. Therefore, he assumed the deficiencies of the young woman so that she would take notice of the likeness and thus would be reassured. And he prepared to take her back to the kingdom, in accordance with the command of his father.

[5] But after the son conveyed her over the water and pointed out to her the kingdom of the father and the way unto the father, the deceiver pursued, in order to hold her back. And so, there was a great battle on the shore-of-the-water where the way unto the kingdom was located. And the son armed himself with weapons and engaged in combat with the deceiver so that the deceiver would allow the young woman to continue on unto the father. And when they fought, the son vanquished the deceiver and bound him inescapably with iron shackles. But while the deceiver was being bound beneath the waist, he wounded the son, who died soon after the deceiver was [completely] bound and sent into the lake of fire. [6] The young woman—seeing that the son of the king had died for her sake, and having become completely certain that all his claims were true—claims that he proved through his death—remained there in mourning. And on the location of his death she built a small house, and she hung in it the son's weapons in order that her espoused one, who loved her to the point of dying [for her], would never slip from her memory.

[7] Hence, when in this way she was crying out unto God from her heart, she said: "O King, my Betrothed, who could not lie, told me that you are the one who sent him and are his father and that he has no other father than you, who are God, and that he has a virgin-mother in the likeness of my nature. If, then, you who are God willed that this son be born of a virgin without [the contribution of] a male seed and that he die for me: cause him to live for my sake, since he has led me in vain from the desert if I am not to enjoy him." Etc. [8] And, accordingly, the son was resurrected by the father, [and] the bride still clings to him, always cherishing the memory of the faithfulness of his death. For her love is nourished by the food of her memory of his death, and she is kept incorrupt and chaste by [the memory of] this supreme faithfulness. But although the bridegroom is alive, he is with the father. And just as he is from the father and the virgin, so also he begets from his virgin bride, whom he loves, co-heirs—[begets them] through the spirit-of-his-love, which his bride has, even as by the father, who is in Heaven, [and] through the spirit of the father's love he himself was

begotten in this world from a virgin.

[9] Now, the bride sends to the bridegroom, every day, (*a*) the fruit of her womb and (*b*) her co-heirs, in and through whom she progressively ascends unto the kingdom. She adorns them in conformity with the weapons of her bridegroom and his likeness, so that they may be pleasing to the father and may be introduced into the kingdom bearing weapons of triumph and the signs of a victor and of protection. Hence, this sign [of victory] is placed on those who are about to die— [placed] before their eyes (Exodus 12: ... that both door-posts be dabbed with blood, etc.).[2] This is done until the number of the elect will have been fulfilled.[3] This number is analogous to the parts of the bride's body, in which resides the bridegroom's spirit, so that the bride belongs only to the bridegroom [and] so that the bride's members are her members in such a way that by means of the bride, who is the bridegroom's, her members are also the bridegroom's members.

The foregoing is a likeness of Christ and the Church, His Bride.[4]

PART TWO
The Illustration regarding Christ and the Devout Soul Is Explained

[10] From this illustration, O Devout Soul (you who are the bride of Christ), you ought to take note of the fact that your Bridegroom—God and man—was sent into this world by the Father in order to disclose to you the truth concerning your origin. [He was sent in order to] teach you that you are in the hand of the Deceiver [and] in order to make faith known to you, and to inflame your desire of arriving at the Kingdom of life, for which Kingdom the King of Life adopted you. And [you ought to notice the following: viz.,] that for the purpose of your knowing how much your Father in Heaven loved you, He gave His only-begotten Son to you as your Bridegroom; and in order that the Son could be your Bridegroom and that you could love Him, the Father willed that the Son be born of a virgin and be altogether lovely. And He charged this same Son with loving you very tenderly and with attracting you through love into coming to the Father by following Him.

[11] The Son, obedient to the Father in all respects, came and instructed you concerning the truth. He disclosed for what reason you were adopted. And because it was difficult for you to believe, He made Himself your physician and your very friendly servant so that because of wondrous healings you would begin to love Him and to believe. And it came to pass that with difficulty He overcame your reluctance, so that you recognized that He loves you. But when you saw that He loves you, you doubted whether He might be feigning. For you saw yourself as shameful because of your associations with the Seducer and as one-eyed and as infirm, etc. Therefore, in order that you might be assured of His love, He took upon Himself these same infirmities in order to console you. And because love now began to be embraced [by you], the Son willed to be obedient to the Father and to draw you by the cord of love into following [Him], in accordance with the [text]: "Draw me. We will run after you …," etc.[5]

[**12**] And so, He brought you with Him by way of the washing-of-water through which one exits from the insular restriction of this world. But the Deceiver—he who is a very envious evil spirit—followed you and held you back so that you could not follow your Bridegroom. Hence, in order that the Bridegroom would be obedient to the Father and would show by experience that everything that He preached to you was true, then although He knew that at the hands of the Prince of the world, the lying Deceiver, He would suffer many things—even unto death on the Cross[6]—He engaged in combat with him. He conquered by dying, by offering Himself for you with tears and with a loud cry.[7] This voice was heard in Heaven. (Apocalypse 12: "I heard a loud voice …," etc. "Now is salvation made …," etc.)[8]

PART THREE
The Christian Soul Is Aroused unto Contemplating the Death of Christ, unto Sharing in His Suffering, and unto Mortification [of the Flesh]

[**13**] Therefore, O Christian Soul, if today you will hear His voice, do not harden your heart.[9] For for your sake He cries out, and because of His reverence He is heard.[10] Consider carefully that He engaged in combat for your sake, that He fought very faithfully and very steadfastly, that in order to conquer He died, etc. Consider who this Bridegroom of yours is; consider that He is altogether lovely, wise, virtuous, noble, etc., [and] that the anniversary of His death must be celebrated. Note that the memory of His death is to be unceasingly cherished in your heart, for you will not find another such spouse. See how it is that chaste women mourn their [deceased] virtuous spouses and how it is that after the mourning they forget [them] with shameless ease, etc. [**14**] Arouse yourself to compassion when you hear that the Lord, your Bridegroom, suffers. Which handmaiden—who if she saw

her noble mistress laboring—would not be motivated to labor similarly?[11] Etc. If Christ, who was sent for your sake, was not able to return to the Father unless He suffered (as [we read] at the end of Luke),[12] then consider that, rightly, you ought to suffer in order to enter into the House, or Kingdom, into which you were not born. What a shame it is [for you] to return to the Lord, who is pierced with mortal wounds from war, and [for you], being an unwounded soldier, to wish to co-reign with Him. Paul, reflecting on these matters (Philippians 3), wanted to have a co-partnership-of-suffering with Christ,[13] etc.: if we suffer with [Him], we shall reign with [Him].[14]

[**15**] Therefore, a soldier of Christ[15] ought to lacerate his own flesh and [to do] this by mortifying the desires of his flesh, etc. For if you, who are infirm and of this world, wish to be of sound body, then you must excise the rotten segments of flesh, etc. For [even] a thief allows his hands to be cut off rather than to lose his life. Therefore, a Christian ought to have endurance amid all hardships. He ought to nourish this endurance with the bread of the memory of Christ's endurance amid tribulations, poverty, disdain, etc.

NOTES TO *Paradigma Filiae Adoptivae*

* Sermon LIII.
1. This day was Good Friday.
2. Exodus 12:7.
3. Cf. Apocalypse (Revelation) 21:27.
4. The Canticle of Canticles (Song of Solomon) is often thought of as depicting the spousal relationship between Christ and the Church. In the parable above, Nicholas uses the word *"amor"* for *love*.
5. Canticle of Canticles 1:3 (Song of Solomon 1:4).
6. Philippians 2:8.
7. Hebrews 5:7.
8. Apocalypse (Revelation) 12:10.
9. Hebrews 3:7-8. Psalms 94:8 (95:7-8).
10. Hebrews 5:7.
11. Cf. II Timothy 2:3.
12. Luke 24:26.
13. Philippians 3:10.
14. Romans 8:17.
15. II Timothy 2:3.

Tu Es Christus*
("You Are the Christ.")[1]
[August 1 (?), 1454; preached in Brixen][2]

[1] "Simon Peter said: You are the Christ, the Son of the Living God" (Matthew 16).

Everyone who acknowledges that Christ is the Son of the Living God is called Peter. Peter's faith is the Church's faith. Every believer is within the Church, which was established upon Peter.[3] We must take note of how it is that the Church is in Peter. For, to begin with, there is one faith, viz., that Christ is the Son of God; in this faith believers are united as one Church. Peter is the primary believer, the primary priest, the primary high-priest, and the chief of the Apostles. Whatever the Church has, in its unfoldedness, is found in Peter antecedently and in an enfolded way. (As regards this topic, see elsewhere.)[4]

[2] Consider carefully that in the Gospel the following is said: Jesus (who fed 5,000 people from 5 loaves of bread and fed 4,000 from 7 loaves)[5] instructed His disciples to beware of the leaven of the Pharisees[6] (i.e., of their teaching, which He calls leaven). Thereafter, coming into Caesarea Philippi, He asked His disciples: "Who do men say that the Son of Man is?"[7] Christ had previously done miracles and had previously warned that [the Disciples] should beware of the teaching of the Pharisees. And subsequently He posed His question—not as one who was ignorant but as one who wanted to hear Peter's confession [of faith]. He began [by asking about the belief of] others; and then He came [to asking about the belief of] the Apostles. Accordingly, the text indicates that [the Apostles] replied as follows: "Some [say that You are] John the Baptist. Others [say that You are] Elijah. Still others, [that You are] Jeremias or one of the prophets." Notice that these [others] understood Him to be the Son of man. But why does He call Himself Son of man? Be aware that He wanted to bring them to the place that the Son of man would be recognized [by them] to be the Son of the Living God. He is not called the Son of some father, as Simon is named "Bar Jona." For although He was the Son of man, nevertheless He was without a father who was a man. And in this regard you know from elsewhere[8] that the reason He did not have a father on earth was in order to be the Brother of all those who with Him would have the same Father in Heaven. Accordingly, He says elsewhere: "He

who does the will of my Father, he is my [brother and my sister and my mother]."[9] This doing of [the Father's] will is the having of the Father as one's own Father.

[3] Likewise, be aware that in Christ there are seen enfoldedly and unitedly all the things that in all the saints are seen separately and partially. For example, by virtue of the holiness of [Christ's] life, John the Baptist seemed [to some] to have arisen.[10] To others it seemed that in Christ there was the spirit of Elijah; but to still others, the spirit of Jeremias; to others, the spirit of some other prophet. Infer therefrom that the spirit of Christ enfolded the virtue of all the saints. Therefore, after Jesus heard the Apostles reporting about others, He asked them the question: "Who do you say that I am?" It was as if He were to say: "Some judge me, insofar as I am human, to have a spirit like that of other human beings. Nevertheless, they cannot find any of the saints to whom to liken me. Hence, what judgment do you have of me?—you who have been with me from the beginning and who have heard me not in an intermittent way as have others but continually. Moreover, I have revealed profound mysteries to you but not to others." Thereupon, Simon Peter, replying, said: "You are the Christ, the Son of the Living God." The *Disciples* had been asked; but the *chief Apostle* answered, as being their spokesman and their leader, etc. Consider how great and divine and how clear this answer was: [viz.,] the declaring to be the Son of God Him who calls Himself, and acknowledges Himself to be, the Son of man—Him whom all [other] men regard (not withstanding His miraculous works) as purely a man, though a man like the prophets!

[4] Likewise, [consider] that the one who professes that Christ is the Son of God is blessed. For this [professing] cannot occur apart from the Father's being revealed. "No one comes to me unless my Father draws him," etc.[11] For the revealing of the Father occurs only when the Father, whom we say to be God, reveals Himself as Father. And this [revealing] can occur only in and through the Son's being revealed [as Son of God]. As Christ replied to Philip, who asked to be shown the Father: "He who sees me sees the Father also."[12] For the Son cannot be seen unless the Father is seen in Him, since the Son is the Son of the Father. Nor can the Father be seen except in the Son—as Christ says elsewhere[13] that no one sees God except the Son and him to whom the Son reveals [the Father]. Just as the Father reveals the Son, so too the Son reveals the Father. But you might ask: "In and

through whom is the revelation made?" I reply: "In and through the Holy Spirit." For when someone reveals the secrets of his heart, i.e., reveals himself, he speaks. But speech makes someone manifest only in and through a spirit of truth. Otherwise, if there were lacking a spirit-of-understanding infusing itself into [another's] rational soul, you would be speaking to someone ignorant and deaf.

[5] Furthermore, note that the head of the Church [viz., Peter] reveals to the Church those things which the Heavenly Father reveals to him above flesh and blood.[14] For of himself [Peter] can speak of human things; but in him the Spirit of the Father speaks of divine things. As Christ says: "You [Disciples] are not the ones who speak; rather, it is the Spirit of your Father who speaks in you."[15] And this is true of the Apostles and of those sent by God (as the successors of the Apostles are supposed to be). For when Christ spoke of Heavenly things, He stated that the words were of His Father, who is in Heaven [and] who spoke in Him as one who sends [an envoy speaks] in and through the envoy, or apostle. What ought all preachers to speak except the words of the bishop who is supposed to send them? What [ought] all bishops [to speak] except the words of Peter's successor [viz., the pope], who sends them? What [ought] Peter's successor [to speak] except the words of Christ, who sends him? What [ought] Christ [to speak] except the words of God the Father? Hence, every word in the Church is nothing but the word of God. And he who speaks not the words of God but his own words is not in God's Church (in which there is only God's word and spirit, enlivening the intellect) but is a schismatic and a heretic and a divider. (Satan, the Divider, is the father of a lie;[16] Christ is Truth.[17]) Hence, [those who are divisive and schismatic] are not of Christ's Church but are of "the assembly of the evil spirit" (and [this assembly] is called the assembly of the wicked.[18]). And Paul says that such individuals adulterate the word of God.[19]

NOTES TO *Tu Es Christus*

* Sermon CLXII.
1. Matthew 16:16.
2. This was the feast-day of St. Peter.
3. Matthew 16:18.
4. Sermons CLX and XCVI.
5. Matthew 16:9-10.
6. Matthew 16:6.
7. Matthew 16:13.
8. E. g., Sermon XXII (**37-38**).
9. Matthew 12:50.
10. I. e., Christ seemed to be John the Baptist, who was presumed to have arisen.
11. John 6:44 (not an exact quotation).
12. John 14:8-9.
13. Matthew 11:27.
14. Matthew 16:17: "And Jesus, answering, said to him: Blessed are you, Simon Bar-Jona; for flesh and blood has not revealed it to you but, rather, my Father who is in Heaven."
15. Matthew 10:20.
16. John 8:44.
17. John 14:6. I John 5:6.
18. Psalms 25:5 (26:5).
19. II Corinthians 2:17.

Dominabuntur Populis*
("They Shall Rule over People ....")[1]
[October 28, 1456; preached in Brixen][2]

[1] "They shall rule over people, and their Lord shall reign forever" (Wisdom 3 and in the office of the mass of the Apostles).

I say that those who are signed with the Cross shall rule over the peoples of the Turkish army—an army gathered from the many peoples of the Tartars, Saracens, and apostate Christians. And the Lord—i.e., Christ crucified—shall reign forever over those who are signed by the Cross. For every power that is opposed to Christ will be eliminated. For it will be necessary that all things be subject to Him. Christ's Father, our God, has given all kingdoms to Him; however, Christ did not yet [during His earthly sojourn] have complete possession, but He will have it before the end of the world.

[2] Let us take up the text that is before us, from which text we have drawn our theme-topic, and let us see who are the victors who shall be crowned. The souls of the just, says [the text],[3] are in God's Hands, and the torment of death does not touch them. First of all, take note of the text, [which indicates] that the virtue of justice makes men just and releases souls from contact with the torment of death, for the souls of the just are in God's Hand. One is just through justice; only through justice is he-who-is-just that which he is. For apart from justice it is not possible to be just, even as apart from whiteness it is not [possible to be] white. Therefore, justice is the Hand of God; for the soul of the just man is in justice—i.e., is in God's Hand, or Power. [3] There is one Absolute Justice, which saves all who are just. There is one Hand of the Almighty;[4] it conserves in immortality all who are just. For what is the Hand of God except immortality? Therefore, a soul that is just dwells amid immortality; for the just shall live forever,[5] because the torment of death cannot touch them. O how splendid is that Power which keeps the soul free from all corruption!

[4] Accordingly, every mortal sin is opposed to justice. Justice is life. As long as the life of the soul is present in the body, the body does not putrefy; and justice is present in the soul as life is present in the body. When a thing is as it ought to be, it exists justly. (If someone builds a house by doing all that is specified in the plans for the house, he is said to have constructed the house rightly and justly.) Therefore,

the rational soul is called *just* when it is as it ought to be; for, indeed, reason lives within that soul, and the soul does not turn away from reason because of whatsoever horrible things. [5] Courage is present within justice, and vice versa. For justice enfolds within itself all the other virtues. Nothing is a virtue unless justice determines it to be a virtue. Justice says that one who is stationed in the line of battle ought to be courageous. Hence, courage has from justice the fact that it is a virtue. Similarly, self-control, gentleness, and the other virtues [owe to justice their being virtues]. All the virtues are immortal because justice, in and through which they exist, is immortal.[6]

[6] We say that justice distributes to each thing that which is that thing's own.[7] Since God, who gives all things, *is* Justice, He distributes all things in justice. (His Goodness and Being are the same thing as His Justice. For as because of the fact that He is good He imparts Himself, so because of the fact that He is just, He distributes being to each thing.) Justice in number, weight, and measure[8] is envisioned [in our text]. Intellectual justice is a living set of balance-scales. Only man, through his intellect, invents just weights-and-measures of things by means of scales. Therefore, the intellect is a judge, or a living set of balance-scales.

[7] If we consider the place and the site of things, we marvel at the divine balance-scales, or the divine justice, which gave to each thing that thing's own place. The fact that earth is heavy and that fire is light is due to justice. Therefore, earth rests content with the fact that it is earth, because it has this [condition] from justice. The situation is similar with respect to all creatures. Hence, justice makes to be content. When there are disputes, justice settles them, because in no respect can any thing seek more than the justice that is due it. The rational soul is rational owing to justice, even as earth is earth owing to justice. Absolute distributive justice, which distributes form, and conformity to form, also distributes—to reason—*freedom*.[9] [8] It is *just* that intellectual substance is free. In every created thing there is weight, through which it is borne to its own place—as, in the case of fire, lightness leads to an ethereal location. And when a creature is thus borne by its own weight, it claims for itself a place of rest, thanks to its justice. Likewise, then, the intellectual nature has weight, through which its moveable freedom is led unto due rest. And this weight is a love of things eternal; and this [kind of love] is nothing other than a love of justice, which is eternity. Therefore, he who prefers things eter-

nal to things temporal, and prefers what is incorruptible to what is corruptible, is moved by an intellectual weight unto a place of rest—viz., unto immortality.

[9] Because God is Justice, He is the place of rest and of immortality. He is said to dwell amid immortality[10] because He is so just that He is Justice itself. It is not torment for a just man to suffer on account of justice. For this suffering constitutes his being strengthened in justice, [and] justice gives being to the just man. A soul which knows what is just can conform itself more and more to justice. Therefore, only an intellectual substance can be increased [in justice] without end. Skill is increased by continual practice; an artisan's skill is increased by the artisan's applying his craft. Similarly, the intellect has its own intellectual justice, which is continually perfected by just exercisings. [10] It is *just* that God, who is Truth, be believed. So he who is just lives by faith.[11] Hence, by means of faith his soul becomes more just; and, for this reason, when he works works of faith (because justice prescribes his doing so), he is strengthened in immortality. Justice prescribes that the Son of God be believed and that no teaching except the teaching that is from God can lead the soul to rest. Hereby, then, it is evident that in us justice is the weight of the intellectual nature. And through justice we draw near to faith in order that we may be justified by means of it, i.e., in order that the initial justice [of believers] may increase through just exercisings.

[11] In the son of an artisan the artisanship is present in potentiality, but it cannot become actual except by the enlightenment of him who has the artisanship in actuality. Similarly, the initial justice cannot become actualized except by means of the enlightenment of a teacher who possesses the art of justice. And so, Christ, who possessed the Art of Justice—indeed, who was that Art—came in order that those who would acknowledge Him to have, and to be, the Art of Justice and who would accept Him as their teacher would be able to increase [in justice] to the point of becoming sons of God[12]—i.e., to the point of obtaining immortality and absolute justice. For Absolute Justice is the place of rest for everyone who is just. The place of just souls is the Hand of God, or the Conserving Power of life.

[12] Consider carefully the fact that the human soul consists of its own four elements. For the soul is immaterial, [and] its elements are immaterial. For we know by experience that the human soul is an immaterial power that makes use of a fourfold movement: viz., of

desire, of anger, of reason, and of free will. And because the soul is of an intellectual nature, it suffices to direct these four movements intellectually, by intellectually moderating the impulse of each movement. Now, the moderating of the movement of desire is called *temperance*; and the moderating of the movement of anger is called *courage*; and the moderating of the movement of reason is called *prudence*;[13] and the moderating of the movement of free will is called *justice*. **[13]** Hence, the intellect is like a living fountain of a paradise—[a fountain] from which four rivers flow. And [the intellect] sets a proper measure[14] so that the four rivers that flow from it in order to water the paradise (i.e., the man) do not overflow and do not, through overflowing, do the opposite [of what they should do]. The first river, which correlates with prudence, is the river Phison (for prudence finds the right measure). And the river Gion correlates with temperance (which safeguards the proper measure). And the river Euphrates correlates with justice (which distributes [the measure]). And the river Tigris is courage (which defends [the measure]). **[14]** Pay attention to the fact that prudence is the pilot of the virtues;[15] it says "I have found the proper measure." Temperance says "I wanted this," and it safeguards it. Justice distributes to itself and to others that which temperance safeguards concerning the proper measure. And courage defends [the measure]; for many untoward events happen to the thus-distributed measure, and courage is the mode of defending the measure.

[15] The river Phison, or prudence, is discernment with regard to a knowledge of good and evil. It is a deep, long, and wide river. The depth is the memory of things past; the width is the understanding of things present; the length is the foreseeing of things future. The river Gion, or temperance with respect to sensual desires, likewise has three [components]:[16] viz., astringency, which is sober-headedness with regard to tasting; coolness, which is chasteness with respect to touching; and deliberateness, which is modesty with regard to behaving. **[16]** The river Euphrates, or justice, is the fixed disposition (*habitus*) that renders to each his own; and it has three [components]: because the river is gentle, justice is natural; because it is clear, justice is from law; because it keeps itself within its banks, justice is from custom. We say that justice applies to superiors and to equals and to inferiors. The river Tigris, or courage, is the confronting of things dangerous; and it has three [components]: viz., a stony bottom (i.e., it has confidence in confronting the disturbances of the surges); and there is patience in enduring [the surges]; and it has swiftness, which is perseverance in continuing onward.

[**17**] Our soul is seen to be a living ray of divine light. Hence, the ray—because of the strength of the light that is in it—purifies, enlightens, reconciles, strengthens.[17] In purifying, it keeps to the proper measure of temperance; in enlightening, it keeps to the proper measure of prudence; in reconciling, it keeps to the proper measure of justice; in strengthening, it keeps to the proper measure of courage. The virtues are seen to be present in the soul. They correlate with the properties of the elements:[18] temperance correlates with the decorative dryness of *earth*; prudence correlates with the clearness of *water* with respect to the intensity[19] [of light]; justice correlates with the subtlety of *air* as regards air's soothingness; courage, or steadfastness, correlates with the forcefulness of *fire* as regards fire's action. [**18**] It seems, too, that the rational soul, or the intellect, is subsequent to the First Cause but prior to what is caused. [The situation is] as if [the rational soul] were at once both caused and cause, as if the First Cause had caused it with a close likeness to itself by conferring on it the nobility of being a cause. Hence, from itself it exhibits a *material cause* when it indues itself with the fixed disposition of temperance; it exhibits a *formal cause* by putting on the fixed disposition of prudence; it exhibits a *final cause* with respect to the fixed disposition of justice; and it exhibits an *efficient cause* with respect to the fixed disposition of courage.[20]

[**19**] And note that the simplicity of the soul is so great that each virtue is in each other virtue. For when the soul puts on the fixed disposition of temperance, then [it also puts on the fixed disposition] of the other virtues. For there is no temperance apart from prudence, justice, and courage. As the virtue of prudence is not a true virtue unless it is temperate, just, and courageous, so too justice is temperate, prudent, and courageous, [and] courage is prudent, temperate, and just. For according to Gregory:[21] without prudence courage is not courage but is [only] rashness. Therefore, all the virtues are united. In this regard see Bonaventure, in his book of illuminations.[22] [**20**] Moreover, be aware that none of the virtues suffice for happiness unless an infused virtue, viz., love, is present. For as prudence is the form of the human virtues, so love forms the virtues so that they are formed with a divine form, which alone is accepted by God. Hence, justice that is not formed by love is not true and living justice but is rather an image-of-justice that falls short of justice.

[**21**] Truth alone is abiding. Therefore, he who puts on true and

living justice obtains immortality. For true virtue is divine and immortal, and it manifests immortal life. For the being of true justice does not depend on the one who is just (i.e., on the subject) as the being of whiteness does depend on the white subject, [i.e., on the white object]. And so, through the death of one who is just his soul (viz., the subject of justice) does not die; but, assuredly, if a white object is destroyed, the whiteness, which depends on a subject, [i.e., on an object], is destroyed. Likewise, it is not the case that together with a dead man, there dies his rational spirit, which does not depend on a subject; on the contrary, [its subject, the body, depends on it]. [22] Behold, because the soul[23] is capable of receiving true and perpetual justice and because it is the subject of divine justice, it is unceasing. Therefore, in order that God—who is a just Judge and who is His own Justice—might show the glory of His justice, He created the intellectual nature, which alone is capable of receiving justice. And it is necessary that the intellectual nature be the subject of unceasing justice, so that there is [in the intellectual nature] a capability for justice with regard to reward and to condemnation. Accordingly, the intellectual nature that is rewarded is rewarded with an eternal inflow of divine justice; and the intellectual nature that is damned is punished with an eternal condemnation on the part of justice.

[23] Moreover, consider that we say unfittingly that the soul is in the body. For we ought rather to say that the body is in the soul. Our text states[24] rightly that the just have seemed to the eyes of the unwise to die. These unwise men think that justice ceases to exist when the just man is dead. And note, as Paul says, that we are transformed into the same image, as by the Spirit of the Lord.[25] Hence, we are conformed to virtue in such a way that under the influence of the Lord's Spirit, or Love, (which in-forms and enlivens justice, whose garment we wear) we are strengthened in justice by a continual inflow and we always put on justice's immortality—as if justice were always elevating unto its own splendor the soul that is habituated by it. By comparison, an object always infuses into a mirror its likeness, so that the likeness is continuously produced in the mirror. And a sunbeam is continuously produced, so that in it is formed the brightness of sunlight. And so, the virtues are called flowers and fruit, as it is written: "My flowers are the fruit of honor and of riches," etc.[26] Likewise, in God, the Son is begotten today and eternally,[27] so that He is to the Father as brightness is to light and so that He is the figure of the Father's substance,[28] as says the Apostle.

[24] Next, direct your attention to the text, where it says that when the just suffer torments in the sight of men, their hope is full of immortality.[29] We read that the Machabees and others had this faith: [viz.,] that those who die for the Law's justice obtain immortality. For (in believers) justice, by means of a certain divine impulse, brings it about that those who strive for justice have hope of immortality. For how could one who dies on behalf of justice be left without a reward from justice? But there is no reward where there is no understanding; nor is there understanding without existing and living. Therefore, it is impossible that a believer who hopes for immortality should not obtain immortality from justice. (On account of justice he suffers even unto death.) The hope of those who are just is steadfast, but that of the godless will perish.

[25] Next, note that to suffer for the sake of justice is [to suffer] for the sake of a better disposition. For example, gold, in order to be made of greater value and to be made purer and of better quality and more noble, is put by a master artisan to the test of fire; for the purer the gold is, the more choice it is.[30] Therefore, he who wishes to be loved by God bears patiently his being tested, since he knows that he will display greater worthiness of being chosen. For whom God loves, He chastens.[31] Therefore, every believer who is just rejoices when the fire of tribulation comes, since he knows that he is loved by Justice, which is God. And a very good likeness is [that of] the burnt offering that is consumed as a whole by fire. And so, it is more acceptable to God than is another sacrifice of which [only] portions are burned.

[The text] adds [a statement about] how the just are endowed, because they shall shine [as the sun] …, etc.[32]

Let these points have been made thus cursorily regarding the foregoing [topic].

NOTES TO *Dominabuntur Populis*

* Sermon CCXLVIII.
1. Wisdom 3:8: "[The souls of the just] shall judge nations and rule over people; and their Lord shall reign forever."
2. This was the feast-day of St. Simon and St. Jude.
3. Wisdom 3:1.
4. II Machabees 6:26.
5. Wisdom 5:16.
6. Wisdom 1:15.
7. Cicero, *De Finibus Bonorum et Malorum*, V, 23, 67. See also Augustine's *De Libero Arbitrio*, I, 13, 27 (*PL* 32:1235).

In the two sentences that follow in Cusa's Latin text above (viz., at **6**:2-6 of the printed edition) I have discretionarily repunctuated the printed text (as is inferable from my translation). Furthermore, the textual note for **6**:5 should be corrected to read: **6**:4 Sicut: Sic *p*. (The correction of this note, however, has no bearing on my translation.)

8. Wisdom 11:21.
9. It is noteworthy that Nicholas speaks of *reason* as free.
10. I Timothy 6:16.
11. Romans 1:17. Habacuc (Habakkuk) 2:4.
12. See Nicholas's *De Filiatione Dei*.
13. The Latin word *"prudentia,"* itself a translation of the Greek word φρόνησις, may be here translated also as "practical wisdom." The four cardinal virtues in Classical Greek civilization were wisdom (σοφία, theoretical wisdom), temperance, courage, and justice. *Wisdom* came to include both φρόνησις and σοφία.
14. Bonaventure, *Collationes in Hexaëmeron sive Illuminationes Ecclesiae*, VI, 12 (Vol. V of *S. Bonaventurae Opera Omnia* (Quaracchi, 1891), p. 362[b]). An English translation of this passage may be found in *The Works of Bonaventure*, Vol. V: *Collations on the Six Days*, translated by José de Vinck (Paterson, NJ: St. Anthony Guild, 1970), p. 100. See also Augustine's *De Beata Vita*, IV, 32 (*PL* 32:975). Both Augustine and Cusa use *"modus"* ("proper measure") in the sense of a *mean* between extremes.
15. Bonaventure, *loc. cit.*
16. Regarding this section see Bonaventure, *Collationes in Hexaëmeron, op. cit.*, VI, 15-18 (Quaracchi edition, p. 363[a]). *Collations on the Six Days, op. cit.*, p. 102. The names of the four rivers are taken from Genesis 2:11-14.
17. See Bonaventure, *Collationes in Hexaëmeron, op. cit.*, VI, 20 (Quaracchi edition, p. 363[a]). *Collations on the Six Days, op. cit.*, p. 103.
18. Bonaventure, *Collationes in Hexaëmeron, op. cit.*, VI, 21 (Quaracchi edition, p. 363[b]). *Collations on the Six Days, op. cit.*, p. 103.
19. Here (at **17**:10) I am following Bonaventure's text, which has "cum intensione lucis" instead of Nicholas's "cum tentione". (Nicholas is here borrowing from Bonaventure.)
20. Bonaventure, *Collationes in Hexaëmeron, op. cit.*, VI, 22 (Quaracchi edition, p. 363[b]). *Collations on the Six Days, op. cit.*, pp. 103-104.

21. Gregory the Great, *Moralium Libri sive Expositio in Librum B. Job*, Book XXII, Chapter 1 (*PL* 76:212 CD).

22. Bonaventure, *Collationes in Hexaëmeron, op. cit.*, VI, 13 (Quaracchi edition, p. 362^b). *Collations on the Six Days, op. cit.*, pp. 100-101.

23. Here (at **22**:1) I am reading (with the Paris edition) "anima" in place of the manuscripts' "animam".

24. Wisdom 3:2.
25. II Corinthians 3:18.
26. Ecclesiasticus 24:23.
27. Hebrews 1:5.
28. Hebrews 1:3.
29. Wisdom 3:4.
30. See Sermon CCXLI: *Suadeo Tibi Emere a Me Aurum Ignitum et Probatum*.
31. Proverbs 3:12.
32. Matthew 13:43.

Multifarie Multisque Modis*
("On Many Occasions and in Many Ways ....")
[December 25, 1456; preached in Brixen]

[1] "On many occasions and in many ways God, who once spoke to the fathers in and through the prophets, most recently spoke to us in and through His Son, whom He has appointed Heir of all things [and] through whom He made also the world."[1]

The Apostle, wanting to explain the Scriptures to the Hebrews who were converted to faith in Christ (By means of the Scriptures they understood that the Mosaic Law is not comparable to the Christian faith), invalidated all the considerations (known to be twelve) with which the Jews were endeavoring to justify their intent to adhere to the Law of Moses. And he begins with the basic point that the Son of God, in preference to the angels, ought to be believed. And by means of the Scriptures he proves that Christ is God's Son. Hence, it is evident that he wrote this letter to Hebrews who had accepted Jesus as the Messiah, or Christ—[a belief] that is presupposed [within the letter].

[2] Now, [the Apostle] speaks profoundly when he begins [by saying] "on many occasions and in many ways ...," etc. God speaks only once; and this speaking in the different ways through which He spoke is varied. The act of speaking is an unfolding of a mental word. God's creating and His speaking are one and the same thing for Him; for "He spoke, and they were made," says the Prophet.[2] By way of illustration: in one who is writing a letter, speaking and writing so coincide that that-which-he-writes he says and that-which-he-says he writes. And because that which he writes is not other than that which he says, they are one and the same thing in substance. But in form they are different; for the form of speaking differs from the form of writing.

[3] Elsewhere I have by means of the illustration of writing presented from time to time the understanding that I have regarding a word; but there is no harm in my repeating the illustration once again for the sake of those who did not at those times hear it. So let it be the case that Aristotle wants to disclose a conclusion that he has in mind—viz., [the conclusion] that there is one Governing Principle. (This is the conclusion of his *Metaphysics*.) On many occasions and in many ways he *implicitly* articulates this conclusion by means of many premises that are in different books, book-sections, and book-chapters. But

finally he renders *explicit* that conclusion which he had in mind—[doing so] at the end, that is, of Book XII. This final, abbreviated word is a conclusion that contains within itself all that either was previously said or that can subsequently be said. In this [word] Aristotle's meaning (*mens*) is contained truly, purely, [and] openly, with fullness of perfection in every respect. He who receives this abbreviated word receives Aristotle's meaning [*mens*] into his own understanding, and [his understanding] becomes Aristotelian.

[4] Therefore, let it be the case that Aristotle stands for God and that the books of the *Metaphysics* are nations, the treatises are regions, the chapters are human beings succeeding one another in time, and the concluding word—i.e., the abbreviated word—is the man whom we call Christ. By means of this illustration Christ ought to be said to be the true Son of God. For in Him is present the Word begotten from God the Father; in this [Word] are contained fully and perfectly the [Father's] entire wisdom, mind (*mens*), intent, truth, concept (and whatever can be said in this regard). And just as one who accepts [Aristotle's] conclusion by faith has no need to trouble himself with the premises, so one who accepts Jesus as the abbreviated Word of God[3] has no need of troubling himself with legalities, which are but premising steps to this concluding [Word]. Accordingly, it is evident that the word in the Son is that which ought to be believed. And faith frees from all toil of study and enlightens the intellect—just as the conclusion enlightens, so that the intellect sees what was meant by the one speaking in and through the premises. So, then, by means of this illustration an explanation of many of the Gospels and the Epistles is apparent. For those who by faith accept the word that is in the Son receive unto themselves the mind [*mens*]-of-God,[4] which is in the Son. And so, they become Christ-like and, likewise, sons of God (analogously to what was said about [minds that become] Aristotelian).

[5] Moreover, Christ, the Son of God, is the Heir of all things[5]—even as the abbreviated word (i.e., the conclusion) "inherits" (i.e., possesses) the mind and all the mind's books, [book]-sections, and [book]-chapters. And all these things are subject to the mind insofar as it is master of them all; and they have nothing of the true and of the good unless it was given to them by the mind. And the mind precedes them all, because it is prior to all the books. And by means of the mind, and on account of it, all the books have been written; and in the mind they are that which they are. You will be able to understand, in a similar

way, how that which Paul says in Hebrews 2 is true, [viz.,] that Christ is He on account of whom all things exist and by whom all things exist.[6] And [you will be able to understand, in a similar way,] his saying that Christ is the First-begotten[7]—and all other such things.

[6] Now, if you consider carefully, [you will recognize the following]: because God created all things in order to manifest His glory, all things have their final goal only by way of Christ. For God is unknown to all except to the Son, who alone knows the Father and who with reference to Himself shows the Father to others. Thus, [Christ] said to Philip, who asked to be shown the Father: "He who sees me sees the Father," for the Father is in the Son.[8] It is as if a conclusion were to say: "he who sees me with the eye of the intellect, sees my father, viz., the intellect that begot me." For in the word the begetter of the word is seen. Therefore, the glory of God would have remained unknown if there had not been a Revealer. Thus, Christ is the Perfection of every creature and is the Door[9] by which one enters unto the vision of [God's] glory. And this is what is meant [by saying] that He opens the heavens, which were closed to all,[10] and that He has the key of David the Prophet,[11] and that He releases the seals of the closed book,[12] and all other such things.

[7] Someone might perhaps say: "As indicates John the Evangelist,[13] no one has ever seen God. And the only begotten Son of God, viz., Christ, revealed this fact. How, then, is the Invisible revealed?" I answer: To reveal God is the following: viz., [to show] that God [both] is and is not something visible. And this [pathway] is [that of] mystical theology, through which we enter negatingly into the darkness wherein God dwells—[enter] by denying of Him all that is known and all that is nameable. Accordingly, it was revealed that he who worships something visible does not worship God. Rather, since God is supposed to be worshiped, and since that which is altogether unknown cannot be worshiped, it was subsequently revealed that God, who cannot be seen by means of physical eyes and with the certainty that results from seeing, must, in order to be worshiped, be seen by the mind's faith. Therefore, it is shown how the Invisible is approached, viz., by faith. And the faith is the following: [viz.,] that Christ, the Son of God, is the Revealer of *our* God and of *His* Father. In our vision of God there is a sufficiency of happiness. As Philip said: "Show us the Father, and it suffices us."[14] (About this [point] I have often spoken [already].)

[8] You might ask: "Since God is ineffable, how is it that we name Him *true, just, good*, etc.?" I reply: We call God by those names that represent for us that toward which we are especially inclined according to the inner, invisible man. Analogously, if the eyes of all men were to name God, they would name Him perceptible Light. For they are especially inclined toward light, since from light they have directly the fact that they are eyes [that see] and since they are nourished by light, without which they do not see. And, in like manner, each thing is inclined—as toward [what is] the best [for it]—toward that from which it directly has its being, even as a child [is inclined] toward the mother from whom he exists and by whom he is nourished. And so, a child qua child has only his mother as "god". But since the inner man is inclined toward truth, justice, goodness, life, reason, knowledge, and since in all these things [it is inclined] toward the One in whom all these things are [one and] the same thing, the inner man worships this One as God. [And] it names Him by the foregoing names, which signify Him from whom the inner man exists and by whom the inner man lives and is nourished.

[9] From the aforesaid it is evident that the inner man was directly created by God, toward whom it is inclined; and it names Him by the names of its inclinations' natural desire. Hence, although God is unnameable, nevertheless the intellectual desire that is expressed by intellectual names leads the soul, by means of the names for the soul's desires, unto the Ineffable Fount of good. The situation is similar to that of a [very small] child to whom the proper name of his mother is not known. He nevertheless is directed to her by certain appellatives known naturally to him: e.g., *mothering, milk-giving, feeding, nourishing*, and the likes. By means of these [natural names] he knows his mother, whose proper name (whether, [for example], she be called Barbara or Catherine) he does not know and never will know unless it is divulged to him when he becomes competent.

[10] Moreover, note the fact that the life toward which the inner man is especially inclined is [one that is] true, intellectual, just, and good. For truth, as object of the understanding, is eternal; a similar thing holds for justice, for goodness, etc. And so, we apprehend the fact that from the natural inclination of our reason we are inclined toward that life which is present in those things that are eternal. And so, in accordance with our intellectual nature we exist directly from Eternal Life (which is God), toward which we are inclined. And

although God is beyond every nameable thing, nevertheless we ascribe to Him the names of our [intellectual] spirit's desires. For just as by all our desires we are inclined, in accordance with the inner man, only toward Him from whom we exist, so by means of all the names that signify our desires, we intend to signify only God. For the desire is directed toward the Best, than which nothing better can be thought. And we call God *that than which a better cannot be thought*[15]—or, indeed, *Him who is better than can be thought.*[16] And things that we do not desire we say to be alien to God. For example, we do not call God evil or death or weakness or malignant. Rather, we ascribe these [attributes] to God's adversary, viz., Satan.

[**11**] I have made the foregoing points in the preceding manner as a way of understanding the fact that God is doubly revealed to us—[revealed] (1) above all understanding through Christ by the light of faith and of grace and (2) by the light of nature, through the inclination of our inner man. But by the light of nature [God] is revealed to us positively, as if God were Life, Light, Goodness, etc. And by means of this revelation we speak of God and worship Him and formulate prayers [to Him]. However, the affirmations that are thus made about God are not, in a proper sense, names of God; rather, they are names for our spirit's desires. Hence, they are not as true as are negations. For example, the [negation] "God is not life" is truer than is the [affirmation] "God is Life." For the former says that God is more than life; and so, the latter says of God less than ought to be said of Him. Therefore, perfect knowledge cannot naturally be had of God by way of affirmation, which does not attain unto Him. Nor [is it had] by the mystical way of negation, which, although loftier, indicates what God is not rather than what He is and which falls short of a face-to-Face manifestation. Hence, it is necessary that revelation and grace be added to nature in order that a face-to-Face vision may be attained. This [vision] consists of a knowledge that renders one happy and fulfilled. Only Christ can impart to us—from out of the fullness of grace and of knowledge—this [revelation] that concerns a knowledge of God His Father. Here [during this lifetime it is imparted] in a dark manner[17] in and through faith; in the domain of the living[18] [i.e., in Heaven, it will be imparted] really and truly and face-to-Face.

[**12**] Therefore, there are four levels of our knowledge of God: [**the first** is], namely, *natural* [*knowledge*], which we elicit from our rational spirit's desires. [**The second** is] *mystical* [*knowledge*]. This

mode is situated in a higher light in which there is revealed to the soul that God is above everything that is expressed by the spirit's names for its desires. This level guides by means of negation, which is rife with affirmation. Because of the negation's latent rifeness with affirmation, we can name [the negation] a mystical or a hidden mode of knowledge. For example, when we say that God is unnameable, we deny of Him everything nameable, and we tacitly affirm that He exceeds all nameable things. This [mystical] mode adds to the previous mode the light of a higher revelation.

[13] Next, there is **the third level**—[that] of the manifestation of God's Face, which remained in darkness in the second mode. And [here] there is light that illumines the darkness unto which the second stage leads. And this light that illumines the darkness is the true light that, in this world, illumines the darkness of ignorance—as the light of the moon illumines the darkness of night. However, the faces of things remain darkened amid this illumination, because the light illumines (in the way it does) by means of faith and is to some extent similar to that light of the sun which illumines by way of the moon, where the sun's light is present unsteadfastly.[19] Moreover, the illumination is obscure and not bright: it does not expose to cognition a distinctly brightened face but [only] a bedarkened one. And faith waxes and wanes, as does [the crescent of] the moon.

[14] But in the steadfast, heavenly domain the Light of the Sun of Justice[20] illumines in and through itself, as in the Apocalypse John saw;[21] and [that Light] discloses the Face of God truly, as it is, without shadow and obscurity. [This knowledge] is a knowledge of God as God is. It is, furthermore, **ultimate knowledge**, which is [knowledge] of God's Quiddity. Now, God's Quiddity exceeds all measuring on the part of that knowledge which is not Quiddity itself. Therefore, since only in the case of God is the quiddity of a thing identical with the thing's knowledge, then since the Quiddity of the Infinite God is not impartible or multipliable, neither is the Knowledge that *is* His Quiddity [impartible]. Accordingly, God alone knows Himself quidditatively. [This is to say] that God alone *is* His Knowledge. And so, Paul maintained that in the domain of the living[22] [i.e., in Heaven] he would know God as he himself would be known. Although I have expounded this [topic] more deeply elsewhere, nevertheless it can be understood even now as follows: viz., that Paul will know God face-to-Face, just as Paul himself is known [face-to-face] here below. But

[he will] not [know God] according to God's inner Essence and Quiddity, because in accordance with *that*, Paul himself was not known by any others; for no man knows another's essential quiddity. Hence, face-to-Face knowledge is knowledge that satisfies desire—just as a drink satisfies one who is thirsty—even though, [in desiring God], the one who imbibes[23] does not know the quiddity of that which he is imbibing: he is satisfied that that draft is nobler than he can apprehend and that it refects better than he can conceive and that it would not satisfy him or make him happy if it were of lesser nobility.

[15] Furthermore, consider—as you have heard elsewhere—that the fact that God's Quiddity is incomprehensible is necessary for our happiness. For, as Anselm rightly says, God is better than can be thought;[24] and so, He is incomprehensible. For if God were only a good that could be thought, [i.e., comprehended to some extent], then since no such good is maximal in being and in power (because that good which exceeds thought would be greater [than this good]), this [good] would not be God, who cannot be greater. Therefore, it is evident herefrom that nothing can be better than God and that the good that is apprehended by our thought or measured by our thought is a lesser [good] than is the [good] that exceeds our thought. Hence, God is that Absolute Good that is greater than can be thought. And so, God is unknown according to His Quiddity, or Essence, for His Essence is that already-mentioned Excellent Good. And this is the Good that (as Christ taught) is predicated truly only of God, who said, "No one is good except God alone."[25]

[16] And note that this [super-excellence of God] is necessary for our happiness. For all that which is grasped by the intellect increases the intellect's desire to understand. Now, if God were grasped by the intellect, there would increase in the intellect [both] the power to understand and the desire to understand; and, [in that case], the [intellect's] power of understanding would be greater than God is understandable. Thus, God would not make [the intellect] happy or would not still its desire. Therefore, He would not be God. Now, because the intellect wants to be happy, it wants only God, who always nourishes it and who can never be deplenished, so that of His Greatness there is no end,[26] wherefore He is Infinite, Immeasurable, and Incomprehensible.

Let these points be recalled in the foregoing way because of the solemnity of [today's] feast.[27]

[17] Returning, therefore, to the text of the [Pauline] epistle [of

Hebrews], let us ponder its words. It says: *"on many occasions and in many ways God, who once spoke to the fathers in and through the prophets ...."*[28] Every articulation is an unfolding of an inner concept, or word. And because the essence of [God's] word can never be unfolded, God speaks on many occasions and in many ways—[speaks] by means of His creation—so that through such variety the simplicity of His word, as well as the fecundity of the simplicity, is better unfolded. By way of illustration: the power of a simple sunray is of inexpressible fecundity; and in order to show this fact on many occasions and in many ways, the sun shows its power in the generable things of this perceptible world. [The sun shows it] even above oppositeness when it hardens clay but melts snow and wax. Therefore, just as in the variety of the powers of the things produced from the earth we experience the inexpressible power of the sun in its ray, so through the prophets we experience the inexpressible power of God in His word.[29]

[**18**] [The story] is told of there being a certain tree in the East, i.e., in Paradise—[a tree that is] the sun's. It has within it the sun's entire power, [and] the poets write that [this tree, when addressed,] gives answers. All other trees, by means of their powers, proclaim and express—each in its own way—only the power of their god, viz., the sun. But according to the poets' account, the one tree that is the sun's own has within itself all the power [of the sun]; and its proclamation and expression embody the fullness of the power of god its father, viz., of the sun. The situation is similar with respect to God and His Son, Jesus, in whom is present the fullness of God's power. And [Jesus] is the Word who enfolds within Himself the power of—and all the words for—all other things.

[**19**] *"Most recently He spoke to us in and through His Son, whom He has appointed Heir of all things [and] through whom He also made also the world."*[30] Note [the Apostle's] saying that the Son is He whom [God] has appointed as Heir of all things. [It is] as if he were to say: "the Father's Son is the Heir of all things." Now, Christ has been appointed Heir of all things. And so, the Son is considered to be the Heir, in whose power are whatever things are the Father's. Accordingly, Christ says to the Father: "All things that are Yours are Mine."[31] But the Father has nothing that the Son does not have from the Father in conformity with eternal begottenness. Likewise, [Scripture speaks] in another way: "The earth is the Lord's and the fullness of the world ...," etc.[32] And just as the Father is Lord of all

things, so also the Son is Lord of all things, because to the Son is given all power in Heaven and on earth.[33] Furthermore, [the Scriptures say that] the Son is the Lord of all creation because He is the Firstborn of every creature.[34] For [He is] the Wisdom of the Father,[35] through which Wisdom God made also the world.

[20] Moreover, note that there are not two Lordships—[that] of the Father, who created all things, and [that] of His Wisdom, through whom He created all things.[36] Rather, [there is but] one Lordship. For just as Wisdom is of the nature of the Father, [and] just as a word is of the nature of the intellect, so the Lordship of the Son [is of the nature] of the Lordship of the Father. Thus, just as they both have one [and the same] nature, so too [they have one and the same] Lordship and Power. And because the Lordship in the Son is from the Father, [the Son] is called the Appointed Heir. By way of illustration: just as an heir has from the father the same dominion, but [has it] by way of succession, so also does the Son [of God have the same dominion]. In other words, [the Son] is appointed Heir of all things inasmuch as He is King and Lord not only of one nation but of all [nations]; for the ends of the earth are His possession.[37] Hence, Christ, who is the King of the kings of the earth, will inherit the whole earth, which will be subject to Him, acknowledging Him as King and as Son of God.

[21] And, lastly, [Christ] is Inheritor of all goods in the future world, as Paul sets forth farther along [in the Book of Hebrews].[38] For all goods, which are God's, are possessed by Christ—even as the members of the body are possessed by the spirit, which rules over the body. Christ is Inheritor of all goods; for through inheritance His mystical Body grows and is increased, so that He gathers unto Himself whatever good there is in the universe. For every rational nature that partakes of Wisdom is an inheritance of Wisdom; for [the nature] serves Wisdom and can produce the good fruits of Wisdom. Therefore, every rational spirit that is like a field in which the seed of Wisdom is present is subject to Wisdom. For [this rational spirit] is the seed of Wisdom, which has sown the field; and it is the good fruit of Wisdom, because it is the fruit of the seed. And so, Wisdom rightfully gathers unto itself the fruit of its seed. And so, those who come will come in exultation, carrying their bundles while entering into the mystical Body of Christ, i.e., into the Church Triumphant. And Christ teaches [all of] this when He explains that the Kingdom of Heaven is like a net cast into the sea, which net gathers many fish;[39] and from among them

the good ones are culled out, etc. The gathering of the good [fish] into one [batch] signifies that these good and tasty fish pass over, like tasty food, into the oneness of the body of the Church, which is composed of the gathering that is the Body of Christ.

[22] There follows [in the Book of Hebrews]: "... *who since He is the brightness of His [Father's] glory and the Figure of His substance, upholding all things by the word of His power, making purgation of sins, is seated at the right hand of His majesty on high ....*"[40] The brightness of glory is wisdom. Of what great glory Solomon was is shown by his wisdom, which was appropriated in the orderedness of his actions. The sun's brightness exhibits the glory of its splendor. And just as a sunray is from the sun's splendor and exhibits the splendor's glory (since without the ray the sun's splendor is not visible), so [a similar thing is true] of the Son of God, who, qua Wisdom of the Father, illumines. And as the ray [of the sun] is coeval with the sun, so the Wisdom [of the Father] is co-eternal with the Father and is the Figure—or Disposition or Image—of the Father's substance (even as a ray [of the sun] is an image of the solar substance). Hence, consider that the Son is the Father's natural Image, which is signified by the symbol *substance*. [The Son is] not a constructed image, which is an image not of the substance but of accidents, as a carved image or a depicted image only imitates the original by way of accidental features.

[23] "... *upholding all things by the word of His power.*" Understand this [as follows]: as by its power sunlight sustains all the things that are situated in the sun, so the Word of God sustains, by His power, all things that are in God. An emperor's word conveys the commanding power of the emperor, and his authority is manifested through his word.

"... *making purgation of sins.*" A word purges the darkness of ignorance, and it enlightens the soul. This [quoted phrase about purgation] is [significative of] removing sins and of purifying. And there is nothing other than the Word of God which can make a purgation in the soul.[41] Since the Word of God *is* God, it alone can penetrate the soul and thereby illumine [the soul], having dispelled the [soul's] darkness. By analogy, sunlight penetrates sight and expels darkness and causes sight to exist actually and causes the eye to be living, i.e., seeing.

[24] "... *He is seated at the right hand of the majesty on high.*" You can construe this [text as saying the following]: that the Son of man, who is also the Son of God, holds a position on high at the right

hand of [God's] majesty—even as a judge occupies a very eminent seat of majesty above those who are to be judged. "Right hand of majesty" signifies executing power—as if to say: 'No one can resist Him (1) whose judgment brings with it its being implemented and (2) whose judgment is a scepter of the kingdom'—about which [scepter one reads] farther down [in the Book of Hebrews].[42] Subsequently, the Apostle [Paul] declares Christ's excellence to be above [that of] all the angels, because [Christ is] the Son. As [Paul] says: "*... being made much better than the angels to the extent that He inherited a much better name than they [had]*."[43] Christ inherited the name "Son" because He is the Heir of all things and because an heir of all things is signified by the name "son". To inherit the name "Son" is to be preferred to all creatures.

[25] "*For to which one of the angels did He [viz., God] ever say "You are my Son; I have begotten You*"?[44] [The Apostle] pursues this [theme] unto the end of the letter [to the Hebrews], showing that the Scriptural texts that are found in the [Books of the] Prophets concerning the Messiah give to Christ the name "Son of God" and the name "Immortal King whose years will not fail."[45] Now, regarding that which the Prophet said in the name of God—[viz.,] "*Today I have begotten you*"[46]—I recently explained that [this] is a continuous begetting, prior to all time. If "today" and "have begotten" are considered together, they are seen prior-to-time, where the present and the past can coincide—[two modalities] that cannot coincide within time.

NOTES TO *Multifarie Multisque Modis*

* Sermon CCLVIII.
1. Hebrews 1:1-2.
2. Psalms 32:9 (33:9).
3. Romans 9:28. Cf. Sermon XXIII (38:3-4).
4. Cf. I Corinthians 2:16.
5. Hebrews 1:2.
6. Hebrews 2:10.
7. Hebrews 1:6.
8. John 14:8-10.
9. John 10:9.
10. Cf. Luke 4:25-26.
11. Apocalypse (Revelation) 3:7.
12. Apocalypse (Revelation) 5:5.
13. John 1:18.
14. John 14:8.
15. Anselm of Canterbury, *Proslogion* 2.
16. Anselm of Canterbury, *Proslogion* 15.
17. I Corinthians 13:12.
18. Psalms 114:9 (116:9).
19. Nicholas is aware that the moon reflects the light of the sun. However, he elsewhere maintains that the moon has also a light of its own. See *De Docta Ignorantia* II, 12 (165).
20. Malachias (Malachi) 4:2.
21. Apocalypse (Revelation) 21:23.
22. See the reference in n. 18 above.
23. Psalms 33:9 (34:8).
24. See the reference in n. 16 above. Unlike Nicholas, Anselm himself does not conclude that God's nature is incomprehensible in the sense of being knowable only symbolically. See my article "Nicholas of Cusa's Intellectual Relationship to Anselm of Canterbury," Chapter 3 of Peter Casarella, editor, *Cusanus: The Legacy of Learned Ignorance* (Washington, DC: The Catholic University Press of America, 2005).
25. Mark 10:18.
26. Psalms 144:3 (145:3).
27. This sermon was preached on Christmas Day.
28. Hebrews 1:1.
29. See the reference in n. 2 above.
30. Hebrews 1:2.
31. Nicholas is here alluding to John 17:10, without aiming to quote it exactly.
32. Psalms 23:1 (24:1).
33. Matthew 28:18.
34. Colossians 1:15.
35. I Corinthians 1:24.
36. Colossians 1:16.
37. Psalms 2:8.

38. Hebrews 1:8-14.
39. Matthew 13:47-48.
40. Hebrews 1:3.
41. At **23**:10 of the printed edition of the Latin text I am considering the word "per" as deleted, as does also the Paris edition.
42. Hebrews 1:8.
43. Hebrews 1:4.
44. Hebrews 1:5.
45. Cf. I Timothy 1:17. Hebrews 1:12. Psalms 101:28 (102:27).
46. Hebrews 1:5.

Puer Crescebat*
("The Child Grew ....")
[December 26, 1456; preached in Brixen]

[1] "The child grew and waxed strong, full of wisdom; and the grace of God was in Him." Luke 2 and in the Gospel-reading [for today].[1]

If you consider [the matter] rightly: the child Jesus was truly a child. For He is called a child because of His purity; for no child ever was or ever will be as pure as He was, whose father was God and whose mother was the Virgin. All things that are said of Jesus are predicated of Him truly. For example, He is called the true Light,[2] the true Vine,[3] and, likewise, a true child.[4] Because He was a child, He grew and became stronger in terms of physical strength but not in terms of wisdom (because He was full of wisdom) and not in terms of God's grace (because that [grace] was present in Him in all its fullness). [2] Nevertheless, elsewhere [in Luke] it is said that He advanced in age and in wisdom.[5] It is not the case that [in Him] the fullness of wisdom was increased in degree. The wisdom did not increase, because He, being full with true fullness, was [completely] full of wisdom. Rather, as His humanity advanced in age (i.e., as it tended toward manhood from childhood), He became of a more advanced age. It is not the case that *humanity [as such]* grew in age; it does not increase in age, because it is free of time. Rather, the individual, who is subject to time, became older.

[3] Accordingly, absolute humanity, through which every human being is a human being, does not admit of greater and lesser degrees, for it is the true substantial form. Likewise, true, absolute wisdom, which is not at all an accident, also cannot admit of greater and lesser degrees; rather, [absolute wisdom] is fullness of wisdom and is absolute maximality. However, insofar as a man partakes of wisdom by means of his intellectual nature, which is an image of wisdom, he can advance and become wiser and more capable [of receiving wisdom]. Nevertheless, he will never become Wisdom itself—even as a white thing can be made whiter, but it never becomes whiteness [itself]. [4] In Christ, therefore there is considered to be divine wisdom, which is called by the Apostle *divinity*. [The Apostle] says that this [wisdom] dwelt embodiedly in Christ.[6] That is, [it dwelt in Him] fully and perfectly with every kind of measure of length, width, and

depth[7]—according as these measures are enfolded in a body. And this is [the Wisdom] through which God made also the world;[8] and [this Wisdom] is the Word of God. From the beginning [this Wisdom] was present fully in Jesus, because Jesus is Wisdom Incarnate.

[5] It is as if someone were to consider [an instance of the element] earth to be turned into water and were to consider that in the transformation there was produced unmeltable ice. (Ice is reported to have been produced [here in Brixen] this past night.) Ice is the coldness liquefied. This coldness is united to the water in the ice in such a way that it is true coldness and is inseparable from the ice. For it is impossible that there be ice without there being coldness. By contrast, water can exist without its being in [the form of] ice; and in that case the water is also without true coldness, and one sample of water is colder than is another. [6] Now, maximal coldness, which is posited as being present in ice, is not an unfitting likeness of unfading wisdom or of an immortal and eternal nature. For coldness preserves from corruption; therefore, in itself it is stable and incorruptible. And just as the nature of water can partake variously of coldness, so too the intellectual nature, being like water, can partake variously of wisdom, which is not embodied in it and which does not indwell it essentially or incorporatedly except in the case of Jesus, in whom the intellectual nature is inseparable from true wisdom, which indwells that nature incorporatedly.

[7] Now, when we consider the human nature in Christ separably [from the wisdom]—(in the case of every man human nature can receive an increase in wisdom)—then we say that the true human being Jesus advances in wisdom, which indwells Him. Likewise, if we were to consider water separably [from coldness], we would say that it increases in coldness, although as it is present [inseparably] in ice it does not increase [in coldness]. Or possibly we say [that Jesus] advances [in wisdom] in the following sense: Just as a wise man advances in eloquence, so that he [better] expresses his wisdom to those who hear him, so the infant Jesus, later an adult, advanced [in the ability to speak], so that He [better] conveyed to us His wisdom. [8] Furthermore, consider the fact that water is not essentially cold, because warm water is also water. However, ice is seen to be essentially cold in a certain sense—not only because there can be no ice unless it is cold but also because in a certain sense [the coldness of ice] is unqualifiedly maximal and is formative of the ice, so that if there were no [coldness], there would be no ice. Understand that I am speak-

ing by way of an illustration [i.e., hypothetically]. For there is not positable any coldness that is unqualifiedly maximal in terms of its actuality and power. Therefore, although in this theoretical way ice is essentially cold, nevertheless the water of [which] the ice [is composed] is not [essentially cold].

[**9**] So let it be the case that accidental coldness is united to essential coldness in such a way that water's coldness (which by way of participation it has from absolute coldness) passes into a union with maximal and absolute coldness (in which it exists inseparably) and that [the water] becomes ice. In that case, the creature is united in a certain way to its creator, because in a certain way absolute coldness creates the coldness in water not from something else but through the infusing of its own image and likeness. [**10**] In a similar, although remote, way human reason—which is created from Absolute Reason, which is called Logos—is, in the soul of Jesus (at the time of His conception[9]), united to the Word, or Wisdom, or Absolute Reason. And by means of the soul the entire human nature [of Jesus] is united to its Creator, even as in ice the coldness of the water [is united to] its creator, viz., to absolute coldness; and the entire nature of water (which is one [and the same nature] in every instance of water) is likewise united to absolute coldness.

[**11**] And [to see] that the production of this ice is in a certain way like the begetting of Christ, pay attention to my having said about water that is—in being made from the transformation of [the element] earth—such that it is not water *before* it is ice. The ice is produced in a certain way as is Christ in the Virgin, [for] He was not a human being *before* He was united to the Word. But if it is difficult for you to envision how it is that, in the transformation of earth into water, ice is produced at the same time, then take the example of lukewarm water (which is reckoned [in an analogical way] as blood) into which there comes coldness (i.e., [into the blood there comes] a permanent nature, viz., an intellectual spirit). And by the very fact that [the water] becomes cold (i.e., [analogically, the blood] becomes a man) [the water] is formed into ice at [one and] the same time [as it becomes cold] (so that, [analogically, the blood together with the intellectual spirit] is Jesus)—as we experience if lukewarm water is exposed to the wind at this [wintry] time [of the year].

[**12**] And there is another such likeness. For just as a spirit, i.e., a wind, *from* the North (as Job 37 says)[10] or *of* the North (as [is said] here: "Arise, O north wind and come ...," etc.)[11] or from the East—[a

wind that] conveys coldness in its power—congeals the pure water of a living fount and forms by means of its infused coldness ice that cools: so the Holy Spirit—conveying in His power the Word of God, or Wisdom of God, (as [says] Job 37: "when God blows there comes frost")[12]—congealed the pure blood of the Virginal fount and by means of the infused Word of God formed Jesus in Mary, from whose womb came the ice (Job 38).[13] Similarly, the angel said to the Virgin: "The Holy Spirit shall come upon you ...," etc.[14]

[13] [Furthermore,] the text says: "And the grace of God was in Him."[15] It is as if there were said: "water of its own nature is not ice; but because there is ice, then it is a result of the power that is present in the water by grace and as a gift." Likewise, it is assuredly true that the human nature in Jesus is, by way of the intellect, united to the Word only by means of the power of the Most High—[a power] that is present in Jesus by grace and as a gift. And if you consider [the matter] carefully, [you will see that] in that unique sonship by which Jesus is the Son of God and of man, grace coincides with nature. For sonship results either from grace alone (as occurs in the case of adopted sons) or from nature alone (as occurs in the case of procreated sons) or from both grace and nature. And so, Jesus is the son of God and of man. [He is] the true natural Son of God the Father, from whom He is begotten; and [He is] the true natural son of the Virgin Mother, from whom He is begotten; and, [thus, He is] both the Son of God and of the Virgin by both nature and grace.

[14] Accordingly, the Father said: "This is my beloved Son, in whom I am well pleased."[16] [Jesus is] indeed a natural Son, because [the Father] says "my Son." [He is] a Son by adoption, because [the Father] says "in whom I am well pleased." Augustine meant something similar when he said: "Whatever befits the Son of God by nature befits the Son of man by grace."[17] For the fact that the Son of Mary is also the Son of God without confusion of the divine and the human natures is not due to nature alone. For according to nature the Son of man ought not to be the Son of God, since the nature of God is distinct from the nature of man. Nor [is that fact] due to grace alone, since in that case He who is the natural [son] of man would be only the adopted Son of God. And so, it is necessary to infer, as concerns Jesus's sonship, that nature coincides with grace inasmuch as He who is the natural Son of God and of man is also—with respect to the fact that He is in this way [i.e., naturally] a son of man—the adopted-Son-of-God, whom God anointed above His fellow-men.[18] Thus, the natural Son with

respect to His divinity was with respect to His humanity made an adopted son, viz., Blessed Jesus. And I think that if this understanding were made known to unbelievers who do not agree that a man can be God, they could be readily brought into the Catholic Faith.

[**15**] By still another illustration you may apprehend the coincidence [in Christ] of the sonship of nature and the sonship of adoption. Let it be the case that there is a king who has a fierce enemy and who has an only son. And let it be that he sends the son into the world, commanding him that, in lowliness, he put on the guise of servants and learn the art of soldiery. Then while the king's son is in the world in the guise of a servant, the adversary of the king does not cease to attack. The king, in order to repulse the adversary, causes there to be proclaimed that he will adopt as his son, and will appoint as heir of all [his possessions], anyone who conquers the adversary. The king's son, who is unrecognized by all, comes in the clothing of a servant and conquers the king's adversary. [Thereupon,] he who is also the natural son will become the adopted son, and he who was the heir by nature is also made the heir by adoption. In an analogous way, Jesus, the Son of God, put on the form of a servant,[19] and He learned service [to God] and learned to suffer (as Paul says);[20] and, at length, He merited, as a result of His triumph [through suffering], to be exalted in accordance with the promises of the Father, so that He was the Heir to all things.

[**16**] And so, Paul says that God appointed Jesus as Heir to all things.[21] Hence, consider that He who conquers the Adversary[22] is adopted as Heir; and, similarly, the victorious [believers] will be co-heirs with Christ through God's appointing. And this inheritance is by means of adoption, so that just as Christ is Heir by choice, and is Heir by grace because of His triumph (for He of whom it is written "the Lion of the tribe of Judah conquered"[23] conquered the Prince of [this] world,[24] the Prince of darkness,[25]), so too each one [of us] who conquers the power of darkness[26] (against which is our constant struggle, as says the Apostle[27]) will be crowned. And John in the Apocalypse saw what will be given to him [who overcomes]; and he describes it variously in accordance with various [kinds of] victory.[28] [**17**] But since there is but one Kingdom of God, every victor will be an heir of the Kingdom, and each [victor] will steadfastly possess the Kingdom of immortality—as if immortality were a kingdom and were given to each one who has merited to see God and has merited that [that] vision and knowledge furnish eternal life and eternal gladness. Therefore, just as one beautiful face can be seen by countless [individuals], so too the

fact that the vision of beauty furnishes gladness and delight (which are the life of the spirit) transforms the sense [of sight] of each one who sees [the beauty]. Although one [individual] sees better and more keenly than does another because on the basis of a better victory he has thus merited to see, nevertheless there is one face, or one kingdom of beauty, which is present completely in each and every [beholder]. And, analogously, the victorious [believers] will arrive at becoming sons of God by adoption.

[**18**] Yet, every adoption [of a believer] occurs by way of the adoption of Jesus; for there can be no more excellent adoption than is that which happens in the case of one's own [natural] son and which proceeds from unblemished justice. Hence, Christ says: "Have confidence. For I have overcome [the world]."[29] All who overcome overcome by means of that confidence . [They overcome] by means of confidence in Christ the King, who was anointed above his fellow-men [and] who is the Leader of an army [and] under whom, alone, all victorious [believers] serve as soldiers. He who is the Captain has handed down the rules for victory—[rules] that [Christ's] soldiers must abide by if they want to overcome. And in that case *they serve under Him*, because they obey His command and authority. Moreover, there are rules of the Gospel that promise assured victory. Thus, victory is had only through Christ, who *teaches* the way and who *shows* the way by His deeds.

[**19**] But no one can attain unto the natural sonship that is also in Jesus. For according to it He is the Only Begotten [Son][30]—He who according to sonship by adoption is the First-born [Son].[31] And keep in mind how it is that yesterday[32] I said that the Heir to all things is identical with the Son of God, who possesses all things. And I said that Christ is the Head of the Church[33] and of the army of heirs; and by His merit all who strive lawfully[34] are made co-heirs with one another. And so, [they are] also [made] sons, as says the Apostle: "if an heir, then a son."[35]

[**20**] See how it is that the Son of God assumed the form of a human being in order by this means to merit to be an heir and in order to have many brethren as co-heirs. It is as if the Son had said to the Father: 'I do not want to be Heir unless I merit to be Heir, so that I will possess the inheritance not only because of the fact that I am the Son but also on the basis of merit'; for the latter is the more noble. It does not avail for anyone to be a son unless he is tried and is proven suitable to be the king's heir. And so, [God the Son] did not assume any

other nature than a human nature, because that is the nature by means of which He could earn merit. [**21**] Therefore, He assumed a human nature as an instrument for earning merit. For in an angelic and immortal nature He could not have been faithful to the point of death[36] and could not have merited, through death, to obtain many brothers who were likewise faithful to the point of death.[37] And so, He assumed a human nature, as Paul is seen to show in Hebrews 2.[38] And this fact must be kept in mind in order that the mystery of the Incarnation may be better grasped, etc.

NOTES TO *Puer Crescebat*

* Sermon CCLIX
1. Luke 2:40.
2. John 1:9.
3. John 15:1.
4. Cf. Acts 4:27.
5. Luke 2:52.
6. Colossians 2:9. I Corinthians 1:24 and 1:30.
7. Ephesians 3:18.
8. Hebrews 1:2.
9. See Sermon XVII (**11**), where Nicholas maintains that Jesus was a complete human being from the moment of His conception. Thus, He is the smallest human being of all (*homo minimus*). In Nicholas's day the Church did not teach that *each* human being is a human being from the moment of conception. Accordingly, Nicholas sees Jesus as a special exception.
10. Job 37:9.
11. Canticle of Canticles (Song of Solomon) 4:16.
12. Job 37:10.
13. Job 38:29.
14. Luke 1:35.
15. Luke 2:40.
16. Matthew 3:17.
17. See Augustine, *In Joannis Evangelium Tractatus* 82.4 (*PL* 35:1844). Nicholas here *alludes* and is not attempting to quote Augustine exactly.
18. Psalms 44:8 (45:7).
19. Philippians 2:7.
20. Cf. Hebrews 5:8.
21. Hebrews 1:2.
22. I Peter 5:8.
23. Apocalypse (Revelation) 5:5.
24. John 12:31 and 14:30 and 16:11.
25. "… the Prince of darkness": i.e., the Devil.
26. Colossians 1:13.
27. Cf. I Corinthians 15:30-31. II Timothy 4:7-8.
28. Apocalypse (Revelation) 19:11 – 20:10.
29. John 16:33.
30. John 1:18.
31. Colossians 1:15.
32. Sermon CCLVIII (**5**:1-2).
33. Ephesians 1:22.
34. II Timothy 2:5.
35. Galatians 4:7. Romans 8:17. Nicholas here *alludes*; he is not attempting to quote exactly.
36. Philippians 2:8.
37. Apocalypse (Revelation) 2:10.
38. Hebrews 2:10-18.

Loquere et Exhortare
("Speak and Exhort....")*[1]
[January 1, 1457; preached in Brixen][2]

[1] "Speak and exhort and rebuke, with all authority." Titus 2 and in [today's] office of the mass.

Paul teaches me by means of Bishop Titus what the nature of my [ecclesiastical] office is: viz., to speak in church, to exhort, to rebuke. And the first [of these] is supposed to take place for the purpose of instructing; the second, for imitating; the third, for correcting; and they [are to be done] with all authority. Now, Paul teaches at the end of the epistle [to Titus] that he who is not corrected by means of three warnings is to be shunned as being a heathen and as being one who is excommunicated and is a heretic. Note [the word] "authority": if I am to speak, then there must be present those to whom I speak. Likewise, if I am to exhort or to rebuke, [there must be present those whom I exhort or rebuke].

[2] What, then, [is to be done] about those who despise [the admonition and the admonisher]? After the words of our theme-text Paul says: "Let no one despise you"[3] Indeed, even as he commands me to speak, to exhort, and to rebuke, with all authority, so he commands all those who are entrusted to me not to despise me when I rebuke. Hence, one who does not want to hear the word of God is seen to despise [God's word]. Contempt is a mortal sin. Therefore, if one who hears but does not obey is to be shunningly regarded as one who is excommunicated, then all the more [is] one who is unwilling to listen to admonitions and exhortations [to be shunned]. How do [such ones] presume to approach the sacrament of the Eucharist?—[I mean] those who despise acceding to the words (1) by means of which the grace of salvation is ministered and distributed to those present and (2) by means of which the nourishment of life is ministered and distributed through the living word of God. The Eucharist is a sacrament of the word. For the feeding of the spirit by faith is arrived at under the forms of bodily feeding. This [faith is faith] that the word of God is the nourishment of the life of a rational spirit. He who does not deign to receive into his rational soul the word by way of its articulation—how does he rightly believe that the Eucharist is the sacrament-of-grace of the nourishing word? [The situation] is seen to be like the following: [it is] as

if someone wanted to be a Platonist on the basis of inspecting a book of Plato's but did not deign to listen to Plato when he was speaking *vive voce*.

[**3**] I ask: how does the Eucharist become for you the living Bread[4] if you will not have been taught by the word itself? Indeed, the living word in the sermon makes the Eucharist tasty to you. The Eucharist will not become food for the rational soul except through the illumination of the word: otherwise, that delicious savor remains hidden from you and you will not know how it is that it contains all succulence.[5] One who is unknowing partakes of the succulence as a carnal man rather than as a spiritual man; for his spirit discerns nothing of it, nor will he ever be able, of himself, to discern it unless he be instructed. [The situation is] as if to someone born blind there were said when wheaten bread was presented to him: "Eat this bread and you will become exceedingly lovely and perfectly complected in countenance." The blind man would scarcely esteem these words, because he would not understand [talk about] the beauty of color. Rather, in order for him to appreciate[6] this gift, you would need to open his eyes. And he, in seeing beautiful colors and in believing that he would obtain such [a lovely complexion], would eagerly eat that bread which would furnish the coloring. Yet, of himself he would never come to this [awareness]. And unless he were enlightened [through sight], he would partake [of the wheaten bread] without the delight of the promise of color. Analogously, it is the case that the enlightenment which comes through the word is necessary for all who are to consume the sacrament of the Eucharist with delight and with inner desire and devoutness; otherwise, [i.e., apart from the enlightenment, the Eucharist] is approached without fervor—as often happens.

In the foregoing way I have set forth the foregoing points on this first day of January in order that those who seldom or never listen to the word of God may know that they, as being despisers of the word, are to be excluded from the Eucharist—as elsewhere I have quite often admonished.

[**4**] However, the Apostle says: "the grace of God our Savior has appeared ...," etc.[7] He intends that Titus instruct the people as follows: viz., that there has appeared the grace of God our Savior—[the grace] that in the subsequent chapter he calls the kindness, and the humaneness, that Christ is.[8] Herefrom you know (in conformity with today's Gospel-reading) why His name is "Jesus"—[viz.,] because He is the

Kindness of God our Savior. God is Savior, and Jesus is His Salvation. God is truthful, and Jesus is His Truth. God is gracious, and Jesus is His Graciousness. God is kind, and Jesus is His Kindness. God is wise, and Jesus is His Wisdom. God is omnipotent, and Jesus is His Omnipotence, or His Power. God is Creator, and Jesus is His Creation. God is Teacher, and Jesus is His Instruction. By way of illustration: Suppose someone were to point to a book of Plato's that contained in it Plato's complete teachings and were to say: "Plato is the teacher, and this is his teaching." Or [suppose] he were to say in pointing to a sculpture of a lyre, painstakingly produced: The lyre, in the artistic skill of the sculptor, is the instructor, and this [product] is its instruction."

[5] And, in sum, Jesus is He in whom human nature has obtained all that which it desires and all that which we attribute to God. Human nature desires Happiness, which God is. The human nature in Jesus obtained Happiness because it apprehended God. And Jesus the Son of man obtained happiness in such a way that He not only has it but also can impart it. Adam obtained a soul that was alive with a rational life, which is the happiness characteristic of this world and is the image of eternal happiness. But he did not obtain happiness in such a way that he could impart it; for he received this gift-of-reason only for himself. However, he received human animality for the purpose of imparting it, because he received a [procreatable] animal nature. [But] he did not in this way receive the image of God, or the image of Wisdom. However, Christ, the Second Adam,[9] received the nature of Wisdom, or the essence of Wisdom. [He did] not [receive] an *unimpartible* image [of Wisdom]. And so, He was made into a Spirit that enlivens all those who receive Him.[10]

[6] Moreover, consider that Paul says "kindness appeared."[11] For Jesus is the Manifestation of God, inasmuch as He is the one in whom are enfolded all the things that are God's or that can be attributed to God. [He is], as it were, the Manifestation of the vessel of God's treasure—[a vessel] that contains in itself all the things that are God's, even as the Apostle says that all the treasures of God's knowledge and wisdom are hidden in Him.[12] Therefore, Jesus is the Appearance, or Revelation, or Manifestation, of the Hidden God.[13] And note that I said that He is God's Creation; for God is the Creator, but Jesus is the Creation. For only in Jesus does the power of the Creator appear; for in Jesus the omnipotence of the Creator is revealed.

[7] God creates all things by means of Creation. But Creation is Jesus, by whom God also made the world,"[14] as a painter paints by means of the art-of-painting, which is called depiction. Therefore, let it be the case that a painter, by means of painting, passes on to one of his paintings the skill-of-painting by which he paints all things[15]—as a father, by procreating a child, passes down to him by nature the power of procreating. In an analogous way God the Father, by creating, united to this same Son of His the art-of-creating through which He created Jesus, the Son of man. So Jesus is God's true Creation, in whom the Creative Power, or Creative Art, or Creation, is "creature-fied" [i.e., is made to be a creature]—as I said recently[16] about ice that it is coldness liquefied. Jesus went forth from God [both] by way of nature and by way of art. [It was] by way of nature because from the *substance* of the Father He is the Son, is God from God; [it was] by way of art because He was *created*. And, in this way, the [Eternally] Begotten [Son of God] is *created* [as a human being], and the Natural [Son of God] is *produced* [as a human being]. Furthermore, in the Sonship of Jesus there coincides all sonship—[sonship] of nature and [sonship] of grace. Whatever is produced through an art is produced by grace, because it is produced only by means of the free will of the artisan.[17] Thus, creating is from grace. And so, the Creation in the case of Jesus, [i.e., in the case of a created human nature that is hypostatically united to the divine nature], enfolds [both] nature and art, in that [the Creation] is the Father's Art, while being also the [natural] Sonship of the Father and the [natural] sonship of the mother, [Mary].[18]

[8] Now, in order that you may understand the Apostle—to the effect (1) that through Jesus there is Resurrection unto immortality and (2) that He is the Seed through which all nations of the earth will be blessed and (3) that by nature and by grace He is the Resurrection: although quite often I have touched upon these topics, nevertheless I think it still useful to recall them [now]. Therefore, note that father Adam, in begetting a natural son, [Cain], imparted to him at the same time the power of begetting. For since Adam was mortal and could not by his own power exist always, he sought (when naturally aroused) to be renewed in and through offspring. And because they, too, were mortal as was he, their father: he passed on to these same offspring, at the time [of begetting them], the same power of begetting, so that in this way he would, because of the reoccurrences, never perish. So Adam lived in all his offspring, and he is renewed in and through every procreation. Hence, humanity—which is the same as *of Adam-ness*[19] (for

"*adama*,"[20] like "*humus*," is a word for earth)—is one [species] in all human beings. In all [human beings humanity] is from one [and the same human being]. Accordingly, in all of Adam's descendants, the [specific] humanity is not aged but is always renewed.

[**9**] Now, humanity encompasses all human beings. For example, as Adam is alive in Peter, his successor, so too are all who are enfolded in Adam. But all human beings are enfolded in Adam as in the father of all. Thus, in each human being there is present the humanity of all the human beings—[the humanity] that is enfolded in Adam. In every man descended from Adam, Paul saw "that old man," who is Adam. [It is] as if we were to say that in all vines the first vine is alive with a vegetative life. For vine-sprouts are cut off from the first vine and are planted. From them come [new] vines, and from these latter [come] still other vine-sprouts, and so on, so that there are no vines unless the first vine lives in them. Nevertheless, because of the variation in the soil and in the location and the likes, [the vines] do not [all] produce the same fruit or produce fruit that is of the same quality. We must think in an analogous way concerning human beings. Hence, the culling of seed from Adam and his descendants is the culling of a portion [of the seed] in whose power is the flesh, i.e., the carnal, or animal, life. [In its power] is not the rational life, which alone is said (in man) to be the life through which man is distinguished from other [animals].

[**10**] And so, Moses says that life was given to man through the breathing-in of a rational soul, or rational spirit.[21] And such [a soul] is not in the power of the seed and is not divisible into more than one but is an image of Eternal Wisdom. And so, the things that in a father are from [the father's] reason are not imparted to the son in procreation. Likewise, [those features] that belong to an art are [also not imparted]. For example, a grammarian does not beget a grammarian. And so, Paul calls a human being [insofar as he is descended] from Adam *animal*, because by virtue of the fact that a human being is from Adam he does not perceive the things that are of God.[22] For only the rational spirit, which is only from God, can perceive these things. But in Jesus this seed from Adam—[seed] that enfolds all men—has obtained blessing and immortality. For [in Jesus] the humanity is united to the Son of God, and the mortal son from Adam is united to the Only-Begotten Son of God.

[**11**] Moreover, consider that there is one only-begotten Son of God. For if because mortal Adam could continue to exist only through

such [procreational] renewal he begat descendants who had the power of procreating on and on, then since God is immortal, He begets only a single, immortal Son, in and through whom He embraces His own immortality[23] most delightfully, just as a father in and through his son [embraces] his own life. For a man who lives in and through his children has joy (Ecclesiasticus 25).[24] So too, our Heavenly Father—who grants to Adam reproductive power so that Adam may be glad [at the prospect of] living in and through his son—cannot be sterile, as points out Isaias.[25] Thus, He is not deprived of that eternal joy; rather, He is always begetting a Son,[26] in and through whom He embraces Himself with very delightful love. Without this delight that He takes in His knowledge of Himself, apprehension of Himself, and embrace of Himself, God would lack a fatherly state of mind and could not be utmostly happy. This Only-Begotten Son of God assumed from the Virgin Mary the humanity of Adam according to the flesh. In her are enfolded Adam and all those who are in his power. And so, the Only-Begotten Son is as the true Vine,[27] which was a sprout taken from Adam and which grew in the earth of the Blessed Virgin—[grew] into the true Vine, bearing true fruit.

[12] Now, truth is incorruptible. And so, the humanity, or *of Adam-ness*,[28] in Jesus is united to Immortality, or Son of God. Therefore, rightly, all nations of the earth (i.e., of Adam) will be blessed in Christ,[29] in whom [Christ's] humanity obtained the blessing of continuance—[continuance] not only unto the fourth and the fifth generation but forever. And from this blessing comes the resurrection of mortal man unto immortality. This [resurrection] will occur after the begetting and propagation of Adamic life ceases. For when begetting and when the renewal of humanity by way of succession and propagation cease, Jesus will come in an immortal humanity—[come] raising the dead. As a result, just as mortal humanity existed in temporal succession, [so too] thenceforth—when heavenly motion and temporal succession thus cease—[it will be] resurrected unto an immortal, steadfast life apart from procreation.

[13] And next we must consider that there is another blessing—[one] that pertains to man's rational spirit. This blessing comes by grace; through grace man's spirit, which is the image of Wisdom, is joined to its Exemplar, viz., to Eternal Wisdom. Through Eternal Wisdom [man's] spirit is made happy, and through his *spirit's* happiness, the *whole man* [is made happy]. And [this blessing] is called the

blessing of believers, the father of whom is named Abraham.[30] Similarly, the intellect in Christ is united to Eternal Wisdom, so that His humanity obtained, through this [uniting], the grace of Sonship with God. Through Sonship [Christ's humanity] was transformed into something better, and it obtained fullness of grace and of blessing—[a fullness] that suffices for all [believers]. And, thus, Christ is the one in whom are enfolded all the blessings of the sensual life that derives from Adam and of the rational life that derives from Abraham. Not through anyone else except through this Son-of-man-and-of-God can a man obtain salvation and live with [both] the life-of-man and the life-of-God according to the spirit (which is from God).

[**14**] Therefore, in and through Christ believers are transformed into sons of God. Since on the basis of Christ's merit this transformation is accomplished by the gift and grace of God, with man's merit concurring: not all [men] who shall arise will be transformed[31] so as to become, in the resurrection, Christlike. Rather, each [*believer* shall be transformed] in his own order, as he has merited[32]—first Christ, then those who are Christ's. And this transformation by means of which a believer passes into becoming a son of God through Christ is called Abraham's blessing, i.e., the blessing on the part of the father of believers.[33] For just as Adam is the father of men, so Abraham is the father of men who believe in God. Accordingly, Luke in his genealogy of our Savior calls Jesus the son of Adam, whereas Matthew [calls Him] the son of Abraham.[34] Furthermore, Abraham's blessing, which is the blessing of believers, pertains to the seed of Abraham that is present in Christ, in whom all believers obtain the blessing of resurrection together with transformation. Hence, the Apostle says: "All shall arise"—namely, Adam and all his offspring, whether before or after Abraham—"but not all shall be changed."[35] For only believers, who have hoped in the Lord, [will be changed]. They are called by Abraham's name, seeing that he was found to be so faithful as regards the sacrifice of his son [Isaac] that his seed as present in Christ rightly obtained the final and maximal blessing. Christ was prefigured in Isaac, since Christ was found to be truly faithful to, and obedient to, the Father even unto death on the Cross. By participation in Christ all believers in God—whether they be before or after Abraham—shall not only arise but also be changed. For they shall be Christlike sons of God.

[**15**] And if I rightly understand Paul, who says "all shall arise," then man will not live in the general resurrection unless Jesus [lives],

who is the Resurrection and the Life.[36] Although saints are those who do not experience corruption, nevertheless they will not any the less therefore need Christ, the First-begotten from the dead, who by His own power by which He arose causes them to pass from death unto life. And this resurrection is not due to our merit or to the merit of anyone. Rather, the Father gave all men to His Son, who is also the Son of man. And [the Son] does not allow them—because they are of the same [human] nature [as is He]—to be reduced to nothing. Instead, [He causes] them to come before His tribunal and to be judged, so that His majesty is manifested. Therefore, those who shall arise unto the judgment of condemnation will go unto punishment, according as they have merited it. But those who will arise unto eternal life will be transformed into Christlikeness; they shall be like Him, so that in them all Christ will be all things.[37] Hence, this transformation is called regeneration in Christ.[38] [It is the time] when the old man[39] crosses over into [being] a new creation that is conformed to Christ.[40]

[**16**] Furthermore, the Apostle Paul takes up—at this point and in the following chapter of the Letter [to Titus]—how it is that the foregoing [transformation] occurs. For on the basis of Christ's merit it occurs through the laver of renewal by the power of the Holy Spirit, who is given abundantly to those who receive Christ.[41] Now, those who receive Christ are described in the Letter [to Titus]. In particular, they are those who receive Christ's instruction and leave behind worldly desires and live soberly, justly, and piously in this world. [Christ], by His own blood, has redeemed these men, who are practicers of good works.[42]

Let the foregoing points have been stated in the way they have been, so that somehow you may apprehend (in accordance with today's Gospel-reading) that Christ is the True Savior and the True Jesus[43] and the True Word that encompasses all men. He encompasses *some* as those who are to be damned by a sentence of condemnation; He encompasses *others* as those who are to be mercifully rewarded by a sentence of absolution.

[**17**] Moreover, because the Father has given all things to the Son, He allows nothing to be outside [the Son] or to fall away toward nothing. All things exist in the Son; but in Him believers not only *exist* but also *live* with a rational life and *understand* truth, by which truth they are made eternally happy. Now, take note of the fact that we [believers] shall live in Christ. And this [living in Christ] is nothing

except that Christ shall live in us, [as] He says in John 14: "Because I shall live, you too shall live."[44] [It is] as if the hand were to say, "because I shall live, you, my fingers, shall live"—or as if a true vine were to say, "because I live, you, my sprouts, shall live."

[18] **At one time** Paul is seen to say that just as the life of the Father is hidden in the life of the Son, so our life [is hidden] in Jesus,[45] seeing that Jesus is Son of man, or Son of Adam. For each descendant of Adam can be named Adam, or man—these being the same thing. And Jesus is called the Son of man (as is every descendant of Adam) and is called the Last Adam.[46] For the life of Adam is hidden in Him, where it is thenceforth immortal and not able to procreate. And so, [Jesus] is called the Last Adam. And, hence, we sang today in the introit of the mass: "Unto us a child is born, and unto us a son is given."[47] Accordingly, [Jesus] is given to us as a Son, because our [Adamic] life is hidden in Him.

[19] **At another time**, Paul is seen to say that Jesus is hidden in us. [For Paul] says: "I do not live, but Christ lives in me."[48] And Christ is begotten in us by God's word, which enters through the ear and is conceived in the intellectual spirit by faith; and it grows until Christ is begotten in us. In this way Christ is hidden in Christians, whose life is hidden in Christ. [20] The word of God begets wisdom in the soul. That is, [the word] begets itself, because the word of God is the wisdom of God. The rational soul harbors this [word] as its secret [possession]—even as the Prophet hid the words of God in his heart in order that he might live.[49] And so, if you rightly consider the fact that Christ is hidden in us, it is the fact that He is conceived in the rational soul as a seed of life—[a seed conceived] by means of the word [of God], [a seed conceived] in order that [the word] may grow there [within the soul] and in order that Jesus, who is the Wisdom of God, may be begotten [in the soul]. And in Jesus, as in the offspring of our spirit,[50] there is present the hidden life of our spirit. And the soul in which there is present only God's will is referred to by Jesus as His mother (Matthew 12).[51]

[21] Moreover: "Where your treasure is, there is also your heart."[52] However, the treasure of the rational soul is only the word of God, or the wisdom of God. Our heart, i.e., our affectional life, is hidden in this treasure. And, thus, the soul is hidden in its Treasure, which, [in turn], is hidden in the soul. But in this world we cannot experience this fact. And so, the Word-made-flesh (John 14) says: "The world

does not see me, but you see me; because I live you also shall live. On that day you shall know that I am in my Father and that you are in me and that I am in you."[53] **[22]** [Jesus] had said earlier that the Son is in the Father and that the Father is in the Son.[54] And, accordingly, I understand that he in whom Jesus is invisibly hidden in this world—in him [Jesus] will be manifested on the day when hidden things shall be revealed. And we shall know Him who was hidden in us—[shall know] how it is that He is in us and that we are in Him. For as life is in the body, so [Christ] is in us; and as the body is alive by means of life, so we [are alive] in and through Him. And the Father is present in Christ as the intellect [is present] in its word and its reason. And Christ is in the Father as reason is in the intellect.[55] Indeed, he who has Jesus within himself has [also] God the Father, in Jesus, and has the saints, who are present in Jesus. And in that [believer] God and Jesus and all the saints are present. Whoever has Jesus has the Treasure-of-the-good, in which are all [goods]. And so, he is happy with utmost happiness.

[23] Perhaps someone will say:

> From the things that have been said, it seems that in the whole of human nature there is nothing but one Adam and one Christ. For what are human beings who derive from Adam except Adam-thus-unfolded-and-multiplied? As Paul states in Acts 17: from one [man] all [men] are multiplied.[56] Similarly, number derives from the power of oneness; nevertheless, in number there is only oneness that is unfolded. Hence, in all the descendants of Adam there is Adam himself as renewed; and the descendants have from Adam all that they are; and they are in him and he, in them. And this [mutual presence occurs] with respect to Adam's nature, which is of the earth and of this perceptible world; and in Hebrews 12 [Adam] is called the father of the flesh.[57]
>
> Likewise, with respect to the immaterial, intellectual nature that is present in a man ([and] without which a man is not a man), it seems that there is nothing but one Christ. For Christ is the Wisdom of God, from which Wisdom there emanates the spirit of understanding[58] that is infused into the sensory nature that is propagated from Adam. Hence, in Christ Jesus there is one wisdom, which is united to Adam's nature [and] which is unfolded in every man—just as there is one wisdom that makes all [wise men] wise by unfolding its power and imparting itself. (For example, Plato's wisdom unfolds itself and imparts itself and in this way multiplies itself in his disciples, in whom there is but one Platonic wisdom that is unfolded and multiplied.)

[24] To the foregoing [assertions] I respond [as follows]:[59] To one who seriously considers [the matter] there comes to mind that God (who is called the Creator of all) created all men in creating Adam. In Adam He created all men, because He created Adam as the father of them all. In Adam's fertility all future men are enfolded in a potential way, just as the future is enfolded in the present. However, the fertility of the species is unfolded through individuals, seeing that the species is the nature and that, considered in and of itself, is uncontracted[60] to *mode*. But in the unfolding of the fertility, [the species] becomes of a determinate mode. [It is] as if the unfolding were not possible apart from a contraction-made-determinate. This [determinate contraction] is called a mode of the nature (i.e., of the species)—just as the unfolding of oneness does not occur apart from a determinate number. Analogously, the one species, or one specific nature, that was in Adam is unfolded in his many descendants, who are of the same species. But the specific nature that was created in Adam—[created] with fertility—was sent to the earth, as Moses reports [in Genesis]. In order that on earth [the nature] might be *Adam*, it was determined to a certain mode, so that it would be "thus and so." But the "thus and so" is not impartible [to another individual] even though the *nature* that is present in that individual, and in that way, *is* imparted [to another]. By way of illustration: this particular candle is not impartible; for this one thing cannot at the same time be both one thing and more than one thing, although the fire with which the candle burns is impartible to another [candle]. Now, even as the fire that is imparted is not some other fire (even though it is received only in another candle), so too a son (to whom a father has imparted his own nature and not a different nature) is not the father but [is someone] other [than the father].

[25] Similarly, there is but one Adam, if we are referring to the species created in him; but there are many sons, [or descendants], if we are referring to the individuation, or reception, of the species. The case is similar as regards the Spirit that is from Eternal Wisdom. For there is [but] one Wisdom that is united to the humanity in Christ. This Wisdom illumines every man—even as one face that shows itself in all mirrors multiplies its appearance [*species*]. The [face] is determined in different ways in the different mirrors, which capture its image. Analogously, let it be the case that the light of a candle is, as it were, the image of the light of Wisdom and that by means of the lit candle (i.e., [symbolically speaking], by means of the man who is alive with a sensory life) that illumining light (viz., the image of Wisdom) is present. [And let it be] that, as a result, not only does the candle burn but it also enlightens itself by means of a *living* light of knowledge, so that

it knows those objects toward which it directs itself. Such a light shines forth in different ways in the different candles since it is received in different ways in the different burning [candles]. Thus, no candle shines as does another; rather, [it shines] either more dimly or more brightly [than the others]. But because the light is a living, intellectual light, then when the light is instructed, it can eliminate the dimness and the causes of its dimness. For we see that the intellect has found ways of pruning burning candles that do not shine brightly. And so, if a candle were alive with an intellectual life, it could—through Wisdom's teaching—prune away its impediments.

[26] Note, furthermore, that the rational soul is like a mirror that receives into itself the Face-of-God that is imprinted on it, as says the Prophet.[61] But every image in a material mirror is directed toward its exemplar. If you look into a mirror, your image appears. It is directed toward you, the viewer, and not at all toward anything else. And we see by a [comparative] similarity that even when the mirror is destroyed the image [still] aims to return to its exemplar and aims not to get divided into pieces but rather to return as entire. So too, the image of God in the soul does not aim to impart itself to anything else but aims to return to its Creator. And the wings of its returning are love. But if it does not return, it is because of the fact that it is held back by love of the world and is inclined [toward the world] through inordinate desire, which predominates in this world.

[27] Furthermore, consider carefully that Christ is the Father of spirits (as Paul is seen to call Him in Hebrews 12)[62] and is the Exemplar of our rational spirit, which is an image of Christ. And, hence, just as Adam, the father of the flesh, lives in and through his descendants {for as is said in Ecclesiasticus 30:[63] "The father is dead, and, as it were, is not dead; for he has left behind one who is like himself. While [the father] lived, he saw [the one to be left behind], and he rejoiced in that one; and when [the father] died, [the father] was not sorrowful"}, so the delights of Eternal Wisdom are [the delights of] being with the children of men.[64] The latter are called men because in them is present the light of Wisdom's life. For what was made was, in Him [i.e., Christ], Life; and the Life was the Light of men.[65] And this [spirit of ours] is a rational spirit, whose father is Christ Jesus, the Word of God. Accordingly, just as a father rejoices in his children,[66] so Christ [rejoices] in His spiritual children. And He loves them because they are His children; and He lives in them as their Father; and they

[live] in Him because their spirit has no place to return-to other than to its own Exemplar, because it has the Fount of its life from nowhere else than from its own Father, or Wisdom.

[**28**] Now, the world shall pass away together with its lusts, because flesh and blood shall not possess the Kingdom of everlasting life. And the old, earthly Adam will be transformed as a whole into a Heavenly Adam, because the corruptible shall put on incorruption,[67] and what is carnal shall become spiritual. And Christ shall reign. All men are in Him, and He is in all men. And by means of Him all men are in God, and God is in all men. And [by means of Christ] all the saints are in each [saint], and each [saint] is in all saints. And this [state of being] is [constitutive of] the Kingdom of peace and of joy. In the kingdom of the flesh all men, who are in Adam their father, are in each descendant of Adam, so that each man is a [determinate] mode of human-nature-as-a-whole, which in its oneness enfolds all its modes and encompasses all individual men. Similarly, in the Kingdom of the spirit each [spirit]—qua son, having in himself the Father of spirits— has, enfoldedly in and through the Father, all saints. And he, [in turn], is present in the saints, so that there is present full joy and so that the Kingdom [of the spirit] is eternal. Eye has not seen this [Kingdom], nor has ear heard [of it], nor has [a true envisioning of it] descended into the heart of man. For the things that God has prepared for those who love Him are greater than are all things sensory.[68]

NOTES TO *Loquere et Exhortare*

* Sermon CCLX.

1. Titus 2:15: "These things speak and exhort and rebuke with all authority."

2. This was the day (in the Church calendar) commemorating Christ's circumcision.

3. Titus 2:15.

4. John 6:51.

5. Wisdom 16:20.

6. Here (at **3**:16) I am reading, with mss. *D* and *L* and with the Paris edition, "magnificaret" in place of "magni faceret".

7. Titus 2:11.

8. Titus 3:4.

9. I Corinthians 15:45.

10. I Corinthians 15:45.

11. Titus 3:4.

12. Colossians 2:3.

13. Isaias (Isaiah) 45:15.

14. Hebrews 1:2. Jesus is God's "Creation" in the sense that His human nature was created and was united to the divine nature of God the Son, who is not created but is eternally begotten by the Father.

15. Nicholas elsewhere, too, uses the illustration of a portrait that is alive. See *De Mente* 13 (**147-149**).

16. Sermon CLXIX.

17. "… is produced only by means of the free will of the artisan": i.e., it is produced at the discretion of the artisan or artist.

18. Jesus, as being the God-man, has God as the Father of His uncreated divine nature; and He has Mary as the mother of His created human nature—an Adamic nature assumed from her.

19. Here (at **8**:18) I am construing the manuscripts' "adeitas" as "Adaeitas", even as one construes "Ade" as "Adae" ("of Adam").

20. The word "adama" is a Hebrew word meaning *earth*.

21. Genesis 2:7.

22. I Corinthians 2:14.

23. I Timothy 6:16.

24. Ecclesiasticus 25:10.

25. Isaias (Isaiah) 49:21.

26. Nicholas subscribes to the orthodox theological view of the eternal begottenness of God the Son from God the Father.

27. John 15:1.

28. Here (at **12**:2) I am construing "adeitas" as "Adaeitas" ("of Adam-ness" or "Adam-ness"). See n. 19 above.

29. Psalms 71:17 (72:17).

30. Galatians 3:7-8.

31. I Corinthians 15:51 (Vulgate version, whose reading differs form that of other translations of the Greek texts.)

Notes to Loquere et Exhortare

32. I Corinthians 15:23.
33. Romans 4:12.
34. Luke 3:23 and 38. Matthew 1:1.
35. I Corinthians 15:51.
36. John 11:25.
37. I Corinthians 15:28.
38. Titus 3:5.
39. Colossians 3:9-10.
40. II Corinthians 5:17.
41. Titus 3:5-6.
42. Titus 3:8.
43. The name "Jesus" means *Savior*. Matthew 1:21.
44. John 14:19.
45. Cf. John 14:10 with Colossians 3:3.
46. I Corinthians 15:45.
47. Isaias (Isaiah) 9:6.
48. Galatians 2:20. Nicholas is here *alluding*, not quoting exactly.
49. Psalms 118:11 (119:11).

50. Nicholas here, as Meister Eckhart in his *Rechtfertigungsschrift*, teaches that Christ is born in the human soul. See Rudolf Haubst, *Die Christologie des Nikolaus von Kues* (Freiburg: Herder, 1956), pp. 30-38.

51. Matthew 12:50.
52. Matthew 6:21.
53. John 14:19-20.
54. John 14:10.

55. Nicholas here (as in *De Docta Ignorantia* and elsewhere) distinguishes between *ratio* (reason) and *intellectus* (intellect). See Hermann Schnarr, *Modi essendi. Interpretationen zu den Schriften De docta ignorantia, De coniecturis und De venatione sapientiae von Nikolaus von Kues*. Münster: Aschendorff, 1973.

56. Acts 17:26.
57. Hebrews 12:9.
58. Job 20:3.

59. The following section is important because it makes clear Nicholas's Thomistic-Aristotelian position as regards the ontological status of universals.

60. Here (at **24**:10) I am reading, with mss. *D* and *L*, "incontracta" ("in" *supra lineam in D*) in place of "contracta" in V_2. The former reading is obviously correct.

61. Psalms 4:7 (4:6).
62. Hebrews 12:9.
63. Ecclesiasticus 30:4.
64. Proverbs 8:31.
65. John 1:3-4.
66. Ecclesiasticus 25:10.
67. I Corinthians 15:53.
68. I Corinthians 2:9.

Sermon CCLXXXVI: Pange, Lingua, Gloriosi Corporis Mysterium*
("Sing, O Tongue, of the Mystery of the Glorious Body.") [1]
[June 16, 1457; preached in Brixen] [2]

[1] "Sing, O tongue, of the mystery of the glorious Body and of the precious Blood that the Offspring of the noble womb, the King of the nations, shed for a ransom of the world."

I realized that something had to be said expressly about the Eucharist. And although to repeat those things which you have often heard would not be useless, nevertheless I have chosen to explain a hymn, so that our remembrance may be focused on it and so that this assuredly glorious hymn may afford me what to say. First of all, let us consider that we are conducting this celebration on the solemn[3] feast-day of the instituting of the sacrament of the Eucharist, i.e., [of the sacrament] of good grace.[4] For [the Eucharist] is a vessel of grace. Just as a gomor is a sufficient measure for manna (for [a gomor of manna] was sufficient for each individual, [according to] Exodus 16),[5] so this sacrament [of the Eucharist] contains fullness of grace that is sufficient for all. And [the sacrament] is the golden urn that contains manna (Hebrews 9) [and] that is placed within the Holy of holies. Everything that God, in His mildness, has prepared for him who is needy is grace and is contained in this sacrament. It is indeed grace; for it cannot be procured by any meritorious work or by any payment. Hence, since it is a sacrament that contains within it Christ, who is the Treasure of goodness and of all longing, it is rightly called a Eucharist.[6] About this topic consult very extensively Albert, *Summa on the Sacrament of the Eucharist* (at the beginning).[7]

[2] The soul, nourished by the flesh of Christ and satisfied by the wine of His blood, speaks to the outer man: "O you tongue belonging to the perceptible flesh, sing of the mystery of the glorious Body and of the precious Blood of Him who is present mystically in the sacrament—[the Blood] which the King of the nations (who is the Offspring of the noble womb of the Virgin Mary) has shed for a ransom of the world." [The hymn] says "mystery"—"*mistirium*" in Greek[8]—because the Blood is present in the sacrament only mystically (howbeit truly), because is not perceptible by any of the senses. Therefore, [the Blood] is exceedingly hidden. [It is] as if beneath the outward form of the wine

I were to see, with the intellectual eye, the very noble Blood—[to see it] not because it is present in the *power* of the wine (as if I were to see a baby lamb in the power of a sheep) but [because] it is *truly* and *actually* present by way of transubstantiation. As an illustration: when Christ turned water into wine:[9] if in a human way we intellectually examine the ordering, [we see that] the substance of the water was transformed into the substance of the wine before [changes in] the odor, color, taste, etc., happened to the substance. At that time [before the accidents changed], the transubstantiation would have been known by faith alone—[known] because of the fact that He who is Truth[10] would have said just that. Therefore, let it be the case that He would not have permitted the water's accidents to depart from the substance but that when the transubstantiation occurred—[occurring, though,] before, in the order of nature, the accidents of the water were corrupted and [occurring] in such a way that the accidents would have remained without corruption—the substance would have been that of wine, but [appearing] under the accidents of water. [In that case], the senses, which make inferences *a posteriori*, would deny that this [substantial change] was real. But the intellect, strengthened by faith [and] believing the word insofar as [it was that of] the Son of God, would have affirmed that the substance is that of wine [appearing] under the accidents of water.

[3] Yet, why is there in the sacrament so hidden a mystery? Surely, [it is] so that we may be taught that by faith we arrive at inner matters, even though the senses gainsay [this fact]. For outer matters, which pertain to the perceptible world, are steadfastly opposed to the things that are of faith. And so, faith has merit where experience not only fails to aid it but even opposes it. This faith overcomes the world.[11] And so, because of the merit of faith there are some things that are seen and other things that are believed [without being seen]. And when those [unseen] things are believed on the basis of the authority of the speaker, then [it is because] we believe that He who speaks is the Son of God and is that Truth which is not of this world but is from above.[12]

[4] Next, pay attention to [the passage, where [the hymn] says that [Christ's] Blood was shed for a ransom of the world. In this [passage] we must note that the merit of Christ's shedding of Blood is the payment with which the [Heavenly] meal of refection is purchased. For the shedding of the sensory life, which life is in the blood, has mer-

ited eternal life—as you know from elsewhere.[13] Moreover, note that [the one who] has shed [His Blood is] a King. A king is a public person who enfolds in his royal power all his subjects. Therefore, there is merited for all of them as much as each of them needs. [It is] as if they were all captives and were condemned to death and as if the king were to give himself over to death for the redemption of them all and as if at his ultimate departure, [i.e., at death], he instituted a sacred sign of this love. Analogous [to this sacrament] is our sacrament [of the Eucharist].

[5] There follows [in the hymn]: "Born for us [and] given to us from an intact virgin, and having dwelt in the world: He ended, in a wondrous orderedness, the time of His sojourn, [during which time] the seed of His word was sown." Christ was born for us and given to us—according as we sing: "From an intact Virgin a Child is born to us, and a Son is given to us."[14] For just as by means of divine power the virginal substance was transformed into the Son, so too by divine power the substance of the bread is transubstantiated into the Son. But the transubstantiation is marvelous because while there remains the outward form of the bread, together with those features that accompany the substance of the bread, the bread's substance passes over into the substance of the Son. However, in the case of the Virgin, the virginal substance did not keep its form but [kept only] its substantial being, or essential being. For the Son is of the same essence and humanity as His mother. Nevertheless, He has His own form, into which the virginal flesh was transformed.

NOTES TO *Pange, Lingua, Gloriosi Corporis Mysterium*

* Sermon CCLXXXVI

1. These words are from the hymn by Thomas Aquinas. See Matthew Britt, editor, *The Hymns of the Breviary and Missal* (New York: Benziger Brothers, 1948).

2. This was Thursday, the feast-day of Corpus Christi.

3. In Medieval Latin the word "sollemnia" was used sometimes as a neuter plural and sometimes as a feminine singular. I am construing it as feminine singular.

4. Etymologically, the word "eucharist" means *good* (εὐ) *grace* (χάρις).

5. Exodus 16:16-18.

6. See n. 4 above.

7. Albertus Magnus, *Liber de Sacramento Eucharistiae*.

8. Re "*mistirium*": more accurately, μυστήριον (*mysterion*).

9. John 2:1-9.

10. John 14:6.

11. I John 5:4.

12. John 8:23 and 18:36.

13. "… as you know from elsewhere": e.g., from Sermons CLXXXIIA (**6**) and CLXXXVI (**10**).

14. Note Isaias (Isaiah) 9:6.

Sermon CCXLIX: Ostendite Mihi Numisma*
("Show Me the Coin ....")[1]
[October 31, 1456; preached in Brixen]

[1] "Show me the coin" (Matthew 22 and in the Gospel-reading [for today's mass]).

You have heard frequently that the words which Christ spoke were enlivened by the Divine Spirit. For the words of Jesus are as Jesus, who appeared in the perceptible nature of human humility. Divinity, in all the fullness of its power, indwelt this nature. Thus, in the simplicity of Christ's human speech lies hidden the Divine Spirit that surpasses all understanding and from whose fullness every intellect can receive the nourishment of life; for [Christ's words] are the words of life eternal.[2] Each person, to the best of his ability, (1) can draw from the river of the Spirit-of-living-water that flows from the center of Jesus's humanity and (2) can fill his vessel, viz., his intellect's capacity. And the living water never ceases to flow, so that everyone who thirsts comes to the health-giving waters and drinks [of them]. Thus, let us suppose that in this short Gospel-reading of ours there lies hidden a treasure, and let us dig it up as best we can.

[2] To begin with: if we observe carefully, [we see that] truth and semblance contend [with each other]. On the one hand, there is the Kingdom of truth, from which the Teacher of truth came and taught the way of coming to the Kingdom.[3] On the other hand, there is the kingdom of the semblance-of-truth, from which come the Pharisees, the hypocrites, and the Scribes, who teach that the kingdom consists in the letter [of the Law], in ceremonial observances, and in shadowings [of the truth].[4] The Kingdom of truth is the Kingdom of the true God; the kingdom of the semblance [of truth] is the sophistical kingdom of this world. Now, the adversaries of Christ admit that Christ teaches the way of God in truth, and, yet, they admit it deceptively. [3] And the following is the reason why truth suffers persecution by hypocrites: viz., because they have attempted to eliminate Christ from the kingdom of semblance; for just as light by its advent expels darkness and discloses things that are hidden, so truth does to semblance [the same thing]. The Pharisees knew that if the ceremonial observances of the Law are nullified—observances which are shadow[s] and semblances—then their kingdom and belief would fail. And so, they resisted Him who

wanted to introduce truth. But they were deceived, for truth could not be eliminated even by the bodily death of Christ. Rather, by the testimony of His blood truth was exalted. For he who bears witness to the truth by his own blood—than which witness there can be none greater—teaches the truth by means of dying. Therefore, from the Gospel-reading we are taught that Christ, who is God the Father's Logos, or Word, was not able to be stymied by human reason, in spite of the fact that He suffered violence in order that truth might be exalted. Therefore, He allowed Himself to be tested [by deceitful questions] in order that the adversaries of truth might be instructed about the truth.

[4] Now, in this Gospel-passage the Savior teaches that justice is that which proceeds along the way of truth. [He teaches] this by the statement which He made when He said "Render unto Caesar the things that are Caesar's and unto God, the things that are God's."[5] Nothing other than truth is a just and right way. A true way is just and right. A true way does not lead to a false and erroneous end but leads rather to a true place of rest. Therefore, justice is the true way to God, who is the end-goal of all [that we find] desirable. He is called Truth by the intellect, which seeks the true, and He is called Goodness by the affection, which seeks only the good.

[5] True justice consists in giving to each thing that which is its own[6]—to the world that which is the world's, to God that which is God's. But what should precede justice? An examination of its assured basis! And so, the Teacher of truth said: "Show me the coin." For He was going to render a judgment about the coin. Similarly, he who is supposed to give to each what is its own ought to examine what it is that he has for distributing. [6] And because by means of a coin we are taught that an image is impressed in accordance with the plan of the minter, let us consider that we are a coin and that our nature has, as impressed on itself, an image in accordance with God's plan for us. A coin is made only by an intellect, to which a body and the instruments belonging to the body minister. A human being is made only by the Intellect that is God, to whom minister the intelligences and the heavens subject to them. Pure Intellect impresses on us only its own image, through which image we are intellectual beings. Thus, we have a life-of-reason, by virtue of the image of God. In accordance with the justice and the judgment of Christ we are supposed to render this life to God, for it is an image of God.

[7] We are taught that to the temporal world the world's own

tribute ought to be rendered temporally. For to God [we ought to render] the [rational] spirit that we have from God, [and] to the earth [we ought to render] that which we have received from Adam; to the world we ought not to render our spirit. Those render their spirit to the world who deliver up their reason to their senses, whose god is their belly.[7] Reason ought not to be subjected to the senses but ought to rule over them with discernment, even as we ought to [have mastery over] the world: we ought to eat, but with discernment; we ought to drink, but with discernment; to sleep, but with discernment; to be angry, but with discernment. For the appetite ought to be governed by law and discernment. This is the justice which gives to each thing what is its own. And he who serves justice is on the way to a peace that surpasses all understanding.[8]

[8] Let us, then, proceed to the text. It says that the Pharisees went away and took counsel [among themselves] in order to ensnare Jesus in His speech.[9] It seemed to the Pharisees that one who gives to God his tithes and first-fruits[10] ought not to give tributes to men; but to others it seemed that tributes ought to be given to the Romans because the Romans fought militarily on behalf of them all. [The Pharisees] wanted to ensnare Jesus in His speech—[so] that He would speak either against those who were zealous for keeping God's Law or against Caesar. They sent [to Him] their [disciples], together with the Herodians[11] (for Herod was the established king, who was in charge of tributes). They come to Jesus and begin with praise, lest He believe that they have come with the intent to ensnare Him in His speech. And they say: "Master, we know that You are truthful and that You teach the pathway of God in truth and that You are not concerned with [the rank of] anyone, for You do not regard [with favoritism] the person of men."[12] The following characteristics pertain to every teacher: viz., that he be truthful and teach the truth and not be a respecter of persons. [9] And note that a teacher who is Christlike ought to teach the pathway of God in truth and ought, in doing so, to fear no one. A teacher who speaks to pilgrims-on-earth qua pilgrims-on-earth ought not to busy himself with anyone except insofar as he shows [to that other person] the way-of-God in truth. For every pilgrim, since he does not have here below a lasting city,[13] tends toward God by way of the corruptible and mortal world. And he needs only one who points out the true way, so that the latter will teach [him] this way in truth. For the [human] spirit's desire aims at and seeks only the Good, which is God; but [the spirit] wanders from the pathway unless a guide

is present. Now, there is but one Teacher who comes from God and who knows the way to God. He taught this way in truth, so that all who proceed along it come, without doubt, unto God. Christ, our Teacher, taught the way by His word and His example. And one who accepts Him apprehends the way, the truth, and the life—which is God.[14] And note that Christ was willing that the tempters set forth these words (although [they did so] with the intent of deceiving) in order that they would be able to react to His answer only with bafflement.

[10] And there follows [in the text]: "Tell us, then, what seems to You to be right. Is it lawful to give tribute to Caesar or not?"[15] It is as if they were to say: 'You are not concerned with [the rank of] Caesar, since You are not one who shows favoritism of persons. However, if You say that tribute is to be given to Caesar, You seem to be one who favors his person and You seem to speak against the liberty of those who keep the [Jewish] Law.' Next comes: "Knowing their wickedness, He said: 'Why do you tempt me, you hypocrites?'"[16] Lo, the Master (who knows all things), knowing their wickedness (because they tempted Christ as to hypocrisy), names as hypocrites those whom the Gospel-writer calls Pharisees. They tempted Christ with regard to hypocrisy when they praised Him in order that, as a hypocrite, He would show Himself to be so apparently truthful that He would not worry about speaking against Caesar, thereby looking for favor with them. But He confounded them when He said: "Show me the coin of tribute." In order to confound them, He commanded to be shown a coin, so that [they would be confounded] by their reactions and by the products of their own utterances. Note the coin of tribute that was then commanded and examined: "They offered Him a denarius."[17] A denarius was a coin of tribute that enfolded, in worth and value, ten nummi.[18] [11] "And Jesus says to them: 'Whose image and inscription is this?'" Lo, a denarius of tribute was engraved with the image of him to whom tribute was due, and the inscription provided the name of, or knowledge about, the image. "They say to Him: 'Caesar's.'" There follows the judgment: "Then He says to them: 'Render, therefore, unto Caesar the things that are Caesar's and unto God the things that are God's.'" He says: "Render," because the image and the inscription showed that the denarius came from Caesar, whose image it bore. Therefore, it was Caesar's. And so, the fact that Caesar's *own* is rendered to him was just. To Caesar tribute is given when there is returned to him his denarius, which went out from him, so that it comes back to him as tribute. [Jesus] says: "... and to God the things that are

God's." For tithes and first-fruits belong to God, who gives all things, so that this portion is returned to Him. Hence, because of the tribute that is owed to Caesar there ought not to be taken away from God what is *His* own. "And hearing [this], they marveled and, leaving Him, went their ways."[19]

[12] Let us now, with an eye to our edification, return to reflecting on the Master's teaching. We have as a *thesis* that there can be no erring in judgment when there is shown that thing about which a judgment is sought—in accordance with the text "Show me the coin of tribute."

Corollary: If a losing party to a dispute has, on his own behalf, adduced all [the evidence], then he is defeated on the basis of what he [himself] has adduced. [This point] is attested to here: "And they offered [Him] a denarius."

A *further corollary*: The judgment that to each his own be rendered is a just judgment. [This point] is attested to here: "Render unto Caesar the things that are Caesar's and unto God the things that are God's."

[13] With respect to the first point [viz., the thesis], we must know that by means of a clear manifestation of the essential meaning of a name, all doubt is settled; for a thing's quiddity coincides with the truth and oneness of that thing. And so, its truth is manifested when its truth is explicated. In regard to all law, no doubt remains when there is known the quintessence of the matter with regard to which there is a question. There was a question about paying tribute. And because there could be many methods of paying tribute: when the method is restricted to monetary payment, then when the coin is exhibited, its image and inscription resolve the doubt. [14] Thus, if the question is raised as to whether it is permitted that a Christian serve the world and its prince, then doubt is immediately removed when the coin and its inscription are exhibited. For we know that we, being a coin of Christ's, bear Christ's image and inscription—as the name "Christian" teaches. Accordingly, we belong not to this world but to Christ. Suppose you are a monk and you ask whether you are permitted to dwell in community with other human beings. And you adduce in this regard certain appealing aspects of this world (as the Jews were able to adduce on their behalf the command of a prince of this world, viz., Caesar). If an arbiter asks you to show what a monk is, then the question is answered. For the text of the Council—the canon "Placuit" ([Causa]

XVI, questio 1)—says: 'It was agreed that a monk live in accordance with the etymology of his name ...,' etc.[20] If you are a canon[21] and you ask whether you are permitted to live without a rule, without restraint, according to your desire, just as before you were a canon, then bring to the fore what a canon is, and you will find that you are a regular—i.e., that you ought to live in accordance with the rules of the [Church] fathers and in accordance with the regulations of the saints [and] in all honorableness [and] under obedience—and that you ought not to mistreat person[s] or misuse things.

[**15**] If you are a presbyter and you ask how you should conduct yourself, the essential meaning of the name "presbyter" resolves the doubt, since you ought to show to others the way of salvation. If you are a rector, you ought to regulate and to see to it that there occurs nothing that is not correct. If you deviate to the right or to the left, you are not rectifying but are veering from the way that is straight. If [the several of] you are inhabitants of the state and you ask how you ought to live, I say that [you ought to live] in conformity with the essential meaning of the word "state," which indicates "a oneness of citizens." But oneness is present in concordance. Concordance is a harmony of different things—as, for instance, in a pipe-organ or in a harp. [Other examples are]: as one [bodily] member is subject to another [bodily] member and as a more perfect member suffers together with a less perfect member (as the whole body suffers with the foot if the latter is injured, and suffers even more with the eye, because the eye is still more necessary to the whole [than is the foot], ..., and so on). If you are a judge, you ask what you are supposed to do. Render a judgment! And if in rendering a judgment you are not reversed, you have acted correctly. If you are a lawyer, defend the just cause of your client. If you are a secretary and a scribe, do this job and not something else. [**16**] If you are married, do that which the essential meaning of "marriage" indicates. Every question concerning marriage is resolved through the essential meaning of the name "marriage." For marriage is a uniting together: a man and a woman are adjudged to be a couple. You, who are bound [to a spouse], are not permitted to be joined to someone other [than your spouse]; nor is your spouse [so permitted]. Just as in the marriage the husband is as *form* and *head*, so the wife is as *matter* and [*the trunk of*] *the body*.[22] Hence, although form is of more worth [than is matter] and although the head is higher [than the trunk of the body], nevertheless they could not be presumed to be able to exist without matter or a body. Etc. If you are a

ruler or a teacher, act in accordance with the name "ruler" or "teacher." For rulership is not for destruction but for orderly social interaction, even as the role of teacher is instituted for [giving] instruction. If you are an attendant, it is fitting that you attend obediently; if you are a servant, render service [obediently]. And so on.

Herefrom you know that with regard to a thing of which there is doubt, the essential meaning of its name shows the solution.

[17] Secondly comes the corollary that with a just judge a judgment is rendered from [the losing party's] own adducings [of evidence]; for we read that a denarius was proffered. With the name "denarius" there comes a perfect unfolding of the rationale. For when metal is brought forth from a mine, it is purified by fire and, at length, is engraved and imprinted. The imprint shows the quiddity and the value of the metal, so that if the metal is shown [to someone], there is no need [for him] to ask what its value is, because all things are evident from the exhibiting of the metal. If there is a question regarding a sin against the Law, and if the Ten Commandments (*decalogus sive decenarius*) are shown, all [answers] are exhibited. By comparison, if there is a question about number, and if the number ten is exhibited, then the question is resolved, because every number is unfolded from the number ten.[23] If there is a question about a sin that is against custom, and if the explication of [the meaning of] "custom" is exhibited, then there is no need of anything else. Therefore, a judge does not, in order to render a legal decision, need anything except a full exhibiting [of quiddity]. Indeed, this is the point that is being made: [viz.,] that the losing party who adduces everything is condemned by a just judge on the basis of what is adduced [by him himself]. And note that the exhibiting [of quiddity] is so effective that even in this present world with a judge who can be fooled, the judgment is safeguarded by the exhibiting. For there is no other quiddity of the thing-to-be-judged than the definition of the essential meaning of the name. Hence, the definition is manifested when the true essential meaning is unfolded. Therefore, the exhibiting [of the quiddity] teaches the judge to define.

[18] Thirdly, within the essential meaning of the name ["justice"], there comes [the theme of] distributive justice. Distributive justice gives to each thing that which is that thing's own—to Caesar the things that are Caesar's, to God, the things that are God's. For the question was about the tribute to be given to Caesar. And by means of the showing of a coin the Jews were convinced that the image and the

inscription were Caesar's and that for this reason there ought, as tribute, to be rendered to Caesar the coin of tribute, in accordance with the essential significance of the name [of the imprinted image]. (Caesar embodies the truth-of-the-image placed in the coin of tribute.) Therefore, [Jesus] judged that those things which are Caesar's are to be rendered to Caesar; and He added: "… and the things that are God's, to God." For although He was not seen to be expressly asked whether they ought to render anything to God, nevertheless He was implicitly asked this. For it seemed to the [Jews] that the descendants of Abraham should be free and should not pay tribute to a man but, in accordance with the Law, should be obligated only to God.

[19] Christ wanted to render a judgment from the fact that the Jews themselves showed that they were subject to Caesar, whose image and inscription the denarius (which was in use) displayed. Moreover, in accordance with this subjection they were obliged here on earth to pay tribute to Caesar as to their overlord, to whom tribute is due. Nevertheless, they were not for that reason free from the Law of God. For one ruler is the Heavenly Ruler, to whom obedience is owed before all else; a different ruler is the earthly ruler, who must also be obeyed in his own way. For that which was accidental[24] with regard to number, viz., Caesar's image and inscription, was of this world; but the substance of the metal was from God. If, then, because of something accidental [the Jews] were obliged to pay to Caesar a tribute of accidental things, then [we are obliged to pay] to God a tribute of substantial things. For we are obliged to render to God not only external and accidental goods but also all that we *have* from Him and all that we *are* from Him.[25]—to wit, our *being*, *living*, and *understanding*. Therefore, we know that we ought to render to the world *its own* in such a way that we do not take away from God *His own*; likewise, we ought to render to God His own in such a way that we do not subtract from what is owed to the world. Hence, you are not permitted to renounce what is necessary for life in this world; rather, you are required to give to the world that which is its own and to give to God that which is His own. And this is a primary teaching that we will be able to elicit from the Gospel-text.

[20] A second teaching is that in this Gospel-reading we are instructed that we ought to overcome the temptations of this world—[instructed] by the fact that God commands that a coin be shown to Him. For when the leaven of the Pharisees[26] (i.e., the leaven of arro-

gance and hypocrisy) assails us and we purpose to detract from the truth and to obscure it, then God (who is Truth) is tempted, as is Christ here [in the Gospel-passage]. And so, there ought to come to mind the fact that Christ commanded that a coin of tribute be shown to Him. For we are unwilling to obey the Law of God because we imagine that we are doing other works that are better or imagine that we are not obligated to this observance of the Law. But when we look to the coin, we know (because it will be detectible there) that we have been imprinted with the image of God and the inscription of Christ, and we know that we cannot escape obedience to, and observance of, [God's] Law. [**21**] Hence, we must take note of the fact that our substance is God's coin. For in accordance with the image of God we are that which we are. And for this reason the likeness in us of the Son of God—[a likeness] which is the image of the Living God—receives from God the Father (who has made us to be like the Son) the imprint of its being. And because through sin we became servants of the Prince of this world,[27] this image of ours—defiled and unrecognizable on account of the contracted rust—was cleansed and reformed by the true Image of God, [viz.,] the Son of God. The Son has redeemed us and has transferred us from this kingdom of servitude-to-sin unto His own Kingdom, in order that we may be heirs of God and joint-heirs with Christ.[28] And He has given us the inscription of freedom, so that we are His. And just as He is Christ, so we are Christians; and as He is Heir, so we are joint-heirs; and as He is the natural Son, so we are sons by adoption.

[**22**] This, then, is the coin that we must show. And we males can show ourselves in no other way than as a coin of true gold—and you females, in no other way than as a coin of pure silver. If thus we show ourselves, we render to God the things that are God's and we remit to the world what was its own. When we men are tempted, let there come to our mind what kind of men we should show ourselves to be before God's tribunal. For if our coin is not a pure coin of true gold that has a pure image of God and an inscription of Christ our Redeemer, then we shall not be rendering to God that which is God's. And for this reason we shall not be received into His eternal and incorruptible Tabernacle: [viz.,] because we do not show [ourselves to be] a coin of pure and true gold. [**23**] Now, true [gold] does not admit of anything's being admixed. So if you are a sinner or if you have added something from other, more imperfect, metals, and if you have adulterated the purity of your gold and have changed the image of the Creator into an image of

the creature[29] or have lost the inscription of Christ the Redeemer and [now] bear the inscription of the Prince of this world, to whom you have dedicated yourself: your money will be valueless in the Kingdom of God, where there can be nothing that is diminished, defiled, or corruptible. Nor will you be able to deceive God, since He is a Refining Fire.[30] For in the fire gold shows whether it is true gold. If it is true gold, it endures in the fire and seems to be turned into fire. If it is false gold, it gives off smoke, and its loveliness is transformed into blackness, and its cohesiveness is transformed into ashes.

[24] Similarly, if the temptation comes for you to purchase the Devil's merchandise with God's coin (in this case the weight of the money is diminished, or the image is destroyed), resist, lest you become defiled. But if the image on your coin becomes defiled, learn from the minters and goldsmiths how to remove the blemishes and how to make [the coin] shine anew: viz., heat it with the fire of your spirit's affliction. However, [do so] without a fire by which the metal is melted, i.e., [do so] without despair. And from that fire in which you are heated, throw yourself into the salty and corrosive water of tears, and wipe [them] away with your hands—i.e., with rigorous and vexatious works of penance such as fastings, abstinences, and so on. Then polish and dry [the coin] with soft cloths—i.e., with works of mercy—and the clear image will return, and the Devil's inscription will be blotted out, and the Savior's inscription will reappear. [25] And note that although the weight of the gold does not return with the cleansing, so that sometimes quite a bit is lacking, nevertheless if [the gold coin] is cleansed, it will be accepted in proportion to its value according to weight. But if by very effective cleansing in the fire of love the gold is caused to be made more excellent than other gold, then its brilliance makes up for [the diminished] value due to its [lost] weight. Hence, although lost virginity is irrecoverable, nevertheless by means of the fire of penance the value of the gold can be recovered, as in the case of St. Afra,[31] etc.

[26] Notice, then, that your coin remains gold; and in accordance with its value expect a measure of glory. Apocalypse 6: "... two pounds of wheat for a denarius and three times two pounds of barley for a denarius."[32] Here you have one man's denarius compared to two pounds of wheat and another's denarius compared to six pounds of barley. So too the weight-of-glory of two [persons] can be equal to the weight-of-glory of three [persons]. Therefore, you are worth as much

as you have. And unless you adduce the gold-minted coin of the King of that Kingdom, you will not be received for lodging, since another currency is not known. [**27**] There are many lodgings in the house of the Heavenly King.[33] As in a large city some lodgings are for the poor, some are for citizens, some for merchants, some for nobles, some for princes: so too *there* [in the Kingdom of Heaven] there are different quarters. For example, suppose that your coin is of true gold but that the gold is not durable and is lackluster (as are the florins from Geldern[34]). That is, suppose that apart from the fire-of-improvement you are only a true professor of Christ and only a member of the lowest order of Christ. In that case, you will be received into good lodging, where you will obtain, to full satisfaction, all things for your gold. [But] if your gold is of a better quality because it was made better through suffering and the fire of tribulation, you will be received, in your ordering, in a [correspondingly] fitting fashion. If in triumph over the flesh you have arrived as a virgin, you will present a different gold—[the gold] of noble crowns. If you are a preacher, you will likewise present gold of good quality. If you are a martyr, who because of great love have given your life, if you have improved your gold by means of fire, so that you present great and noble things, things of best gold: you will be received into the quarters for triumphant princes.

[**28**] Therefore, we must labor to accomplish, with singular strength and with profit, the task entrusted to us. [We must do so] in order to merit to enter into joy. We are profited when we direct our attention to the origin of gold—in particular, to how from black and ugly ashes hidden in the hills (i.e., in our first parents) God has brought gold to light through successive veins. [And let us note] how it is that by His wondrous graciousness He has brought to those foul ashes the fire of His love and has by the power of His omnipotence elevated us unto His own image and has granted to us to be as ones who have incorruptible gold within our rational spirit. [This rational spirit is] the image of the oneness and trineness of God, so that our one soul is memory, understanding, and will, so that we gather into ourselves God the Father (through memory), God the Son (through understanding), God the Holy Spirit (through will and love).[35] Etc.

[**29**] Next, we must see to it that we strongly preserve our gold-piece's durability and constancy amid all adversities—whether we pass through fire or through water. And, moreover, [we must preserve] the luster of our gold-piece by means of honesty (without deceit); and

[we must preserve] its malleability, so that we not be inflexible but rather be capable-of-change and be compassionate, etc. And [we must preserve our gold-piece's] weightiness by means of seriousness-of-moral-conduct and humility-of-spirit. No metal is as heavy and as without a clang as is gold. Therefore, in a "golden man" much humility is required as is also suffering without complaint.

And the foregoing [considerations] relate to males.

[**30**] But as for women,[36] who are considered as a coin of silver:[37] they ought to pay attention to the things already said about a coin of gold. For there is one [and the same] image and inscription in women as in men. And their silver-coin is not of less value than is a gold-coin; rather, it is white-gold.[38] For such very precious, very pure silver is incorruptible, solid, weighty, bright, appealing. Therefore, let women beware lest their silver-piece become mixed with quicksilver, which is unstable and continually changeable. For in that case [the coin's] solidity very readily disappears into the changeability of the quicksilver. ([See] Proverbs 7, where [you will read] about the wandering woman.)[39] [**31**] Let women beware lest they become mixed with heavy, crude, and impure lead. For a woman at leisure loses her splendor and falls into idleness and vice (just as iron, when one works by means of it in a plow, remains shiny; [but] when it is put away, it becomes soiled with rust). [Jeremias] calls these [women] *reprobate silver* (Jeremias 6: "Call lead consumed in fire reprobate silver.")[40] Let them beware of a mixture of tin, because tin has the nature of corrupting other metals, and it is not easily separated [from them]—just as when a woman mixes the preciousness of chastity with shameful licentiousness. (Isaias 1: "Your silver is turned into dross.")[41]

[**32**] Therefore, let [a woman] be busy, so that her silver may well retain its image [and] so that she may keep the image clean and pure and bright. Let her be gracious and compassionate so that the malleability of her silver not become too great amid temptations. Let her preserve well the balsam of the fragrance of a good reputation. Let her not be quarrelsome; for good silver does not offend by its clang. Let her take precautions to safeguard her silver so that it not come into contact with anyone, since it leaves black streaks.[42] If you have defiled your image, purify [yourself]—(Proverbs 25: "Take away the rust from silver and there shall come forth a pure vessel"[43])—according as was said earlier[44] about men. Do not believe that in the Kingdom of Heaven your [silver] coin has less value than does a gold coin, because

the value of both coins is the same: for in the Kingdom of Christ there is no distinction between male and female.[45]

[**33**] Note, then, (1) that there are but few coins—whether of gold or of silver—that are pure and unmixed and (2) that a good coin does not long pass through the world without becoming worse. From this [fact] accept the teaching (1) that few are elect but many are called[46] and (2) that it is scarcely possible for a human being not to defile himself if he lives in the world for very long. Hence, we have need of considerable and attentive safeguarding. Silver is white through modesty and chasteness; it is pure through innocence; it is sonorous through acceptable behavior; it preserves its good scent through conduct of good repute; it firms up the strength of jasper through helping neighbors, through graciousness, and through beneficence.

NOTES TO *Ostendite Mihi Numisma*

* Sermon CCXLIX
1. Matthew 22:19.
2. John 6:69.
3. Matthew 22:16. John 14:6.
4. Matthew 23:13-33.
5. Matthew 22:21.
6. See Sermon CCXLVIII, endnote 7.
7. Philippians 3:19.
8. Philippians 4:7. Regarding justice, see the reference in n. 7 of Sermon CCXLVIII.
9. Matthew 22:15.
10. Deuteronomy 12:6.
11. Matthew 22:16.
12. *Loc. cit.*
13. Hebrews 13:14.
14. John 14:6.
15. Matthew 22:17.
16. Matthew 22:18.
17. Matthew 22:19.
18. A nummus was a Roman coin of lesser value than a denarius (as the text above indicates).
19. Matthew 22:22.
20. Not an exact quotation. *Decretum Magistri Gratiani*, "Placuit" = Pars II, Causa XVI, Questio 1, Canon 1. [See Aemilius Friedberg, editor, *Corpus Iuris Canonici* (2nd edition, Leipzig, 1879 (Vol. I), column 761.]
21. Here the English word "canon" (Latin: *canonicus*) refers to an individual who holds the *office* of canon. In the immediately preceding sentence the English word "canon" (Latin: *canon*) refers to a regulation.
22. See Ephesians 5:23.
23. Cf. Cusa's *De Coniecturis* I, 3. See also *De Mente* 15 (158). *De Filiatione Dei* 4 (72:19-26). *Apologia* 16:25 – 17:1.
24. Here "accidental" is used in the Aristotelian sense, which contrasts *accident* with *substance*.
25. Here (at **19**:18) I am reading (with the Paris edition) "ipsius" in place of "sui".
26. Mark 8:15.
27. The Prince of this world is the Devil. Cf. John 12:31.
28. Romans 8:17.
29. Romans 1:23.
30. Malachias (malachi) 3:2. Cf. Hebrews 12:29.
31. St. Afra, born in Germany, was a sacred prostitute in the temple of Venus. She was converted to Christianity and was martyred, around 304, when she refused to sacrifice to pagan gods.
32. Apocalypse (Revelation) 6:6.

33. John 14:2.

34. Geldern is a city in Germany, in the vicinity of Düsseldorf.

35. The significates of the terms *"memoria," "intellectus,"* and *"voluntas sive amor"* are Augustine's symbolisms for the Trinity. Thinkers such as Anselm and Nicholas of Cusa borrow them from Augustine's *De Trinitate*.

36. Here (at **30**:1) I am correcting the printed edition of the Latin text, which has "quod"—whereas *Codex Vaticanus Latinus* 1245 has "quo ad", which is to be taken as "quoad".

37. See, below, sections **30** and **32** for an additional clarification that shows that Nicholas is not here minimizing the value of women (silver) in comparison with the value of men (gold).

38. Cf. the further sections indicated in n. 36 above.

39. Proverbs 7:10 ff.

40. Not an exact quotation. Jeremiah 6:29-30. Nicholas wrongly has "Jeremiah 5," which the editors of the printed edition of the Latin text correct. (See *Codex Vaticanus Latinus* 1245.)

41. Isaias (Isaiah) 1:22.

42. Silver, when worn ornamentally as in a bracelet, can leave black smudges—especially if the wearer perspires.

43. Proverbs 25:4. Not an exact quotation. The editors of the printed edition of the Latin text rightly correct Nicholas's "Proverbs 26" to "Proverbs 25".

44. See sections **24** and **29**.

45. Galatians 3:28.

46. Matthew 22:14.

Qui Me Invenerit*
("He Who Finds Me ....")
[September 8, 1458; preached in Bruneck][1]

[1] "He who finds me shall find life and shall have salvation from the Lord"[2] (Proverbs 8 and in [today's] reading of the office of the mass).

Solomon [in Proverbs 8] speaks of wisdom,[3] which he shows to have preceded all created things by virtue of the fact that all [created] things were created by means of wisdom; therefore, wisdom was prior to all [created] things and, hence, is eternal. However, he says that Wisdom was *conceived*.[4] This conceiving I understand in the way in which the intellect conceives, or begets from itself, an internal word. By way of illustration: If someone were at first to have found a *number* and by means of that number were to have numbered all things. That number would have been a conception of reason or of intellect. And because it would have existed prior to everything countable, it [itself] would not have been any of the countable things. Hence, [it would not have been] either time or an aeon or an age or a duration or a substance or a quantity or any of all things countable. For the beginning of things countable is [itself] none of all the countable things, i.e., is none of the things originated from itself.

To number, [or count], is to use reason. All well-made things are made through [the use of] reason. Thus, Solomon here says that God created all things by means of reason, or wisdom. For to weigh,[5] to measure, to determine, to order, to place—[activities] which, as regards creatures, we experience as having preceded the situating of the universe—these [activities] were first conceived of in and by reason. And when all things sprang forth into existence, they all existed with respect to a single law: viz., that heavy things are at the center, light things are at the circumference, and in-between things are in the middle. Heavy things were in [preconceiving] reason without heaviness, and light things [were there] without lightness; and [in reason] all things were nothing but reason. But when by way of creation they went out [from reason] in order to become creations, some were made to be *perceiving* creatures, others were made to be *intellectual* creatures, others to be *living* creatures, and so on. For reason so required it.

By way of illustration: In the simple conception on the part of a painter's reason there is an [envisioned] man. In this conception the foot does not exist in the way that feet exist; nor does the hand exist in the way that hands exist; instead, all [bodily members are] the one noncomposite reason. But when the man is portrayed, then although he is patterned after that immortal conception, nevertheless reason requires (1) that his head have its own distinct form [and that the head] be proportioned to the body and (2) that his foot [have its own distinct form], (3) and so on. Moreover, if the portrait is to be a good one, it must be produced by [the use of] reason, so that the wisdom and reasoning of the painter-who-has-the-perfect-artistic-skill shine forth clearly both in the image as a whole and in each part of the image.

Therefore, wisdom, or reason, is that without which nothing was made and in which all things are life itself. For example, in that reason, time is eternity and—to put the point summarily—the creature is the Creator.

Now, all things exist through that through which they come into existence. Hence, it is evident that everything that exists as something well-made exists in and through reason, as Solomon rightly asserts.[6] For the counsels of wise men, as well as good governance, which conserves the state, have their goodness from no other place than from reason. If [governance] veered away from reason, [the state] would go to ruin. Therefore, wisdom furnishes life and duration to all [living] things.

[**2**] Of all the created things that are present in the perceptible world, only man is capable of true wisdom. Animals thrive through much skill, in order thereby to stay alive. For example, they hunt in order to keep living. But that hunting reaches its goal in the sensory life, toward which it is ordered. Man, however, has a twofold pursuit: one that is animal, another that is intellectual. For he undertakes pursuits in order to survive at the animal level but also in order to find delight and vitality at the intellectual level. Delight is [his] life's moving-force. Accordingly, as Aristotle rightly said,[7] we know by experience that we have a natural desire to know and (2) that we have sight (a) not only in order to obtain those things that conduce to a conserving of this life (b) but also in order to know the differences among things. And men who are men of reflection know what great delight there is in apprehending truth.

Solomon declares that wisdom delights to be with the children of men.[8] For all things were created to the end that the Creator be glorified. And so, wisdom delights to be with the children of men because then [the Creator] is known and is glorified. Therefore, the apprehending of wisdom is the apprehending of our goal and is happiness and is eternal life, for it is the apprehending of the Omnipotent Art and of the Art of Immortal Life. It is as if some mortal man were to obtain an art that would furnish immortal life and immortal joy. Solomon rightly said: "He who finds me shall find life and shall have salvation from the Lord."[9] Accordingly, wisdom can be found when it is sought as life; for unless it is thus sought, it is not found as life. The following is wondrous: [wisdom] is found in such a way as it is sought. If, then, you believe that you cannot live without wisdom and that you would rather die than not to obtain it (even as a man would rather be dead [or non-existent] than to be devoid of reason or to be a stone), you accept all the counsels for finding it. And you keep all the commandments, even if they seem very difficult; and you abstain from all uncleanness and malevolence. For you know that wisdom does not enter into a malicious soul.[10] And you very strictly observe all the Gospel's precepts, the observance of which precepts gives promise of an indwelling wisdom.

[3] But who is this Lord about whom Solomon speaks when he says (in the words of our theme-text):[11] "... and shall have salvation from the Lord"? Assuredly, it is He who is the Savior and who is called the Lord Jesus; for Jesus, the Savior, saves. He who seeks salvation in and through wisdom has salvation from Jesus. For Jesus is Wisdom Incarnate, or Wisdom Humanified, by whom God made also the world.[12] Jesus, the Son of God-the-Creator, has the same creative art, or omnipotent art, as the Father has. The Father, [who is] Intellect, had eternally creative wisdom, i.e., the creative art. Through the creative art [the Father] created, in the temporal dimension, the man Jesus, whom He summoned to this art. All [other] men partake of a likeness of the creative art; but Jesus obtained the art itself. And this gift that the Father gave Him is greater than all [other gifts]; for [Jesus received it] not in part and not in a certain measure but in fullness, so that whatever He saw the Father doing He Himself could also do. Just as a fleshly father begets by nature a son and together with this [begetting] endows him with the same nature of begetting, so God the Father created Jesus and together with this [creating] endowed Him with the same art of creating. For just as the Father enlivens those whom He wills to, so He gave to the Son the gift of being able to enliven those whom He would will to.[13] And because [the Son] came in order to teach us the way unto apprehending His Spirit (viz., the Spirit of wisdom and of immortality), we are to have salvation from Jesus, as from

[Him who is] the Lord of salvation.

Now, here [in the theme-text] we read [in a symbolic way] about the glorious Virgin. For he who will find her as the Mother of salvation will find in her life and will have salvation from the Lord Jesus, the Savior, her ever-blessed Son.

[4] Because [in what was said] previously there is contained [the idea] that man is capable of wisdom, which furnishes immortality, you might wish to know how you can experience this fact. I answer: in many ways; for you have a spirit that is free and that does not pursue out of necessity works of nature and of the flesh. [Our] animal body, too, desires the things that other animals desire: viz., to eat, to seek pleasure, and so on. [Our rational] spirit [sometimes] forbids [these things] because the works of the flesh are often contrary to cleanliness and to religiousness and to custom; and mortification and fasting and modesty [are required] in works-of-animality—[animal actions such] as urinating in public, seeking [inordinate] pleasure, etc. And, hence, reason [sometimes] forbids that a man pursue animal activities. Moreover, in a spirit that abhors sins and things unclean we experience there to be a capability for wisdom and for immortality. For [such a] spirit is inclined toward things that are incorruptible, and it embraces them, as we see in the case of the arts. For example, it embraces the immortal art of numbering as it is handed down in [the Arabic art of] reckoning; and [it embraces the art] of measuring [as it is found] in geometry; and so on. And [our spirit] could not do this unless it had a soul that could turn itself from the particular corruptible things that we have experienced unto the universal rational ground of such [experienced things] and thus could come to acquire the art. Now, to be able to turn toward the universal ground of particulars is a sign that the soul that is able to do this is not bound to the corruptible bodily instrument, as are the organs of the senses. And so, [the soul] is capable of knowledge and of the arts and of wisdom—[things] that are separated from corruptible particulars. And, hence, the soul does not perish when the body perishes, since it is not dependent on the body. For example, sight perishes when the eye, to which it is bound, is destroyed; [yet,] since the power [of sight] still remains in the soul, the soul could see if the eye were restored.

[5] Moreover, we experience that imagination is a higher [power] than are [the powers of] the senses. For we *imagine*—even when the object is absent—more subtly than we perceive. Nonetheless,

the imagination often errs concerning truth, as when we imagine that people at the antipodes fall.[14] Hence, there is a more subtle power that corrects the imagination—viz., reason, which tells us that that falling would be [comparable to] something heavy's ascending. Accordingly, [reason] infers that they can no more fall than we can ascend. Yet, inferential reasoning is often mistaken, and intellectual vision corrects these errors, as is mentioned briefly in [my] short work *De Beryllo*. And because our soul has an eye through which it beholds its Beginning—which precedes all contrariety and, therefore, all corruption—it is incorruptible. Corruptible things are attained by a corruptible eye; composite things [are attained] by a composite [eye]; material things, by a material [eye]; and like is attained by like. Similarly, incorruptible things are seen with an incorruptible [eye]; incomposite things, with an incomposite [eye]; immaterial things, with an immaterial [eye]. Herefrom you know that the intellect is incomposite and incorruptible. For it sees the First Beginning, which is simple and indivisible by any creatures' means of division. And in the First Beginning the intellect sees all originateable things. But the First Beginning is not any of all the originated things. [I have discussed] this [topic] in that same work, [viz., *De Beryllo*].

[**6**] Moreover, in accordance with the teaching of our Savior, the soul by means of the fixed disposition of faith sees farther than does the intellectual nature; and [this] is the farthest point unto which the intellect can be elevated. And miracles are what attest that by means of faith the intellect can proceed to, and can work, all faith-related things. [**7**] And so, one-who-considers-[the-matter] can easily understand that the intellect is not the faculty of sensory perception. For we perceive many things that we do not understand, and vice versa. Moreover, with our eyes closed and at a time when we are hearing nothing, we can understand. And so, hereby the soul senses that it is bound to the body. But [the soul] through its own essence [and] as it is in and of itself (i.e., insofar as it is separated from its [activity of] enlivening the body) is in a certain way free from *particular* contractedness and beholds *universal* contracted-principles and is capable of receiving wisdom and immortal life.

[**8**] When the intellect beholds the cognitive power of the senses, [it sees] that (1) insofar as [that power] is dependent on the [sensory] organs, it fails[15] when the [sensory organs] fail but that (2) insofar as [the cognitive power] is a power of the soul, it does not fail. For if

the [sensory] organ is restored [to health, the soul] senses as at first, without a new power-of-sensing's being created. Similarly, [the soul] sees what happens in the case of the imaginative power: viz., that if the [sensory] organs are less well adapted, then the rational soul imagines less clearly. And [the soul] sees that for a time a man loses his memory if the [sensory] organs are obstructed but that he later recovers it. So the power-of-remembering remains in the rational soul even though it [temporarily] ceases its activity, which it cannot engage in without the suitable [sensory] organs. Just as a writer cannot write without a pen, so the rational power ceases its activity when the [sensory] organs fail; but it remains in the intellect. Hence, in its own [manner of] viewing, the intellect does not use the sensory organs when it beholds intelligible objects. Rather, it uses sensory organs only when [it views] perceptible objects. The case is similar as regards objects of imagination, since [these objects] are of a perceptible nature. The case is also similar when [the intellect] makes rational inferences and is influenced by reason. For it makes inferences among the things that it draws from percepts; for in these instances it uses the organs-of-sense, which are subtle in varying degrees and which in varying degrees are suited to being exercised. However, as regards the [intellect's] viewing of intelligible objects (which, because of their extreme simplicity and because of the incontractibility of that [intellectual] nature, which is not bound [to the senses], are not signifiable by means of any sensory [organ]): [the intellect] does not use any sensory organ but uses only its own simplicity of nature—[a nature that is] similar to the intelligible objects. Hence, this power of intellectual vision[16] does not fail to be present in the intellect. And since [this power] does not depend on there being a [sensory] organ, nothing can keep it from being able always to see unobstructedly. Analogously, if the eye and the soul's visual power were [one and] the same thing, viz., the soul itself, then the faculty of sight would never undergo detriment as a result of the deblilty or the indisposition of the [sensory] member.

[**9**] Moreover, consider that the intellect examines reasons and judges which reason is true and judges which reason substantiates [belief in] immortality and which does not. Therefore, [the intellect] sees its own immortality when it sees that one rational consideration comes nearer to apprehending immortality than does another and that by means of one rational consideration immortality shines forth more precisely, and is shown more precisely, than by means of another rational consideration. However, the intellect could not make this

judgment if it did not at all see its own immortality. Accordingly, the intellect sees that it is immortal when it sees that by no formable, or articulable, reason is its immortality so able to be made evident that it could not better and more precisely be made evident and be established. Therefore, [the intellect] makes judgments about reason on the basis of its intuition of immortality rather than, vice versa, making judgments about immortality on the basis of rational considerations. And if some argument were to substantiate [the doctrine of] immortality, nonetheless this [confirmation] would not be known unless the intellect judged the argument to be sound. Nor would the intellect by means of this judgment be considering only the argument but would also be considering truth; according to the conformity-with-truth found in the argument, the intellect would judge the argument to be correct [or not correct]. Therefore, it seems, once all these considerations have been rightly weighed, that the intellect sees—not by means of an argument but in and of itself—that the nature of its own simplicity is incorruptible.

[10] Next, consider that this intellectual power does not at all derive from a [human] procreator. For if it were from a [human] procreator, it would conform to the nature and the condition of other things that derive from the procreator. For example, just as the eye is related by nature to color and just as the senses are related by nature to their objects, so we would have to say of the intellect (1) that it would not be free with respect to willing, remembering, and understanding but that it would be necessitated by its nature or (2) that it could be compelled by another man. [But] we experience to be the case the opposite of these [assertions], because [the intellect] is free to love and to will and to understand, etc. Moreover, [the intellect] does not grow feeble, as do the senses; and so, it is not derived from what is mortal and corruptible. For we see that those who are elderly [still] flourish in understanding and in wisdom when their senses become weak. Moreover, a man reaches his full capacity, and reaches his limit, with regard to those [powers] that he has from his procreator; for at times he does not want either to see or to hear those things that he sees or hears. However, the situation is not this way with regard to understanding and willing; for he would always want to understand better that which he understands and would always want to love more fully that which he loves; and so on. And the entire world does not fully satisfy him, because it does not completely fill up his desire to understand—as a single object satisfies the senses. Therefore only God satisfies the intellect. The intellect has

its being from God and is an image of God. For the living image [of God, viz.,] the intellective life, can obtain rest not in and through itself and not in and through some other thing but only in and through its Exemplar as in and through its Beginning, Cause, and Truth.

[11] Furthermore, if the soul were from a [human] procreator, all its works would be natural, and it could do no moral work, i.e., could have no justice, no practical wisdom [*prudentia*]. Thus, a father does not beget a child who has practical wisdom through the father's own practical wisdom; and the child is not by nature practically wise. Rather, the child has from God a spirit that is capable of having immortal virtue because [the child's spirit] is from the Immortal Father. If a man were by nature virtuous, then every man would be virtuous, even as every man is capable of laughter. The intellectual nature is immaterial and, hence, is not procreatable. For if it were procreatable, it would also be corruptible—just as when from bread flesh is produced,[17] the specific form of the bread is corrupted, and flesh is generated. However, the specific form of an immaterial nature cannot be thus corrupted, as can the specific form of a corporeal nature, which nature has a substratum (*subiectum*), and a matter, that admits of different specific forms. Furthermore, the final and most potent reason that the rational soul is not from a procreator is that [the rational soul] has a goal-for-the-sake-of-which-it-exists that is higher than [it would be] were [the rational soul] to be [only] the form of man: viz., [it has the goal] of understanding God and of loving God, etc. Therefore, the intellect is from the Creator.

[12] How, if the soul is created, is it from God's essence? Solution: As claims Avicenna, [God] does not act or create through any accident,[18] since there is nothing accidental in Him, who is altogether simple.[19] For He does not act as fire acts by means of heat; rather, He acts in the way that heat, of its own essence, makes-warm. Yet, [in acting], He does not impart Himself by way of contractedness, since He is simple and unintermixable and not able to be participated in—even as the sun's ray cannot possibly be commingled with anything that could besmudge it. Accordingly, God remains independent (*absolutus*), and He creates by His will—just as a king, by his will, creates officials and just as he moves all things by an immovable law. And when [the king] makes individuals to be officials and administrators, he impresses on the administrators—[impresses] by means of his will—a likeness of his authority, so that they are partakers of his *impe-*

rial likeness, while the unparticipated-in *imperial [exemplar]-truth* remains in him. (By analogy, if a seal were to impress its likeness on wax, the letters in the wax would not be, in an unimpartible way, of the essence of the letters of the seal. Rather, they would be the likes of the essential letters.) For God impresses *likenesses* of His exemplars [*rationes*]. Similarly, He imparts to intellectual natures [likenesses] ..., etc.[20] And note that since God is, in an actual way, infinite liveliness, a likeness of His infinity is present in the intellect in the way in which the likeness of infinity is capable of receiving the liveliness. Likewise, a likeness of eternity (which exists as a whole in an actual way at once)[21] [is present in the intellect in a way in which the likeness of eternity is capable of receiving the eternity]. And so, to be able to *understand* ever more and more, without end, is a likeness of Eternal Wisdom. And from this fact infer that [the intellect] is a living image that conforms itself to the Creator unendingly. And so, [the intellect] is teachable, etc., as you know from elsewhere.

NOTES TO *Qui Me Invenerit*

* Sermon CCLXXXVIII.

1. This was the feast-day of the birth of Mary, the Mother of God.
2. Proverbs 8:35.
3. Nicholas later (at **3**:5-8) identifies wisdom with Christ, who is Wisdom Incarnate. See I Corinthians 1:24. Nicholas follows Ausgustine in maintaining that all who seek wisdom are either knowingly or unknowingly seeking God, who in the person of the Son is Wisdom.
4. Proverbs 8:24.
5. Here (at **1**:22) I am using the one English verb "to weigh" as a translation of the Latin words "appendere seu ponderare".
6. Proverbs 8:27-30.
7. Aristotle, *Metaphysics*, opening sentence.
8. Proverbs 8:31.
9. Proverbs 8:35.
10. Wisdom 1:4.
11. Proverbs 8:35.
12. Hebrews 1:2.
13. John 5:21.
14. Cf. *De Docta Ignorantia* II, 11 (**161**). The antipodes Nicholas thinks of as the region diametrically opposite to Europe and, thus, as at the bottom of the earth and on the other side. The earth he regards as sphere-like but not as a nearly perfect sphere. The imagination envisions people at the bottom of the earth as falling off, as falling away. But from the viewpoint of those living at the antipodes, what to us seems like their falling would be to them an ascending. And so, they can no more "fall" than we ourselves, living where we do, can ascend. Note Augustine's alternative discussion in his *De Civitate Dei*, XVI, 9 (*PL* 41:487-488).
15. Here (at **8**:3) I am adding, with the Paris edition, the word "deficit".
16. Regarding Nicholas's various uses of the expression "*visio intellectualis*" (e.g., at **5**:10) and its cognates (as here at **8**:29), see Klaus Kremer's "Der Begriff visio intellectualis in den cusanischen Schriften," *Mitteilungen und Forschungsbeiträge der Cusanus-Gesellschaft*, 30 (2005), 201-230.
17. Nicholas here is alluding to the facts of the digestive process.
18. Nicholas here means "accident" in the sense of Aristotle's distinction between substance and accident.
19. "… who is altogether simple": i.e., who is altogether incomposite.
20. That is, just as God imparts to all objects their respective essential form, so He imparts to the rational soul, in creating it, its very rationality, its very intellectuality, which is a likeness of the Divine Reason, the Divine Intellect.
21. The allusion here is to Boethius's well-known definition of "eternity" as "the complete possession—at once and as a whole—of endless life." *De Consolatione Philosophiae* 5.6 (*PL* 63:858).

Suscepimus, Deus, Misericordiam Tuam*[1]
("We Have Received Your Mercy, O God ....")[2]
[February 2, 1455; preached perhaps in Brixen][3]

[1] "We have received Your mercy, O God, in the midst of Your temple."

[This] is the introit of the mass on this feast-day of purification. And in the introit of the mass for this Septuagesima Sunday[4] there is said: "The sorrows of death surrounded me, the sorrows of Hell encompassed me, and in my affliction I called upon the Lord. And from His holy temple[5] He heard my voice." Where we are heard, there we receive mercy. The place in which the Lord's mercy is received is His temple. God's mercy is God. God's place is His temple. Of what kind is that Temple which receives God, since God—of whose magnitude there is no end[6]—is not contained in a place?

Mercy is a grace. But by nature God cannot be in a finite place; for since no place is deprived of quantity, it is limited by, and proportioned to, that which has location. But of the infinite to the finite there is no proportion.[7] Grace (*gratia*), though, we understand to be [one and] the same thing in many things. For example, a king's favor (*gratia*) can be toward his many servants; and this fact is not other than that the many [servants] are in the king's good graces (*gratia*). The fact that God, by grace, is in many saints is the many saints' being in God's grace. That the many saints have love is that the Holy Spirit is in the many saints. "He who abides in love abides in God and God in him."[8] There is a coinciding of a saint's abiding in God and God's abiding in the saint.

Yet, since God's grace is His goodness and is His essence (*essentia*), God is not present through grace where He is not present through His being [*essentia*]. Nonetheless, God is not received, as grace, in all existing things. No existing thing would exist if God—who is the very being of every existing thing—were not in it. Hence, since He is the Creator of all things, He is present in all things as the Originator is present in the originated. And this presence is [the same thing as] all originated things' being present in their Originator—even as for the soul to be in the body is for the body to be in the soul. And although God cannot hate any of the things that He has made, nevertheless He can love one more than another. (Similarly, a father, by nature, does not hate any of his children, since he is the father of them all; nonetheless, he can love one child more than another.) Moreover, God gave the Law for the following reason: viz., that we might know whether He loves us and whether we are in His grace. For He says: "I love those who love me."[9] If you wish to be loved, then love.[10] Therefore, God created a nature that is more lovable than other natures because it is more like Him. (Similarity is lovable.[11] For example, we love ourselves in our likeness.) And that nature is the one which was created in such a way that it is able to love God.[12] [2] But love does not exist without knowledge. Therefore, that nature must be capable of [apprehending] God by way of knowledge in order to be able to taste the pleasantness of the Lord,[13] whom it ought to love. For nothing unknown can be loved.[14] Hence, [that nature] must be an intellectual nature. Therefore, intellectual nature is the temple in which God can be received with respect to mercy and love. And this [receiving occurs] when that nature loves God. God, who is Love,[15] is received in the intellectual nature's fire-of-love .

Love is noble and free. Therefore, the intellectual nature must be noble and free in order to be able to love its God truly and nobly. Hence, if God is loved truly, then He, who is Love, cannot but be in the one who loves [Him]. He who loves a material object harbors that object in his love. But because that object is not love, it is not present in the one who loves, although the one who loves [it] harbors in himself a love for it. Hence, the object is present in the lover in its image and likeness and not in truth. God alone is in a true way present in intellectual love. Accordingly, God alone satisfies one's love. For since that which is loved besides God reaches the lover only in a likeness and an image, it cannot satisfy. For intellectual love finds its rest only within truth. Therefore, those shadowings and befigurings of divine love torment and inflict sufferings rather [than bringing rest]. Thus, it is evident that the temple of God is the intellectual spirit that exists in love.

[3] Note that when one-who-loves harbors within himself an image of the object loved, then this [state] is nothing other than his having become transformed into a likeness of the object loved. And so, when we love base things we are transformed into base images. But when we *understand*, we transfer the thing understood into our [likeness], so that by us it is rendered intelligible. For we remove from it all sensory properties so that it may be free [of them] and pure, in order that we may apprehend its truth.[16] And in this way, when it is understood, it is made a part of the intellectual nature. Hence, if you notice

carefully, [you will see that] the mind that loves God (whom the one not knowing Him does not truly love) is transported unto God. This [transporting] can occur only if God is somehow transported unto him. And since God is Love, the mind cannot know God and fail to love Him; thus, there cannot be true knowledge of God where there is no love of God. Therefore, in every [unregenerate] sinner there is an ignorance of God.

Moreover, consider that, in the mind, likening and being likened coincide, just as do the mind's understanding and its loving. For the mind, apart from desiring, does not understand; and apart from understanding, it does not desire. Therefore, the mind is a source of understanding and of affection. The mind is a simple, very noble power in which the act of understanding and the act of loving coincide. Furthermore, that power which the mind is is a living, contemplative, and uniting power. For in and of itself it unites all things; and, at the same time, it is united by all things. For spirit is a uniting power, even as in us there is a certain spirit that unites, within itself, all bodily members and that unites itself to them all; and it is the locus of the [rational] soul, or the mind. Similarly, the mind is the locus of God. Hence, the mind is in between God and [other] creatures—analogously to spirit's being in between body and the [rational] soul (which we call mind). And just as the locus of the life of the spirit is the soul, so the locus of the life of the soul is God. And just as the locus of the soul is that uniting spirit, so the locus of God is the intellect, or mind.

[4] Therefore, we must take note of the fact that, in this body our intellectual soul, insofar as it is intellectual, is not in its proper place—although it is in its proper place insofar as it animates. And we can grasp this point by means of the following consideration: We do not understand the [pure] truth. And since the intellect was created for understanding—just as sight was created for seeing and the ear for hearing—the reason that the intellect does not understand the pure truth is that it is not situated in its proper place, i.e., in the intellectual heaven or in God. For there it cannot fail to understand, even as sight that is in a healthy eye cannot fail to see. But if sight were not in its proper place, viz., in the eye, or if the eye were not in its proper place in the body (but were in another place), then sight would not be effective in its operations. The case is similar as regards the eye of the mind, i.e., as regards the intellect. Likewise, too, the soul does not love the Supremely Lovable, viz., the Absolute Good, but loves other things that fall short of the Absolute Good, because the soul does not have its

perfect operation as long as it exists outside its proper place. But because, with respect to its role of animating, the soul is in the body as its proper place, this place was assigned to it for its benefit, not for its detriment. And so, in the body the soul is not altogether outside its proper place; hence, it can to some extent love God and seek after truth. By comparison, sight in an infirm eye is in its proper place, where it enlivens the eye; but it *is not* in its proper place, because its proper place is a healthy and perfect eye. Accordingly, to some extent, although imperfectly, sight [in an unhealthy eye] discerns visible things, [doing so] by surmising rather than by knowing.

[5] Moreover, from our commotion and turmoil and restlessness we apprehend that we are outside of our proper place; for every thing that is in its proper place is at rest. Moreover, we apprehend that in our proper place we are incorruptible, as are other things—for example, the stars, etc. And this is the reason that we are by nature moved toward God: [viz.,] because *there* we obtain rest and incorruptiliblity. Hence, sin is contrary to our nature. For it originates when out of free choice we move away from God. Furthermore, sin withdraws the soul away from its natural movement and natural end. Analogously, weight that is accidental[17] to a fire draws it downward, as when it spreads and attaches itself to the heavy wood in a roof. When the wood falls in conformity with the direction of what is heavy, the fire, too, falls with it in the direction of the earth's center. Accordingly, the soul in Hell is like fire that adheres to a heavy, imperishable material. The fire always seeks to move upwards, but because of its union with what is heavy and earthly, it is held down contrary to its nature. Therefore, the prison, or locus, of the celestial spirit is downwards and is unnatural and forced, and earthly.[18]

[6] Furthermore, consider the fact that a humble soul is, in proportion to the depth of its humility, capable of attaining unto the Most High God. For humility is a deepness and an emptying-out. Now, you can experience whether or not God dwells in your soul as in His holy temple—[dwells in it], that is, if your soul is rid of sin. (For then God dwells in it.) But sin works three ills in the soul: from the arrival of sin the soul is (a) darkened, (b) besmirched, and (c) saddened. As, then, a bride who has lost her groom is dressed in black [and] does not bathe but, instead, besmirches herself and grieves: so a similar thing happens to the soul, God's betrothed, because of the loss of her Spouse. This loss occurs on account of sin, which splinters the marriage because of

spiritual fornication or [profane] love. But when the Spouse comes, all sins are removed. If, then, the soul senses within itself the brightness of the light of divine grace (which illumines the conscience in such a way that the soul can detect its sins, which previously it failed to see because light was lacking), then God is present. (For sin is like a blotch that darkens the soul's sight, just as a dark blotch on the eye darkens the eye's sight.) For when the [sinful] soul begins to see how dissimilar it is to its God, its Spouse, and when its blotches are washed away and cleansed away (tears of contrition conduce to this [cleansing]), then there follow joy and gladness and relief, which result from God's presence.

[7] And in the reading of [today's] office the Prophet Malachias explains the foregoing manner of purification. He saw, in his spirit, the Lord's coming. For when the Lord comes into His own place, or temple, He comes as a refining fire and as a herb used by fullers. And He shall sit in the soul and shall refine and cleanse the silver and shall refine and cleanse His ministers, the sons of Levi, as gold and silver. And they shall offer sacrifices in justice ..., etc.[19] And we must note that the Prophet [Malachias] places the sign of purification in a sacrifice pleasing to God.[20] [He does so], that is, when, [in the text], the sacrifice in justice follows after purification. [This is a sacrifice] such as was characteristic of the holy fathers, etc. And thereupon the soul will be able to say with just Simeon, who in the tempel took the Savior [as a child] into his arms: "Now You send Your servant away [in peace], O Lord, ...," etc.[21] [8] But if you ask how a sinful soul can help itself prepare a dwelling-place for God, I answer that [it can do so] in the manner in which the prophet [states]. (We learn of this manner in the introit of today's Septuagesima mass.) For [the prophet] says: "The sorrows of death surrounded me, and the sorrows of Hell [encompassed me] ...," etc.[22] "And in my affliction I called upon the Lord ...," etc.[23] For when true mindfulness of death and true belief in the torments of Hell completely surround and distress the soul, then the soul, unfailingly viewing itself amid unspeakable future afflictions as if they were present ones, has only God as its refuge. God is the sole and unique hope of those who grieve. Thereupon [the soul], by means of prayer, summons God to its aid. All things yield to prayer; and by means of prayer God is drawn from Heaven in order to come [to give aid]. But if someone maintains that he has true mindfulness of death and a real belief in the punishments of Hell—but he is not contrite—then he is a liar. For true mindfulness of death puts the soul into a state

of grief than which there is no greater grief; and it brings the soul, together with the body, into a state of agony. And when the soul is in that agonous state, a mortal sweat breaks out; and the soul, seeing that only God is its refuge, recurs to Him in its agony; and it commends itself to the Savior and prays more protractedly, as we have an example in Christ.

And in order that we may be distressed much more greatly than Christ was placed in agony, we ought to supplement the grievous mindfulness of death with [a mindfulness] of Hell's punishment. For Christ did not fear Hell's punishment, which we sinners ought to fear. Hence, when fear of death and when dread of infernal punishment come upon us, we will be covered with the very dense darkness of sorrow, and wailing [will] cause tears that are both very moist and very warm to exude from the internal arteries of life and from the marrow of the bones. Therefore, we ought—even now, at every moment of the light, and of the gladness, of [this] sensory life—to begin to be mindful of that dark time. For the song of gladness, the Alleluia, [will] cease because the lament of death is approaching. [We ought to be thus mindful] so that, thereby, having been crucified with Christ,[24] we may merit to arise with Him unto the life that itself is everlasting gladness.

[**9**] We must note that the Prophet likens the Lord's coming unto us to a refining fire and to a fuller's herb which bleaches garments. This [likening signifies] nothing but that the grace of God purifies hearts and souls. Now, the Prophet means that grace refines silver and gold and purifies by refining in the fire of love. Hence, the soul is compared to gold and to silver. Therefore, the soul is as silver and gold, i.e., as select-metal that has been purified for receiving the impression of the divine form; and from the divine form a denarius, i.e., a coin, is made. For the soul is like silver in one respect and is like gold in another. In the respect in which the soul is silvery it draws near to corruptible metals and can be called *reason*, which is near to corruptible sensory-images. For in reason there is the imprint of the Divine Word—[a Word that] clarifies all the things by means of reason. But the other, the golden, aspect [of the soul] is near to eternity and to incorruptibility. In that aspect is the form of divine life; and [that form] is the impressing which produces the imprint of the omnipotent Father-Creator. And the union of the silver with the gold has within it the figure of the Divine Spirit, who unites all things.

[**10**] Now, the Gospel of [this] Septuagesima Sunday says that

God gives His imprint to His servants—[gives it] by grace, not in accordance with merits. But to give this is to manifest value in the soul, which is stampable, and imprintable, with divine glory. For in the Kingdom of Heaven gold and silver that are without the imprint of that King have no value. Participation in the Kingdom is acquired in accordance with the value of the coin; and it makes no difference—when in that world gold and silver are refined—whether [the refining] is done with protracted and low heat or with brief and intense heat. For the Lord is good; and without envy He gives payment of the reward.

[**11**] Today the Church sings: "An elder, [viz., Simeon], carried the child [in his arms], but the child directed the elder."[25] Therefore, we must consider that Christ is in a place. For in accordance with His humanity He is in a place, but in accordance with His divinity He is not. But because Christ, who is God and a man, is one Christ, He cannot be seen either in a place or apart from place, and it is necessary to see Him in a coinciding of being-in and being-apart-from. And something similar seems to be the case, to some extent, with each human being. For from a mind and something animal Peter is one man. In accordance with his mind he is not delimitedly in physical space; in accordance with his animality he *is* in space. Hence, although mind is in union with that which is animal, and although animality is united hypostatically to mind, nevertheless mind is not therefore contracted to the location of the animal component [of the man]. For mind remains free [of spatial dimensions]. And while the body exists in this [or that particular] place: the mind illumines within itself all things; it ascends to Heaven through prayer; it journeys to Rome; it is in a piece of wood by seeing the image that the sculptor wants to make from it;[26] it is in a lump of clay by seeing the vase that the potter wishes to fashion from it. But the mind is not there as in a location; for if it were [there] as in a location, it could not be elsewhere. For it could not be in different places at the same time. Therefore, it is not there spatially but [only] in thought. For by means of thought the mind is where it thinks—even as by means of enlivening [a body], it is where it enlivens. And when the mind thinks one thing, it cannot at the same time also think another thing, because it directs itself completely to the one thing that it thinks. And it does not have such great power that it can direct itself at the same time to another thing. Analogously, sight is free to direct itself to different visible things, but it cannot actually direct itself at the same time to different things. But God is of infinite freedom and power; at one and the same time He beholds, and directs

Himself to, each and every thing.

[**12**] And this is the difference between our finite mind and God's Infinite Mind: viz., the difference between the finite and the infinite. For although our mind is not contracted to place and time, neverthelesss it is not altogether in every respect free of spatial and temporal quantity. Rather, it is, as it were, on the horizon where contractedness begins and absoluteness ends. Hence, that which is purely absolute, or infinitely absolute, cannot be captured by a perfect mental concept. For if the mind were to conceive perfectly of the infinitely Absolute, it would conceive at [one and] the same time of all things in the Absolute.[27] Similarly, if the mind were to conceive perfectly of Socrates, it would conceive at [one and] the same time of each and every [characteristic] belonging to Socrates. And if [the mind were to conceive of] place in an absolute way, it would conceive of each and every thing that has location. And if [it were to conceive of being in an absolute way, it would conceive of] each and every thing that exists and of [each and every thing that] can exist. Accordingly, the mind does not conceive of the absolute except with reference to the contracted, even as it does not conceive of the contracted except with reference to the absolute. So it does not conceive of either of them precisely. For the mind likens to itself the things that it conceives.[28] But since the mind is neither altogether absolute nor altogether contracted, but is contracted in contrast to what is absolute and is absolute in contrast to what is contracted, it conceives in a way such as it itself is.

Now, the role of our mind in this small world, or microcosm, is like the role of God's Mind in the large world, or universe. For [our mind] is at one and the same time in each part of the body and in no [part of the body] spatially. (Similarly, God is everywhere in the universe but is nowhere spatially; rather, He is [in the universe] through His power, His being, and His presentness.) For our soul is in terms of its power in each part of the body—[is there] wholly and undividedly. For wherever the body is touched [the touch] is felt, and [this] sensing occurs on the part of the soul. Where there is the power of sensing, *there* there is the soul's being. Where there is being, there is presence. In a similar way, God—the King of kings, to whose dominion all things are subjected—is (through His being and through His power, by which He governs all things) in the universe as a King in His kingdom. For His activity proceeds from His being. But He works all in all.[29] Therefore, He is with all things by means of His being. And so, He is present to all things. For if His being were not present to beings, how would [these beings] *be*? Therefore, you know that in Christ there must be considered to be, at [one and] the same time, a *human mind* (with respect to the microcosm, or small world, that is named "Jesus"); and you know that [in Jesus] that mind is united hypostatically to the *Divine Mind*, which must be considered as the Mind of the universe, i.e., of the large world). [The situation is] as if someone were to conceive of the soul's power—insofar as it is the visual power in the eye—to be [symbolically] *Jesus*. For that [visual] power is united to the rational power, which is in the whole man and in his every part. This [rational power] is like unto God, or Absolute Reason, or the [Absolute] Word. Hence, insofar as the [visual] power is in the eye, it is in a place; [but] insofar as it is united to the rational power, it is not in a place, because that [rational power] is everywhere, governing all things, and is nowhere spatially. In this way, Jesus was today carried in the arms of the aged [Simeon], and he worked all things in Simeon and in the universe, as the Church sings: "An elder carried a child [in his arms], but the child directed the elder." Etc.

NOTES TO *Suscepimus, Deus, Misericordiam Tuam*

*1. Sermon CLXXII. The fuller title is "Suscepimus, Deus, Misericordiam Tuam in Medio Templi Tui."

2. Psalms 47:10 (48:9).
3. This was the feast-day of purification.
4. This is the third Sunday before Lent.
5. Psalms 17:5-7 (18:4-6). Not meant to be an exact quotation.
6. Psalms 144:3 (145:3).
7. *De Docta Ignorantia* I, 3 (**9**) and II, 2 (**102**). *Apologia* 32:7-8. *De Visione Dei* 23 (**100**).
8. I John 4:16.
9. Proverbs 8:17.
10. I John 4:7-8.
11. *De Visione Dei* 15 (**70**).
12. The nature alluded to is human nature.
13. Psalms 33:9 (34:8).
14. Augustine, *De Trinitate* 8.4.6 (*PL* 42:951) and 10.1.2 - 10.2.4 (*PL* 42:973 - 975).
15. I John 4:8 and 4:16.
16. Here Nicholas endorses the theory of abstracting, whereby empirical concepts are derived by the mind's abstracting essential features from sense-data.
17. Nicholas, of course, is using "accidental" in the Aristotelian sense that alludes to a non-essential property of a thing.
18. Here (at **5**:21-22) I leave aside the words "contra naturam," which the editors supply from the Paris edition.
19. Malachias (Malachi) 3:2-3.
20. Here (at **7**:10) I am reading "Deo" in place of "Dei", in accordance with the correct surmise of the editors.
21. Luke 2:27-30.
22. Psalms 17:5-6 (18:4-5).
23. Psalms 17:7 (18:6).
24. Galatians 2:20.
25. Cf. Luke 2:27-30.
26. Here (at **11**:21) I am reading "eo" (as do the editors of the Latin text) in place of "ea".
27. See *De Possest* 41: "Bernard: When I consider that we are unable to conceive of any thing as it is *able* to be conceived, it is clear to me that we are unable to conceive of God, who, assuredly, is not able to be conceived unless all that is able to be conceived is actually conceived."
28. *De Mente* 7 (**100**) and 9 (**125**).
29. I Corinthains 12:6.

Sermon IV: Fides autem Catholica*
("The Catholic Faith")
[May 27, feast day of the Trinity,1431; preached in Koblenz]

[1] "Now, this is the Catholic faith: that we worship one God in Trinity and Trinity in oneness" (from the Athanasian Creed).

The saints say that man fell from a state of innocence through the sin of his first ancestors and that, [as a result], darkness arose in the intellect and that greediness and coveteousness arose in the will. But since man as recreated and regenerated was supposed to be restored and made righteous, his soul (in accordance with its higher part, which consists of the image of the Trinity) has to be made righteous by means of the three theological virtues.[1] Hence, just as the image of creation consists of a trinity of Persons and a oneness of Essence, so the image of re-creation consists of a trinity of fixed dispositions [*habitus*], together with a oneness of grace. Now, by means of these three fixed dispositions the soul is brought unto the Supreme Trinity in accordance with the three traits ascribed to the three Persons. Faith guides unto the *supremely true* by means of believing and assenting. Hope guides unto the *supremely difficult* by means of relying-upon and expecting. Love guides unto the *supremely good* by means of desiring and loving. Faith assents to God; hope trusts in God; love loves [God]. Faith [is centered] in the intellect or reason; hope [is centered] in the irrascible [nature]; love [is centered] in the desiring [nature]. Faith pursues God in the present; hope accompanies God into Heaven; love embraces God forever.[2]

[2] And because, in accordance with the chosen theme, my sermon is on faith, and because the foundation of our salvation consists in faith, and because faith is a gift of God ...:[3] let us pray ..., etc. [3] "Now the Catholic faith ...," etc. My sermon to you, O Christians, is about a most serious matter, viz., about faith. It is not about just any kind of faith but is about the orthodox Christian faith, which is so great that it overcomes this world ....[4] Since faith is the power by means of which those things that pertain to the foundation of religion are steadfastly believed (*Sentences*, Book III),[5] I must first speak about the nature of faith and about faith's disposition—[doing so] in accordance with the beginning of our theme: "*Fides*." Secondly, I must deal with the topic of the nature-of-faith as it applies to the Catholic faith, which

is the belief that there is one God who exists in trinity, etc., ...[6] And, thirdly, [I must deal with the topic] of the works of faith insofar as they are in our power; ([as it says] there [in the Athanasian Creed]: "... [that] we worship ..."[7]). For [faith] is the just man's life: "The just man lives by faith" ...;[8] and "he who believes in me has life eternal ...."[9] Therefore, in order that someone live by faith it is required that faith be [in-]formed [by love] and not be dead faith, because "faith without works is dead, even as is the body without the spirit ...."[10] For faith's work is through love ....[11] And by faith hearts are cleansed ....[12] Since the effect of faith is so great, then (as will be evident a bit later) if we reverence it, we must attend to it with diligent care and must keep it in mind, lest we err and declare falsely that we are Christians, although we are not, and lest we lose the very great benefit of faith.

PART ONE
The Nature and Disposition of Faith

[4] As regards the first part, let us say with the Apostle that "faith is the substance of things to be hoped for, the evidence of things that do not appear."[13] For faith is the underlying foundation for the spiritual edifice of grace and glory. Faith is—ontologically, not chronologically—the first *habitus* of the virtues. Through faith's assent the things to be hoped for are in us. Faith persuades the mind, because it inclines the mind toward believing things that do not appear. It manifests by its own light past, present, and future things that do not appear.

[5] First of all, it was said that faith is a virtue. Hence, William of Paris in his [work] *On Faith and the Laws* [states] that to believe the improbable is characteristic of power and strength.[14] For what is pleasant and useful presents itself forcefully to the will; and the uprightness of the one who possesses [these characteristics commends itself] to our love, so that pleasantness and usefulness make the object that has them desirable *per se*. Similarly, evidence and truth bring it about that they themselves are things believable *per se*, because they impose confidence [*fides*] and credibility; hence, it requires no effort to believe them. But when improbable things are believed, the belief is due to the strength of the believer and not to the fact that what-is-believed imposes itself. Just as what is bright is to sight, so what is probable is to the intellect and what is pleasant and useful is to the affections. Just as what is dark is to sight, so what is improbable is to the intellect. It

requires no effort to see what is bright, since what is bright is in no way opposed to sight but, rather, imposes itself. The case is similar as regards believing that which is probable. The fact that fire ignites dry wood does not require much power, because [dry wood] is igniteable; but much power is required if [the wood] is green. Similarly, our loving what is pleasurable, useful, or pleasant approximates [fire's] igniting what is igniteable. For pleasantness, usefulness, and splendor are three kinds of immaterial fire; and in human souls they produce three burnings: the lust of the flesh, the lust of the eyes, and the pride of life[15]—i.e., licentiousness, greed, and haughtiness. The ignorant are consumed by these three. As dry wood is consumed by a material fire, so the ignorant are consumed by means of an immaterial fire—[consumed] from the time of the original corruption, not from the time of the first creation.

Probability is a diffusion of dim and weak immaterial light; and so, it does not stabilize—as does the evidentness of truth, [which] strongly penetrates the intellect's certitude, fixes it, and renders it secure. And just as the will has concerning itself the aforementioned three immaterial fires, so the intellect has the two aforementioned illuminations of probability and evidentness. And so, from this [consideration] it is evident that to believe improbable things is characteristic of the strength and robustness of our intellect, even as to love things that are hurtful and vexing is characteristic of the strength and robustness of our affection. [6] Now, the light of strong faith is required; it penetrates the darkness of the many improbable things that pertain to faith, and it illumines them. And so, it is evident that our initial faith is a grace and is clothed with glory; and without faith glory has no place. And if it is needful that the whole man be religious, given that he wishes to obtain glory, then especially the head, viz., the intellect, must be religious through faith. For just as, necessarily, the will will struggle against itself if it strives to arrive at glory, so too the intellect will, necessarily, do the same thing. And as regards its operations, the intellect makes war only on believing. *Believing* and *reflecting* and *considering* approach the intellect forcefully, and the intellect receives [them] nonvoluntarily, but not as things demonstrated. Likewise, [the intellect receives] things that have been proved, because, necessarily, it assents [to them]. But knowledge involves a deliberate investigation from books and from teachers; and so, it can be partly the result of effort and partly not, etc.

[7] Believing, [which is] the foundation of true religion,[16] has,

as opposed to itself, an array of disputings, dissuasions, contradictions, as well as of improbability. This improbability is directly contrary to [religious belief] because where reason founders [because of the improbability], faith bridges the gap ....[17] For faith is faith regarding things unseen ....[18] Now, every war must be waged with warlike power, because without power one does not triumph. Therefore, faith is a power. [8] [We can discern that] in faith not all things are manifested, because if they were, there would be no dissension, no heresy. No one contradicts [statements] that are manifestly true, because where there is manifest truth, there is no power [to contradict]. Therefore, there is a power of faith on the part of a believer, because there is no evidentness with regard to the things believed. [9] Each thing is believed through persuasion. But God is believed in and through faith, without persuasion and proof. [Faith] honors God supremely in that it believes Him quite readily. Every [form of] superstition and idolatry, every sect and every faith weeds out with the sword and fire those who blaspheme their God or gods. Therefore, the Catholic faith teaches that God is believed-in without proof and without evidentness.[19] [10] The intellect, because of its weakness, seeks props and means of proof, as if supporting itself by the aid of a cane while ambulating from one conclusion to another. But he who believes by his own power does not need a prop; and he believes the more strongly. [The situation is] comparable to a lover who loves his beloved by his own power more than because of the things that accompany his beloved; otherwise, his love, if it were lured away from [focusing on] the beloved, would be crooked and bent.

[11] An intellect that looks for proofs is like a seller who looks for a guarantee of payment and who, otherwise, does not believe. A heathen demands such a guarantee before he believes; but a Christian, knowing that a guarantee is wrested from God because of a deficiency of belief, does not demand a guarantee in order to believe in God, for a guarantee is deemed to be a sign of unbelief. Because of these props derived from proofs and guarantees, the intellect is judged to be infirm—just as a man, because of his many props, is judged to be weak on his feet. Now, canes do not cure one who is infirm; similarly, guarantees do not heal the intellect; hence, they also do not make the intellect strong. Faith is not to be sought by means of signs (as the Jews [sought it]) nor by means of wisdom or art (as the Greeks [sought it]) but, rather, as a result of virtue. For it is known more certainly by virtue than by art. Art is as a painting that displays the outer form; virtue is

as a scent and a flavor that manifests inner [aspects].

[12] The closer that light is to the sun, the more noble it is; the more diminished it is and the more distant it is from the sun, the more ignoble it is. A similar [truth holds] regarding the heat of fire. Similarly, through grace faith descends from God as light from Light; probabilities descend through a distant light. Therefore, God's Light is more noble than is light that is reflected from creatures. Hence, "every best gift and every perfect gift is from above, coming down from the Father of lights."[20] Accordingly, those things that are given beyond nature are stronger than are natural things, for they conduce to happiness. Hence, nothing is more certain than is faith. [13] Therefore, faith is a general good that is freely given by the grace of generosity and of beneficence. And it is a power holding the intellect upright and securing it, making it to stand by itself and to walk rightly along the pathway of salutary truth and without the maintenance or support of canes. Faith protects the intellect against the darts of disputings and against [the need for] props; and it gives the intellect support against the impulses and concussions of contradictions and opinions and against the severity of its own infirmity and sluggishness. And faith is a light of the intellect that triumphs over the natural lights of the senses—as is evident, in the sacrament of the altar,[21] wherein the senses are triumphed over by faith. In this sacrament we believe in worthy God without any guarantee, and we believe in Him by means of the virtue of obedience. And this [believing] is the foundation of religiousness. And just as the intellect is the nobler part of the soul, so its religiousness—in regard to the works of God and in regard to honoring Him by faith—comes first. And no belief that demands more, viz., [that demands] guarantees, is worthy to be called faith.

[14] Now, the generation of Christians, which obediently suppresses its understanding and believes, obeys, and honors [God], is not a perverse generation that seeks a sign[22] but is a people given to worshipping God. With head bowed, i.e., with the intellect bowed, it adores God. And so, faith descends from the Fount of life and enlivens the head of man, i.e., his intellect. Habacuc 2: "The just man lives by faith."[23]

[15] *Whence the error against faith*: The error against faith arises first of all from the fact that someone does not believe anything unless he understands, for he thinks that his intellect is capable of understanding all possible things. However, the human intellect is measured and delimited by God, its Creator, who set the bounds of its

capability. A second cause [of error] is a turning away [from faith], as when one who loves something discards it and turns to something else. A third cause [of error] is the grossness of the intellect, just as one who has a thick and turbid eye does not see a hair. And so, he claims that there is no hair there where acute vision [detects it]. As Aristotle says: The inexperienced observe as one who is far distant.[24] It is necessary, then, to believe the learned and experienced. Moreover, there is a further folly: wanting the intellect to grasp things impossible for it [to grasp]—analogous to wanting to see with a human eye as with an eagle's eye. Or again, there is the additional folly of those who want to have proofs [that serve] as stairs for ascending unto the Infinite One. Likewise, another cause [of error] is the sin or the neglect by which divine aid is not sought for [believing] the things that ought to be believed. For light does not enter in where someone sets up a barrier. Isaias says: "Your sins have divided between you and your God."[25] As a result of these errors such great darkness is produced in the intellect that the Sun of justice[26] does not illuminate the darkness unless the night recedes.

[16] Now, faith is God's light and grace; it is not naturally present in [anyone], for nature works according to the manner of one who is a servant without freedom. For example, fire does not act in one way on one thing and in another way on another thing; rather, it acts in equal ways [on both]. Hence, too, even faith would be equally in all [individuals, if it were a natural endowment]. Moreover, because faith is a divine light that descends from God and that [does] not [arise] from things, there will be one true faith that descends from the one God—just as the vision from one eye extends itself unto many objects outside itself, and just as the rays of the one sun illuminate many objects. Moreover, there is one faith common to all believers, just as the articles of faith are common to all Christians. Now, all men are bound to a single divine worship that is owed [to God]. Therefore, there will be a single faith. And whatever is counter to this divine and owed worship and to [this] one faith is an error that is to be extirpted by fire and the sword.[27] All men, as creatures of one Creator, agree in their essential nature; likewise, they agree also in the divine worship [that they owe]. With respect to the basis of their subjection, all subjects are acquainted with their master, although they obtain different duties in the court of this same master. The situation is similar as regards faith.

[17] Now, a sign of belief is that you extend to God obedience and worship—[doing so] out of love that is upright and pure, for [such love] is freely given and does not result from fear of punishment or from shame or from hope of reward. For upright and pure love is a sign that you believe Him to be good and to be worthy of your love because of His goodness. And in one who thus believes, there is most pure and most sincere love, as well as actual and most pure worship. And the love is voluntary because it is freely given; hence, it deserves a reward. And there is room for a reward in that situation only because of the preceding gift. But he who loves for another reason ([e.g.,] out of hope or of fear or because of a reward) is not, properly speaking, rewarded (for, in that case, his love seeks something outside of God), but he is given his wages, not a reward.

PART TWO
The Things That Are To Be Believed by the Catholic Faith

[18] Whatever things are to be believed about God are present in Him either *per se*, without respect and comparison to other things, or they are not. (1) [Exemplifying] the first [alternative] is our believing that He is Oneness, Trinity, Equality, etc. (2) [Exemplifying what is present] comparatively [is] our believing that He is Powerful, Wise, Kind. (3) In these [comparative conceptions] other [ideas] are included, as, for instance, His being called Father, Creator, Light, Leader, etc. From belief of these three [kinds] arise all the aspects of divine worship. Out of the loftiness of [His] wisdom arise [our] honoring, venerating, purifying, sacrificing, and adoring. These are nothing other than our inner and outer subjection and the humbleness with which we believe, with complete justification, that we are subject to Him as regards our being saved or lost. Herefrom come (a) bowing, genuflecting, prostrating, etc., and (b) petitions (which we most devoutly and with humble submission deliver into His power) and (c) venerating (by which we fearfully and only as cleansed and purified approach Him for serving Him and approach holy places, holy men, the relics of the saints) and (d) the attending to divine matters in silence and with lights and ornaments, etc.

Wisdom produces fear and shame, blushing, dread, etc. For when you believe that God knows all of your affairs better than do you, what are you if you are[28] without shame and fear? But if you were not to believe that He sees all things, you would be a heretic (even though this [proposition] is not listed in the articles of faith). For of any two opposites of which the one is a heresy, the other is, necessarily, an article of faith. Therefore, it is an article of faith that God sees all things and that nothing is hidden from Him. Something similar holds regarding other [attributes]. From out of God's goodness, or loving-kindness, there arise, in our worship, thanksgiving, blessing (i.e., the summoning of good things), praising (i.e., a magnifying of the Creator), glorifying (which is preaching, proclaiming, disclosing, making-known). Glory is renown that is splendid, sublime, wide-spread. From out of God's loving-kindness, or mercy, there arise, in our worship, hope-of-pardon and thankfulness. The latter includes within itself (a) prayer for mitigating and removing evils, (b) prayer for obtaining good things, (c) affliction (for example, fasting and other forms of mortification), (d) sacrifice (for example, both spiritual and corporeal alms-[giving]).

[19] It is now evident that he loves God most purely who believes (1) that God is the Supreme Good and the Creator of all good and (2) that the entire universe (from top to bottom) has, comparatively, in a certain shading, a very faint trace of that Goodness. Accordingly, God is not loved purely unless He is known or believed to be thus. [20] Now, the articles of faith have been handed down to us in a fixed number for the purpose of our apprehending and believing [them]; and no one is excused from believing them. Moreover, no one, if he is of sound reason, has the excuse to offer (on grounds of his incapability) that he cannot with a general sense of credulity believe to be true all that is contained in the sacred writings and all that men who were instructed by the Spirit of God taught—and [that he cannot believe] to be true of God all that the Prophets believed about Him and that the saints believed had to be imitated. Those who are not of sound reason neither believe nor disbelieve. Thus, it is evident that the community of men is required to believe in a general way the principles of faith without contradiction or inconsistency. However, one departs from faith in two ways: when one does not believe to be true the faith which the Catholic Church preaches (or in some such way) and when one stubbornly disbelieves it or believes something contrary to it or dissents from one article in particular. And so, in regard to what is believed there is no difference between whatsoever simple individuals and those who are well-instructed; for in his own way each of them believes equally but rightly, because the simple man believes generally, whereas the well-instructed man believes particularly.

[22] The basis of faith is the fact that God exists. Moreover,

thereafter [comes the principle] that there is one Originator, because every multiplicity has prior to itself oneness. Furthermore, nothing that is first is compatible with anything else's being first; and two contraries are always preceded by another thing. This [assertion] goes against the Manichees, who posited two principles: one of light and the other of darkness.

[23] *What things faith is like.* Faith is like the ark of the testament, for in Exodus 25 it is said that the propitiatory does not exceed the arc. Likewise, propitiation is had by faith and never without faith. Faith is like a star of the firmament and a star of the sea, because the star shows to sailors the port of safety. And it is like the morning star that precedes the sun of justice[29] and like the star in the East that led the three kings to Christ. Faith is the foundational stone on which the Church is built. (Matthew 16: "On this rock ...," viz., the rock of faith, because Peter confessed his faith: "You are the Christ, the Son of God," etc.)[30]

[Faith], which comprehends all kinds of magnificent things, is like a mirror—because the Divine Majesty is attained through faith, the mirror without blemish (Wisdom 1)[31]—and is like the right eye. The left eye is reason, which makes judgments only about natural objects; the right eye is faith, which determines all things, both natural things and miraculous things. Now, someone who has lost his right eye is useless for combat. For his left eye is covered by his shield; and if he has no right eye, he can see nothing. Similarly, without faith no one engages without danger in the combat of spiritual war.

[Faith], is like a ring adorning a finger. In a similar way, faith adorns reason that is betrothed to God. (Osee 2: "I will betroth you to me in faith.")[32] And faith is a silver ring, because it gleams by way of true knowledge and resonates by means of confession. (Romans 10: "With the heart one believes unto justice; with the mouth confession is made unto salvation.")[33] Moreover, faith is like the king's flag, which during the battle exhibits the king's presence, in order to terrify the enemy. In a similar way, faith frightens the spiritual enemy (I Peter 5: "... whom resist, you who are strong in faith").[34] And just as the [king's] flag is placed in the citadel of the city, so faith is situated in the citadel of the mind. (Isaias 11: "The Lord has raised a standard unto the nations.")[35] Furthermore, faith is a military shield, placed on the left side, that protects the heart from injury (Ephesians 6: "In all things taking the shield of faith.").[36] Likewise, faith is like the sun's rays, because without candlelight the sun is seen by means of its own rays; similarly, God is seen without proof, by faith alone. Hence, Ambrose [writes]: "In matters of faith we believe the pastors, not the dialecticians."[37] And because with respect to its own disk the sun is not seen except by an eagle, so God is seen only by a soul that is very devout and that is elevated by wings of contemplation. A blind man does not see the sun, but he believes him who does see it; and he does not see the pathway, but he believes the dog that guides him; furthermore, he does not see the pit [in front of him], but he believes his cane, which touches it. Similarly, the simple ones who do not see ought to believe those who do see, viz., the bishops. O how great the danger is if a blind pastor leads someone who is blind! (Matthew 11: "If the blind lead the blind, ..." etc.)[38]

Or again, faith is like a sacramental pillar, like spiritual dawn, and like first light. It is like the pillar that led the people of Israel out of Egypt and that was a light for them; similarly, faith lights [the way] for believers. Moreover, just as dawn is detestable to thieves, so faith is detestable to demons. And faith is like the first created primordial light, which as first-born ought to be blessed, etc.

PART THREE
The Works of Faith

[24] True confession ought to be [made] in faith—lest it say something other [than in faith] and live otherwise [than in faith]—so that the faith may be living faith and not dead faith. A fictional object is not really a thing, even as a dead man is not considered to be a man. Moreover, a depicted lion and a forged denarius exist fictively, not truly. (Corinthians 1: "They profess that they know God; yet, they deny [Him] with their deeds.")[39] Such [false professors] are like a chimera. True faith is a good denarius, one that is good for purchasing Paradise; and true faith is a real tree that produces leaves of divine love and leaves of beneficial confession, flowers of honorable conduct, and the fruit of good works. Furthermore, faith ought to have magnificent devotion; for when natural reason fails, faith trusts in God alone, even as aged Abraham believed God, who promised that from his aged, barren [wife] there would be born a seed in and through whom all nations would be blessed (Genesis 15). Thomas did not have such faith, because he wanted to touch ..., etc.[40] As regards such faith St. Gregory says: "Faith does not have merit ...," etc.[41]

Likewise, great faith ought not to fail during hardship; rather, it ought to grow stronger. (Matthew 4: "If you have faith as a grain of mustard ...," etc.)⁴² The more a grain of mustard is threshed, the more vigorously it thrives. Such was the faith of the martyrs, who through faith conquered kingdoms. (I John 5: "This is the victory that overcomes the world, viz., your faith.")⁴³ Peter, who when he saw the strong wind was afraid, did not yet have faith. (Matthew 14: "Why did you doubt, O you of little faith?")⁴⁴ Likewise, when the righteous who lack faith see the strong wind, they immediately waver and sink into the sea of despondency, which is a dead sea, in which nothing can live. Faith is great through its continuedness and uninterruptedness, just as in the case of the woman who was in Cana of Galilee. (Matthew 15: "O woman, great is your faith.")⁴⁵

[**25**] Likewise, [there are] three creeds: that of the Apostles for instructing in the faith, the Nicene Creed for explaining the faith, the Creed of Athanasias for defending the faith. Moreover, faith is supposed to have universal perfection; i.e., [there ought to be] twelve articles of faith, even as there were twelve Apostles, each of whom laid down an article. Not only are we to believe God—to believe, i.e., that those things that He speaks are true (as also Peter, etc., is believed) but we are to believe in God (as Augustine claims); i.e., in loving-belief we are to go unto Him and be incorporated into His members. Bad and simulated faith (as states Ambrose in his book *On Faith*) is like mixing gypsum with water—a mixture that deceptively resembles milk.

Jottings on Faith and Reason

[**26**] Ramon: "Faith is a good *habitus*, [i.e., fixed disposition], that comes through God-given goodness, in order that through faith those objective truths which the intellect cannot attain may be apprehended."⁴⁶ Faith is great with respect to magnitude; and so, the more of faith there is, the better faith is. Now, a Christian believes more greatly about God because he believes that God is trine and one, incarnate, etc., and believes in the seven sacraments. However, the Incarnation and the like seem to an unbeliever to be things impossible. The intellect can have a fixed disposition (*habitus*) for faith and a fixed disposition (*habitus*) for knowledge. And it has a fixed disposition for faith in order to acquire a fixed disposition for knowledge. As Isaias says: "Unless you believe, you will not understand."⁴⁷ Accordingly, a Catholic can understand more about God than can an unbeliever. Faith is a power accompanied by righteousness (*iustitia*), since it is right (*iustum*) to believe about God those truths which the intellect cannot

attain. The Catholic faith asserts more true things about God than [any] other faith; therefore, it is a truer faith. Faith together with hope and love produce delight.

[27] Faith is a fixed disposition by which a Catholic believes that there is clarity in divine matters, so that it prepares a light for the intellect, in order that the intellect may understand clearly, and not confusedly, acts of divine reasoning and, thereby, may understand the agent and the doable [act]. The Catholic faith says that God can, in and of Himself, act to the extent that He can exist, because "with God all things are possible."[48] The faith of unbelievers says that this [viz., what is claimed by Catholics] is impossible; therefore, [the faith of unbelievers] denies the [doctrine of] the Trinity. The Catholic faith is a better means for the intellect to be illumined for attaining the loftiness of God, even as air is illuminated by the light of the sun, so that our visual power can see color and shape. Faith is tranquility of the intellect as a result of believing; but it is a secondary tranquility, because the primary tranquility comes from [the act of] understanding. Nevertheless, faith is superior to [the act of] understanding, because faith believes more greatly than [understanding] understands. To understand occurs with effort and by stages; however, faith is not [like this]. Faith has the enlightenment of truth, which elevates the soul; and it has the correctiveness of authority, which secures the soul. Both of these [characteristics] come through Christ, who is the Splendor and the Word.

Jottings on Proving the Trinitarian Faith

[28] The initial considerations for proving the truth of the Catholic faith are rather general: [viz.], (1) that [the Catholic faith is] God's instruction, God's words, and (2) that in its precepts there is nothing except what is honorable and fitting, in terms of every law. There is (3) the death and martyrdom of the martyrs, (4) the unwaveringness amid suffering, (5) the wisdom infused generally by the Holy Spirit. There are (6) the miracles, (7) the resuscitation of the dead by the power of this faith. And there is a greater miracle: [viz.,] that at many turns persecution is instituted by emperors and tyrants for the purpose of removing [faith] from the world, but faith has always increased between the hands of raging tyrants.

[29] In the Trinity there are three persons of the divine nature. The first Person is from no one; the second Person exists from the first

person through begottenness; the third Person exists from the first two through being breathed out. This trinity does not preclude a oneness of essence or the essence's simplicity, immensity, eternity, unchangeableness.

Rationale for the Trinity: He who would believe that God is not able to impart Himself supremely would deny in Him power. He who would believe in this [ability-to-impart] but would say that God was unwilling to do it would deny His mercy. He who would confess God's ability and willingness but would say that He lacked the knowledge would deny His wisdom. Therefore, since He was able, willing, and knew how to, He ..., etc. Dionysius: It is the nature of the good to flow forth. The Father is the Fount of goodness from which the Son flows forth; and through liberality and loving-kindness the Holy Spirit emanates from both [the Father and the Son]. The Trinity is evident in the Scriptures. Isaias [says]: "Holy, Holy, Holy"; and there is added: "Lord God"—in the singular.[49] In Genesis [we read]: "Let us make man according to our image"—["image" being used] singularly.[50] In the Psalms [we read]: "May God, our God, bless us,...." etc.[51]

Jottings on the Principal Names of God

[**30**] There shines forth in creatures a trace of the Trinity: In the magnitude of creatures the power of the Father shines forth; in the arrangement of creatures the wisdom of the Son shines forth; in the equipping of creatures, the goodness of the Holy Spirit shines forth. In every individual thing there is oneness, beauty, and usefulness; and likewise, there is being, power, and operativeness. In the sun there is being, splendor, and heat; in the soul there is memory, intellect, and will. As regards the three hierarchies [of angels]: they are a trinity. And in each hierarchy there are three orders.[52] A trinity is there present in oneness (and it is generally present in all creatures), because "there are three ...," etc., as you know from elsewhere.[53] [**31**] An abstract essential name is not taken as a designation of a Person [in God]. Hence, the following [statement] is false: "An Essence begat an Essence." However, concrete essential names are rightly [taken as designating the Persons in God]: for example, "God from God." There are two principal names of God: viz., "He who is" and "the Good." By means of the first name there is signified God's absolute, infinite being. By means of the second name there is indicated the divine being qua Cause; for God made all things on account of His goodness. By means of the [grammatical] neuter-gender, substantive things are expressed;

by means of the masculine gender the person [is signified]; by means of the feminine gender things conceptual are expressed.[54]

Jottings on the Manner of Knowing That the Incomprehensible God Is One and Three

[**32**] Those who are willing to say something deeper about our comprehension of God [say] that although faith does not have merit, etc., nevertheless when faith comes first it is elevated by means of understanding—just as if water were mixed with olive-oil, then the olive-oil of faith would be enhanced by the water of understanding. However, as Augustine says, the human mind's acuteness is weak; the mind is not established in such excellent light unless it is cleansed by the justice of faith.[55] Bernard: "God is present in non-rational creatures in such a way that, nevertheless, He is not apprehended by them. He can be apprehended cognitively by all rational creatures. But by good men only is He apprehended through love."[56] We can know about God *what He is not* but not *what He is*, for He is great without quantity, good without quality, etc.[57] In Heaven God is known in terms of His essence—known in proportion to the worthiness of one's merits. Hence, Augustine [says]: "We shall behold the essence of Your majesty—each one [among us beholding it] clearly to the degree that he has lived purely here below."[58] There is an illustrative example in the case of the ocean, which offers itself to sight but, nevertheless, cannot be seen in accordance with its entire scope. And this fact obtains both because of the breadth of the ocean and because of the disproportionality of our sight to so vast a surface. Keep the following in mind: Here on earth we can know God with respect to the fact *that He is*; in Heaven we can know Him *as He is*;[59] but neither here nor there can we ever know *what He is*, because He is incomprehensible.[60]

[**33**] Now, those who will to arrive at a knowledge of God must first of all cast off the darkness of sins and must put on the armor of light. They must cast aside considerations of natural reason, which are as the light of decaying wood giving light at night but of no use during the daytime. They must set aside mutable goods and cling to the Immutable Good. Thereupon, [a believer] attains a knowledge of God either through infusion or through rational inference or through [a consideration of] creatures, which are a mirroring of the Creator in the present era, just as God is the Mirror of creatures in the future [age]. At times God is known as is wine, which is known by our hearing of it, by

our seeing it, and by our tasting it. You know of [God] by hearing of [Him] from a preacher. When theologians read [of Him, they know] by sight. When good men love [Him, they know] by taste. "Taste and see that the Lord is sweet."[61] According to Dionysius, God is known through eminence, so that when power is found to be in a creature, supreme power is to be ascribed to God—and similarly regarding other [attributes]. Although all things are in God, from God, and through God, He is incomprehensible on the basis of [inferences] from creatures. For He walks upon the wings of the winds, i.e., above the understandings of angels.[62] Furthermore, recall to mind how Augustine, seeking God, asked of the earth whether it was God and asked of the air [whether it was God]. They replied: "He made us," etc.[63]

[34] In God power, being, might, wisdom, etc., are the same thing. God is infinite to such an extent that if there were infinite worlds, He would fill them [by His presence], because He has, and can have, no end. Rather, although delimiting all things, He Himself is undelimitable, because He is not absent from any place nor is He localized at any place. Wherever He is present, He fills all things. And before the creation of the world He existed in and of Himself, even as He exists today. Through nature He is everywhere; through grace He is present with those who are good. "He who abides in me and I in him brings forth much fruit."[64] Likewise, through His glory He is present, in what is reasonable, as truth; present, in what is desirable, as goodness; present, in what is emotional, as graciousness. Similarly, through union He was united, in the Virgin's womb, to human nature—[united] in the tomb to His flesh; united in Hell to His soul. He exists in and of Himself as Alpha and Omega; He exists in the world as a king in his kingdom. He reigns and commands everywhere ([says] Bernard). He reigns over angels as Comeliness (insofar as He is Truth) and as Tastiness (insofar as He is Goodness). He reigns over the Church as the head-of-household [governs] the household. He reigns over the elect as Liberator from evils; over those who are good He reigns as Helper; over the reprobate, as Terror and Horror; over the believing soul as King in His kingdom, as Fount in His gardens, as Light in darkness, as a ruby in a ring.

Moreover, God is eternal. No time or measure of time befits Him, who is without beginning and end. Pope Leo [writes]: Nothing can be added to or subtracted from the simple nature of Divinity, for [that Nature] is always that which it is. Living and understanding are proper to it and are co-eternal with it and are the same thing as it. Yet, [that

Nature] is manifold in its gifts. The excellence of the Divine Worthiness is so great that the mind that endeavors to conceive of God fails, since He is incomprehensible. The senses do not perceive [Him], since He is invisible. The tongue does not explain Him, for He is ineffable. Place does not confine Him, because He is undelimitable. Scripture does not explain Him, since He is inestimable. Might does not attain Him, for He is inaccessible. And because there is no comparative relation of the finite to the infinite,[65] creatures cannot apprehend Him. He alone is omnipotent; He alone is omniscient; He alone knows Himself; though He is the Worker of miracles, He is quiet in His workings.

[**35**] Every multiplicity is originated from what is one. Every order has an *earlier* and a *later*. Everything imperfect takes its origin from what is perfect. Every union of different things has as the cause of its persistence some one, ultimate thing that we say to be God. And because this God is most powerful, most wise, and most good, He *is able to*, He *knows how to*, and He *wills supremely to*, impart Himself. But this [imparting] is a giving of the fullness-of-His-majesty to another. Therefore, from eternity God the Father begot a co-equal Son, to whom He imparted the essence of His divinity. Isaias [says]: "Shall I, who bestow on others [the gift] of begetting, be barren?"[66] This is most perfect begetting, where the Begotten One is in every respect like Him who begets. And so, power is ascribed to the Father; wisdom, to the Son. And the Father is said to have made all things in wisdom[67]—i.e., by means of Wisdom, which is the Son. The Son is the Image-of-equality, begotten of the Father; man is a created image that imitates; the world is a created image that represents and that is a mirroring of the Creator. As the Apostle [says]: "Now we see through a mirror."[68] The world was made in the likeness of God because God had no other exemplar than Himself. Properly speaking, the corporeal creature is a vestige of God, a likeness of the immaterial Creator. [According to] Ezechiel: "You [were] a seal of resemblance ...," etc.[69]

Furthermore, emanation in the case of God is twofold: one kind is by means of nature, and it is a begetting; the other kind is by means of an act of will, and it is fittingly called procession but is properly called breathing forth. Now, the Holy Spirit is Love; accordingly, He proceeds by means of a volitional act from both [Father and Son]. From the Father He proceeds mediately and immediately: immediately from the Father and also mediately, because the Son breathes forth the Holy Spirit, and the Son has this [assignment] from the Father. The

Holy Spirit is Essential Love insofar as He is one God with the Father and the Son. Because these three [Persons] are one in essence, they love one another with an Essential Love, a name given to the Holy Spirit. Moreover, the Holy Spirit is Personal Love, because He is the Bond between the Father and the Son. The Father and the Son love each other with a Love that proceeds from them—a Love which is the Holy Spirit. The Holy Spirit is called Love in the sense of exemplar-cause. For not only is the Holy Spirit the Efficient Cause of the freely-given love that is in us but also He is the Exemplar and the End-goal [of such love]. The love that is present in us comes from the Holy Spirit as Efficient Cause, insofar as He is God. Or again, the Holy Spirit is said to be the Love—in the sense of Exemplar-Cause—by which we love God and our neighbor, even as Love (i.e., the Holy Spirit) proceeds from both [Father and Son]. But at times "love" is construed formally in the sense of inherence—as when love of virtue is said to be a fixed disposition in the soul, a disposition by means of which we love God and our neighbor. According to this mode the Holy Spirit is not called love.

NOTES TO *Fides autem Catholica*

* Sermon IV.
1. "... the three theological virtues": viz., faith, hope, and love.
2. Hugo of Strassburg, *Compendium Theologicae Veritatis*, Book V, Chap. 18. [Falsely ascribed to Bonaventure, this work is found in Vol. VIII of *S. Bonaventurae Opera Omnia*, edited by A. C. Peltier (Paris: Vivès, 1866). The cited passage is on p. 178.]
3. Ephesians 2:8. *Decretum Magistri Gratiani*, Part III, De Consecratione, Distinctio 4, Canon 145 ("Gratia"). [See Aemilius Friedberg, editor, *Corpus Iuris Canonici* (2nd edition, Leipzig, 1879 (Vol. I)), column 1408.]
4. I John 5:4. *Decretum Magistri Gratiani*, "Sciscitantibus"; Part II, Causa 15, Questio 8, Canon 5. [See Aemilius Friedberg, editor, *Corpus Iuris Canonici* (2nd edition, Leipzig, 1879 (Vol. I)), column 760.]
5. Peter Lombard, *Sententiae*, Book III, Distinctio 23.2 (*PL* 192:805).
6. *Decretalium D. Gregorii Papae IX Compilatio*, Book I, Titulus I ("De Summa Trinitate et Fide Catholica"), "Firmiter", etc. [See Aemilius Friedberg, editor, *Corpus Iuris Canonici* (2nd edition, Leipzig, 1881 (Vol. II)), columns 5-6.]
7. See this present sermon's opening quotation.
8. Habacuc 2:4 (Habakkuk 2:4). Hebrews 10:38. *Decretum Magistri Gratiani, op. cit.*, Part II, Causa 24, Questio I, Canon 29 ("Ubi sana ....") [Friedberg, *op. cit.*, Vol. I, column 977]. See also Part II, Causa 33, Questio III (Tractatus de Penitencia), Distinctio 4, Canon 11 ("In domo ...") [Friedberg, *op. cit.*, Vol. I, column 1233].
9. John 6:47. *Decretum Magistri Gratiani, op. cit.*, Part II, Causa 33, Questio III (Tractatus de Penitencia), Distinctio 2, Canon 14 ("Karitas ...") [Friedberg, *op. cit.*, Vol. I, column 1194].
10. James 2:26. *Decretum Magistri Gratiani, op. cit.*, Part II, Causa 1, Questio I, Canon 28 ("Fertur ...") [Friedberg, *op. cit.*, Vol. I, column 370]. *Decretum Magistri Gratiani, op. cit.*, Part II, Causa 33, Questio 3 (Tractatus de Penitencia), Distinctio 2, Canon 40 ("'Si enim, omnis,' inquit ...") [Friedberg, *op. cit.*, Vol. I, column 1203, lines 15-16].
11. Galatians 5:6. *Decretum Magistri Gratiani, op. cit.*, Part II, Causa 28, Questio I, Canon 4 ("Uxor ...") [Friedberg, *op. cit.*, Vol. I, column 1080]. *Decretum Magistri Gratiani, op. cit.*, Part II, Causa 33, Questio III (Tractatus de Penitencia), Distinctio I, Canon 52 ("Potest fleri ...") [Friedberg, *op. cit.*, Vol. I, column 1171].
12. Acts 15:9. *Decretum Magistri Gratiani, op. cit.*, Part III (De Consecratione), Distinctio 4, Canon 150 ("Verus ...") [Friedberg, *op. cit.*, Vol. I, column 1410].
13. Hebrews 11:1.
14. William of Paris (i.e., William of Auvergne), *De Fide et Legibus*, Part I, Chap. 1. [See Vol. I (Paris, 1674) of *Guilielmi Alverni Opera Omnia*, p. 2^b, lines 15-13 from bottom. (Reprinted in Frankfurt a. M., Germany by Minerva Verlag, 1963.)].
15. I John 2:16.
16. This idea is repeated in section 13 below.
17. Nicholas, in his text, refers to Gratian's *Decretals*. The passage corresponds to *Decretum Magistri Gratiani, op. cit.*, Part III (De Consecratione), Distinctio

Notes to Fides autem Catholica 113

2, Canon 69 ("Revera ...") [Friedberg, *op. cit.*, Vol. I, columns 1339-1340]. But the words "ubi ratio deficit, fides supplet" are not found there. See, rather, Augustine, *Sermo* 190.2.2 (*PL* 38:1008).

18. *Decretum Magistri Gratiani, op. cit.*, Part II, Causa 33, Questio III (Tractatus de Penitencia), Distinctio 4, Canon 11 ("In domo ...") [Friedberg, *op. cit.*, Vol. I, column 1233]. Also note Hebrews 11:1.

19. Distinguish "without evidentness" from "without evidence." What is to be believed is not self-evident; rather, it is supported by some measure of evidence.

20. James 1:17.

21. "... in the sacrament of the altar": i.e., in the eucharist.

22. Matthew 12:39.

23. Habacuc 2:4 (Habakkuk 2:4).

24. Aristotle, *De Sophisticis Elenchis*, 1 (164^b26-27).

25. Isaias (Isaiah) 59:2.

26. Malachias 4:2 (Malachi 4:2).

27. This idea reached its extreme in the Spanish Inquisition.

28. Ms. Vaticanus Latinus 1244 here has "es" (vs. "est" in the Heidelberg Academy's printed text).

29. See n. 26 above.

30. Matthew 16:18 and 16:16, respectively.

31. Wisdom 7:26 (not Wisdom 1).

32. Osee 2:20 (Hosea 2:20).

33. Romans 10:10.

34. I Peter 5:9.

35. Isaias (Isaiah) 11:12.

36. Ephesians 6:16.

37. Ambrose, *De Fide ad Gratianum Augustum*, presumably I, 13, 84 (*PL* 16:571).

38. Matthew 15:14 (not Matthew 11).

39. Titus 1:16 (not Corinthians 1).

40. John 20:24-25.

41. Gregory the Great, *XL Homiliae in Evangelia*, Book II, Homilia XXVI, 1 (*PL* 76:1197C).

42. Matthew 17:19 (not Matthew 4).

43. I John 5:4.

44. Matthew 14:31.

45. Matthew 15:28.

46. Ramon Lull, *Liber de Praedicatione* (edited by A. S. Flores), 3rd Part of 2nd Part of Distinction I (De Novem Virtutibus, Deductis per Principia), section 5. [See Vol. III in the series *Raimundi Lulli Opera Latina*, edited by F. Stegmüller (Palma of Majorca, 1961), p. 243.]

47. Isaias (Isaiah) 7:9.

48. Matthew 19:26.

49. Isaias (Isaiah) 6:3.

50. Genesis 1:26.

51. Psalms 66:7 (67:7). The word "bless" is used singularly: "benedicat" (in Latin translation).

52. Cf. Cusa's *De Ludo Globi*, II (77-78).
53. I John 5:7-8.
54. Cf. Thomas Aquinas, *Summa Theologica*, I, 31, 2, ad 4.
55. Augustine, *De Trinitate*, I, 2, 4 (*PL* 42:822). In citing Augustine, Nicholas was influenced by Hugo of Strassburg's *Compendium Theologicae Veritatis, op. cit.* [n. 2 above], Book I, Chap. 16.
56. Bernard of Clairvaux, *Sermones de Tempore*, "De Laudibus Virginis," Homilia III.4 (*PL* 183:72D-73A). Nicholas, in citing Bernard, was influenced by Hugo of Strassburg's *Compendium Theologicae Veritatis, op. cit.* [n. 2 above], Book I, Chap. 16.
57. Augustine, *De Trinitate*, V, 1, 2 (*PL* 42:912). See also Hugo of Strassburg, *Compendium Theologicae Veritatis, loc. cit.*
58. Cf. Augustine, *De Civitate Dei*, Book XXII, Chap. 29 (*PL* 41:796-801). See also Hugo of Strassburg, *Compendium Theologicae Veritatis, loc. cit.*
59. I John 3:2.
60. Hugo of Strassburg, *Compendium Theologicae Veritatis, op. cit.* [n. 2 above], Book I, Chap. 16. See also Cusa, *Sermo* XXXII (1:7-16). Cf. his *Sermo* XXIX (11:22-23).
61. Psalms 33:9 (34:8).
62. Psalms 103:3 (104:3).
63. Augustine, *Confessiones*, X, 6, 9 (*PL* 32:783).
64. John 15:5.
65. Hugh of Strassburg, *Compendium Theologicae Veritatis, op. cit.* [n. 2 above], Book I, Chap. 16.
66. Isaias (Isaiah) 66:9.
67. Psalms 103:24 (104:24).
68. I Corinthians 13:12.
69. Ezechiel (Ezekiel) 28:12.

Gaudete et Exsultate*
("Be Glad and Rejoice ....")
[November 1, 1453; preached in Brixen]¹

[1] "Be glad and rejoice, for your reward is very great in Heaven" (Matthew 5).²

The Gospel-[text]³ is the Lord's Sermon-on-the-Mount that was delivered to His disciples separately [from the multitude]. [2] "Jesus, [as we read,] seeing the multitudes ...."⁴ As a man He saw the multitudes; i.e., He saw a collection of men. But as God He saw individual members of the multitude at once, and He saw the hearts of each one. And as a man He who as God was everywhere ascended the Mount. And when He sat down when teaching as a teacher, His disciples drew near to Him in order to be closer to His word. This was the reason for the incarnation of the Word: [viz.,] so that He could be approached and heard. And opening His mouth as a man, He taught them as a teacher, uttering, in particular, human words in which the power of the word of God was present. Now, He uttered those words—located throughout three chapters in Matthew's Gospel⁵—which describe a man who is perfect in moral conduct. Hence, He concludes His sermon [by saying]: "Whoever hears these words of mine and does [according to] them, him will I liken unto a wise man ...," etc. (Matthew 7).⁶

[3] And we must consider that the Word of God creates wisdom in the souls capable [of receiving it], for He is Wisdom. Now, Wisdom is the Power of Omnipotent Reason. For all things are present in Eternal Reason as in their Cause; and as they are present there, they cannot be comprehended, although they can be seen from afar. Hence, that Infinite Reason, which enfolds all things, is the Light that shines in darkness, and the darkness did not comprehend it.⁷ For it is incomprehensible by darkness. All philosophers-who-want-to-know sought this Light (which is the Formal Cause (*ratio*) of things), because to know is but to apprehend a thing in its Cause (*causa*). This Cause is not contingent but is necessary; moreover, it is not [simply] universal but, rather, is so universal that it is most particular. And it is only God, who is the Word, etc.

[4] And note that God created the earth, and the capability in it, in order that by His Word He could make man from it. He breathed into man a spirit, and in this spirit of life He created a capability for wis-

dom. Hence, the Wisdom of God created the soul of man in such a way that the soul is like a suitable tablet wherein Wisdom could form a likeness of its own Reason, in conformity with which it created. Therefore, in man's spirit is created a wisdom that is like Eternal Wisdom, even as from earth there is created a man similar to Wisdom's conception [of man]. [The situation is] as if a painter, in accordance with his conception, were to paint a man and then were to impart to this same man the art of painting. Or, again, [the situation is as] if a father who is a painter were to beget in accordance only with his own design a son from a mother (even as a painter in accordance only with his own design paints from colors) and thereafter were to breathe into him a certain power that was capable of receiving his art and thereafter were to form in that spirit, which was capable of art, a likeness of his own art.

[5] And, likewise, preaching or teaching has a similarity to creating: when God creates, He calls unto Himself all things, but they approach Him in different ways. By comparison, when I call all men unto me by means of a single word, viz., "Come!," then my singular-calling summons all in equal measure. But since those whom I summon are many, one [of them] cannot occupy the same spot as another, but each one [comes] in the order that is his. Similarly, Paul says that in the resurrection the dead are called to life with a single summons; but each one arises in his own order.[8] A similar example [is that] of the sound of the trumpet in the army: The one sound of the trumpet is heard by all [the soldiers]. But at this sound of the trumpet one [soldier] sets out to ready the horses; another [soldier sets out] to collect his gear; another, to load the chariots; another, to gird on his weapons, ..., etc. In a similar way, Wisdom, by means of a single word, summons unto itself all souls in order that they may be filled by His riches. But each soul comes in its own order. [There is] one teacher, [but there are] many students. A plurality [of things] is not without otherness. Accordingly, students come to their teacher in different ways; and their souls come by different pathways unto Wisdom.

[6] Now, the spirit that was breathed into the body by the Creator was not from the earth but was from the Creator only and from no material. In a similar manner faith is created initially in the soul by the grace of God from no pre-existing thing. (For faith does not presuppose anything except the authority of the one from whom it comes.) Thereafter, the believing soul is fit for receiving wisdom, etc. And note that the inner man[9] has as its abode the spirit-of-life, which is capable

of faith and of wisdom—just as the outer man has earth as its material and just as the body's sensible soul is capable of receiving that spirit-of-rational-life. [I do] not [mean] that the sensible soul is the material from which the rational spirit is created; rather, it serves as a place capable of receiving the rational spirit. Likewise, the spirit-of-life serves as a place capable of receiving faith; and faith is the ground of wisdom. Wisdom presupposes faith. As Isaias says: "Unless you believe, you will not understand."[10] [7] The spirit-of-life is free, and faith is created in it with the spirit's freedom being preserved. For a soul is not made to be believing unless it wills to be. It is capable of receiving faith; but it is not constrained to receive it, as clay is constrained to receive the form that the potter wishes [it to have]. Hence, it is necessary that the soul, which cannot be compelled, be summoned and guided. Thus, the Word was made flesh in order to be able to be approached and to be heard and in order for men to be led from the darkness of ignorance to faith. And the manner of drawing [men] to faith is [the following]: to work miracles—those things which are above man—in the sight of man. Hence, Christ worked in this way so that He could implant wisdom after faith had been received.

[8] Now, [Christ] said: *"Blessed are the poor in spirit, for theirs is the Kingdom of Heaven."*[11] Consider how it is that Christ begins to speak of that spirit which is capable of receiving the Kingdom of Heaven. For the Kingdom of Heaven is nothing but wisdom itself. Through wisdom all kings rule. Therefore, to have wisdom is to have supremacy over all kingdoms. Now, the Kingdom of Heaven is the supreme kingdom; for higher things rule over lower things. All the visible things of this present world are subordinate to celestial influence; and they are moved in accordance with the movement of that celestial kingdom, even as in accordance with the movement of the sensible soul's desire all of the soul's corporeal and visible members are moved. [9] But that spirit which is to be a possessor of wisdom must be poor; for unless it is poor and beggarly, it is not capable of receiving that gift. For example, it is necessary that the eye, which is supposed to possess the kingdom of things visible, be altogether impoverished and have nothing of all visible things; otherwise, it cannot freely make judgments as regards everything visible. Likewise, the intellect is poor in order to be rich, for it must possess none of the things intelligible, so that it can arrive at the kingdom of wisdom. Accordingly, that spirit which abides in earthly and carnal affections and in earthly and carnal delights is not capable of attaining wisdom, because it has

not yet rid itself of all that it possesses. Such [an undivested spirit] cannot be a disciple of Christ, who is the Wisdom of God.[12] And take note of the coincidence of poverty and riches. For the poorer the spirit is, the more capable it is of attaining wisdom and the happier it is; [and] the happier it is, the richer it is. Poverty of spirit coincides with riches.

[10] And take note, [furthermore, of the following]: unless the spirit altogether divests itself even of worldly knowledge, it is not capable of attaining wisdom. For one who is wise must become foolish in order to be wise.[13] He becomes foolish when he despises all that which the world judges to be wisdom. For the wisdom of this world is foolishness with God.[14] But when someone wants to be wise in the sight of God, he must abandon the wisdom of this world. Now, the children of this world are wiser in their generation than are the children of light.[15] Hence, he who leaves behind this worldly wisdom is regarded as foolish, even as all the martyrs, who despised this worldly wisdom of living in sins, were regarded as foolish.

[11] There follows in the Gospel: *"Blessed are the meek, for they shall inherit the earth."*[16] Note that Christ calls them all blessed. His words, then, must be understood in accordance with this [rubric]. For to possess the Kingdom of Heaven is the reward of him who chooses poverty, just as he who humbles himself will be exalted.[17] Exaltation coincides with humility; the Kingdom of Heaven coincides with poverty.[18] And if someone is poor in spirit and is meek, then together with the earth, which he inherits, he obtains also the Kingdom of Heaven. For riches can flow to us without our setting our heart on them. Thus, we still remain poor in spirit while inheriting the earth. Hence, properly speaking, someone is not meek unless he is poor in spirit. For, otherwise, how would someone meek be blessed, as someone poor in spirit is blessed? Therefore, he is not meek who does not yet have poverty of spirit. As long as in his spirit there is such aggression that he does not want to believe but wants to pursue the movement of anger and spite, and as long as he does not know how to overcome evil with good, he is not poor [in spirit]. But the meek are those who inherit the earth, because they do not hurl words and are not disturbed by words but restrain themselves, etc. Moreover, it is generally thought that the meek lose all their possessions, as if they were careless; but Christ teaches us [about] a coinciding: [viz.,] that to be meek is to inherit.

[12] *"Blessed are those who mourn, for they shall be comforted."*[19] One who is poor in spirit is meek. And because he who is meek

overcomes evil with good, there is mourning amid this triumph. Christ strengthens us, [telling us] that we ought not to be withdrawn on account of mourning, because the reward amid mourning is comfort. For when we mourn, we wash away sadness, and comfort ensues. Mourning is a medication of the aggrieved soul: it purges of things grievous and unnatural. And after the soul is purged, it begins to hunger and to thirst for its food, viz., for justice, just as after the body has been evacuated and purged, it recovers its appetite. And so, consider the fact that mourning ought to be so intense that it purges to the point of inducing hunger. For as long as hunger for justice and thirst for justice do not ensue after mourning, the purifying does not suffice. Therefore, one must repeat this purifying as many times as it takes for this sign [viz., hungering and thirsting for justice] to appear.

[13] There follows [in the Sermon on the Mount]: "*Blessed are those who hunger and thirst after justice, for they shall be filled.*"[20] Note that justice, which coincides with wisdom, is the nourishment of the healthy soul. Wisdom orders all things and places one thing *above*, another *below*, and gives to each his own;[21] and so wisdom is justice. For wisdom judges all things; and judgment proceeds from justice, which is also wisdom. Therefore, to hunger for justice is to savor wisdom. For to hunger after obedience and after compliance with God's commandments, etc., and to do all that God commands, is to hunger after justice. And in this hunger there shines forth wisdom, without which there would not be such hungering. A soul that has not been purified hungers only for injustice, viz., for alien goods; and it desires those things which *just reason* forbids, as does the corrupt appetite of one who is sick. However, a purified soul hungers for those things which just reason dictates; and so, it hungers for justice, which is the light of reason-that-is-just.

[14] Take notice of the fact that the Kingdom of Heaven and the inheritance of the earth and the being filled, and the other [rewards] that follow [in the Sermon] express an unnameable happiness by means of a likeness that can be grasped. Yet, the blessed state of feeling full will not be had unless a state of hunger precedes it; otherwise, it would not be pleasant to be filled with food but would be loathsome. Nor would the delight be complete unless [the food] were your due. For he-who-hungers craves food that is suitable for himself and that is in his power [to obtain]. And this food will be given to him if, being a just man, he hungers justly. Thereupon, justice dictates that this [suit-

able food] be given to him—as Christ teaches us that a father does not give a scorpion to his hungry son who is asking for bread but, rather, provides suitable and right food.[22] And the right food for the intellectual soul is wisdom, which is justice. **[15]** Be aware that the food that is ours feeds us more agreeably because we obtain it by right, not by grace. (As we say: 'Fire, although small, quite properly heats and is worth gold.') And this food is called a reward because justice is that which can satisfy us with the food of utmost happiness. But if the food were not owed to us, because we did not earn the having of it, it would not be for us a very succulent food that would accord with our free nature but would be, instead, the food of servants (who possess nothing by right but who are possessed) rather than the food of sons (who are heirs by right). However, take note of the coinciding of justice and of grace. For the Kingdom of Heaven is a grace with which justice coincides, because it is a gift, and a gift is from grace. But since [that Kingdom] is a food that makes one happy and that contains the satisfaction of desires, it is not *just* that it be given to those who do not desire it and do not hunger for it. Therefore, those who hunger after justice deserve to obtain the gift of being filled satisfyingly. Consider this point carefully.

[16] But no one who is not merciful can hunger after justice, for hunger for justice is a sign that mercy is present. Justice is as bread in which there is moistness, without which the bread does not nourish. The moistness is mercy. The severity of justice does not nourish, but justice tempered with mercy does. Therefore, justice coincides with mercy, or grace.

Hence, there follows [in the Sermon on the Mount]: "*Blessed are the merciful, for they shall obtain mercy.*"[23] Justice requires that you do to another that which you would want done to you.[24] But there is no one who does not wish to be shown compassion and mercy. For those who mourn seek thereby to be shown mercy. If, then, after having been purified through mourning, one hungers for justice: whether the hunger is true hunger is proved by mercy. For it sometimes happens that hunger and appetite return to those feverish ones who have been purged—[returns] as if they were well, but they are not. And the instability of their appetite shows that the appetite does not result from health but from sickness. Hunger for justice is proved in the following way: If the sweetness of mercy comes to be present, so that where previously you were miserly but now you are generous in almsgiving and so that you rejoice in being able to display works of mercy in order to be justified, then the appetite results from healthiness. But if you hunger for justice and to be justified but do not have compassion on the wretched but have your earlier inflexible and hard heart, then the hunger does not result from healthiness but, rather, you hunger unstably for justice, and your appetite will not continue on; instead, it will be marred from your uncleanness of heart, and your illness will recur.

[17] Hence, in order that [the illness] not be feared to be going to return, the heart must be clean. And so, there follows [in the Sermon on the Mount]: *"Blessed are the clean of heart, for they shall see God."*[25] They have a clean heart who hunger and thirst after justice. A sign of this [hunger and thirst] is that they are merciful. And then there is a sign that they are wholly[26] healthy—[a sign] in the eye of their mind, whose gaze is directed only toward that for which there is hunger, viz., toward Justice, which is God. And for this reason they shall see God. And consider the following: that to see God is to obtain mercy and to be filled and to inherit the earth and to attain the Kingdom of Heaven. Keep in mind that God is not visible to the outer eyes, which are capable of seeing only corporeal and temporal objects. Rather, [He is visible] to the eye of the heart, and this eye is the intellect. And He is visible to the eye of the intellect only in accordance with the condition of [this] world—i.e., only symbolically.[27] However, in the next world, which is the world of truth, God is seen in accordance with the condition of that world, viz., in truth. This present world is not present in truth but is present in an image. The Apostle says: "The fashion of this world passes away."[28] Hence, truth can be seen only in a figure and in an image. But because truth is present in the next world, where the figure passes away, Christ says that those there, who will have a clean heart, shall see God. Now, He uses the word "God"; and God is Truth; and He says "they shall see …," etc. Therefore, those who have departed from this world and who did not beforehand have a clean heart shall not see God. Hence, it is necessary to have a clean heart here, so that there God can be seen.

[18] And keep in mind that Purgatory does not purify the heart or mind that is turned away from God and turned toward creatures; rather, [it purifies only the heart] that is turned toward God but that is not yet completely pure, etc. And, for this reason, mourning is a more effective purifier than is the fire of Purgatory, because it purges the mind of all disease and blindness. Such is not the case with Purgatory; rather, Purgatory only clears up sight. Now, he who sees

God [will] thereupon have peace. Hence, there is added [in the Sermon on the Mount]:

[19] *"Blessed are the peacemakers, for they shall be called the children of God."*[29] For he who has arrived at cleanness of heart is a peacemaker; and this is a sign that his heart is clean, [viz.,] that he is a peacemaker. For if he does not take offence: not only does he not take offence at the fact of whatsoever injuries' being inflicted upon him, but he even wishes every good on his enemies and on those who are harming him. Such a man has no stain in his heart but, instead, is of pure heart, from which only godly things can go forth. He has God ever before his eyes, and he does not judge himself to be harmed but judges that all things result in good for him[30] and that gracious deeds are to be done to those-who-harm-him, who are trying him, so that as someone tried and found to be peaceable he may be made more like God, who does not withhold even from those who are evil that which He has granted to be done from heaven by the sun and the rain for the life of those who are good. Therefore, in the future age they will obtain sonship with God, i.e., with the King of peace, and they will obtain this new name [of "sons of God"]. For since the sons of Satan take their name from Satan, who is the prince of divisiveness, (for [these sons] are thieves, robbers, hateful, envious, angry, etc., which [conditions] are sins that exclude one from peace), so too the sons of the Prince of peace,[31] (who is God) will be called sons of God.[32] For God is Absolute Peace. Hence, [believers] are God's sons and heirs and will possess the inheritance of peace, which is eternal rest. But one who is peaceable is tested amid adversity. Hence, [Christ] adds [in the Sermon on the Mount]:

[20] *"Blessed are they who suffer persecution for the sake of justice, for theirs is the Kingdom of Heaven."*[33] Note that the Kingdom of Heaven belongs to those who, having been tested by persecution, have been found to be peaceable. When Christ was mistreated, He opened not His mouth,[34] because He was peaceable. But He says that peacemaking is tested by 'persecution for justice's sake.' For he who suffers willingly and readily all persecution in order that God, who is Justice, may be glorified—he is a son of God and an heir to the Kingdom. Hence, these are the ones who are poor in spirit, whose is the Kingdom of Heaven. Therefore, all these [sufferings] are required for poverty of spirit; and so, the poverty is only poverty of spirit. Indeed, this poverty of spirit cannot be true poverty unless in it is found each of the things that are expressed serially by the Savior and the Teacher of truth. The Teacher adds the reason that these things are so:

[21] Blessed are you disciples *"when men shall revile you and shall persecute you and, though lying, shall speak all [manner of] evil against you for my sake."*[35] It is as if He were to say: 'if the poor in spirit are blessed, then you are blessed when you suffer persecution.' For suffering for justice's sake amid persecution is the utmost sign of poverty of spirit. For by seven trials one is tried, as gold is tried in seven ways [in order to determine] whether it is true gold; and if it holds up under the seventh test, then its authenticity has been proved. Poverty of spirit is gold and is tried by seven temptations and fires; and the last trial is persecution, by which martyrs, having been tested, are found to be true paupers in spirit. Hence, Christ speaks of the manner of persecution: first, when [believers] are reviled; secondly, when they shall be persecuted from city to city; and, thirdly, when men, who are lying, shall say all [manner of] evil against them and [shall do] this on account of me, who am Justice, etc. Note [the following]: those who suffer persecution by revilings, by defamation, or otherwise: if they suffer these things for the sake of truth and justice (because Christ is Truth and Justice), and if those who speak evils are lying, then those who suffer are blessed. Note that [Christ] says: "Blessed are you." By the fact that someone suffers persecution he is blessed, with respect to God.

[22] [Christ] concludes: *"Be glad, therefore, and rejoice, for your reward is very great in Heaven."*[36] Note that [Christ] says that one is to be glad, and to rejoice amid persecution and tribulation—even as the Apostles, being glad, departed from the judgment hall, where they were condemned to death for the truth's sake, being glad because they were counted worthy to suffer reproach for the sake of Christ,[37] who is Truth. Therefore, the greater the joy amid persecution, the greater the reward. For the reward begins in this life, i.e., with this present joy; and it is continued in eternity. If there is joy in death, then there can never be sorrow. For nothing is more frightful than is death, and [nothing is] more removed from gladness [than is death]. Accordingly, if there is joy in death, then it is evident that there is never going to be sorrow. Therefore, [Christ] says, "Be glad"; and He adds, "Rejoice"—as if to say: 'Be glad as much as possible, for very great is the reward for that gladness which you shall have amid tribulation.' He says that [the reward] is very great, because in place of temporal gladness He gives eternal gladness.

[**23**] Take note of the fact that justice is the reward and that justice-with-mercy is an abundant reward. With Christ there is abundant mercy; for the abundance is mercy, which exalts itself above judgment.[38] And pay careful attention to the fact that the reward is Abundance itself: God is the exceedingly great reward, as God said to Abraham.[39] An abundance that is infinite is exceedingly great. And so, be aware that we are transferred unto an [infinite] abundance, so that we may attain, with abundance, that unto which we aspire, viz., the enjoyment of God, who is forever blessed. Be aware also that this Sermon [on the Mount] extends throughout three entire chapters in Matthew and is a most perfect teaching for him who hears [these words] and who acts [according to them]—as Christ says at the end [of the Sermon], where He likens such a man to a house founded on solid rock, and where He likens one not acting [according to His words] to a house founded on sand.[40]

And if anyone considers [the Sermon on the Mount] carefully, [he will see that] the entire Sermon is enfolded implicitly in the [verse]: "Blessed are the poor in spirit, for …," etc.

NOTES TO *Gaudete et Exsultate*

* Sermon CXXXV.
1. This was the day of All Saints.
2. Matthew 5:12.
3. Matthew 5:1-12.
4. Matthew 5:1.
5. Matthew 5-7.
6. Matthew 7:24.
7. John 1:5.
8. I Corinthians 15:22-23.
9. Nicholas follows Augustine, who held that the outer man consists of the body, together with the outer and the inner senses, whereas the inner man is the rational soul, i.e., is reason or mind or the *imago Dei*. Note also II Corinthians 4:16.
10. Isaias (Isaiah) 7:9 (Old Latin version). *De Docta Ignorantia* III, 11 (**244**).
11. Matthew 5:3.
12. I Corinthians 1:24.
13. I Corinthians 3:18.
14. I Corinthians 3:19.
15. Luke 16:8.
16. Matthew 5:4.
17. Luke 14:11.
18. We must keep in mind (as we here see clearly) that the verb "coincides with" does not mean "is identical with."
19. Matthew 5:5.
20. Matthew 5:6. The word "justitia" (in the Vulgate) is translated in the Douay-Rheims version by "justice". The corresponding word in the Greek text (δικαιοσύνη) is translated in the King James version by "righteousness".
21. Cicero, *De Finibus Bonorum et Malorum*, V, 23, 67. See also Augustine's *De Libero Arbitrio*, I, 13, 27 (*PL* 32:1235).
22. Luke 11:11-12.
23. Matthew 5:7.
24. Matthew 7:12.
25. Matthew 5:8.
26. Here (at **17**:7-8) I have corrected the printed text's "integrae" to "integre".
27. Here the reference is to I Corinthians 13:12, where "in aenigmate" is translated (in the Douay-Rheims version) as "in a dark manner." I here translate Nicholas's "in aenigmate" by the English adverb "symbolically," a word that expresses his meaning more accurately than does the expression "in a dark manner." See *De Docta Ignorantia* I, 12 (**33**) and III, 10 (**241**).
28. I Corinthians 7:31.
29. Matthew 5:9.
30. Romans 8:28.
31. Isaias (Isaiah) 9:6.
32. Romans 8:14. II Corinthians 6:18. Galatians 4:5.
33. Matthew 5:10.

34. Isaias (Isaiah) 53:7.
35. Matthew 5:11.
36. Matthew 5:12.
37. Acts 5:41.
38. See Psalms 129:7 (130:7). James 2:13.
39. Genesis 15:1.
40. Matthew 7:24-27.

Trinitatem in Unitate Veneremur*
("We Worship Trinity in Oneness.")[1]
[May 23, 1456; preached in Brixen][2]

[**1**] "We worship Trinity in Oneness." ([Words found] in the Creed.[3]

Aristotle said that the First Cause is trine since it is efficient cause, formal cause, and final cause. The one Cause is trine, or tricausal: it is the First Efficient Cause, the First Formal Cause, the First Final Cause. There cannot be three First Causes, because prior to all plurality there is oneness. Therefore, the First Cause will be tricausal. The Efficient Cause is not the Formal Cause or the Final Cause; likewise, the Formal Cause is not the Final Cause. Therefore, they are [seen to be] distinct Causes when we view them in their hypostases. But when we view them in their primacy, they are [seen to be] one [and the same] Cause.

[**2**] Plato said[4] to Dionysius the Tyrant that all things are present with the First King and that all things happen for that King's sake. Perhaps Plato meant the same thing as Aristotle said, viz., that the First Cause is trine. Because by "the First King" Omnipotence is understood, [the First King] is the Efficient Cause. And because [Plato] says that all things are present with the First King as in a cause, [the First King] is Formal Cause, or the Form-of-forms, which enfolds every formable form. Next, Plato says that all things happen for that King's sake; thus, [that King] is Final Cause. That which exists is not impossible to exist. Hence, a thing has from an Omnipotent Cause—which causes the possibility of being—the fact that it is possible to exist. But the fact that a thing that is possible to exist is made actually to exist is derived from an Art, in which all forms are present; and the Art is a Formal Cause. But that which finalizes the causal power of the Efficient [Cause] and the Formal [Cause] is the Union of possibility and actuality.[5]

[**3**] Analogously, a potter produces possibility in [a portion of] earth by adapting the earth so that it is capable of receiving a form. Then he exhibits the intention to make such and such a jar, whose form he conceives in his mind. Thereafter, he *unites*, by means of motion, the *possibility* that is in the [portion of] earth (so that it can become a jar) and the *form* that he has in mind. Hence, in a single [artisan]-mastery these three are present.[6] However, the potter does not produce the

possibility *ex nihilo*, as does the First, Omnipotent Cause, [viz., God].

[4] Moreover, note that final cause is twofold: the one cause defines and completely plans the work and is called the subjective end; the other is the actual accomplishment of the work and is called the objective end. Now, with respect to the First Trine Cause: it is the Final Cause, which causes union [of possibility and actuality] and which is the Cause of the work in that it works all things for its own sake, i.e., in order that its glory may be manifested. [The situation is] as if a potter were to make a beautiful artifact for the purpose of displaying his glory, because he wanted to manifest his admirable artisanship.

[5] From the Gospel of John we know that the Father and the Son and the Holy Spirit are called by our Teacher, [viz., Jesus], *Givers of life*. For [Jesus] says: "As the Father gives life, so He grants also to the Son to give life."[7] And subsequently He says elsewhere: "It is the Spirit who enlivens."[8] Let us seek, then, in [the phenomenon of] enlivening a certain gusto of the Most Blessed Trinity. God is a trine and one Enlivener. Now, it is necessary that that which is to live optimally have this [gift] from the First, Enlivening Cause. But present in the essence of the best life there is, necessarily, *living*—together with *knowledge* and *delight* (or gladness). For one who lives [but] who does not have knowledge of his life does not at all live perfectly; rather, he is as someone sleeping or as an eye situated in darkness. He who is alive and knows that he is alive is not without delight and joy.

A rational spirit has from the Enlivening Father (whose image [that spirit] is) its possessing a vital nature. From Wisdom, or the Word, or the Son (who has the words of an enlivening life), the rational spirit is formed, or illumined, so that it actually lives and so that it understands that it understands and lives. (The same thing is true of the intellectual nature, in which to exist and to live are to understand.) From the Holy Spirit, who enlivens, the rational spirit has gladness and joy, because it has a vital nature and understands that it is alive. Therefore, God creates the vital nature with a rational life; God illumines it so that it sees itself to be alive; God renders it happy and glad.

[6] I want still further to investigate the Trinity—[to do so] from [a consideration of] the image of the Trinity. The intellectual spirit, created in the image of God, is king of the heavens. In its kingdom is found a heaven in which all things are present, and the heaven is called *memory*. Moreover, there is found a heaven in which distinguishing and selecting are done, and it is called *knowledge*. And there is a heav-

en of delights, and it is called *will*. In the first heaven of the kingdom of our mind all things are present, since memory is the image of the eternal God. (Mind takes its name from this heaven, since mind (*mens*) is called mind from its remembering (*memoria*).) Therefore, all things are present in memory, which is the mindfulness of Him who is all in all.[9] In the second heaven [of our mind] all things come into light in order to be measured. (And mind takes its name from this heaven, because mind (*mens*) is called mind from [the activity] of measuring [*metiri*]).[10] In the third heaven are present delights.

So the [three] heavens are [three] kingdoms of the mind. In the first kingdom mind has a treasure of riches; in the second kingdom mind enumerates and selects; in the third, it finds delight. Memory, insofar as it is mindfulness of eternity, has within itself truth, justice, beauty, and whatever such things are everlasting and eternal. In the second kingdom [mind] makes judgments about what is just, true, [or] beautiful. And unless the first kingdom conveyed to mind truth, justice, and beauty, mind would not have that whereby to judge something as just, something as true, something as beautiful. In the third kingdom [mind] delights and rejoices that it has found the just, the true, the beautiful. Mind, then, endeavors to equalize the [three] kingdoms. For knowledge is begotten of memory. And if mind could understand to the extent that the capacity of memory is extended, then there would result supreme delight and [supreme] joy and eternal happiness. For, in that case, mind would know God, who is hidden in His image (viz., in memory) as an original is concealed in its image.

[7] God is omnipotent. Omnipotence enfolds all things. And we can name it Eternity, which in relation to creation is a Beginning-without-beginning, in which all [created] things are enfolded. And because [the Beginning] is omnipotent, it begets from itself a Knowledge of itself, or a Light. For it would not be omnipotent if it were ignorant. And because it produces from itself a Light in which it sees itself, this Light has in it Omnipotence, whose Light, or Substantial Form, it is. Therefore, from these [two]—viz., that the *Omnipotent Beginning* has *Knowledge* that it is all things—there proceeds [*Eternal*] *Happiness*, or Eternal Joy.[11]

The Omnipotent Beginning is the first kingdom, in which all things are present in an enfolded way. The second kingdom is the kingdom of Sonship or of Form or of the Word or of Knowledge, in which all the things that are present in the first kingdom ([viz., the kingdom] of the Father)—present as in Eternal Memory—are unfolded (as from the treasury of Memory) into the Light, where they are all distinguished. In the third kingdom, viz., the kingdom in the Holy Spirit, all things are present as things embraced with joy and love (as being things eagerly sought and gladly found); and it is a kingdom of gladness and of happiness.

Combine with the foregoing points those which you find in Book One of *Learned Ignorance*[12] and in my other sermons for this feast-day.

NOTES TO *Trinitatem in Unitate Veneremur*

* Sermon CCXXXIII.

1. This title is taken from the Pseudo-Athanasian Creed called, from it opening word, the *Quicumque*. It was composed by an unknown author some time between 430 and 500 A.D. If the Latin title here used were to stand alone, without a context, it would be translated as "Let us worship Trinity in Oneness." But Nicholas explicitly mentions that he is drawing the wording from the Creed. Since, in the Creed, the present subjunctive of *"veneremur"* is to be translated into English by the indicative mood, the indicative is appropriate in the translation of the present title. See n. 3 below.

2. This was the feast-day of the Trinity.

3. "Fides autem catholica haec est, ut unum Deum in Trinitate, et Trinitatem in unitate veneremur, neque confundentes personas neque substantiam separantes ...." See n. 1 above.

4. Plato, *Epistola* II (312 E). See also Nicholas's *De Beryllo* 16.

5. Because in this paragraph Nicholas is alluding to the Trinity and the persons of God, "Cause" and "Art" have been capitalized.

6. That is, the three things that are present in artisanship are possibility, form, and union.

7. John 5:21.

8. John 6:64.

9. I Corinthians 15:28.

10. See Nicholas's *De Mente* 1.

11. The image of the Trinity here alluded to is trine image of omnipotence, knowledge, and joy.

12. *De Docta Ignorantia* I, 7-20.

Spiritus autem Paraclitus•
("But the Spirit, the Paraclete ....")
[May 25, 1455 (Feast-day of Pentecost); preached in Brixen]

[1] "But the Spirit, the Paraclete, whom the Father will send in my name—He will teach you all things and will bring to your mind whatsoever I shall have said to you."[1] [Text found] in the Gospel.

[2] First of all, we must attend to the fact that God is the Creator of all visible things and all invisible things. For since whatever things the perceptible world contains are finite, they cannot exist of themselves. For the finite can exist in a way different from the way it does exist; and so, its *being* is not eternity, which cannot exist in a way other than it does. Nor is [the world's *being*] infinity or absolute necessity. And so, if that which is not eternity itself were to exist from itself, it would exist before it existed—[something impossible]. Thus, then, we come, necessarily, to a Beginning of all finite things—[a Beginning] which is infinite ..., etc. ([I have written] about this matter elsewhere.)[2] Therefore, there must be a single Beginning of all things—(an assertion that even the pagan philosophers make). Hence, the Apostle Paul said to the Romans that God had manifested Himself to them through visible things.[3]

Secondly, we must consider that since God is the Beginning, He is Pure Intellect.[4] For we say that Intellect is that power which from out of itself begets and produces. For example, it is the Beginning of movement. For it did not have the beginning of movement from elsewhere; thus, it is the Beginning [of movement], since it is the First Beginning. And because Intellect, since it is the Beginning, produces from itself movement: we [ourselves], who have intellect, experience that we discover, of ourselves, arts that were not previously seen and known; hence, we know that new things are made by the intellect and not by some lesser power. (For intellect begets of itself an understanding-of-itself, which it loves.)[5] Hence, the Intellectual Beginning is an Omnipotent Beginning.

[3] Now, omnipotence begets from itself an understanding of itself; from these, [viz., omnipotence and understanding], there proceeds most glorious happiness. For how could omnipotence be omnipotence if it did not know itself? And how could sight be omnipotent if it did not see itself? But if sight is omnipotent, then there is

nothing that is beyond its power. So if omnipotent sight begets of its own power the seeing of itself, then there arises supreme happiness and delight. For omnipotent sight cannot fail to be content, and at rest, when it sees itself; for nothing can be more desirable [for it]. Hence, the Omnipotent Intellect, which begets of itself an Understanding of itself, is happily at rest.

Now, from Omnipotent Intellect that understands itself there proceeds Omnipotent Glory. But Omnipotent Intellect can beget from itself an Understanding of itself only if [the Understanding] is equal to the Omnipotence. For from Omnipotent Intellect there cannot be begotten a lesser than it. For [omnipotence would] not [be] omnipotence unless it begat what is equal to itself. Now, Omnipotence is Pure Intellect; accordingly, the Begotten Intellect, [or Understanding],[6] cannot be lesser. Otherwise, it would not be *of an Omnipotent*[7] *Intellect* but would be *of a lesser intellect* than an Omnipotent Intellect. And because it must be the case that the Begotten Intellect is Omnipotent, the Begetting Omnipotent Intellect begets—i.e., understands, i.e., sees—itself both in itself and in [the Intellect] begotten from itself. And the Begotten Omnipotent Intellect sees within itself the Begetting [Omnipotent Intellect]. [4] And in this way Glory arises, proceeding from them both. For Begetting Omnipotence cannot, without Infinite Glory, see Omnipotence that is begotten from it. Nor without Infinite Glory can Begotten Omnipotence see within itself Begetting Omnipotence. And when viewing its Begotten [Omnipotent Intellect], the Begetting Omnipotent Intellect has Infinite Glory only if the Begotten [Intellect] also has this same [Glory]. Hence, there is one Glory of Begetter and Begotten. Therefore, the Glory of the Omnipotent Begetting Intellect and of the Omnipotent Begotten Intellect cannot exist unless it is Omnipotent and Intellectual and Equal to the Begetter and the Begotten. This [Glory] can also be called Goodness or Love or Delight or Gladness or Joy, etc.[8] For if Supreme Intellectual Beauty begets from itself Knowledge-of-itself, or Equality-with-itself—i.e., [if it begettingly reproduces] its Intellectual Beauty—then from the beholding of its Beauty in the Begotten Beauty, and from the beholding by which Begotten Beauty sees within itself all the Beauty of the Begetter, there arises the true Glory of them both.

By analogy, the vain glory of a corruptible and sensory beauty arises if an especially beautiful father begets a son equal to himself in beauty. Then when the father beholds in the beauty of the son his own beauty, and the son beholds in the beauty of the father his own beauty, there arises a certain glory, by means of which the father and the son glory[9] vainly in the excellence of each other's beauty. For glory—whether true glory or vain glory—does not exist without knowledge. As long as a beautiful woman does not know that she is beautiful, she does not glory in her beauty. But when she sees in a mirror (in the likeness begotten from her) that she is beautiful, she begins to glory vainly, etc. Therefore, glorying is a loving of excellence. But without knowledge there is no love.

[5] Now then that we know to some extent that God the Father is Purest Intellect that begets from itself an Understanding[10] of itself, from both of which there proceeds Infinite Glory: we ought to consider how it is that God is a Beginning that is above all intellect. Because we judge all things with our intellect and because we judge not to exist that whose existence we cannot apprehend with the intellect: we assert to be the case that among existing things intellect is the supreme thing, as among things hot, fire [is supremely hot]. Accordingly, we ascribe to God intellectual being, even though He excels all intellect. Moreover, He is said by Jesus (in John 4)[11] to be Spirit—viz., the Most High Spirit, which is Intellectual Spirit. And from the nobility of intellectual being (*qua* being that first goes out from God, its Beginning,) we endeavor to make a surmising concept of God Himself. [We do so] in the likeness of someone who from a close *image* ascends [mentally] to the *original*.

[6] Now, we experience in our own case that our intellectual nature seeks, with all concern, to make known the glory that it possesses by virtue of understanding. And for this reason those-who-rejoice seek out, and desire [to have], others who will rejoice with them—as Christ illustrates as regards joy over finding a lost son, a lost sheep, and a lost coin.[12] And, in general, on account of our desire that our glory and gladness be made known, the possession of any benefit is not gladdening apart from company. And the intellect cannot make known its glory unless it summons, for a sharing, other intellects to which it endeavors to impart itself so that in this way other individuals may in their own intellects taste of the glory which it itself has within itself by virtue of understanding. Similarly, we deem that God Almighty does all things in order that the riches of His glory may be made known and may be appreciated—as the Apostle [Paul] indicates in many passages.[13] And in this regard consider the text in Ephesians 3, where he says:

> But to me, the least of all the saints, is given the following grace: [viz.,] to preach among the Gentiles the unsearchable riches of Christ and to enlighten all men as to what is the dispensation of the mystery that was hidden from eternity by God, who created all things in order that the manifold wisdom of God might be made known, by the Church, to principalities and powers in Heavenly places, according to the eternal purpose which He made in Christ Jesus our Lord, in whom we have boldness and access with confidence by means of faith in Him.

Lo, according to Paul, all created things have come about—and Christ, too, has come—in order that God's manifold wisdom may be made known. And in Romans 3 it is said that God made Christ to be [our] Propitiator through faith in His blood—[doing so] in order to show His justice.[14] So too, all the works of a rational creature ought to be done in order to glorify God—as in I Corinthians 10 the Apostle commands when he says: "Do all things unto the glory of God."[15]

[7] Therefore, God wills to be known. Hence, all things exist to this end. And for this reason man was created, as Paul says in Acts 17.[16] And God looks down from Heaven [to see] whether man understands, and He inquires after Him, as the Psalmist says.[17] And because it is the case that man was created in order to know God, man's happiness, peacefulness, restfulness, repose, eternal life, glory, and supreme good consist in his knowledge of his Creator. And the manifesting of God's glory is nothing other than the manifesting of all good, as [we read] in Exodus 33.[18] And hence it is that all men by nature desire to know.[19] For they came into the world in order to seek and to know God. Indeed, by means of this knowledge the desire-to-know is fulfilled. Wherefore Jesus taught us that the intellect's eternal life is this: [viz.,] to know God (John 17).[20]

[8] But there cannot enter into the heart of man anything that is like God, as Paul [says] somewhere earlier [in Corinthians].[21] (Now, man's heart is the soul's [faculty of] reason). And the senses cannot arrive at anything which is such that it would render the intellect happy. Therefore, man cannot by any of his own powers come to a knowledge of God, for in the human intellect there is only that which comes to it by way of the senses.[22] Therefore, although man was created in order that the riches of God's glory might be made known to him, and although this [manifesting was] for the purpose of his praising God's glory, nevertheless [he was not created] in such a way that of his own powers he could arrive at this [state of knowledge]. For God Himself remains hidden from the eyes of all the wise, and God is called

hidden by the Prophet.[23] Something excellent that is perceptible corrupts the senses more quickly than it is apprehended successfully by the respective sense. Similarly, God, who is excellent, is not seen by the intellect. Rather, [He is seen] even less than the brightness of the sun [is seen] by the eye, although nothing is more visible than is [that] brightness, which imposes itself on the eye. But because the [sun's] excellence does not meet with a very strong power in the eye, the eye's light[24] is dimmed rather than [the sun's light] being apprehended. Eternal Wisdom is a Light in which there is no darkness.[25] Likewise, created-reason is a light, because it is an image of that [Uncreated] Light. But the Infinity of the Light of Wisdom cannot be apprehended by that discriminating created-light. Instead, it is rather the case that created-reason is dimmed than that it takes in the infinite brightness of Wisdom. Hence, of Wisdom it is written: "Man shall not see me and live."[26]

[9] Therefore, God's riches would be small if they could be grasped by creatures; and His Light would be small if it were directly visible by a created intellectual eye. Accordingly, God in His glory[27]—which as it is [in and of itself] cannot be manifested as visible (because [that glory] infinitely exceeds the power of all creatable sight)—willed to manifest the riches of His goodness and mercy in the best way in which creatures could apprehend them. Therefore, He created a creature to whom He gave intellect, through which intellect the creature could arrive at knowing that God (although incomprehensible) is his Creator. (By analogy, man's sight arrives at the fact that the brightness is the sun's but that this brightness is not fully apprehensible.) But because the weak light of nature cannot fully attain to a vision of [God's] glory, God willed to manifest the *riches* of the glory [that is present] in this infinity-[of-glory]. And He retained for His infinite generosity the prerogative of granting to His creature the power of attaining the *riches* of His glory within the Light of His glory. For He added to the light-of-nature, which [now became] perfectly disposed for receiving [that super-added light]. For in this way the treasures of His goodness and mercy are manifested when by the gift of our most merciful King we are freed from the failing, and the impoverishment, of our nature and are made rich by means of His gifts. Thus, in regard to the attaining of happiness, no one can ascribe glory to himself but [can ascribe it] only to His Creator. For the Most Glorious King—being ever-willing to show the grace of His mercy to those[28] whom He

called unto the showing of His glory, in order that they might experience it—gives them gifts from His treasure, according as He sees each of them to be deserving. Therefore, [the following] will redound to manifesting our great God's glory: [viz.,] that He can always make known through gifts the magnificence of His mercy.

[10] Similarly, [the following] redounds to showing God's glory: [viz.,] that man, who without free choice could not have been a noble creature of God's, was able to err and to sin. For since the ability to sin contributed to the nobility of free choice, then by the marvelous providence of God it happened that this ability redounds to a manifesting of God's glory. For since God is a very noble King who wills to manifest His nobility in and through His servants, He created intellectual natures, which alone can be capable of serving Him. For only these [natures] can hear and obey the commandments of Wisdom. [God] did not will to have ignoble servants, who, being compelled in the manner of beasts of burden, bore their burdens under the yoke of necessity. Rather, [He willed to have] free and noble [servants] who by free choice and loving affection would freely offer themselves for the keeping of His commandments. And there followed that those who were able to serve by free choice were also able to choose not to obey and thereby to sin against the King. But this ability to sin was turned by the King into a manifestation of His very great graciousness and mercy, so that when He would show the grace of forgiveness to those sinners who were truly contrite and humble in His sight, He would make known His mercy, unto the praise of His glory. In the case of the unrepentant the situation is similar, with regard to the showing of His justice unto the praise of His glory.

[11] Thus, then, our God ordained all things in the best way in which to show the riches of His glory. Therefore, everyone who turns to the visible works of God sees in each and every one of them that a manifestation of God's glory shines forth. And when [anyone] ascends from visible things to invisible things, he discovers that in the invisible things the glory of God shines forth more brightly. And these men have been called lovers of wisdom, or philosophers. Turning to intelligible things by means of perceptible things, they disparage all the delights of this world and discard corruptible pleasures and corruptible lusts of the flesh in order more freely to attain unto things incorruptible. And they turn to the immortal virtues.

Now, although God had manifested His great glory to them by

means of visible and perceptible things, they nevertheless did not glorify God as having manifested these things to them for the praise of His glory.[29] Rather, they continued in vanities, seeking their own glory—as if on their own they would have come to a knowledge of the truth. And they were puffed up because of their knowledge, and they were full of vain glory. And so, ascribing to themselves the praise that they were supposed to have given to the glory of God, they became foolish, though esteeming themselves to be wise (as Paul shows [in his letter] to the Romans).[30] Thus, when Adam—who wanted to ascend, by means of his own knowledge, unto God's likeness—thought that he had found life, he found death. And this is the outcome of all those who have endeavored to ascend unto happiness by their own ingenuity. For all [these] men found no knowledge in their possession; instead, they became vain in their thoughts.[31] For they did not know that happiness is a grace of God and that it can be obtained not by means of their own ingenuity but only by the gift of God. And [they did not know] (1) that every human endeavor to obtain happiness is supposed to be nothing other than for the praise of God's glory in regard to everything that He created and (2) that conformity to the life-of-reason obtains that gift of God's mercy [and] grace—through which [gift] those who are clothed with the light of glory obtain happiness.

[12] The foregoing is the ignorance in which those who sought God were kept until [the time of] Christ. For they did not know the means of arriving at an apprehension [of happiness]. This means is only God's grace, diffused by the Holy Spirit, in the hearts of those who believe and hope.[32] Therefore, Paul says in Romans 11 that Christ has concluded all in unbelief in order that He might have mercy on all.[33] And so, he adds: "O the depth of the riches ...," etc.[34] Therefore, the [Holy] Spirit, the Paraclete, is He who alone teaches all truth. He is given to those who are called to eternal life. For He is sent unto our soul's [faculty of] reason and reveals [to it] truth and remains forever in it. Since He is the Spirit of life, He ever enlivens—just as the Light of life, [viz., Christ], ever enlightens vitally those who receive [Him]. Hence, this knowledge is obtained from revelation on the part of the Incarnate Word of God. For God's word, which is sent by the Spirit, nourishes the intellect. By way of illustration, a teacher who wants to display the glory of his fertile intellect does so by means of his word. By emitting this word, he sends it into his student's conception, [thereby] giving to him a [cognitive] sharing in his own intellect. (For otherwise one man's spirit could not manifest itself to another man's spirit.)

In a similar way, God reveals to an intellectual creature a knowledge of Himself only through His word—[doing so] by means of the Spirit of truth. For the inner Word is a perfect likeness of its Father, i.e., of the Intellect that begets this [Word] from itself. And by means of the Spirit, which is Love, the Word conveys a knowledge of the Father to that intellectual spirit to which it wills to manifest itself. Hence, the Word reveals—to that spirit to which it is bound by the Spirit of love—the Father, who is present in the word. Therefore, angelic spirits cannot know God the Father except by means of the Holy Spirit, who is united to their spirit, in which the word is present—and, in the word, the Father.[35] But because human nature has an intellectual spirit, to which God planned to manifest His glory, and since this [manifestation] is not possible apart from revelation: it was necessary that the Word of the Father put on human nature (just as a teacher's word [puts on] a vocal, or sensory, nature) so that thereby in the word of a man who was a Teacher the word of God could be conveyed to mankind by means of the Spirit. Hence, the gift by which the Spirit is given to us—and [by which], in the Spirit, the Word [is given to us] and [by which], in the Word, the Father [is given to us]—is the maximal manifestation of God's grace and wisdom, unto the praise of His glory.

[**13**] And note that God the Father manifested His glory supremely in that creature in which the Word put on a human nature in order to reveal the Father. For if you consider that a man can come to a knowledge of God's glory, i.e., can come to his own happiness, only by means of the Son's (i.e., the Word's) revelation, then you see rightly that the man who is the Father's Word is the one without whom it is not possible to come[36] to happiness. Hence, Christ Jesus—the Word of God and the Son of man—is the Intermediary without whom God's glory cannot be manifested. Therefore, [Christ] is the Fulfillment, and Perfection, of creatures. Therefore, Paul rightly says that in this Mediator are hidden all the treasures of God's wisdom and knowledge.[37] By way of illustration: in the words of a teacher's instruction there are hidden, beneath the perceptible sounds, all the treasures of the teacher's knowledge and wisdom; and by means of such words his students are enlightened in spirit in order to be able to be brought to a knowledge of the hidden treasure.

Jesus rightly said that the Father had given Him that which is greater than all. For the Father gives by means of one Spirit various gifts: to one [man He gives] prophecy, to another the interpretation of languages, etc.[38] But the gift given to Jesus is greater than all other gifts. For Christ's Spirit, or Gift,[39] enfolds the excellence of all other gifts. For [Christ's Gift] is, without measure, altogether full and perfect—to such an extent that [the following is true]: the Gift that God gave to our Teacher, [viz.,] Christ, is of such great fruitfulness (as regards the knowledge that makes a man happy) that every man who hearkens to [this] teaching can obtain happiness. And the Gift is such that, as it were, the Son—who alone is the Father's heir, because of the Father's love for His Son—imparts to others who are capable of receiving it the art by which He is the Beloved Son, in order that they too, by means of that knowledge, may become beloved sons of [this] same Father. (By way of analogy: from the perfection of a teacher's art all his students can be instructed, so that whichever [of them] grasps the meaning of his words can likewise become a teacher.)

Accordingly, the nature of the human intellect is teachable; and Christ, our unique Teacher, is the Word-of-the-Father, who speaks (as one sent by God) the things that God speaks within Himself. And [Christ does this] not unto His own glory and praise but unto His Father's glory and praise. [And Christ] teaches (1) His own way of life and (2) the art-of-happiness by which He came to happiness and glory in preaching and in working and by which eternal life is truly possessed. [The situation is] as if some natural father were to pass on to his son (who had reached adult age) a secret art together with assured instructions. [It is as if] through this art the son could free himself from a miserable and needy life and could live splendidly. [And it is as if the father] were to give to the son the power to impart [that] same art to all who (1) would honor and love the father and honor and love the son as the father's son and also (2) would adhere to the instructions that he had given to this same son of his.

[**14**] Thus, then, it is evident to some extent that the Son of God, [i.e.,] Jesus, is necessary for us, since without Him we would all remain ignorant of the art by which one arrives at happiness. For only Jesus Himself is the Most High, in whom God shows all the riches of His glory altogether perfectly. Moreover, [Jesus is necessary for us] because preaching (in which the glory of God is manifested) does not suffice for our obtaining the spirit of glory, or gift of glory, with which our nature is clothed-upon in order to be made happy. Rather, purification and adaptation of our spirits to the receiving of the light of glory [are needed], so that in this way the exceedingly great glory of God is shown in Christ Jesus with regard to the restoration of the fallen and

the justification of the wicked. For the Spirit of Wisdom cannot enter into a servile spirit bedarkened with sins or into a soul of evil intent. For the spirit is not capable of wisdom unless it is pure and clean and altogether free of, and purified from, every alien desire. For as long as the spirit is bound to shameful affections, it is powerless to receive wisdom. For it must so cling to the Spirit of truth that it is made one Spirit with it[40]—something that is not possible if it is shackled to worldly servitude. And so, our Teacher was to purify and enlighten us not only by His teaching but also by His merit, so that in that way the glory of God was manifested supremely and most perfectly in Him. For the Father did not spare His very beloved Son; and the Son gave Himself over to death in order that we might receive purification-of-soul by the merit of His blood. Thereupon, God maximally showed the praising of His own glory in order that we would praise His infinite love and would see very clearly that He alone is the one to whom all glory is due, since He is our Creator and Redeemer. Whatever we are, we are from Him, because we are redeemed by His most innocent and most precious blood.

Moreover, consider that in order for us to give praise to His glory, it is fitting (1) that we rightly recognize our indisposition for happiness-in-His-presence and is fitting (2) that we need the grace of redemption and (3) that we seek that [grace] with all our devotion. And [when these conditions are met], then we are giving glory to God in a way that is worthy. Now, the more we recognize our baseness, the more [we give glory to God]. And yet, we believe steadfastly that God can, in accordance with the greatness of His glory, conform the body of our humility to the Body of the brightness of His Most Beloved Son.[41] And we hope that this [transformation] is going to occur—on the basis of the merit of Christ's suffering—when we walk that pathway by which Christ entered into glory. For in that case we shall be moved by the same Spirit as was Christ—[the Spirit] that leads to the Father and to eternal life.

[15] I think that this evangelical teaching is elucidated, especially by the Apostles, in Sacred Scripture, which speaks of the Spirit, who is not of this world (where truth is absent) and whom neither the world nor any of the wise of this world know. In this [Spirit] we were baptized with the baptism of Christ when we received faith in Him.[42] For faith is that which alone is able—through the Spirit of Jesus, who dwells in us through our faith[43]—to strengthen the weakness of our spirit and to give strength for all things. For our spirit can become a

beholder of majesty only by means of the indwelling Spirit of God's Son. This [Spirit] dwells in us because of the faith which we have within our spirit—[faith] concerning Jesus, [faith] that He is God's Son. Through [our] love [this Spirit] becomes one Spirit with our spirit, provided that our faith is [in-]formed by love. By means of this faith we anticipate in this world the happiness that we shall obtain in reality when our Jesus—whom here we have received by faith—will have appeared to us visibly.

Furthermore, note that the art of arriving at happiness is, practically speaking, nothing other than that we keep to the way that Christ kept to. Therefore, if we have faith that Jesus is the Son of God and that no one is happy unless he is a son of God: then if we believe this unhesitatingly, we have the faith (1) through which we overcome the world and all the wise and (2) through which we shall attain unto happiness. For since we have accepted as most assuredly true this one thing—[viz.,] that Jesus is the Son of God—we do not doubt (1) that all of Jesus's words are so steadfast that heaven and earth shall pass away sooner than will one iota of any of His words[44] and (2) that all His promises about the Eternal Kingdom are beyond doubt. So, then, it will not be possible [for us] *not* to keep His commandments, [even] to the point of [being put to] death [because of keeping them]. For He teaches that to-obey-unto-death is to-enter-into-life.

[16] Therefore, he who believes that Jesus is the Son of God and that the sacred Gospels are true has Him in whom his spirit most agreeably finds consolation. (For just as there is no comparability between the Son of God and the sons of men, so there is no comparability between the teaching of Christ and that of the philosophers.) [Such a believer] sees that the whole of Sacred Scripture serves the gospel and that the entire teaching of the philosophers is empty and vain and without an enlivening and delighting spirit. He will clearly learn by experience that through the certitude of faith one arrives at love for God and that together with love that is rooted in faith there comes an intellectual vision, i.e., knowledge. For by means of love a living faith proceeds continually onwards unto seeing and unto knowing. For a loving spirit in which Jesus dwells because of our faith is caught up unto a *beholding*—[one] that is a foretaste of the eternal bliss that we await.

The teaching of Jesus is that without *faith* it is not possible to arrive at happiness. Next, [He teaches that] without *love* it is impossible for there to be true faith. Hereafter, there follows that such a believer comes to a *knowledge* of that which he has received by faith. And not only (1) does he believe that he believes what is true but also (2) he knows that faith is true faith and that through faith he will arrive at happiness, as says Wisdom 3: "Those who trust in Him will understand the truth, and those who are faithful in love will rest in Him."[45] Hence, he who chooses not to *believe* unless he *knows*, thereby giving priority to knowing: such a man remains in darkness, because his knowledge cannot ascend to God unless his spirit is strengthened by faith in Jesus.

[**17**] But how it is that the foregoing teaching of Jesus's is found in Sacred Scripture is itself found in another sermon [of mine] for this day.[46] But for now let it suffice to have said the following: [viz.,] that the [Holy] Spirit, the Paraclete, will bring to mind all the things which the Word of God speaks.[47] [This bringing to mind] is the gift by which our rational spirit sees in itself (i.e., sees by means of its rational faculty) that that which the Word of God speaks is true. By way of illustration: when a teacher sets forth a true mathematical proposition, then if one of his students has the gift of understanding, he quickly sees in his own reason the truth of the proposition that was set forth. And [this truth] is sweet and pleasing to him. And so, [in a corresponding way], the Spirit from whom [a believer] has the foregoing gift of understanding is rightly called Comforter, or Paraclete. For He aids the spirit that is still bedarkened with the darkness of ignorance, and He brings to its mind an evidential ground; and from this bringing-to-mind there arises great consolation. But he who has not yet received this gift of understanding does not apprehend the meaning of the words or feel the consolation, i.e., the nourishment.

Now, the Spirit that gives understanding proceeds from the Father, who is Pure Intellect[48] from whom comes every best gift and every perfect gift.[49] And because [this Spirit] is the Spirit of truth[50] (or of an understanding of the words), it is the Spirit of Jesus, who is Truth and who is the Word of God. Therefore, this gift of the Spirit of truth proceeds from the Father and the Son (i.e., from the Word) and is sent from the Father in the name of the Son; for it is sent in order that the Word be understood. Therefore, it is sent in the name of the Son in order to prompt an understanding of Jesus's words. Hence, there is written in Wisdom 9: "Who will know Your thought unless You will give wisdom and will send Your Holy Spirit?" etc.[51]

NOTES TO *Spiritus autem Paraclitus*

* Sermon CLXXXVII.
1. John 14:26. See my n.1 in Notes to Sermon XXXVII.
2. *De Docta Ignorantia* I, 6. *De Possest* 3. *Cribratio Alkorani* II, 2 (**90**). These passages, together with the text above, are as close as Nicholas comes to giving *arguments* for God's existence. See my *Nicholas of Cusa: Metaphysical Speculations: Volume Two* (Minneapolis: Banning, 2000), pp. 52-60.
3. Romans 1:19-20.
4. "… is Pure Intellect": or, "… is Pure Understanding".
5. Throughout this sermon Nicholas signifies in a twofold way. On the one hand, he is referring to God's Triunity by means of the words "Omnipotence," "Understanding," and "Love." On the other hand, he is using these words with their common significations. Sometimes a single word plays upon both significations at once. Accordingly, it is not always clear whether or not to use capitalization in the English translation.
6. Throughout this section Nicholas uses the one Latin word "*intellectus*" both with the sense of the English word "intellect" and with the sense of the English word "understanding." The latter English word is ambiguous, since it can be used to stand not only for the act of understanding but also for the faculty of understanding (i.e., for the intellect). Nicholas's use of "*intellectus*" is ambiguous in this same way. Only the context can serve to disambiguate the meaning.
7. Here (at **3**:22) I am reading, with the Paris edition, "omnipotentis" in place of "omnipotentiae".
8. These words are construed by Nicholas as names for the Holy Spirit.
9. In this example of the father and the son, as well as in the subsequent example of the beautiful woman, the idea contained in the signification of the Latin verb "*gloriari*" and the Latin noun "*gloria*" is more like the sense of our expressions "to take pride in" and "a taking pride in."
10. See n. 6 above.
11. John 4:24.
12. Luke 15:11-24; 15:4-6; 15:8-9—respectively.
13. E.g., Romans 9:23. Colossians 1:27. The indented text below is from Ephesians 3:8-12.
14. Romans 3:25.
15. I Corinthians 10:31.
16. Acts 17:24-27.
17. Psalms 13:2 (14:2).
18. Exodus 33:18-19.
19. Aristotle, *Metaphysics*, opening sentence.
20. John 17:3.
21. I Corinthians 2:9. See also Romans 11:33-34. Nicholas makes the point that man can have no conception that corresponds to God's nature as it is in and of itself. All knowledge of *what* God is is symbolical.
22. Here Nicholas shows the influence of Aquinas's theory of knowledge. See pp. 121-139 of my *Nicholas of Cusa: Metaphysical Speculations: Volume Two*

(Minneapolis: Banning, 2000). For an alternative view see Klaus Kremer's, "Erkennen bei Nikolaus von Kues. Apriorismus – Assimilation – Abstraktion," pp. 3-49 in his *Praegustatio naturalis sapientiae. Gott suchen mit Nikolaus von Kues* (Münster: Aschendorff, 2004). In this same volume see also pp. 103-146 ("Das kognitive und affektive Apriori bei der Erfassung des Sittlichen").

24. Plato, Augustine, Anselm, and others teach tat the eye emits an invisible ray that meets with the light of day (or other external light), making possible the actual seeing of visible objects.

25. I John 1:5. Cf. John 8:12.

26. Exodus 33:20.

27. Literally: "God's glory ...."

28. Here (at **9**:28) I am surmising "illis" in place of "illos".

29. Romans 1:21-23.

30. *Loc. cit.*

31. *Loc. cit.*

32. Romans 5:5.

33. Romans 11:32.

34. Romans 11:33.

35. See my n. 51 in Sermon CLXXXIII.

36. Here (at **13**:8-9) I am reading, with the Paris edition, "pervenire" in place of "perveniri".

37. Colossians 2:3.

38. I Corinthians 12:4-31.

39. "Gift" is a name that Medieval writers often use for the Holy Spirit. See n. 5 and n. 8 above.

40. See *De Filiatione Dei*, Nicholas's treatise on a believer's deification, a believer's becoming a son of God through Christ.

41. Philippians 3:21.

42. Nicholas accepts both the view that baptism removes the guilt of original sin and the view that faith is a gift of God (Ephesians 2:8).

43. Ephesians 3:17.

44. Matthew 5:18.

45. Wisdom 3:9.

46. "... for this day": viz., the feast-day of Pentecost. See Sermon XXXVII.

47. John 14:26.

48. "Pure Intellect": or "Pure Understanding." See n. 4 and n. 6 above.

49. James 1:17.

50. John 14:17 and 15:26.

51. Wisdom 9:17.

Qui Me Invenerit Inveniet Vitam
et Hauriet Salutem a Domino*
("He Who Finds Me Shall Find Life
and Shall Acquire Salvation from the Lord")[1]
[September 8, 1455; preached in Brixen][2]

[**1**] "He who finds me shall find life and shall acquire salvation from the Lord" (Proverbs 8).

[**2**] Today the Church reads these words from the Book of Solomon. And because they are read aloud for the honor of the glorious Virgin's birth, they are likewise in this way set forth for our instruction.[3] For we sons of Eve are exiles in this world; we are sons of the mother who brought death into the world because she chose what was beautiful in appearance and because she preferred her own desires to the commandment of the Giver of life. Therefore, with groaning and weeping we seek in this vale of tears a mother who will turn the curse of Eve into a blessing, who will feed us sons of Eve with the milk-of-her-breasts, the stream of Heavenly life. Accordingly, to us who are wailing to be fed, the Mother speaks as follows: "He who finds me [shall find life] ...," etc. She means not *life* but (a) the vessel in which there is life and (b) the stream that flows with life, from which stream salvation from the Lord can be drawn forth.

[**2**] We must consider that although Solomon spoke of the Creator's wisdom, by which the Creator made the ages and is delighted to be with men,[4] nevertheless among all the works of God, the Virgin Mary came into this world in order to manifest His glory. First of all, we must reflect on the fact that there cannot be a world unless there is a beginning; and there can be only one Beginning. And because that Beginning is without a beginning, it is eternal, or Eternity. From that [Beginning] there does not naturally come a world. For by nature sameness of species is preserved; for example, man begets man. Now, God, or Eternity (which is also Oneness), is not more than one; for, [were Eternity more than one], God would cease to be Eternity, or Oneness. And because He is *actually* everything *possible*,[5] He cannot be multiplied or increased or decreased. Therefore, since creatures do not proceed from this First Beginning by way of nature or of necessity, they proceed by way of art (for there are no other modes [of their originating]), although we can say that in God art coincides with

nature. For the art of the Creator is not of a different nature but is of the nature of the Beginning. This art is eternal, since Solomon says that it is from eternity.[6] Therefore, the Eternal Art is from Him who is eternal; and there cannot be more than one eternal thing. Hence, the Art, i.e., the Wisdom of God, is Eternal God from Eternal God.[7] This Art, by means of which God the Father made all things,[8] is apprehended in terms of orderedness. For Wisdom is established (*ordinata*)—as we find in today's reading. But Art acts freely [and] not by necessity, as does nature. Therefore, the First Beginning cannot be understood to be perfect unless He is [understood to be] triune—i.e., [unless we understand] that in Him is Capability, Knowing, and Willing.

[3] Now, God created all things for His own sake in order to manifest His glory. And so, Solomon says that the Wisdom of God delights to be with the sons of men.[9] For the sons of men were created by God so as to be capable of wisdom, so that they would see in God's Wisdom the glory of Him who created all things so wisely and orderedly—and so that by means of things that are caused they would contemplate the Cause. And since Wisdom, while remaining in itself, transfers itself to the souls of the saints: choosing to perform a very perfect work, He determined from eternity to descend unto human nature. And because that Eternal Art willed to unite Himself to a human nature, He ordained for Himself from eternity a mother by means of whom He would assume a human nature.

Take note of our wondrous God, who from eternity foreordained for Himself a temporal mother! Eternity creates for Himself a mother from whom He would be begotten! [Analogously, it is] as if a knowledge of philosophy were eternal and as if there were to be begotten a man who would have the entire art of philosophy, to which art nothing could be added. In that case, there would not be one art that was eternal and another art that was begotten. A similar situation would occur if philosophy were a self-existent art (not an accident),[10] so that (1) the one begotten would be both a philosopher and a man (and qua philosopher would be of one nature and qua man would be of another nature; and the temporal nature of the man would exist in the eternal nature of the art of philosophy) and so that (2) philosophy would be the creator of that man.

[4] We rightly marvel at the glorious God—[marvel] in and through Mary, who is not the mother of a human being without being also the mother of God, because she is *theotocos*.[11] For she is the

mother of Christ, (1) who is a human being (*homo*) in such a way that He is the Wisdom of God the Father [and] (2) who is the Son of God in such a way that He is also the son of a human being [*homo*]. Therefore, Eternal Wisdom created for Himself a mother. What can be thought to be more wondrous [than] that what-was-originated would be the mother of the Unoriginated? Christ, the Son of God, is, *apart from a male seed*, the son of Mary; and, nevertheless, He is *of the seed* of Abraham according to the flesh.[12] What can more profoundly be said, surpassing all understanding, [than] "apart from a seed but of the seed"? [He was] born of a woman who was a virgin—[born] of a woman (for He was of the seed of Abraham) who was a virgin (for [He was conceived] apart from a male seed). In Adam there was present Eve, who was a woman;[13] she is the mother of all those who are alive according to "Adam," i.e., according to the flesh. In Mary Christ was present; He is the father of all those who are alive according to the spirit. Eve came from a male without coming from a male seed; Christ came from a female without coming from a male seed. Eve came from a male without there being lust of the flesh; Christ came from Mary without there being lust of the flesh.

NOTES TO *Qui Me Invenerit Inveniet Vitam*

* Sermon CCIII.
1. Proverbs 8:35.
2. This date was the feast-day of the Virgin Mary's birth.
3. Cf. II Timothy 3:16.
4. Cf. Proverbs 8:31.
5. This is the theme of Nicholas's *De Possest*, written in 1460.
6. Proverbs 8:23.
7. Nicholas is here alluding to God the Son's begottenness from God the Father. In Medieval theology God the Son is called the Wisdom of the Father, the Art of the Father, the Word of the Father, the true Image of the Father, etc.
8. Colossians 1:16.
9. Proverbs 8:31.
10. The word "accident" is here being used in the sense of the Aristotelian distinction between substance and accident.
11. "Theotocos" is the Greek name used (in the Chalcedon Creed of 451) for Mary with respect to her being the *God-bearer*, or *Dei genetrix*.
12. Cf. Romans 1:3.
13. Genesis 2:23.

Maria Optimam Partem Elegit*
("Mary Has Chosen the Best Part ....")[1]
[August 15, 1446; preached in Mainz][2]

[1] "Mary has chosen the best part, which shall not be taken away from her." Luke 10.

We celebrate the feast-day on which—in and through the most glorious Virgin Mary, who is our most gracious advocate—our human nature was exalted above all the choirs of angels unto the Heavenly kingdoms, unto the Son. We come together today in *this* place praising her in order that through [this] Mother of mercy we may merit to obtain *in Heavenly places* kindness from her and fellowship with her. Let us who salute her implore her that for the sake of our edification I may be able to say something worthwhile about her assumption.

[2] The words of the theme-text can be applied to the rational spirit, which has chosen the best part, even as [this same] Gospel-passage befits [our present] feast-day in terms of its gist. For if to sit at Jesus's feet and to hear His word and to devote oneself to the one necessary thing and to choose that part is something so perfect that it shall never be taken away, then if this [verdict] holds true in the case of Mary Magdalene,[3] [as it does], it is also altogether true in the case of the Mary who is Theotocos, i.e., the God-bearer. Hence, according to this reasoning we can consider, for our learning,[4] that the end-goal of our intellectual nature is to obtain *happiness*. But *choosing* precedes the happiness; for we must obtain happiness intellectually; hence, choosing precedes. But that which is altogether unknown cannot be either chosen or desired. Therefore, *enlightening* precedes choosing. In accordance with these three [considerations] let us elicit something [for our present edification].[5]

I

[3] Now, first of all, with respect to enlightenment: the learned ought to elicit from the words of Christ a certain deep teaching, viz., that our rational spirit partakes of the form of Divine Reason, which is called *Word* or *Logos*. And, accordingly, from the Source of this divine light (which enlightens every man who comes into this world)[6] we sense (by means of the power of apprehending through innate desires) that in us are present those things which the Incarnate Word declares that He *is*:

viz., Truth, Life, and the Way.[7] For if Divine Reason—in whose image our rational faculty was created and from which it has the light-of-reason—declares that it is these things, then it is not strange that with great desire we are inclined toward *truth* (i.e., toward true and unfailing *life*) and that eternal law (which is the *way* to truth and to life) is present in us as in its own image.

[4] But our faculty of reason, which is a light from Divine Light, shines forth in the darkness of this corporeal and fleshly substance, so that its immaterial nature cannot be apprehended amid the corporeal shadow. Yea, rather, our rational spirit exists as if in a fleshly prison[8] and is able to seek immaterial nourishment only through the windows of the body. Therefore, since all its nourishment is taken in by means of what is perceptible, the nourishment remains disproportionate, so that it is not nourishment that is true and vital and formed in the way that the rational spirit requires. Hence, reason, which is embodied in flesh, cannot attain in truth that which is sought—just as the eye [that is looking] through an impure medium (e.g., colored glass) also cannot attain the truth of the object.

[5] God, taking account of this ignorance, sent Absolute Reason (i.e., His Word or consubstantial Son) into the flesh in order that we might be instructed as to how we would be able to attain the desired truth and life, which are not present in this world. And [His Son] teaches us about this [attainment]—[teaches us] in a clear and simple and concise manner in this Gospel-passage. There He instructs us that the rational soul that was in Martha and that was in Mary can have a twofold endeavor in regard to seeking truth or life or the way: thus, [the rational soul] is nourished in spirit either by means of the multiplicity of frequent endeavors or with respect to a single endeavor. [The endeavor] that occurs by means of multiplicity is perturbing and temporal and does not have truth, life, or the way, because truth is abiding and undisturbable. Moreover, that which is supposed to nourish the [rational] spirit with incorruptible life cannot be divided into a plurality-of-things, [for] plurality is beset by a troubling unsteadfastness. Therefore, to be busy with the frequent ministering of many things is not to proceed on the pathway of the eternal and incorruptible law.

[6] Hence, since a plurality of things brings disquietude to the [rational] spirit, which seeks peace, a single thing is necessary in order that the spirit may choose. For what is *one* is unifying and, hence, enlivening and eternalizing. Therefore, reason, which can choose

either the part that is centered on what is lower (as concerns the attending to multiple affairs, which cannot be multiple without division and which, accordingly, are disquieting) or can devote itself to what is higher, (as concerns the One, which is the Self-existent Beginning that is eternal and at rest, free of all disquietude. If [the rational spirit] chooses the one necessary End, it chooses the best part, in which it will rest eternally [and] which will not be taken away from it. Indeed, since things that are more-than-one are things that are multiple, they can exist neither from themselves nor through themselves; nor can they find rest in themselves; for that which is One [and] Necessary is the *Beginning* of plurality. For that which is necessary for the existence of a multiplicity of things is One Thing, without which there could not be a multiplicity.

[7] Therefore, the One Thing that is necessary for positing a plurality of things is the Cause—the Beginning, Middle, and End—from which, through which, and in which the many exist.[9] Therefore, it is not the case that to be troubled with many things is rightly to proceed unto rest; for the many have nothing from themselves; rather, the *One* alone is their rest. But since only the *One* is the rational spirit's termination of desire, it is that which is so necessary that only in it, qua in what is absolutely necessary, can the rational spirit happily rest as in the Beginning, Middle, and End of it and of its desire for truth, life, and eternity. For only then does the [rational] spirit turn back upon itself with a complete turning. For in this way it attains its end not, as it were, in something else—as does he who seeks his end in a plurality. For this latter [individual] cannot find his end except in something other than [the true end] itself. And, hence, he finds [the end] only as existing otherwise than it does [in and of itself]; and, thus, [his finding] is defective and disquieting. However, he who seeks his end-goal in the One Necessary Thing finds it not as it is present in something else but as it is present in the One Necessary Thing.

[8] The *one* attains itself unfailingly only in the One Thing, which is necessary for it, through which Thing it is *one*. By way of illustration: The form of a signet-ring in wax can attain itself unfailingly only in the ring of which it is the image. For only *there* does it attain its own measure in truth. For, indeed, the exemplar is the true measure of the exemplification. And just as a student is perfected when he is made like his teacher, and just as then he attains rest, so our reason is perfectly at rest in the One Necessary Thing, viz., in Infinite

Reason, because [*there* it is present] not as in [some] other [reason] but as in our own [Source of] reason. For when [our reason] shall appear as resting in that [Infinite Reason], [our reason] will be like that [Infinite Reason]—as we are sufficiently instructed from the teaching of the saints.[10] [9] And we, as being those who are instructed from this teaching of Christ's, will now be able to grasp with ready discernment all the philosophers' deepest laborings, which seem to students to be especially difficult. For, indeed, the Platonists (as is evident from Plato's book the *Parmenides*) after turning away from multiplicity toward the One, professed that the One is Absolute Necessity and is the Ground (*ratio*) of all existing things. For all things exist insofar as they are one, as states Boethius[11] regarding oneness and the *one*. And as Dionysius says toward the end of *The Divine Names*: the absolutely One is all things unitively.[12] For, as Cause, [the One] enfolds all things.

[10] The *one* precedes all things, as our ordinary German language teaches us. For before anything that is expressible we always put a oneness. For example, we say "one man," "one essence," "one congregation," "one substance," "one quantity," "one angel," "one virtue," and so on.[13] Hence, after "one" we have everything expressible. Through the [One], from the [One], and in the [One] all things partake of One in their own way; the One is ineffably and inco-ordinately[14] exalted above all things.[15] Therefore, whatever is named is less than it. Similarly, whatever part of a city is named is less than the city, since with the name of the city there come, implicitly, all the things that are in the city. Likewise, whatever part of all things [is named is] less than the One.[16] Hence, Martha, who by means of many ministerings went off into many things, was rightly perturbed, since all things exist only by means of the One.

[11] Since the one is one, it cannot exist from another, because before all otherness there is oneness, so that otherness is a falling away from oneness, or a defect in the approach to the *one*.[17] Therefore, the *one* acts as one. That is, just as the characteristic of heat is to make-warm and the characteristic of cold is to make-cold, so the characteristic of *one* is to unite. Hence, for the *one* to act is for it to summon the not-one unto the *one's* oneness. Now, of its own nature *one* is unmultipliable, because twice one is not one but is other than one, viz., two. Therefore, when *one* summons what is not-one (i.e., what is pure nothing) unto its own unattainable oneness, then a creature rises up in [the *one's*] likeness. Thus, you have [the following truth]: because

there is one thing, there are all things. And so, one thing is necessary for all things. Thus, then, that which has nothing at all of oneness—viz., what is altogether nothing—comes, by means of the *one's* omnipotence, to be a likeness of the *one*. Therefore, because any creature can exist only if it is one, it is found in the likeness of the Absolute and Super-exalted One.

[**12**] Yet, multiple creatures cannot have one and the same degree of likeness, because *one* is unmultipliable. Therefore, each creature in its own individual manner is found to exist in a likeness of the Absolute One. But since [these] multiple creatures are found to exist only in a likeness of the Absolute One, they will be compatible in their differences of individuality. And this [compatibility] constitutes the world's harmony. Therefore, just as every creature has from the One that it is one, so it also has [from the One] that it unites. Hence, every activity of creatures is likewise found to exist with [a degree of] likeness [to the One's activity]. When heat heats, it summons to itself that which is not-hot. But since [heat] cannot [cause] what is not-hot to attain unto an identity with heat's unattainable oneness, there arises [in the not-hot] a likeness [to the hot]. The case is similar as regards the intellect: since its operation is to summon what is not-intellect unto a oneness with itself, [that which is not-intellect] is found to arise with a [degree of] likeness [to intellect]—and so on, in the case of all natural and all constructed objects.

[**13**] Hence, the wondrous teaching of Christ is this: [viz.,] that whoever wishes to seek truth not tire himself with a multiplicity of objects so that, for example, he seek [to know] what the sky is, what the earth is, etc. For if all these things are considered in and of themselves, there will be found in them, qua multiple things, nothing of the true; rather, there is [only] a mental disquieting when, after infinite tiring efforts, [the seeker] finds that he has arrived at nothing precise but has wasted his time. However, when amid all [these] things he turns his attention to the One, then he finds that the One is the Absolute Necessity of all the things. For, as Dionysius says: because there is the Absolute One, there are all things.[18] For [the reason that it is] the Cause of [all] causes and of all being is only that it is One. Hence,[19] because [the seeker] attains the One, the Necessary Cause of all things, he seeks peace and rest in all things. He uses rightly the book written by God's Finger, viz., [the book of] the created world. He knows that every creature is a likeness of the One. He knows that the one heaven, when sum-

moned forth from the not-one, arose in a likeness of the Absolute One. And [he knows] that the more [the heaven] was elevated away from the not-one, the closer it drew near to the One in terms of likeness.

[**14**] [The seeker] rests at the feet of the sensory world in order to hear what the Rational Spirit speaks in and through it. For he sees in each creature—as in a likeness of the One—the One Necessary Thing, and he chooses it. He sees here one tree and there one stone and here one animal and there one star. Hence, he readily understands—since these all agree only in terms of their oneness—that, accordingly, they all derive from One thing, from which they have the fact of their being united in regard to [being] one. And since there can be only one One, all things have their oneness from the one [Oneness]. But since a tree is not a star or a stone, then there does not belong to the essence of the One that the One be a tree or a stone or any other nameable thing. Rather, the Absolute One is prior to everything nameable. And everything nameable has a mode[20] in which it is named one, because it does not attain the unmultipliable One unto which it is summoned. Hence, with respect to likeness it is the case (1) that the one heaven is a likeness-of-the-One such that it is called heaven and (2) that one man is a likeness-of-the-One that is called a man and (3) that one essence is a likeness-of-the-One that is called an essence and (4) that one power is a likeness-of-the-One that is *thus* called [i.e., is called a power].

[**15**] Accordingly, the point of ready accessibility to difficult matters is this: [viz.,] that since we know that present in all things there is One Necessary Thing and that all things are in its likeness, we are at ease and we hear how it is that in and through our reason all things speak of the One and how it is that all things endeavor to express the One through a likeness but that, nevertheless, they cannot do so, because the likeness always falls short of the One. Thus, our intellectual power, which is inclined toward the true, turns toward the One's truth, equality, and highest likeness. And [the intellect] attains the One (which is unattainable because it precedes everything understandable and effable) in and through a highest likeness of equality with (the truth about) the One. For the truth about the One is a supremely precise likeness. Hence, this preciseness, which can be called truth, is that by means of which our intellect desires to attain the Absolute One. We are disposed toward truth, because truth is the highest equality with the One. For example, when it is said of gold that it is true gold, then [the gold] admits of nothing other than gold. Hence, the true is a highest

equality, and highest likeness, that admits of no otherness.

[16] Hence, when we attain the One in Truth (which Truth is also called Logos, or Word, or Son), then we attain the One as it is—[attain it,] that is, in a precise Likeness.[21] And so, to attain the One is to attain it as it is attainable *by the intellect*, although in and of itself [the One] surpasses every intellect. And when [the One] is thus attained by the intellect, then the intellectual life, which cannot then perish, is at rest in Truth and is made happy in Truth. And so, the part[22] of the One Necessary Thing that is chosen will never be taken away from this soul. Moreover, since the sacred text of the Gospel[23] instructs us that Mary sat at the feet of Jesus and heard His teaching, we ought to infer from this [passage] that these words of Christ were [spoken] in order that he might *instruct* Mary, who [elsewhere] is said to be an illumined tower. [The words were meant to instruct her] that [our rational] spirit—which desires, with respect to the inner desires of its nature, the immortality of the intellectual life—is like an illumined tower. [It is like this] when it has been instructed [and] when it knows that that which it seeks is One Thing, which is not found in a discrete plurality, although without the One there could not exist anything.

[17] By analogy, suppose that the living eye wished to seek the true source of its life in order to know from whence it truly is alive. [In order to do so,] the eye ought not to turn toward any other one of the members of the body, as if the eye had life from that member. For no such member is the cause, or basis, of the eye's life, even though the members might seem to persuade the eye that they give life. For example, the hands, which administer food, [might therefore seem to be persuasive]—as might also the stomach, which digests, and the mouth and the teeth and all the other members that seem to work cooperatively so that the eye might be alive. But, indeed, none of these rather distinct living members are the true life of the eye; instead, in their own way they are partakers of the eye's true life. Each of them has life in its own way after the fashion of the life-source toward which they [all] are turned and in which they rest [and] which they all serve. For together with the eye they are alive by means of one life, viz., the soul. Accordingly, if the eye were to judge that the source of its life is in these several members, and if it were to find that the life in them is perturbed, it itself would be perturbed to have judged that the true source of its life is in corruptible things.

Hence, when [the eye] sees that the hand becomes lacking in life because the hand withers and when it sees that nevertheless it itself is still alive, then it knows that the life of the [bodily] members depends on a truer life that does not fail in its own true being, even if the member perishes. Therefore, [the eye] turns toward the one life by a partaking of which the entire life of the members is that which it is. [The eye turns] as if toward the singular and necessary cause [of the life] of all living members. In particular, [it turns] toward the soul, and it chooses the soul as the best part. [The eye turns toward the soul] as toward the true source of its life, and it cherishes the soul and loves it as being the source of its life. And life is not taken away from the eye as long as the eye remains united, in a oneness, to the life of the soul. And thereupon the eye recognizes that the living members—such as the living hand, the stomach, etc.—have the state of being alive for the purpose of being useful to [the source] of their life, not for the purpose of conferring life.

[**18**] The intellect is present in man as God is present in the world; for the intellect is not imbedded but is independent. The one intellect summons all things unto itself in order that they may live in the oneness of its life. But its oneness is unmultipliable. Therefore, all the members of a man, by partaking in their own way of the intellect's life, have life in the likeness of the intellect's life. Now, the intellectual life of the soul imparts itself in an equal way [and] as something one. But in the different members it is found in various degrees of likeness. For [it is present] in one way and very obscurely in strands of hair and in nails [of the fingers and toes]. [It is present] in another way, and somewhat more obviously, in the hands—and present still more apparently in the eyes. The Absolute One is related in a similar way to all the members of this present world, each of which members in its own way is one in the likeness of the Absolute One. And just as one intellect enfolds, in its oneness, all things unitedly in its own way, viz., intellectually, so the Absolute One [enfolds] all things unitedly in an absolute way. And just as from the things unfolded by the intellect we are led in a unitive way unto the enfolding, so that to some extent we can attain [a knowledge of] the oneness of the intellect, so from the many onenesses [of the things in the world] we are elevated in a unitive way unto [a knowledge of] the Absolute One, so that as a result we arrive at the One Necessary Thing, which is the Best because of the fact that it is the Super-exalted One. For it is of the nature of the good to *summon unto itself* and to *make good*. Because the good is one, whose nature is to unite: the Best is the Absolute One, which is exact-

ly and supremely and perfectly identical [to the Best].

[**19**] If, then, Mary Magdalene,[24] seated at Jesus's feet, came—as a result of having heard His words—unto a choosing of the Best in her own way, viz., as Mary Magdalene: how excellently the Virgin Mary, when elevated above all the heavens, was brought to a choosing of the Best—she who merited to be the mother of Jesus and of the Word and Light and Reason and Truth! O how highly above all intellectual visions she saw that One Invisible [Being], and how she tasted, with a healthy palate, of the one Fount of life! If David was elevated to the point of having said "Taste and see that the Lord is pleasant!"[25] then, as is right, the higher [the Virgin Mary] was than all the prophets, the more perfectly she saw and tasted of Him with whom is the Fount of [all] good, Him who alone is the One Good that all things seek. Therefore, she chose this best part, which shall not be taken away from her, since to choose is to unite.

[**20**] Therefore, Mary's power-of-choice, viz., her intellectual spirit, was united to the Best. Therefore, her soul cannot be turned away from the Best, which is worthy of choice in and of itself [and] which is the Cause of her choice. If all things naturally seek the good, then after the intellect has intellectually chosen the best, it can never fail to keep choosing it. But it chooses intellectually when it has intellectually foretasted that the Best is the One Necessary Thing. Now, this tasting comes by way of an administering of a refection to the life of the [intellectual] spirit. This [refection] occurs by means of an enlightening from the word-of-God, which *enlightens*—as Mary Magdalene was enlightened while she sat listening to Jesus's word. Hence, although many daughters, or rational souls, who were enlightened by the word of life by way of choosing the Best have gathered riches: only that most enlightened-Tower—Mary, the God-Bearer—surpassed all [souls], so that with respect to excellence there rightly befits *her* that which the Gospel states that the sinner Mary Magdalene obtained.

This [suffices] as regards the first part [of the sermon].

II

[**21**] In the second place, our text from the sacred Gospel can be construed [in such a way] that it expresses the vital endeavor of every Christian. And this [endeavor can be construed] in a manner such [as Mary's] or in a similar manner [to hers]. For after Jesus had entered into this world as into a certain town of the universe, He was received

in a house of the town, viz., in the Church, which is called His house. Now, in the house where Jesus was received there are two sisters, who symbolize [two] endeavors of the Christian man. Although these [endeavors] are different [from each other], nevertheless they occur in the same house of the two sisters: the one endeavor concerns love of neighbor; the other concerns love of God. As regards love of neighbor, the endeavor is symbolized in Martha, who received Jesus and who was busy with much serving. Hence, the works that we do for Christ—whom, in and through our neighbor,[26] we feed, give drink to, [and] visit—are works-of-Christians that are pleasing to God. For [they are] works of mercy done to our neighbor [and] done in love for Christ's sake.

[22] But [these works] produce very much perturbation because disinclination of mind is sometimes present during the ministering. Or [there is perturbation] because of the flesh's weakness or because of a lack of supplies to be ministered or because of the insistence and disobedience of those to whom one is supposed to minister or because of many other obstacles that often cause disturbance. For example, there are instances of bodily fatigue; there is listlessness, is lukewarmness, and so on. Nevertheless, that [kind of] life is pleasing to God and is quite meritorious in proportion to the degree of love that the one who does the works has. And [that kind of life] ought to be the life of those who wish to make progress as Christians. For according to Gregory[27] it is necessary that Christians prove themselves in the field of actions by means of physical and spiritual works of mercy and necessary that they busy themselves with much serving of Christ by means of such holy endeavors. [It is necessary] in order that hereby they may arrive at a Christ-like fixed disposition, viz., humility and gentleness of heart, so that they can turn completely to the Best and to the One Necessary Thing once the perturbations are overcome and the hardships are dissipated.

[23] Secondly, there is the life that follows the foregoing life. [It involves] a clinging solely to God by means of godly love—after, indeed, [there are ended] the labors of the active life, in which through righteous endeavors one has subdued the flesh and has, from the benefits conferred on him by God, shown himself merciful to his neighbor in terms of love. As a result, the following have no place in him: neither greed nor pride nor lust nor gluttony nor sloth nor anger nor envy.[28] Rather, [there has place] only the humble desire to arrive at the sabbath-

-of-rest [and] to be free of labor in this world and to see that the Lord is pleasant.[29] For at that point, having become of firm disposition in the sweetness of holy prayers and having in remorse of heart left behind the cares of the world [and while dwelling] only in love for God, he aims with the eye of his mind at the joy of happiness, [and] he foretastes it with great fervor of desire; [and] in ecstasy he elevates himself sublimely unto it, insofar as [this elevation] is granted by Divine gift. This [attainment] is the best part of the Christian life—a part that will not be taken away. For [the attainment] is begun here on earth and is perfected in eternity. But it is begun here below by sitting at Jesus's feet and meditating on Jesus's humility—by meditating on how He entered into this world and walked in it, not [by meditating] perfunctorily but by putting on that form [of Christ-like humility] and by receiving in the ear of our heart Christ's word.

[24] Now, the word that emanates from the Godhead is not of this present world but is of the other world, so that a contemplative who is thus inflamed with the desire for happiness posits his entire course of conduct in Heaven. For when in this way [the contemplative] yearns for Heavenly things—[yearns] with his whole heart and from out of the warmth of love—then his heart is expanded, and, by the attestation of his consciousness, God is sensed to be present and God is seen spiritually with the eye-of-the-soul, which is the intellect. For where He is fervently desired, He is present; and there he makes His abode[30] and conveys Himself unto those holy souls. From this pleasing visitation—by which, as a sudden flash of lightening, [God] shows Himself to be present—there arises an elevation of the mind. And [the contemplative] begins to become drowsy between the arms of his Beloved, so that he clings not only delightedly but also tightly to the Beloved. Thus, he is drawn away, as if by a certain force, from the perception and the memory of all visible things. And he almost forgets himself,[31] in accordance with the Canticle: "I sleep, and my heart watches, like one who is drowsy but not yet asleep."[32] And this love for God, when it is grounded in understanding, intoxicates the mind and glues the mind to God, once it is free from outer objects. And the more robust the love and the more lucid the understanding, the more strongly [the love] wrests the mind [away from the world and] unto itself—until the point, at length, that [the mind] casts aside all that is beneath God and remains dwelling as if amid gleaming light.

[25] The mind, by itself, can just barely think of few things.

[But] when it is lifted upwards by a flash of Heavenly light, then it sees many things at once in proportion to its being loftily elevated beyond itself. And because the body is a load upon the mind and presses it down,[33] and because the affairs of this world call the soul back toward itself, [the soul] cries out with Paul: "O wretched man that I am! Who shall free me from the body of this death?"[34] For the contemplative soul will suddenly lapse back toward lower things and [will] be [now] fed from the memory of the [lofty] things that it has agreeably seen. In this way devout men attain slightly and privily some measure of the uncircumscribed light; and, according to St. Gregory,[35] they return, sighing, to their own darkness. And at this stage different kinds of devoutness manifest themselves: viz., joyous shouting, intoxication of spirit, melting, and spiritual delight. Thereupon, one comes to mental alienation—at times because of the magnitude of the devotion, at times because of the magnitude of the amazement, at times because of the magnitude of the exultation—so that the man's mind does not apprehend itself but, rather, passes over into alienation because it is elevated beyond itself. For the flame that has increased beyond human measure melts the mind of man like wax, even as the brilliant light beclouds the sight. And oftentimes because of the stunningness of the Heavenly beauty [the mind] is alienated due to the magnitude of its exultation when it tastes of the inmost [delights] of Heavenly sweetness. And [the soul] is led unto alienation-of-mind because of its excessiveness of joy. And as long as we do not detect these [states] in ourselves, we are [in a lower state of] loving less intensely, since these [previous states] result from ardent love.

[26] Now, these stages of contemplation can be detected from the Gospel-passage. For the lowest stage of [the heart's] expansion is detected in the sitting at Jesus's feet. For love caused [Mary] to sit and to be prepared for receiving the word of her Beloved. The second stage of the mind's elevation is observed in the fact that [Mary's] mind was nourished by the word of life[36] and was uplifted so that it beheld the true Life.[37] The third stage of separation [from the world] is observed in the choosing of the Best. For the mind to which Heavenly Life was shown, passed over into alienation from itself by choosing that Best Life.

[27] However, among all men Mary the God-Bearer had the best part in respect both to the active [life] and to the contemplative [life]. For she was most holy, because she was a tabernacle sanctified for the

Most High. Hence, she was the true "Martha" who welcomed the Word of God into her house and who was busy with much serving and who performed works of mercy in the highest degree. For these works [of mercy] have degrees because of their greater [or lesser degree of] love or because [they are done] for one who is more needy or for a needy one who is more worthy or because of the greater effort spent or because [the work is] more necessary and less indispensable; therefore, all these [factors] came together in the highest degree in the Virgin Mary. For in her was the greatest love, [and] she aided Him who was the neediest of all creatures, because no one among wayfarers was poorer than was Jesus. [And] she aided a pauper who was most worthy, because no one is a more worthy mendicant than was Jesus. For a work of mercy is greater if it is done for a bishop rather than for a layman—assuming that both are equally needy. Hence, the greatest work [is that which is done] for God. [The Virgin Mary] engaged in the maximum act of mercy. For, as an instance of good works: [through giving birth] she gave God as a ransom for wretched captives. [She gave Him] as a provision for the hungry, as a reward for those who labor, as medicine for the sick. And along with Him she gave the Kingdom of Heaven. She did works of mercy that were not of a dispensable kind but that were of a necessary kind. She made for her Son, who was very poor and a pilgrim, a tunic embroidered with her own blood. She lodged Him in the core of her womb; from her own body she fed Him and gave Him milk to drink.

[**28**] Moreover, Mary was, in all excellence, the contemplative about whom the beloved in the Canticles is seen to say: "Who is she who goes up by way of the desert …?," etc.,[38] and "Who is she who comes forth as the morning rising …?," etc.[39] and "Who is this who comes up from the desert, flowing with delights, leaning on her beloved?"[40] But after she had tasted, with an intellectual tasting, the agreeableness of the One—[tasted, with the intellect, of this pleasantness] more deeply and more lucidly than all others—she passed beyond all contemplation. For God can be loved most greatly only when He is attained most greatly by the intellect.

Although some men might, in a rapture, at some time taste of the [refreshing] moistness that comes down into their mouth from the head of the divinity, nevertheless their stomach cannot take it in, because their mind is occupied with cares and is through its memory beclouded with images. [Their mind] does not return to its full powers because it is drawn away by desires. Moreover, it fails to turn back toward itself through a desire for eternal salvation. And if it does turn back [toward itself], this [movement] occurs with great difficulty, since it did not previously taste rightly and fully of the pleasantness of the Lord, (as Gregory, in his *Moralia* [speaks] about this matter).[41] However, Blessed Mary tasted fully [thereof], being inflamed with eternal desire that was free of satiety. She hungered and thirsted more and more for the apprehension—in an eternal embrace—of such a great good. Hence, [her desire] was always increasing; and so, the best part, [viz., the apprehension,] was never taken away from her.

This [suffices] as regards the second part [of the sermon].

III

[29] Thirdly, the Gospel-passage can be construed [as teaching] that Jesus discloses to us what we are to expect after this present lifetime. Thus, then, with regard to the words of our theme-text, a threefold understanding will suffice us for now, although many other [construals] can be given.

In the theme-text [the name] "Mary" is mentioned. The interpretation of "Mary" is *enlightenment*, so that, therefore, we may infer the enlightenment of an inquiring intellect—even as we touched upon in the first part [of the sermon]. Next, there is said: "She chose the best part," so that we may infer what ought to be more choice-worthy for a Christ-like affection; and we touched upon this [topic] in the second [part of the sermon]. Lastly, there is added [in the verse]: "… which shall not be taken away from her." And in accordance with this [portion of text] we ought to infer what the outcome of the journey of our soul will be with respect to the soul's powers—i.e., with respect to the intellect [and] the affections. Let me now add a few things about this [topic].

[30] Accordingly, we know, first of all, that works of mercy that are greatly troublesome are not found in the Kingdom of the next world—[a Kingdom] that is a Kingdom of peace. For *there* no one is needy. Hence, all the works that can be done in this present world—no matter how praiseworthy they are—do not continue on [in the next world] but rather cease. And eternal peace is not at all bestowed on account of these [works], since they contain nothing of the eternal. Rather, only love—whose works are signs—is that which neither falters nor fails when the works cease; instead, [love] is of the same domain as is the immortal soul, which it does not forsake, since the

soul is rooted in it.[42] For just as the life of the soul gives life to a man, and just as the life of a man is rooted in the life of the soul, so love is the life of the soul. And the life of the rational soul, insofar as it is rational, is rooted in love.

[**31**] But love is a power that unites the soul's affections to the *soul's own life*, which is the One, the True, and the Good. (Similarly, the *life of the perceptible body* consists of a union with the sensing soul. This bond [of union] is called love.) Hence, powerlessness to perform works of love does not hinder the union of the soul with the soul's own life. But he who wills to attain love must know where he ought to look for the life of the soul. For if [only] he can find that [life], he can but love it. And, hence, the Gospel-text teaches us that only One Thing is Necessary in order for all things to be that which they are or that which they desire to be. If after this One Thing is known it is chosen, then this [choosing] occurs because of love and a loving will. Thereupon, the one who is choosing is united to the One Thing and will never be separated from this Thing best-chosen by him.

[**32**] Hence, from this Gospel-text we know that the soul which does not turn to the One Necessary Thing and choose it, but which turns to whatever other things, will never be at peace. For whatever things [the soul] chooses other than the One cannot bestow on it a restful life, since they do not have it to give. There is but one Fount-of-life that can give [life] abundantly. But whatever is chosen other than the One Necessary Thing will be taken away. And death for the loving soul is this: [viz., the condition that obtains] when the beloved is taken away—even as death for sight that sees occurs when the visible object is taken away. For then the eye sees nothing—not because the eye has been blinded but because what is visible has ceased for it. Similarly, the stomach does not cease desiring food when food is taken away; however, the stomach is afflicted the more greatly because it is hungrier and has less food. Likewise, the absence [of what is true] or the turning away from the true is the death of the intellect, because [the intellect] does not have that on which to feed.

[**33**] Thus, then, in accordance with the fervor of its love the soul is joined to its own Life, which, since it is the unfailing Fount of life, shall not be taken away from it. Now, since the soul obtains happiness in proportion to its degree of love, it is self-evident that the Virgin Mary obtained happiness more than did all other spirits. For, as God attested through the angel, she obtained full grace by means of a very

deep partaking of the absolute fullness of the Incarnate Word within her. And for this reason the saints continue to chant her praises. Jerome, writing to Paula and Eustochius, speaks as follows: "If any saints have obtained grace so that they were conveyed to the Heavenly homeland with triumph by means of hymn-singing choirs of angels, then such an accompaniment was not lacking to Mary, whom, we are to believe, a multitude-of-Heavenly-spirits—terrible as an army set in array[43]—led into the palace of Heaven."[44]

[34] Albert,[45] says a similar thing, when he tells of the privileges of other saints: [there were those] who foreknew of their death (e.g., Martinus), [those] who died without pain (e.g., John), who were immediately assumed into Glory, who did not experience corruption [of body], etc. The Ark of the Testament, in which was manna, etc., was made of pieces of setim wood,[46] which are not corrupted. This [Ark] befigures Mary, whom John in the Apocalypse saw in Heaven, etc.[47] Hence, as David led the Ark in triumph,[48] so too we are to believe that Christ led the Ark of His resting place, in accordance with this [text]: "Arise unto [your] resting place—you and the ark of your sanctification."[49] If the saints obtained crowns and golden wreaths, etc., then in all [these respects] Mary was exalted above all [these saints]. And in the Apocalypse John saw this great sign in Heaven: [viz.,] a woman clothed with the sun [and] having the moon under her feet [and] crowned ...," etc.[50]

(Here let there be added a pleasing contemplation of Mary's death and of her ascension, through choirs of angels, to the point where the Queen stood at [God's] right hand in the gilded clothing of eternal glory.[51] Christ, her ever-blessed Son, leads us to her, at her entreaty.)

NOTES TO *Maria Optimam Partem Elegit*

* Sermon LXXI.

1. Luke 10:42: "But one thing is necessary. Mary has chosen the best part, which shall not be taken away from her."

2. Monday, August 15, 1446 was the feast-day of the Assumption of Mary.

3. Nicholas here wrongly supposes that Mary the sister of Martha is Mary Magdalene.

4. Romans 15:4.

5. The three topics are enlightenment, choice, and happiness. Three other topics are (1) the rational spirit's choosing the best part; (2) the Virgin Mary's choosing the best part; and (3) the intellectual nature's obtaining happiness.

6. John 1:9.

7. John 14:6.

8. The notion that the body is a prison for the soul is the Pythagorean theme of σῶμα σῆμα, a theme picked up by Plato.

9. Colossians 1:16-17.

10. Cf. I John 3:2. See also Nicholas's *Sermo* IV (**32**:26-28), which makes clear his view that we will never (not even in Heaven) know *what* God is. In the passage above, Nicholas is teaching that the believer's reason will one day be a closer "mirroring" of the Divine Reason. Yet, this mirroring yields only a finite image, which is infinitely other than the mirrored Infinite Reason.

11. Dominicus Gundissalinus. See *Die dem Boethius fälschlich zugescriebene Abhandlung des Dominicus Gundisalvi De Unitate.* Edited by Paul Correns. [Beiträge zur Geschichte der Philosophie des Mittelalters, Vol. I (1891), Heft 1], p. 3, lines 8-9.

12. Pseudo-Dionysius, *De Divinis Nominibus*, XIII, 2 [*Dionysiaca*, Vol. I, p. 540 (*Patrologia Graeca* 3:978)].

13. Nicholas is alluding to the German word "ein" (and its endings)—a word that both (1) means *one* and (2) functions as the indefinite article. For example, "ein Mann" can mean either *one man* or *a man*. Sometimes nowadays "ein" will be italicized in order to show clearly that it is being used as a numeral and not as the indefinite article—should the use not be immediately clear.

14. "… inco-ordinately": i.e., disproportionally.

15. In this section Nicholas alludes to God, who is supremely one, who is Infinite Oneness. Yet, Nicholas is also, at the same time, speaking of oneness and one in a non-theological sense, i.e., in the ordinary sense.

16. By "all things" Nicholas here (as also elsewhere) means all finite things, all things other than God.

17. See n. 16 above.

18. See the quotations from Pseudo-Dionysius that are found in Nicholas's *De Li Non Aliud* 14 (70), my edition.

19. Here (at **13**:16) I am reading, with the Paris printed edition, "Hinc" in place of "Hic".

20. Here (at **14**:17) I am reading, with the Paris printed edition, "modum" in place of "modo".

21. II Corinthians 4:4. Colossians 1:15. Christ is the perfect Likeness of the

Father qua God.

22. God has no parts. We apprehend God as having aspects, attributes.

23. Luke 10:42 and surrounding sentences.

24. See n. 3 above.

25. Psalms 33:9 (34:8). Cf. I Peter 2:3.

26. Matthew 26:31-46.

27. Gregory the Great, *Moralium Libri* (= *Expositio in Librum B. Job*), VI, 37, 59 (*PL* 75:763C).

28. This is a listing of the seven deadly sins as found in the High Middle Ages. This list has several variants. Sometimes the capital sins are numbered at eight.

29. See n. 25 above.

30. John 14:23.

31. Nicholas is influenced by Pseudo-Dionysius partly by way of Hugh of Balma. See *Hugh of Balma on Mystical Theology: A Translation and an Overview of his De Theologica Mystica*, edited, introduced, and translated by J. Hopkins (Minneapolis: Banning, 2002).

32. Canticle of Canticles (Song of Solomon) 5:2. Nicholas is *alluding to* this verse rather than attempting to quote it exactly.

33. Wisdom 9:15.

34. Romans 7:24.

35. Gregory the Great, *In Ezechielem Prophetam*, II, 2, 12 (*PL* 76:955AB).

36. Cf. John 6:69.

37. John 14:6.

38. Canticle of Canticles (Song of Solomon) 3:6.

39. Canticle of Canticles (Song of Solomon) 6:9.

40. Canticle of Canticles (Song of Solomon) 8:5. Here (at **28**:6) I am reading, with the Clementine Vulgate Bible, "deliciis" and "innixa" in place of "deliciarum" and "enixa".

41. Gregory the Great, *Moralium Libri, op. cit.* (n. 27 above); see, perhaps, Book XXXI, Chapter 12, n. 19 (*PL* 76:583-584).

42. Ephesians 3:17.

43. Canticle of Canticles 6:3 (Song of Solomon 6:4).

44. This passage comes not from Jerome but from Paschasius Radbertus. The letter was falsely ascribed to Jerome: *Epistola Beati Hieronymi ad Paulam et Eustochium de Assumptione Sanctae Mariae Virginis*.

45. Pseudo-Albertus Magnus, *Mariale*, chapters 169-172.

46. Exodus 25:10. Hebrews 9:4.

47. Apocalypse (Revelation) 11:19.

48. II Kings (II Samuel) 6:12-17.

49. Psalms 131:8 (132:8).

50. Apocalypse (Revelation) 12:1.

51. Psalms 44:10 (49:9).

Tota Pulcra Es, Amica Mea*
("You Are All-fair, O My Love.")[1]
[September 8, 1456; preached in Brixen][2]

[**1**] "You are all-fair, O my love, and there is no blemish in you ...."

Since we are celebrating the joyous birth of the glorious Virgin and are singing the [foregoing] thematic words, our sermon will be about beauty. [**2**] To begin with, there comes to mind the statement of Dionysius (where he discusses beauty):[3] viz., that we are to note that in Greek the word for the good is "*kalos*" but the word for the beautiful is "*kallos*"—as if the good and the beautiful were cognates. Now, "*kalo*" in Greek is "*voco*" in Latin, for the good calls [things] unto itself and attracts [them], as does also the beautiful. Furthermore, the beautiful is called "*formosum*" (from *forma*) and "*speciosum*" (from *species*) and "*decorum*" (from *decorum*, or *decet*, for that which is fitting is comely and beautiful).[4]

[**3**] Now, if we are attentive, then with our more immaterial powers-of-sense, with which we pursue teachings, we [will] arrive at things beautiful in their own way. For we say that color and shape have beauty and, likewise, that a sound, a song, and a spoken word have beauty. Thus, sight and hearing attain unto beauty in some measure. [But] we do not call an odor beautiful or a taste beautiful or sensations of touch beautiful. For these senses are not so similar in nature to the rational spirit; for they are merely brute-senses, or animal-senses. Now, all of man's senses—because of their union with the intellectual spirit—are more noble than are [the corresponding senses] in brute animals. For the quite noble power makes what is united to it noble, even as sunlight illumines the air. Now, the senses that are the more discriminating have a closer union with the intellect. Hence, sight is attracted by beautiful form and color, as hearing is by beautiful harmony. And this [fact] is true in the case of man because reason, which takes pleasure in proportions, shines forth in these senses in a more proximate way. And so, things proportioned and well ordered—i.e., where a unity of proportion or of harmony shines forth amid the plurality—are pleasing.

[**4**] The same Dionysius says[5] that the form [*ratio*] of beauty consists in a certain agreement of different things with one another. He writes[6] that there are certain divine processions into creatures whereby creatures are perfected into a divine likeness since the processions

go forth in a formal way (just as from what is at first hot other things [are made] hot). Now, the first procession, which occurs with respect to the mind, occurs in accordance with the apprehension of what is true. Next, that [apprehended] truth glows and is received under the aspect [*ratio*] of the good; and, thus, at length, desire is directed toward it. For a twofold apprehension must precede the motion of desire: [there is] one apprehension that occurs on the part of the speculative intellect [and] is apprehension of what is true *simpliciter*; [there is] another apprehension that occurs on the part of the practical intellect [and occurs] through a further consideration of the true under the aspect of the good. Only then does there arise the motion of desire-for-the-good. [5] And Albert [Magnus] adds—over and above Dionysius (whose words these are)—the example that just as the art of medicine does not obtain its effectiveness-in-working unless it is aided by the power of nature, so too desire is not moved unless it is guided by an apprehension of the true.[7] To the apprehension of the true there corresponds the procession of light; to the apprehension of the true under the aspect of the good there corresponds the procession of the beautiful; to the motion of desire there corresponds the procession of the loveable—according as Dionysius treats of these in ordered relation.

[6] And Tully in Book One of his *Moral Obligations* defines the *beautiful qua intrinsic goodness* as, namely, that which draws us by its own power and attracts us by its worth.[8] Hence, we must consider that the beautiful, in its essence, includes three things: [First, it includes] excellence of form (whether substantial or accidental form) with regard to the parts of the material object that are proportioned and delimited. (E.g., a material object is called beautiful because of excellence of color as concerns its proportioned members.) Secondly, [beauty includes] the fact that it draws desire toward itself. (The beautiful has this characteristic insofar as it is something good and is an end-goal.) Thirdly, [the beautiful includes] the fact that it gathers all things together. (And this is said with reference to the form, whose excellence makes [the object] beautiful. But beauty in and of itself is that which through its own essence both is the cause-of-beauty and produces all beauty. [7] Therefore, the beautiful and the intrinsically good are the same thing by reason of their subject. But they differ by reason of the fact that, in general, the essence of the beautiful consists in the excellence-of-form in the parts that are proportioned to the material object—i.e., in the different material objects or the different actions. [But] the essence of the intrinsically good consists in the fact that it

draws desire unto itself. According to Dionysius beauty and the beautiful are identical in God. For in God Beauty is supreme-and-primary beauty, from which emanates the nature of beauty in all beautiful things. [In God Beauty] is the Form of beautiful things; for it makes all beautiful things beautiful, even as whiteness [makes all white things] white. The essence of God—which *is* God—is, according to Albertus [Magnus], supreme-and-primary Beauty.

[**8**] In everything beautiful there are present agreement (i.e., proportion) and manifestness. Agreement is present as subject; manifestness is present as essence. Virtue has within itself manifestness, through which it is beautiful. Even if virtue were unrecognized by anyone, nevertheless it would still have a proneness for coming to be known manifestly. Accordingly, Tully called the intrinsically good *beautiful*. [**9**] The beautiful, through the essence of its subject, is joined with the good. And so, all things desire beauty. It is of the essence of the good that it be the goal of desire, moving desire toward itself. And so, the [following] definition is given by the Philosopher: the good is that which all things desire.[9] The *intrinsically* good adds to the [concept of the] good the idea that the good draws us by its own power and worthiness. The *beautiful* further adds, to certain well-proportioned things, a certain illustriousness and manifestness. Hence, there befits beauty—qua an end and qua a good—to call things unto itself. [There befits beauty]—qua form—to unite things to itself; for it properly befits form to unite, because form unites multiple potencies of matter and confines them in one thing. Insofar as beauty is an end, it summons unto itself. Beauty that depends only on one form is of more perfect beauty than is that thing whose beauty is produced from more than one form. For the more something receives its perfection from fewer things, the more noble it is.

[**10**] Next, Dionysius deals with the fact that the beautiful (which is convertible with the good) is the cause of all the movements of spirits—which, indeed, are moved by desire. Therefore, properly speaking, desire is on the part of a spirit. When the beauty of the good is shown to an angel, he attempts eagerly to reveal it and to return as quickly as possible to enjoying it—so that in this way the circle is closed. The showing occurs in the center. The descending of the revelation is the movement, by means of a straight line, toward the extremes—i.e., is the way of providence. Then the return is like a sideways movement, so that in the beauty of goodness the circle is com-

pleted. Just as someone by whom a treasure is discovered shares his delight with a friend as quickly as possible and then returns to counting and enjoying the treasure, so angels move circularly—in a straight direction and [then] in a bending direction—as do souls, which likewise move by a great number of motions.

[11] When the sun illumines sight so that by means of the sun sight sees colors, then if sight wishes to gaze upon the light of the sun, it turns away from all colored objects. Similarly, the soul, because of the light of the active intellect, sees particular things. And when it wishes to gaze upon the light itself, it turns away from particular things and likewise returns to the primary light. According to Albertus [Magnus] this is a circular movement.[10] For sight is comparable to the intellect; the light of the sun is comparable to the light of the active intellect; things understandable are comparable to colors. [12] The movement due to the beauty of the First occurs in a comparable way, as does the return to the First. For by means of the power of the divine light that glows within the active intellect, the active intellect *makes* all things.[11] Therefore, after the possible intellect has received the light of the active intellect and turns its gaze away from particular things back onto itself, then from the fact that it has received that which has furnished to it actual being, it reflects on the First in accordance with its understanding.

[13] The movement of all sensing things is from the beautiful unto the beautiful. The same fact holds true of all progressions, positionings, lives, senses, [as well as] of the soul, of nature, of smallnesses, largenesses, proportions, mixtures, properties—and of all things. For whatever is from the beautiful-and-good is also in the beautiful-and-good and turns toward the beautiful-and-good. And whatever all things are and become, they are and become on account of what is good-and-beautiful. And all things look toward it and are moved by it and are encompassed by it; and on account of it and through it and in it is every beginning from which instances are derived.

[14] And [Dionysius] concludes by saying: "Now, to summarize: all existing things are [from] the beautiful-and-good; and all nonexisting things are super-substantially in the beautiful-and-good, and the latter is the beginning and the end of all things."[12] And, later, [Dionysius states]: "Therefore, the beautiful-and-good is apprehended by all as desirable and lovable; and through it and on account of it inferior things love more excellent things by way of turning [toward them]. And things socially equal love similar things; and more excellent

things provide for, and are joined by love to, less excellent things. And individual things love one another by reason of their constancy and contiguity; and whatsoever they do and will, they do and will out of desire for the beautiful-and-good."[13]

[15] He concludes as follows: "Furthermore, we will say confidently, on a very firm basis, that even the Author of all things, because of His great goodness, loves all things, makes all things, perfects all things, encompasses all things, and turns all things [toward the good]."[14] Amply and with multiple terms, that great Areopagite teaches us that the good (which all things seek) and the absolutely beautiful (which *is* beauty) are one and the same thing. He sets out the properties of absolute goodness, exemplifying them by [the illustration of] the sun. And then he turns his attention from perceptible light to intelligible light, noting how it is that that light affects intellectual spirits after the fashion of the sun's affecting the sensory nature. Assuredly, all the things that he writes about the beautiful are themselves beautiful.

[16] Let us note how it is that by means of our more immaterial senses, viz., sight and hearing, we arrive at the final stage of the resplendence of the beautiful, so that the intellectual spirit is moved by wonder. And [the intellectual spirit's] potency is stimulated so that that spirit proceeds to the act of hastening intellectually toward the beautiful at which it has arrived, to a very small extent, by way of the sense [of sight or of hearing]. (By comparison, he who with the tip of his tongue has made contact, foretastingly, with what is sweet is moved to take his fill of it.) For all things seek the good, which is also the beautiful; and they turn toward it—each thing in accordance with its own nature—either in terms of their existing or in terms of their being alive or in terms of their being intellects. [17] Now, because the intellectual nature partakes intellectually of the nature of the beautiful-and-good (since this is its form), it can be nourished and kept alive only by the in-flow of the beautiful-and-good. Therefore, its life consists in the good-and-beautiful, which it beholds and tastes intellectually.

[18] Now, in all things that flourish by means of reasoning we experience there to be a power of judgment that is concerned with the beautiful. For example, [these rational beings] call this circular shape beautiful, that rose beautiful, this piece of wood beautiful, this song beautiful. Hence, unless the judge, i.e., the intellect, had within itself a representation-of-beauty[15] that enfolded all perceptible beauty, it could not judge between beautiful things, saying this one to be beautiful, that

one to be more beautiful. Therefore, the intellect is a certain universal beauty or universal representation of [perceptual] representations, since the [perceptual] representations are contracted beauties. And as fire enfolds within itself the form and nature (*species*) of all hot things, so the intellect is a power that enfolds all intelligible forms [*species intelligibiles*].[16] For intellectual nature—which is the first irradiation of the beautiful, in that it is the image of God, who is Beauty itself in an antecedent way—enfolds within itself [conceptually] all the natural instances of beauty that are unfolded in the universe through their specific forms. [**19**] Absolute Beauty, which is God, beholds itself and is ardently filled with love for itself. For the Fount of all beautiful things, a Fount that all beautiful things rightly call their Father—how could it be Supreme Beauty if it did not know itself to be beautiful? (For the intellect is more beautiful than are the senses.) Therefore, Infinite Beauty cannot fail to know itself. Hence, if Beauty beholds (i.e., understands) itself, then only Infinite Love can follow therefrom. Here, then—where the *Fount of Beauty* begets *Understanding of Beauty*, from both of which comes *Love* [*of Beauty*]—is a Trinity in the oneness of the essence of Beauty.

[**20**] This eye of ours sees itself only in the reflection of a mirror. By contrast, the spirit does not see other things unless it first sees itself, for through itself it sees other things. Similarly, if sight, which is in the eye, were the intellect, it would first see itself and would [then] see other things within itself. For the intellectual nature knows that it is intellectual (otherwise, it would not be intellectual); and this knowing is its seeing itself. And after [seeing, or knowing, itself], it intellectually sees within itself other things, even as within themselves the senses arrive perceptually at perceptible things. [**21**] Therefore, Beauty, which is alive with divine and eternal life, which is Life itself, which is God, willed to make manifest its glory, which is a form of beauty. And [Beauty did] this because Beauty is Goodness. Now, the good diffuses itself. Similarly, Beauty—summoning unto itself not-being in order that not-being would manifest Beauty's glory and would partake of Goodness and Beauty—created all things. Beauty attracts unto itself. Therefore, as regards everything attracted from not-being by Beauty: insofar as from not-being it approaches Beauty, it comes from not-being unto being. Hence, there is not anything that is devoid of beauty, just as there is not anything that is devoid of goodness. [**22**] Therefore, form, which gives being, is only a partaking of beauty. Hence, the gradations-of-beings accord with their resemblance to beauty. By means

of accidental beauty—at which we arrive by way of the senses [and] which is present in the outward appearances and outer shapes—we arrive at the beauty of substantial form. All existing things are works on the part of Absolute Beauty; these works are formed in the likeness of Absolute Beauty. And this formation is their attractiveness.

[**23**] The Prophets say that the Israelites sat in the beauty of peace.[17] Elsewhere we read about the beauty of justice.[18] David says that the beauty of the field is with God[19] and that praise and beauty are in His sight.[20] From these [verses] we can infer that in the Kingdom of Beauty are present (1) all the beautiful things that exist and can exist, (2) the beauty of all the *being* of all existing things, the beauty of all the *life* of living things, and the beauty of all the *intellect* [of things that have intellect]. For just as in oneness every number is present in an enfolded way, and just as in number all proportion and all intermediateness are present enfoldedly, and just as in proportion all harmony and order and concordance [are enfolded]: so too, for this reason, [there is enfolded in oneness] all beauty, which shines forth in the ordering and the proportion and the concordance. [**24**] Hence, when we say that God is One, this One is Supersubstantial Oneness itself, which is also Beauty, enfolding in itself all things beautiful. We say that God is Light in which there is no darkness.[21] Therefore, that Light is nothing other than Oneness; and if there were a simple name that signified Light that is Oneness, then [that name] would befit God. In this name would be enfolded all beauty—viz., [both] that which is something material in beauty (e.g., proportion) and that which is something formal (e.g., splendor). The former [would be enfolded] because [God is] Oneness; the latter, because [God is] Light.

[**25**] What are the powers of the heavens except instances of beauty within the Kingdom of God? Power is great insofar as it is beautiful. Things ugly do not belong to the Kingdom of Beauty. Souls' defects are only ugly blemishes that deform their beauty and that are not derived from Beauty; for from Primary Beauty there can emanate only things beautiful and good. Loveliness comes from the Giver of form; defectiveness comes from the recipients. [**26**] If the eye looks unto the Kingdom of Beauty, it sees the beauty of all beautiful things, in such a way that the beauty of the one thing does not displace the beauty of another thing. For beauty is not quantitative or small or large; rather, small things and large things are beautiful through beauty. If in the Kingdom of Heaven the beauty of the Kingdom [of Heaven] is

seen, or if the beauty of the hierarchy of the Church Militant is seen, then the beauty is seen there in its purity, above all contractedness due to place or time. In the Kingdom of Beauty the beauty of the truth of things, the beauty of places, of locations, and of all things is only spiritual and eternal. The beauty of innocence, the beauty of purity, of adolescence, of manliness, of chastity, of courage, and so on, are not commingled domains but are beautiful and well-ordered domains in the Kingdom of Heaven.

[**27**] The many mansions in the Kingdom are the beautiful virtues. In these mansions are placed the beauties of virtuous spirits, each spirit being in the region that befits it because of its imitation of virtue. For the twelve tribes of *Israel* (i.e., of *those who see God*) in the kingdom of *Jerusalem* (i.e., of the *vision of peace*) have, in the one kingdom, seats divided in accordance with the tribes; and there they are nourished by beauty in accordance with the beauty of virtue.

[**28**] In this beautiful world (which because of its beauty is called a cosmos) the intellectual spirit pursues the beauties of the virtues, with which it adorns its natural beauty. Love is the end-goal of beauty, which wishes to be loved. God is Beauty itself, because He wills to be loved. But beauty, which is lovable in and of itself, *is* love; and so, without love no one will see Absolute Beauty. [**29**] Our earnest desire ought to be to ascend from the beauty of perceptible things unto the beauty of our spirit—a beauty that encompasses all perceptible beauties. And from our beauty let us ascend admiringly unto the Fount of Beauty, to whom our beauty bears a likeness. And let us leave behind all things ugly, i.e., all sins. For our spirit attests that sins are hideous. (This testimony is called conscience.) And let us amidst our beauty aspire with continuous love to be conformed to the Fount of Beauty. For living, intellectual beauty, by beholding (or understanding) Absolute Beauty is brought to it by means of indescribable desire. And the more fervent its desire, the closer it approaches and the more and more it becomes like the Exemplar. For the desire, or love, continually transforms the one-who-loves into a likeness with the Beloved. And this ascending occurs by means of the attracting power of beauty, i.e., of God's glory. (For there is glory only in royal beauty.) To be amid glory is to be in the visual presence of beauty and to be united to it in love.

Let these things now have been said in the foregoing way regarding beauty.[22]

[**30**] But our theme-topic—"You are all-fair ...," etc.—must be

expounded as regards the soul: in all its powers and in its entirety of, and fullness of, perfection the soul comes from the vale of sorrows without blemish. The Bridegroom, who is Absolute Beauty, welcomes her with a very beautiful word, viz., by calling her His love. For the soul that loves Beauty so greatly that she gives her entire self to Beauty, so that no blemish is found in her—such a soul comes as the beloved into the embrace of Beauty. Therefore, these five words ["Tota pulchra es, amica mea"] can be interpreted broadly as words of the King of Beauty, who wills to have nothing short of the entire soul—beautiful in every respect [and] languid in her whole being because of love—as the most elect beloved-one only of Himself.

[**31**] Next, the words are applied to the glorious Virgin Mary, who assuredly, more than all other women, was totally and most perfectly beautiful in every manner of beauty. From the origin of her being, she gave herself, as bride, to Absolute Beauty. She was attracted—as the beloved, and over and above all other women—unto Supreme Beauty. Since she possesses the beauty of all the virtues, she drew nearer to the throne of the King of Beauty than did all other daughters of Jerusalem who, in the distribution of allotted duties, hold a seat in the circuit of Jerusalem. She approached as being the mother of the true King Solomon, viz., of the Beauty of eternal peace. Let us approach her with movements of devotion, so that she, being conscious of our weakness, may pray for us to her ever-blessed son, Jesus.

NOTES TO *Tota Pulcra Es, Amica Mea*

* Sermon CCXLIII.
1. Canticle of Canticles (Song of Solomon) 4:7. In the printed edition of Nicholas's Latin text the full sermon title, which I have abbreviated, is "Tota Pulchra Es, Amica Mea, et Macula Non Est in Te."
2. This was the feast-day of the Virgin Mary's birth.
3. Pseudo-Dionysius, *De Divinis Nominibus*, 4, 7 (*Dionysiaca*, Vol. I, p. 180).
4. The Latin words all indicate loveliness, attractiveness, comeliness, congruence, and the like. A free translation would be: " ... is called well-formed (from *form*) and lovely (from *appearance*) and decorous (from *congruence* ...)."
5. Pseudo-Dionysius, *De Divinis Nominibus*, 4, 7 (*Dionysiaca*, Vol. I, pp. 183-184.)
6. Pseudo-Dionysius, *De Caelesti Hierarchia*, 1, 1 (*Dionysiaca*, Vol. II, pp. 727-728. Nicholas borrows from Albertus Magnus, *Super Dionysium De Divinis Nomniibus*, Chap. 4, Section 71, *solutio* [p. 181^b in Vol. 37 (edited by Paul Simon, 1972) of *Alberti Magni Opera Omnia* (Münster: Aschendorff)].
7. Albertus Magnus, *Super Dionysium De Divinis Nominibus*, Chap. 4, *loc. cit.*
8. Cicero, *De Officiis*, I, 6, 18. Cicero's use of the word "*honestum*" can be translated by "an intrinsic good," "what is good in itself," "what is intrinsically valuable," "what is morally good," and the likes.
9. Aristotle, *Nicomachean Ethics*, A, 1 (1094^a2-3).
10. Albertus Magnus, *Super Dionysium De Divinis Nominibus*, Chap. 4, Section 103, *solutio* [p. 202^b in Vol. 37 (edited by Paul Simon, 1972) of *Alberti Magni Opera Omnia* (Münster: Aschendorff)].
11. The active intellect makes concepts from perceptual images by way of abstraction. Nicholas takes this view from the tradition of Albertus Magnus, Aquinas, and Aristotle.
12. Pseudo-Dionysius, *De Divinis Nominibus*, 4, 10 (*Dionysiaca*, Vol. I, p. 198 (in the translation of Ambrose Traversari)).
13. Pseudo-Dionysius, *ibid.* (*Dionysiaca*, Vol. I, pp. 199--200).
14. Pseudo-Dionysius, *ibid.* (*Dionysiaca*, Vol. I, pp. 200-201).
15. That is, unless the intellect had within itself a concept of beauty ....
16. The intelligible forms are concepts.
17. Isaias (Isaiah) 32:18.
18. Jeremias (Jeremiah) 31:23, as worded in the Vulgate Latin text.
19. Psalms 49:11 (50:11), as worded in the Vulgate Latin text.
20. Psalms 95:6 (96:6), as worded in the Vulgate Latin text.
21. I John 1:5.
22. That is, let what has now been said about beauty suffice.

Non Sumus Ancillae Filii*
("We Are Not Children of the Bondwoman ....")[1]
[March 27, 1457; preached in Brixen]

[1] "We are not children of the bondwoman but of the free [woman], by the freedom by which Christ has made us free."

The feast today is one of a certain gladness and is called *Laetare Sunday*. It is [also] called *Rose Sunday* [and] *Loaves of bread Sunday*. You know the reasons [for these epithets].

I

[2] We can rightly name [this] Sunday from "*laetitia*" because in the Epistle for [today's] mass the Apostle expresses for us those things that are joyous. For he says: 'Rejoice, O barren, for our mother is she in whom barrenness is fecundity—just as in Mary virginity was fecundity, because she brought forth a blessing for all nations. For the faith which in the case of Mary brought about these things is barren. **[3]** In the intellect there is a certain fountain-like fecundity; for [the intellect] begets streams of reasons by means of which it imparts an intellectual likeness of itself. For its fecundity shines forth in its reasons, which are lovely and good to the extent that the intellect shines forth in and through them. However, faith is barren, for it has no children, i.e., no reasons; and the more reasons it would have, the more diminished it would be.

[4] So faith is barren; but when we rightly consider it, [we see that] that barrenness is fecundity. This fact is evident in the case of Abraham and Sarah, where by faith in the promise, there was born by natural means Isaac, who otherwise [than by faith] could not have been born. And in that seed was present a fount of blessing; and later it was present in Jacob. For the Apostle declares [in the Epistle] to the Romans that not only the children of Sarah but also the children of Rebecca were children of the promise.[2] Likewise, it is also evident [that this blessing was present] in the case of Zachary and Elizabeth[3]—and, at length, last of all and most perfectly, in the case of the Virgin Mary, where faith gave to us Christ. **[5]** And take note of the reason that Scripture says that Christ came in the end-time and in the fullness of time.[4] For in the Virgin Mary this fecundity of faith reached its highest and final level, beyond which there is no other level. This [level] is of such great perfection that it enfolds within itself the entire fecundity of faith; for it is the form and exemplar whereby faith regenerates a son of man and elevates him in proportion to his ability to believe—[elevates him] even unto the form of God.

[6] In the case of Abraham faith culminated in a begetting on the part of one who was barren, who begat a child promised to her by God, whom she believed. In the case of the Virgin Mary faith culminated in the begetting of the Son of God—[God] whom Mary believed. Behold, how fecund is that barren mother-of-faith, [Sarah], from whose fecundity all the children of Israel have proceeded and continue to proceed![5] These [descendants] see God [both] here and in the future—here in a dark way,[6] there face-to-Face. [7] Now, note well that in the barrenness of faith there is very great fecundity. For example, as say those physicians who are called empiricists: at times certain herbs produce wondrous cures. Indeed, we experience this [fact about herbs] to be true; for instance, [we experience] that scammony purges cholera. However, no reason for this can be given, since the effect proceeds from a hidden and special property; but he who trusts the authority of him-who-is-experienced discovers this fact to be true, even though no rational consideration is persuasive thereof. And from these medicines we experience greater-effects, and more assuredly reliable[7] effects, than we do in cases where the physiologists, through exploratory reasoning, concoct a remedy.

[8] Therefore, faith (1) that the Incarnate Word of God cures all lassitude of soul and (2) that causes the soul to renew its youth, i.e., its innocence, and (3) that always keeps the soul in [a state of] innocence is like a proven remedy that has this [set of effects] from a special property. And if someone believes this [claim] to be true, then he will find, by experience, that he is happy. This finding is a *seeing*, which is a more reliable state than is *reasoning*. [9] And so, it is evident that in the barrenness of faith, from which seeing follows, there is greater fecundity than is present in that which, on the basis of many rational considerations, is asserted to be fecund. And, indeed, in the case of the children-of-promise experience has taught that faith has brought about the outcome. Note very carefully that the promise is the word of God. God is truthful and faithful. Hence, he who has the word of His promise rests assured. This word saves him who believes in Christ, who is the Promise[8] and the Word. The [one who believes] will obtain God's sonship, because sonship is promised to believers,[9] and sonship *is* the promise.

[**10**] Pay attention to the difference between Sarah's faith and Mary's faith. For the fact that an elderly woman believes that by the grace of God she still can conceive from an elderly man in accordance with the pleasure of the flesh has no comparison with the faith of the Virgin, who believed that apart from a male seed she could conceive a son by the gift of the Holy Spirit of the Most High. Of what great fecundity was that promised seed—in barren Sarah—is evident. For, as said the Prophet,[10] and as Paul states in the Epistle,[11] many more were procreated from her who was barren [than from her who had a husband]. For on account of the grace of the promise the blessed seed was, [in the case of Sarah], turned into a living and fecund fount—more so than in the case of fecund Hagar, the bondwoman. For the descendants of Isaac increased innumerably. Similarly, spiritual fecundity, as symbolized in barren [Sarah], is immeasurable. For John of the Apocalypse says that he saw a multitude that no one can number—[a multitude] which, in the vision, followed from out of the tribes of Israel. [**11**] Moreover, note (in accordance with the lovely gloss[12] on this passage to the Romans[13] concerning the fact that Abraham believed against [all] hope and was justified) that just as Abraham was justified because he believed that through his seed Christ would come according to the flesh, so we too are justified who believe that Christ has come and that God has raised Him from the dead. Hence, we do not have doubt about [our] resurrection and glorification on the basis of justification by faith.

[**12**] I understand, then, that we who are not descended from the bondwoman Hagar (for he who is born from a bondwoman is a servant, [since] the offspring follows the womb)[14] are from barren Sarah, our mother, who is free. Through her we are children of the promise,[15] which is faith. And so, we are not brothers of Ismael (who was born in bondage and according to the flesh and in a natural way). For we are not bound to the servitude of the Old Testament, viz., to circumcision and to ceremonial observances and to the law of works. For in accordance with the promise we are brothers of free Isaac and are born of faith. [**13**] Hence, the promise made to Abraham, the father of faith, culminated in Christ, who was promised to Abraham; that is, [there was promised] that Christ would come from Abraham's seed. Therefore, it is evident that the promise-of-faith stops with Christ not in order that there cannot be someone greater [than Christ] but [because the promise] is fulfilled in Christ, than whom nothing greater can be thought.[16]

[14] Likewise, note that Abraham, who believed the foregoing, was justified by Christ, for his faith ascended all the way unto Christ. Therefore, all justification by faith is perfected in Christ. Therefore, one errs who thinks that he can obtain justice[17] on the basis of a faith that does not accept Christ. Hence, in the Gospel there is rightly said that Christ is the son of Abraham,[18] for He is the Son promised for Abraham's seed. And, likewise, Christ is promised to us believers; i.e., it is promised that He is to be born spiritually in our spirit by means of the seed of faith. For He is born in us when His life is hidden in us.[19] For just as because of Abraham's faith Christ, according to the flesh, was in his seed, so through faith Christ was spiritually in Abraham's spirit. For in spirit Abraham desired nothing except Christ. Therefore, Christ, who was yet to exist from Abraham according to the flesh, was in a real way present in Abraham's thought and spirit. And so, Abraham was *just*, because God's justice was in him. [15] Christ is the true Justice that justifies everyone who is just. Thus, in every believer who is justified by faith it is necessary that Christ be present, who alone is the justification of those who are just.[20] This justification is received when one takes account of the merit of the suffering by means of which when [Christ] obeyed[21] the Father He merited eternal life for all those who accept Him by faith. Because they believe Christ, Christ makes them to be sharers of the merit of Him who justifies everyone who is justified. Therefore, Christ is the Liberator, who frees the sons of God[22] and of the promise from all bondage of the Prince of darkness[23] and of death.

[16] Pay careful attention to the fact that Abraham had two sons. One was born according to the flesh; the other, according to the promise. One was born by natural means; the other, through the grace of faith. The son who [was born] according to the promise propagated from himself the people of *Israel*—i.e., *the people who saw God.*[24] Hence, all who arrive at seeing God are sons of Abraham according to the promise. And the promise was fulfilled in Christ, who was promised in and through all the sons of promise. (For they all have the name of promise from Christ, who was promised in and through them. Indeed, Christ *is* the Promise.) Therefore, the sons-of-Abraham in whom Christ is present through faith—these are the true sons of the promise. They are born not according to the flesh but through faith.

[17] Therefore, the mystical Body of Christ is the Promise, i.e., the Seed, in and through which all the nations of the earth will be

blessed. Thus, it is evident that only Christians are sons of Abraham according to the promise. The true names "Israel" and "Jerusalem that is from above" befit them—i.e., [the names] "the vision of God" and "the vision of peace."[25] All other sons are called sons of Abraham (i.e., sons of the father of many nations),[26] according to the flesh; these sons do not arrive at the things that are of the Spirit of God. Consider the Apostle, who says that Jerusalem that is from above is our mother,[27] i.e., is [the mother] of Christians. And this mother is faith. In the present [world, faith is] a symbolic seeing, but in the future [world there will be] a face-to-Face seeing. Moreover, faith is from above because it is a grace of God.

Let these points suffice with regard to the first topic.

II

[**18**] The second topic concerns the rose. We ought to know that by means of the rose—which [at today's feast] the pope carries with honor and gives to one who is quite noble—the Roman Church symbolizes for us spiritual joy. For at the beginning of planting, the rose was hidden in the rose-cutting;[28] and in the springtime it comes into the visible world. [The new rose is] not another rose than what it was in potency; but [it now exists] in a different way. For what is intellectual takes on visible form when it is seen by the intellect, which saw the bush in the seed and saw, in the bush, the blossom—and [which saw], speaking generally, in the potential the actual and in the present [condition] the future [condition]. Hence, when the rose that comes from potency to actuality is visible, then the rose-cutting ceases its activity; and so, the rose is the end-product of the planting of the rose-cutting. [**19**] In the rose there are two things, viz., beauty and fragrance. Beauty nourishes the eyes; fragrance nourishes the sense of smell. Hence, by means of the rose we are given to understand that a certain immaterial beauty nourishes the eye of the mind, viz., the intellect, and that [a certain] immaterial fragrance nourishes the olfactory power of the mind, viz., the will, or the affective power.

Now, this immaterial beauty is an object that makes the intellectual spirit cling tightly to it; and [this beauty] continuously infuses a likeness of itself, so that it makes the [intellectual] power to be like itself. We see that the beauty in things turns the eyes to itself and in a certain way binds immovably to itself the beholder, so that he cannot look away. [**20**] Lo, how greatly pleasing is the beauty of innocence, the beauty of life, the beauty of courage, the beauty of honorableness, the beauty of glory, the beauty of honor, the beauty of orderedness, the beauty of customs, the beauty of virtue, and so on. And since all of these are beautiful because of beauty, how greatly pleasing can be true Beauty itself, which has no admixture of the impure and imperfect. No one can [adequately] express this fact. [Yet,] he easily understands [it] who considers that the ornate cosmos—or something perceptibly beautiful that has a sizable admixture of impurity and imperfection—is [greatly] pleasing. Now, no beautiful thing in this world has all possible beauty; and so, [it] is imperfect. However, Ineffable Beauty—the Fount of everything beautiful [insofar as it is beautiful]—has within it all beauty in an eternal and infinite perfection.

[**21**] Secondly, there is in this world nothing that so resembles a feast for the spirit as does a fragrance, which is an invisible aeration and thus is more nearly immaterial than are all other nutrients. Now, a fragrance nourishes; for it is written that certain men in India are nourished by, and live from, fragrance. Therefore, fragrance that so greatly delights us arouses us to draw it unto us. And when it is drawn unto us, it begets enjoyment in our natural spirit. For it very greatly comforts our nature. Hence, that [analogous] fragrance that nourishes our rational spirit with gladness is pleasant, pure, true, and unmixed, and is pleasantness itself.

[**22**] Our spirit, or mind, is rightly made happy by God's beauty and pleasantness. God is Goodness itself. Hence, by means of the goodness of beauty (which unites the mind to itself) and the goodness of pleasantness (which is drawn-close by the mind) the mind will live in perpetual gladness. But the Medium of the coinciding in which the beauty and the pleasantness of the intellectual life coincide is the Word-of-God made flesh. Through this [Medium] the happy man is united with God, who is Beauty itself; and through this [Medium] the happy man is nourished with divine pleasantness.

[**23**] Thus, since this rose symbolizes Christ's humanity, in which is present Beauty itself and divine Pleasantness, and since Christ's humanity is no longer corruptible, because it is glorified and hence is completely separated from death and corruption: the pope carries a golden rose (i.e., one that is incorruptible and very precious), so that we are elevated from a corruptible rose unto that incorruptible [Rose] and are elevated from the visible [rose] unto the eternal and invisible [Rose] that bestows immortal life and that is the Paradise-of-delights for our mind.[29] [**24**] Therefore, to the [golden] rose [carried

by the pope] chrism is applied in order to denote Christ; and balsam is added because of its very pleasant fragrance, which the gold does not have, although it well has the shape of a rose. Paul said: "We are Christ's fragrance."[30] For those who convey the word of God convey Christ; and by preaching the gospel they spread the fragrance. If they live like Christ did, then they *are* His fragrance; for he who pursues this fragrance will come to this Rose.

Let the foregoing things have been said according as God has given [them] for an increase of our gladness. He who desires to know more concerning the symbolism of the rose will be able to read the *Rationale regarding Divine Matters*[31] and other writings of the learned.

III

[25] There is a third topic concerning the third name for [this present] Sunday, viz., "[Loaves of bread Sunday." This name is given] because the Gospel-reading [for today] speaks of loaves of bread.[32] So let us consider that the Word of God, who preached to the people about eternal life, willed to inform even the simple people [of the following]: that he to whom God is merciful and to whom He disposes to give the Kingdom of eternal life—[to him] the Word of God can give living food, even as here below He gave, by the power of God, food to the hungry when there was more [food] than it took for the feeding. [26] Today's feast is joyous because if [when] we are hungry because of abstaining from vices, we find here below in our desiring spirit [that] there is someone who can feed [us] and who is merciful, so that He permits no one to perish on this pilgrimage, then how much more abundantly will the Word of God feed [us] in the Heavenly Land of plenty! By means of this Gospel-passage of ours[33] we see, in [right] order, that the word of God nourishes first through our hearing [and] then through our tasting. We saw earlier that it nourishes through our sight and our sense of smell. By reference to these four senses let us infer four stages of spiritual contact. Every sensing is a certain touching. The intellectual nature is nourished by the word of God—i.e., is nourished by its authority [and] by its succulence. [27] Here it is relevant to consider in what condition, in relation to us, ought to be the spirit that is to be fed in this way. For our inner man, in order to apprehend the word, ought to have (1) ears that are open and receptive and (2) a strong and clear auditory spirit. Hence, since the word of God is intellectual bread, we ought to take note of the condition of the bread.

[28] The bread is Sacred Scripture. And he who is to draw nour-

ishment from the bread must chew it and must moisten its dryness with his own moisture in order in this way to [be able to] swallow it and be nourished. Scripture ought to be greatly broken into smaller sections and greatly ground up as if by teeth. And [this breaking-and-grinding] is called *searching*; for the Savior says "Search [the Scriptures] ...," etc.[34] Now, vital nourishment is elicited if one comes to Scripture's center; for its deepest [center-point] is Christ, who is Living Bread.[35]

[**29**] And consider that the one to be fed must introduce salivary moistness into the bread that has been broken down [in chewing]—[must do so] if the bread is to provide him with nourishment. This moistness is the humility of faith. Thereafter, the word is conveyed into the stomach of memory, and there it is cooked by the heat of love. Next, the *spiritual* (which befits the spirit) is separated from the *perceptible*, i.e., from the letter.[36] And this separation is made by the very subtle mesentery veins; they are the spiritual senses. And in the liver there is made a distribution to all the [bodily] members, i.e., to all the powers of the soul. [**30**] All these things occur by themselves without our paying attention if only we are healthy, so that our soul has healthy senses and instruments—i.e., healthy spiritual organs. If [the soul] lacks teeth, or if the teeth are dull or unfit for chewing, [or] if the mouth is dry, [or] if the tongue is infected, [or] if the stomach is weak, [or] if the liver is infected, then the word will not nourish the spirit.

[**31**] The word of God[37] gives wholesome bread; but the Evil One gives the bread of death. The word of God gives the bread of nature. Genesis 3: "In the sweat of your face ...," etc.[38] Ecclesiasticus 33: "Fodder and a rod and a burden are for an ass; bread and correction and work are for a slave."[39] By "ass" and "slave" the body is understood; by "fodder" and "bread" the food of nature and the necessity of sustenance [are understood]. By the other [two] things [are meant] (1) an affection for mortifying [the flesh] and (2) the engaging in labor. Consult Mauritius's *Distinctions* as regards *bread*.[40]

[**32**] Likewise, we must carefully consider the fact that Christ ministers the bread of life. As has been said very wisely, let Christ be conceived of as Virtue. In that case, the persuasion that leads away from the lusts of the flesh and leads unto a love of the immortal virtues is the ministering of the bread of life for the intellectual spirit—[the bread of life] that the Word of God ministers. And [the Word] distributes one bread unto a thousand who are hungry, because, in them all, there is one faith, one spirit, one baptism.[41] Even as they are *just* by

means of one justice and through one justice have been called from injustice unto justice, and even as by one heat [they have been brought] from coldness into warmth, so all who are just are the body of a single justice—of which body justice is the form, or life. The case is similar as regards truth and life; for there is one divine life that enlivens all the spirits of [all] the just. And [the just] are one body that is alive with one divine life, which is the Word of God, i.e., Christ.

Our having touched upon the foregoing topics in the foregoing way suffices for our better understanding the things that follow, in John 6, regarding the Living Bread, which enlivens all who partake of it.[42]

NOTES TO *Non Sumus Ancillae Filii*

* Sermon CCLXXV.
1. Galatians 4:31.
2. Romans 9:8-10.
3. Luke 1:5 ff.
4. Galatians 4:4.
5. Nicholas does not mean that all the natural descendants of Abraham are saved. He means that all men of faith are saved. These are called children of Abraham, the father of faith (Galatians 3:7). Abraham and many of his natural descendants were saved by looking forward to Christ, even as Christians are saved by looking back on Christ. See section **14** below.
6. I Corinthians 13:12.
7. As regards the translation of "*infallibilius*" and its variants, see pp. 10-12 of my *Hugh of Balma on Mystical Theology: A Translation and an Overview of His De Theologia Mystica* (Minneapolis: Banning, 2002).
8. II Cor. 1:20. N.B. In the Latin text above (at **9**:10) I am repunctuating the Latin sentence so as to read: "… est promissio et verbum. Assequetur filiationem …." This punctuation is permitted by both manuscripts (viz., *Codex Ashburnham* 1374 in Florence, Italy and *Codex Vaticanus* 1245).
9. II Corinthians 6:18.
10. Isaias (Isaiah) 54:1.
11. Galatians 4:27-30.
12. Origen, *Commentarii in Epistolam ad Romanos*, IV, 6. See n. 19 of Sermon CCLXX, as regards an English translation.
13. Romans 4:18-22.
14. "The offspring follows the womb" ("*Partus sequitur ventrem*"). That is, the offspring follows the mother. In other words, if a mother is a bondwoman, then her neonate is born into bondage, irrespective of whether the father of the child is a bondman or a free man.
15. Galatians 4:28.
16. St. Anselm's formula ("God is Something than which a greater cannot be thought," from *Proslogion* 2) is here applied by Nicholas to Christ, who, according to Orthodox theology, is God.
17. Nicholas uses "justice" ("*iustitia*") in the sense of *righteousness*.
18. Galatians 3:7.
19. Colossians 1:27. Cf. therewith Colossians 3:3 and John 6:54.
20. I Corinthians 1:30.
21. Philippians 2:8.
22. John 1:12.
23. Satan is the Prince of Darkness (and the Prince of Death). Cf. Colossians 1:13.
24. Nicholas here unfolds the meaning of the name "Israel".
25. "Jerusalem" means "possession of peace," and "Israel" means "seeing God."
26. "Abraham" means "father of many."

27. Galatians 4:26.
28. Usually, not a rose-seed but the "cutting" from a rose-plant is planted in order to grow new roses.
29. Christ is this Rose. Traditionally, Song of Solomon (Canticle of Canticles) 2:1 has been construed by Christian orthodoxy as signifying Christ: "I am the rose of Sharon ...."
30. II Corinthians 2:15.
31. Guillaume Durand, *Rationale Divinorum Officiorum* (Nürnberg, 1494), Book VI, section entitled *de Quarta Dominica Quadragesimae et Feriis*. In particular, see folio CXCIII^v.
32. John 6:5-59.
33. John 6:5-59.
34. John 5:39.
35. John 6:41.
36. That is, the meaning is extracted from the written words.
37. See n. 21 of Sermon CCLXIX.
38. Genesis 3:19: "In the sweat of your face shall you eat bread ...." These words were said by God to Adam and Eve after they had sinned and immediately before they were expelled from the Garden of Eden.
39. Ecclesiasticus 33:25.
40. Mauritius Hibernicus, *Distinctiones*. The editors of the Latin texts here refer to *Codex Cusanus* 27.
41. Ephesians 4:4-5.
42. More literally: "In the foregoing way [we] have sufficiently touched upon the foregoing matters, so that in John 6 the items that follow [there] regarding the Living Bread, which enlivens all who partake of it, are better understood.

Beati Qui Habitant in Domo Tua*
("Blessed Are They Who Dwell in Your House ...")
[November 1, 1456; preached in Brixen]¹

[**1**] "Blessed are they who dwell in Your House, O Lord; they shall praise You forever and ever."²

First, the Prophet excludes an error as regards happiness; secondly, he describes the happiness of the saints. [**2**] All (even the philosophers) who speak about happiness understand happiness to be a perfect good. And so, in [this] good there is a contentment of desire. Now, whatever admits of greater and lesser degrees cannot be that perfect good. For in the case of things that admit of greater and lesser degrees we do not arrive at an unqualifiedly maximum or at an unqualifiedly minimum—i.e., at that than which a greater or a lesser could not be posited. Nonetheless, we can arrive at that than which there is not *actually* a greater or *actually* a lesser. Hence, the perfect good, which is unqualifiedly maximum in being and possibility, cannot at all be of the nature of things that admit of more and less.

[**3**] Therefore, all those were mistaken who situated happiness in things temporal or in riches or in knowledge or in the virtues;³ for these things admit of more and less. And so, the Prophet David rightly indicates⁴ to be mistaken those who call the people who have these things *happy*. For it is not true. Rather, the people who have the Lord as their God are happy. Hence, it is not at all possible that there be [true] happiness in this world, where no one can arrive at the unqualifiedly perfect either with respect to purity or with respect to constancy. [**4**] Nor can the opinion of the Platonists be true. They said that souls which are divested of a body are happy but that after the course of years [these souls] re-enter bodies and are enveloped in their former conditions of unhappiness. But, [in fact, such souls that are free of a body] would cease being happy. For a nature that lacks reason has, as the scope of its desire to exist perfectly, only the here and now. However, a *rational nature*, which surmises about what is universal, has as the scope of its desire perpetuity and all time; and if it were ever deprived of its desire [to exist perfectly], it would not be happy. Nor could a [rational] soul be happy if it were ignorant of its inconstant state or if it had foreknowledge of its fall [back into a body]. [**5**] Moreover, Christ eliminates this error [of Plato's] when He says: "Whatever comes to me I will not cast out."⁵ Furthermore, since the saints cling

to God with the intent of never being separated from Him, how is it that Divine Justice would separate Himself from them? Thus, they are mistaken who say that happiness is not an abiding good. And this point [the Prophet David] makes in [the words of] our theme-verse: "they shall praise You forever and ever."

[6] Man has the prerogative that among animals he alone is capable of happiness. The Epicureans and the Saracens (and all who place happiness in food, drink, and sexual pleasures) speak against this prerogative; for other animals agree with man in [having] these [appetites]. And, for this reason, the Apostle says: "The Kingdom of Heaven is not meat and drink ...," etc.[6] In the hierarchy of nature man is higher than all other things—in accordance with [the verse]: "You have subjected all things [under his feet]," etc.[7] Now, the lower does not perfect the higher; moreover, (as is self-evident), abstinence, continence, temperance, etc., would not be virtues if the opinion [of the Epicureans and the Saracens] were true.

[7] Secondly, as regards the description of [the saints'] happiness, our theme-text touches upon three things: viz., state-of-being, location, and role.[8] The state-of-being [of the saints] is perfect, because there is happiness and because they are all happy. For [the text] says: "Blessed are they who ...," etc. According to Boethius happiness is a perfect state with a complete assemblage of goods.[9] Of this state-of-being, and of happiness, a sequence of the Gospel speaks, in which [passage] the Gospel mentions three things regarding the saints: viz., their number and character, their reward and happiness, their merit and holiness.[10]

[8] To begin with, there are seven orders of saints: some of the saints are saints from the beginning of the world, viz., (1) the [good] angels. Other saints are found in the Old Testament, viz., (2) the Patriarchs and (3) the Prophets. Others are found in the New Testament, viz., (4) the Apostles, (5) the martyrs, (6) the confessors [of Christ under persecution], and (7) the virgins. And in accordance with this [set of distinctions the text] posits seven beatitudes by means of which these orderings are distinguished.[11] An eighth beatitude—viz., "Blessed are they who suffer persecution ...," etc.—is common to all [these orderings of saints]: Consider these [orderings] further, according as [they are discussed] in the sermons of Aldobrandinus of Tuscania,[12] and consider further the beatitudes according as [they are discussed] in my other sermons for this feast-day.[13]

NOTES TO *Beati Qui Habitant in Domo Tua*

* Sermon CCL.

1. This was the Feast-Day of All Saints
2. Psalms 83:5 (84:4).
3. Plato was thought—in accordance with one interpretation of his *Republic*—to have regarded a life of virtue not only as a necessary condition of happiness but also as a sufficient condition thereof. Nicholas considers it to be the former without being the latter.
4. Psalms 143:15 (144:15).
5. John 6:37.
6. Romans 14:17.
7. Hebrews 2:8.
8. The saints' state-of-being is one of happiness. Their location is the House of the Lord. Their role is to praise God.
9. Boethius, *De Consolatione Philosophiae*, Book III, Prosa 2 (*PL* 63:724 A).
10. See the list of beatitudes in Matthew 5. The *number* of saints Nicholas immediately designates as being constituted by seven groupings.
11. Nicholas means to correlate the seven groups of saints with the seven beatitudes. But since he does not do so expressly, we cannot know how he would have envisaged the correlation, since none is obvious.
12. See n. 2 of Sermon CCLXX.
13. See Sermons X and CXXXV.

Sermon CCXLVI: Michael et Angeli Eius*
("Michael and His Angels ....")[1]
[September 29, 1456; preached in Brixen][2]

[1] " Michael and his angels fought with the Dragon ..." (Apocalypse 12).

This feast-day of the angels is called the feast-day of Michael. For "Michael" means "he who is like God" or "he who is as the Ruler." Michael, who is a defender of God's honor, is rightly called a prince. Everyone who is puffed up with pride exalts himself against God; hence, Michael cast out from Heaven *Pride*, which is called the Devil, the Dragon, or Lucifer. The Dragon, or Serpent, deceived our First Parents; for he motivated in them pride, with the result that through disobedience they desired to be like God.[3]

[2] He who thus motivated was for this reason cast out of Heaven by Michael—[cast out] because he placed his throne in the North[4] and willed to be like the Most High. Ascending by pride, he placed his throne in the North, and the *ascent* to the North is a *fall*. For the more someone ascends to the North, the more he recedes from the middle of the heavens, from the sun, and from the zodiac (i.e., from the way of life), toward death and toward the cold and the frozenness of vital movement. [3] Michael was rightfully put in charge of the Church, for the regimen of the Church consists of a humbling and of a ministering and of an orderliness (which orderliness does not occur apart from obedience). Orderliness is a divine splendor; obedience is a sacrament of sacred orderliness. All multiplicity is present in an orderly way; without orderliness multiplicity neither exists well nor can exist. For multiplicity falls short of *one* and of *being*. For each thing *exists* insofar as it is *one*. Therefore, the existence of multiplicity is found only in a union. But what except orderliness unites the many? For the many have an ordered relation to the *one* so as to exist; in and of themselves they cannot exist as many. But order requires proportion and harmony. And, indeed, the Church's governance, which is diffused from one unto many, depends upon hierarchy and divine governance, whose likeness it bears.

[4] Yet, in the following way understand how it is that we arrive at some knowledge of the existence of angels, or intellectual substances. For all nations, alike, maintain that intellectual substances exist. First of

all, [this claim is made by] the Bible's sacred books, which precede all other books. (Abraham preceded all who wrote in Greek; similarly, Moses was prior to Plato and to Socrates.) The philosophers speak of intelligences (which Moses calls angels) when they claim that all things arise from the movement of the heavens. [5] However, life is not from heavenly bodies, for material power is directed toward material objects. Therefore, something that executes the vital movement in a material object is not from the material heavens but is from a mover of the heavens. Therefore, just as the movement of *material* objects derives from the movement of the heavens, so *vital* movement derives from a mover of the heavens. But since vital movement is movement toward a goal, it is from an intelligence, which moves [it] toward the goal. Therefore, there are intelligences, which are movers of the orbits.

[6] The zodiac is said to be the place beneath which the planets are moved. The zodiac is said to be alive. Therefore, there are as many intelligences as there are different motions in the heavens. And if each of the stars has its own movement, then it also has its own mover, or intelligence, from outside itself. For, as a rule, it is true that if two things are found in combination, then if one of them is found [also] existing separately, then both of them are found existing separately. For example, with regard to the color dark-grey: because white is found [existing separately], black is also found [existing separately]; (for dark-grey contains both colors). Similarly, human nature enfolds within itself a spiritual nature and a corporeal nature. And the corporeal nature is found, qua separated, in earth, in metals, and in other things; therefore, the spiritual nature is found as existing separately, i.e., as an immaterial, or an intellectual, nature. Now, an angel is a separated, immaterial substance.

[7] In every movement that relates to a species we see a concordance. For example, the species of horses is a single species, and all horses have from the oneness of the species a single specific movement. And so, an intelligence presides over that species; the intelligence moves in a uniform way that [specific], or formal, set of equine characteristics. Therefore, we find from the uniformity of the regular specific movement an intelligent mover, without which there would not be a single species, power, and activity. [8] Every species, which consists of what is indivisible, is a domain over which there presides an intelligence, or an angel, that is as a god in his kingdom. Every man, on account of his perfection, is as a species. For Hermes Mercurius

Trismegistus, writing to Asclepius, called humanity a genus [and] called men species.[5] Certain men say that the text has come down to us not rightly translated in this respect. Nevertheless, we see that the rational soul (without which a man is not a man) is not from traduction[6] but is, in the case of each man, from the Creator (who is the Creator of [all] species). Therefore, we know by experience that in man intellect[7] presides over reason's movement, for rational movement is from intellect. [**9**] But unless our intellect (which in the bodily state is subject to sins) were directed by a separate intelligence, it would always follow [the influence of] the bodily passions. Therefore, there is an angel who moves us upwards so that we may desire things of an intellectual nature; and the angel stimulates rational motivation for things eternal. There is another motivation, [viz., that which is] from our animal nature, to which nature things earthly are pleasing; and the Prince of Darkness stimulates this motivation. And in us is this conflict, because we experience reason and the senses as subject to opposing princes and as waging war with each other incessantly.

[**10**] Moreover, law is ministered by angels. There is law with respect to specific nature. Each specific nature has its own laws; and the angel who presides [over that species] governs [the nature] according to the laws. The law is God's spirit, or God's providence. An angel is the one who proclaims, and executes, the law. And [reference to] his manner [of doing so] is inserted, to some extent, into the introit of the mass: "Bless [the Lord] all you His angels, you who are mighty powers for proclaiming His voice," etc.[8] For just as the voice of an emperor is sent to his subjects in a letter, and just as in the voice his word is present, and in the word his spirit, which informs and enlightens the subjects as to what the intent of the emperor is: so the writing, or the missive, that contains the word can be called a messenger or an angel. But the word and the meaning in the word can be called the spirit that motivates in accordance with God's providence. Accordingly, an angel is the one through whom God proclaims and ordains all that He wills. Angels are bearers of the eternal law and of God's will, and they are executors of the divine ordinance.

[**11**] God is a Spirit.[9] In every angel there is a receiving of the intent of the Spirit that God is. Therefore, an angel is like a living and intellectual book-of-law, or written-tablet-of-law, that contains the writing, or imprint, of God's intent. [An angel is] like an intelligent envoy to creatures, or speaker to creatures, so that [rational creatures],

which cannot see into the mind of the Invisible God, may by means of a sign receive enlightenment as to God's intent. **[12]** I mean this in regard to angels' names, which are names of roles, as concerns angels' being ministering spirits.[10] Just as we call a burning candle a light because we receive from it illumination, so angels take their names—one being called Michael, another Gabriel, a third Raphael, a fourth Uriel—from their role, because in accordance with the meaning of their name they minister to us such divine gifts. Just as in a king's court the attendants have names (because one attendant is the cupbearer of the king, another is the king's food-server, another his porter, and so on), so the names of angels end in "el"[11] (El is God) because angels are attendants of the King of Justice,[12] who is called El and Elohim.

[13] But if those [angelic] spirits are considered in and of themselves [and] not as attendants, then they are unknown to us. We know someone from his role; for example, we say "I know him" because I know him to be the king's cupbearer, because I know him as cupbearer. But if the role is removed, I do not know him—with respect, that is, to his being an image of God. For an image is not known unless its exemplar is known.[13] Hence, an intellectual nature is apprehended by us only by means of a likeness. For, as Dionysius teaches us, our visible sun (which in Greek is called Helios) summons all things unto itself, so that it infuses into them its power; and all things receive [this power] in accordance with their capability. **[14]** Now, visible objects that are generated because of the approach of the sun's ray show what the wondrous power of the sun is. For the sun's inexpressible power is received in the best way in which it can be; but it is received in different ways. For all the power of the sun is received in each thing contractedly.[14] In each apple the power of the tree is present contractedly (although it is present in one apple in one way and is present in another apple in another way); the case is similar with respect to each pear and to other things. Analogously, the whole power of the sun is present in the tree and, by means of the tree, in the fruit. Accordingly, the whole power of the sun's influence is received in each [tree] in accordance with the nature of the receiving-tree. Similarly, in every moveable[15] thing motion is received in accordance with the condition of the moveable thing: in one moveable object it is received in terms of location; in another, with respect to growth; in another, with respect to perceiving, etc.

[15] Now, the species receive a universal power in the way that species do, and by means of the species individuals [receive that power] in an individual way. In each individual the power of the species shines forth completely [and] in its own way, i.e., more perfectly or less perfectly in conformity with the individual contraction [and] in accordance with the individuation and determination—as one face is present completely in each mirror in conformity with the disposition of the mirror, [so that it] is present in one mirror more brightly, in another more dimly. Analogously, the Sun of Justice,[16] which is an intellectual Sun, diffuses (in its Kingdom, which is above all the senses) the light of understanding and the warmth of love; and the intellectual species receive the influence in accordance with their capability. (For the intellect is higher than are number and reason, and it is immaterial; for the intellect separates, and abstracts, intelligible forms from matter, so that it makes them to be forms that are understood within the intellect—as we experience in the case of our intellect. For that which is universal is present in the intellect. Matter individuates the form and contracts[17] it.) And by means of this inflowing of the rays of the Intellectual Sun we behold intellectual natures ([viz., angels]), which are noble and Godlike and are like living, clear mirrors. [The situation is] as if a mirror-image were alive and as if the mirror were clear by virtue of the fact that it is an image of God, who is the Sun of Intelligence.) All things are formed by means of this Sun, for Intelligible Being is the Source by means of which all things receive form.

[**16**] Hence, by virtue of the fact that [an angel] is an intellectual spirit, he is a divine ray. And because he is an image of the light of the Intellectual Sun, he has in himself a likeness of all formable species. For the Intelligible Being that is the Sun [and] the Source of light and of species is received [by each being] in its unique way: seraphically, cherubically, thronically, and so on.[18] Visible light is received in a diaphanum—in one diaphanum simply and closely, and the light is called the color white. In another diaphanum the light is received more distantly and is called blue; in another, still more distantly and is called red; and so on. And in this way nine orders of color are produced from the various modes of receiving. Therefore, in a certain comparable way: as nine discrete colors are produced from the different receptions of light (none of which colors appear to exist outside the region of the domain of visible things), so there are nine discrete choirs of intellectual spirits [i.e., angels] because of the different receptions of the intellectual light, and [these choirs] are apprehended only

in the domain of intellectual beings, i.e., in the intellectual world.

[17] The Gospel says that the angels [who preside over] believers see the Face of the Father, who is in Heaven.[19] Therefore, angels are like clean eyes of the heart. For a mirror, if it is not clean, ceases to be a mirror in its operation; so too, unless the eye is clean it does not see. Therefore, angels are very clean intellectual eyes. And just as sight vitally delights in visible beauty, which it seeks in all its meanderings, so the intellectual nature by means of its sight (viz., its intellectual sight) seeks to see the Giver-of-form, than whom nothing is more beautiful [and] in whom it finds rest. **[18]** A face is [i.e., symbolizes] knowledge; by means of the face we recognize men. To see the Face of the Father of the intellectual nature is to understand (or have knowledge of) the Fount of one's life. Every intellect desires to know the Cause-of-all-things, which we call *God*; and so, [this knowing] is the apprehending of Him than whom nothing is more pleasant or more delightful. But this seeing occurs by means of the manifestation of the Son of God, because only the Son knows the Father and because all others who know [the Father] know [Him] from the Son's revealing [Him].[20] For (as says the Son) the Father is hidden.[21] And so, the Word of God, or Son of God, is the Mediator for all rational spirits. Through the Son of God all things attain ultimate happiness and the goal of their desires.

[19] From the foregoing point let us come next to the reason for the strife between Michael and the Dragon, according as we read [of it] in Apocalypse 12. For the Dragon, or that old Serpent (viz., the Deceiver of [our first] parents), Lucifer, Satan, the Devil, gloried over his natural gifts and placed his highest happiness in self-love—[doing so] up to the point of contempt for God. Thereafter, he elevated himself (together with those [angels] whom he attracted unto his side) against God, to whom he willed to be similar by means of a natural ascent. He supposed that apart from merit and grace, and apart from the Son of God's teaching and manifesting, he could by his own natural means arrive at a vision and an apprehension of God's glory and could be happy. And because, afterwards, God created [other] *free* intellectual natures, He created them in that way so that they would not eat of the Tree of knowledge by feeding themselves from their own fruit of presumption but would serve [Him] in humility, relying on the grace of the Son, or Word, [of God]. Through the Son He showed that the work of redemption (which excels the work of creation) would be completed. And He showed that the Son would lead every intellectual nature to happiness and to fellowship with Himself when the Son by His own merit would convey those subject to Himself unto the King of Justice and would bring them to an inheritance of the vision and enjoyment of God. [20] But the Dragon, contending that he had no need of the Son's grace and merit but that his own nature sufficed, elevated himself (contrary to obedience) by [presuming] to make himself equal to the Most High. And in doing so, he sinned mortally. For as much as he could, he presumed to remove from God His glory—glory which is God Himself—and in this way to slay God and to reduce Him to naught. (By comparison, he who arrogates to himself a king's glory destroys the king qua king and slays him.) Thereupon, Michael, together with those who sided with him, took up battle, saying: "Who is like unto the Lord?"[22] And he cast Pride out of the Kingdom of Heaven. Thus, Lucifer fell from Heaven and from the height of unchanging Wisdom; and there remained to him [only] the mundane knowledge that is characteristic of this world unto which he was cast.

[21] Self-love fell from Heaven, and this love pervades this present perceptible world, and it deceived our [first] parents. And Satan, who is the Prince of this world,[23] is the ruler over this [domain]. Therefore, woe to the earth and to the sea!, etc.[24] For where self-love (to the point of contempt for God) holds sway, *there* there is eternal woe, because the inhabitants do not obtain happiness and their [true] end. Instead, those who in this way love themselves more than they love God end in self-hatred. For the damned could not in this world love themselves so much that they would not out-weighingly hate themselves after passing from this world. This is the punishment deserved by those who posit themselves as the goal of their movements; for they will be tormented with eternal hatred for themselves.

[22] And note with regard to this battle that it was fierce. For the power of the Devil reared itself against the power of our Christ. And because of this [rebellion] there arose a turmoil that was opposed to well-being, to virtue, and to the Kingdom of God, in which is present the power of Christ. But Michael, together with his [forces] took up the defense of Christ's power, which the Dragon warred against; and he obtained victory by the merit of Christ. And the [Scriptural] text tells us this when it says: "they overcame him through the blood of the Lamb and through the word of the testimony; and even unto death they loved not their lives."[25] That is, they battled for, and were prepared to

die for, the Word. **[23]** In this [text] we must note that the angels who were fighting triumphantly for Christ merited to be confirmed steadfastly in grace, because they preferred to their own lives God's honor. However, the fact that they were victorious results from the merit of Christ's shedding-of-blood. For Christ merited that those who to the point of death contend on behalf of His honor not be overcome by Satan but, rather, overcome Satan. For Christ Himself overcame Satan, and Christ has power over him. Therefore, the Dragon is conquered by the virtue of Christ: Christ's virtue is His obeying even unto death and His seeking not His own honor but God's honor. Thus, Christ's merit assisted the angels from the beginning, even as [it assisted] the holy fathers who preceded Christ's coming in the flesh. (By comparison, a reliable and trusted guarantor frees a debtor [of his debt] immediately upon his assuming the [debtor's] debt, even though he actually pays off the debt later, at the prescribed time.)

[24] And so, note that the Word of God, i.e., Christ's Power, is the royal power of the blessed [angelic] spirits. Accordingly, I said previously that the [good] angels execute the authority of the Word of God. An when Christ was led to His suffering, He attested that angels are in His power.[26] They battle for Him when He wills [for them to]. Hence, Christ is called an Angel, [or Messenger], of great counsel;[27] for He is the one who by His counsel directs the [good] angels in every respect. **[25]** From the [aforesaid] victory there followed gladness. For the text says: "Be glad, you heavens and you who dwell in them!"[28] For turmoil, or rancor, among brothers (this results from hatred and envy on the part of those who love themselves) was cast out of that Kingdom, where there is only peace. For Christ, our Peace,[29] holds the eminence there. And because this turmoil was cast out of Heaven, it descended unto the dwelling-place of men, who inhabit the sea and the earth. And so, in this world there is impermanence, pain, woe, death, and all other such things that are troubling.

[26] But the text indicates that the Devil has great anger because he knows that he has [only] a short time; for he is not ignorant of the fact that his dominion will be cast off. Hence, when Christ came to the world in order to instruct us regarding Satan's wickedness and in order to teach us [to do] battle to the point of triumph: the Devil said, in and through those whom he possessed, why he had come to torment them ahead of time (as if in that case there would not be a definite time at which [he and his followers] would be ejected from this world. And

Christ allowed them [viz., those whom the Devil possessed, to dwell] in the desert and in places where they would not harm men. [**27**] Moreover, note that just as in Heaven the angels, who were created at [one and] the same time, came to eternal gladness by means of triumph over the Dragon, so too human beings, who come into the world at different times, are by means of victory adapted so as to merit to be assigned to the celestial army. And to all of [these] assigned elect there will come the power of Christ for the purpose of *judging*—[judging] together with the [good] angels.[30] And [Christ] will cast out the Dragon together with all the apostate spirits; and those who have received counsel of the Devil [will] also [be cast] out of this world into darkness, so that there will remain only the power of our Christ, to whom all things are subject. And the earth will be freed from that woe, because the earth will be new and purified.

[**28**] In the meantime, the Dragon persecutes a woman, viz., the Church of Christ. And note that the persecution occurs in order that the Church (or "Jerusalem") may be restored in Heaven. Persecution descended when Lucifer and his angels were overcome [by Michael]; and so, [the Church] will be restored by means of an on-going battle. For unless the Evil One is conquered, no one will ascend unto the place from which he, the Devil, fell. And the angels who are among the loyal combatants [and] who in Heaven always behold the Face of the Father: just as from the beginning they fought against the Dragon, so they do not cease [to fight], so that the number of the expelled [evil angels] may be replaced.[31] This number [of replacements] will be taken from human beings, in whom there is the capability of becoming citizens of Heaven because of their intellectual nature, which derives from the Kingdom of those who are incorruptible, i.e., from the Kingdom of Heaven.

[**29**] And so, the Devil was not cast out of the world; rather, he fell to the earth, to the place of human beings, so that he persecutes a woman, viz., the Church, i.e., the Mother of Heavenly wisdom. [In the text] the offspring is called male[32] because male strength is triumphant over Lucifer. By means of this persecution soldiers are made noble [and] worthy of the Kingdom of Heaven—just as peasants and farmers because of their strength and virtues and loyalty are elevated all the way to the emperor's court, where they are made noble if they strive lawfully.[33] And they become citizens and members of Caesar's family.

[**30**] At times there comes to my mind why it is that the end of

the world is delayed. For many saints have previously surmised that the Day of Judgment ought to have come already. These saints saw from the triumph of the martyrs that the Heavenly Jerusalem was greatly increased [in number of inhabitants]. And from the fact that it grew so greatly from the beginning they surmised that it ought very soon to be completed. Yet, because ardor ceased with the ceasing of the emperors' persecution and because almost all men yield to the temptation of the flesh, the establishing or restoring of the City of Jerusalem, i.e., of the vision of God (a vision which is a peace that surpasses all understanding[34]), is delayed. [**31**] For no one except a crowned king[35] can be the living [corner]stone of this edifice.[36] However, unless one strives lawfully, he will not be crowned.[37] For the Kingdom of Heaven suffers violence, and the violent bear it away.[38] And those bearing it away are those who by means of violence conquer the Evil One. Therefore, when the end of the world approaches, there will be very great persecution, in order that the number of the predestined may be filled up quickly.

[**32**] Now, John is seen to describe, in the [Book of] the Apocalypse, the disposition of this warfare on the part of the Church—[to describe it] even to the point of the construction of the new City of Jerusalem. And we have great strife with spirits, with the world, and with the flesh. And at different times the mode of the strife differs. And so, [John] depicts the different battles with their different modes by means of figures and symbols. And one who with this supposition enters into the intent of that book will find sweet pastures.

Let these thus-expressed points be now sufficient.

NOTES TO *SERMON CCXLVI*

* Sermon CCXLVI.
1. Apocalypse (Revelation) 12:7.
2. This was the feast-day of St. Michael the Archangel.
3. Emphasis here must be place on the words "through disobedience." For there is a rightful desire to be Godlike. See I John 3:2.
4. Isaias (Isaiah) 14:12-14.
5. *Apulei Platonici Madaurensis Opera Quae Supersunt.* Vol. III: *De Philosophia Libri*, IV, 21 (p. 42). Edited by C. Moreschini. Stuttgart: Teubner, 1991. [Contains the *Asclepius*.]
6. Augustine and other Church Fathers raised the question as to whether an infant's soul is passed down from his parents (as is his body) or whether the soul is created anew by God. In the end, Augustine accepts the doctrine of creationism and rejects that of traducianism.
7. Nicholas here (and subsequently) uses "*intelligentia*" as a synonym for "*intellectus*". Note, for example, Sermon XIX (**6**:9-10): "… supremam intelligentiam sive intellectum …." Cf. Hugh of Balma, *De Theologia Mystica*, text edited and translated into French by Francis Ruello (Paris: Cerf, 1995-1996, two vols.). Vol. 2, "*De Via Unitiva*," **84**:20 (p. 136): "… remoto omnis imaginationis, rationis, intellectus vel intelligentiae exercitio …."
8. See Psalms 102:20 (103:20).
9. John 4:24.
10. Hebrews 1:14.
11. The Latin word-stem of <u>angeli</u> and the Greek word-stem of ἄγγελοι both end in 'el'. (Transliterated, 'ελ' is 'el'.) In the Latin manuscript Vaticanus 1245, which the editors of the printed Latin text are following, 'el' is not capitalized in either of its two instances.
12. See Malachias (Malachi) 4:2: "Sun of Justice."
13. Cf. Cusa, *De Possest* 38:13-14 (Latin text in my *Concise Introduction to the Philosophy of Nicholas of Cusa* (Minneapolis: Banning, 1986; second printing 1994)): "Non enim potest se causatum cognoscere causa ignorata."
14. "… contractedly": i.e., in a restricted, delimited way.
15. "… moveable": i.e., changeable.
16. See n. 12 above.
17. See n. 14 above.
18. Nicholas is here alluding to the orders of angels: cherubims, seraphims, thrones. Regarding the hierarchy of angels, see Nicholas's *De Ludo Globi* II, 77-78. As regards Nicholas's referring to God as Infinite Sun, see *De Coniecturis* II, 13 (**136**).
19. Matthew 18:10.
20. Matthew 11:27.
21. Matthew 6:18.
22. Isaias (Isaiah) 40:18.
23. John 16:11.
24. Apocalypse (Revelation) 12:12.
25. Apocalypse (Revelation) 12:11. The point of view of the Apocalypse is

future. The text that is alluded to signifies not that the good *angels* "loved not their lives even unto death" (for angels do not die) but that the redeemed human followers of Christ, who side with the Archangel Michael, are such as have not, and do not, love their own lives more than they love God.

26. Matthew 26:53.

27. Isaias (Isaiah) 9:6. The Latin word and the Greek word for angel (see n. 11 above) signify *messenger*.

28. Apocalypse (Revelation) 12:12.

29. Ephesians 2:14.

30. Matthew 19:28. Wisdom 3:8.

31. Nicholas borrows from Anselm's *Cur Deus Homo* the doctrine that the places of the fallen angels will be filled by redeemed human beings. See *Cur Deus Homo* I, 16-18.

32. Apocalypse (Revelation) 12:13.

33. II Timothy 2:5.

34. Philippians 4:7.

35. See Hebrews 2:9.

36. See I Peter 2:4-5.

37. II Timothy 2:5.

38. Matthew 11:12.

Nos Revelata Facie*
("We, with Unveiled Face ....")
[November 1, 1456; preached in Brixen]¹

[**1**] "With unveiled face beholding the glory of the Lord, we are transformed into the same image from glory to glory, as by the Spirit of the Lord" (II Corinthians 3).²

Since I spoke yesterday³ (in accordance with the Gospel-text) about the denarius that had Caesar's image, and since I did not fully explain the notion of God's image [in us], I will now take for our consideration the words of the Apostle that seem to be the words of all saints if someone were to ask them what they are now doing. [**2**] For they would reply: "With unveiled face" (i.e., face to Face and not by means of a symbolism)⁴ "we are beholding the glory of the Lord." For beholding, or contemplating, or seeing, is a very perfect activity that renders happy our supreme nature (viz., the intellectual nature), as also Aristotle shows.⁵ However, Aristotle himself does not speak of the glory of the Lord. In this [present Biblical] passage we understand this glory to be the glory of Christ, who exists in the glory of God the Father.⁶ For to see the glory of God and of His Son is the ultimate goal of creation, as you know from elsewhere.

[**3**] Now, the saints say that they are beholding the glory of the Lord; for this vision always transforms into the same image, from glory to glory. For those who behold are transformed continually into the image of the object, being transformed as by the Spirit of the Lord. For it is the spirit that is transformable, but [it is transformable] only by the Spirit of Him into whose image the transformation is made. (By analogy, when the affection of a lover is transformed into affection for the beloved, this happens by virtue of the beloved's spirit's attracting unto itself the lover's spirit and transforming it, so that in the lover there lives only the beloved.) [**4**] But this transformation [of the saints] is always new. For [the saints'] love never ceases but is ever increased, since the Beloved One is always pre-eminent, so that He is loved more [and more]; for He can never be loved to the extent that He is lovable,⁷ since He is Absolute Love. Correspondingly, the transformation never ceases. Therefore, those-who-are-beholding pass over—continually and eternally—from glory unto glory, since Absolute Maximality, in and of itself, always [and] incomprehensibly holds the

pre-eminence and attracts.

[5] Let us speak, then, about God's having given something of the image into which saints are transformed. And let us first of all consider Moses's having told of God's having said "Let us make man in our image and likeness."[8] The Apostle says that the Son of God is the Image of the Father,[9] just as Moses, too, writes that Adam begat a son in his own image.[10] Therefore, the true Image of the Father, who is Creator of the heavens and the earth, is His Son, who is the Splendor and Figure of [the Father's] substance[11] and who is a spotless Mirror[12] of the Father's majesty. Now, man was *made* in the image of the Creator. Therefore, man is not a true image, as is the Son, but is *created* in God's image. [6] Now, "image" signifies an express likeness of the original of which it is the image. Therefore, when the human mind is created, the Creator creates it by means of His true Image, viz., the Son. (The human mind elevates man above all things that lack a mind, and by means of its perfection it bears a quite close imprint of its Cause.) As the Apostle says: through the Son, as through the First-born prior to all created things, God also made the world.[13] Therefore, the Father looks into the Mirror of His majesty, [viz., the Son], when He creates mind.

[7] And in order that you may understand what I mean, consider [the following]: A painter wishes to paint his own portrait on a polished tablet[14] and can do so only with respect to his image. He has a mirror, and [in it] he views his image as very perfectly containing his face qua representation of the whole face. And he endeavors to paint another image—like that [mirror-image]—on the tablet, which is mirror-like, i.e., polished. But because the tablet, although mirror-like, is not a mirror, it does not receive the face as does the mirror; rather, it copies the mirror-image, which is itself an image. The image in the mirror is the result of nature; and this is because the appearance [in the mirror] has gone out from the being of the face. [8] For the being [of the face] is, because of being's goodness, so fecund that it begets from itself a similar appearance. And the [human] will does not, as a source, share in this [begetting]; for even if the acts-of-will of the painter were excluded, this begetting would still occur by nature. But when begetting occurs by nature: will, or love, arises from both [the painter and his image]. For the painter loves his "son" (or image); and from the painter and the image there proceeds love, or union.

In an analogous way, the Son of God the Father is the true Image (or true Figure) of God the Father's substance. That is, the Son is the

Brightness (or Mirroring) of the Light that the Father is. Thus, these names coincide.[15] Moreover, the Son exists by nature from the Father, because by virtue of the fact that [God] is Father, the Son [of God] is begotten without an accompanying act of will. And from the Father and the Son there proceeds the Holy Spirit ([i.e.,] Love, or Union), so that the Holy Spirit is not the Image of the Father but proceeds from both [the Father and the Son].

[9] Now, the works which God the Creator works outside Himself are the works of a God who is three and one. Hence, they are works that are done not with the will's acts being excluded but with the will's active cooperation—(just as a painter paints his own face on a tablet only with his will actively cooperating). For, as the Prophet says, "just as He willed [to do, so] He did."[16] And consider, next, that when a painter wills to paint something (e.g., a certain past scene), he looks unto his visualization of the thing to be painted, and he paints a picture in the likeness of the idea that he views within himself. But if the intellect were to undertake to paint the art-of-painting, it would not paint in particular anything that could be painted. For [it would paint] not the heavens, not the earth, not an animal, and not anything visible; rather, [it would endeavor to paint] the intellectual nature, which alone is capable of art. And the intellect would imprint on the painting the principles of the art-of-painting, so that [the painting] would be an image of the form of the art-of-painting and would be a visible representation of all the forms that could be perceptibly painted.

[10] Similarly, when God creates this or that, He looks at His Word, or Mental Concept.[17] But when He creates mind, i.e., an intellectual nature, He does not look unto some particular mental concept, i.e., unto some [aspect] of the Son; rather, He looks unto the Art itself, i.e., unto the Son Himself insofar as the Son is, in regard to the totality of the Father's perfection, the Father's truest Image. For mind is an image of God's universal Art. For the Son of God, or Word of God, is the Art through which God made the world. But the Creative Art is begotten from the fecundity of God the Father's Infinite Intellect. Therefore, the [human] mind is not bounded but is elevated above all [else] that is contracted. Mind is as a form created in the image of the Divine Art; this form, in its intellectual fecundity, enfolds the forms of all perceptible things.[18] [11] Therefore, when from nothing mind is called forth unto being the image of the Creator, when from nothing it first approaches the image, it arrives at the potentiality of being an

image—so that it is like a seed in which the image, not yet actually present, is present potentially, as manhood is present in the potency of boyhood. And when [the image] passes from potency into actuality, it is transformed—(1) as boyhood is continuously transformed when it is moved toward manhood and (2) as the potency-of-knowing is continuously transformed, from glory unto glory, in a student, so that he becomes a teacher. But this transformation is caused by the teacher's spirit, which is *actually* knowledgeable; it moves the spirit of the student from potentiality unto actuality. Analogously, the image [of God, viz., mind,] is led from potentiality unto the point at which it is completely actualized—led by the tutelage of the Word of God.

[**12**] And note that in II Corinthians 4 Paul is seen to speak to some extent of the manner in which the image [of God] is perfected [in us], when he says that "God, who commanded light to shine out of darkness, has shined in our hearts to give the light of the knowledge of the glory of God, in the face of Christ Jesus."[19] And he adds: "We have this treasure in earthen vessels in order that the excellency may be of the power of God and not of us."[20] Accordingly, the power of God elevates with respect to excellence, viz., elevates from potency unto actuality—just as the power of the sun elevates from potency unto actuality a tree that is present in a seed that has been flung to the earth. So our mind is a likeness of the Son of God's Image.[21] This likeness does not yet appear [in us] in actuality; but when the Son of God shall appear and we shall see Him, then by means of that seeing we shall pass over into that same image, because we shall be like the Son.[22] [**13**] Hence, in our mind we find a seed of the Divine Image, because we are capable of knowledge, of wisdom, of foresight, of governance, and of virtue—things which supremely befit God but befit no creature that is without a mind. Thus, just as God enfolds all things divinely, so mind enfolds all things intellectually.[23] Therefore, God alone can be present in the mind as an original is present in its image. And the more the mind is perfected in the just-mentioned things that have a likeness to God, the more the image [that the mind is] is perfected and the more clearly God shines forth in it. For as Augustine said:[24] the soul is an image of God by virtue of the fact that it is capable [of receiving] God. For unless an image were to receive, in an express likeness, the original of which it is an expression, it would not be its image.

[**14**] Hence, note that our mind is an image of God's beauty;[25] and so, it enfolds within itself all perceptible beauty, which is lower

than God [and God's beauty]. A similar point holds as regards all other things. Moreover, if you consider carefully: if mind is removed, there is no perceptible beauty, no discrimination of things, no ordering; in the perceptible world all these result from mind's judgment. And so, mind is not of the region of this world; rather, its perfection is higher than the world, and when mind looks at the world, it looks downward. And when mind turns its gaze back upon itself, then once the turning back is accomplished, mind finds that there is nothing of the beautiful and the lovely that it does not see to be present in itself [26] as in the form of all [perceptible] forms.

[**15**] Many things remain to be discussed here. These have been partly dealt with elsewhere. Still, we must not neglect the following thing: [viz.,] that in the mind there is freedom of choice,[27] so that the mind has within itself the origin of its acts and so that (according to Damascene)[28] mind controls its own works. Mind has this freedom because it is created in the image of God. And one who carefully considers [the matter] sees that the First Cause has placed in mind a likeness of Himself as Cause, so that mind is a living image, or a caused cause. And it is not possible that mind's excellence be [adequately] articulated. But Augustine sufficiently explains the way in which an image of the Trinity is present in our soul, and [this explanation] has often been repeated by me.[29]

Let the foregoing [remarks] suffice, in view of the shortness of time.

[**16**] Now, we ought carefully to safeguard this treasure which we carry about in earthen vessels.[30] And we ought always to retrieve it from the earth, in which it lies hidden—[to do so], for our profit, by imitating Christ (our Teacher) and all the saints who have gone before us in every circumstance. And we ought to beware lest we ever assume the image of the Beast and assume its figure, or characteristics.[31] For those who, after having blotted out the image of God, take on the image of the Anti-Christ (i.e., of the Serpent and Dragon) incur God's wrath; and day and night they shall never have rest. But those who, having spurned the image of the Beast and its characteristics, bear the image of the Word of God: in the future [they shall have] eternal life and eternal joy (according as is written in Apocalypse 20)[32]—even as shall all the saints, whom today we are commemorating in order that by their intercession we may merit to be in their company and to be joined to Christ, our Lord, who is forever blessed.

NOTES TO *Nos Revelata Facie*

* Sermon CCLI.

1. This was the Feast-Day of All Saints.
2. II Corinthians 3:18. Almost an exact quotation. The word "*omnes*" is omitted by Nicholas.
3. Sermon CCXLIX.
4. I Corinthians 13:12.
5. Aristotle, *Nicomachean Ethics*, X, 7 (1177^a12-18).
6. Matthew 16:27.
7. *De Visione Dei* 17 (75).
8. Genesis 1:26.
9. Colossians 1:12-15. II Corinthians 4:4.
10. Genesis 5:3.
11. Hebrews 1:3.
12. Wisdom 7:26. Nicholas also uses the mirror-metaphor at *De Visione Dei* 15 (67) and 8 (32) and 12 (49). See also *De Filiatione Dei* 3 (67) and *De Aequalitate* 12.
13. Hebrews 1:2. Colossians 1:15. Ecclesiasticus 24:5.
14. Cf. *De Mente* 13 (148-149).
15. "… these names": viz., "true Image," "true Figure," "Brightness," "Mirroring."
16. Not an exact quotation. Psalms 113B:3 (115:3) and 134:6 (135:6).
17. *De Visione Dei* 11.
18. The human mind enfolds the forms of all perceptible things in that it has the *power* to abstract a concept from particular sensory images. See *De Mente* 4 (77-78), where Nicholas refers to the *vis iudiciaria*, etc.
19. II Corinthians 4:6. Nicholas's text here differs slightly from that of the Vulgate: whereas Nicholas (at **12**:6) has "faciem", the Vulgate has "facie". The difference makes no difference to the translation (although "facie" is grammatically the better reading).
20. II Corinthians 4:7.
21. That is, our mind is a likeness of the Image that the Son of God is. (The Son of God is the perfect Image of the Father. We are an image of this Image.)
22. I John 3:2.
23. See n. 18 above.
24. Augustine, *De Trinitate*, XIV, 8, 11 (*PL* 42:1044).
25. See Sermon CCXLIII.
26. Here (at **14**:13) I am reading "ipsa" (with ms. Eisleben 960) in place of "ipso" in *Codex Vaticanus Latinus* 1245 and in the printed edition of the Latin text.
27. See Sermon CCXLVIII, endnote 9.
28. Saint John of Damascus, *De Fide Orthodoxa*, Book II, Chapters 25-27 [pp. 194-195 in Vol. I of *Sancti Patris Nostri Joannis Damasceni Monachi et Presbyteri, Opera Omnia Quae Exstant*. Paris: Delespine, 1712]. See also Vol. 37, pp. 255-259 in Frederic H. Chase, Jr., translator, *An Exact Exposition of the Orthodox Faith* [*Saint John of Damascus: Writings* (New York: Fathers of the Church, 1958)].
29. See Augustine's *De Trinitate*.

30. II Corinthians 4:7. Believers are themselves the earthen vessels to whom Nicholas is referring.
31. Apocalypse (Revelation) 20:4.
32. Apocalypse (Revelation) 20:4 – 21:4.

Qui Credit in Filium Dei*
("He Who Believes in the Son of God ....")
[April 13, 1455; preached in Innsbruck]

[1] "He who believes in the Son of God has God's attestation within himself." ([Verse contained] in the Epistle of John).¹

The Gospel of this same [writer]—[a Gospel] that is read today—states toward the end that the whole of the Gospel was written in order that we would believe that Jesus is the Son of God.² And [the Gospel] adds what we shall obtain as a result of our [believing]: "... in order that, believing, you may have life in His name."³

[2] Now, consider, first of all, that God's attestation is present in everyone who believes that Jesus is the Son of God. "Faith comes by hearing";⁴ and so, it needs an attestation. For certainty does not result from hearing. For unless that which is said is manifest either to the sensory eye or to the intellectual eye, it does not have within it a warrant for belief [*fides*]. For the statements made can be either true or false or doubtful. But faith, which unhesitatingly is supposed to affirm to be true the things it has heard, is, necessarily, free of the false and the doubtful. *Seeing*, then, is the certainty of all the senses, just as we are taught in the Gospel. For [Doubting] Thomas did not believe the report of the Apostles without his having *seen* and having *touched*.⁵ For it happens that sight is sometimes mistaken—as when a stick [partly] in water seems broken but the sense of touch discloses the mistake. Moreover, sometimes *one* thing seems, to the sense of touch, to be *two* things—as when a pea is touched with two fingers that are crossed and to the sense of touch there appear to be two peas, though there is only one. Accordingly, touch discloses the mistake of sight, and vice versa.

Thus, [Doubting] Thomas wanted to see and to touch, in order not to be mistaken. But certitude is referred to as seeing. So Christ said: "Thomas, because you have seen me, you have believed."⁶ Now, He does not say "[because] you have touched" but says "[because] you have seen." For to see is to apprehend in the highest degree of certitude. Believing (*fides*) that arises in this way, [viz., from seeing], is [but] small faith and is of little merit. For that which is seen cannot fail to be believed; and so, to believe to be true that-which-is-seen is of little merit. For what would the one [who sees] merit more than all others, since, like him, there is no one who, [upon seeing], would not believe? This belief (*fides*) does not result from any strength, or victory, over what impedes [belief]. And so, Christ said: "Blessed are those who have not seen and [nonetheless] have believed."[7] For great is that faith which is supported by no visible evidence; and so, those-who-[thus]-believe merit to obtain happiness.

[3] There are some things that are declared by a teacher, but yet the students do not believe the teacher unless [the bases for these declarations of his] are shown to the intellect. An instance would be when an inference is set forth—for example, that there is [only] one world—[and] the inference is not believed unless it is shown by evidential considerations to be true. The intellect sees in the evidential considerations the true inference and believes. There are other things which cannot be shown true either to the sensory eye or to the intellectual eye—e.g., the inference that the true man Jesus is the true Son of God. Now, although many evidences are educed for proving [this point], nevertheless it is not possible that all the evidences prove to be anything other than surmises.

In particular, in the Epistle [of John] there are said to be three[8] who give an attestation on earth and Three who give attestation in Heaven.[9] And although the Three in Heaven agree, so that there is [but] one attestation of all Three, nevertheless all of these attestations in Heaven and on earth do not establish the truth in such a way that faith is lessened because of certitude; rather, faith is increased because of the attestation. As regards Jesus: by means of *water* there came to be publicized that He was the Son of God. For John the Baptist baptized in water for the following reason: [viz.,] in order to get to know, and to make manifest, Jesus, who would come for baptism.

Moreover, *blood* likewise attests; for a knowledge of Him comes not only by water but also by blood. For He shed His blood in support of those claims which he asserted to be true. Among these claims was the following principal claim: viz., that He was the Son of God who was sent by the Father for the salvation of the world. Furthermore, the *Spirit* attests that Christ is Truth. For after the Apostles received the Spirit of truth, they became witnesses to Christ's being the Truth.[10] And this is the case because in and through them there spoke only the Spirit that they [had] received and that the Father [had] sent in the Son's name. And, hence, [that Spirit] is called the Spirit of truth because Christ, in whose name the Spirit was sent, is Truth. And in the case of all those who were baptized and who believe, the Spirit was the one who attested. Likewise, there are Three in Heaven[11]—the *Father*, the *Word*, and the *Spirit*—who attest. And the attestation is [but] one—

as when the Father said from Heaven "This is my Son," and the Spirit descended upon the Son and remained.[12] These are the attestations that cause faith to be greater and that rightly oblige us to believe that Christ is the Son of God.

[4] However, after faith has been received because of the foregoing considerations, the believer experiences *within himself* God's attestation. For as John the Baptist said, he who receives [divine attestation] knows that God is truthful.[13] Jesus said to the Father as regards His own believing disciples: "The words that You have given me I gave to them. And they received [them] and now know that I have gone out from You. And they have believed that You sent me."[14] See how it is that after the reception of faith, which is preached by means of words,[15] there arises the knowledge that comes from faith. This fact is ascertained by experience. For example, believers who have born witness by means of their own blood possess within themselves God's witness; otherwise, they would not joyously have accepted death in order to declare their faith. For if they had not had within themselves God's attestation, how would they have been made witnesses by means of their blood? For a martyr is a witness.

[5] Moreover, consider that conscience is said to render an attestation, as Paul and John the Evangelist say. For if we who are believers seek to know for sure whether Christ is the Word of God, and if we see clearly with our inner eye Christ's commandments, then we discover that in all the commandments of Christ there is contained only that which the Lord speaks in our respective conscience. However, we do not doubt that the word that speaks in us who have a clean conscience is the word of the King of kings, who is Justice and Truth and who commands our reason and enlightens it so that it may see that that which Christ commands is true and just. Hence, each good man endeavors to conduct himself in such a way that he is found to be obedient and blameless before the word-of-God, which he hears in his conscience, which is the spirit of the intellectual ear.

[6] Many law-givers have endeavored to explicate the [divine] word by means of laws, so that laws are certain expressions of God's word, or of eternal reason. By means of laws [these expressions] command that conscience be in-formed as if by God's word, which is unfolded in the laws. Thus, by means of the written Law and as a testimonial to the fact that the Law is holy, Moses referred the people to the word-of-God that was within those to whom he made the Law

known. It was as if God's word were the judge of all laws and were not a word to be sought at a great distance either above or below or beyond-the-sea but were a word that in us speaks to the rational soul by means of the ears of conscience. However, although that [Mosaic] Law explicated the authority of [God's] word in many respects that have to do with the well-being of groups of people living in this world, nevertheless it did not explicate the highest happiness. For this latter is not of this world but is of the world of [God's] word. And so, with respect to Christ's law,[16] in which eternal life is promised, temporal life is counted as nothing. For [Christ's law] teaches not only that we ought patiently to bear mistreatment and to pray for those who persecute us but also that we ought to do good to our enemies, being, as they are, those whose persecution and enmity redound to our acquiring happiness.[17] And if anyone is a believer (i.e., is one who believes that Christ is the Son of God), then he has within himself God's attestation that Christ's commandments can be only God's word and the fulfillment of the Mosaic Law and the ultimate and consummate perfection of all the laws that could unfold our inner word. What faith is more perfect than is that faith which overcomes the world?[18] What law is more perfect than is love?[19]

[7] The Jewish people, if they kept the Law, believed that God is truthful. God promised to them the choice-land of Canaan and the goods of this present world. And in order that [the people] be made fit to obtain [the fulfillment of] this promise, the Law was given. On its observance depended the assurance of their obtaining that which was expected [by them] because of their belief in the promise. However, all the laws of the world, as well as the legalisms which Moses unfolded, do not suffice for eternal life, which we desire as our ultimate happiness. For our faith and expectancy, as regards the promise of the holy land, has not issued forth from this perceptible world, where there is nothing eternal but where all things are temporal. Therefore, in order to obtain this eternal life, it is necessary [for us] to have faith such as overcomes this world, so that the things of this world are trampled on and trodden under foot; and it is necessary that the [requisite] law be altogether perfect. Yet, what law is good except that law which proceeds from love?[20] And the more love that [that law] has, the better it is. Therefore, the law that is most perfect love is immutable and eternal and is not of this present world.

[8] Now, since [this latter law] can be observed always by a

rational spirit, the rational spirit can always live by means of observing it. Therefore, by faith the [rational] spirit is disposed to the grace of happiness and is formed by love. For that which is altogether unknown is not loved.[21] Faith removes ignorance so that love can have room. Therefore, the deeper and more certain our faith is, the more capable of love is our spirit. So if we believe that Christ is the Son of God, then we do not at all doubt that His words are the words of God the Father, who sent Him. And [we do not doubt] that, therefore, they are words of truth, so that heaven and earth shall pass away but not those words.[22] And [we do not doubt that] God, the Giver of life, has by means of His Son spoken to us only[23] life and words of eternal life.[24] If, then, we believe that Jesus is the Son of God, we have the faith that overcomes the world and the faith through which we are most certain that we shall obtain [fulfillment of] the promise of eternal life if we keep His commandments. And lest a multitude of commandments make it impossible for us to have faith in [the fulfillment of] the promise, there is only one commandment, viz., love, as said the Apostle.[25] That [commandment] concerns, first, *God* and, secondly, *one's neighbor*.[26] And as far as concerns one's neighbor, it is a commandment like the commandment to love God, as our Teacher has taught us.

[9] But the fact that all things proceed on the basis of faith is best considered by each person on the basis of the following [judgment]: If the faith that Jesus is the Son of God is great and perfect, so that there is no doubt at all in this regard (even as [such faith] was present in the holy Apostles and holy martyrs who declared their faith by their own blood): then because that believer does not at all doubt, he does not sin. For he knows with undoubted certainty that sin inflicts eternal death if [the sin] is mortal sin. Accordingly, the believer would sooner die a temporal death than sin mortally. Moreover, he very patiently endures with joy all the maltreatments of this world, knowing the following words of Christ to be free of doubt: "Be glad and rejoice, you who suffer mistreatment, for your reward in Heaven is very great."[27] And he knows that those who seemed in the eyes of the foolish to die, live in glory.[28] Therefore, the true Christian overcomes the world. For poverty, which is an affliction to the sons of this world, is pleasing to the sons of light. For this world's poverty holds for him the riches of the other world, toward which he is hastening in order to remain there. Similarly, the troubles of this world hold, for the believer, the joy of the next world; and this world's death holds the life of the other, eternal world. Lo, how wondrous is the power of

faith, which in all hardship finds consolation!

[**10**] And one who considers the foregoing things says:

> Who would not love God, who has given us such a Teacher, through whom God has revealed to us such great secrets, unknown for generations? Who would not love such a Teacher, who taught us by means of a single word, viz., "faith," that we can ascend (even above all understanding) unto all things and can happily obtain the things that we desire? Who would not love supremely that Teacher who—since He could not disclose to us the things of faith except by means of our hearing [them]—assumed flesh and conformed Himself to our nature in order in this way to preach to us about faith and to transfer us from a corruptible life unto eternal life? Finally, who would not love that Teacher who—since He could not show to the eye the truth of the Gospel—resolved doubt by means of visible miracles and supernatural works and, at length, after all the signs and miracles by which He confirmed His preaching, furnished *such* an attestation to the truth, [an attestation] than which none more assuring could have been given to us? For to give His life for this purpose—[to give it] by means of a most shameful death—was the ultimate attestation.

If, then, He loved us to such an extent that He gave His own soul, or life, for us in order in that way to strengthen faith in us, how is it that we do not love that Teacher supremely? In that manner He loved us antecedently and above all other things. [This] Teacher died for us not only in order to remove from us all doubt about His teaching and to make us certain that He is the Word of God but also in order to cleanse us (who were unjust and incapable of happiness) by the merit of the shedding of blood, which [that] Innocent Lamb shed most abundantly in that sacrifice, when for our sakes He obeyed the Father on the altar of the Cross.

Wisdom is the life of the intellect. It does not enter into a soul that is intent on evil.[29] as is the soul of every man born from Adam—as we experience in the case of lust, which is a certain dark shamefulness that is not capable of wisdom. Because of the merit of the Crucified One, we are freed, through faith, from this evil intent. How is it that we do not love Him by whose grace alone, we can be saved? For He merited exaltation not only for Himself but also for all those who are made partakers of His merit. But He willed that [the following] be made partakers: [viz.,] all those who received Him by faith—the sacramental sign of this faith being baptism.

[**11**] Today's office begins: "As newborn rational babes, be desirous (without guile) of milk."[30] And in the epistle of Blessed

Peter—from which epistle [today's] introit is taken—there follows next: "... so that thereby you may grow unto salvation, if you have tasted that the Lord is sweet."[31] Accordingly, Blessed Peter desires that we Christians ought to be as is He who set aside all evil intent and all guile—as well as dissimulations and envies and evil-speakings—[32] [and become] as are newborn rational babes. We must take cognizance of this [point of Peter's]. For infants, who do not yet have the use of reason, have none of these [failings]. Rather, rational men become as newborn infants when they set aside all evil intent and all deceit, etc. Accordingly, those who have become newborns-in-Christ are like newborn infants. But this [statement] refers to the fact that the newborn-in-Christ are *rational* infants. For where there is no use of reason there is no faith. Therefore, the faith by which we are born [again] as Christians converts us to the likeness of babes, or innocents. Hence, Jesus said: "Unless you become as a small child, you shall not enter into the Kingdom of Heaven."[33] By the gift of original justice, or original innocence, as concerns his rationality: Adam was able to obtain eternal life in Paradise. But because he lost original justice, or original innocence: when presumptiveness arose in him (for he willed to become like God by means of knowledge, and he despised the pathway of innocence by transgressing against the precept): arrogance precluded him from attaining divine life. Thus, in Adam—[who was originally] a man perfect and having the use of reason—there was, prior to his sin, innocence with regard to reason. We see the likeness of this [condition] in the innocence (prior to actual sin) of those who lack the use of reason, [viz., infants].

[12] Moreover, note that we cannot be restored to being able to receive enlivening grace except by that very lofty faith which humbles, even to the point of death, the intellect and all the senses. For, in the case of [our having that faith]: if we come to taste the Lord's sweetness, then we [come to] desire [this] Food-of-life[34] in order to grow. Now, a mother does not deny her baby milk; rather, she feeds the innocent child from herself as one who puts her own life into the food, while the child's innocent-helplessness remains. Similarly, the Word of Life, through which we are reborn, nourishes our soul with itself in order that the soul may grow unto salvation. Analogously, a student desires his teacher's instruction, which he has tasted and found to be pleasing. And as long as the teacher sees that the student is without evil intent and without reluctance [and is] as an innocent child who is obedient and desirous of the milk of nourishment, the teacher nourishes

the student's intellect by means of his own master-knowledge in order that the student may grow in learning and in wisdom. But whenever the teacher experiences that the student, through the arrogance of his own presumptiveness, becomes someone who contradicts him and resists him and under-rates him, then he permits the student to be governed by the student's own judgment, and he ceases nourishing him. In that case, [the student] becomes froward[35] and does not attain to the likeness of the teacher who is perfect; rather, his own presumptiveness leads him to [a state of] ignorance, which is the death of the intellect.

[**13**] Now, John's Epistle says: "Whatever is born from God overcomes the world. And this is the victory that overcomes the world: [viz.,] our faith. But who is he who overcomes the world except him who believes that Jesus is the Son of God?"[36] Note that if we are reborn, so that we are sons of God, then we have overcome the world. And this victory consists in faith. (How this [point] is [to be] construed is mentioned earlier.)[37] Note (as [I stated] on Easter Sunday)[38] that faith in the Resurrection has God's attestation, which, within ourselves, we experience to be true. For no one denies that God exists and that He is this Rewarder. So he who dies for God's sake can be rewarded only if he is enlivened with an intellectual life. For one who would be unaware of the reward would not be rewarded. To live is, for the intellectual nature, to understand. Therefore, the one [who is rewarded] understands that he is rewarded; and so, he lives by means of an intellectual life that is without end. Now, 'how it is that we merit by the death of Christ to be resurrected' was spoken of on Easter Sunday.[39] And [the following] is a lovely contemplation: [viz.,] how it is that our soul—by discarding freedom of choice (which is the life of the rational spirit) by subjecting itself to the governance of God's word,[40] which was explained to us by Christ—dies unto itself. For in that [soul] there rules only the word of God, which enlivens and nourishes, [to the end] that through faith it happens that the word of God is made manifest to us by means of the Son. And by dying in this way, [that soul] enters into life.

[**14**] The Gospel [says]: "Now when it was late ...," etc.[41] In the Acts of the Apostles we read that Christ showed Himself alive by many proofs.[42] For without various perceivable showings [the Apostles] were not able to have faith in His resurrection. Therefore, [Christ] showed that He was the one who [had] died on the Cross—[showed it] first because of the fact that, although the doors were closed, He stood in their midst and said: "Peace to you." And He showed them His

hands and His feet. The proof of the Resurrection was wonderful. For He who entered when the doors were closed, i.e., He who stood in the midst of the disciples and spoke and showed His hands and feet: how He came into their midst without being seen—whether through the door or from elsewhere—they were not able to know. For God's ways are without restriction.[43] As Mary said: "In what way shall this be done?"[44] The angel answered that [it would be done] by the power of the Most High. This [power] is omnipotent and is not restricted; rather, [God does] as He wills to. Free will is unrestricted when, as in the case of God, the will *is* power.

[**15**] Now, [as risen, Christ] spoke [to the disciples] those words which He was accustomed [to speak]. And [He spoke those words] in the way in which He was accustomed to—[doing so] in order to make Himself manifest by His speech. And lest [the Apostles] would think it impossible for one who was crucified to be alive, He showed His wounds, by means of which they would recognize that the same one who was alive was the one who was crucified. This is marvelous: [viz.,] that He showed Himself to be alive, with His mortal wounds remaining. By means of death, Life showed that it was alive! And this [disclosure] is nothing other than a disclosing that death is nothing but the separation of the living soul from the body. Hence, wounds do not cause death, though they do remove from the body the fitness for a vital movement of harmony and connectedness. But the separation of the soul causes death in an incidental, [i.e., non-essential], way. So if the separated soul were to return to the body, the body would [once again] be alive because of the soul's presence.

[**16**] [Doubting] Thomas did not believe the words of [those] Apostles who reported to him that they [had] seen Christ.[45] Instead, he wanted to have stronger proofs than [come] from the seeing of one who appears while the doors are closed. It is as if [Thomas] were to say: "Perhaps it was an apparition, which was deceiving the eyes. And so, unless touch judges together with the eye, I will not believe." It is as if he were to say: "There can be no mistakenness if they both, [viz., sight and touch], agree in their judgment"—just as [I stated] above [that] Jesus rendered Himself palpable and visible in order that faith in the Resurrection might be instilled in the unbelieving. So there is resurrection; and the body of the resurrection is then of a nature [such] that it is subject to that Godlike will, which is the spirit's power over it. For just as the spirit wills to, so it can [effect] in the body to which it is united.

When [the spirit] wills [for it to be the case, then the body] will be invisible and impalpable; when [the spirit] wills [for it to be the case, then the body] will be visible and palpable. When [the spirit] wills, [the body] will have the form of a stranger;[46] when it wills, [the body will have the form] as of a gardener.[47] Or if it wills to appear in another form of light, it will so appear. These things are true at the time the soul is glorious. At that time, [the soul] has such a body [as was just described]; and at that time, it has obtained in Heaven its full power.[48] Therefore, it has that [power] even over its own "earth," viz., its body. And so, the body is moved according to the governance of the will. But if the soul has not obtained glory, then the body and its weight are not subject to the governance of the soul's will; rather, the heaviness of the body rules. This [heaviness] drags the soul down to the lower parts of the earth into a dark place, [far] removed from all joyous gladness of rational light.

[17] Furthermore, consider that before the showing of His hands and feet, Christ pronounced peace, which is the preaching (of peace and of grace) that precedes faith. (For the soul must be at rest and at peace prior to the reception of truth. For anger hinders the soul from being able to discern what is true.) Next, because of unobstructed faith in the Resurrection there arises joy in one's vision-of-the-Lord, which is a seeing, by faith, beneath the visible signs.

[18] To repeat, there follow, [in the Scriptural passage, the words] "Peace to you." This [peace] is a confirming, or subsequent, grace and is a blessing for one newly born by faith—even as in [the Book of] Genesis a blessing ensued.[49] Subsequently: just as, in the Word of God, the Father speaks (or sends forth) His word, so in the believer the word of the Lord is present; and the believer is sent and moved by the word. Hence, of him who is supposed to be an envoy of [God's] Word, there is required that he be alive with the life of the spirit of God's word. And so, an in-breathing follows,[50] as in the case of Adam's being created.[51] Therefore, [God] breathes-in the spirit so that it is now born into a living soul in such a way that the believing soul is made alive; for faith without life is a dead faith. But [faith] is shown to be living faith when it pursues works of life, i.e., when it keeps the commandments of God's Word. And so [Jesus] said: "Receive the Holy Spirit. Those whose sins you forgive are forgiven them; and those whose sins you retain are retained for them."[52] It is altogether true with regard to every sin against one's neighbor that every believer can forgive a sin that [another] believer has committed against him. And if he who has

sinned is [indeed] a believer, then because of that forgiveness, he obtains forgiveness with God. If [the believer who is sinned against] does not forgive [the other believer] but retains [the sin], then [the sin] is retained with God. But [in that case] he himself who retains does not obtain forgiveness of his own sins. For the Lord's Prayer makes clear that he who forgives will be forgiven.[53] But the foregoing [Scriptural] passage—insofar as it concerns those who are properly sent (i.e., concerns envoys-of-the-word who are sent), e.g., the Apostles and their successors—has a further interpretation: viz., that sinners are subject to the envoys' judgment and that [the envoys] cannot be mistaken [in their judgment]; for [the envoys] bind and loosen by the power of the Holy Spirit.[54]

[19] First, we must take cognizance of the fact that God worked all things for His own sake.[55] For He wanted to show the riches of His glory.[56] And for this reason He created a rational creature, or intellectual creature, so that He could show to it the riches of His glory. (Only this [creature] can perceive God's glory, by means of an intellectual tasting.) For true and incorruptible glory, or grace, can have a place of manifestation only in the intellectual nature. Analogously, he who is a noble king shows his magnificence only to those whom he deems to understand what royal magnificence is supposed to be. Moreover, no one who has precious pearls sets them before swine;[57] rather, he displays them where they [and their value] are known. Therefore, God created three natures: one that is altogether beyond time, viz., *angelic nature*; and another that is within time, viz., *animal nature*; and a third that is in between, viz., *human nature*, which through its intellect is associated with angels and through its animal nature is associated with beasts. Now, God willed that man, because of his intellect, be the goal of all corporeal natures and that He Himself be the Absolute Goal of all intellectual natures. And so, understanding is [given] only to the end that God be known—as if the imperial power of magistrates were present in a kingdom in order that the emperor's power would be known. And [suppose that] a king is known only by the imparting of his grace and mercy in a case where only out of grace and graciousness he elevates a faithful servant from the lowest rank to [the state of] co-reigning with him; and the more people to whom he can impart grace, the more he shows the riches of his glory. In similar fashion, God willed to create man, who is the lowest of the intellectual natures, in order to manifest in every possible way the riches of His most excellent glory when He would elevate him unto partaking of His Infinite Kingdom.

[20] God was not pleased that man [viz., Adam] fell into sin (as is mentioned in Romans 3).[58] Nevertheless, God permitted man, who was predestined to glory, to fall unto a very far separation from Him. [He permitted it] in order to be able further to show—in the most perfect way, to one returning—the riches of His glory and mercy, so that He might also recall this man unto a sharing of His Kingdom and might show him the unspeakable riches of His mercy. And so, God permitted predestined man to fall to such a depth that it was impossible for him, by himself, to rise again and to come to a tasting of divine mercy—[a tasting] by means of which he would be eternally delighted. And God permitted this [falling] in order that when He would restore man, He would show His infinite treasure of love and mercy. Thus, for the restoration it would be necessary that His Son put on—without any partaking of sin—the form of man the sinner and thereby restore [human] nature by means of a humiliating sacrifice even to the point of [undergoing] a most shameful death. Hence, in this way it happened that man, who was restored by a grace than which there is none greater, was justly made an heir of God on the basis of the merit of the Restorer. By way of illustration: if a king were to give his only son in order to redeem his opponents and if he were, by grace, to admit the redeemed to succession with the real son, then those who have been admitted would lay claim, justly, to the inheritance to which they would have come by grace. Therefore, being justified by grace is a manifestation of unspeakable riches. Understand [the point] rightly with regard to those who are predestined to glory. Now, in order to show His mercy, [God] does not permit-to-fall those whom He has foreknown;[59] but [in order to show His] justice, [He does permit to fall] those who are children of unbelief.[60]

[21] Hence, we must observe that through the Redeemer of nature man is made capable, by means of the Redeemer's merit, of tasting of the riches of God's glory. Now, these riches are eternal life. But for man to arrive at this [state], he must by faith be strengthened in his power. For faith makes the impossible possible; and it is necessary that faith lead [one] to [a state of] innocence, as [indicated] above. Next, we must consider that there is but a single faith by which it is possible for us to arrive at eternal life. And that [faith] is [the faith] which overcomes the world. Through it man is enlivened by dying. And so, he is raised up from death by a faith that mortifies—as [was explained] above, etc.[61]

NOTES TO *Qui Credit in Filium Dei*

* Sermon CLXXXVI.
1. I John 15:10.
2. John 20:31.
3. *Loc. cit.*
4. Romans 10:17.
5. John 20:24-29.
6. John 20:29.
7. *Loc. cit.*
8. "... are said to be three": viz., the Spirit and the water and the blood. I John 5:7-8.
9. *Loc. cit.*
10. I John 5:6.
11. Here (at **3**:39) I am considering the word "qui" to be deleted (as does also the Paris edition).
12. Matthew 3:126-17. John 1:32.
13. John 3:33.
14. John 17:8.
15. Faith comes by hearing. Romans 10:17.
16. I Corinthians 9:21.
17. Matthew 5:43-44 and 5:10-12.
18. I John 5:4.
19. I John 5:3.
20. Romans 13:10. John 13:34.
21. Augustine, *De Trinitate* 8.4.6 (*PL* 42:951); 9.3.3, first sentence (*PL* 42:962); 10.2.4 (*PL* 42:974).
22. Matthew 24:35.
23. Here (at **8**:14) I am correcting Nicholas's text (as does the Paris edition) so that it reads "non ... nisi".
24. John 6:69.
25. Matthew 22:36-40.
26. *Loc. cit.*
27. Matthew 5:12.
28. Wisdom 3:1-2.
29. Wisdom 1:4.
30. I Peter 2:2. Nicholas misremembers the Scriptural passage. In I Peter 2:2 "rational" goes with "milk", not with "babes".
31. I Peter 2:2-3.
32. I Peter 2:1.
33. Matthew 18:3.
34. John 6:48 and 6:51.
35. I Peter 2:18.
36. I John 5:4.
37. "... is mentioned earlier": viz., in section **9** above.
38. Sermon CLXXXV.

39. See n. 38 above.

40. Here Nicholas makes clear that by "discarding freedom of choice" he means '(freely) submitting one's will to the will of God,' so that he prays with Christ: "Not my will but Thy will be done."

41. John 20:19: "Now when it was late that same day, the first of the week, and the doors were shut, where the disciples were gathered together, for fear of the Jews, Jesus came and stood in the midst, and said to them: Peace be to you." (Douay-Rheims Bible).

42. Acts 1:3.

43. *De Filiatione Dei* IV (**77**) – V (**80**).

44. Luke 1:34-35.

45. John 20:24-25.

46. Luke 24:18.

47. John 20:14-15.

48. "Omnis potestas" here does not signify that the soul obtains all power (the prerogative only of God). Rather, it signifies that the soul obtains all *its* power—i.e., all the power assigned to it by God, the Creator.

49. Genesis 12:1-3.

50. John 20:22.

51. Genesis 2:7.

52. John 20:22-23. Not an exact quotation.

53. Matthew 6:12.

54. Matthew 18:18.

55. Proverbs 16:4.

56. Romans 9:23.

57. Matthew 7:6.

58. Romans 3:10.

59. Romans 11:22-23. God does not permit the good angels to fall; and He brings it about that elect men do not remain fallen.

60. Ephesians 5:6.

61. See n. 40 above.

Non in Solo Pane Vivit Homo*
("Man Does Not Live by Bread Alone ....")[1]
[February 23, 1455; preached in Brixen]

[1] "Man does not live by bread alone but by every word that proceeds from the mouth of God."

Consider the fact that with respect to the intellect man is said to be fed by a word. Jesus said to Peter "Feed my sheep."[2] Therefore, to feed is to enliven by means of the word of God. A teacher feeds his students with a word. A word is light from light. A vocal word is a lamp of light, as the Prophet says: "Your word is a lamp for my feet."[3] By means of the light that is in it the word illumines and gives understanding to children. Therefore, the intellect is fed by means of a word.

[2] Let us consider, then, the man who is fed with bread and the man who is fed with words. He who is fed with bread takes the bread and grinds it between his teeth. He sends it, once ground, into his stomach; and [the stomach] makes it moist and causes it to gurgle and to be parted, so that what is fine is separated from what is gross. And after the first parting is finished, another one subsequently occurs. And this [subsequent parting] casts off what is gross from that which is finely-textured, in order that the latter can become more finely-textured. Then a third time [the stomach] parts and separates. Fourthly, the food is prepared so that it turns into the nature of the one who is fed.

In a similar way there occur the separatings of the things that are supposed to nourish the intellect. For the first refining of things is done by the senses; for the [sensible[species[4] retain, once the gross materiality is detached, the immaterial aspect of the objects. A further refinement is done by the communal sense, or imagination. A third refinement is done by the faculty of reason, where the intellect finds its refined nourishment, viz., the intelligible form, or intelligible species,[5] which it turns into the intellectual nature. Therefore, the word, or logos, is form that nourishes. A vocal word is as a heaven in which reason, possessing all the things in [that] heaven, is seen to speak of all [these] things. And all things are present in [reason's] word as things signified are present in a sign. Furthermore, a certain religious man said that there is a sixth sense, and he named it speaking; for we speak of whatever things we conceive.[6] A word is bread for the soul and is a seed of life or a wheatan grain-of-life that contains the power of nourishing. In the vocal word there is present the [intelligible] form, or the light of reason; and by means of degrees of abstraction[7] with respect to the perceptual and the imaginative powers the form is brought unto the rational power so that there it may be refined as is gold.

[3] Now, by means of abstractive "digestings" there are removed all the things that surround the [mental] food—things, that is, which are incidental features of it and are separable and corruptible. For [the intellect] is not nourished except by pure and simple, incorruptible and steadfast truth. The pure quiddity and incorruptible essence, having been abstracted by reflective attention, nourishes the intellect, just as the perceptual image of a beautiful color nourishes the eye. The perceptual image of a beautiful color delightfully nourishes sight. But the abstracted form-of-beauty—through which everything beautiful to sight or delightful to the senses is beautiful and which shines forth contractedly[8] in the senses—is the nourishment of intellectual sight. And unless beauty were free from, and separated from, everything beautiful, it would not be a simple and incorruptible and delightful meal for the intellectual, incorruptible soul. We are nourished by the things of which we are constituted. Corruptible food is not suited for that which is incorruptible. Hence, the reflection of beauty in beautiful things that are corruptible does not nourish [the incorruptible intellect]; rather, only the truth that shines forth [nourishes it]. Therefore, truth's reflection is freed, [by abstraction], from everything in which its trace appears—[freed] in order that by means of a purified likeness [and] without a symbolism or a sensory image it can be seen by the intellect, which is not yet fully freed of all animating contractedness.

Analogously, if someone seeks to view his own true face amid multiple images and befigurings of it, then he frees from all material contractedness the form or figure [of it] that he finds in the different materials. For example, in a golden sculpture [of his face] he does not focus on the gold; and in a clay sculpture he does not focus on the clay. Nor does he look at the largeness or the smallness [of the portrayal] or at any such thing. Rather, from the different contracted faces he turns—as purely and simply as he can and by way of abstracting[9]—to the one face that is common [to the different images]. In this [one face] he reduces to a unity all the differences among the contracted images. And because the face of himself which he is seeking is only a true and *living* face, he does not find it—as he wanted to see it—in the purified perceptual image and symbolism. Rather, by means of a closer resemblance he beholds the *liveliness* of his face—just as from the configuration of an image someone detects an unportrayable mirth or mourning.

[**4**] We must reflect on the fact that our intellect is nourished by intelligible species, just as sight is delighted by the seeing of what is beautiful. Bread, which is not alive, enlivens (as Christ here[10] says); and a word, which is not alive, enlivens. For just as the soul is aroused by a beautiful object so that it is gladdened and exhibits its gladness, so the intellect, [when aroused] by its most enjoyable object, exhibits its life. Hence, when the object that is loved is offered to thought, the object arouses gladness. So too, love enlivens, and the object that is presented in the word enlivens. Hence, the arousing of gladness is the infusing of life. Therefore, the intellect is moved continuously [and] vitally and gladly when its most desired object is ever-present to it. But this [state] cannot occur as long as the intellect is not free from its mortal body, a concern for which keeps the intellect back from such contemplation. Consider that the life of our intellect is an image and a likeness of the Life from which it exists. For there is as much difference between the intellect's life and the Divine Life as between the light of the sun and depicted light, or between real fire and depicted fire. For God is the Sun of Justice[11] and a Consuming Fire,[12] infinitely transcending an image. Therefore, in this world we are nourished in a way that befits our nature, viz., by a shaded light of truth, or a shaded word of truth.

[**5**] Consider carefully that because the intellectual nature is incorruptible it does not need food—as does a corruptible animal—in order not to perish. Now, a man, after all sorrow, returns to [a state of] gladness as to a form of life in whose absence he does not care to live. (For a man thinks it better for him not at all to exist than to exist amid continual sorrow.)[13] Similarly, I esteem gladness to be a sense of life, as it were. For through this spirit, or warmth, [of gladness] a man senses that he is alive. But to be alive and not to sense that one is alive, [i.e., not to have a sense of gladness], is[14] rather to suffer a wretched life. [A man] suffers in that he desires especially to feel good. Accordingly, consider a life that is without sensing or without gladness to be a life without form, i.e., to be lacking the form of life. [**6**] And because nothing except love (*amor seu caritas*) begets gladness, love is the spirit of life. Now, love proceeds only from a being-known; for that which does not exist or (if it does exist) is not known cannot be loved.[15] Moreover, knowledge is knowledge of a thing; knowledge of a thing is begotten from the thing; from both [the thing and the knowl-

edge of the thing] there proceeds love. Therefore, if the thing is love and if the knowledge [of the thing] is the knowledge of the love, then the love that proceeds from these two is a spirit that supremely and unfailingly gladdens and enlivens the spirit that tastes of that gladness.[16] And so, a love that never fails nourishes [that spirit]. And this nourishing is perfectly captured in a likeness: [viz.,] the way in which the sight of the beloved nourishes the [visual] sense of the lover. And so, the Teacher of truth says that eternal life consists in the eternal vision of God, who *is* Love.[17]

[7] And note that there can be only two [specifics] which are sought: viz., *whether it is* and *why it is*. For love that enlivens is love that proceeds. Therefore, the goal of every intellectual investigation is to arrive at love, i.e., at the enlivening spirit which derives from the aforesaid [love and knowledge of love]. *Whether it is* has to do with *being*, which is from the Father. Hence, in every investigation as to *whether* [something] is, only the Cause-of-beings, viz., the Father-Creator, is sought. And in every investigation as to *why* [something] is, only the Cause-of-knowledge—i.e., the Father's Son, Word, Form Wisdom, or Absolute Knowledge of things—is sought. But if we arrive at the Form of being and thereby at the Form of knowing, then there arises, by way of procession, the Form of delighting.[18] The Form of being, the Form of knowing, and the Form of delighting are not different forms; rather, that which is the Form of the forms of being is also the Form of the forms of knowing and is the Form of the forms of delighting. Nevertheless, the Form of being begets from itself the Form of knowing—[doing so] in the Form of forms. For knowledge is begotten from being, and the origins of being are the origins of knowing; and in the Form of forms the Form of delighting proceeds from the Form of being and the Form of knowing.

Hence, in order that our intellectual spirit may arrive at the Enlivening Spirit with respect to *whether* [that Spirit] is, [our spirit] needs only perceptual cognition, through which it senses in and of itself, without weariness, perceptible objects. And thereupon it turns in wonderment to seeking *why* that which it senses is. For example, [our spirit] uses sensory sight in order to see all that it senses. For example, if it senses an odor, then it hastens to see, with sight, what is disseminating the odor; and if it hears a sound, it endeavors to see from whence the sound originates—and so on. (In a similar way, sight inquires, out of curiosity, from whence an external perceptible object originates. And unless sight detects [this origin], it does not judge that

[it] senses as perfectly as could be sensed.) And so, [sight] is, as it were, the form of the senses. Therefore, as regards that which is sensed, we inquire by means of reason why it is. And the eye (or the sight) of reason is the intellect. Hence, [our spirit] is not content unless it sees with the intellectual eye why [the external perceptible object] is, even though that object be sensed and attained by means of many methods. But when there is seen the Quiddity of quiddities, or the First Cause, of that which by way of the senses has come to be known, then there follows an embracing on the part of the soul and an adhering and attaching, or a love. And from the ever-present object our spirit is enlivened with the motion of gladness, as is mentioned above.

[**8**] Note that you are supposed to conceive of a difference between our intellect and the Divine Intellect. For we understand only that toward which we turn [our attention]. For our actual power of understanding is only finite. And so, it can actually understand only that toward which it unifiedly turns—just as sensory sight [can see only that toward which it unifiedly turns]. For a finite power, because of its weakness, requires that it be unified; for a unified power is stronger than one that is dispersed. Now, the more unified a power is, the simpler and more acute it is. For example, a flame of fire comes together in a sharp tip; and where the fire is more unified, it is the stronger as regards heating. Now, because God's intellect is not finite but is infinite, it understands, in and of itself, each and every thing at one and the same time; and it sees in the way that is spoken of in [my] *De Visione Dei*.

[**9**] Consider that this [present time] is the acceptable time,[19] in which all things receive renewal. And at this time children are put into schools and those who wish to make progress in the requirements of the Christian religion ought now to pay attention to the day of salvation.[20] For man's life on earth is a warfare.[21] But for Christians [life on earth] is a contending with spirits, in order that through triumph Christians may be received into the place of the spirits and may possess, in the Kingdom of Heaven,[22] the inheritance which had been possessed by those spirits who are adversaries of our salvation. Now, Christ's every action is our instruction. And so, He is the Way, through which we are to walk in following Him; He is the Truth, whose teaching is infallible; He is the Life, unto which we aspire.[23] And since He was the Son of God, He showed in Himself how we too could become sons of God. For as many as received Him, to them He gave the power

to become sons of God.[24] Therefore, it is first necessary to be renewed in mind and spirit and to be reborn. And this rebirth or renewal of the inner man is accomplished by faith through the cleansing of the outer man in the sacrament [of baptism]. For through faith we receive strength that is superior to the strength of unclean spirits. And this is the case because through faith the power of the Creator of the universe dwells in us and because through faith there is given to us a good spirit, which will lead us unto a good land where there is a joyous [and] incorruptible dwelling-place [and] where gladness is the food. Therefore, once we have been regenerated through the most sacred sacrament-of-faith, viz., baptism, by which we have made a profession [of our faith] and in which profession we ever persevere: then because of the old man[25] who clings to us, we must often purge away, and rid ourselves of, encroaching uncleanness—even as a tree, once planted in good soil, is every year pruned and trimmed and even as from our field, which of its own nature produces thistles and thorns, we must remove the weeds so that the field produces grain that is good and plentiful.

[10] Now, the Christian religion consists in the worship of one God, who is worshiped by every rational soul. [It is] a very stringent and very perfect religion, even though its precepts are but two: viz., to love God and to love one's neighbor.[26] For in love is contained the whole of the Christian religion's law. Nevertheless, in order that we may indeed fulfill this law, all the other prescriptions and the observances found in the Gospel have been written down. This religion was revealed to us from Heaven by the Word who put on our nature, [viz.,] by our true Teacher, Christ Jesus. And just as the disciples of St. Benedict are those who embrace and keep his Rule, so [the disciples] of Christ [are those who embrace and abide by] love. But in love are included faith and hope; and love cannot be true love unless all the virtues are included in it.[27] The Rule of St. Benedict is not other than love; nor is the Rule of St. Francis, nor that of the regular canons, etc. Rather, all these rules are methods for more easily acquiring love.

[11] Hence, with regard to every rule there must be a leader or a chief among those who profess [the rule]. In him the observance of the regulations must especially be found. By word and example he is to preside over others and is to visit his subordinates every year. And such a one is the pope, who succeeds Christ, as an abbot is a successor of St. Benedict. There can be one general abbot over many other priories,

just as the pope is over the priests whom he takes unto himself so that they may be co-workers—as Christ, when He saw the great multitude and the few laborers, took the disciples as His co-workers. Now, the pope is a shepherd who, as the vicar of Christ, is obliged to visit the flock and his entire Church. In the pope the law of Christ is especially to shine forth by word and example. He is as the instrument of Christ—as a servant is the instrument of his lord. But the pope ought to be a faithful servant, knowing and complying with the will of the Lord. Accordingly, a bishop ought to be someone learned and someone who knows the Lord's will, which is written down in the holy Scriptures, viz., in the Old Instrument and the New Instrument[28]—which contain God's final will and testament.

This visitation through which individuals are visited individually occurs by means of the sacrament of penance, in which oral confession is necessary so that the [the priest] may know each's disposition and may reform each one. And these days [of penance, confession, and reformation] are days of visitation, i.e., of salvation, just as a physician or one who has a remedy visits in order to heal ..., etc.

NOTES TO *Non in Solo Pane Vivit Homo*

* Sermon CLXXIV.
1. Matthew 4:4.
2. John 21:17.
3. Psalms 118:105 (119:105).
4. A sensible species is a perceptual image.
5. An intelligible form or intelligible species is a mental concept.
6. Cf. Anselm, *Monologion* 10.
7. Here and in section **3** below, Nicholas attests to the fact that his view of perception is Thomistic. See also n. 24 of my Notes to Sermon XXXVII and n. 12 of my Notes to Sermon CLXIX.
8. "... shines forth contractedly ...": i.e., shines forth in a restricted way.
9. See n. 7 above.
10. "... as Christ here says": i.e., as is said by Christ in the text that Nicholas takes as this sermon's theme, viz., Matthew 4:4.
11. Malachias (Malachi) 4:2.
12. Hebrews 12:29. Deuteronomy 4:24.
13. This view of Nicholas's is opposed to Augustine's verdict as found in *De Libero Arbitrio* III, 7, 20-21 (*PL* 32:1280-1281).
14. This text of Nicholas's is corrupt, as the editors recognize. At **5**:11 I am reading (with the Paris edition) 'est' in place of 'sed'.
15. See n. 14 of my Notes to Sermon CLXXII.
16. Here Nicholas is indirectly alluding to a trinitarian motif: God is trine, since He is: (1) Love, (2) Knowledge of Love, and (3) Love that proceeds from Love and Knowledge of Love.
17. I John 4:16.
18. See n. 16 above.
19. Cf. II Corinthians 6:2.
20. *Loc. cit.*
21. Job 7:1.
22. Nicholas holds Anselm's view that redeemed men replace the fallen angels. See Anselm's *Cur Deus Homo* I, 16-18.
23. John 14:6.
24. John 1:12.
25. Romans 6:6. Ephesians 4:22-24. See n. 14 of my Notes to Sermon CLXXII.
26. Matthew 22:35-39.
27. See my article "Die Tugenden in der Sicht des Nikolaus von Kues. Ihre Vielfalt, ihr Verhältnis untereinander und ihr Sein. Erbe und Neuansatz," *Mitteilungen und Forschungsbeiträge der Cusanus-Gesellschaft*, 26 (2000), 9-37. [A diagram appears on the two unnumbered/misnumbered pages following p. 37.]
28. The allusion here is to the Old Testament and the New Testament.

Beatus Es, Simon Bar Iona*
("Blessed Are You, Simon Bar-Jona")[1]
[June 29, 1457; preached in Innsbruck][2]

[1] "Blessed are you, Simon Bar-Jona." [This text is contained] in the Gospel whose reading you have just heard in a certain measure.

"Simon" means *obedient*; "Bar-Jona" means *son of a dove*. For the soul that obeys with such obedience as results from dove-like simplicity is blessed—even as is the rational soul that obeys out of faith. *That* [soul] can be called *Peter*, i.e., *knowing*. For it is necessary that a happy soul be a knowing soul; for a soul that cannot be knowing—as [the soul] of a beast is [not knowing]—cannot obtain happiness. For happiness consists in knowledge. For example, a stone, even if it had incorruptible being, would not be happy, because it would not know that it had [incorruptible being]. Only a nature whose being is to understand and to know is capable of happiness.

[2] However, the knowledge that makes one happy does not arise from perceptible things or from the power of the created nature. For [the knowledge that makes one happy] is knowledge of the Beginning. Nothing can know its own beginning—i.e., know whence and how it came into existence—except by revelation. A child placed on an island during infancy would not in and of himself come to know his father and the manner in which he himself was born. [Similarly,] the intellectual nature knows its own beginning [only] by revelation. And its knowing is its being. And so, when it understands, it has within itself the beginning of its being; and so, it exists amid immortal happiness. By way of illustration: if a certain pond—being established within its own limits [and] having arisen from a living fount springing up within it centrally—were of an intellectual nature and were to know that within it there were the living fount from which it emanated, the pond would be happy, because it would know that it had incorruptible being.

[3] Now, we know from the Gospel that Christ is the Revelation of the Beginning, i.e., of the Father. [He is Revelation] not in the way that ordinary people conceive of seers and prophets as making revelations but in the way in which the Son, who is the Image and Form of the Father's substance,[3] reveals. John [the Baptist], the last priest of the Old Testament, first revealed Christ.[4] Peter, the first [priest] of the New

Testament, likewise revealed Christ but on the basis of revelation from the Father.[5] Accordingly, the whole of the Old Testament concludes with the revelation of Christ; and the whole of the New Testament begins with it. Hence, by means of John and of Peter, the Heavenly Father first drew all men unto a revelation of His Son. Jesus well said: "No man can come unto me unless my Father draw him."[6] However, no one can come to the Father except by the Son's revelation.[7] Therefore, if we accept the fact that Peter's confession (viz., that Christ is the Son of the Living God)[8] was revealed to him by the Father, then we are blessed. For Peter confesses that Jesus is the Christ, the Son of the Living God; [and] Christ says that this is a revelation from the Father.[9] If we admit the former, then the latter is certain—since the Son of God, who is Truth, has spoken it.[10]

[4] Now, if the Father reveals to Peter hidden truth, how is it that He would not reveal to His Son all things? Consider, then, as you very often have, [the following]: he who acknowledges that Christ is the Son of God surely believes in Him and believes that He was sent by God the Father and that He speaks God's words. Surely, he does not sin, because he keeps [Christ's] commandments. Who would not keep the Son of God's commandments, which promise eternal life and promise that to die to this world is to live in the Kingdom of God?[11] Therefore, a sign that someone readily sins is that he does not believe in Christ as the Word of God. But if someone truly believes, then he has within himself the word of God, because there speaks in him only Christ, whom he obeys [and] who is the King who rules him and leads him to the promised inheritance of life.

Note that the Church is founded on Peter's confession. For the Church is the mystical Body of Christ,[12] which has existing within itself Christ the Son of the Living God. In this Body is the full power of binding and loosening;[13] this power in Christ is from the Father. For just as Christ, the Incarnate Word of God, includes within Himself all the power of the Father, so the word of Christ in Peter includes all the power of Christ. I say "word of Christ" insofar as Christ is understood as existing mystically and really. For insofar as "Christ" is construed in a mystical sense, i.e., [is construed] as designating the Church, which is the mystical Body of Christ: in this Body Peter, being the Head, has all the power of the Body because [He is] the rector who governs by means of the revelation from the Word of God. Moreover, Peter has the full power of Christ in order to be able to build the Church, which was not yet built. Even as Christ said "Upon this rock

I will build my Church," so by the word of Christ Peter builds and governs the Church. This is to say that Christ builds the Church by means of Peter and that by means of Peter he governs the Church once it has been built. Furthermore, "Peter" stands for every believer, for every believer has only Peter's faith. Therefore, from Christ we are called Christians; from Peter we are called believers. In Peter there is the enfolding of all believers and there is every principality and there is all power of binding and loosening. And so, he is called blessed. And no one can be blessed unless he follows our patron saint Peter, who is the patron saint of every church and of this church of ours in Brixen.

NOTES TO *Beatus Es, Simon Bar Iona*

* Sermon CCLXXXVII.
1. Matthew 16:17.
2. This was the feast-day of the Apostles Peter and Paul.
3. II Corinthians 4:4. Colossians 1:15. Hebrews 1:3.
4. Matthew 11:13 and 3:13-17. John 1:35-37.
5. Matthew 16:15-17.
6. John 6:44.
7. John 14:6.
8. Matthew 16:16.
9. Matthew 16:17.
10. That is, if we acknowledge that Jesus is the Son of God, then we will admit that Peter's revealing of this fact is from the Father, because Jesus (who is the Son of God) tells us that the revelation is from the Father.
11. See Romans 6:11.
12. Ephesians 1:22-23.
13. Matthew 16:19.

Ecce Ascendimus Hierosolymam*
("Behold, We Go Up to Jerusalem.")[1]
[February 27, 1457; preached in Brixen]

[1] "Behold, we go up to Jerusalem." Luke 18 and Matthew 20.

First of all, we may note (as does Tuscanellus, in a sermon for this day, [a sermon that concerns Christ's] summoning of His apostles),[2] that God does some things by Himself—for example, creating, healing, and judging. For He wills to be loved, to be desired, and to be feared—to be loved because He is the Giver of being, to be desired as Physician of the soul, to be feared as Judge. [God does] other things by intermediaries because, on account of orderliness, it is fitting that one creature depend on another. Thus, God governs corporeal creatures by means of immaterial creatures. We experience in our own case an example of this fact. For by itself (i.e., by its nature) the soul enlivens and in-forms the body; however, it shares with [various] powers the moving of the body. For example, by means of the visual power [the soul] moves the eye to seeing; and by means of the power to advance, it moves the feet to walking. Similarly, the pope does by himself some things that he reserves for himself [to do]. He does other things by means of envoys and ministers [both] (1) so that the order of dependence is preserved and (2) for the sake of the union of different things and a sharing among different things. Likewise, Christ, as Head of the Church, took twelve apostles into a portion of His concerns; and through them, to whom He revealed secret matters, He visited the world.

[2] Secondly, according to this same Aldobrandinus of Tuscania,[3] we may note that Jesus foreknew whatever things were going to befall Him. Jesus foreknew all things because He had God's knowledge. Now, God [foreknows all things] because He is present in the universe analogously to the way the soul is present in the body (and the sensitive soul[4] senses all things, including even whether a hair is plucked out). And so, God, who is purest Intellect, knows all the things that are in the universe, since they are present in Him. Therefore, all things are open to His eyes.[5] [3] But God's seeing is His existing, with which living and understanding coincide. Therefore, whatever things either exist or live or understand are present in God's seeing, even as an animal's living members are present in its vital being. If whiteness were an intellect, would it not see and understand all white things,

which are present in it and which have from it their being white? The case is similar with Absolute Being, which is Intellect.[6] Since it is the Form of forms, which gives being to all forms: that which it gives by means of Intellect, it also understands; for Absolute Being's understanding is its giving being. For the Creator is like Sight that creates by seeing. Therefore, He sees all things, because His seeing is the creature's existing.[7]

[4] As Artisan of all things, God knows the species and forms of these things, even as a writer [knows] the letters formed by himself, of which he is the cause. God is the Life of all existing forms, since the forms of all existing things are alive in God; for the perfections of effects are present in their cause in a more noble way [than they exist in the effects]. Just as from God there proceed sensing, living, understanding, and reasoning (which are creatures' perfections), so in God there are present, altogether perfectly, every act of understanding of an angel or act of reasoning of a man [and] all sensing and being of a creature. Therefore, God knows, in a more perfect way, all that angels or men know or can know. He works all in all.[8] And so, He not only knows generally but also knows each thing individually; for otherwise His knowledge would not be perfect. Hence, in God's knowledge—from which proceed all general knowledge and all special knowledge—are enfolded all the modes of knowing.

[5] Hence, necessarily, God knows at once all things universally and each thing individually. For in God all perfections of knowing are *united*, even as in a human being the particular powers of sense, which are united in the communal sense, are *separated*. And if by a unique act the communal sense were—through itself and without a sense-organ—to reach to all the perceptible objects of the particular senses, then at one and the same time it would touch, see, hear, and taste all things. Similarly, God views all things by an incomposite viewing. He sees in the point-of-eternity all the things that are future to us. For all temporal things are enfolded in that [point], just as each number [is enfolded] in the simple power of oneness. The point-of-eternity is like a seed that enfolds in its own power all time. Hence, he who sees the [seed-of-eternity's] power sees in the seed each and every thing that can be temporally unfolded from it—just as he who views the power of a grain of mustard sees in that [power] all the things that can be temporally unfolded from [that] grain. Regarding this topic, enough is found elsewhere, including in the book concerning the Icon of God's vision.[9]

[6] You might assert: "Admittedly, God knows good things because He is good [and] because from Him come all good things. But since evil is nothing, and since oftentimes not to know evil is better than to know evil, it seems that God does not know things evil. For example, that Christ foreknew the bitterness of His death rendered Him heavy-hearted. But it seems that it would have been better that He would not have [fore-]known."

I reply that the Glorious God knows [both] good things and evil things, because otherwise He would not know perfectly. Analogously, an eye knows [both] light and darkness; for it would not know light unless it also knew darkness. A painter recognizes his own painting; and if someone were to mar it with an ugly color, he would also recognize [this condition]. God, by the Hand of His Omnipotence, painted [into existence] all creatures; and on them all He impressed His likeness, as if [impressing] very beautiful colors. But the Devil marred [the paintings]. God knows of this [marring]. Just as He knew that after a man sowed good seed, the enemy oversowed tares,[10] so too [He knows of] sin and evil. Even though according to fact[11] [evil] is not anything, nevertheless it is known.

[7] Now, God knows future evils. I call [them] *future* with respect to us, for God's knowledge, which is beyond time, is neither past nor future. We see that a skilled physician and a skilled astronomer make predictions about death and about eclipses—foreseeing future things by means of sure inferences. How is it that these things could be unknown to God, with whom the Form of all things is present?

Now, there might enter into someone's mind the thought that God created man infirm in order, on account of the defect, to be desired as Physician—as was spoken of in the initial topic [of our sermon]. I respond that God did not create defect or infirmity or death but that—should these come about as a result of man's freedom—He reserved unto Himself a remedy, so that man would not on account [of that defect] always languish as infirm, through his own fault. In a similar way, the father gave to the prodigal son the portion [of his inheritance].[12] And because without the father the son might possibly waste his portion and become destitute, the father reserved unto himself [resources] from which he could once again support the son if the son returned. The son, [having become] impoverished and famished, desired to be fed, and he did not know where [he could be fed] except in his father's house. He returned and was received with joy. This

Gospel-story satisfactorily answers the objection.

[8] From the foregoing [considerations] and from our theme-text we can infer that Christ foreknew all the things that were going to befall Him (as John the Evangelist says[13]). Thus, Christ's suffering and death were so consummate that (1) they would enfold in themselves, intensely, the full bitterness of death and, consequently, (2) His merit would be consummate and would make satisfaction for all (as elsewhere I recall my having extensively discussed);[14] for the reward of death's bitterness is life. Now, there was consummate bitterness present in the death of Christ, who saw that the bitterness of death would come upon Him in the way it was going to come. (No one else can foresee the [distress of his death].) And so, [Christ's death] enfolds all the pain of all who die. Therefore, Christ's death is a reward for all those to whom merit is imparted. Therefore, take note of the mystery that the Savior was, for this reason, necessarily God and man. [He was] God in order that nothing of the future would be hidden from Him with respect to His suffering of a most horrible death; [He was] a human being in order that He would be able to die.[15] And, thus, Christ's death would be a meriting-of-life that would be sufficient for all who through His death could merit from God eternal life.

[9] Hence, the question (which is commonly raised) of whether God could have saved man by another means can be answered as follows: Since that thing is possessed more joyously which is acquired as one's due because of merit: eternal life, which ought to be obtained on the basis of merit so that nothing pertaining to happiness should be lacking to it, could have been obtained only as God ordained. And because He ordained in such a way that Christ would die, it was necessary that Christ die and in that way enter into glory—as Christ Himself informed two disciples (Matthew 16) before His death and on the day of the Resurrection on the Road to Emmaus.[16] For in such a way He was made to be our justification, so that the imparting of [His] merit through grace is our righteousness. And we can request of God our Father that He give us the Kingdom-of-life because of the merit-of-our-Christ that is reckoned as ours. And I regard this [transfer of merit] as the supreme mystery of the Cross and of [Christ's] death. For I believe that Christ has the Kingdom on the basis of merit. And those to whom Christ, out of grace, imparts merit [also have the Kingdom]—[having it] both because of the grace of association[17] and because of the merit of Christ's suffering. Therefore, in everyone who is to be

saved grace concurs with justice. Analogously, when the pope confers a benefice on someone, he does this out of the fullness of grace, because he can confer it or not confer it; however, the one on whom he confers it has the benefice by entitlement. (About this matter you have elsewhere heard extensively.)[18]

[**10**] Nevertheless, note one [more] thing: [viz.,] that only the death of Christ was able to merit eternal life, because [only] a consummate death merits immortal life. No other martyrs merit by their death eternal life; for each death of each [of the martyrs] falls short of the maximum and is infinitely distant from being a consummate death, which alone merits maximal life, viz., eternal life. However, the death of martyrs attests (1) that they are Christ-like and (2) that they exist in the grace that makes one pleasing [to God] and (3) that therefore they are justified and sanctified by the merit of Christ's death—[merit] imparted to them by way of grace.

[**11**] You might ask, in addition: "Given that Christ's death explains all things, how does it show that Jesus, who is Son of man, is the Son of God?"

I reply that a certain very eminent ancient teacher, an expounder of Paul's letters ([but] whose name I still have not been able to discover),[19] has taught me that Christ's death thereupon showed Christ to be the Son of God. For Christ died for His enemies and in order to strengthen in us, by the witness of His blood, the words of life. And since God is Absolute Goodness, then He who is so good that He dies for the salvation of His enemies is rightly called—since a better man cannot be posited—the Son of Goodness, which is God. [**12**] Christ Himself said that no one has greater love than does he who lays down his life for his friends.[20] And so, he who [dies] for his *enemies* exceeds all [others in love], so that there cannot be a greater [love]. Now, love than which there cannot be a greater is unqualifiedly maximal and, hence, is divine. Thus, Christ's works, which issue from maximal love, show which spirit—because it is divine—is of Christ. Therefore, since the spirit of a Christian is of the Spirit of Christ, it does not render evil for evil but renders good for evil [and] love for hatred. Christ rightly reproved His disciples who wanted to requite, with fire, an affront.[21] He asked: "Do you not know of whose spirit you are?"[22] And so, keep in mind that Christ's death on behalf of His enemies is an attestation that Christ is the Son of God.[23]

NOTES TO *Ecce Ascendimus Hierosolymam*

* Sermon CCLXX.
1. Luke 18:31. Matthew 20:18.
2. Nicholas here refers to the sermons of the Dominican lector Aldobrandinus de Toscanella (Aldobrandino of Tuscania, Italy), who flourished during the second half of the thirteenth century and whose monastery is presumed to have been in Viterbo. He is also sometimes referred to as Aldobrandinus Lombardus. See Tommaso Käppeli, "La tradizione manoscritta delle opere di Aldobrandino da Toscanella," *Archivum Fratrum Praedicatorum*, 8 (1938), 163-192. Josef Koch, pp. 55-67 of his *Cusanus-Texte. I. Predigten. 2./5. Vier Predigten im Geiste Eckharts* [Sitzungsberichte der Heidelberger Akadamie der Wissenschaften. Philosophisch-historische Klasse, 1936/37. 2. Abhandlung]. Heinrich Pauli, "Die Aldobrandinuszitate in den Predigten des Nikolaus von Kues und die Brixener Aldobrandinushandschrift," *Mitteilungen und Forschungsbeiträge der Cusanus-Gesellschaft*, 19 (1991), 163-182.
3. See n. 2 above.
4. Nicholas here alludes to the Aristotelian-Thomistic distinction between vegetative, sensitive, and rational souls.
5. Hebrews 4:13.
6. Here the allusion is to God, the Supreme Intellect and Divine Mind.
7. Cusanus, *De Visione Dei* 12.
8. I Corinthians 12:6.
9. Cusanus, *De Visione Dei* 7 and 12.
10. Matthew 13:24-30.
11. Nicholas here seems to be distinguishing with Anselm (*De Casu Diaboli* 11) what is said *secundum rem* and what is said *secundum formam*.
12. Luke 15:11-32.
13. John 18:4.
14. The printed edition of the Latin texts here cites Sermons XXVII, XXVIII (**3-4**), and CLXXXV (**4-8**).
15. Although here (as also in other sermons) Nicholas is influenced by Anselm of Canterbury, he here takes an importantly different tac. See also the text marked by n. 23 below. As regards, more generally, the relationship between Nicholas and Anselm, see my "Nicholas of Cusa's Intellectual Relationship to Anselm of Canterbury," Chapter 3 of Peter Casarella, editor, *Cusanus: The Legacy of Learned Ignorance* (Washington, D.C.: The Catholic University Press of America, 2005).
16. Matthew 16:21, John 12:23-33, Luke 24:13-27.
17. Cf. John 15:15. James 2:23.
18. The printed edition of the Latin text here cites Sermon CLXIX (**3**).
19. The printed edition of the Latin text here cites Origen, *Commentarii in Epistolam ad Romanos*, IV, 10. For an English translation by Thomas P. Scheck, see Vol. 103 in the series *The Fathers of the Church*. Washington, D.C.: The Catholic University of America Press, 2001.
20. John 15:13.
21. Luke 9:52-54.
22. Luke 9:55.
23. This argument is interesting because it is very uncommon.

Confide, Fili. Remittuntur Tibi Peccata Tua*
("Be of Good Cheer, Son. Your Sins Are Forgiven You.")[1]
[October 31, 1451; preached in Trier]

[1] "Be of good cheer, Son. Your sins are forgiven you." Matthew 9 and in the Gospel-reading [for today].

[2] As Hilary says,[2] whatever things Christ did He did to the end that He might show Himself to be [both] God and a man. Now, here in this Gospel-passage we are clearly taught that Christ healed the man with palsy—[healed him] to the end that He might show Himself to be God. Now, take note of the words and of the symbolical meanings. For the Scribes maintained that Christ had blasphemed because He said "Your sins are forgiven you." And for that reason Christ arranged the course of events in such a way that from them the people would understand that he who ascribed to himself the forgiveness of sins and was not God would be a blasphemer. For elsewhere the text states that the Jews said of Christ "He blasphemed" because He called Himself the Son of God. For it is blasphemy to ascribe to God that which does not befit Him. It does not befit the Creator that He be a creature. [The Jews] saw the creature; and they knew that the creature whom they saw with their eyes could not be God. And so, it is blasphemy that what is visible be ascribed to the Invisible God.

[3] Thereupon Jesus said: "What is easier to say ...," etc.[3] Behold, He implied that he who of his own power can command a maladie to disappear can also forgive sins. Therefore, He said: "in order that you may know ...," etc.[4] Lo, we must take note of what was said. For no one was healed except in order that we might know that the Son of man has [power on earth to forgive sins], etc. Therefore, He commanded the man with palsy: "Arise, ...," etc. And note that not only was [the man with palsy] healed at Christ's command but that at Christ's command he was strengthened: he who had been accustomed to be carried on a bed [now] carried his bed! Etc.

[4] "And the multitude, seeing [it], feared and glorified God who gave such power to men."[5] Note: The man with palsy was healed to the end that it might happen that the people would come into a fear of God and would, as a result of the fear, come unto glorifying [God] because of the fact that He gave such power to men. [The text] says "to men." But note [what is said] there: only Christ

was present [as Healer]; yet, [the Scriptures] say "to men." And this [usage occurs] in order that we may know that human nature can be united to divine power. For in Christ the human nature is united to the Divinity. [Human] nature is [essential] humanity [*humanitas*],[6] which encompasses all human beings. Therefore, when [God] gave [power] to the nature [qua nature], He gave [it implicitly] to all human beings. [**5**] Hence, note that "just as in Adam all die, so in Christ all shall be made alive."[7] Insofar as our nature is from Adam it is not uniteable to Divinity—even as darkness is not uniteable to light, [the two] being unable to be mutually compatible. With respect to Adam the nature is said to have originated from the earth, which is opaque and dark; with respect to Christ [it is said to have originated] from lustrous Heaven. With respect to Adam [human] nature is a seed of death and of infirmity; and as such it is not uniteable to life, because ashes return to ashes.[8]

[**6**] Now, in its own eyes [human] nature is not weak, because it does not perceive itself to be weak. A man is not weak who in his own judgment does not deem himself to be weak—even as a man born paralytic or blind has no knowledge of [having] an infirmity. No one can be acquainted with *what blindness is* unless he is acquainted with *what seeing is*. Hence, with respect to Adam [human] nature is like a blindness in which we are born and from which there can result dangers that can betake those who are blind (e.g., a fall into a ditch, etc.). With respect to Christ there is the possibility of seeing. [**7**] But note that human nature—insofar as it is like *rationality's being present within animality*—is like a light in a lamp. Thus, the rationality works by means of the animality, just as a lit and shining candle [works] by way of a lamp. And when reason follows [the lead of] the animality, [then the situation] is as if (1) a lamp were [made of] transparent but colored glass and (2) as if the candle-light were to shine accordingly.[9] Thus is [human nature] with respect to Adam. However, insofar as the *animality is present in the rationality*—as a wick is present in a lit candle—so is [human nature] that way with respect to Christ. For Christ is only Word and Reason and Light-that-enlightens, etc. Human nature with respect to Adam uses reason as it uses a candle in a lamp, and it inquires by means of discursive reasoning that befits it in accordance with the animality. Human nature with respect to Christ uses animality—in order to reason—as the flame of a candle uses the wick in order to burn and to give off light.

[**8**] Note that within our reason there is present an intellectual power. It is the power by means of which a man can know the mechanical arts and the liberal arts. This power has always been present in the soul. However, the soul was ignorant of its own power—e.g., [ignorant] that it could come to possess the art of planting crops.[10] There came [one day] a person who in the first place had this art from himself and who passed it on to others. And the people said: "Blessed be God, who gave this power to men." A similar thing holds true of the art of healing, of the art of writing, etc. [**9**] Thus [it was that] Jesus came, who had from Himself all knowledge—and every art—of all knowable things. Among these arts is the art of enlivening. For all other arts—[both] mechanical and liberal—are ordered toward life. Therefore, the art of enlivening includes all [other arts]. And Christ had from Himself this art of healing and enlivening and of imparting Himself to others.[11] And just as He was the Son of God, so too all those who received Him, in and through His teaching, were made sons of God. "For as many as received [Him] ...," etc.[12] And this art is faith, so that you will *obtain* in the measure that you are able to *believe*. In this world right faith is the perfection of all unwavering [faith].

[**10**] Furthermore, take note of [the following]: that just as when a blind man bumps his head against a wall, he experiences that pain has befallen him because of his blindness, so because of the power of seeing, he experiences joy when he not only avoids danger but also sees light that is delightful to all. Accordingly, human nature of itself is as an eye. With respect to Adam it is like the eye of a mole; with respect to Christ it is like the eye of an eagle.

NOTES TO *Confide, Fili*

* Sermon CVIII.
1. Matthew 9:2.
2. Hilarius, *De Trinitate*, IX, 5 (*PL* 10:284B).
3. "What is easier to say?" : 'Your sins are forgiven you' or 'Arise, and walk'." Matthew 9:5.
4. "But in order that you may know that the Son of man has power on earth to forgive sins …" (Matthew 9:6).
5. Matthew 9:8.
6. Christ had a particular human nature. But his human nature was a perfect human nature, was the perfection of human nature. Nature and person are distinct. A person has an individuated, numerically distinct human nature. However, this individuated nature belongs to the species human nature, to human nature as such. Accordingly, Nicholas writes in Sermon CCLX (**28**): "quilibet homo est modus totius naturae humanae, quae in sua unitate omnes modos complicat." See my n. 51 in the endnotes to my translation of Sermon XXII [*Nicholas of Cusa's Early Sermons: 1430-1441* (Loveland, CO: Banning, 2003), p. 375].
7. I Corinthians 15:22.
8. Genesis 3:19.
9. That is, the light that shined through the glass would be colored in conformity with the color of the glass.
10. Cf. *Cribratio Alkorani*, II, 2 (**93**).
11. Here (at **9**:6) I am reading, with the Paris printed edition, "vivificandi et communicandi se" in place of the manuscripts' wording: "vivificandi se et communicandi".
12. John 1:12: "But to as many as received Him He gave the power to become sons of God—to those who believe on His name."

Ubi Est Qui Natus Est Rex Iudaeorum?*
("Where Is He Who Is Born King of the Jews?")[1]
[January 6, 1456; preached in Brixen][2]

[**1**] "Where is He who is born King of the Jews?"

In addition to what I have elsewhere[3] indicated in regard to this feast-day, when on this feast-day I preached in various places, I will now add a further explanation of the theme-topic. The wise men did not doubt that the King of the Jews was born, but they asked where He was. *That [Jewish] people* had the King of kings (who dwells in Heaven) as their King: He governed the same Jews through Moses and the Prophets. And subsequently He who spoke to the people through Moses and the Prophets said: "Here I am."[4] And He was seen on earth, and He conversed [with men],[5] according as He had foretold that He would come. Hence, the Magi, who because of the star did not doubt that He who was going to come was already born, asked where He was. [**2**] Certain men who study the religious sects say that the sects can be foreseen from important and rare combinations of the planets (especially of Saturn and Jupiter). Among these sects, they call the Christian sect (which is of hidden wisdom) the sect of Mercury; for it is possible (1) that a combination that signifies a sect occur in regard to the configuration, or constellation, of the nature of some planet and (2) that in accordance with this [occurrence] sects are made. For example, one sect is that of Saturn; another is that of Venus. For [the astrologers] say that the sect of the Jews is of Saturn, the sect of the Arabs is of Venus, the sect of Christians is of Mercury, etc. And they say that the Magi were able to foresee, from the configuration of the important combination [of planets], that a King and Leader of a sect was born and in what region He was born. Nevertheless, [they did not foresee this] exactly or [foresee] in what town or in what house. Likewise, Messahalla[6] writes that the ancients noted with respect to the first appearance of [the constellation] virgo that a virgin ascends who suckles a child whom the nations would worship. And according to those [who study the sects] these astrologers [i.e., the Magi] came in order to see on earth, with their sensory eyes, Him whose constellation they had previously seen in the East, from whence they had come.

[**3**] However, we [Christians] do not take seriously these conjectures. [Rather,] we consider the Magi to have been led by a visible sign

(in the form of a star) that preceded them. By means of this sign they were made certain that there was born He from whom comes all wisdom, He who is to be sought, known, and worshiped by all the wise of this present world. [4] Now, the words of our theme—[words] which are presently to be expounded—can (according to Meister Eckhart, [in his Commentary] on John) be construed first of all attributively.[7] [It is] as if there were said: the King of the Jews, who has been born, is, in an unqualified sense, *Where* or *Place*. [It is] as if the wise men had said: that King who has been born is God, who is the Place of all things. For, similarly, all who are wise have seen that God is Place. For all things are at rest in their own place; and outside of their own place all things are in a state of unrest because they are not at the place toward which they tend. Just as Solomon saw that all rivers return to the place from which they go out,[8] so all things return to the Place from which they have gone out. Now, all things, insofar as they *are*, are from *being*—even as white things are from whiteness, and good things are from goodness, and true things are from truth. Therefore, the Being from which all existing things have gone out is the Place to which all things tend. For from the fact that all things, when outside their own place, are in a state of unrest and tend toward their own place and return to their own place and in their own place are safeguarded and are safe and are at rest: God can be called, not unfittingly, *Place* (not simply in the way in which the meaning of the word is understood [by us] but above the mode of our weak power-of-conceiving. Thus, John, in the Apocalypse, mentions that the Word of God said: "I am the Alpha and the Omega, the Beginning and the End."[9] But End, Rest, and Good are the same thing.

Now the Psalmist in many places, and Augustine throughout the course of his *Confessions*, and other men as well, state that God is the Locus of the soul.[10] Now, God is the one from whom all things receive their existence. For those-things-which-are-not God calls unto Himself in order that they *be*. But being is that to which all things are called in order to *be*; and outside of *being* things are in a state of unrest. For things that do not exist desire only to exist—[which is a state] in which they are at rest. Therefore, because [of the foregoing truths], *being*, which is the beginning of all the things that exist, is [also] the end—the place (or the resting-place) of all things. As we see in the case of all things made by art or by nature: they are then, [when once made], at rest in being. For example, when a house is brought into existence by the art [e.g., of carpentry], it remains and rests without changing.

But if it lacks having been colored or painted, then although it is unchanging qua house, it is moved toward the being that it lacks, viz., toward being colored; after it has received color it is at rest, and all prior changing ceases.

[5] And consider that the locus of time is eternity, or the *now*, or the present moment, and that the locus of motion is rest and that the locus of number is oneness, etc. For what except the present is seen to indwell time? For time flows, and its flow is only from being unto being. This being is the present, or the *now*—even as we say that we have the *now* from time alone. There are not many *nows*, but there is only one. For *now* does not pass over into the past; nor can "now" be predicated of the future. Therefore, the *now*, from which and to which all time flows, is the being (*essentia seu esse*) of time that we name "today," or "eternity," or "now," which always remains in an unchangeable way. Hence, the *now* of eternity is eternity itself, or being itself, in which there is the being of time. And God is eternal: He is His own eternity. For we give the name "eternity" to the beginning and the end of being and, likewise, to the locus of time. [6] And it seems to me that when we look at motion, we find therein only rest. For everything that moves is moved from a state of rest unto a state of rest, just as time [is movement] from *now* to *now*. Moreover, rest (with respect to which motion occurs) is only singular—just as there is not more than one *now*. Therefore, rest is the permanent being of motion. Therefore, whatever is moved is moved from being-at-rest unto being-at-rest.[11] But this permanent and sempiternal being of motion is Rest, which is God. For he who takes cognizance of the coinciding of beginning and end and of the fact that, in the Absolute End, the end-from-which and the end-to-which coincide—he sees the truth of this [claim].

[7] The case is similar with respect to number. For number proceeds from the *one* unto the *one*; and there is no other being of number than the *one*. And there is not a plurality of *ones*; rather, there is [only] one *one*. Therefore, oneness—which is also being (*entitas seu essentia*)—is one: it is the beginning, and the end, and the locus, of all beings and of every numerable number. Hence, God—insofar as He is the being of numerable beings—is called Being or Oneness or the one God, who is His own Oneness. [8] Likewise, reasoning is the movement of the rational spirit from truth unto truth. And there is only one Truth; and God is called Truth, because He is the Rest, or Locus, of the forms of reasoning, i.e., of the forms of intellectual inferences.

Likewise, conceive in a similar way of other things; and you will find in the variety of names only that this same God is the Locus, or Rest, for all things. He is the Beginning of all creatures—[a Beginning] which coincides with the End of all creatures. But with regard to these modes of speaking you must always beware lest you believe these terms to be precise when we speak of what is ineffable.

[**9**] Now, Paul said that in God we exist and move,[12] for we are pilgrims. Now, a pilgrim (*viator*) takes his name from the pathway (*via*) and is a wayfarer (*viator*). Therefore, as regards a wayfarer who walks along, or moves along, an infinite pathway: if it is asked where he is, it is replied "on the pathway." And if it is asked where he is moving along, it is replied "on the pathway." And if it is asked from where he moves, it is replied "from the pathway." And if it is asked to where he is headed, it is replied "from the pathway to the pathway." And in this manner the infinite pathway is said to be the Locus of the pilgrim and is God.[13] Hence, that Pathway in the absence of which there is no pilgrim is that beginningless and endless Being from whom the pilgrim exists and has all that he is as a pilgrim. But the fact that a pilgrim begins to be a pilgrim on the Pathway adds nothing to the Infinite Pathway and makes no modification in the perpetual and unchangeable Pathway. [**10**] Accordingly, take note of the fact that the Word of God says that He Himself is the Way.[14] You can understand this to mean that a pilgrim on the Pathway (i.e., in the Word of life) is a truly living intellect; the pilgrim is, and is called, a pilgrim from reference to this Pathway, and on it he moves. For if movement is a being alive, then the pathway of movement is life. Thus, the Pathway of the living pilgrim is a Living Pathway. From the Living Pathway a living pilgrim has the fact that he is a living pilgrim. And the Living Pathway is his Locus; and he moves on it and from it and through it and unto it. Hence, the Son of God rightly says that He is the Way and the Life.[15]

[**11**] But note, furthermore, that that Way which is also Life is also Truth. For a living pilgrim is a rational spirit that takes living delight in his own movement. For he knows to where he tends. For he knows that he is on the Pathway of life. But this way is truth. For truth is the immortal and very delicious food of the pilgrim's life; for the living pilgrim is nourished from that from which he has his being. Therefore the Living Way, which is also Truth, is the Word of God, which is also God and is the Light of men who walk on the Pathway. For the one who is walking needs no other light in order not to walk in dark-

ness, as if he did not know where he were headed. Rather, the Way that is the Life and the Truth is also the Light that illumines; and the Light is a Living Light, because it is the Light-of-life that manifests itself.

[**12**] There is one entrance of all men into this world; but men do not all live in equal ways. For although men are born naked as are other animals, nevertheless by means of the human art-of-weaving men are clothed, in order to live better. They make use of cooked foods and of a house and of horses and of many such things that art has added to nature for the sake of living better. From inventors we have these arts as a great present and a great gift, or favor. Hence, since many men live miserably and in sorrow and in hovels, suffering many things, whereas others live happily and nobly in abundance: we rightly infer that man, by means of some grace or art, can arrive at a quiet and joyous life in excess of what nature grants. And many men by their own intelligence or by divine illumination have invented various arts for living better. For example, [there are] those who have invented the mechanical arts and the arts of sowing and of planting and of engaging in commerce. And [there are] others who have drafted the rules of statecraft and of buying-and-selling and who have learned the ethics of habituating themselves—through *mores* and customary practices—up to the point of taking delight in a virtuous life and up to the point of governing themselves[16] peacefully. Nevertheless, not all these arts are of service to the spirit; rather, they hand down surmises about how in this world a virtuous life and a life worthy of praise can be led in peace and quiet.

[**13**] To these arts there is then added religion, founded on divine authority and divine revelation. Religion prepares a man for obeying God out of fear of Him and out of love for Him and for one's neighbor. [It prepares us] in the expectation of our obtaining friendship with God, the Giver of life, so that we may obtain a long and peaceful life in this world and may obtain in the future world a joyous and divine life. Yet, in the midst of all the kinds of religion that fall far short of true life there is revealed to us the way to eternal life—[revealed] by Jesus, the Son of God, who has taught us what the Heavenly life is which the sons of God have and has taught us *that* and *how* we can arrive at sonship with God. For just as the art of living well in this present age has been handed down in various ways by various men-of-talent, and just as an art that has been produced from keener reason is a more perfect art, so too religion that has regard for the future life and that arranges the present life in relation to the future life was handed

down in various ways by the prophets who foresaw the future from afar. And because no one saw the future life except by way of surmise, only He who came to us from God or from that future, Heavenly life—[only He who came] with our nature—could perfectly teach [us] religion or the way to Heavenly life. This individual is our Jesus, who came from Heaven in order that we might have life and might live through Him more abundantly than through nature. [For] He began to show by His works, and to teach, how this [obtaining] could occur. And He said: "He who follows me does not walk in darkness but will have the light of life."[17] Therefore, He who was also the Way of nature was the Way of obtaining grace.

[14] And so, Jesus is the place where all movement of nature and of grace find rest. Christ's word, or teaching, or commandment, or pattern-of-movement, is the way unto the vision, or the apprehension, of eternal life, which is the life of God, who alone is immortal.[18] Accordingly, it is a life that is more abundant than is a created nature's life. Hence, by himself no one can come to the way-of-grace that leads to the Father; rather, one must go unto that life by way of the door. Now, Christ says that He is the Door[19]—He who is also the Way. A Christian (who is a believer, having faith that works through love[20]) has entered through the door and is on the pathway. The door is faith; the pathway is love. Hence, faith in Christ—faith in-formed [by love][21]—is both the door and the pathway. And so, the Word of God the Father summons from *not-being* to *being* and, in the end, to such being as lives with an intellectual life, because it understands itself to exist. But through grace the Word-made-flesh summons this intellectual being unto fellowship with Himself, so that [this being] may taste, in the Paternal Fount, the agreeableness of its own divine life, which is imparted to the sons of God.

[15] Let us construe the words "Where is He who is born?" in another way, interrogatively[22]—[construe them] in such a way as to mean that the wise men sought the Child-King (a) in order to worship Him, because He is God, and (b) in order to see Him, because He is a human being. Let us, then, first ask: "Where indeed is the God who was made a human being?—where with respect to His divinity?" And since we know, to begin with, that God is He of whose magnitude there is no end[23] and know that, for this reason (as Solomon says in II Kings 8), the heavens of heavens cannot contain Him,[24] then [we know that] He is not located in any place. [16] Since we wish to investigate where

He is, let us first note, in accordance with Meister Eckhart, that we can see better where He is not.[25] Let us say that He is not present in anything that contains defect, deformity, evil, privation, or negation. For [these features] are privative and deny that something is the case (even though they affirm something to be the case in addition to their depriving and denying). But God is Complete Being; of His fullness all existing things partake in order to exist. (For God is Being itself, to which no being can be lacking—even as to whiteness nothing white can be absent or lacking. And so, God is not a part of the universe but is prior to, and superior to, the universe. For to a part of the universe the being of the other parts is lacking.) Thus, no negation or privation befits God; rather, to Him, and to Him alone, the negation of a negation is proper. This [double negation] is the quintessence and peak of very pure affirmation, in accordance with the [Scriptural text] "I am I who am" (Exodus 3).[26] Now, God cannot deny Himself (Timothy 2).[27] But if something were lacking to Him or if He were lacking to anything, He would be denying Himself to be *Being*. Hence, God is present in all things and in no thing. For He is present in each thing insofar as the thing is *something having being*; but He is present in no thing insofar as the thing is *this* being.

[**17**] This [latter claim] seems to me to be nothing other than [to say] that God is, as it were, the Form of forms, the Absolute Form (or Absolute Being), which gives being to forms. Thus, Moses calls Him the Former of heaven and of earth. For God is not heaven or earth or any such thing. For heaven has its own proper form, which gives to it celestial being; this form has being from the Form of forms. Thus, God, who forms all things, is Being, which gives *being* to all forms. These latter forms give *this* being or *that* being.[28] But God cannot be the form of the heaven—[a form] which is constituted by the differences of the heaven from what is not the heaven. Hence, to that form, so constituted by differences, there is absent the being that does not constitute it [to be the form of the heaven]. However, to Absolute Being, which is God, no being is lacking. Therefore, God is the Being of all being, just as the being of oneness is the being of all number. But just as oneness is not either the number two or the number three, so God is neither heaven nor earth. Oneness is the beginning and the end of the number two. For two is terminated in oneness; if oneness is removed, two ceases to be. Likewise, God is the Beginning and the End of all things; that is, He is the End of which there is no end; i.e., He is an Infinite End.

[18] Therefore, if God is present only in being, then it is the case, as Meister Eckhart says, that He is not present in time or in division or in succession or in quantity or in anything having more or less or in anything differentiated or in any created thing insofar as it is *this* or *that* or in any property—although He is present in *all* things insofar as they are beings, just as whiteness is present in all things insofar as they are white, but it is not present in them insofar as they are temporal, quantitative, differentiated, or this or that (e.g., are pieces of wood, are stones, etc.). For God is He-who-is, and "Being" is His name, and He is Being itself, which all things seek. [19] And it seems to me that to say that all existing things, insofar as they exist, are in Being, which is God,[29] is nothing other than to say that God, who is Being itself, is in all existing things insofar as they exist. For how could [these things] *be* if Being were not present in them? But Being, which is present in all existing things, is present in each existing thing uncontractedly to this or that. Thus, through Being all existing things are that which they are. For if Being were present in the heaven contractedly—i.e., were in the heaven qua heaven—it would not be in the earth. And how could the earth *be*, [if it were] without Being? So Being is present in all things and in no thing—in all things insofar as they *are*, and in no thing contractedly insofar as the thing is *this* thing.

Now, the heaven is this thing and not that thing; for it is not Absolute Being but is something contracted and delimited. For if it were uncontracted and undelimited, if it were infinite, then it would no more be *this* than *that* but would enfold the being of all things in equal measure, because it would be the power-of-being of all things existing and possible to exist. God is present everywhere and nowhere, as Augustine (in *On True Religion*) says about truth.[30] God is present everywhere, i.e., in every place—but is not present locally and contractedly. Rather, while He is in every place, He remains free from all place, because He is in every place non-spatially. [20] For He is present in the *being* of place, because the *being* of place is present in Him; and He is not present in place, although He is not absent from the *being* of place. By comparison, the being of a hand is present in the being of all the fingers. For all the fingers take their being from the fullness of the hand's being; and unless the being of the fingers were in the being of the hand, the fingers would not *be*. For a finger that is separated from the hand's being is not a finger. A finger is not the hand; yet, the finger's being derives from the hand's being. Therefore, the hand's being is not in the finger qua finger or in the thumb qua thumb or in the index-finger qua index-finger. For if the hand's being were in the thumb qua thumb, the index-finger would not be from the hand's being. For the hand's being would not enfold the being of all the fingers if it were contracted to the thumb. Hence, in order that the hand's being can furnish being to all the fingers, it is uncontracted to any [particular finger]. By means of this example of the hand's being you can help yourself pass over [reflectively] to the being of the universe and from the universe unto the Cause of the universe's being—just as if you were to look from the hand's being unto the cause of the hand's being, viz., the intellect, which is the beginning and the end of the hand's being.

[21] By means of the foregoing illustration you will be able to assist yourself in many respects as regards the familiar question wherewith one asks: "Where was God before He created heaven and earth?" The question presupposes something false: viz., that *where* or *place* existed when it did not exist and that there was a time before time existed. For since place and time do not exist prior to the creation or prior to heaven and earth,[31] the question presupposes what is false. Hence, if to the question "Where was God before He created heaven and earth" the answer were given that 'it is not the case that He was' (meaning thereby that if He had been, He would have been in time, for *was* is a mode of time which did not yet exist): then the answer would not be absurd. For it is as if one were to ask: "Where was eternity when there was no time?" The question is foolish, because it implies the contradiction that eternity is not eternity because it is temporal. For if eternity would have been somewhere, it would have been at a place and at a time. [But] place and time cannot contain what is immense and eternal; and they did not exist prior to heaven and earth.

[22] Thus, to the question "What was God doing before the creation of the world?" (a question that Augustine treats in Book XI of the *Confessions*) and to the question "Why didn't God create the world earlier?" one may reply: the question presupposes something false, viz., that when the world did not exist, there was an earlier. For without time there is no *earlier*, since earlier and later are temporal differentiations. And because there was no *earlier*, God did not create at an earlier time. If it is asked "Did not God exist earlier than the world?" the answer is given: "If 'earlier' is a temporal differentiation, then the question implies a contradiction." Likewise, the question "Why didn't God create time earlier?" presupposes a genuine contradiction, viz.,

that there both was and was not time. Similarly, if someone were to ask "Where was God prior to the world?" this [question] presupposes something false, viz., that outside of being there is being, that outside of God there is uncreated location.

[23] Moreover, if it were asked "Did the world, then, exist from eternity?" we could answer, in one way, that God and the world were present in the same *eternal now*. For the world began not in another eternal now but in the same eternal now in which God is present; for that *now* is without beginning and end and is God. Furthermore, we can say that because God is Eternity, then insofar as time derives from Him (and, thus, the temporal world is, and always was, from Eternity, i.e., from God), the world was *always*, i.e., *at every time*. Indeed, it was never true to say that the world *did not* exist. For at any time that it could possibly be said that the world was not in existence, the world *was* at that time. And although *was* is from Eternity, it is not eternal, because it is time. Moreover, it is a case of false imagination [to imagine] that between the *eternal now* (from which time flows forth) and time a certain delay intervenes. For it implies a contradiction [to assert] that there is a delay without there being time. Between eternal being and temporal being no delay intervenes. This [statement] is the same thing as if we were to say: between God's Being and the world's being there is no intermediary. And if you consider the matter rightly, [you will see that] the question as to whether the world existed from eternity implies a contradiction. For it presupposes that what is temporal and originated can be non-temporal and without a beginning.

[24] You might assert: "The temporal world is not eternal, even though it flows forth from eternity. How is it, then, claimed by the wise that the world has *always* existed?" I answer:[32] "[It is so claimed] because 'always' is taken to mean 'for all time'." You might respond: "So there was always time?" I answer: "Yes. For [to say] this is not to say anything other than that time was at all times or that time was always time." You might ask: "If the world has existed always, why is there said that 7,000 years have not yet elapsed since the world began?" I answer that *always* is not eternal[33] and is not without quantity; for it is not without time, and its measure is said to be comprehended by 7,000 solar revolutions. You might say: "I imagine that more years [than 7,000] have passed." I reply that the imagination does not get beyond quantity and that there cannot be posited a quantity than which a greater quantity cannot be imagined. Now, the imagination

errs when it imagines the quantity of the heavens to be something convex in such a way that someone sitting on the convex perimeter could extend his arm. So, too, I say to be similarly false the act of imagination by means of which someone imagines the world to be capable of being larger. For he conceives that between God's greatness, of which there is no end, and the finite magnitude of the world there can be an intermediate magnitude—something that is false. Similarly, I call false the imagination by which you imagine that there is time prior to *always* and that prior to *time* there is motion, which cannot exist except temporally. Hence, the prophet, who, as regards the past, expresses a determinate quantity of time, discloses to us that our imagining [there to have been] a period of time longer [than 7,000 years] is in error.[34]

[**25**] You might ask: "Wasn't God able to create the world earlier?" I reply that this question, like the others already posed, implies a contradiction, viz., that it was possible for there to be a creature prior to creation. Hence, just as no quantity, however great, exhausts infinite magnitude, so no time, [however great, exhausts] eternity. Accordingly, God's infinite and eternal power, which can accomplish that which God wills to, is not rightly conceived when such a question is formed. For the question presupposes (a) that one who is omnipotent cannot accomplish whatever He wills to and (b) that God is not God. Hence, to the [foregoing] question the Prophet rightly responds: "He did as He willed to."[35] And in prayer we acknowledge that His will is done in Heaven and on earth.[36] So, then, say: "If He had wanted to, He could have." Likewise, if you were to keep on asking "Why didn't He will to create earlier?" you will say that the question implies a contradiction. For it presupposes that free will is not free. Hence, there is no other [correct] reply than that the will of God is free and that His freedom counts as a reason. As regards these questions, see Augustine, *Confessions*, XI. These questions are to be left aside because they do not edify.

[**26**] Returning, then, [to the principal issue], let us ask: "Where is, or where dwells, God?" For as regards this question, being and dwelling coincide in God. Now, God is said to dwell in the highest places (Ecclesiasticus 24)....[37] He dwells in Heaven, as the Psalmist says: "I have lifted up my eyes unto You, who dwell in Heaven."[38] And He dwells in our midst (Exodus 25: "He dwells in their midst.").[39] He dwells in a cloud or in a dark cloud (Exodus 20: "Moses approached the dark cloud in which God was present.").[40] He dwells in holy

[places] (The Psalmist: "You, O Praise of Israel, dwell in the holy place.").[41] He dwells in light inaccessible (Timothy 6).[42]

[**27**] Let us now ask in a moral sense:[43] "Where is He who is born King of the Jews?" And let us draw our answer from the things that we have said. For grace imitates nature (grace is super-added to, and superimposed upon, nature), just as art imitates nature, as best it can. To begin with, God is not in time. Therefore, those who embrace temporal and ephemeral things—as if in them were present He whom all things seek—are deceived. Thus, being divided among themselves and clinging to (a) what is successive and (b) to corporeal quantity and (c) to an image that does not go beyond the bounds of quantity and (d) to things that admit of more and less, they do not attain God, who is infinite and who is free of all these things. But he who desires to come unto God must seek Him in lofty places[44] and in most lofty places, in the heavens, in the place in-between, in very secret places, viz., in a dark cloud and in dark mist. And he must become holy and free of the earth and of earthly affection; he must become saintly and a son of Israel, [a people] that dwelt[45] in the light, casting aside works of darkness.

[**28**] Moreover, Tusculanus[46] (in his sermon on this feast-day [of the Epiphany], the theme of which is the one we have set forth) says that each corporeal creature, since it is finite, has a place in which it is conserved; for example, a plant [is naturally found] in the earth, a rose in a thorn-bush, fish in water, birds in the air. But an immaterial creature is not in a place, because it is neither circumscribed nor conserved by place. (Understand [this point] with respect to physical place.) Thus, [even] if the material world did not exist, an immaterial creature could, nonetheless, exist. Things eternal—as are Father, Son, and Holy Spirit—are not in a place but rather surround and encompass all places. For just as that which is located at a place is conserved by the place, so place is conserved by God. [**29**] Now, God is said to be in a place because of certain effects that He causes there. Thus, He is present in the world on account of the [good] deeds of pilgrims and is present in Hell on account of the punishment of the damned and is present in Heaven on account of the joy of the blessed and is present in the mind on account of the consolation of companions. Accordingly, He is said to be in the world.

That which is originated cannot exist without its origin. A branch does not yield fruit independently of the root. A bodily member does not have movement in the absence of the heart's beating. The heavenly bodies do not shine in the absence of the sun. In this [same] way, no creature can function apart from God. "Without me," says the Son of God, "you can do nothing."[47] And John says: "Without Him nothing was made."[48] So, then, [God or the Son of God] is said to be in the world insofar as He causes in creatures their power-of-activity. "He was in the world, and the world was made by Him."[49]

[**30**] God is present in Hell for the torment of the damned; but He is not afflicted by Hell's fire, which operates by divine power. For [that fire] is the instrument of the Judge's justice, and the capability of suffering from that fire is present in no one except in him who is guilty—even as the servants of a judge have power only over wrongdoers. Hence, the fire of Hell does not act except against sin. And so, the penalty corresponds to the guilt, in which there are three things: the fervor of sin, to which the fire corresponds; the stench of sin, to which brimstone corresponds; and the disorderedness, to which the fury of the torment corresponds. Regarding these [three features] the Psalmist [says]: "fire, brimstone, and storms of winds …," etc.[50]

[**31**] In Heaven [God] is always the joy of the blessed; and unless they were to see God through their essence, they would not have the glory of happiness. Hence, their entire happiness consists in [that] vision. And St. Peter says that the angels desire to gaze upon God.[51] And of this joy Christ says, "No one shall take your joy from you."[52] [**32**] Likewise, [God] is in the mind because of the solace of friends. For although friends exist in a certain equality,[53] nonetheless the Son of God, who was exalted in His majesty, emptied Himself and humbled Himself[54] and was made humble in His humanity. Accordingly, He says: "I will now call you not servants but friends."[55] Now, friends associate with one another. Thus, the Son of God associates with us and dwells in our flesh and is at rest in our mind. Our association with Him does not have bitterness or boredom but has, rather, gladness and joy.[56]

NOTES TO *Ubi Est Qui Natus Est Rex Iudaeorum*?

* Sermon CCXVI.
1. Matthew 2:2.
2. This was the feast-day of the Epiphany.
3. Sermon CLXXI and elsewhere.
4. Isaias (Isaiah) 58:9.
5. Baruch 3:38.
6. The editors of the printed Latin text point out that Nicholas's reference should be not to Messahalla but to Albumasar. See their note for **2**:16-19.
7. That is, instead of asking a question ("Where is He who is born King of the Jews?"), the verse ascribes an attribute ("He who is born King of the Jews is *Where*"). Nicholas goes on to treat the text as an interrogative (**15**:1-2) and as having a moral sense (**27**:1-2).
8. Ecclesiastes 1:7.
9. Apocalypse (Revelation) 1:8 and 22:13.
10. Psalms 70:3 (71:3) and elsewhere. Augustine, *Confessiones*, I, 1, 1: "... fecisti nos ad te, et inquietum est cor nostrum, donec requiescat in te" (*PL* 32:661).
11. Here (at **6**:9) I am reading, with the Paris edition, "quietis" in place of "quietum".
12. Acts 17:28.
13. John 14:6: "Jesus saith to him: I am the Way (*via*) and the Truth and the Life."
14. *Loc. cit.*
15. *Loc. cit.*
16. Here (at **12**:25) I am surmising "ipsos" in place of "ipsum".
17. John 8:12.
18. I Timothy 6:16.
19. John 10:9.
20. Galatians 5:6.
21. *Loc. cit.*
22. See n. 7 above.
23. Psalms 144:3 (145:3).
24. III Kings (I Kings) 8:27.
25. Meister Eckhart, *Expositio Sancti Evangelii secundum Iohannem*, 1·38 [*Die lateinischen Werke*, Vol. III, edited by Karl Christ and Joseph Koch (Berlin: Kohlhammer, 1936), paragraph **206** (p. 173, lines 12-16)].
26. Exodus 3:14.
27. II Timothy 2:13.
28. See Cusa's *De Dato Patris Luminum*, 2 (**98**).
29. The expressions "Being," "Being itself," "Absolute Being," "Pure Being," are capitalized in the English translation in order to indicate that Being is God, that God is Being. Nicholas takes this point from Eckhart.
30. Augustine, *De Vera Religione*, 32, 60 (*PL*34:149). Augustine makes this point about oneness and not directly about truth.
31. Augustine, *Confessiones*, XI, 10, 12 – XI, 14, 17 (*PL* 32:814-816). Meister

Eckhart, *Expositio Sancti Evangelii secundum Iohannem*, 1:38 [*Die lateinischen Werke*, Vol. III, edited by Karl Christ and Josef Koch (Berlin: Kohlhammer, 1936), paragraph **214** (p. 180, lines 3-9, and pp. 182-183)].

32. Literally: "It is answered [by me] ...."

33. Nicholas is here distinguishing *existing eternally* from *existing forever*, i.e., from *existing for all time, existing everlastingly*. Likewise, the Scholastics distinguished between *aeternitas* and *sempiternitas*.

34. See, for example, the definite periods of time mentioned in Genesis 6-11. Cf. Luke 3 and Matthew 1.

35. Jonah 1:14.

36. Matthew 6:10.

37. Ecclesiasticus 24:7.

38. Psalms 122:1 (123:1).

39. Exodus 25:8.

40. Exodus 20:21.

41. Psalms 21:4 (22:3). Not an exact quotation.

42. I Timothy 6:16.

43. See n. 7 above.

44. Ecclesiasticus 24:7.

45. Here (at **27**:19-20) I am reading "habitabant". In the printed edition of the Latin text: in the note for this line, but not in the text itself, the spelling "habitabunt" needs to be corrected.

46. That is, Aldobrandinus of Tuscanella (late thirteenth century).

47. John 15:5.

48. John 1:3.

49. John 1:10.

50. Psalms 10:7 (11:6).

51. I Peter 1:12.

52. John 16:22.

53. Aristotle, *Nicomachean Ethics*, IX, 12 (1171^{b}33-34).

54. Philippians 2:7-8.

55. John 15:15.

56. Wisdom 8:16.

Hoc Facite in Meam Commemorationem*
("This Do in Remembrance of Me.")
[May 30, 1456; preached in Brixen]

[**1**] "This do in remembrance of me."[1] (The sacrament of [our] remembrance of Christ.)

We are obliged to have Christ with us in memory. And this [Eucharistic] sacrament, in which Christ is present, has to do with this precept. Hence, just as we are obliged to have Christ in our memory not in the way that perceptual forms are reposited in memory (for we have neither seen Him nor heard Him nor touched Him) but only insofar as we have received Him by faith as the true Son of man and the true Son of God, so He is truly present in the sacrament [but] not[2] spatially or extendedly or as having color. And just as by faith He is truly seen to be present in our memory, so [by faith He is] also [seen to be present] in the sacrament.

[**2**] By way of introduction, [we can say] that after man was created, then at length—where the light was [shining] in darkness without being comprehended—[3] a people was chosen from the seed of Abraham. This people was oppressed in the darkness of Egypt, from which region it was led through the Red Sea into the wilderness. *There* [this people] entered into a covenant with God; and a promise was made to them that if they kept the law of the tablets, they would be led to a land where there was an abundance of all the foods that they could wish for. They received many sacred signs of this promise. But manna was the consummation of the sacred signs. By means of it the delights of the Land of Promise were prefigured. And that which under the form of manna they foretasted by faith, they obtained in reality in the Land of Promise. In an analogous way this [Eucharistic] sacrament is the true manna, and the Kingdom of Heaven is the Heavenly Jerusalem, where indeed all things are [delightful] to the eye, because the vision of God [is present there], as is also the happy enjoyment of the Good.

[**3**] Let the reflection that can be made in regard to this sacrament be touched upon, to some extent, for the sake of our devotion—even though the reflection cannot be fully conceptualized or written down. And first of all we need to note that Christ's entire teaching is [directed toward] saving the soul. And because the rational soul has a weakened intellect and has corrupted affections (since men love the

darkness of sensuality more than the light of reason), Christ taught that the intellect is saved by faith and that the affections are saved by love. Now, the faith that frees the intellect is that than which there can be no greater faith, viz., [the belief] that God exists, who spoke to us most recently in His Son, Jesus, as Paul states.[4] The love that repairs the affections is the love than which there can be none greater—[a love] which [God] manifests in His Son, Jesus. And because God the Father is truthful, the words of His Son, Jesus, are true, for they are [the words] of the Father.[5] But the words of Jesus contain the gospel, for they declare to us that for God (since He is the Omnipotent Creator) nothing is impossible[6] and that He is a bountiful Rewarder of believers, giving what is eternal in place of what is temporal.

Now, Jesus's love is [manifest by His] willingly undergoing the most horrible of all horrors on account of His love for God and love for His neighbor. The sacred sign of this love is obedience. For to obey [God's] commandments is a sign of love; to obey unto death is the sign of perfect love. Therefore, obedience is a sacrament of love, because it is a sign of a sacred thing. Accordingly, the Apostle said to the Philippians: Christ "became obedient unto death."[7] And Christ Himself said that He died out of love, because no one has a greater love.[8] But the fact that Jesus is He who is Truth and is such that he who does not believe Him will not see life (as He says in John 3)[9]—this fact Jesus showed by means of many miracles, which were sacraments, or sacred signs, that He is the one in whom is God the Father.[10] Therefore, He says: "if you do not believe me, believe my works."[11] [It is] true that the ultimate witness to this fact was His shedding of blood, when He bore witness by means of His blood. For example, He said in the presence of Pilate that He was born for this purpose and had come into the world in order to bear witness to the truth.[12] And His witness strengthens and nourishes the truth.

[4] Hence, the Eucharist is a sacred sign of this [witness]. For it is the remembering of His death insofar as His death nourishes and strengthens the truth. Moreover, it is a sacred sign of His supreme love. For Christ loved His own unto the end,[13] as He showed at the Last Supper. Therefore, because all [the other] things would not have measured up to most perfect love were He not to give Himself for all men, Christ in this way handed Himself over [to death] for us—as if Life,[14] by dying, were to impart Himself in order to enliven us. Of His [love and death] this is the wondrous sacrament; for He took His own [Eucharistic Body] in His hands and broke it and distributed it. It was

as if the Living Bread[15] broke itself and distributed itself in order that those to whom He distributed Himself would live and that He Himself in distributing Himself would die. Hence, the Apostle said that the eating of the Body of Christ in the sacrament is the declaration of His death.[16] For by thus dying He remade us by means of His death. According to the Gospel His death merited the reward of life (with respect to [our] condition of death). For to lose in that way one's temporal life, or soul, is to find it in the Kingdom of Heaven, or of Immortality. But His death was consummate: it merited as much as all [other] men could have merited by dying. Therefore, He acquired merit for all men. Similarly, by dying, He imparted life to all who were capable of receiving it. Moreover, the [Eucharistic] sacrament is [a sacrament] of sonship, which is attained by means of perfect faith. For in the truth of this sacrament all doubt about sonship with God is removed. For if bread can pass over into becoming the Son of God, then so too [can] man, who is the purpose of the bread.

[5] Next [comes our] reflecting on a final consolation that we mortals can receive by means of this transubstantiation by which, through death, we are transferred through death from mortal nature unto immortal [nature]. For death will not have dominion over us, who have put on Christ.

The difficulties concerning the way in which the bread is turned into the Body of Christ are seen to be able to be conceptually cleared up, to some extent, as follows: Christ said that the words which He speaks (in John 6) are spirit and life.[17] But that which He says—[viz.,] "This is my Body"—must be construed in a spiritual sense. A spiritual, [i.e., immaterial], body is not attained by any of the senses. A material body is seen to be distinguished from a spiritual body as *body belonging to the category of quantity* and *body belonging to the category of substance*.

[6] Dionysius affirms that in each thing there is *essence, power*, and *activity*.[18] In the essence are enfolded the power and the activity. Now, Dionysius calls essence *ousia*, which we call *substantia*. And so, I construe essence as substance, just as also in the new translation[19] of Dionysius's [works the word] "substantia" is placed where in the old [translation[20] there is the word] "essentia". Now, to begin with, from the essence is begotten the power; and [from these] there proceeds the activity. Hence, the essence, or substance, even of a material nature— for example, of earth or of water or of fire—is like [that] of a spiritual,

[i.e., immaterial, nature]. For [the essence] is not attainable by any of the senses.

Next, we must consider that in the turning of one thing into another thing, first [the one] essence is transformed into [the other] essence; subsequently [both] the power [is transformed] into [the other] power and the activity into [the other] activity. For instance, when Christ by the word of His power turned water into wine,[21] the essence of the water was first turned into the essence of the wine; subsequently [both] the power of the water [was turned] into the power of the wine and the activity of the water [was turned] into the activity of the wine.

[7] Therefore, let it be the case that water is turned into wine—i.e., that the essence of the water is turned into the essence of wine—without the power of the water being turned into the power of the wine and without the activity of the water being turned into the activity of the wine. It is true that after the transformation there is not water but there is wine, even though the power and the activity remain as they were before the transformation. And in each part of that water's power and activity there will be present the real body-of-wine. I am speaking of body insofar as it is the essence, or the substance (insofar, that is, as it belongs to the category of substance). And if the real wine could speak, it would say: "This is my body." And that body-of-wine would enfold all the things that are of the essence of wine.

In a similar way I consider the Body of Christ to have an essence, a power, and an activity; and, likewise, I consider the bread to have an essence, a power, and an activity. And [I consider] the essence, or substance, of the bread to be turned by the Word of God into the essence, or substance, of the Body of Christ—with the bread's power and its activity remaining as they were prior to the transformation of the essence. And because the bread's essence is in each part of the bread (because each part of the bread is bread), then after the transformation of the bread's essence into the essence of the Body of Christ, the essence of the Body of Christ will be in each part of the bread. Accordingly, the essence will be present in each part in such a way that it is true to say that there are present there all the things that belong to the real essence of the Body of Christ. Hence, whatever the real essence, or substance, of the Body of Christ enfolds within itself is present there essentially and really. Now, substance is prior to accident. Therefore, since the Body of Christ is present there only substantially, it is not there extendedly (as Henry of Ghent [rightly] maintains in his *Quodlibeta*).[22] Hence, that essence is incorruptible and is inaccessible to any of the senses. Here [on earth] it is apprehended by the eye of the intellect only by means of the light of faith. But by means of the light of glory it is seen as it is—[seen] by those who have obtained [eternal] happiness.

[8] And in a certain way there is seen to be a difference between the Body of Christ as it is present in Heaven and the same Body as it is present in the sacrament—just as [there is a difference] between fire that is giving off light and heat and fire into which the essence of earth has been turned. For example, if the essence of a flintstone were transformed into the essence of fire, then fire would be hidden invisibly beneath the coldness and opacity of the earthy nature of the stone. Now, the essence of fire insofar as fire gives off light and heat is not a different essence from that of fire insofar as fire lies thus hidden [within the flintstone]. Rather, [they are one and] the same essence and are equally real. Nevertheless, in the first way fire is present in its own kingdom together with its power and its activity; but in the second way it is not [present in its own kingdom] but is outside its kingdom. Hence, just as fire hiding beneath the form of a stone does not do the works of fire unless it is separated, by an intellectual nature, and joined to what is ignitable: so also the Body of Christ does not work works of life unless by an intellect with faith-informed-[by-love] it is separated from the signs (beneath which it lies hidden) and is joined to a spirit that is capable of being enlivened. Now, *that* spirit can be enlivened which is prepared for *receiving*—even as wood that is free of mud and freed from cold water is ignitable, or capable of becoming inflamed.

Furthermore, by means of this [Eucharistic] sacrament you will be able to see, to some extent, that the Word, or Power, of the Heavenly Father is united to the human nature without the Father's being united to the human nature. For the Father is like unto essence, the Son is like unto Power, and the activity is like unto the Holy Spirit—as says Dionysius.[23] Similarly, in the bread there are essence, power, and activity—in the likeness of the Trinity. Now, the power of the bread is found in the sacrament, which is composed of quantity, and [this power] is united to the other accidents; but the essence of the bread is not present. Likewise, the Power-of-God, which is the Word of God, is united to the human nature; the Father [is] not [united thereto].

[9] Moreover, at this point, you will be able to see that [a believer's] human nature (*homo*) passes over into Christ, because the essence

of the body of a blessed man [i.e., of a redeemed man in Heaven] passes over into the essence of the Body of Christ,[24] just as a grain of wheat passes over into bread. For [in Heaven] believers are like grains of wheat that pass over into Living Bread. And since the humanity (*humanitas*) of each [believer] is one [and the same in species] but Christ is no longer dead, then when the mortal nature becomes immortal in Christ,[25] it is transformed. By way of illustration: the essence of a finger passes over into the living essence of the body; yet, the finger's power and activity remain. (For it is not the case that because of the [passing-over] the finger does the works of the eye or of the foot rather than of the finger—even though the finger is alive with the life of the eye and of the foot, since there is [but] one life of all [the bodily members].) In a similar way, the blessed man's [i.e., the Heavenly man's] power and activity do not pass over into being Christ's power and activity; rather, these remain [as themselves], just as in the sacrament [the power and the activity of the bread and the wine remain as themselves]. Nonetheless, the essence [of a redeemed individual in Heaven] passes-over in such a way that it becomes [one and] the same Body with Christ (even as the essence of a grain of wheat passes over into bread) and in such a way that it is enlivened by the same spirit. Yet, the power and the activity remain (even as the power of each grain of wheat remains in the bread), so that [each believer will] experience in himself—in accordance with his power and activity—his happiness differently from other [believers]. For each one is to receive his own reward according to his own doings.[26] In accordance with the passing over of the essence, there is one essential reward for all [believers]; in accordance with the power and the activity, there is a different reward for each [believer].

[**10**] A certain learned[27] man understood the matter in the foregoing way. In my judgment he was unfairly criticized by others.[28] For [even] Blessed Ambrose understood Paul in the foregoing way—[understood Paul thusly] in his Letter XVII to Herennius, which begins [with the word] "*Poposcisti*". In this letter Ambrose makes, among other very lovely [statements], [the following] inference:[29] "Therefore, we are not seated in Heavenly places[30] but are seated in Christ and in the flesh of Him who alone is seated, as the Son of man, at the right hand of the Father." By way of [further] illustration, you have understood Augustine similarly. He said that Christ is the Food of grown men. This Food is not changed into the partaker, but rather it changes partakers into the Food.[31] I understand in a similar way the

Gospel-passage about the Living Bread—in particular, where Christ said, "He who eats of me lives by me."[32] And Paul says, "We many who partake of one bread and of one cup are one body."[33] Hence, even as many hosts, or pieces of [consecrated] bread, are transformed into the one Body of Christ[34] through the same Word by which God made even the ages[35]—[the Word] that alone can transform nature—so the same [Eucharistic] Body is present in the many men who partake of it. For just as the same life of the soul is present in the many [bodily] members that partake of it, so the same life of the Food-of-life is present in the many who partake of that Food-of-life.

[11] Certain men have said that in this sacrament are present [*both*] the Body of Christ *and* bread—[a view] that [we] moderns do not admit.[36] For in that case Jesus would not have said "This is my Body" but [would have said]: "This [bread] is [my] Body."[37] Nevertheless, the understanding of the Ancients can be admitted, for "bread" names a thing which is such that it has essence, power, and activity. And although [in the sacrament] the essence does not remain: from the fact that the power and the activity remain, the name "bread" still befits it. Hence, with respect to the fact that the essence of the bread becomes the essence of the Body of Christ, we speak of the *Bread of Life* or of *Living Bread*. It turns a partaker into itself, making him to be possessed of its own Life, which is immortal; and the partaker is assumed [into this Life]. For the essence of the bread is not destroyed; rather it passes from being a mortal nature into being an immortal [nature]. And insofar as the power and the activity remain, the name "bread" is used. Hence, if someone were to name the sacrament, [i.e., the host], consecrated *bread*, he would be seen not to veer [from the truth]. Accordingly, when a man is beatified [in Heaven], his mortal body becomes an immortal body, viz., the Body of Christ, wherein death is swallowed up in victory.[38] But the [body's] power and the [body's] activity remain. Therefore, in view of the aforesaid understanding, that man is named as he previously was (e.g., "Peter"), supplemented by [the name] "Christian".

[12] Therefore, Christ is not present in the sacrament extendedly and, hence, not spatially. For substance, considered qua substance, is not at a place.[39] Hence, it does not remain present there with the corrupted forms under which it is contained. (Yet, as says the Solemn Doctor [of the Church],[40] the substance is not corrupted.) For "there" indicates *place*. And since the substance is not at a place except by

means of the forms: then after the forms become corrupted, it is not present *there*, i.e., at a place. Consider that Paul said: "You will show the Lord's death until He comes."[41] And Christ says: "I will raise him up on the last day."[42] And elsewhere [He says]: "I am the Resurrection and the Life; he who believes in me ...," etc.[43] Note that by means of this present sacrament the death of Christ is declared to be our enlivenment. And the truth of this fact will be evident at His coming. For, as Paul says, "It does not yet appear [what we shall be] ...," etc., "but when He shall appear, we shall be like Him,"[44] since we, as resurrected, shall pass into immortality. As [Jesus] says, they shall go unto life.[45] This going [unto life] is a being changed from a mortal nature into an immortal [nature]. Therefore, as long as Christ does not appear, we shall not obtain in our body resurrection unto life. Therefore, this present sacrament of the remembrance of [Christ's] death prefigures [our] resurrection unto life. Accordingly, we pray after the communion-celebration of the mass: "Cause us, we ask, O Lord, to be filled with the eternal enjoyment of Your divinity—[the enjoyment] which the temporal reception of Your precious Body and Blood prefigures." And if you rightly consider [the matter, you will see that] this sacrament is a sacred sign of that regeneration about which there is said: "When in the regeneration the Son of man is seated ...," etc.[46] That is, [Christ] will then co-enliven us and will conform us to Himself.

NOTES TO *Hoc Facite in Meam Commemorationem*

* Sermon CCXXXV.
1. Luke 22:19. I Corinthians 11:24.
2. Here (at **1**:11) I am supplying the word "non," which is missing from the printed edition of the Latin text but is found in *Codex Latinus Vaticanus* 1245.
3. John 1:5.
4. Hebrew 1:2.
5. John 12:49-50 and 14:10.
6. Matthew 19:26. Mark 10:27. Luke 18:27.
7. Philippians 2:8.
8. John 15:13.
9. John 3:36.
10. John 10:37-38.
11. *Loc cit.*
12. John 18:37.
13. John 13:1.
14. John 11:25.
15. John 6:48 and 6:51.
16. I Corinthians 11:26.
17. John 6:64.
18. Pseudo-Dionysius (Dionysius the Areopagite), *De Caelesti Hierarchia*, XI, 2 (*PG* 3:284). *Dionysiaca*, Vol. II, p. 930.
19. "… the new translation": i.e., the translation by Ambrose Traversari. See *Dionysiaca*, Vol. II, p. 930.
20. "… the old translation": i.e., the translation by Eriugena. See *Dionysiaca*, Vol. II, p. 930.
21. John 2:1-11.
22. Henry of Ghent, *Quodlibeta*, I, Quaestio 6. (Paris edition, 1518. Reprinted in Louvain, Belgium by Bibliothèque S. J., 1961. See Vol. I, f. 3^v.)
23. See n. 18 above. Nicholas seems to assume that the order in which Dionysius mentions *essence, power,* and *operation* is meant by him to correspond to the order Father, Son, and Holy Spirit—whom the former concepts symbolize. Dionysius does not explicitly make such a correlation.
24. Nicholas makes the point that the resurrected bodies of believers will be like the resurrected Body of Christ—will be one in essence with Christ's Body. Similarly, each believer's human nature will be assumed into Christ's human nature, thought without losing its individuality. All human natures are of one and the same species. See especially Nicholas's *De Docta Ignorantia* III, 8 (**227-228**). See also Romans 12:5, I Corinthians 12:27, and I Corinthians 15:44.
25. I Corinthians 15:53-54.
26. Matthew 16:27. II Corinthians 5:10.
27. "… a certain learned man": viz., Meister Eckhart. See Eckhart's *Rechtfertigungsschrift*, IX, 39. In particular, see p. 54 of A. Daniels, editor, *Eine lateinische Rechtfertigungsschrift der Meister Eckhart* [Beiträge zur Geschichte der Philosophie des Mittelalters, Vol. XXII, Issue 5 (1923)].

28. Nicholas is aware that he himself is venturing into a theologically difficult area, so that, as he realizes, he must exercise special caution in articulating his points.

29. St. Ambrose, *Epistola* LXXVI, 8 (*PL* 16:1261C). Not meant by Nicholas to be an exact quotation.

30. Ephesians 2:6.

31. Augustine, *Confessiones*, VII, 10 (*PL* 32:742). Not meant by Nicholas as an exact quotation.

32. John 8:58.

33. I Corinthians 10:17. Not meant by Nicholas as an exact quotation.

34. Romans 12:5.

35. Hebrews 1:2.

36. See Nicholas's Sermon CLXXXIII (**12**).

37. In the Latin text that corresponds to the present English sentence Nicholas uses the masculine pronoun "*hic*" ("this") to stand for the masculine word "*cibus*" ("*bread*"), whereas in the previous clause the neuter word "*hoc*" ("this") stands for neuter noun "*corpus*" (*Body*).

38. I Corinthians 15:54.

39. A thing's place, according to Aristotle, is an accidental feature of the thing.

40. Henry of Ghent is called *doctor solemnis*. Regarding the present passage, see the reference in n. 22 above.

41. I Corinthians 11:26.

42. John 6:40 and 6:44.

43. John 11:25.

44. I John 3:2. Nicholas seems here to misremember the location of the text, which is not Paul's but John's.

45. Matthew 25:46.

46. Matthew 29:28.

Qui Manducat Hunc Panem*
Vivet in Aeternum
("He Who Eats of This Bread Shall Live Forever.")
[June 5, 1455 (Feast-day of the Sacrament); preached in Bruneck]

[**1**] "He who eats of this Bread shall live forever."[1]

We must note, in addition to the other things that are contained in [my] other sermons for this feast-day,[2] that the Bread of Life[3] is an incorruptible food. Now, it is God alone who inhabits immortality, as Paul says[4] in I Timothy 6. But we say that God is in Heaven; yet, we ought to understand His habitation to be *immortality*. Hence, because, in the case of God, inhabiting and having are *being*, God *is* Immortality. [The notion of] infinite life cannot be better expressed than by "immortality"; for not to be able to die is maximal life, which cannot be greater or cannot be lesser; and so, it is infinite. God is the Infinite Treasure of Life.

An intellectual nature is not alive unless it has wisdom. The Intellect that is Wisdom itself is alive with an infinite life. Now, the All-Wise One nourishes by means of His own Word those whom He calls to fellowship and to a partaking of enlivening wisdom. Christ is the Bread of Life[5] and the Word of the Father.[6] And so, He nourishes with eternal life because He is the Eternal Word of God-the-Enlivening-Father. Christ is the Enlivening Word of the Enlivening Father, who enlivens by the sending of the Enlivening Spirit that proceeds from the Father. In the Books of Wisdom[7] it is shown that wisdom is glorious and never fades and that it gives immortality and is better than all riches and that it incomparably surpasses whatever can be thought of. Wisdom furnishes right judgment. Justice is perpetual and immortal (because it is the fruit of wisdom); thus spoke the wise man in Wisdom 1; and in Wisdom 5 [he said] that the just shall live forever.[8]

[**2**] Accordingly, wisdom furnishes immortality—a fact that you will be able to pursue, in the following way, by means of a likeness to sight: The intellectual eye is to the sensory eye as a real object is to its likeness. None of the senses are more noble than is sight, even as no power of the soul is more noble than is the intellect. Sight lives from light and by means of it: for if light is removed, sight cannot see; and its seeing is its living. Likewise, whatever sight seeks comes to it by means of light. Wisdom is related in a similar way to the intellect.

Hence, the wise man says in Wisdom 7 that he esteemed wisdom in preference to light, since the light of wisdom cannot be put out;[9] for [wisdom] is the brightness of eternal light and the unspotted mirror of God's majesty and the image of His goodness.[10] [And he says] that together with wisdom there came to him likewise all goods.[11] And just as light that is pleasing to sight descends from the fount of perceptible light, viz., the sun, so wisdom [descends] from the Creator of the sun. Hence, the wise man says: "Send me wisdom that is seated by Your throne."[12] Just as without perceptible light sight is altogether without the activity of life and cannot arrive at the truth that it even has being,[13] so without immaterial, or intellectual, light the intellect cannot have the activity of life or cannot taste of life, for without the activity of its life—viz., [the activity of] understanding—the intellect cannot understand that it is alive. Wisdom is the light of truth. Just as what is visible is not seen without light, so truth [is not seen] by an intellect [that is] without wisdom. Sight says that nothing is comparable to light; for if in sight's purview all objects were visible, still without light they would be, for sight, as if they did not exist. A parallel point holds true for all intelligible objects in the absence of intellectual light.

The Word of God conveys truth to the believing soul; the Word is Wisdom; truth is the nourishing object. Similarly, light conveys color to sight, and color is the object that nourishes sight. Colors derive only from light; similarly, the truths about things are only from Eternal Wisdom, for Wisdom[14] is the Mother of all [truths] (Wisdom 7).[15] Truth is a perpetual food that remains forever—[a food] that is seen only by means of wisdom. Therefore, Wisdom enfolds within itself all that our spirit desires. And just as color in and of itself is light, so too truth, in and of itself, is Eternal Wisdom. Hence, light is the true nourishment of sight, and whatever nourishes sight is, in its origin, only light. And Wisdom is the true nourishment of the intellect; whatever nourishes the intellect is in its origin only Wisdom. Without light sight is in darkness in the distress of death; similarly, without intellectual light the intellect is said to be in darkness and in the distress of death.

[3] The Christian faith in the soul is like sight. But if a Christian is separated from God by sin (for our sins separate [us from God], as says the Prophet),[16] then his sight is in darkness. Unbelief is as blindness in the soul. Hence, a pagan without actual sin[17] does not suffer as much as does a Christian who is a sinner. For [the unbeliever] does not have sight but is as one who is born blind, who does not suffer from a longing for sight, which he has never had—as does the Christian [suf-

fer, who cannot see because of the darkness].

You have healthy sight; and so, you judge yourself to be, in comparison with the man born blind, rich. For you would not want to lack the power to see any given thing whatsoever; for you have experienced the pleasantness of sight's life and the delightfulness of light, and you cannot prefer to light any of the objects which you have ever seen. (Ecclesiasticus 11: "Light is sweet, and to see the sun is delightful to the eyes.")[18] Similarly, he who has tasted of wisdom with his intellect knows that wisdom surpasses all that can be understood; and he knows that to understand wisdom is, for the intellect, supreme delight and immortal life. No man is found who would choose to lack intellect in exchange for all the things of the world. And because without wisdom an intellect is not a living intellect, an intellect cannot be happy without wisdom. Wisdom alone is the life that enlivens the [intellect]. Every man is satisfied with his [having] intellect, so that he can be made happy. But he seeks wisdom in order to be happy; for he who discards wisdom and learning is unhappy (Wisdom 3).[19] Wisdom is unitary; it makes happy every intellect [that possesses it, and] from it each intellect takes as much as satisfies it. By analogy, there is a unitary sun, whose light is sufficient for all eyes; and there is one Fountain[20] from which many who are thirsty drink as much as satisfies each of them. The Word of God, which speaks about itself in the Gospel, is the Father's Wisdom, which nourishes *qua* Living Bread, so that one who eats of it lives eternally.

[**4**] Moreover, we must consider (1) that Christ said "My flesh is meat indeed, and my blood is drink indeed"[21] and (2) that elsewhere there is said: "She fed him with the bread of life and of understanding; and with the water of wholesome wisdom she gave him drink."[22] For all the ways of feeding our bodies ought to be understood spiritually with regard to the feeding of souls. For all these [Scriptural] words [about taking nourishment] are spirit and life if they are understood in a spiritual sense. Hence, whatever refects the body—whether meat or bread or honey or blood or wine or water—is said to be the word of God if [the signification] is applied figuratively to the refection of the rational soul. For Truth says that man does not live by bread alone but by every word that proceeds from the mouth of God.[23] [Both] material bread and the word of God feed a man, who consists of a body and a rational soul. The Word of the Lord is the Lord's wisdom. Thus, the wise man says in Wisdom 9: "O God of our fathers and Lord of many mercies, [You are the One] who has perfected all things by means of

Your word; and by Your wisdom You have appointed man."[24] Therefore, by the word of God, i.e., by His wisdom, there is nourished the part [of us that is] capable of receiving wisdom, viz., the rational soul. Now, Christ is an Envoy, who spoke not His own word but the word of God. And because He *is* the Word of God, He is also our soul's Living Bread and the Image of God-the-Father's Goodness.

[5] The wise man teaches us that we ought to seek to obtain wisdom. He states in Wisdom 6: "The beginning of wisdom is a very real desire for learning. The care, then, of learning is love; and love is the keeping of wisdom's laws. And the keeping of her laws is the firm foundation of incorruption, and incorruption brings [one] near to God. Therefore, the desire for wisdom brings [one] to the everlasting kingdom."[25] Thereafter, in Chapter 7, he says (1) that he desired wisdom so fervently that he esteemed all else, in comparison to it, to be as nothing and (2) that he loved wisdom more than health and comeliness and (3) that he purposed to have wisdom instead of light.[26] And he called unto God, and the spirit of wisdom came upon him.[27] And then together with wisdom there likewise came all goods, although he did not know that wisdom is the Mother of all [goods][28] For wisdom's treasure is infinite; those who have availed themselves of this treasure have become partakers of God's friendship.[29] From these [texts] we are taught how it is that one comes to wisdom, which is not obtained except by the gift of God. Furthermore, [we are taught] that God gives wisdom only to one who seeks it with utmost desire and that such desire can be present in a man only if he desires wisdom's learning and only if he loves wisdom and keeps wisdom's laws. Moreover, [we are taught] that observance of [wisdom's] laws keeps the soul from corruption so that the soul may be fit for receiving wisdom. For [wisdom] will not enter a soul that has evil intent, as says Wisdom 1. And he who keeps her laws and loves her more than health and beauty, or comeliness—unto him she descends, once invoked. For, as [the wise man] says in Wisdom 6, "she is readily seen by those who love her, and she is found by those who seek her."[30]

[6] Furthermore, we must consider the fact that St. Dionysius, in his *Ecclesiastical Hierarchy*, speaks of this sacrament [of the Eucharist]. And he calls it both the sacrament *of communion* (i.e., *synaxeos*) and the *consummate sacrament*. It is called the sacrament of communion because it is a fellowship, a communing, a gathering. For, as he says, "every sacrament is instituted to the end that it gather our

lives (which are splintered in many directions) into that unitary state in which we are joined to God. And by means of that divine gathering of our divided affairs God bestows on us [that gift] of His which is truly one: [viz.,] undivided fellowship and oneness. And so, we say that other sacramental signs by which fellowship of this [kind] is bestowed on us are, assuredly, made perfect by means of divine and consummate gifts."[31] And after many [other statements the wise man] adds (1) how it is that this sacrament is conducted and (2) that one bread broken by the priest is distributed to many, so that many are gathered into unity with, and fellowship with, the Body of Christ. Something similar is the case with the one chalice, which is distributed to each [partaker]. (On this topic see that very divine teacher.)[32] And you will find this sacrament of communion to be a sacrament *because* it makes us members of unitary Jesus, if only we abide by His teaching and imitate His life. Hence, this is the sacrament of the mystical Body of Christ, which was freed from the power of the Prince of this world[33] and which put on Heavenly comeliness in order to obtain an incorruptible life.

The Word of God, which assumed our nature, nourishes us if we arrive at participation in His mystical Body, of which this [eucharist] is the sacrament. For so great is the power of the Word of God's union with the humanity of Jesus[34] that it can admit all Christians to participation and partnership and can unite them to itself. And the ones capable of [this] union are believers who have faith [in-]formed by love.[35] For Christ prayed that just as His humanity was united to God, so too [we who are] His own would remain united to Him, so that all believers might be one with Him and so that this [togetherness might occur] by means of a consummate and very perfect union.

[7] Now, this is a sacrament[36] of consummate union with respect to eternally enlivening life. In the foregoing regard, note the conclusion of the mass, which indicates that this temporal reception of the sacrament prefigures that eternal [reception]. And if you consider the matter more deeply, [you will see that] the passing from this world to eternal life is a passing from faith to sight. For faith is a symbolical beholding of [that] vision which [in Heaven] occurs in truth and face-to-Face. And so, it is evident that this [sacrament of the eucharist] is the sacrament of sacraments and that with respect to it there is consummation of faith. For by means of it the future life, which is signified by all the sacraments, is received, although [this reception] is not apparent as long as the soul is present in [this] mortal body. Wherefore, Christ said that the one into whom He is incorporated by faith does not

die. This incorporation is expressed [symbolically] by the eating [of the eucharistic bread]. Indeed, Christ says that the [partaker] lives even if he has died and that he passes, in the course of temporal death, from death unto life. For faith is potentiality; seeing is actuality. Faith is of this present world; actuality is of the future world. And in the actuality there will be found only that which was present in potentiality.

Faith is received in the soul by means of the word,[37] and it *conveys* by causing the intellective soul to pass from death unto life. The death of the intellect is ignorance, since for the intellect to be alive is for it to understand. For when the word of wisdom enters the intellect, it causes the intellect to pass from ignorance to wisdom, from death unto life, and it slays ignorance in order that in the intellect there may live only wisdom, imparted by the word of wisdom. This wisdom is life that remains, for wisdom does not die by virtue of the body's death (as not only our saints teach but also Plato, in the *Phaedo*, and other philosophers). Similarly, faith—which holds that the word that is received is God the Father's word, as uttered by the Son—causes the soul to pass from an ignorance of God unto God's wisdom. And so, faith puts to death those things which are of the flesh and are of an ignorance of God; and it conveys the sensual life unto its own spiritual life.

[8] Most sweet Jesus, I—a humble sinner who am present on this holy [eucharistic] feast-day on which is celebrated the remembrance of the mystery [*sacramentum*] of our enlivenment—contemplate how it is that nothing can be more desirable than life. I call *true life* [life] which is not without gladness. We supremely love (*diligimus*) true life, which life can be called love (*caritas*). For what is more lovable than love [*amor*]?[38] If, then, life is loved above all [other] things, it is assuredly lovable above all [other] things. Hence, a life that is not lovable above all [other] things is not loved. Therefore, the life that is lovable above all [other] things is a life full of gladness. For true gladness-of-life is always and forever lovable. Now, if someone were to ask me whether I would prefer not to live rather than to live with the life by which irrational animals live, I would sooner choose not to live. For such a life is not the life of a rational spirit. And so, [a rational spirit] does not deem life that is without reason to be true life. Therefore, I desire only a perpetual rational, or intellectual, life.

But how can a rational, immortal life be given to me unless I am fed? For I see that nothing can live delightedly unless it is fed. For that which does not have from itself its *being* cannot from itself have the fact *that it is conserved in being*. My rational life does not have from itself the fact that it exists, for it is neither infinity nor eternity.[39] For if it were infinite, it would not have received an increase. But I was once a child in understanding, and my use of reason increased. Because I know that I have [the power of] reason, I am aware that I have free will and great desire but little power. (Reason does not have from itself the fact that it exists, for how could it have given to itself *being*?) Therefore, O my God, my rational spirit was created only in accordance with the will of Your omnipotence. Therefore, my rational life must be nourished by You, my God, from whom it has the fact that it is life.

[**9**] But what refects the rational life except intellectual food, which is undiminishing Wisdom, viz., that Word which has called my spirit into being? Therefore, that Word is Infinite Reason; it has called my reason from nothing into rational being. Therefore, only Wisdom—through which I am that which I am—can conserve my reason from all corruption and death. So when You, O Wisdom, call me in order that I may live, You speak in me. And when, in order to discern the voice, or word, I turn toward the one who is calling me: I am turning toward my Life, and I am nourished by Enlivening Wisdom. For what is it to see Creating Wisdom speaking in the intellect except to apprehend within oneself the Fount of Life by means of a tasting of unspeakable sweetness? O Lord, just as by means of Wisdom[40] You have called all rational spirits into being, so You call and speak to them all so that they may live. One Word speaks to them all and calls them to partnership with that Eternal Wisdom, through which they have that which they are. And those who hearken (to the one who calls) turn, so that they all discern that Word which speaks unto them. Therefore, all [those] rational spirits hear one Word, and they turn toward seeing and apprehending the Fount of Life.

[**10**] O Most Sweet Jesus, You have taken on my nature in order that I, who have not heard You speaking Your word and wisdom in Heaven, might hear you on earth and might see that in Heaven You are calling to me on earth. I was unable to hear the word[41] of God in this world, which does not apprehend truth. But the Word of God *is* Truth. The Word put on the passible human nature of this world in order to summon me and in order that I could hear the word of God in the voice of a man. Now, You, O God, are not able to be seen in this world. And so, You declared to me by means of Your word that if here below I will

hearken to Your word, I shall in Heaven, where Truth reigns, truly apprehend You and see You. But this seeing is nothing but a tasting within oneself of Uncreated Wisdom, which alone is Enlivening Life. Therefore, a man who arrives at seeing within himself the Word of God will be Your partner. One-who-believes-You will discover this fact because by the Father You were sent as one declaring and preaching what is true. And no one who trusts in God will be able to be deceived. You have left us this sacrament as a memorial of this promise—viz., [the promise] that one who believes You and follows You will arrive at partnership with You. By means of this sacrament we come into partnership with You. We believe that You, who are one, are partakable by many. By faith we see—beneath the perceptible signs—the nourishment for our rational life, and by faith we consume the food of eternal life. We know that faith is, in this world, that which seeing will be in the next world; for truth that is the object of faith and truth that is the object of the seeing are a single Truth. Here below [that single Truth] is obscured by sensory signs; in Heaven it is bright and face-to-Face. To You be praise and glory forever.

[11] Moreover, I say that this sacrament is a new testament through which the covenants of peace between God and man are confirmed. In this regard we must note that Hermes Trismegistus[42] writes that by man a spirit is bound to a graven image and inhabits it. And he says that the Egyptians discovered that art, and he maintains to be very highly wondrous the fact that man makes gods for himself. Eusebius, in Book 5 of his *Preparations for the Gospel*,[43] addresses here and there the topic of this encapturing. Surely, it was done by faith. Likewise, similar things are done by means of certain incantations that magicians believe in. For by faith a magician is strengthened in his own spirit with power over the created spirit that he commands. Analogously, through words an enchanter commands the soul of a serpent; and since the serpent knows that it must obey the command of the enchanter if it hears his words, it stops up its ears in order not to hear—as the Prophet David says.[44] [It happens,] then, [that] by faith the spirit of a man prevails over the spirit, and prince, of the air,[45] so that it binds that spirit with respect to a material object—[binds it] by virtue of the fact that the man submits himself to that spirit as to a god, and the spirit does not do its own will but does the will of the man. For the spirit obeys in order thereby to possess him whom the spirit is seen to obey and in order to receive honors as a god. In that case, it is evident that if an evil and deceiving spirit is by faith thus summonable, then an

enlivening spirit is by faith more (and more truly) summonable into our spirit than is a slaying spirit. The enlivening spirit lives and speaks in us, [and] the spirit of our soul will cling to it more strongly than a graven image [clings to] an evil spirit.

[12] Moreover, this union [of our spirit with God] occurs by means of an evoking, or invoking, when we abide by the art handed down by Christ, viz., the pacts and the observances of His commandments [and] a love also of purity. Magicians who wish to summon a spirit to instruct them enter into a covenant with the spirit by means of certain pacts (as in Judges 8, where they struck an agreement with Baal),[46] and they abide by the precepts of that spirit, and they do not transgress the physical purifications, the ceremonies, and the regulations—on the grounds that these are things sacramental. Thus, we are taught throughout the entire course of the Bible (1) that God is summoned by certain covenants and pacts and (2) that as long as these covenants, ceremonies, and sacred [regulations] were observed, God kept His word and, when invoked, was present and hearkened. But when [the people] did not keep the covenants, the Spirit of God turned away from them—as [we read] in Deuteronomy 29 and in many passages of the Bible and throughout almost all of the Prophets. After these [goings on] Jesus, the Son of God, came. He taught us that we can call forth unto ourselves an abiding and eternally enlivening Spirit. And He gave us, by His word and example, precepts and the manner in which this [summoning] can be done. Thus, if we have faith-of-attaining such as He had it,[47] and if we do as He taught and did, then without doubt we shall obtain such an indwelling Spirit.

[13] Furthermore, consider the fact that the covenants, pacts, promises, and oaths concerned a certain unnamed contract: "I give [this] in order that you give [that]"; "I do [this] in order that you do [that]." And [these contracts] had to do with the goods of this perceptible world. For all worship of the gods or of the God of gods was brought under a pact, so that by reason of the worship men obtained the goods of the earth. Hence, the worship consisted in certain sacred objects that were material because material things were expected in return (as is shown by the pacts between God and Abraham (in Genesis 17) and by other, later, pacts made [by God] with Abraham's seed [and] written about throughout the whole of the Old Testament). Christ alone, when He came, declared that God is Spirit and that He is to be worshiped in spirit.[48] Hence, He disclosed the meaning of the Scrip-

tures and a spiritual understanding [of them]. And He instituted spiritual worship and promised a spiritual reward, viz., eternal life, which is given to our spirit by the Spirit that is God. And Christ preached that the Kingdom of Heaven is not of this world. For He taught that man can, by undoubted faith, arrive at all that his spirit desires, so that faith prepares our spirit's capability of receiving God's Spirit.

[14] Therefore, God's promise, revealed by Jesus, is that by faith believers obtain the blessing that was on Abraham and obtain [God's] Spirit (Galatians 3).[49] And these [gifts result] from God's legacy, in which we are called unto an inheritance and, hence, unto sonship, because a son is an heir. And [all of] this [occurs] through Jesus, the Son [of God]. John 1: "But as many as received Him" (viz., Jesus, who is also the Word of God—i.e., whoever receives God's word,[50] preached by God's Son, Jesus), "to them God gave the power to become His sons (viz., God's sons) if they believe in Him."[51] Therefore, he who believes that the man Jesus is the Son of God has faith that a man can be a son of God and that he himself, since he is a man, can obtain sonship with God.

But as for a believer's obtaining that for which he hopes: [Christ] said that this [obtaining] comes about through love; for love on the part of such a believer occasions the Spirit-of-God's descending upon the zealous soul. Now, faith ought to be consummate faith;[52] and, likewise, love [ought to be consummate love]—as ought also love for one's neighbor, [a loving that reaches] to the extent that it does good to one who does injury [to it]. [This love of neighbor] is to the end that it may merit to possess the Spirit of the Father,[53] even as Christ possessed this Spirit, which is the Spirit of spirits and which is consummate virtue. (Colossians 1: "It was pleasing [to the Father] that in Him [viz., Christ] all fullness of the Godhead dwell.")[54]

About the immediately foregoing [topics I will speak] at another time. But, [for now], keep [the following] in mind: When a fleshly man becomes regenerated in spirit (and [this transformation] happens on the basis of that spiritual law which is consummate law), then through renunciations and through covenants [made] through the intermediary of a priest, acting as Christ's representative, [the regenerate man] makes a contract with God. And in the sacrament of baptism this faith and these pacts are accepted, so that if the baptized individual abides by the pacts, he obtains the promise: viz., "Where I am, there will be also my servant."[55]

[15] But [in Scripture] we find, first of all, God's revelation. Next, we find that mediator (between God and men) to whom the revelation was made for the purpose of making a contract and covenants. Next, we find signs of the pacts and of the covenant. For example, God first manifested Himself to Abraham (Genesis 17), saying: "I am God Almighty. Walk before me, and be perfect, and I will make my covenant between me and you, and I will multiply you exceedingly."[56] And a sign of the pact, viz., circumcision, is added in the same text. Hence, the pact was that (1) God would be the God of Abraham, and (2) Abraham would have Him as His God and would worship Him and (3) would carry the sign of this pact (viz., circumcision) in his flesh. Abraham and his seed [would keep this pact], under penalty of death [for not keeping it]. Behold, the penalty of not keeping the pact between God and Abraham and his seed was the penalty of death! Abraham believed that the one who spoke to him was God; and so, he believed Him and received revelation. And he was made a mediator between God and his whole household and family, since [these latter] entered into that covenant and all the males were circumcised. In this way Moses received revelation and was made a mediator between God and the people of Israel (Deuteronomy 5).[57] So, too, Christ is the Mediator between God and men, as Paul says[58]—[the Mediator] not of a single people but of all [peoples].

[16] The Tables of the pact between God and the people—the pact made by means of Moses [and] about which things [we read] in Deuteronomy 9—are in the ten commandments, or ten articles, that are written on the Tables. And the writing is called the old testament and also the instrument of the pact. In that contract there was introduced into the written pact that which was natural. For *reason*, from itself, has all the [same] articles, with the exception of the commandment about the sabbath day.[59] And because the law of nature was neglected and was effaced through abuse (for men followed their lustful passions and by sensual motion were led in accordance with the desires of the flesh), it was renewed through the Tables and introduced into the explicit pact.

To Abraham it was commanded that he walk before God and be perfect. And in these few words are enfolded the laws of nature; for [the command] to walk [uprightly] before God, and in this respect to be perfect, contains everything. For he who walks before God and is perfect is moved by reason and does not deviate from it. He knows that God (who declared that He is the Almighty) is one God, that He is to be believed and worshiped, and that to another individual there is not to be done that which one would not want done to himself.[60] These things—which were of the law of nature—were incumbent on Abraham and his seed on the basis of the pact. However, the pact added a special obligation, [assumed] by choice, which was free. And because of the pact [choice] was restricted to an observance of the law of nature, so that it would no longer use its freedom-of-transgressing. And [the requirement of] circumcision was put into the pact as a sacred sign of the foregoing professing [of God on Abraham's part].

Now, Moses received nothing but this same [covenant]; yet, [he received it] explicitly in the Tables of the pact.[61] And [the requirement concerning] the sabbath is seen to have been added as a sacred sign of that pact, as Ezechiel 20 [states]: "I gave them my sabbaths as a sign between me and them."[62] Hence, Moses himself and the prophets after him caution that the observance of the sabbath is in every respect to be kept. Thus, circumcision and sabbath-[keeping] are seen to have been instituted as a confirming sign of the pacts between God and Abraham's seed.

[17] Now, Christ the Mediator between God and men, affirmed that the pacts between God and man exist in the way in which Abraham and Moses [attest]. But through Christ a spiritual understanding was made manifest. In this respect He became the Mediator of a new testament. For God willed that all the pacts-of-nature—which were unwritten but which were renewed in the Tables [given to Moses]—be received with a spiritual understanding. This understanding is an enlivening spirit and a word of God that nourishes [our] soul with perpetual life. Hence, the sacred sign of this new testament, or new pact, is seen to be the eucharist. For Jesus says: "This chalice is the new testament in my blood."[63] For in this sacrament the Word of God is *by faith* taken into our nature as a way of nourishing our rational soul, even as after death the Word of God is expected [to be apprehended] in person. Therefore, the covenant of the new testament is between the soul and the Word of God. It was not a different covenant from[64] the covenant between God and Abraham (and his seed), but it was concealed. For in the motion of the sensual nature and in the promise of happiness from temporal things there was concealed and veiled the motion above nature and the promise of an eternal, supra-temporal, happiness—even as in the corruptible writing of the Tables there was concealed[65] the incorruptible spirit-of-understanding of God's word, [a spirit] which no one can investigate on his own [or] without that

Teacher in whom the Word of God is present.

Accordingly, we must believe of Jesus that He is the Word of God, or Son of God. For he who does not believe the Son will not see eternal life (John 3).[66] For the Son is the Mediator of a better testament, of a new testament (Galatians 3 and Hebrew 8 & 9 & 12)[67]—the Mediator, i.e., between God and man. [He is the Mediator] by means of the covenant by which the soul believes that He has the words of eternal life.[68] The soul which receives this [covenant] as the word of God obtains all perfection—I mean the soul which receives it in the way in which someone very hungry [receives] very tasty food with respect to which he does not doubt that he will have life and gladness. The sacrament of this covenant is the eucharist, which was instituted in memory of the Mediator and of the covenant, when our Teacher and Mediator said (as the Apostle Paul tells us): "Do this in memory of me."[69]

[18] Consider how it is that God gave to our intellectual nature two gifts: viz., the ability to hear about his glory and the ability to see it. The ability to hear about his glory befits us insofar as we are inhabitants of this world, where darkness reigns and where we are as far distant from God as Heaven [is distant] from the earth—[where we are] in a region far from the Kingdom of the glory of Light and Truth. To-be-able-to-see befits us insofar as we are approaching Heaven and are translated from earth unto Heaven, i.e., translated from this world unto the Kingdom of Glory. But because the ability to hear about the Kingdom of God is in us, then—because that which we hear is a word—we can hear a word about the Kingdom. But only God can speak to us about His Kingdom, which is known only to Himself,[70] since no one else knows the glory of His Kingdom except Him who is His own glory. (Similarly, no one knows what is in a man except the man himself and one to whom he discloses it.) Therefore, God gave us the ability to believe. For unless we had the ability to believe the word of God, we would not be able, through hearing, to apprehend His glory. Therefore, without faith [on our part] nothing of God's invisible glory could be revealed to us. Accordingly, God gave our intellect the ability to believe, in order that by means of belief the intellect might, through our hearing, apprehend the revelation.

[19] Now, one-who-is-unwilling-to does not believe; rather, only he-who-is-willing-to [believes]; moreover, the will is free. Therefore, it is in our power to be able to believe or not. So when we choose to believe, we submit ourselves to the word—[doing so] in the

case both of the intellect (which we reduce to servitude) and of the will. Therefore, to believe is (as Augustine states in *On the Predestination of the Saints*)[71] to think with assent. For in believing, the intellectual eye assents to the ears; i.e., sight assents to hearing. By analogy, in a true relation with a beauty that is not seen, I think of the beauty with assent. But it seems that believing is not simply a hearing or a seeing on the part of the mind. Rather, it is inferior to sight and superior to hearing. For we do not assent to all that we hear; nor do we see everything to which we assent. Instead, when we believe things that we have heard, we assent to things that we have not seen.[72]

And note that only by faith was glory able to be revealed to our intellectual nature, which is incapable of having a vision of the glory. Hence, every intellect, if it has something of the light of reason, is able to believe. For *acute* sight is not required for this [believing]; rather, a *modicum* of [sight] suffices. And so, those individuals who are simple are suited for [the act of] believing, for they have more ready hearing [but less acute sight]. (We experience in ourselves that those who are more focussed on seeing are less fit for hearing, and vice versa. But it is necessary that every student first of all listen attentively; next, he must consider attentively the things he has heard—in order, lastly, to view in himself the truth of what he has heard. He who altogether lacks the light of reason cannot believe, because he cannot think and assent.) Therefore, to small children and to the simple-minded—who are more suited for believing than are the wise and knowing ones of this world—are revealed those things which are of the Kingdom of God. But [these things] remain hidden to the wise, as Jesus says.[73] Hence, in order that the revelation be apprehended, a man must become as a little child,[74] and one who is wise must become as one who is foolish.[75] That is, it is necessary that he deem all knowledge by which he presumes to know something about the Kingdom of God to be foolishness. (For there has never entered into the mind of man anything like the Kingdom of God.)[76] And at this point, the man submits himself to the Kingdom of God, in order to apprehend.

[20] The word of God is His Omnipotent Word, of which Moses and all the prophets spoke and wrote.[77] For what else is found in all of holy Scripture other than the power of God's word? For all the holy writers and prophets attested that the word of God is that through which God works all things; and they acknowledge that they are messengers of the word for the sake of revealing it to the people that was called unto a vision of God—a people named Israel. But Jesus is the

Messenger, or Envoy, of God. In Him is the word of the Father; in all other messengers there is the word that comes from the Word of God. [These] other messengers and prophets spoke in conformity with what they heard; for none of them saw God in the way that the Only Begotten [Son] revealed Him. But Jesus [spoke] in conformity with what He saw. Therefore, all the other prophets give testimony of the greatest Prophet, Jesus, that His word is the word of the Father. (For "prophet" means "one who sees.") Among the prophets one is greater than another. Therefore, we were bound to arrive at one who is the greatest of the prophets (whom Moses foretold that God would raise up). For in all things that admit of more and less we come to a maximum.[78] But Jesus, the highest of the prophets, spoke of the things that He saw of the Kingdom of God; [He spoke] not through revelation (as did the others) but through Himself [i.e., through direct knowledge]. But the others, who [spoke] by means of revelation, [spoke] only by revelation on the part of the Word of God that dwelt bodily in Jesus. Therefore, through the Incarnate Word, which is named Jesus, they were all appointed to be prophets. Therefore, let us praise the marvelous graciousness of God, who gave us the ability to believe that His Word put on a human nature in order to preach to us of His Kingdom and [in order][79] that we might be able to apprehend this Word within ourselves and in this way obtain the happiness [*felicitas*] that comes from seeing.

[21] Hence, since happiness (*felicitas*) is only a grace that is added to nature—[a grace] that was not known and that was preached by Jesus and His apostles[80]— it is evident that the philosophers were deficient in [their understanding of] happiness. Nevertheless, it can seem to someone that Aristotle [rightly] touched a bit upon [this notion] in Book 10 of the *Ethics*, where he said that the happy life is higher than the human life. As he says:[81]

> It is not the case that a man *qua* man will live [happily]; rather, [he will live happily] insofar as something divine is present in him. And the more this [divine state] differs from something composite, the more this activity [viz., happiness] differs from that activity which accords with another virtue. Therefore, if mind is something divine in relation to man, then the life that accords with mind is divine in comparison with [purely] human life.

These things Aristotle [says]. And *there* he seems to mean that the activity in accordance with mind is a most joyous happiness. This [activity] is contemplation, with respect to which we are like God.

Now, he calls this [contemplating] mind *divine, immortal,* and *incorruptible*; it excels, in value and in virtue, whatever things are of man. It is true that Aristotle speaks of other *virtues* that accord with what is composite and that he speaks also of another *happiness* that accords with what is composite. And he says that all these virtues (except for the mind's virtue, viz., contemplation) accord with man and with what is composite. But he speaks of another happiness that accords with mind and with separation [from the body]; in that passage he understands happiness to accord with the activity-of-mind that is contemplation. Now, he understands (1) that our mind is divine with respect to our other [properties] and (2) that our mind has a distinct and natural activity, viz., contemplating, and (3) that our mind, by means of its natural functioning (viz., its very joyous contemplating), obtains ultimate happiness.

In this [latter regard Aristotle] errs. For just as it is delightful to see light with the sensory eye but, nevertheless, light cannot be seen except by means of its ray's entering into sight that is strong and capable (by means of which power-of-sight it is seen): so also Absolute Truth, which is Infinite Light, is not contemplatable apart from the Light of its glory. Hence, since happiness is a perfect [state], and since all the things that belong to [the state of] happiness are perfect (as Aristotle himself admits in that passage), then there is no happiness without perfect contemplation of Truth. But that Light will be seen perfectly only by means of its own light. And this light of its glory is given, by grace, to a mind capable of receiving it.

How our mind becomes capable of receiving this grace, and how our mind can obtain it, we know from the revelation of Jesus, our Teacher.

NOTES TO *Qui Manducat Hunc Panem*

* Sermon CLXXXIX.
1. John 6:59.
2. This was a feast-day of the eucharist.
3. John 6:48.
4. I Timothy 6:16.
5. John 6:48.
6. John 1:14.
7. I. e., in the books of Proverbs and of Wisdom.
8. Wisdom 1:15 and 5:16.
9. Wisdom 7:10.
10. Wisdom 7:26.
11. Wisdom 7:11.
12. Wisdom 9:4.

13. Here (at **2**:21) I am *not* following the editors of the Latin text in adding "nec". Nicholas is distinguishing between a thing's existing and its both existing and living. (Stones, for example, exist but do not live.) A man may have sight but not be able actually to see because there is darkness. In that case, his power of sight exists, or has being, but is not active, is not "alive"—to use Nicholas's terminology.

14. Cf. n. 5 of Notes to Sermon CLXXXVII. See also n. 40 below and n. 51 of Notes to Sermon CLXXXIII.

15. Wisdom 7:12.
16. Isaias (Isaiah) 59:2.

17. Actual sin is distinguished from original sin. The former is personal sin; the latter relates to inheriting a sinful human nature. The comparison in the text above is purely hypothetical and rhetorical, since Nicholas does not believe that there is any human being (except for Christ and for infants) who has not sinned actually and personally. Indeed, an unbeliever's unbelief is itself a sin, since it is a failure to acknowledge God as Creator and Redeemer. With regard to small children there may be a very brief time-span, maintains Nicholas, between the child's reaching the age of accountability and his actually committing sin. See Sermon CXC (**9**:15-20)).

18. Ecclesiastes 11:7 (not Ecclesiasticus, as Nicholas writes).
19. Wisdom 3:11.
20. Psalms 35:9-10 (36:8-9).
21. John 6:56.
22. Ecclesiasticus 15:3.
23. Matthew 4:4.
24. Wisdom 9:1-2.
25. Wisdom 6:18-21.
26. Wisdom 7:8-10).
27. Wisdom 7:7.
28. Wisdom 7:11-12.
29. Wisdom 7:14.
30. Wisdom 6:13.
31. Pseudo-Dionysius, *De Ecclesiastica Hierarchia* (*Dionysiaca*, Vol. II, pp.

1162-1164).

32. *Loc. cit.*

33. "... the Prince of this world": viz., the Devil. John 12:31 & 14:30 & 16:11. The Resurrection freed Christ's Body from the Prince of this world. Acts 2:24-30.

34. N.B. Nicholas speaks of the Word of God's union with Jesus's humanity, not with universal humanity (i.e., not with human nature as such). When he speaks of one human nature in all men, he means one specific nature (i.e., one nature in species). See Sermon CCXXX (**10**:8-9): "... ut ... una natura specifica inveniatur in multis hominibus."

35. Galatians 5:6.

36. Here (at **7**:1) I am reading, with the Paris edition, "sacramentum" in place of "sacramenti".

37. Romans 10:17: faith comes by hearing; and hearing, by the word of Christ.

38. Nicholas does not here distinguish between his use of "*caritas*" and his use of "*amor*". As often, he uses these words interchangeably.

39. See n. 2 of Notes to Sermon CLXXXVII and the text that it references.

40. Christ is the Wisdom of God (I Corinthians 1:24) and is the Word through which God created all things (Colossians 1:16). Christ's word is supposed to dwell in believers in all wisdom (Colossians 3:16).

41. See the references in n. 14 above.

42. Hermes Trismegistus is an enigmatic figure who was sometimes regarded as a god, sometimes as the son, or grandson, of the Greek god Hermes. Not only was he sometimes regarded as a Greek but also sometimes as an Egyptian. Some stories make him a contemporary of Moses. In the Middle Ages a series of writings (the *Hermetica*) came to be grouped under his name. The best-known of these is perhaps the *Asclepius*. Trismegistus was known for his interest in magic. Nicholas may have borrowed from Augustine much of what is said in the passage above. See Augustine, *De Civitate Dei*, VIII, 23-24.

43. Eusebius of Caesarea (ca. 269-340 A.D.) wrote *De Evangelica Praeparatione* (*Preparation for [Believing] the Gospel*). Book V deals with beliefs in magic. See the translation by Edwin H. Gifford, *Eusebii Pamphili Evangelicae praeparationis libri XV* (Oxford, 1903).

44. Psalms 57:5 (58:4).

45. Ephesians 2:2.

46. Judges 8:33.

47. Here (at **12**:24) I am reading, with the Paris edition, "eam" in place of "eum".

48. John 4:24.

49. Galatians 3:14.

50. See the references in n. 14 above.

51. John 1:12.

52. James 2:22.

53. According to Nicholas, however, believers do not have the Spirit of the Father (i.e., the Holy Spirit) in the same way as does Christ, who, as Son of God, is He from whom (together with the Father) the Holy Spirit proceeds.

54. Colossians 1:19.

55. John 12:26.

56. Genesis 17:1-2.
57. Deuteronomy 5:4-5.
58. I Timothy 2:5.
59. Here Nicholas endorses the concept of there being a natural law. And he indicates clearly that the natural law is the law of reason (since by nature man is a rational animal).
60. Tobias 4:16.
61. Exodus 20.
62. Ezechiel (Ezekiel) 20:12. Not (meant by Nicholas to be) an exact quotation.
63. Luke 22:20.
64. Here (at **17**:17) I am supplying "quam", which I regard as tacitly implied by "aliud".
65. Here (at **17**:23) I am reading, with the Paris edition, "occultabatur" in place of "occultatur".
66. John 3:36.
67. Galatians 3:19-20. Hebrewe 8:6 & 9:15 & 12:24.
68. John 6:69.
69. I Corinthians 11:24.
70. *De Docta Ignorantia* I, 26 (**88**). *What* God is is known only to Himself. We "know" only symbolically what He is.
71. Augustine, *De Praedestinatione Sanctorum*, II, 5 (*PL* 44:963).
72. Hebrews 11:1.
73. Matthew 11:25.
74. Matthew 18:2-3.
75. I Corinthians 3:19.
76. I Corinthians 2:9.
77. John 5:46.
78. *De Docta Ignorantia* I, 6 (**15**).
79. Here (at **20**:32) I am adding "ita" before "quod".
80. John 13:17.
81. Aristotle, *Nicomachean Ethics*, X, 7 ($1177^{b}27$-31).

Erunt Primi Novissimi, et Novissimi Primi*
("The First Shall Be Last and the Last First.")[1]
[February 6, 1452; preached in Louvain]

[1] "The first shall be last and the last first." Matthew 20 and in the Gospel-reading [for today].[2]

[2] Christ said to Peter that those who have left behind all things and have followed Him will in the renewal [of the world] be seated as judges. And their judgment will be that each one will receive according to his [proper] reward. And [Christ] said that a reward is what [each rightly] expects as compensation for leaving behind—for His sake—the things that are of this world. And so, one man has left behind a field; another, his father. And according to what he left behind he will receive [a reward] in corresponding measure; nonetheless, [the reward is] always one hundredfold.[3] And because everyone who has left something behind has left behind that which he possessed, he will receive—in place of the possession that he left behind in the sensory life—an eternal possession in the intellectual life in place of the temporal [possession].

[3] "And the last shall be first." For he who is last is at the rear. He who for Christ's sake is found in *this* world to be at the rear will *there*, in the renewal, be first. And so, the judgment of these [believers] is said to be that [each] one [of them] will receive—in proportion to what he has left behind—that which is eternal, in lieu of that which was temporal. And out of love directed toward Jesus he has come to leave behind, for Jesus's sake, his love for this world. Therefore, since he loves greatly, many sins are forgiven [him].[4] [4] And because Christ said that the last shall be first and the first last, He added an illustration—according as He says in the Gospel-passage that the Kingdom of Heaven is like a landowner ..., etc.[5] And consider the fact that Christ gives an example of this [teaching]—[an example] with respect to time. (In terms of time we understand [the notions of] *earlier* and *later*.) He offers as a lesson [the teaching] that lateness of time does not militate against [one's receiving] the compensatory reward, since the places [reserved] for the elect are not removed because of the multitude of those who are called—even as, among the elect, many who are later in time will be prior in terms of reward.

[5] Consider [Jesus's] illustration of those laboring in the vine-

yard—how it is that preachers and purifiers-of-the-Church who come at the last hour can deserve to be rewarded together with the first ones, who planted the vineyard. And this [arrangement holds true] even though it is not to their credit that they were among the first ones. [Jesus] compares with the first-comers these [late-comers], who have as an excuse for their lateness that they were not hired [earlier]. For no one is supposed to engage in cultivating a vineyard unless he is sent to cultivate it and is hired. And so, since[6] it is not his fault that he cultivates [the vineyard] less, the landowner cannot give him less of a wage. And in [not] doing so, [the owner] does no injury to the others, to whom he gives what is owed them by mutual agreement.

[6] We must take note of the fact that the Kingdom of Heaven is a reward. As God said to Abraham: "I will be your Reward."[7] Now, Abraham is the father-of-faith for all believers who believe in God. As the Apostle James says: they, not wavering in faith, will receive that which they seek.[8] That which is desired will be received in accordance with the measure of faith and not in accordance with the expending of physical labor. But since God is the Reward of believers, God is seen to be likened, in the Gospel-passage, to the silver coin, [the denarius], that is given to them all. In the case of the denarius we pay attention only to its value; indeed, [the denarius] is an object-of-value that is stamped [with an insignia]. With this denarius we purchase eternal life; for in the Kingdom of Heaven there is only this currency. And whoever does not have it cannot enter into [the Kingdom] or purchase [eternal life].

[7] The number ten (*denarius*) is a number that enfolds within itself everything numerable.[9] The value of the denarius is the measure in terms of which the value of all things is assessed. The value of a horse, the value of corn, the value of wine are assessed in terms of the value of the denarius. The denarius is the implicit enfolding of number, weight, and measure.[10] The text [of the Gospel-passage] speaks of [a wage of one] denarius per day. The denarius per day has the value of the labors for a day. It is necessary to consider the wages in terms of that daily denarius that is asked for the labors.

Now, note closely that, [symbolically speaking], a denarius is given to us for conducting our own affairs. When we are created, we receive a nature that is able to receive impressions and that is an image of the Father's omnipotence. When we are regenerated in Christ, we receive the imprint of Christ—the image, that is, of Christ. When we are called, we receive [His] inscription. And, accordingly, we are from the beginning a malleable and teachable nature.

[**8**] Hence, we are as gold with respect to our intellectual and incorruptible spirit. And we are gold that is alive with an intellectual life—[gold] that can conform itself to all things. (By analogy, if a piece of wax were alive with an intellectual life, it would conform itself to the letters and shapes of things. But because [the wax] is not alive in this way, it is brought into this [state of conformity] by means of a man's outer-directed intellect.) We have this nature from the Omnipotent Artisan, who is all in all.[11] He gives us His own living image in accordance with which we cannot *form* all things, as can He, but can [only] *liken* ourselves, and *conform* ourselves, to all things. Yet, the power-of-likening is oriented only toward the power-of-forming, because the power-of-likening is such insofar as it is a power-of-forming. Thus, the power-of-likening comes to rest only in the power-of-forming.

[**9**] Moreover, from the [Gospel-]text there can be inferred that we too are hired early in the morning and are likewise sent into the vineyard of this world. Thereafter, this nature of ours arrives at the third [hour of the day] when the sun is then higher. The sun shines upon our power and upon the idleness that accords with our nature when we do not act in conformity with that nature. And thereupon we are brought into the state of putting forth intellectual efforts by means of that power. And [this stage of development] can be called the time when discernment begins to appear. And subsequently, as children who are placed in schools, we begin to make progress in grammar. And there begins to appear in us a rational power. And at the sixth hour [we come to possess] higher mental skills such as logical reasoning. And at the ninth hour [we arrive at] philosophical reasoning and at the eleventh hour [we come to] theological reasoning.

[**10**] Likewise, "early morning" [refers] to the first period of time, from after [the birth of] Adam down to the Flood. The "third [hour]" [refers to the subsequent period] down to Abraham. The "sixth [hour]" and the "ninth [hour]" [refer to the period] from Moses, through the Prophets, down to Christ. "Evening" [refers to the period] from Christ down to Christ's second coming. Furthermore, consider the fact that "early morning" can refer to the sensory power; the "third [hour]," to the imaginative power; the "sixth [hour]," to the rational power; the 'ninth [hour]," to the intellectual power; and "evening," to the intellectible (or divine) power. Or again: "first [hour]" can be said

of creation; 'third [hour]" of re-creation in Christ; "sixth [hour]" and "ninth [hour]" and "evening," of progressive works of supererogation.

First you are a human being; secondly, a Christian. Then you are called to this or that [vocation]. (For example, you are a farmer or a vineyard-keeper, or [you are called] to doing something else]. [You are called] in order that you not be idle or in order that you be a member of a religious order. [Etc.]) [11] Moreover, it can be said that first you are something gold; next you are something minted; then you are something inscribed. For a denarius is valid and true [currency] if it has all these [three] features: viz., true gold, a true image, and a true inscription. Now, God is the Truth of the [human] denarius. A denarius that is a true denarius in accordance with the nature of incorruptible gold is from the Truth that is the Father. With respect to the image [the denarius is] from the Son, who forms all things. With respect to its "roundness" [the human denarius is] from the Holy Spirit, who contains all things within His eternity; for the Spirit is that which contains all things.

[12] Note that God can be considered to be the Worth of all things that have any worth. In this way He is a Reward and is as the Value of money. Next, God gives to his servants a denarius each day; to some of them, because He wills to,[12]   [He gives an equal amount, though they have come later], etc. And in His Kingdom only that money has value [as currency]. With that money each person in the Kingdom can live and can purchase an inheritance of the Kingdom— [an inheritance] that is [constituted by] the King's love [for him] and the King's grace [toward him].

And at this point [in our reflection] we must rightly consider the fact that individual [members of the Kingdom] receive individual denarii as concerns what is basically essential. However, individuals differ [from one another] as one star differs from another star in its accidental features, etc.

NOTES TO *Erunt Primi Novissimi, et Novissimi Primi*

* Sermon CXVIII.
1. Matthew 19:30.
2. See Matthew 20:16. Nicholas, however, actually quotes from Matthew 19:30.
3. Matthew 19:29.
4. Cf. Luke 7:47.
5. Matthew 20:1: "The Kingdom of Heaven is like unto a landowner who went out early in the morning to hire laborers into his vineyard." Etc.
6. Here (at **5**:10) the microfilm of ms. V_2 reads illegibly. I am surmising "ideo cum" in place of "conductus".
7. Genesis 15:1.
8. James 1:5-6.
9. See *De Docta Ignorantia* II, 6 (**123**). The Latin word "denarius" can signify either the number ten or the Roman coin that originally had a value of ten donkeys. Nicholas here trades upon this double signification.
10. Wisdom 11:21.
11. I Corinthians 15:28. Cf. Colossians 3:11.
12. Matthew 20:15.

Ubi Venit Plenitudo Temporis*
("When the Fullness of Time Was Come ....")[1]
[December 29, 1454; preached at Innsbruck]

[1] "When the Fullness of time was come, God sent His Son."

Paul disclosed to the Galatians the true liberty that we have from the gospel and from faith in Christ. He declared that Christians are not under obligation with respect to the legalisms that are contained in the Law and with respect to ceremonies and circumcision and the other things. For faith justifies. But in this fourth chapter Paul inserts the likeness that was read in today's office: "As long as the heir is a child …," etc.[2] [Thereby] he wanted to say that in our predecessors (viz., in the believing sons of Abraham) we were as children, although we were heirs. And in that condition there is no difference between heir and servant, even though [the former] is lord of all. For such an heir is under tutors and guardians until the time prescribed by the father. Similarly, when we were children we were serving under the elements of this world.[3] Hence, [Paul] calls ceremonial things "the elements of this world."

[2] Elsewhere [Paul] speaks as if at the time of the Law we were under a pedagogue.[4] For a pedagogue is assigned to a child in order to guide him in learning. And the lad does not know where he is being led or why; but, like a captive, he obeys out of fear of punishment. And [Paul] says that [the son] serves the elements, which are, as it were, starting points, or "the letter." For elsewhere [Paul] says that the letter kills but that the spirit enlivens.[5] And *that* is the difference between the Old Testament and the New Testament; for the New Testament understands [that which the Old Testament does not]. And so, to act in accordance with one's understanding is to be at liberty. Someone who does those things which his intellect tells him ought to be done cannot say that he serves as a servant. But he who is compelled to keep the Law out of fear of punishment fulfills the Law in a servile way out of fear and out of forced obedience. (He does not understand this Law, because in those things which he does there are certain secret aspects and aspects hidden from the intellectual eyes. These aspects are revealed at the appropriate time; but at first they are known only obscurely.) By comparison, a child who is subject to a pedagogue fears the rod [and] with effort combines the elements of letters and learns grammar. He does not then know of what use it is. But when he arrives

at adulthood, he experiences the fruit [of his efforts]; and he no longer serves grammar and the elements [of writing]. Rather, he applies his mind freely to the spirit of the words, i.e., to the significations of the words. And he is concerned not with the words but with their meanings. He pursues truth, by means of which he is at rest, once it has been apprehended.

Therefore, all engagement with the elements [of writing] tends only toward truth. Once truth has been apprehended, there is no need to insist on the shapes and forms and articulation of the letters. The case is similar as concerns the Law and Christ, who is Truth.[6] For a fullness renders otiose that which is but partial; thus, truth renders otiose [the Law's] befigurings. The spirit [of the Law renders otiose] the letter [of the Law]; and the end-goal [of the Law renders otiose] those things that are a means to the end. Hence, Paul adds that that time when we were servants under the elements of this world (i.e., under perceptible signs, which are of this world) was like unto our servitude. For we were children and were imperfect; thus, the time was not yet full and complete. But when the fullness of time arrived, there came Fullness and Perfection: i.e., the Son of God was born of a woman, etc.

[3] Note [the following]: As the entire time prior to Christ is seen to be a time of truth's being formulated, as it were, insofar as truth lies hidden beneath the writing [of the Old Testament] and is not seen even though it is whole and complete, so the promise of divine life was hidden beneath the promise of sensory life—hidden as beneath elements and signs and shapes. Similarly, the truth of the New Testament is not different from the truth of the Old Testament. Rather, the same truth is one that is hidden [in the Old Testament] as in the womb [and] is not yet understood or seen [and] is one that [in the New Testament] is born and made visible, since the veil of the writing has been removed. Furthermore, note that truth is perfected in us in four stages: something that appears in the distance is first seen to be a certain thing; then when it comes nearer, it is recognized to be an animal; then when it comes still closer, it is seen to be that which has the appearance of a human being; and when it comes into our presence, then we first recognize who it is, viz., our father or our son or someone else. In a similar way, prior to the Law truth appeared, by means of nature, at a distance and in terms of confused being. Subsequently, when an angel gave instruction and ministered the Law (as [attested] in [the Book of] Acts),[7] truth was revealed, as it were, not as some entity or other but as a living being. Thereafter, it was revealed more specifically (viz., as

a man) through the Son of God. The fourth stage still remains [to arrive], so that [at that future time] we may see truth without a revealer and may know it as it is.[8] And this [fourth stage] is the last and perfect [stage], where the intellective soul finds rest as in its goal.

[4] Therefore, we turn our attention to the fact that the intellectual nature is the only nature that is capable of true life. For nothing can understand itself to be alive except the intellect, which alone has the characteristic that it is like sight. It is not like sensory sight, which sees other things but not itself; rather, it is like living sight that sees itself and that sees, within itself, all things. Therefore, only the intellect, as being a living image, is capable of relishing life in and of itself, i.e., [of relishing] true life, of which it itself is the image. For inasmuch as an image that is alive with an intellectual life knows itself to be an image, it knows that within it is the Truth and Exemplar and Form that gives being to it, with the result that it is an image. And this [Form] is the image's true life, which is present in the image as truth is present in its image.[9] Next, an intellect that understands itself to be a living image has from God the power to liken itself more greatly to its exemplar and, thus, has the power to approach closer and closer to greater union with its own object, viz., with truth, so that it may be more pleasantly at rest. For an image that knows itself to be an image cannot have rest apart from Truth, of which it is the image. Rather, it dwells in error and confusion and death if it is separated from that influence which gives to it vital, intellectual being; nevertheless, as concerns the pleasantness of its life, it remains as a dead image, as does a real eye when in darkness.

[5] Moreover, God, who, because He is good, willed to manifest the riches of His glory,[10] created all things for the sake of the intellectual nature, to which alone there can be a manifesting; for only the intellect has an eye that can behold truth. Now, God can manifest, by means of all His riches, nothing but truth. And so, lastly and subsequently to every [other] creation, He sowed a divine seed, viz., the intellectual nature (as it is beautifully revealed in Genesis that He placed man in charge of all [other] created things). In man He placed a living image—[doing so] by means of in-breathing, so that in that way we might understand the difference between the intellect and other creatures, since that in-breathing was the breath of life.[11] And from that breath the soul was made to be alive, in conformity to the divine life, which understands itself to be alive. And through this

breath man was made to be a living image of God.

[6] Now, we experience within ourselves that this living, wondrous power, [this] divine seed, is like a living image. For we are creators who make likenesses. Just as God the Creator creates and forms real things by understanding them, so we produce from our intellect the likenesses of things; and by means of the arts [and crafts] we show that we are makers of likenesses. And just as God actually enfolds within His own being all the things that exist or that can be made, so [our] intellect enfolds *within its power* all the likenesses of all things, and it unfolds by *making likenesses*, and this [making of likenesses] is the act of understanding.[12] Now, many stimuli are given to the intellectual nature in order that that seed may be stimulated and may sprout up, yielding cognitive fruit, in order that God may show the riches of His glory. Hence, God has given, and continues to give, many free gifts to men. They are gifts of the spirit, because God, who is Spirit, gives them to our spirit. And they are illuminations, and instances of grace, that tend only toward bringing it about that the grain not remain in potency in the earth but be stimulated to bear fruit.

[7] Therefore, to that soul in which this seed is present by nature, God speaks through the Holy Spirit or an angel. [He speaks] in these days, and lastly, through His Son, whom He has appointed heir of all things.[13] For the more actualized the intellect is, the more truly it possesses and comprehends. But an intellect that is altogether actualized, so that nothing more can be added [to it] since it actually understands everything that can be understood: this intellect[14] is attracted to [union with] Infinite Actuality, which is God; and as being an heir to all things, it possesses all things. [It possesses them] not as a child who is under a tutor but as an heir who after a definite period of time will actually possess all things. And this [heir] is Christ, because, as Paul states in Hebrews,[15] He was anointed above His fellow-men. Therefore, the true heir is that man [Jesus], whose human intellect is altogether actualized and enfolds within itself all things and possesses all things, because of its supreme union with the divine intellect. In Christ, then, there is fullness of perfection by means of the image's union—in the supreme degree [and] in such a way that it cannot be a greater union— with its Truth. And unless the union were a personal union, it could be greater. For the two natures in a man—viz., the soul and the body—are united in such a way that one man is constituted from the union, with the result that the sensory life exists only in the rational life.

(Otherwise, there would be not a man but a beast.) But the rational soul does not have a corporeal nature but is a seed of divine life and is a likeness of the Word, which is Absolute Reason; to this likeness the animal nature is united hypostatically.[16]

[8] Moreover, in all men there is found a grace that is a certain light and liveliness given by God to the soul. On account of this gift (because it is the gift of God) all men are made content by it with themselves. But Christ's intellect obtained the fullness of all grace because there remained nothing that was not given [to it]. Hence, Christ's intellect (in which the life of the animal nature from Adam was subsumed) was subsumed not in its own person but in the Word of God (i.e., in the Power through which God made even the ages) as what is attracted is subsumed in that which attracts it (as you know from elsewhere[17] about iron and a magnet). Likewise, you know that the Son of God, Heir of all things on account of the fullness of grace, is not an heir such as the sons by adoption are. These latter are called[18] to be partial heirs or joint-heirs or heirs together with the true Son.[19] But [Christ is Heir] both by grace and by nature. For [in Christ] grace, which is such that it cannot be greater (because it is full—indeed, because it is fullness), coincides with nature.

[9] And consider attentively that Paul instructs us as follows: because we have in us the Spirit of the Son—in that we cry out "Abba, Father"[20]—then just as we are partakers of the Spirit of the Son, so we are also co-heirs. But the Son Himself, as true Son, is the true Heir, whereas we, as participants, are adopted sons.[21] For adoption is the grace of sonship, or the partaking of sonship. And we are co-heirs. This partial inheritance is expressed for us by [Christ] our Teacher, who said that in His Father's house are many mansions and that He would go to prepare and arrange them for us and would go to prepare a meal for us and to feed us by ministering to us.[22] As Heir to all things, Christ shares [His inheritance] with us as with adopted sons, giving [us] mansions and food after the fashion of [one's bequeathing of] possessions belonging to this present world. By comparison, certain principates are as domains of the elect where the first-born son is heir to the principate, and he gives to his other brothers mansions and food or [other] necessities. Consider, then, carefully Paul's text about the Jews' serving under the elements—[serving], to wit, not as the heathen by worshipping visible things and the heavenly bodies (for then they would have been serving the elements). Rather, the Jews were serving under

the elements by observing new moons, sacrifices, etc. And they were heirs. Nevertheless, they did not know from these elements that they were sons of God and heirs of the Kingdom of Heaven. For just as they were serving under the elements of the world, so they were also expecting to inherit the earth.

[10] Furthermore, consider the fact that [Paul] says that God sent His Son, made of a woman and made under the Law.[23] Understand that of a woman, or mother, He was made a human being in order that through the sending of the Son of God into our nature—[a nature] that He received from His mother—we might receive adoption as God's sons. For just as the Father Himself sent the Son into the nature that is from the mother, so we understand that the nature that is from the woman is able to be united to the Son, who is from God. [Paul] says that [Jesus] was made under the Law—[meaning], to wit, that He was circumcised and was offered [to God] in the temple in accordance with the precepts of the Law. For it was supposed to be known that He was the Son of Abraham, whose sons are recognized in this way. And so, He was made under the Law not as one who needed to keep the Law in order to be purified but so that He might free those who were under the Law. For He came as Fullness of grace that frees from all servitude. And in Him the requirements of the Law reached their completion. As He said: "I have not come to destroy the Law but to fulfill it."[24] Hence, as representing the person of all, on behalf of all those who possess Him by faith, He fulfilled the Law as Mediator between God and men.

[11] Note carefully regarding the Spirit: viz., that we who have received through Christ (whom we received through faith) adoption as sons of God have received in our spirit the Spirit of the Son. This Spirit gives us the boldness to cry out "Abba, Father."[25] For unless God had sent into our spirit (in which Christ dwells through our faith) the Spirit of the Son, we would not have the boldness to cry out unto God as unto our Father; neither would the Jews say "Abba" nor we Latins "Pater". Therefore, faith in Christ is proved to be in us if we have Christ's Spirit, which is the pledge that we shall obtain true sonship with God as His adopted sons. For as our pledge we have the Spirit, who leads our spirit unto what is perfect. That Spirit is as heat, or love, that strengthens and purifies and illumines. We see that nature is strengthened by faith in a new and most famous Physician who heals by His touch. Hence, if we have the Spirit of God's Son, that Spirit purifies us, as the spirit of grape-juice causes the grape-juice to ferment and by

means of the warmth distills by expelling everything that is not of the nature of wine. And it does this in order to turn the grape-juice into wine (as you know from elsewhere).[26]

[12] Note that miracles done by the saints were done in the Spirit of the Son of God. Peter said: "In the name of Jesus, arise and walk!"[27] And if amid incantations an evil spirit works because of faith the wonders that are signs of the power of the Prince of this world [viz., Satan],[28] then the Prince of the future age [viz., Christ] works in us, because of our faith, much more strongly by His own Spirit those things that are above nature. If, then, we say that we are believers having true faith that is [in-]formed [by love],[29] and if we have the Spirit of God's Son, through whom God works all things, then none of the opponents of the Word of God (viz., evil spirits and sinners) will be able to withstand us. [13] Moreover, we will be able to experience in ourselves whether or not that Spirit indwells us—[to experience it] provided that we delight in following Christ by means of good works [and] provided that in our movements we walk as pilgrims who follow Christ. For the movement in our reason comes from our spirit. Therefore, if our soul is moved by a good spirit, viz., by the Spirit of truth and of Christ, then we follow Christ, and we joyfully suffer all things for God's sake, humbling ourselves and being obedient [even] unto death. Christ said: "Do as I have done; for I have given you an example," etc.[30] "Take my yoke upon you, and learn of me. For I am meek and lowly in heart, and you will receive rest for your souls," etc.[31]

[14] Note, as you know from elsewhere,[32] that grace and the Spirit of the Son of God are the life of the soul, even as the soul is the life of the body. And although the soul does not always infuse a cheerful life into the whole body, nevertheless [the lack of gladness] occurs not because of the soul but because of the indisposition of the body. Likewise, the body is purified by the soul in order that it may better receive the inflow of the soul's life. Similarly, the soul, too, must be purified in order that it may take into itself the inflow of divine life and divine grace. And thereupon we will be able to experience [both] the joyous life of our soul and the good spirit that indwells that life—even as someone cured of lethargy senses life and experiences, when the offending humor is withstood, that he has a vibrant soul. [15] From the Gospel take note of the fact that Simon said to Mary: "Behold this [child, Jesus] is set for the fall and for the resurrection of many in Israel

and for a sign which shall be contradicted."[33] The Apostle says that in Christ Himself God is going to judge the world.[34] Similarly, I understand that Christ was placed as a certain sign which is contradicted in that some say that He is good, whereas others say that not He but the Seducer is good. And in Him we apprehend the fall and the resurrection of many in Israel, viz., of believers. For when we believers take as a sign the life and the desires and the movement (that we have in the soul) toward Christ, then we immediately experience whether we are Christlike, arising with Him unto life, or whether we ought to fear ruin and damnation. For Christ alone is the Way to the Kingdom and is the man through whom judgment will be made (1) concerning resurrection unto life on the basis of conformity [to His life] and (2) concerning [damnation] on the basis of a lack of conformity. Therefore, let us act as do goldsmiths, who have in solid-form a sample of perfect gold and who determine, in relation to that sign, the degree of perfection of the gold presented [to them]; and they purify [the proffered gold] until it agrees [with the sample] and is perfect; thereupon it is true and lasting [gold].

[**16**] Consider that as regards him who ought to be free and not a servant: it is necessary that he first pay attention to the fact that every action of Christ is our instruction[35] in order that we may know that we will obtain the liberty of the sons of God if we follow the Son of God. And because the body of the Church has different kinds of members,[36] it is necessary that each member abide in his calling. And so, it is first necessary that you determine whether the spirit of Christ is in you and that until you find that spirit in your particular calling, you not believe it to be present in you. For the life of Christ is the universal pathway on which, however, different people walk. Hence, a Christian priest ought to put on Christ[37] in a priestly way; and someone in a religious order ought to put on Christ in a religious way; and a duke, in a ducal way; and a citizen, in a citizen's way—each in his own order, office, and calling. Christ in one man is not different from Christ in another man. Similarly, there is not a different cloth for a secular leader and for a religious monk; but from the same cloth, made from the immaculate Lamb of God, different kinds of vestments are taken and are to be worn. For the Lord wills it to be thus. For He wills that the vestment be adorned roundabout with variety for the sake of the splendor of His curia, which is the Church militant, etc.

[**17**] Furthermore, the introit of the mass says: "While [all things were in] the midst of silence ...," etc.[38] Christ the Mediator,[39] the

Cornerstone,[40] the Stone cut without hands out of the mountain, etc.,[41] came in the midst of silence, etc.; by this means the respective faith of both the heathen and the Jews is united in the Cornerstone (as [you know] from elsewhere).[42] The case is similar as regards [the expression] "the midst of time"; by means of this [expression] it is understood that [Christ] is coming at the end [of time]. And here [in the present text] it is said that He is coming in the midst [of time—coming] as the End [of time], as the Saint of saints.[43] Thus, [He comes] at the height of [our] ascent and at that point. For He alone is the Most High, unto whom the ascent was made. And afterwards there occurs the descent, etc. And so, [He appears] in the middle [between the ascent and the descent]. But the descent is always steeper, and the ruin swifter, than the ascent. Thus, [it comes] after the middle-point of time when the world is declining.

NOTES TO *Ubi Venit Plenitudo Temporis*

* Sermon CLXIX.

1. Galatians 4:4. The fuller title of this present sermon is "Ubi Venit Plenitudo Temporis, Misit Deus Filium Suum."

2. Galatians 4:1: "As long as the heir is a child he differs not at all from a servant, though he be lord of all."

3. Galatians 4:3.

4. Galatians 3:24-25.

5. II Corinthians 3:6.

6. John 14:6.

7. Acts 7:53.

8. I John 3:2.

9. Throughout this section Nicholas is distinguishing between an image and that of which it is the image. The latter he refers to as the truth of the image.

10. Romans 9:23.

11. Genesis 2:7.

12. These likenesses are concepts, which the mind abstracts from images by means of its assimilative power. See my *Nicholas of Cusa on Wisdom and Knowledge* (Minneapolis: Banning, 1996) and my "Nicholas of Cusa (1401-1464): First Modern Philosopher?" pp. 13-29 in Peter A. French and Howard K. Wettstein, editors, *Renaissance and Early Modern Philosophy* (Vol. 26 in the series *Midwest Studies in Philosophy*). Boston: Blackwell, 2002. See also the different view about Cusa's position on *a priori* knowledge: Klaus Kremer, "Erkennen bei Nikolaus von Kues. Apriorismus – Assimilation – Abstraktion," pp. 3-49 in his *Praegustatio naturalis sapientiae. Gott suchen mit Nikolaus von Kues* (Münster: Aschendorff, 2004).

13. Hebrews 1:2.

14. " ... this intellect": viz., Christ's intellect, which was a human intellect.

15. Hebrews 1:9. Psalms 44:8 (45:7).

16. That is, in man, the corporeal animal nature is united to the rational soul in a oneness of person.

17. *De Pace Fidei* 8. Sermon CLVIII.

18. Here (at **8**:14) I am reading, with the Paris edition, "vocantur" in place of "nominantur".

19. Romans 8:15-17.

20. Galatians 4:6.

21. Galatians 4:5. Ephesians 1:5. Romans 8:15.

22. John 14:2.

23. Galatians 4:4.

24. Matthew 5:17.

25. Galatians 4:6.

26. Sermon LXIX (**67**).

27. Acts 3:6.

28. John 12:31 and 14:30 and 16:11.

29. Galatians 5:6.

30. John 13:15. Not an exact quotation.

31. Matthew 11:29.
32. E. g., Sermon CLXV (**11** and **12**).
33. Luke 2:34.
34. John 5:22.
35. Cf. II Timothy 3:15-16.
36. Cf. Romans 12:4-8.
37. Romans 13:14.
38. Wisdom 18:14-15: "For while all things were in quiet silence and the night was in the midst of her course, thy almighty word leapt down from heaven ...," (Douay version).
39. I Timothy 2:5.
40. Ephesians 2:20.
41. Daniel 2:45.
42. I Peter 2:5-10. Romans 10:12-13.
43. Daniel 9:24.

Sermon CCXLIV: In Caritate Radicati et Fundati*
("... Rooted and Grounded in Love ....")[1]
[September 12, 1456; preached in Brixen]

[1] "... being rooted and grounded in love in order that you may be able to comprehend with all the saints what is the breadth, length, height, and depth ..." (Ephesians 3 and in the office of the mass).

Paul wrote to the Ephesians that he received [instruction] by revelation from on high, in order that he might preach even to the Gentiles the sacrament hidden from the world. Afterwards he added: "Therefore, I ask that you not faint at [my] tribulations [for you]," etc.[2] But in the office of the mass we read: "I beseech you, Brethren ...."

[2] Let us first of all note that God sent Christ—in whom are hidden all the treasures of knowledge and wisdom[3]—for the purpose of manifesting God's own wisdom. And He did so for the following reason: The Wisdom of God[4] is the Former of all created things; for God made all things in wisdom,[5] and all things were formed for manifesting God's glory[6] (as if a very gifted and very skilled artisan were to form all things in order to manifest his artisanship). Therefore, unless [God's] wisdom were known, [God] would be neither praised nor glorified. If, then, the subtle aspects of the art of painting be shown to an ignoramus, the master-painter is not glorified by the ignoramus. A pearl ought not to be cast before swine,[7] where the pearl's value is not at all recognized. And Paul spoke wisdom among the perfect,[8] where, indeed, it was understood. But the human race as a whole was without a knowledge of God, as the Apostle said[9] in Acts 17. And so, the Son of God, who is the Wisdom of the Father,[10] came into the world for the enlightening of men and for dispelling the darkness of ignorance—as here and there the Apostle states.

[3] You have often heard elsewhere that Christ is the one in whom divinity dwells in a bodily habitation[11] and dwells perfectly and permanently. Divinity is present in all creatures, but [in them] it is present by way of participation; in Christ alone it is present fully and wholly. And so, Christ alone—in whom God the Father's omnipotent art is present—was able by His power to manifest in and through His human nature works that can befit only the Creator. Therefore, the Father, wanting to make known from Heaven the riches of His wisdom,[12] created all things and, at length, sent His own Son, by means

of whom we have, through faith, access to apprehending wisdom, in order that we may be able to attain to glorifying God. For in our [human] nature [as it is present] in Christ Jesus we find wisdom in [such great] abundance and flowing-forth that [the human nature] can partake of wisdom for us; and it seeks to do so. Therefore, through the faith by which we believe that Christ is the Son of God we approach Him as Teacher of truth, and we are enlightened to such an extent that, being aroused as disciples, we will come to perfection.

[4] Now, the Apostle [Paul] wrote from Rome this truly marvelous and most pleasing letter [to the Ephesians], declaring all of God's benefits that they received by faith in Jesus. Through faith those who were far from God and from wisdom were brought near, so that [now] they give thanks to God and do not faint amid the tribulations of Paul, the apostle of those [tidings]. [It was not] as if when their teacher was imprisoned,[13] they would depart from the truth or be fearful or doubting. For when someone suffers because of a service rendered for someone else, then it accrues to the glory of him for whom the service is done not to faint but to show himself faithful. When, indeed, a preacher suffers for the sake of the word of God, although he could avoid suffering by consenting to his adversaries, then those who hear him ought rightly to be strengthened; for his sufferings or his acts of martyrdom bear testimony to the truth.

[5] There follows [in the text]: "To this end (viz., that you faint not) I bend my knees to the Father of our Lord Jesus Christ."[14] Note Paul's manner in praying. In particular, each individual ought to bend his knees. And [to do] this is only to bow in the presence of the Father and to humble oneself in every manner of humbling. For the outer man[15] ought to show signs of humility and to bend the physical knees suitably, as the inner man bends spiritual knees. Oftentimes the mind is called the inner man,[16] and the principal member of the inner man is called the heart,[17] because the heart is the seat of life; [and] we call the giver of life—viz., the rational soul—by the name of the physical heart.

[6] Paul says: "... to the Father of our Lord Jesus Christ."[18] The Latin manuscripts have these words, [whereas] the Greek manuscripts have only "... to the Father." And so, some men have thought that [the text] must be understood to mean that the name "Father" is applied not to the Lord Jesus Christ but to all rational creatures. But I deem that not without reason do the Latins construe [the text] as they do, so that we may know that this God is He who is the Father of Jesus

Christ. **[7]** From this [observation] note that our every prayer ought to be referred to the Father of the Lord Jesus Christ. The Church observes this practice; and in the collects [of the mass] are placed [the words] "... through our Lord Jesus Christ, Your Son." Therefore, because, when we pray, we approach the Father through Christ, so that in praying we express our faith, without which faith nothing is obtained: we ought to signify that Jesus is the Son of God and that He whom we call Father is the Father of Jesus. For we know to be true the teaching of Him who said: "If you ask anything of the Father in my name, He will give it to you."[19]

[8] Now, Christ says that God is His Father, and He teaches us to say "Our Father." For there is only one Father and His only Son. Christ, as being the one Son, says with regard to the Father that He is *His* Father. But if all the members[20] of that Son were rational and could speak, they would rightly say with regard to the Father "Our Father." Christ, who is one, would say "My Father"; the members, because they are many, would rightly say "Our Father." But the members would have not from themselves but from Christ the fact that they could say "Our Father." For unless they were members of Christ, who is the unique Son, they could not say "Our Father." Hence, all the sonship of all the sons is from the unique Son, just as the life of all the members of the body is from one life. Therefore, Christ is the perfection [of the members]—i.e., is a totality—that is personal. He is the Son, who *is* also Sonship. But Christians are sons of God *through* Sonship,[21] which, indeed, Christ *is*.

[9] Paul says: "... from whom all fatherhood in heaven and on earth is named."[22] Note that the Fount and Origin of all begottenness and of all unfolding-of-power takes its name from the Father of our Lord Jesus Christ. For only that Father is Absolute Fatherhood, which enfolds in itself all fatherhood that is present in heaven or on earth and that is present in the joining of heaven and earth (i.e., in human nature).[23] For just as Fatherhood, which *is* God the Father, is eternally very fecund and sends forth from itself a knowledge of its fecundity and embraces [that knowledge], so Fatherhood has given to every creature in heaven and on earth a likeness of itself. Thus, there is no creature that does not, in its own way, partake of fecundity, so that it endeavors to unfold fecundity and to rest lovingly in its embrace. **[10]** *That* fecundity is present in angels, in the heavens, [and] on earth. And if the entire perceptible world is considered as a single species, or essence: then the heavens are as a father; the earth is as a mother; [and] from them exist the things that are produced in this world. The philosophers said that intelligences move the heavens and that an intelligence, together with the motion of the heavens, produces living natures.[24] For since a living nature is more noble than is a non-living nature, the physical heavens do not produce life, since the producer is more noble than is the produced. And so, [the philosophers] said that life is produced by an intelligence.

[11] Now, in angels there is fecundity-of-memory, which always bears fruit, so that it knows itself and is in a state of restfulness. The fruit is knowledge and is the restfulness-of-love—just as a living seed (which enfolds within itself a power that is never eternally unfoldable) always by means of unfolding begets fruit, in which one delights. [The situation is] as if one seed, e.g., a mustard-seed, continually expressed its power by producing its yield, and as if the expression would be only the seeing of fecundity in and through the yield. Similarly, the seeing of fecundity in the case of angels is the seeing of *understanding*. The memory, or the paternal fecundity, produces a yield—viz., [the angels'] vision and knowledge of their inexhaustible fecundity—in which yield [an angel] takes delight. And in an angel there is no other fecundity-of-memory than the Creating Father's creation, or likeness. Therefore, the more fruit an angel bears, the more he proceeds to a knowledge of God, from whom is all fatherhood. [12] Moreover, an angel will never be able to unfold his own fecundity so as always to produce new fruit—[viz., fruit] consisting of a knowledge of his fecundity. By contrast, the Father begets anew today[25] (i.e., continuously) the same Son, i.e., the Understanding of His fecundity.[26] (Hence, all things new are delightful, because they bear a likeness to divine begottenness.) So an angel cannot at just any and every moment unfold his fecundity-[of-memory] and his delight in such a way[27] that [these latter are] always new.

Likewise, consider what, in its own way, is the case with our intellectual nature.

[13] Hence, it is evident that the fatherhood that is present in all creatures manifests likewise the fact that a trinity is present in all creatures. Yet, [the trinity] is present to the intellectual nature in an intellectual way only where the intellectual nature has fecundity-of-memory after the fashion of the Father-Creator. In this fecundity-[of-memory] there are likenesses of the Divine Fatherhood; i.e., there are intellectual seeds of the beginnings from which an understanding is expressed. In this understanding the fecundity of the beginnings is

seen. [**14**] And if you consider carefully, [you will see that] there is only *one* Beginning, which is of manifold power. As Paul says in Acts 17, certain wise men have called it a divine seed or a divine offspring.[28] The intellectual nature's memory is like a source or a very fecund divine seed that yields from itself—when it becomes actualized—fruit of understanding (like the fruit of Paradise), in which one takes delight.

[**15**] Note that the Apostle says "... from whom all fatherhood is named,"[29] since the true name [for a thing] is given by the Giver of forms. For a name follows from the form, as you know from elsewhere.[30] Hence, on the basis of the foregoing statement of the Apostle's we ought to say that all names are named from the divine name rather than the converse.[31] For although those who say that we ascribe to God names that are imposed on things do so rightly, nevertheless they do not take account of from whence names are imposed on things. For we read that Adam imposed names on things.[32] Assuredly, there was with Adam divine light by which he was enlightened so that he would know what name would be fitting for each [animal]. [**16**] Hence, just as all fatherhood that is named in heaven and on earth has from the Fatherhood of God the Father that it is thusly named, so all sonship that is in heaven and on earth has from God's Sonship [that it is thusly named]; and all spiration, from God's Spirit; and all oneness, from God's Oneness; and all being, from God's Being; and all life, from God's Life; and all love, from God's love; and so on.

[**17**] But names do not befit God and creatures in the same[33] way. For they befit God as Creator and Originator [but] befit creatures as caused and originated. In the case of God they are [names] only of the infinite simplicity of the Originator, but in the case of creatures they are [names] only of likenesses of [that divine] simplicity. Therefore, every creature consists of *whereby it is* and *what is*.[34] It has *whereby it is* from a likeness to God, i.e., from actuality that is likened to God, who is purest Actuality. [It has] *what is* from potentiality, which in itself is nothing (for all *what is* exists [only] insofar as it exists actually; potential being does not exist [actually]). Thus, every creature is from being and from not-being. *Whereby it is*, i.e., its likeness to God, is being; and so, it is near to God because it is His likeness. However, not-being is near to nothing. As Augustine, too, said: God created two things, one near to Himself and the other near to nothing[35] (for privation is nearly nothing).

[**18**] In [today's] text there follow [the words]:

... in order that He would grant you, according to the riches of His glory, to be strengthened [with] might (*virtutem*) ...

{Elsewhere we read "*virtute*", and [that reading] better conduces to understanding [the meaning of the text].}

... by His Spirit in the inner man (*in interiorem hominem*), ...

{Elsewhere I have read "*in interiori homine*," and [that reading] is more felicitous. The Greeks ought to have that reading. Perhaps the reason that they have the reading that accords with our text [viz., "*in interiorem hominem*"] is that they lack an ablative case [in their language].}

... that Christ may dwell in your hearts by faith.

Let us take note of what the Apostle prayed to happen—i.e., of what he prayed to be given [to him] by the Father according to the riches of His glory. For one who is glorious and rich does not give meager things. Therefore, [the Apostle] asks of the most glorious and most rich Father-of-powers (who gave to His Son power in all fullness) that the power of being strengthened be given to the Ephesians, in order that they might be strengthened by His Spirit (viz., by the Spirit of the Father) in the inner man, [so that] Christ might dwell in their hearts by virtue of their faith. For since Christ is the power of God and the Wisdom of the Father,[36] then if He is to dwell in the inner man, or heart, this abode must be made to be *disposed* and must be strengthened by the power of God's Spirit. For unless God the Father strengthens the soul by means of His Spirit, the soul cannot be capable of receiving God's Son by faith. [**19**] And so, no one can speak of Jesus Christ except by the Holy Spirit.[37] No soul is capable of having Christ dwell in it as God's Son unless the Holy Spirit has prepared [it as] a dwelling-place. For every human spirit in which Christ, the Son of God, dwells passes into sonship with God. Christ *is* Sonship that converts and forms sons of adoption.

[**20**] There follow [in our theme-text for today the words]: " ... being rooted and grounded in love, so that you may be able to comprehend, with all the saints, what is the breadth, length, height, and depth ..."[38] For when the inner man is strengthened by the power of

the Holy Spirit, then the man is rooted in love. For God's Spirit is Love.[39] Therefore, where a man's strengthening-root is a love that will never fail, then in that [loving] union [the man] is [united] with all the saints. For all the holiness that is in all the saints comes only from the love in which [the saints] are rooted. (For the root is hidden in that from which it draws life and the nourishment of life.) Love ministers life and gladness to the root. Therefore, the inner man lives from love by means of the union of his life's root with love—just as the Tree of Paradise [draws life] from the Garden of Paradise, in which it is rooted.

[21] "... and grounded" is said [in today's text], because what is grounded in love is steadfast in order that there may be comprehended what is its breadth, length, height, and depth. These [dimensions] are measures that are found in a complete material object. Now, Paul said elsewhere[40] that in Christ God dwells bodily—i.e., fully and perfectly and in full measure of every kind. [22] Therefore, he who has been made an attainer attains, together with all the saints, what is absolute length, absolute breadth, absolute height, and absolute depth; for the Great Lord, of whose magnitude there is no end,[41] is altogether infinite. Infinite length is length that is also infinite breadth; likewise, infinite height [is height that is] also infinite depth. But there is not more than one infinite thing; therefore, only infinity is the adequate measure of all things that are measurable by any kind of measuring. Maximum and minimum coincide in the infinite.[42] An infinite line, or infinite length, is the form and actuality of all that can be made from a finite line, or a finite length. And so on. Infinite being is *actually* all things that *can be*.[43] Infinite life is *actually* all things that *can live*. And so on.

[23] Hence, God is understood to be the Exactness and Measure of all the things that exist and that can exist. And herefrom it is known (1) that length is breadth, height, and depth and (2) that breadth is length, height, and depth and (3) that height is length, breadth, and depth, and (4) that depth is length, breadth, and height. All of these [statements] mean only that God is understood by the saints to be all in all.[44] [24] And if the aforementioned terms are applied to love, in order to know love's breadth, length, height, and depth: then consider that the inner man is rooted in love after the fashion of an intellectual tree that grows by understanding. (Understanding is the breadth of the tree that is rooted in love.) For [love] is extended to all different places in all their breadth. For nothing is broader than is love, which for the sake of the Creator embraces all created things with a sweet embrace. Love is

not wearied throughout the entire length of days and times; rather, it is more lasting and longer than any length that is measurable by any measure whatsoever. For from end to end,[45] by means of a most pleasant contact, it reaches all things. It most highly ascends to union with God, who dwells in the highest places;[46] and through the mercy of compassion it reaches, by means of its humility, the lowest places and the depths. For there is nothing that can remain hidden from love's warmth.

[25] With regard to love there is not favoritism of persons.[47] There is no king, no matter how great, whom his lowliest servant could not love exceedingly—and vice versa. Love overcomes all [obstacles]. With respect to God's[48] love, [which] adheres to someone indissolubly, [the Psalmist] says: "If I ascend unto Heaven, You are there. If I descend unto Hell, You are there."[49] You never forsake me.[50] [26] Thirdly, the text [of today's mass] can be construed as referring to love on the part of Christ, who indwells [us] through our faith. For a soul that exists in love [and] that has Christ within it comprehends with all the saints what is the breadth, length, height, and depth of His love, through which all the saints have been gathered together so that they exist in sonship with Christ, the Son of God, and so that they are holy in the Holy of Holies. They comprehend that there can be no breadth that is greater than is the breadth of Christ's love, which is of such great [breadth] that it wills the salvation of all of this world's inhabitants—present ones, past ones, and future ones. [Christ's love] expends itself for them all—not only for friends but also for enemies, all of whom such immense love reconciled to God, as much as was possible, by a most generous shedding of Christ's own blood.

[27] How great the *length* of this love, which from sunrise until sunset embraces all men at all the times of [this] world! How great the *height* [of this love], which has united even angels very closely to God! How great the *depth* [of this love], which has drawn even those in Hell unto fellowship with God! Therefore, no measure attains the limit of Christ's love, which has merited eternal happiness for the foregoing and for all who through faith have Christ in their inner man. [28] Hence, if you take note: just as in Adam all die, so too in Christ all will be made alive.[51] Christ's love gathers into one all those who are obedient [and] who have been reborn through faith [and] whom Adam's presumptiveness made hateful[52] to God. Therefore, all the saints, having been gathered by Christ's love [and] having been

rooted in love, apprehend (*comprehendere*) the breadth, length, height, and depth of that love by which they are apprehended [*comprehendi*]. For to apprehend is to be apprehended: to have Christ within oneself is to be in Christ; to possess love within oneself is to be possessed by love. See how it is that the elect return to the Father in and through the one Son of God. Just as there is one earthly Adam, through whom all men have been scattered throughout this world, so there is one Heavenly Christ, who gathers from this world unto Himself the elect and who leads them back to the Kingdom of the Creator.

[29] There follow [in the text for today's mass the words]: "... to know also the love of Christ which surpasses all knowledge, so that you may be filled unto all the fullness of God."[53] Note in what way the Apostle speaks when he wishes for the Ephesians to have the love of Christ which surpasses all knowledge. For super-eminent knowledge of Christ's love seems to be only obedience. For Christ knew that the obedience of love is to such an extent knowledge that he who loved God would know, according to the degree of his love, that God ought to be obeyed. And he who loved God in an eminent way would know that God ought to be obeyed even to the point of death and even to the point of a most vile death. And he would know that from this obeying there would result the fulfilling of all his desires even to the point of God's fullness. Thus, one who is thus obedient and who empties himself will be filled with divinity up to the point of the fullness by which God is full of all glory and happiness. For all who will attain that knowledge of love shall be as is Christ Himself. For they—those who in this way by faith have Christ in the inner man, i.e., in the mind—shall be like Christ when He appears.[54] This Christ the Lord has indeed obtained all the fullness of God.

[30] The Apostle adds: "Now, to Him who is able to do all things more abundantly than we ask or understand, according to the power that[55] works in us: to Him be glory in the Church and in Christ Jesus unto all generations, world without end."[56] After his [previous] prayer [the Apostle now] gives to the Father-from-Heaven glory—as to Him who is able to act more abundantly than we ask and understand, in accordance with His wondrous power, which[57] works in us indeed more than we ask or understand. For in Paul God's power worked abundantly and above all understanding. To God [be] glory in the Church and in Christ, its Head (i.e., in the Church, which is the body of Christ Jesus), unto all generations, world without end (i.e., forever.

For eternity is "world without end." For a *saeculum*, which extends to the longest life of an elderly man, follows after a previous *saeculum*. But *saeculum saeculorum* is a duration that enfolds all *saecula*.)

NOTES TO *In Caritate Radicati et Fundati*

* Sermon CCXLIV.
1. Ephesians 3:17-19.
2. Ephesians 3:13.
3. Colossians 2:3.
4. "Wisdom" is oftentimes used, in the Medieval tradition, as a name for God the Son. See I Corinthians 1:24.
5. Psalms 103:24 (104:24).
6. Psalms 18:1 (19:1). Isaias (Isaiah) 43:7. Colossians 1:16 (King James Version). Apocalypse (Revelation) 4:11.
7. Matthew 7:6.
8. I Corinthians 2:6.
9. Acts 17:23-31.
10. See n. 4 above.
11. Colossians 2:9.
12. Romans 11:33.
13. Paul wrote to the Ephesians from prison in Rome.
14. Ephesians 3:14.
15. II Corinthians 4:16.
16. Romans 7:22. II Corinthians 4:16. Ephesians 3:16.
17. I Corinthians 2:9. Ephesians 4:18.
18. Ephesians 3:14.
19. John 16:23.
20. Cf. Romans 12:4.
21. Romans 12:5.
22. Ephesians 3:15 (Vulgate and Douay-Rheims versions).
23. Nicholas often calls man a microcosm. See, for example, *De Docta Ignorantia*, III, 3 (**198**). Sermon XX (**32** - **33**). Sermon XXX (**8**:1-2). Sermon XLV (**5**:1). Sermon CXXII (**2**:17-18). See also Hugo von Strassburg, *Compendium Theologicae Veritatis*, II, 2 (beginning part). [This work was falsely ascribed to Bonaventure and is found in Vol. 8 of *S. Bonaventurae Opera Omnia*, edited by A. C. Peltier (Paris: Vivès, 1866).
24. See Aristotle, *Metaphysica*, XII, 7 ($1072^a19 - 1072^b13$). See also Nicholas's *De Beryllo* 36.
25. Hebrews 1:5. Psalms 2:7.
26. Nicholas borrows from Augustine's *De Trinitate* the names "Memory," "Understanding," and "Love" as names of God the Father, God the Son, and God the Holy Spirit. Nicholas holds to the orthodox theological doctrine that the Son is *eternally begotten* from the Father. Thus, the Father always understands Himself through the Son.
27. In this sentence I am reading (at **12**:9) "quin" in place of "quoniam"—as does the Paris edition.
28. Acts 17:28.
29. Ephesians 3:15.
30. E.g., *Compendium* 6 (end of **18**).

31. "… rather than the converse": i.e., rather than the Divine Being's being named by the names of created things.

32. Genesis 2:19-20.

33. Here (at **17**:1) I am surmising "eodem" in place of "eo".

34. See Thomas Aquinas, *Summa contra Gentiles*, II, 54.

35. Augustine, in *Confessions* XII, 6 (*PL* 32:828) calls formless matter *prope nihil*.

36. I Corinthians 1:24.

37. I Corinthians 12:3.

38. Ephesians 3:17-18.

39. Cf. I John 4:16. See Sermon IV (**35**).

40. Colossians 2:9.

41. Psalms 144:3 (145:3).

42. *De Docta Ignorantia* I, 4.

43. The Latin here ("Infinita essentia est actu omnia, quae esse possunt") makes clear that Nicholas's point is that God, who is Infinite Being, is *actually* all things that *can be*. That is, his point is not simply that God is all that *He* can be. See *De Docta Ignorantia* I, 4 (**11**) and *De Possest* 7.

44. I Corinthians 15:28.

45. Wisdom 8:1.

46. Psalms 112:5 (113:5) and 122:1 (123:1).

47. Romans 2:11.

48. Here (at **25**:4) I am surmising "Dei" in place of "Deus". The Latin sentence is malformed.

49. Psalms 138:8 (139:8).

50. Hebrews 13:5. Josue (Joshua) 1:5. At **25**:7 of the printed Latin text, I am reading, with the mss., "derelinquis" in place of "derelinques".

51. I Corinthians 15:22.

52. Note Hebrews 1:9. Osee (Hosea) 9:15.

53. Ephesians 3:19.

54. I John 3:2.

55. Here (at **30**:3) I am reading (with the Vulgate) "quae" in place of Nicholas's "quam".

56. Ephesians 3:20-21.

57. Here (at **30**:10) I am reading "quae" in place of Nicholas's "quam".

Quaecumque Scripta Sunt*
("Whatever Things Were Written ....")
[December 5, 1456; preached in Brixen]

[1] "Whatever things were written were written for our learning ..."[1] (Romans 15 and in the reading of the epistle of the Sunday mass).

The Apostle [Paul] taught that each one [of us] ought to please his neighbor unto good, for edification, and that Christ pleased not Himself but that, as it is written: "the reproaches of them that reproached You fell upon me."[2] (Thus spoke the Prophet—in the person of Christ—to God.) Afterwards, [the Apostle] added: "For whatever things were written ...," etc.—as if to say: that which was written about Christ, viz., that He pleased not Himself but bore the weakness of others, [instructs us that] we, too, who are stronger, ought to bear the infirmities of the weak.[3] [2] Moreover, note that it is the opinion of the Apostle that although some things were written about Christ, nevertheless they were written for our learning. For Christ's every action serves as our instruction. And the things that were written about Christ describe a perfect man. And so, from those things we ought to learn in which way to be perfect.

[3] The rational soul, which is like a divine seed, was implanted in Adam, or earth, in order to grow and to be perfected. And so, to Abraham our father—in whom humanity began to have the use of reason and in whom humanity submitted itself to God through faith (as a student [submits himself] to a teacher)—God said: "Walk before me, and be perfect."[4] From that time on, humanity made progress and in Christ arrived at a perfection of the role of teacher. Christ taught us that our perfection consists in imitating God the Father. Therefore, Scripture perfects. [4] Indeed, [the Apostle Paul] speaks as follows: "Whatever things were written were written for our learning, in order that through patience and the consolation of the Scriptures we might have hope." We see that Paul indicates that two things are contained in Sacred Scripture: viz., patience and consolation. And this [containment occurs] in order that we might have hope. For since this life (in which God spared not His own Son)[5] is not without turmoil, we are taught in order that we may conduct ourselves patiently and may make a virtue of necessity and, in so doing, may follow the perfect men Job and the others, about whom it is written [in Scripture]. And [we are taught] in

order that we may, especially, follow Him who is the Perfection of those who are perfect, viz., Christ, who when He was evilly treated opened not His mouth.[6] Furthermore, [we are taught in order that] the Scriptural passage regarding the patience of the saints[7] might be, for us, instruction in patience and in the way in which the saints had this patience.

[5] Likewise, let us further consult the Scriptural passage, which after the mention of patience mentions consolation, as in the case of Job and the others, but especially as in the case of Christ; for "on account of this [patient, humble obedience] God exalted Christ and gave Him a name that is above every other name."[8] From these Scriptural passages we are taught that those who have greater patience expect the greater consolation. Thus, because of the consolation, we will exhibit patience with equanimity; and so, from patience and consolation we shall have the hope of obtaining the reward of saints.

[6] Patience is a virtue which, according to Tully,[9] consists in the fact that over an extended period of time one endures with equanimity difficult and dreadful things because of usefulness and honorableness. Therefore, patience is present amid hardships; and although, properly speaking, patience is a forbearing of harm that is inflicted from an external source, nevertheless it can also have to do with hardship which the old man[10] inflicts, since it [also] concerns temptations that arise from the flesh. [7] For man is of a rational and an animal nature; and the one is from above and the other from below. Accordingly, man is, as it were, of fire and of water. Insofar as he is animal, he is like water; and insofar as he is immaterial, he is like fire. Accordingly, in the order of nature [fire and water] are opposed [to each other]; but with respect to man's constitution they are united. Hence, man is a union of natures that have in themselves different laws and motions. Yet, this union, or love, is in continual conflict. And so, the virtue that pacifies the conflict is called patience. [8] It is a virtue for the following reason: the soul loves the body; and when the soul cannot please the body with regard to bodily desires but, rather, resists the body—which it loves—lest by satisfying the desire of the sensory life the soul lose the rational life: then the soul comports itself patiently. For the soul suffers because it cannot satisfy the one it loves. Thus, when the law of reason commands things that are vexations to the flesh, and when the observer of the law inflicts this vexation on his own body, [doing so, however,] with good intent: then he acts virtuously.

[9] Patience is a virtue by means of which a man governs himself. As our Teacher says: "In your patience you shall possess your souls."[11] Patience can, not unfittingly, be spoken of as knowing how to suffer. Now, consolation coincides with sorrow, even as Christ said that the saints' sorrow would be turned into joy.[12] For sorrow contains within itself joy. Unless in the one who is patient there were joyous consolation, [patience] would not be a virtue. Patience is a noble kind of overcoming, for he-who-bears-with-patience overcomes and plunges the enemies' spears into the enemies' hearts. The-one-who-bears-with-patience conquers the enemy, demons, and himself. [10] The patient soul is like a salamander, which is nourished by the fire of tribulation; and it is like an ostrich, swallowing down a piece of iron; and it is like a piece of gold placed in mortar, where it is purified. Gregory says: "we can be martyrs if we truly keep patience in mind."[13] Therefore, the patience that is written about and the consolation which is subsequently mentioned teach us that we ought to have confidence in our attaining the reward.

[11] The text [under consideration] can also be read with a different punctuation, so that there is said "Whatever things were written for our learning ...," so that then, after a punctuation-mark has been made, there is added "... were written in order that through patience and the consolation ...," etc.[14] Thus, by means of the punctuation-mark the universal [clause] "whatever things ... for our learning" is modified. And, in this case, [the referent] can be only Sacred Scripture, which was written for Christians' learning; and the height of learning is to arrive at true hope by way of patience and consolation. Now, when the Gospel and the sacred books of the Bible speak of *Scripture*, they speak only of the writing that is contained in the canon of the Bible. And if the intent [of a Biblical writer] is [to speak] of another writing, then that [other writing] is *specified*—as Paul in Acts 17 says "... as certain of your poets [stated] ...," etc.[15] [12] Paul prays subsequently that God, the Giver of patience and of solace, grant to the Romans to be of one mind in accordance with the teachings of Jesus Christ—[grant it] in order that they with one mind and one mouth might glorify God the Father of our Lord Jesus Christ.[16] {Unanimity is the rule of Christ's disciples. (John 13: "In this respect all know that you are my disciples: viz., if you love one another."[17] "For we, being many, are one body in Christ" (Romans 12).[18] And when we are gathered together, we more readily obtain what we seek. (Machabees 3: "The assembly was gathered as a large number ready for battle in

order to pray and to seek mercy."[19] Matthew 18: "If two or three of you shall agree ...," etc.[20])} [Paul] uses the words "with one mouth" because every creature obeys God, to whom it gives honor. (For [God] is worthy of receiving glory and honor, because He created all things (Apocalypse 4).)[21] *A fortiori* [God ought to be glorified by all] rational men, who are supposed to imitate angels, who do not cease giving glory to God (Apocalypse 7).[22]

[13] Moreover, do not neglect to note that God is the Giver of patience (of which the Apostle intends to speak) and likewise of solace. Accordingly, the Apostle is not speaking about that patience of which Tully [wrote] in his *On Rhetoric*;[23] rather, he is speaking about that divine patience which motivates a man to desire[24] hardships unto the end that the virtue of patience may increase in him in order that he may be proved. And together with this patience solace increases—as the Apostles went out from the council (when the sentence of death was brought against them), rejoicing because they were worthy to suffer reproaches for the name of Jesus.[25] [14] And because [Paul] prayed for like-mindedness ("... to be of one mind according to Jesus Christ"[26])—i.e., prayed that they conduct themselves in the manner in which Christ conducts Himself toward them—he adds: "wherefore receive one another as Christ has received you"[27] (i.e., he added that one [person] have concern for another). And in this regard there ought to be no difference between those who have come to faith from Judaism and those who have come from paganism; rather, each Christian ought to care about the good of his brother. [Paul] declares[28] that for the sake of the truth of the promise that was made to the Jewish patriarchs Christ came as one sent to them. Christ preached to them, and He received them[29] in order to honor God; but out of mercy He admitted the Gentiles to the same [fellowship].

[15] And note that Paul cites the Psalm: "Therefore, I will give You glory among the Gentiles."[30] Christ gives glory to God the Father among the Gentiles, as also among believing Jews. Therefore, Christ, i.e., His mystical body, is what manifests God and praises Him. Therefore, no nation except the Christian nation rightly manifests God. (A Christian nation is said to *be* Christ because in Him they *are* Him.)[31] Christ manifests; Christ praises; Christ is rewarded—just as if a military general, under whose command the army serves, were to say that he does the things that the army does. [16] And so, note that the prophets took on the person of Christ in representing Him when they

prophesied. For in this way the prophet who said "I will give You glory among the Gentiles" said—in the person of Christ, whom he saw from afar—that he would praise God his Father among the Gentiles. Understand in a similar way the words of the other prophets: [e.g.,] "I have given my face to smiters"[32] and "O God, my God, look [upon me] ...," etc.[33] And consider, with respect to all the prophets when they assume the person of Christ, that they speak as those who represent Christ—as if the Spirit of Christ then possessed them and as if through them the Spirit of Christ spoke.

[17] The Apostle [Paul] concludes his prayer: "May the God of hope fill you with all peace and joy in believing, so that you may abound in hope and in the power of the Holy Spirit."[34] You know that God is a God of patience, a God of solace, and a God of hope. God is the one who alone can fill souls with all peace and joy in believing. For faith is a gift of God.[35] The fact that we believe the truth is not an individual gift of God, because *reason* cannot dissent from truth. But the fact that I believe the one who speaks the truth is a gift of God and is a grace. I say "the one speaking the truth," which truth I do not recognize of myself. For I come to the truth through the word of the speaker; I would not come to this truth unless there were given to me by God that I believe the speaker.[36] [18] [Paul] says next: "... so that you may abound in hope."[37] For [hope is] from the peaceful unity of faith.[38] That is, where faith is filled with peace and joy, it is perfect and vital and [in-]formed [by love]. Herefrom follows the abundance of hope. And the power of the Holy Spirit is present; for faith increases the power of the soul, because faith is the power of the Holy Spirit, whose gift it is. (Romans 8: The Spirit helps our infirmity and asks [on our behalf]—i.e., causes [us] to ask ..., etc.)[39]

[19] "Whatever things were written were written for our learning." Bonaventure in his *Illuminations* likens Scripture to water. According to him the vision of an intellect that has been made learned by means of Scripture is what is meant by "the work of the third day," when God divided the water from dry land and called the gatherings of the waters *oceans* and saw that [the work] was good and said "Let the earth bring forth the green herb."[40] For the fountain that waters the Paradise is Scripture, which waters the earth, wherein is the seed of the Tree-of-life, i.e., of the rational spirit.

[20] If we pay attention, then [we see that] Scripture is as water, which by means of the sun's heat causes there to come more quickly

into actuality that which is present in the potency of the seed that is sown in the earth. And just as the heat of the sun by means of water causes the seed to be fruitful, so God's Spirit, which is called the Spirit of Wisdom, by means of Scripture causes the intellectual seed to be fruitful. For as water is a suitable intermediary between the sun's heat and the earth—and, thus, water is above and below the firmament,[41] so that it is a suitable intermediary that cooperates with the warmth of the sun for enlivening the seed—so, too, Scripture [is an intermediary]. [21] Hence, we ought to take note in Scripture of the fact that the invisible ray of the Sun of Justice[42] and of Wisdom was rendered diffuse on account of our infirmity—we who cannot stand to view it in its brightness.[43] Thus, we are able to apprehend [it only] by means of Scripture's mirror and Scripture's symbolisms and its signs and figures—even as the substantial form that perfects a thing is not visible to the sensory eye and, thus, shines forth in a visible befiguring, so that in this way it is attained in the best way it can be.

[**22**] Therefore, the Apostle rightly said in II Timothy 3 that a Scriptural-text, being divinely inspired, is useful for perfecting the man of God.[44] And the Jews rightly believed that they had from Scripture the life of the soul. Yet, they did not understand this life to consist in the Spirit-of-Wisdom that was hidden in them, viz., the Spirit of Jesus. And so, our Teacher sent them back to search the Scriptures, [and] He revealed that those Scriptures that contain the word of life are about Him (John 5).[45]

[**23**] Moreover, consider that Holy Scripture is as water that is impregnated by the celestial spirit for the fruitfulness of the earth. Nature has made water to be a means whereby the generation that is due to the influence of the heavens can occur on earth. By analogy, the intellectual nature [makes] the Scriptures [to be a means of fruitfulness for the intellectual spirit]. Hence, the Scriptures are from the intellectual nature's art in order that one intellect can impart to another the inspiration of the divine ray, [doing so] for the glory of God and the perfection of the rational nature. [**24**] For [the art of] writing is a means whereby a concept is manifest for the instruction of men (both present and absent) of the past, the present, and the future. For it is necessary that the intellect be informed by means of some experience, so that it becomes fit for inquiring. For example, if I have a seed, I cannot know what will come from it if it is planted, unless experience in the past shows me this or unless it shows someone else who teaches me this.

[25] Man cannot foresee future things except on the basis of a knowledge of things past. And so, a knowledge of things past is necessary for man—just as Ptolemy from the observations of Abrachis and Tymochardis regarding the movement of the planets discovered conjectural rules concerning their future movements;[46] and so on. Therefore, it is necessary that man know past things (and know those things which have been observed for a long time) in order more assuredly to make inferences about future things. And for the following reason the first men lived long lives (as Josephus reports in the *Book of Antiquities*):[47] [viz.,] so that from the long experience of 600 years they could investigate the movement-of-the-heavens and other [phenomena] and so that their experience could become known to their descendants. [26] The assistance of writing was given (by means of which assistance one era is linked to another) in order that by this implement man might in a "mirror," so to speak, see past things and things which are behind him—things from which he profits. And by means of this assistance, viz., writing, one who is physically dead speaks to one who is living and one who is absent speaks to one who is present. For, assuredly, [writing] is a divine device whereby all eras and ages, and whereby the world's learned men who have existed, and whereby divine illuminations and human inventions from earlier times, are still present to each intellect and still vital for the intellect's perfection. For example, the spirit of Paul in his epistles lives on for our instruction. It teaches and perfects us by means of the writing. Something similar holds true as regards all other [writings].

[27] Therefore, whatever things were written for our learning were written in such a way (1) that we are therefrom certain that the spirit of the writer is of an immortal nature and (2) that the life of the spirit does not depend on the written characters but, on the contrary, this spirit gives [life] to the written characters, so that they are Paul's epistle. The case is similar for all writings. Hence, we know that the intellectual spirit is not bound to the written character or to the paper or to a location. Accordingly, whatever things were written for our learning show that the one who is teaching us by means of the writing is an incorruptible spirit. [28] But from the different kinds of teaching we apprehend the different perfections of the [rational] spirits. For example, one teaching is crude and childish, another is more refined; but only in the teaching of Christ do we apprehend that the Spirit of Jesus is the most perfect Spirit of instruction-about-true-and-eternal-life. This Spirit does not teach by means of human *surmisings* but

teaches on the basis of a very certain *seeing*. For those things which Jesus's Spirit saw to be with God the Father, our Originator and Creator—these things are revealed by Him.

[**29**] Hence, all the teachings of whatsoever others, come from hearing and are surmisings. Only Christ's teaching comes from seeing and, thus, is true and certain; and so, it is unchangeable and eternal. For heaven and earth (as He says) shall pass away, but His words shall not.[48] The teachings of all others [besides Christ] are surmises about the teachings of Christ. Among these other teachings there is discrepancy and is unsteadfastness. For surmise partakes of truth to greater and lesser degrees; but it is not truth. About this fact the Apostle speaks elegantly in I Corinthians 1, [when he says], in particular, that the happiness-that-salvation-is is attained not by the prudence of the prudent but by the simplicity of faith, which is esteemed by the prudent of this world to be foolishness.[49] [**30**] Aristotle, not without reason, named [that] book of his which we call *The Book of Physics* "On What Has Been Heard about Physical Nature." [He did so] perhaps for the following reason: that he arrived at very strong certainty[50] only by means of surmising inferences, in the human manner. Hence, if you rightly discern, [you see that] Christ's instruction is a perfection that enfolds all instruction; for it is instruction about the reason for which God made the world.[51] No one ever doubted that every investigation centers on the Cause of things and that if that Cause were apprehended, then there would be had [the fulfillment of] every desire on the part of the intellect; there would be had the ultimate goal: rest and happiness.

[**31**] Therefore, that light of the Word of God illumines all instruction and is not confined. And all the things discovered by the philosophers have no light except from a partaking of that light [of the Word of God]. Hence, the saints' teachings, in which the light of Jesus's teachings is received, are not theirs but are Christ's; for the saints make known no other teachings than Christ's, which they have received. Therefore, just as in their teachings there live only the teachings of Christ, so in their spirit there lives only the Spirit of Jesus. Thus, Paul in this Chapter 15 [of Romans] admits that he can do nothing except that which Christ works in him.[52] Therefore, in the writings of Paul there lives the Spirit that is concealed in[53] him; and [concealed] in him is the Spirit-of-Jesus, the Author of life (even as in the teachings of a student of Plato's Plato the teacher [is present concealedly]).

[32] Regarding the fruitfulness of Scripture and its multiple senses, see Bonaventure, in the [afore-]mentioned place,[54] for he writes subtly. But in order today to minister to the common people something that will serve as needed food, let us by following Scripture's light, which illumines the darkness, investigate other sacred writers in terms of their writings on (1) uncreated foreknowledge, (2) innate conscience, (3) inspired knowledge, and (4) incarnate wisdom.

[33] *About the first [topic], the Book of life*: Luke 10: "Rejoice, for your names are written ...," etc.[55] We ought to see to it that our names are written in the Book of life. For this Book is a Book of joy and of an immortal Kingdom. In this Book are written not [the names of] the lowly but [the names of] kings; for in it God has written [the names of] all those who will co-reign with His Son. Woe to those whose [names are] not written there, because their [names] are in the Book of death! And know that in the Book of life are written down [the names of] those whose life the life of Jesus characterizes. Therefore, there are [the names of] no sinners there, because Christ committed no sin, nor was deceit found in His mouth.[56] [34] It is evident that usurers, fornicators, adulterers, and other [such] ones are not named in the Book of life. Rather, their names are blotted out of God's memory. They themselves are cast out of God's memory (which is life) into outer darkness. (Apocalypse 20: Whosoever's [name] was not found in the Book of life, he was cast into the pool of fire.[57] Those whose [names] are not written in the Book of predestination are written in the Book of reprobation. (Isaias 65: "Behold, it is written before me. I will not be silent but will render and repay into their bosom their iniquities.")[58] Behold, the fact that [their names] have been written shows that they are not so dead that they do not exist but that they are damned.

[35] *About the second [topic]*: Romans 2: "When the Gentiles, who do not have the Law ...," etc., "they show the work of the Law written in their hearts, with their conscience bearing witness to them."[59] Accordingly, no one can excuse himself on the grounds that he does not know the Scriptures, since he has them in his heart. For just as the Ten Commandments are on the tablets in the Ark [of the Covenant] in the Tabernacle, so the natural law is in the conscience. Conscience is in the soul; the soul is in the body. But conscience is destroyed by sin; it is repaired by grace. (Hebrews 8: "I will place my laws in their hearts and will inscribe them in their minds.")[60] [36] In

the Book of conscience is written not only the natural law but also what is done in accordance with it.[61] Moreover, those things which are done in accordance with the law of nature are written [in conscience] with a golden pen; and those things which [are done] against [the law of nature are written in conscience] with an iron pen. (Jeremias 17: "The sin of Judah is written with a pen of iron, with the point of a diamond"[62] (that is, [is written] on an obstinate heart)). And on the Day of Judgment all will read that writing, because the reason for the condemnation will be known to all.

[**37**] *About the third* [*topic*]: II Timothy 3: "All Scripture, inspired of God, ...," etc.[63] Comply with these Scriptures in living rightly—if you wish for [eternal] life. {(Luke 10: " 'Master, what shall I do to have eternal life?' Jesus said: 'What is written in the Law? ...'," etc.[64]) Woe to the transgressors of the Law! (Galatians 3: "It is written: 'cursed is everyone who does not abide in all the things which are written in the Book of the Law and who will not do them.' "[65])} Note that [Paul] uses the word "inspired"; hereby it is evident that [Scripture] was sent from Heaven. And so, just as exiles and pilgrims are consoled by letters sent to them from their homeland by their loved-ones, so [Christ's] beloved-ones [receive consolation] from Divine Scripture. However, the following is a sign that they do not belong to the Heavenly Homeland: [viz., that] they have no interest in the Scriptures and do not comply with them.

[**38**] *About the fourth* [*topic*]: Psalms [44]: "My tongue is a scribe's pen ...," etc.[66] The Holy Spirit is designated by [the symbolism of] the tongue and by the [symbolism of] the pen, by means of which pen the Word (who was conceived in the womb [of Mary]) is being written about. And the scroll that Ezechiel saw:[67] it was written-on inside and out ..., etc. Who could know how much wisdom there is on the inside and how many examples are written on the outside? Nonetheless, we ought always to read [this scroll]; and we shall find [described] in it the lamentation [that is] in the world, the song [that is] in Heaven, and the woe [that will occur] on the [Day of] Judgment.[68]

NOTES TO *Quaecumque Scripta Sunt*

* Sermon CCLIV.

1. Romans 15:4: "For what things soever were written were written for our learning in order that through patience and the consolation of the Scriptures we might have hope."
2. Romans 15:3. Psalms 68:10 (69:9).
3. Romans 15:1.
4. Genesis 17:1. In the printed edition of the Latin text, at **3**:6, I am regarding "ideo", which some manuscripts omit, as deleted.
5. Romans 8:32.
6. Isaias (Isaiah) 53:7.
7. Apocalypse (Revelation) 14:12.
8. Philippians 2:9. Not an exact quotation.
9. Cicero, *De Inventione Rhetorica*, II, 163.
10. Ephesians 4:22.
11. Luke 21:19.
12. John 16:20.
13. Not an exact quotation. Gregory the Great, *XL Homiliarum in Evangelia,* Homily XXXV, 7 (*PL* 76:1263 D).
14. "… in order that through patience and the consolation of the Scriptures we might have hope." Romans 15:4. Note the difference between (a) "Quaecumque enim scripta sunt, ad nostram doctrinam scripta sunt: ut per patientiam, et consolationem Scripturarum spem habeamus" and (b) "Quaecumque enim scripta sunt ad nostram doctrinam, scripta sunt ut per patientiam …," etc.
15. Acts 17:28.
16. Romans 15:5-6.
17. John 13:35. Not an exact quotation.
18. Romans 12:5.
19. I Machabees 3:44. Not an exact quotation.
20. Matthew 18:19-20. Not an exact quotation.
21. Apocalypse (Revelation) 4:11.
22. Apocalypse (Revelation) 7:11.
23. See n. 9 above.
24. Here (at **13**:5) I am reading, with *Codex Vaticanus Latinus* 1245, "desideret" in place of the printed Latin text's "desiderent".
25. Acts 15:41.
26. Romans 15:5.
27. Romans 15:7.
28. Romans 15:8.
29. Here (at **14**:12) I am reading "eos" in place of "vos".
30. Psalms 17:50 (18:49). Romans 15:9.
31. Here (at **15**:7) I am reading the manuscript's word "id" as an abbreviation for "idem". See *Codex Vaticanus Latinus* 1245.
32. Isaias (Isaiah) 50:6. Not an exact quotation.
33. Psalms 21:2 (22:1).

34. Romans 15:13.
35. Ephesians 2:8.
36. Cf. Augustine, *Contra Epistolam Manichaei*, V, 6 (*PL* 42:176): "Ego vero Evangelio non crederem, nisi me catholicae Ecclesiae commoveret auctoritas."
37. Romans 15:13.
38. "... ex pace fidei...." Nicholas uses "De Pace Fidei" as the title of one of his treatises.
39. Romans 8:26.
40. Genesis 1:9-13. Saint Bonaventure, *Collationes in Hexaëmeron sive Illuminationes Ecclesiae*, XIII, 3 (Vol. V of *S. Bonaventurae Opera Omnia* (Quaracchi, 1891), p. 388ª. An English translation of this passage may be found in *The Works of Bonaventure*, Vol. V: *Collations on the Six Days*, translated by José de Vinck (Paterson, NJ: St. Anthony Guild, 1970), p. 184.
41. Genesis 1:7.
42. Malachias (Malachi) 4:2.
43. The ray is invisible because it is too resplendent for the human eye to gaze upon. See Cusa's *Apologia Doctae Ignorantiae* 12.
44. II Timothy 3:16-17. The Apostle says that *all* Scripture ....
45. John 5:39.
46. Abrachis (i.e., Hipparchus, ca. 150 B.C.) and Tymochardis (or Timocharis, ca. 295 B.C.) were Greek astronomers whose observations were used by Ptolemy. See Paul Kunitzsch, *Der Almagest. Die Syntaxis Mathematica des Claudius Ptolemäus in arabisch-lateinischer Überlieferung* (Wiesbaden: Harrassowitz, 1974), p. 160.
47. Flavius Josephus, *Antiquities of the Jews*, I, 3, 9 (p. 18 of Vol. I in the series *Complete Works of Josephus* (New York: Bigelow, Brown, & Co., n.d.). Revised from Havercamp's translation. (No reviser named.) See also Genesis 5. Note also *The Latin Josephus: Introduction and Text: The Antiquities: Books I – V*, edited by Franz Blatt (Kopenhagen: University of Aarhus Press, 1958 [in the series *Acta Jutlandica*, Vol. XXX], pp. 136-137 (= *Antiquitates*, I, 3, 9)
48. Matthew 24:35 and elsewhere.
49. I Corinthians 1:19-24.
50. Re Nicholas's term "infallibilitas" and its meaning see pp. 10-12 of my *Hugh of Balma on Mystical Theology: A Translation and an Overview of His De Theologia Mystica*. (Minneapolis: Banning, 2002).
51. Hebrew 1:2.
52. Romans 15:17-18.
53. Here (at **31**:13) I am reading, with the Paris edition, "in eo latens" in place of "eo latens".
54. See n. 40 above. Saint Bonaventure, *Collationes in Hexaëmeron, op. cit.,* XIII, 2.
55. "... that your names are written in Heaven." Luke 10:20.
56. I Peter 2:22. Isaias (Isaiah 53:9).
57. Apocalypse (Revelation) 20:15.
58. Isaias (Isaiah) 65:6-7.
59. Romans 2: 14-15: "When the Gentiles, who have not the Law, do by nature those things that are in the Law: these, having not the Law, are a law unto themselves. They show the work of the Law written in their hearts, their conscience bearing wit-

ness to them."
    60. Hebrews 8:10.
    61. Here (at **36**:2) I am reading "quod" (with *Codex Vaticanus Latinus* 1245) in place of the printed Latin text's "quodam modo". Moreover, I follow *Codex Magdeburg* 38 in adding "secundum". Thus, I am reading "... quod secundum eam fit."
    62. Jeremias (Jeremiah) 17:1.
    63. II Timothy 3:16.
    64. Luke 10:25-26. Not an exact quotation.
    65. Galatians 3:10. Not an exact quotation.
    66. Psalms 44:2 (45:1).
    67. Ezechiel (Ezekiel) 2:9.
    63. *Loc. cit.*

Non Diligamus Verbo neque Lingua*
("Let Us Love Not in Word or with Lip-Service ....")
[June 8, 1455; preached in Stegen (near Bruneck)]

[1] "Let us love not in word or with lip-service but in deed and in truth."[1] ([Passage found] in [the reading] of the epistle for Sunday.)[2] John says in the canonical first epistle, Chapter 3: "Marvel not, if the world hates you. We know that we have passed from death unto life, for we love the brethren."[3] He says later, in Chapter 5, that the entire world is situated in wickedness.[4] And because true Christians are not of this world[5] (although they are in the world), it is not surprising if the world hates them.[6] For as Jesus says, the world loves that which is its own.[7] Likewise, it is not strange—Jesus says to His apostles—if the world hates you, because it previously hated me.[8]

[2] Now, from the fact that the world hates us, we can know that we have passed from death unto life, for we love the brethren.[9] For this love is a clear sign that we are sons of God, because, as [John] says earlier,[10] in Chapter 1: "he who loves his brother abides in the light."[11] Keep in mind [the following]: when the world hates us who are Christians (even though we love as brothers those who hate us), then we know that we have passed from death unto life. He who does not love abides in death. For example, everyone who hates his brother is a murderer,[12] and such a one does not have eternal life abiding in him.[13] Accordingly, if hatred [works] death, then love works life. But it is necessary that love be perfect, i.e., necessary that we love our neighbor as God [loves] us—even as, also, consummate hatred enfolds murder. For in the will of him who hates is [the intent] that the one-whom-he-hates not live. So, then, this [hate-filled one] is a murderer, even as he who lusts after his neighbor's wife has already committed adultery in his heart, as says the Savior.[14] But Jesus, who is both God and a man loved us with perfect love, because He laid down His life for us; and we ought to do likewise, viz., lay down our life for our brothers.[15] And when we act as we are obliged to act—[obliged] since Christ's every action is our instruction and since we ought[16] to walk as Christ walked (as [John] says earlier[17])—then we know that we have passed from death unto life, because we have perfect love for our neighbor.

[3] Assuredly, he who loves his brother, with whom he has a common Father, viz., God—[he who loves him] because of the fact

that he is his brother [and who loves him] even if the brother hate him—loves God exceedingly. For in that case he loves him on account of God, who is the Father of both; for the love of the brother *qua* brother is related to the Father. And when, like Christ, someone loves even his enemy to such an extent that he dies for him because he is his brother, then he especially loves the Father; for he loves the brother only on account of the Father; therefore, he loves the Father more greatly. Accordingly, he receives the reward of life if he dies for his brother's sake. Therefore, he who loves his brother perfectly has rightly passed from death unto life (for such love is as strong as is death);[18] and so, he [who loves perfectly] has the [same] reward as if he had undergone death for his brother.

However, consider the fact that John does not say "neighbor" but says "brother". For although a neighbor can be called a brother, nevertheless John asserted that a *brother* (rather than a neighbor) is to be loved perfectly—[asserted it] so that we might see that in the love of a brother the love of God the Father is contained antecedently. He who lays down his life (i.e., his temporal life) for his brother overcomes the world. For he chooses to please God the Father, so that he saves his brother[19] even if he must lose his own life thereby. Such a man, by losing this [earthly] life—[a life] called animal from *"anima"*[20]—finds eternal [life]. Hence, note that we are under obligation to lay down our life for our brothers (i.e., for the salvation of our brothers). For in order that [their respective soul] not perish eternally, we ought to undergo temporal death—in the example of Christ, who died temporally in order that we not die eternally.

[4] Next, [John] adds another stage of love, when he says: he who has the goods of this world and who sees that his brother is in need and who closes his heart to him: how is it that the love of God abides in him?[21] For the goods of this world ought not to be preferred to the needs of a brother. Tight-fistedness with regard to the goods of the world, when one's brother is in need [of them], is an evident sign that the [tight-fisted one] is a miser and has not renounced the world. Instead, it is evident that his soul clings to the goods of the world. The law of love does not command that I should give my life in order that my *neighbor* not die *temporally*; rather, in order that [my neighbor] not die *eternally*, I ought rather to choose temporal death [for myself].[22] Next, the law [of love] commands that lest my brother die temporally, I ought rather to choose to lose [those] of this world's goods without which I will be able to continue to live temporally. When I do not do

this, then it is a sign that my life, which I am not required to forfeit [through my sacrifice], clings to the goods of the world, with the consequence that I cannot abandon them. Hence, it is evident that I am a miser and that my soul is glued to the goods of [this] world; and I worship those goods as constituting my soul's happiness. Therefore, I am an idolater; and in me is not love (*caritas*) of God but love (*amor*) of the world's goods.[23] Consider the fact that [John] infers that love for God is not present in one who shuts up his heart to a brother. So if one does *not* shut up [his heart], then love for God is present in his love for the brother—as was said. [5] Hence, [John] concludes [by] saying: "My little children, let us love not in word or with lip-service but in deed and in truth."[24] For he who says that he loves but who does not evidence it in his deeds does not love in truth. Rather, he is a liar and serves as a soldier not under Truth but under the father of lying and wickedness;[25] and he will not see eternal life.

[6] The Gospel instructs us, concerning a dinner, how it is that we are invited to a dinner that has been prepared by a [fellow]-human being [*homo*].[26] For unless a [fellow]-human being prepared and invited, we would not be motivated [to come]. For a human being is motivated only with respect to community with [other] human beings;[27] for [man] is a political and civic animal that delights in community [with others]. But community comes under a single species; for without oneness there is no community. Therefore, the natural desire for community comes under a oneness of species. Accordingly, Jesus, who has made a dinner of eternal partaking, is a man who has prepared so much food that all men would be able to be fed. Hence, He has invited many;[28] an indeterminate multitude has been invited. Now, it can[29] be understood that they are *invited* only if they are invited by *someone*. The Word of God, by which our spirit lives,[30] put on human nature in order to be able to invite man to a meal. [The situation is] as if some new and precious branch-of-learning (*ars*) were to take on human form in order to be able to summon men to its content-of-learning.

[7] Hence, [the parable] describes how it is that those who are invited—those who are entangled in the temporal affairs of this world—make excuses. No one who serves God as a soldier is entangled in worldly affairs;[31] and, conversely, he who entangles himself in the affairs of this world does not pay attention to the things that are of God. If a student's mind is bound to carnal desire, then the student does not hear, with the ear of his mind, the words of the teacher; for he is

mentally distracted and is somewhere else [with his thoughts]. The concern that is in a man for the things that he desires draws his mind toward that which is desired, and it binds [him], with a strong bond, to that desired object. By way of illustration: one who focuses on visible features cannot easily understand a speaker, because his attention is not free but is fixed on visible features.

By way of [further] example: In the case of intense deliberation the mind takes on the form of that upon which it is deliberating; and it cannot be drawn away to other [objects of deliberation] unless it is first freed from the antecedent form—just as matter is not suited for receiving another form except by means of a discarding of its antecedent form. Therefore, in the case of intense and serious deliberation, the bond of love that arises between the soul and the loved-object that is being considered binds together the mind and that object. As Paul says: "he who is joined to a harlot is made one body with her; and he who is joined to God is made one spirit with God."[32] For with regard to God nothing can be considered other than spirit; and so, the loving mind is joined to Spirit, which is God. But with regard to a harlot nothing is considered other than body; thus, mind is made carnal. Hence, it is evident that those who are in this world and who walk amid its delights and who are interested in these delights are such that, although they are called away from the world's meal-of-delights unto the feast of eternal life, they do not hear the one inviting [them]. Rather, they make excuses, on the ground that they have things to do—[things] which are better than the things to which they are called. For they are saying that they are to be excused, at a time when they are not foregoing that which is preferable [to them].

[8] Now, the Gospel mentions worldly transactions that are undertaken with very great concern[33]—for example, as regards pride of dominion (e.g., in acquiring a farm) or as regards greediness (e.g., in the case of five yoke of oxen) or as regards the desire of the flesh (e.g., in the case of [taking] a wife). The Gospel states that all [these transactors] asked to be excused, because of preoccupation, [from coming to the dinner]. For one bought a farm; another, five yoke of oxen; a third married. (That is, according to common parlance, [the latter] procured a wife. For in that contract by which a husband gives himself to a wife and the wife [gives herself] to a husband; the husband procures a wife with his own body, because he gives himself in exchange for her; and, conversely, the wife is said to procure a husband, because she gives herself in exchange for him. And so, neither

of them retains proprietary-right over his own body but transfers it to the other—as, in a purchase, property or dominion is transferred.) Hence, in these business-transactions (which cannot be engaged in without mind, for business-transactions require a mind free [of clutter and preoccupation]) the mind is occupied by the business-dealings and eagerly longs to find out whether it has made a favorable transaction. [The situation is] as if one were to say: since I have made a purchase, then inasmuch as someone strongly desires to see what he has purchased, I am excused if I am interested in seeing it, probing it, and making use of it. Because, then, there results from a business-transaction [the outcome] that [the transaction] renders the transactor so very much concerned and intent: these business-dealings, which are especially prepossessing, do not permit [the transactor] to hear the voice of the inviter [to the feast].

[9] Now, the one who has prepared the dinner wills that it be eaten.[34] At the appropriate time he sends his heralds to summon the invitees. We are invited [to Christ's feast] when we are regenerated through the washing of baptism and through faith. Through servants we are invited prior to our death, prior to our demise; and so, all care is taken. But, at the same time, we all hide behind excuses—we who attend to the engrossing tasks of this world. But those who live in hamlets and villages and who are poor and weak: since they are not transacting business but since, rather, the world has become of no interest to them, they are suited to be led into [the dinner]. And there is no need of an invitation and a summoning, because temporal delights, which they lack, do not have a grip on them. And these individuals can be said to be teachable by God, [and] theirs is the Kingdom of God. (Nevertheless, the dinner is prepared not only for them but also for those who have not yet entered into the City of [this] world[35] but who are still in the cradle [or playpen], as are those baptized ones who have not yet come to use reason or who, if they *have*, have not [yet] sinned actually.) Such ones also come to the dinner but are not induced through rational persuasion but are impelled by the simplicity of faith. For faith does not guide by means of persuasion and reason; rather, it impels[36] [one]—in spite of his not understanding—to undertake the journey. And so, there are those who, in this last way, are impelled; and there are those who are not yet entangled in the delights of the world-community; and there are those who have abandoned the world's delights and are brought in. But entangled in the world's delights are those who, when invited and called, make excuses. And because they adduce excuses,

none of these who are called come to the dinner (as the Gospel states).[37]

[**10**] Please note that eternal life, which is consummate happiness, is always expressed in the Gospel in terms of the sending of God's word into the soul—[expressed], for example, through the sowing of seed in good earth[38] or through the nourishment of a prepared dinner[39] or through a treasure in a field[40] or through a finding of a pearl,[41] etc. Hence, our soul makes itself capable of the grace of receiving into itself the word of God; and the word, once planted in the soul as in good earth, bears fruit. A seed that is in the earth draws unto itself, from the earth, that by which it is nourished and by means of which it grows; suitable nourishment is converted into the vegetative life of the seed's nature. Similarly, the word of God draws from the soul what is suitable to itself, viz., the intellectual power, which is converted to the divine life of the word. And [the word] bears fruit in accordance with the soul's degree of goodness. Furthermore, note that our soul, in comparison with [God's] word, is called *earth*. Accordingly, the word of God is to the soul as the soul is to the body. For the soul is as the seed of life for the body, and it bears the good fruit of life in accordance with the condition of the body. Similarly, the word of God is the soul's seed-of-life, and it bears the good fruit-of-life in accordance with the condition of the soul. Now, the body has within it principles such that it can be enlivened. For otherwise it could not be brought to be actually alive—[brought] by the soul, which is alive actually and which brings into actuality the body's potentiality for being alive. Thus, [the soul] is the prime activator of the organic body, which has, potentially, an animal[42] life. In an analogous way, it must be the case that the word of God is the prime activator of a disposed soul, which potentially has divine life.

[**11**] Now, the disposition that is in the soul is called intellect. For the fact that the soul has the potency to receive the word-of-God (which is life) is due to the fact that the soul can understand. For if it could not understand, it would not be capable of receiving the word. Therefore, there is included in the soul a certain power, or potency, for a receiving of the word, or of wisdom. Hence, in the soul there are certain principles, even as in earth there are certain universal and interfused powers because of which earth is capable of receiving seed; and from these powers the seed draws nourishment and transfers the nourishment unto itself. Hence, from its own universal power the earth produces fruit. But there are thorns, thistles, and hay. (Hay is straw that

grows wild. For the earth produces from itself certain sheaves that grow wild; they are called hay, and they have a certain likeness to grain, but they are not food for the life of a rational animal but are food for beasts.) By analogy, the intellective soul has a power that enfolds universal principles by means of which it unfolds the natural fruit of the branches-of-learning [*scientiarum*]. Now, if good seed is sown in the earth and if the earth is good, then in accordance with the nature of the seed [the earth] brings forth much good fruit. Hence, [analogously], in accordance with the seed of the word, [the intellective soul] produces the fruit of the arts and the sciences. For example, from Plato's word—if it is received and preserved—[there comes] the fruit of Plato's knowledge, so that we may partake of Plato's intellect. And from Aristotle's word [there comes the fruit] of Aristotle's knowledge, so that we may conform ourselves to Aristotle's intellect. And so on. But from the word of God [there comes] a very perfect fruit: viz., an understanding of the most perfect Intelligible Being, viz., God.

[**12**] Moreover, consider [the following]: From the fact that our Teacher, Jesus, speaks the word of God as a seed, insofar as [the seed] falls into our soul: in the word that is received in the soul there is, in potentiality, that of which the seed is [a seed]. (By analogy, in the seed of a tree there is the tree, in potentiality.) Accordingly, in a receiving of God's word in the soul, there is received, in potentiality, the divine understanding [of that] of which the seed is [a seed]. Moreover, in order that a seed in the earth produce fruit, the seed must be activated, in order that the fruit of the seed be brought from potentiality into actuality. For example, the seed of a tree is activated to become like the tree from which it had its being a seed. And this [activation] is wrought by means of celestial heat, from which comes the activation, because [the activation] arises from the movement of the heavens. In a similar way: by means of divine warmth—i.e., by means of Love, or the Holy Spirit—the seed of God's word is activated to become like Him whose seed it is. Therefore, the word of the Son of God, when it becomes active, grows into a likeness of the Son of God.

[**13**] And consider that that very lofty theologian says [the following]: When the Son of God—He who is in us by His word, or seed—shall appear to us, then we shall be like Him.[43] It is as if the *form* of a tree's seed were an *intellectual seed* having an arboreal form (since the form of the tree of which it is a seed would be present in it). In that case, [the intellectual seed] would conform itself to this [arbo-

real form] by passing from potentiality to actuality; and this [transformation] would occur noticeably. Our intellect is like a universal seed for forms [*species*]; and when a certain form appears to it by means of perceptual images, then the intellect is "in-formed" and is made like that [form];[44] for [in regard to this form the universal seed] is brought, by the light of the active intellect, from potentiality unto actuality. But if the intellect, i.e., the power of the soul, is indued with a higher and supernatural power, viz., faith, and if the intellect takes into itself the word of God, then the universal seed for natural forms becomes a divine seed that is formed from the seed of God's word. And so, the [universal] seed for created forms becomes a [divine] seed of the Creator of forms.[45] Therefore, the word of God is a seed, and it turns into itself the intellectual power (which is a seed for forms) so that [that power] becomes a seed of the Form of forms.[46]

In the earth there is a universal power of seeds; and when a seed is sown in it, the seed turns that universal power into itself, so that the power which was earthly accords now with the nature of the seed that was sown in it. Let it be the case, then, that that seed which is strewn into earth is a seed for the fruit of all fruit and, hence, is the seed of all seeds. In that case, it would convert into itself all the seminal power of earth; for the power of that seed would occupy the whole of the earth and would diffuse itself throughout the entire power of earth. In an analogous way, the word of God, received by the soul of a believer, is diffused throughout his entire intellective power; and it draws [that power] unto itself. And in this way intellect comes to be attracted into the word of God, or seed of God, so that it becomes like God, whose seed it has been made by the word.

[14] And note that our Teacher compared the rational soul—which is capable of receiving God's word—to earth, from which seeds draw nutriments. But the nutriments are transformed into the nature of that which is nourished. Hence, the vegetative life, which makes what is potentially vegetable to be actually vegetable, furnishes the earth with plant life rather than the earth's furnishing life. [The vegetative life] attracts in order to enliven; and by nature [earth] seeks to be enlivened. And so, it does not resist, but obeys, the attracting. Similarly, the divine life in the word, or seed, seems to be nourished from the rational soul's power, which passes into the seed. But, nevertheless, this [phenomenon] is nothing but the fact that the vegetative life of the divine seed becomes present in the rational soul's power, which is called intellect.

NOTES TO *Non Diligamus Verbo neque Lingua*

* Sermon CXC.
1. I John 3:18
2. *Loc. cit.*
3. I John 3:13-14.
4. I John 5:19.
5. John 15:19.
6. I John 3:13.
7. John 15:19.
8. John 15:18.
9. I John 3:14.
10. Here (at **2**:5) I am correcting the printed edition of the Latin text so as to read "supra" instead of "Sapientia".
11. I John 2:10 (not Chapter 1, as Nicholas misremembers).
12. I John 3:15. Cf. Matthew 5:22.
14. Matthew 5:28.
15. I John 3:16.
16. Here (at **2**:27) I am surmising "debeamus" in place of "debemus".
17. I John 2:6.
18. Canticle of Canticles (Song of Solomon) 8:6.
19. Nicholas is here speaking of saving the brother's soul, not of saving his temporal life. See the passage marked by n. 22 below.
20. The Latin word *"anima"* is translatable both as *soul* and as *life*. Insofar as the human body is alive, it has *animal* life, i.e., life that is due to the animating (enlivening) soul.
21. I John 3:17.
22. See n. 19 above.
23. Although oftentimes Nicholas uses *"caritas"* and *"amor"* interchangeably—as when he speaks of *caritas Dei* or *amor Dei*, he never speaks of *caritas mundi* but rather of *amor mundi*.
24. I John 3:18.
25. John 8:44.
26. Luke 14:16-24.
27. Aristotle, *De Politica*, I, 2 (1253^{a}2-3).
28. Luke 14:16.
29. Here (at **6**:14) I am surmising "potest" in place of "possunt".
30. Matthew 4:4. Deuteronomy 8:3.
31. II Timothy 2:3-4.
32. I Corinthians 6:16.
33. Luke 14:18-20.
34. Luke 14:17.
35. Nicholas is here alluding to Augustine's distinction, in *De Civitate Dei*, between two cities: the earthly city and the heavenly city.
36. Luke 14:23 uses the Greek aorist imperative ἀνάγκασον, which the Vulgate translates as *"compelle"*. In the passage above, which reflects Luke 14:23,

Nicholas too uses forms of the infinitive "*compellere*". I have translated these forms by "impel," since, obviously, no one is *compelled* by faith. Etc.

    37. Luke 14:16-20.
    38. Matthew 13:3-9.
    39. Luke 14:16-24.
    40. Matthew 13:44.
    41. Matthew 13:45-46.
    42. See n. 20 above.
    43. I John 3:2.
    44. Nicholas here articulates the Aristotelian theme that a passive intellect receives the universal form that the active intellect abstracts from perceptual images. This theme is developed a bit (though never extensively) in *De Mente* (e.g., *De Mente* 4 and 7).
    45. See *De Mente* 2 (62-65), where Nicholas uses the example of a spoon, which is a utensil that represents a new species, one not found in nature. Such artefacts and such new forms are created by the human mind. In this way, the creating mind, notes Nicholas, imitates God's creating of natural forms.
    46. The human mind does not become the Form of forms (viz., God) but becomes like the Form of forms—i.e., becomes Godlike in becoming a son of God (John 1:12), in becoming "deified." See Nicholas's *De Filiatione Dei*.

Suadeo Tibi Emere a Me
Aurum Ignitum et Probatum*
("I Counsel You To Buy from Me Fire-tried Gold.")[1]
[August 28, 1456; preached in Navacelles, France][2]

[**1**] "I counsel you to buy from me fire-tried gold in order that you may be made rich ...."

Because the Sunday Gospel-reading, which speaks of love for God and neighbor, presents itself, and because love for God is the first and greatest commandment and love for one's neighbor is similar to it (as says the Teacher in Matthew 22),[3] I will say some things about love.[4] In every sermon one speaks of love; but enough can never be said about it, because it is the completion of the Law.[5]

[**2**] Christ said that all the laws and the prophets depend on this love of God and of neighbor. Now, the former love (*dilectio*) is a true love and is very great; it is called *caritas*. The latter love is the image and likeness of the former love; and it is called love (*dilectio*) of neighbor. But consider the fact that unless love of neighbor were the image of love for God, it would not have perfection. For nothing is *absolutely* perfect except God, who is Love (*caritas*).[6] Nothing is perfect *by way of participation* except insofar as it is an image of the Absolutely Perfect. Nothing is a befiguring, or an image, except insofar as the truth [of the original] shines forth in it. For an image in which there is no likeness of its exemplar has [in it] nothing of the truth [of the original]. Therefore, a likeness is a true image. Hence, in the image there is nothing except the exemplar in a contracted likeness. [**3**] Therefore, insofar as love of neighbor is like love for God, it fulfills the commandment. For that which appears in love-of-neighbor is a likeness. But the spirit that lies hidden in love-of-neighbor is Love, which that resembling-love [viz., love-of-neighbor] befigures. And so, in the canonical text [viz., Apocalypse 3:18] John instructs us [as follows]: Although without love for God no one can attain sonship, and although no one can even know whether he is abiding in love, nevertheless if he has love for his neighbor, he ought to be certain that he does abide in love.[7] Loving one's neighbor is loving God in and through His image.[8] When I love a human being—who, like me, has God as his Father—I love in him the Father, whose image he bears. Analogously, he who on account of a king loves the son of the king loves, in the son, the father;

and he is pleasing to the father. For he knows that the procreator takes pleasure in his offspring and son, or image, whom the procreator has called to his inheritance and to partnership with himself.

[4] Therefore, he who loves his neighbor not on account of God but on account of something useful or beneficial does not fulfill the commandment; and he abides not in love for God but in self-love, because he loves himself in his neighbor. Thus it is that true works of mercy are holy, for they proceed from a love-for-one's-neighbor in which only God is seen. [5] Moreover, let us note that by means of love we come to a knowledge of God. Although nothing is loved unless it is known,[9] nevertheless God—who because of His infinite knowability is unknowable (as a light, which of its own nature is visible, is on account of its exceeding brightness invisible to our eyes)—is knowable by means of a likeness. For anything that was unknown enters into our knowledge by means of a likeness. (For example, an unknown face becomes familiar through its likeness, which comes unto our eye. Now, we know that God is Love. But love for one's neighbor is a likeness of Love. Therefore, by means of love, as by means of an image and a likeness, we come to a knowledge of God. [6] The Savior made this point when He said: "If anyone loves me ...," etc., "we [viz., the Triune God] shall make our abode with him."[10] And this [abiding] is [God's] remaining in the understanding of the one who loves [Him]. Natural love[11] shows that nothing is more desirable than is love; for if love and harmony are removed, all things fall into disarray. If love and delight are removed, all sensory life occurs in sorrow and in death, and [that life] perishes. Therefore, that which furnishes life with gladness and delight is love, than which nothing more agreeable, nothing better, can be thought. Hence, the Fount of so great a good—from which Fount there flow life and the motion of gladness and delight—is beyond all reach of the senses and is the resting place of all motion and is better than can be thought.

[7] Lo, by means of the likeness of natural love one arrives at a taste of, or a knowledge of, the Love that God is. Moreover, fire, because of its heat and light bears a likeness to love, which in natural things is as heat and in immaterial things is as light. Therefore, by means of the likeness of fire's forcefulness, one ascends (according as Dionysius teaches)[12] unto a knowledge of God. Therefore, the Spirit of Christ, who spoke to John, symbolized love as gold—and not only as gold but as gold heated up, and not only heated up but proven [there-

by to be gold], because [fire-tried gold] makes wealthy. If we look at the sky, we see in the sun all [celestial] power; if we look at the earth, we see in gold all mineral power; if we look in-between, we see in fire a marvelous [in-between] power. We assert that Love has placed its likenesses in these three perceptible materials and that in them its power shines forth. For the light of the sun makes all the stars bright and turns them unto itself, inasmuch as all brightness is enfolded in the sun's power as in a fount; and so, the sun is light firstly and foremostly. Similarly, love diffuses itself throughout intellectual natures and turns them unto itself so that they partake of its nature. This nature is a true light that illumines every spirit—[illumines it] with divine and incorruptible life.

[8] However, it is necessary that things receive, into their inner being, the radiating light ; and, in that case, there remains in them no darkness. For example, the moon, being of earthy nature, does not deeply receive the sun's ray; and so, it remains darkened but is illumined on the side that is turned toward the sun. Similarly, our soul, which is where time and eternity are united (viz., on the horizon of eternity) receives the spirit of Love only in [the soul's] highest power, which is turned toward the Sun of Justice;[13] for like a polished mirror this splendrous, incorporeal surface, [or power], is capable of receiving that radiating [divine light]. Yet, [this highest human power, viz., the intellectual power,] does not deeply receive [the divine ray when the soul is in the state] where it animates flesh and blood. For the sensual man does not perceive the things that are of the Spirit of God.[14] For the perceptible world (to which the old man[15] belongs) neither sees nor knows nor can know that Spirit; rather, that which is reported about Love is foolishness to him.[16]

[9] Apart from the influence of the sun nothing lives. Therefore, all things partake of the motion of life—[partake of it] from the movement of the sun in the zodiac, or circle of life. Some stars do not by means of their own movement infuse the motion of life; rather, in accordance with their power they *dispose* to being alive. Therefore, in the heaven of the intellectual nature there are as many powers as there are stars in the firmament; [these powers] all have light from the Sun of Justice. Without this spirit, [or light], they would be altogether without any adornment and beauty and, likewise, without virtue. For virtue is not present apart from lovely adornment. But only the Spirit of the Sun of Justice effects divine life, which is called "being a son of God."[17]

[10] Likewise, the value of gold enfolds within itself the value of all metals; and the more a metal partakes of gold, the more valuable it is. And [a metal] is incorruptible only to the extent that incorruptible gold is present in it. Nor does a metal have any real value except insofar as it has within itself some gold. Therefore, gold measures the value of metal. Similarly, love measures the value of the virtues, for they have value in proportion to the love that is present in them. Likewise, the action of heat—without heat nothing has life—takes its beginning from fire. Fire is hot firstly and foremostly; and it is of highest activity, penetrating all things and transforming all things into itself. In itself fire is not visible, but it is visible in that which partakes of its nature. For pure fire is not anything that we see; rather, [we see] what is on fire. Analogously, divine warmth, i.e., divine love—unknowable in itself—shines forth in the virtues, which divine love transforms into itself and purifies and renews, as does fire. And so, the prophets spoke of God's spirit (1) as a fire that purifies metal and that separates incorruptible gold from corruptible and combustible sulphur and (2) as the power of the herb used by fullers—[a power] that washes away all uncleanness.

[11] And because the Kingdom of Heaven is only joy and peace in the Holy Spirit,[18] who is Love, Christ is seen to liken [it] (1) to love for[19] a good pearl[20] and, likewise, (2) to a hidden treasure.[21] And here in our theme-text love is likened to fire-tried gold that makes [one] rich. These [examples] are only of (1) possessing all things in one thing and of (2) possessing nothing except that one thing in which are all things. By comparison, in a precious pearl a merchant has all things, because he has sold all his goods and has bought the pearl. Thus, in and through the pearl he has all the things that he wishes to have. (The situation is similar with regard to the treasure hidden in the field and similar here [in today's text] with regard to the fire-tried gold.)

[12] I say that love is like a gem-stone that renders a man invisible.[22] For love, which covers a multitude of sins,[23] covers shame and nakedness; and no blemish appears. Analogously, in a flame of fire a black piece of coal or a black piece of iron appears not black but bright, in conformity with the brightness of the flame. For the brightness covers the blackness. And the fact that [the blackness] is covered is evident; for if [the coal or the iron] is withdrawn from the fire, it again looks black, as it was previously. Something similar is evident in the case of this world's love; for love covers defects. For example, a lover, while he is in love with his beloved, does not see her defects, because he loves exceedingly; but after the love ceases, he sees the defects. As the lyricist said: "If someone loves a frog, he thinks the frog to be Diana."[24] Hence, love covers shame, so that it is invisible to all, as was said about iron in fire. But the world's love does not cover the defect; rather, it blinds the lover, from whom it removes a true viewing, because the lover does not see in accordance with a true judgment of the intellect but sees in conformity with his affection.

[13] Moreover, I say that love can be called a divine elixir. For some men tell of a certain potion that transforms all things into gold. In Arabic this potion is called an elixir. Analogously, love not only covers over but also transforms a son of man into a son of God by making of what is terrestrial that which is celestial. For he who has perfect love has fire-tried gold that enriches. For he is rich to the point that he can purchase the Kingdom of Heaven, since the worth of that gold enfolds the value of the Tree of Life in the midst of Paradise[25] and the value of all the fountains of the waters-of-life in the city of the New Jerusalem[26] and in the entire Kingdom.

[14] Do we not see in the case of the world's love that all things are added to the state-of-love, a state in which all things are the common-property of the loving-parties and in which the one who is poor possesses all the things that the one who is wealthy possesses?—if between the two parties there is perfect love. Now, love makes to be its own son the one who loves it [viz., love]. Even as one who has justice is made to be a son of justice and from justice is called just, and even as one who has humanity is called, from the humanity, a man and is truly that which he is called, so if love is present in our spirit, it makes us sons of love. But God *is* Love. Therefore, through love we are adopted sons, because God Himself loved us before we loved Him.[27] Therefore, He chose us. This choosing is love. So love is the adoption of the sons of God. But a son has the father's inheritance. Hence, each one abiding in love possesses the Kingdom of the Father. Although the Kingdom is one Kingdom, all the sons possess it at the same time, and each possesses it completely. Analogously, all see the [one] Face of the Father who is in Heaven, and each by himself sees it in its entirety.

[15] Therefore, the gold of which [we are speaking] here in our topic—gold which has passed through the fire and been proven—can be understood to be gold that has been fire-tried by the Spirit of Omnipotence. For when the power of the elixir (which furnishes the

power-for-transforming) is added to the gold, it makes the gold fiery; and by means of this procedure we see that this gold, through the fiery spirit that dwells steadfastly in it, becomes possessed of the power of transforming other metals into gold. Similarly, perfect love not only covers shame and weakness, as does bogus love, but transforms into gold-producing powers the powers and operations of lead and of stannum and of copper. Similarly, when a draught of water is given, it is a small work in terms of effort; but love makes it to be a work worthy of the Kingdom of Heaven.[28] Likewise, when vital warmth is joined to human nature, it makes the nature capable of turning food (e.g., bread and meat) into itself. And if [the food] is joined to a fleshly nature, there is a turning of the meat and of the bread into the nature of flesh. Therefore, just as vital warmth is a likeness of the divine warmth that is called love, so [love] gives to the nature to which it is united the power of choosing, of attracting, of loving, and of transforming. Thus, divine warmth, or love, is rightly said to be like gold that is heated by the fire of the spirit of an elixir, in the aforesaid way.

[16] Likewise, when a strong wine's simple and pure spirit—for the more purified and simplified a wine is, the stronger it is—is joined to water, then in accordance with the wine's strength, it transforms into wine the water into which it is poured. Moreover, consider the fact that a fiery spirit is characteristic of good aqua vitae. And so, if into aqua vitae there is put a chemical potion or a spicy [herb], the aqua vitae immediately attracts that [herb's] spirit and enters into [the herb]. For example, place galingale [into aqua vitae] at certain times; the entire power of the galingale leaves the solid substance and ascends into the spirit of the aqua vitae, and the spirit of aqua vitae descends, with its power, into the spirit of the galingale. If later you put a little of this aqua vitae into a jar of wine, the whole of the wine is changed into the taste and power of the galingale. (And if the specimen were a laxative, the wine would become a laxative; and if it were constipating, the wine would become constipating; and if it were an antacid for the stomach, the wine would become such as to be transformed in such a way.) For the spirit, or strength, of the wine is transformed by the spirit of the spicy thing in which is present the fiery spirit, viz., the spirit of the "quintessence." And this [transforming occurs] through adoption in order that there might be possessed the inheritance of sonship with the "father," i.e., the inheritance of the "paternal" power, which extracts [the spicy taste]. [17] A certain devout man called this aqua vitae a heaven, or a quintessence. And, not unfittingly, it is likened to a heav-

en. For there is in that heaven the spirit-of-aqua-vitae, which by its nature, which is called love, attracts every spirit-that-is-capable-of-love; this spirit comes to the spirit-of-aqua vitae, and [this latter] casts out no spirit. And it separates off the corruptible body, which cannot retain the [spicy] spirit. It is as if in the very perfect aqua vitae there were placed various kinds of spices, from which their [respective] spirit would be attracted (with the dead bodies being left behind [as dregs]). It is as if the immaterial power of each [spice] were conserved in the heaven of aqua [vitae], in which each [spice] remains intact with regard to its power and species, even though each kind is united unmixedly with each [portion of aqua vitae].

[18] Moreover, in each power of each species one and the same spirit of aqua vitae is present, binding that power to itself by means of an unseverable union, lest that power ever be separated from the aqua vitae. And the spirit of wine is in that aqua [vitae]; and no power of any kind [of spice] can be attracted except in the aqua [vitae], where there is the kingdom of the spirit of life. And that spirit is altogether unknown. (For although it is called the spirit of wine, because it is extracted from wine, nevertheless that fiery spirit is also extracted from beer and from apples and pears and all things, as giving to every thing power. And so, it would have to be named by all names and by none of them all.) So, too, to some extent (although the comparison is exceedingly lame), conceive of God's Spirit, which we call Love, as the unknown and truly ineffable Creator of every [finite] spirit. And God's Spirit is not attained except by rational spirits, who alone are capable of attaining it and in whom an incorruptible love of virtue brings delight. And this [occurs] in the heaven in which there is the throne of God, even as the spirit of aqua vitae has its throne in its own heaven, viz., in water. But the heaven in which the invisible and unknown Spirit is hidden is the medium through which one comes to union with it and to enjoyment of it. (This [union, or enjoyment,] is also called a seeing.) Similarly, warmth is a heaven, or a throne, of the spirit of sensory life.

[19] But that [incorruptible] heaven is called a heaven of glory. For it is the Divine Light (in which there is the throne of God's Spirit) insofar as a created spirit has access to that Light. Therefore, [that Light] attracts every rational spirit that is in [that] heaven. Now, the spirit of reason is an intellectual power that is free of desire and that indwells each [rational spirit] unconfusedly. This indwelling is, for

each rational spirit, a possessing of God and of eternal life. And so, by means of a likeness you see that God is present in each and every [rational] spirit. And each spirit is most lovingly united with each other spirit through an indwelling love. (The [individual] power of each spirit remains preserved and unintermixed [with that of other spirits].)

[20] Climacus said that love is a fountain of fire: the more it flares up, the more it will inflame one who thirsts. Love of peace [is] the mother of wisdom, the fount of immortality, and the root of glory. The domain of love is hope. Through hope we expect and receive love's reward and retribution. Love and impossibility-of-suffering and the adoption-of-sons differ only in name, as do fire's light and a flame. Consult Climacus in regard to the final stage of the *Scales*,[29] because he spoke as one who understands.

NOTES TO *Suadeo Tibi Emere*

* Sermon CCXLI.
1. Apocalypse (Revelation) 3:18.
2. This was the feast-day of St. Augustine.
3. Matthew 22:36-39.
4. Here Nicholas uses a declined form of the noun "*caritas*". In the opening sentence of this paragraph he uses the noun "*dilectio*". In general, he makes no distinction between the use of these two nouns and the use of "*amor*". Toward the end of **6** and at the beginning of **7** he employs "*amor naturalis*" ("natural love") when speaking of the human love between a man and a woman. But at **11**:2-3 he speaks of love (*caritas*) for a good pearl. And in Sermon I (**6**:15-18) he speaks of God as *amans* and as *amabilis*. (See also Sermon II (**4**:7) and III (**3**:1-6).) Neither Augustine nor Nicholas uses "*amor*" exclusively to signify profane love, worldly love, etc. However, in the present sermon Nicholas does use "*caritas*" (principally) and "*dilectio*" (alternatively) when speaking of God's love for man and of man's love for God. In here preferring the word "*caritas*," he is displaying the influence of the Vulgate-text of I John 4. See n. 6 below. See also Sermon XXXVII (**11**:1-2).
5. I Timothy 1:5. Romans 13:8.
6. I John 4:16.
7. *Loc. cit.*
8. Augustine makes this same point. See his *In Joannis Evangelium Tractatus* lxv.2 (*PL* 35:1809).
9. See n. 14 of my Notes to Sermon CLXXII.
10. John 14:23.
11. Natural love is the harmony, orderliness, affinity, cohesion that pervades the natural world.
12. Pseudo-Dionysius, *De Ecclesiastica Hierarchia*, Chap. 2, section 1 (*PG* 3:393 & 394. *Dionysiaca*, Vol. II, pp. 1113-1114).
13. Malachias (Malachi) 4:2.
14. I Corinthians 2:14.
15. See n. 25 of my Notes to Sermon CLXXIV.
16. I Corinthians 2:14.
17. I John 3:2.
18. Romans 14:17.
19. Here (at **11**:3) I am surmising the preposition "*ad*" in front of "*margaritam bonam*".
20. Matthew 13:45-46.
21. Matthew 13:44.
22. The allusion is to the story of the Ring of Gyges, as told in Plato's *Republic*, Book II (359C – 360B).
23. I Peter 4:8.
24. Hans Walther. *Proverbia sententiaeque Latinitatis Medii Aevi. Lateinische Sprichwörter und Sentenzen des Mittelalters in alphabetischer Anordnung*. Göttingen: Vandenhoeck and Ruprecht, 1966 (Vol. 4), p. 952, entry 28967.
25. Genesis 2:9.

26. Apocalypse (Revelation) 22:1 and 7:17.
27. I John 4:10 and 4:19.
28. Mark 9:40.
29. St. John Climacus. *The Ladder of Divine Ascent*, Step 30, n. 9. Translated by Archimandrite L. Moore (London: Faber and Faber, 1959), p. 262.

Sermon CXCVI: Respice de Caelo et Vide et Vista Vineam Istam*
("Look Down from Heaven, and See, and Visit This Vineyard.")[1]
[July 20, 1455; preached in Brixen] [2]

[1] "Look down," O Lord, "from Heaven, and see, and visit this vineyard" (Psalms 79).

God once planted a choice vineyard. After He had tended to it with much care and it did not bear good fruit but, on the contrary, produced with bitterness wild grapes, the Prophet David[3] asked that a visitor come from Heaven and inspect the vineyard so that it not be reduced to total ruin. And it happened that that Divine Power, through which all pleasantness of life exists, descended from Heaven unto the vine[s] and became the true Vine[4] bearing the fruit of eternal gladness. And from the true Vine there sprung forth, and there spring forth, fruit-bearing sprouts. Now, in order for a vineyard to yield fruit, it must be maintained by means of good and continual cultivating. And hence it pertains to the head of the household to visit often and to see whether the workers cultivate the vineyard rightly. Similarly, to the bishop—who was set over the workers in God's House by Jesus, to whom, as Heir, the vineyard belongs—it pertains to visit the vineyard at times in order to see what those who care for it are doing and to see how they are laboring in the Lord's vineyard, each in the area assigned to him.

[2] By the supreme and universal head of God's House, viz., the Roman Pontiff, I have been set over an area of the God-of-hosts' vineyard—[an area] marked off by certain boundaries and called the Church of Brixen. But I am unworthy to be in charge of workers and to exercise care of the assigned portion in order to see that it is rightly cultivated. Would that I were able diligently to accomplish the assigned tasks! But because I have determined to now begin the visitation with this parish, I consider the words set forth by the Psalmist [as saying] that I must take a pattern from Heaven in accordance with which I may judge whether the vineyard is being cultivated optimally or whether something is lacking to it. For as far as possible we must attend to the church militant in order that it may be conformed to the church triumphant. For just as on the Mount of Contemplation Moses saw an exemplar after whose likeness he fashioned the material tabernacle,[5] so too must it be done by us.

[3] First of all I ask, dearly beloved, that you take note of the fact that we who are called Christians have entered into a certain religious practice that is—assuredly, beyond all conceivable holiness—quite in line with [that of] the Heavenly citizens. For our Teacher, who by word and example taught us this [religious practice], alone knows the disposition of that Kingdom and of its inhabitants. And He descended for our sakes, in order to preach to us about the riches-of-glory of the Heavenly Kingdom and in order to instill in us earthly beings the fire of desire for Him so that it would blaze and would convey us upwards. The special property of heat is to tend upwards; and the special property of divine love is to join hearts to God, who dwells in Heaven. Now, in every founder of a religion there must be found such holiness of life that he is believed. Each person who reflects finds [this point to be true]. For how is it that some people would follow St. Benedict, others [St.] Basil, others [St.] Anthony if they did not believe that by the route by which they were proceeding they would arrive at happiness, which alone all wish for? Hence, faith is that without which no religious practice is accepted; and so, the gateway of Christian religious practice is faith: viz., the faith (which Peter first confessed)[6] that Jesus is the Son of the Living God. Jesus, according to His humanity, is truthful; and, according to His divinity, He is Truth. And according to His humanity He is the Way to life, but according to His divinity He is Life itself,[7] which enlivens all intellectual spirits and makes happy all men who are made happy.

[4] Only Heavenly citizens obtain true happiness. Therefore, the pathway by which Jesus Christ preceded us—Jesus, whose teachings and religious practice we have professed—leads us to the Kingdom of Heaven and to the community of Heavenly citizens. And unless we had this faith as regards Christ, we would not at all be Christians. Accordingly, we ought first of all to believe that Jesus the Son of God is the unique Savior, who in accordance with His humanity aids all those, and intercedes for all those, who call upon Him—[aids them and intercedes for them] with God the Father, in order that they may obtain salvation—and who in accordance with His divinity gives [them] salvation and saves [them]. Therefore, if God alone is the Creator of souls and the Savior of souls, then salvation is not to be sought from anyone other than from God and from Jesus our Savior. Now, aids and intercessions with God the Father are to be sought (1) from Jesus, the Head of religion and of holiness, and (2) from the glorious Virgin and (3) from the saints. Hence, a visiting [inspector] ought to ask, in the first

place, whether every Christian keeps his faith undefiled. For example, if there are those who resort to any kind of words or deeds[8] by which to instill faith-in-a-rescue, then they do injury to the true Savior—as when they promise: "If someone does such and such, he will be freed from his fever or will find love or will obtain wealth."

[5] With full devotion and humility a Christian ought to ask from God—through Jesus Christ and the intercession of the Virgin Mary and of the saints—whatever he needs. And he ought to believe that omnipotent and most gracious God will grant whatever things are for salvation. And if those things that oftentimes are ignorantly asked for are not granted, he ought to express thanks to God, who in accordance with His providence knows that those things are not suitable for the one who is asking. Accordingly, the Apostle James said: "If anyone needs wisdom, let him ask, and it shall be given."[9] Now, the judge who judges as to need is God, who grants only to one who needs [something] with respect to salvation. For example, because forgiveness of sins is necessary for salvation, God never denies it to one who truly and rightly seeks it. Thus, one who seeks it ought to believe that he will obtain it. But one who asks for other things ought to believe that he will obtain them if he needs them for his soul's salvation. Otherwise, he ought not to ask for those things from God, the Giver of every good; nor ought he to hope for them or believe [that he will receive them].

[6] Moreover, in cases where the Church has placed certain forms of prayers in the missal or in the pontifical ([e.g., has placed prayers] against storms, dissensions, ailments, inclement weather, and so on), we ought to stick to these forms. But where [the Church] has placed no special [forms], we ought to take the general [forms] and apply [them] to the particular envisioned-need. Where no general forms are applicable to what is purposed, let us bring forth prayers of our own together with [using] the Lord's Prayer. Now, each person can, with devout intention, extend the Lord's Prayer (which enfolds within itself whatever things can be sought from God) to the particular things that are desired. For example, [suppose that] you want to obtain a condition-of-air that is good for [growing] fruit and you say "Our Father"; and subsequently you add devoutly: "O Lord, You command me to ask of You daily bread, which is always necessary for life. And so, in order that I may acquire it by Your gift, remove inclement weather, hail, excessive rain, aridness, extreme degrees of cold and heat, and other such things." Likewise, [suppose] you wish to ask from God a good

bishop. You premise "Our Father" and add: "Because, O God, You command that all food [that is necessary] for life be sought from You, and because wisdom and Your word feed the soul and are the daily bread of the rational soul: in order, then, that my soul can be nourished by the word of life, give us, O Lord, a good, knowledgeable overseer who loves You—one who will feed us daily and without ceasing." Do you wish to ask God for other things that are necessary for you—such as health, peacefulness, love, and whatever such things? You will be able under the name "bread" to ask God for all that you need. For all that we need comes under the name "bread".

[7] Consequently, superstitions, fortune-tellings, incantations (and all trickeries), divinations, geomancy, nigromancy, pyromancy (and all foretelling) are far from the Christian religion. Likewise, those individuals are far from faith (1) who ascribe to God neglect or meager providence or ignorance or that He distributes goods unjustly, ([distributing] much to one who is evil, little to another who is good, many children to one who is poor, few children to another who is rich) and (2) who blame God (a) because of storms and bad weather and (b) because He allows the young and strong to die, the frail to live, (c) because He creates some as beautiful, others as deformed, and (d) because He is slow to be merciful, and (e) because He permits the Devil to tempt even those who are going to fall. Those who thus rail against God do not have faith, as do those who believe that God neither does nor permits anything without a reason, (though His judgments are a great depth,[10] as in the example of the hermit. See, in Discipulus, Sermons CVIII and CX.)[11]

Therefore, one who comes to this Christian religion must, as the apostle says, believe that God *is* and that He is a Rewarder of all.[12] But he who does not believe that the rational soul is immortal, and that it is of very great dignity insofar as it exists, cannot be called a Christian. For to whom could a reward be made by God if there were no subject capable [of receiving it]—i.e., if the soul were not immortal? But the fact that the rational soul is a noble creature you will infer from the following [consideration]: it is a living image of the Creator; and from its presence the body has all things, viz., life, movement, beauty. In order to benefit the [rational soul], Christ worked thirty-three years and gave His life, which was of more value than are an infinite number of worlds.[13] And He gave His Body for [the soul's] food.[14] God gave an angel as guardian for the [rational soul], and He chose the [rational soul] for His temple.[15] He created [it] to take the place of [fallen] angels[16] and to come to inheritance of the Kingdom of Heaven. Therefore, the [human] soul is of more worth than is anything perceptible and corruptible. (See Discipulus, Sermon CXXXII, and take note of his illustration.)

[**8**] Therefore, each person ought to enter the Christian religion by way of the door of faith, viz., the sacrament of baptism. Hence, in order that this sacrament be accomplished in the right manner, all care should be exercised—[care] especially (1) that midwives, who baptize in emergencies, know the [proper] form and (2) that in regard to this sacrament the Church's prescribed manner be devoutly maintained in all respects. Now, after one comes into the Lord's House (which is called the Church) by means of baptism, one ought to consider that the Christian religion leads us from this world unto the Kingdom of Life. And since there are three things in the world—viz., the pride of life, the lust of the flesh, and covetousness (i.e., lust of the eyes)[17]—then in perfect religion a man ought to be free of these things. And hence in religion there is, against pride, *ordinate obedience*; against lust of the flesh, *chastity*; against covetousness, *poverty*. [These are] in conformity with the Kingdom of Heaven, in which there are supreme obedience, supreme chastity, and supreme satisfiedness (which can be called poverty, or renunciation of the desire of having anything more). Where these three [traits] are most excellently maintained, *there* perfect religion is present. Indeed, these three are of the essence of perfect religion; for those who preserve these [traits] live after the fashion of Heavenly citizens. [**9**] In heart, in mouth, and in deed—i.e., in will, in speech, and in action—they preserve accord. And such accord acquires all things. For it is impossible that the prayers of many persons not be heard. And for this reason we come together in church, praying all together—because our Teacher says (in particular, in Matthew 18): "If two [of you] shall agree concerning any thing whatsoever they shall ask, it shall be done for them by my Father."[18] How much more [is this true] where a multitude come together!

Just as God dwells amid the Heavenly citizens, so Christ dwells amid His own: Matthew 18: "Where two or three are gathered together in My name, I am in their midst."[19] Where *many* [are gathered together this statement holds] all the more true. God readily hearkens to a multitude. In Genesis 18 God said to Abraham: "If in Sodom I find ten just men, I will spare the entire place for their sakes."[20] Moreover, even as in Heaven the saints are nourished [spiritually] by their vision of God, so in the Church they are nourished by a hearing of the word [of God]. For [man does not live] by bread alone ...," etc.[21]

Furthermore, in Heaven all things are [held in] common, and one individual shares with another. For the merit of one increases joy for all. Such was the case in the state of nature prior to the law and in the early Church (Acts 4)[22] and [is the case] now in religions other [than ours].

In Heaven the citizens do not marry; rather, all are totally chaste. The case is similar [for the priests] within religion. Fifthly,[23] in Heaven all offer themselves as a sacrifice to God; similarly, in religion [they offer themselves] through obedience, when they yield up to God their own will. In Heaven the inhabitants obey the divine commands *willingly, gladly*, and *persistently*; within religion the case is similar with a prelate. Obedience is either with respect to precepts or with respect to counsels or with respect to conformity-of-mind. As Paul says: "You will that I do a thing without murmuring."[24] For with murmuring-complaint the devils, crying out, departed at the command of Jesus, etc.[25] Obedience ought to be Heavenlike and joyful. Obedience gladdens a prelate, renders work less burdensome, furnishes assurance to conscience.[26] Obedience ought to be persistent. Bernard [says]: "So as not to lose obedience, Christ lost His life."[27]

[10] Now, in the Christian religion [obedience] is a threefold state: of laymen only or of clerics or of monks. However, in every religion, life must be lived under obedience. For Christ our Teacher became obedient to the Father (1) when He said "not as I will but as You [will]"[28] and (2) when [he was obedient] to the point of death, even death on the Cross.[29] Accordingly, it is necessary that all [Christians] be obedient. Yet, obedience ought to be stricter in the clerical state [and] still stricter in the monastic state. In the first state, [viz., the state of laymen], all three substantial [requirements] are present: [viz., obedience, chastity, poverty]. But [the requirement of] chastity is less strict, for fleshly desire is permitted unless it becomes lust. Hence, a virgin does not sin if she marries in the Lord;[30] and a man does not sin [in marrying] if he keeps his vessel [i.e., his body] in a state of holiness. Thus, the sacrament of matrimony is allowable for them since it takes place without lust and fornication. So too, in this [laical] state poverty (which is the renunciation of personal possessions) is thought to be present when[31] one possesses what is his own and does not take what is another's. In the clerical state chastity is required to be stricter, since in that state even marital union is forbidden. Likewise, [a cleric] cannot call anything his own, although he has the use of those things that belong to the Church and has special administrative jurisdiction [over them]. But in the monastic state neither matrimony nor use in

terms of managing is permitted to every [monk]; rather, [use is permitted] to one [monk] who is in charge, and he manages for the others.

Now, to no one is there granted that he be allowed to misuse what has been granted [him]. For in the laical state both the misuse of marriage and the misuse of things are forbidden. Likewise, in the clerical [state] the misuse of things is forbidden, and in the monastic [state] the misuse of the managing of things is forbidden. Laymen, as long as they do not abuse marriage, are called chaste; and as long as they do not misuse their goods they are called poor and are said to keep the basic requirements of the [divine] ordinance. A similar thing holds true for clerics and monks. But misuse is found to characterize transgressors.

[**11**] Let us now turn our attention [more fully] to the laical state. And first of all we must maintain, as regards obedience, that each [Christian] is obligated to be obedient to Christ (the Head of the [Christian] religion) and to one acting as Christ's representative. For Christ left behind for us the law of the Gospel and He made to be its overseer him who acts as His representative, who makes this law known. And this man, sent by Christ, speaks not his own words but the Son of God's word, which is contained in the Gospel. Therefore, he must be listened to exactly as Christ would be. For Christ said: "He who hears you hears me."[32] And [Christ] speaks of Himself, saying: "The words that I speak are not mine but are His who sent me, [viz.,] the Father. For on my own authority I speak nothing."[33] Therefore, if the words of a priest, or of a bishop, are God the Father's words, made known to us by the Son and recalled by the priest, then they must be obeyed completely. Hence, consummate disobedience—which is [one's] choosing not to obey—excludes [one] from the Christian religion, because [disobedience] is heathen and satanic and is the sin of idolatry. Therefore, the overseers of the Church are to be obeyed as [being representatives of] God. And if any men are obstinately disobedient, they are to be separated off and relegated away from fellowship with others—being considered members cut off from the mystical Body of Christ because of their rottenness.

Therefore, dearly beloved, know the following: that unless you are obedient to those who are set over you, you are not in the Church, in which there is the power of binding and loosening.[34] And unless you believe that your overseer acts as the representative of Christ and that he has the power of binding and loosening on Christ's behalf, you will never obtain sacramental absolution of your sins. Nor [will you obtain] indulgences and remissions, which flow from the [episcopal] chair.[35]

For he who does not believe does not hope. And he who neither believes nor hopes will not obtain. But he who believes that the one [who is ecclesiastically and spiritually] set over him acts as the representative of Christ (because of the fact that Christ said regarding those overseers "He who hears you hears me") will assuredly obtain from Christ all things on account of his faith and trust, which cannot disappoint those who place their hope in Christ. Therefore, let each person be united to his prelate and priest, and let him reverence Christ in and through his priest, and let him receive his priest's words as the words of Christ. Thereupon, through this obedience, he offers himself as a sacrifice to God. [He offers himself] even to the point of the demise of his freedom of choice,[36] when *he* does not live but Christ lives in him;[37] [and] he obeys Christ's will (which the priest communicates to him) without murmuring.

[12] Therefore, when you do the foregoing and are obedient in all respects to him whom God has set over you, then by the hands of [that] prelate you will be led unto the Eternal Kingdom. And, as regards strict judgment, you will not have to answer for anything other than for obedience. For example, if you say "O Lord, I have obeyed you in and through your overseer," then this [obeying] will suffice for your salvation—even if the overseer is going to answer to God for the burdens placed on your shoulders and for the obligations and payments. For, indeed, through the obedience that you give to the overseer, whom the Church backs, you cannot be defrauded [of salvation], even if he imposes obligations other than he ought to. Therefore, for the sake of your salvation the judgment of your pastor is binding on you because of the good of obedience—even if the judgment be unjust. For it does not pertain to you to decide that the judgment is unjust; and you do not have the prerogative of not obeying, if the judgment seems to you to be unjust. For it would not be a case of obedience if it were up to you to decide, regarding the judgment of the pastor, whether [or not] it ought to be obeyed. For the Church takes that judgment for granted; if you obey it, your reward will be great. Accordingly, blind obedience is consummate obedience and very perfect obedience. [Blind obedience occurs] when one obeys without asking for a rationale, just as a mule obeys its master. Therefore, if you see that your bishop does not associate with someone, then do not yourself associate with him. See how greatly those sin who detract from the bishop and speak evil against one who is serving as Christ's representative—especially [if they speak evilly] with regard to the things which he does as bishop.

Let these statements suffice for now.

[13] In addition, because holy matrimony is a sacrament that makes licit what otherwise would be forbidden, we must see to it that the ceremony is rightly performed in accordance with the regulations of the holy fathers. The holy fathers decided that in certain cases marriage cannot be contracted. And although in those times there was a prohibition [against matrimony], as regards blood-relationships and relationships by marriage, down to the seventh degree: nonetheless, nowadays the prohibition is extended only to the fifth degree. Moreover, there are spiritual affinities and matters of public decorum and certain great sins, as well as times when the contracting parties are not free; these [circumstances] hinder the contracting [of marriage]. Therefore, it was ordained that proclamations should be made openly in churches prior to the [marriage] contract, in order that if anyone would know of a hindrance, he could disclose it in due time. Now, because it has not been the practice in this diocese that proclamations be made, many marriages have been found [to have taken place] contrary to the ordinance of the Church. Therefore, I decreed that proclamations be made; and, now at last, by the gift of God, that salutary decree has been accepted.

There still remains that there be enacted the sacred rite regarding the blessings of those who are marrying—a rite that is observed in many churches. Accordingly, I desire that the mode prescribed in my written communications be accepted and observed. For the holy fathers have judged that thus the [ceremony] ought in every respect to be conducted. Therefore, you who propose to contract [marriage], undertake [it] henceforth with faith—[undertake it] after the proclamations and three days before the conjugal union (in conformity with the example of Tobias).[38] Or contract [the marriage] in the presence of the Church at least one day [before the conjugal union]. And, having confessed, receive the (assuredly very fecund) blessing according to the form handed down for laymen. For if you act accordingly, you can hope for enjoyable peace and long life together with all the things that are favorable for sustaining a holy marriage. Therefore, as concerns the observance of this sacrament, it is fitting to be exceedingly watchful that it be adhered to in a holy, pure, and very strict manner and that adulterers (who according to the Law of Moses are to be stoned) not be allowed to defile the communities of Christians who are living rightly. And each [Christian] is obliged to be zealous in this regard and to aid me and my assistants, so that [adulterers] be corrected or so that incorrigible ones be separated [from the fellowship of believers].

Now, one preaches often about the honorableness and mutual love with which married persons ought to live together and raise their sons and daughters in the fear of God. And so, [this topic] may now be passed over.

[**14**] As concerns the point about property, the following is to be observed: [viz.,] that you neither covet what is someone else's nor be enriched through another's loss—but that you live from that which (by the gift of God) is yours and by means of your labors, so that you may be happy. But you should give alms, as Jesus said, from that which is more than you need.[39] Likewise, have[40] in your possession only the necessities of food and clothing, as accord with your status. The remainder belongs to God, who wills that you distribute to the poor. Therefore, whatever things you possess are God's; and inasmuch as they are not anyone else's, He wills that you use them for your necessities and that you distribute among the poor that which remains over and above your needs. Thus, managing is entrusted to you. And you remain poor because all things belong to God, in accordance with whose will you distribute [them]. Hence, so that the concession by which you are allowed to be able to have some things which are yours not turn back against religion (in accordance with which you have relegated from yourself all coveting of your neighbor's goods), guard yourself carefully from becoming greedy and from reassuming *that [earlier] inordinate desiring*. Therefore, lest you become overly eager, do not set your heart, as it were, on desiring to become rich. Otherwise, you will entangle yourself in many useless cares and will pass from one mode of acquiring to another and will forget that you have renounced inordinate desires and will fall into many wearying and useless snares.

Now, because, as regards *acquiring*, a certain mode that is called usury is trouble-free, assured, and easy: many persons latch onto it as a means of acquiring. [But] you, O Christian, flee from it completely. Once [this practice is] accepted, it is abandoned [only] with difficulty. And where it is found, one must attempt with very great determination to root it out, for it defiles not only relatives but also religion; and it harms the state and does very grave injury to love-of-neighbor. Likewise, let each one who has goods that are due to be returned, take care to return them as soon as possible. And he who owes to God and the Church payment of tithes and owes rent to his masters: he must make a certain effort and discharge his debts as soon as possible; for sin is not remitted unless what has been taken is restored. This restitution is, indeed, scarcely made without [great] effort.

[15] Now, the statutes of our religion must be adhered to in every respect. They are contained, chiefly, in the Ten Commandments and, secondarily, in the things added by the holy fathers (especially for you laymen) regarding feast-days and fasts. As concerns feast-days, be careful to observe them, not by acting wantonly or by singing and dancing or by becoming drunk and gluttonous, but by ceasing from manual labor, in order to have time for God and in order to recover your strength, which you depleted through physical laborings. And for this reason beasts of burden ought also to be rested, as Moses commanded.[41] And in this regard you will note four different kinds of feast-days that will be published for you [by me].

[16] Now, as concerns silence (which in every perfect religion is judged to be necessary), some things in regard to the Christian religion are to be noted. For our Teacher, Christ, admonishes us not to spew forth words idly, for all of which we are going to give an account [in the Day of Judgment].[42] Therefore, since an idle word is one that is uttered pointlessly, then (as is evident) silence must be preserved within religion at every place and time when words are not useful and do not edify and do not serve a purpose. And if we are forbidden to waste time spewing forth idle words, then [this prohibition applies] all the more in a holy and religious location and among things divine. Those who belong to religious orders are obliged to keep silent in the house of prayer—and likewise during meals and in their sleeping quarters. So, too, you, who have professed the Christian religion, ought to do nothing other in the house of prayer than pray; and in the house of refection [you ought] to be fed while praising God; and after the meal [you ought] to sing a hymn to God. But if you must speak at mealtime, these [utterances] will be able to be made very briefly [and] without fault-finding. For it is dangerous to say many things while eating. Many talkative people have choked between bites. Likewise, when you go to bed, you ought, after having prayed, to lie down and be quiet and well-up with praise for God.

Religiousness discloses itself in speech. For of what kind each person is, of such things he speaks: either [he is] Heavenly and [speaks of] Heavenly things or [he is] earthly and [speaks of] earthly things or [he is] infernal and [speaks of] infernal things. Speech reveals each person. For of what kind a man's heart is, of such kind are his speech and his deeds. Christ teaches us that sins proceed from the heart, and He gives the example of blasphemy.[43] Just as praisings of God proceed from a celestial heart, so blasphemies proceed from an infernal heart and mundane prattle from a mundane heart. A wife who has an impudent tongue has an unclean heart. The same holds true for husbands and for virgins.

Moreover, we ought not to believe those who make the excuse for themselves that they do not harbor in their heart the things which they bring forth with their mouth. For Christ says that "out of the abundance of the heart the mouth speaks."[44] If someone readily and with joy praises God, he is learning here in this world the language with which he will always speak in the future. As the Prophet Isaias says: "Joy and gladness will be found in her" (viz., in the City of God), "thanksgiving and the voice of praise."[45] He who is of the earth speaks of the earth.[46] And, as John says in the canonical epistle: "They are of the world; and so, they speak of the world."[47] For regarding those who speak often of worldly things: it is a sign that they are sons of this age. However, those who are infernal blaspheme God, as says John in the Apocalypse: "They have blasphemed the God of Heaven because of their pains."[48] Therefore, blasphemers and users of profanity[49] are here learning the language that they will speak in Hell. Hence, Isidore in his *On the Supreme Good* says that evil words ought not to be present in the mouth of a Christian.[50]

[17] A Christian ought to imitate Christ. For as Augustine [says] in *On Christian Doctrine*, no one is rightly called a Christian except him who imitates Christ's ways. In His words Christ kept to the truth; and a Christian is obliged to do likewise. For no one who is a liar is loved either by God or by men. "For, lo,"[51] said the Prophet, "you have loved truth."[52] A genuine florin is of more worth than is a counterfeit one; similarly, a man of truth is of more worth than is a man of lies. The liar has the tongue of the Devil, who from the beginning deceived our first parents by lying.[53] Usefulness is supposed to be connected to truth, so that truth either consoles or admonishes, or either teaches or informs. According to Bernard, Christ (whom we imitate) never uttered a useless word. Nor is it fitting that *we* utter jesting words through which we provoke the elderly or others to anger or to blasphemy; for [in that case] we are guilty of those sins. For those individuals who are damned give occasion ..., etc.[54] And jesting [words] that incite to evil or that entice or that produce excessive delight are to be avoided—especially the mode of joking that produces a lie togeth-

er with an oath [that it is not a lie]. For as St. Thomas holds in [the *Summa Theologica*], IIa – IIae, 98: [the fact of its being a practical] joke does not excuse such a liar from perjury and from mortal sin.

Christ had moderation in speaking, and so [should] you [have]. As a rich man does not spend money unless it is first counted, so let us not speak except with aforethought. Therefore, to our Christian religion it especially pertains to bridle the tongue. For the Apostle James says: "He who esteems himself religious but does not bridle his tongue—his religion is empty."[55] Cato spoke similarly: "I regard the primary virtue to be restraining the tongue."[56] And not without reason do we have one mouth for speaking and two ears for hearing. To have kept silent does no harm; to have spoken causes harm.[57] Talkativeness is a sign of foolishness according to Solomon.[58] Silence is the material of peace. And so, [silence] befits religion. For "by means of very few words a quarrel sometimes grows to be immense."[59]

NOTES TO *Respice de Caelo*

* Sermon CXCVI.
1. Psalms 79:15 (80:14).
2. This date was the Sunday before the Feast-day of Mary Magdalene.
3. Psalms 79:15 (8j0:14).
4. John 15:1.
5. Hebrews 8:5. Exodus 25:40.
6. Matthew 16:16.
7. John 14:6.
8. "… any kind of words or deeds": i.e., incantations, promises, false hopes, and the like.
9. James 1:5.
10. Psalms 35:7 (36:6).
11. Johannes Herolt (Discipulus), *Sermones discipuli de tempore* (Lyon, France, 1529). See principally Sermon CVIII.
12. Hebrews 11:6.
13. See Anselm of Canterbury, *Cur Deus Homo* II, 14.
14. The allusion here is to the eucharist.
15. I Corinthians 3:16.
16. See Anselm of Canterbury, *Cur Deus Homo* I, 16-18.
17. I John 2:16.
18. Matthew 18:19 (not Matthew 8, as the copyist and/or Nicholas misstates and as I have corrected in the translation).
19. Matthew 18:20.
20. Genesis 18:26.
21. Deuteronomy 8:3. Matthew 4:4.
22. Acts 4:32.
23. Nicholas is following Johannes Herolt, whose fifth point he here repeats. See n. 11 above.
24. Philippians 2:14. Nicholas *alludes to* this text rather than *quoting* it.
25. Mark 1:26. Luke 4:41.
26. At **9**:37-38 I am reading (with the Paris edition) "obedientia" in place of "obedientiae".
27. Bernard of Clairvaux, Epistle 42 (33). See p. 126 of Bernard of Clairvaux, *Oeuvres Complètes*, Vol. III, Tome 2 (*Lettres*), in the series Sources Chrétiennes, #458 (Paris: Cerf, 2001). The Latin text is from Jean Leclercq and Henri Rochais.
28. Matthew 26:39.
29. Philippians 2:8.
30. "… marries in the Lord": i.e., marries a (Christian) believer in God.
31. Here (at **10**:19) I am reading (with the Paris edition) "quando" in place of "quamdiu".
32. Luke 10:16.
33. Nicholas alludes to John 14:10.
34. Matthew 16:19.
35. We must remember that in this present sermon Nicholas is addressing the

Church at Brixen during his episcopal visitation of it.

36. Nicholas does not teach that man can lose or can abandon his freedom of will. Rather, he is here alluding to a believer's "surrendering" his will to the will of God, i.e., to a believer's conforming his will to the will of God, to his making God's will for him to be his own will for himself.

37. Galatians 2:20.
38. Tobias 6:18-22.
39. Luke 11:41.
40. Here is an example of an indicative mood ("habes") used imperatively.
41. Exodus 20:10.
42. Matthew 12:36.
43. Matthew 15:18-19.
44. Matthew 12:34.
45. Isaias (Isaiah) 51:3.
46. John 3:31.
47. I John 4:5.
48. Apocalypse (Revelation) 16:11.
49. Here (at **16**:52) I am correcting the printed edition of the Latin text to read "maledici" in place of "maledicti".
50. Isidore of Seville, *Sententiae*, II, 29, 5 ("De Summo Bono") [*PL* 83:629].
51. In the printed edition of the Latin text: add quotation marks around "Ecce enim" at **17**:7.
52. Psalms 50:8 (51:6).
53. John 8:44.
54. Bernard of Clairvaux, passage not found.
55. James 1:26.
56. *Dicta Catonis*, Book I, Couplet 3. Edited by Geyza Némethy (Budapest: Hungarian Academy of Letters, 1895), p. 18.
57. *Dicta Catonis, op. cit.*, Book I, Couplet 12 [p. 19].
58. Proverbs 29:20. Ecclesiastes 5:2 (5:3) and 10:14.
59. *Dicta Catonis, op. cit.*, Book II, Couplet 11 [p. 25].

Assumptus Est in Caelum*
("He Was Taken Up into Heaven.")
[May 26, 1457; preached in Brixen][1]

[**1**] "He was taken up into Heaven, and He is seated at the right hand of God" (end of Mark).[2]

(See, in the *Scholarly History*,[3] the story of Christ's Assumption into Heaven. And for an interpretation, see the illustration mentioned elsewhere, [viz.,] in my sermon [preached] in Erfurt;[4] for [that illustration] is sufficiently suitable.)

[**2**] Mark states that the Apostles did not believe those who saw Christ after the Resurrection. Accordingly, he adds: "*Lastly, He appeared to the eleven [disciples] as they were eating.*"[5] Moreover, Jesus, while eating with them, etc., (as Luke says),[6] reproached [them for] their unbelief and their hardness of heart.[7] For they did not believe those who had seen that He had arisen from the dead. Note that unbelief comes from hardness of heart. Now, that heart is hard which is not pliable and soft and tempered for receiving an impression. [**3**] "Heart" stands for the inner man. Hence, the inner man[8] must be docile; otherwise, it does not receive the form of wisdom. But why are the Apostles called unbelieving and hard [of heart]? Surely, [Christ] permitted them to be such for the sake of a more excellent salvation. For it did not befit our salvation to believe quickly on the basis of those evidences by which Christ showed that He had arisen. For the evidences ought to have been multiple and varied, since, given the form in which He then was, no one [of them] proved that He was Christ. For a variety of God's works, no one of which [by itself] suffices to show His omnipotence, occurs in order that [the omnipotence] may be better displayed.

The text [of Mark] says: "*... who saw that He had arisen from the dead.*"[9] I take [this] to mean that from the condition of the dead (who remain immovably where they are laid) [the Apostles] recognized that Christ had arisen—[recognized it] when He appeared to them alive. That is, [they recognized it] by those works that befit the living; for they saw [Him] walking, talking, eating, and so on.

[**4**] However, He made of them believers. That is, [they believed] that just as from within the womb of the Virgin the divine nature assumed into union with itself a true, living human nature (consisting of a body and a soul), so too the mortal body, which was sepa-

rated from the soul by death, maintained this same union [with the divine nature]. [And] the soul, [also] united to the divinity, reassumed the body from the sepulcher—[doing so] by the power of the divinity once [the body's] mortality was shaken off. Thereafter, [Christ] said: "Going into all the world, preach the gospel to every creature."[10] That is, go once this faith has been confirmed by the Holy Spirit, who will, very shortly, descend upon you (as Luke reports[11]). For no one is suited for preaching the gospel unless he has that Spirit which causes the soul—once all unbelief has been expelled—to be fervent with that divine fervor, so that the soul's words are an expression made ardent by God—indeed, made exceedingly ardent. For by means of the word [the Holy Spirit] breathes firey ardor into the hearts of those who hear [it]. About this fact the Savior speaks: "I have come to send fire on earth; what will I but that it be kindled?"[12] And [this] is the fire of love, when the whole man is fervent with yearning for the Kingdom of eternal life.

[5] "... *into all the world*" indicates that [Christ] willed that all men be saved. And so, in the midst of the world He wrought salvation, so that [the Apostles] would preach as they went circularly from the center to the circumference. In the Church we sing thusly: "Go into the world-orbit ...," etc. Lo, how our King established the fullness of His Kingdom! For He sent His law to the whole world. Therefore, God's Church—whose King, Head, and Teacher is Christ—is not confined to a particular location but is extended unto the ends of the earth, and there is no end of the King's dominion. And if up to now Christ is still not accepted in some region of the world, assuredly He *will be* accepted; for the whole world is His possession. Christ would not have commanded the Apostles (and, in and through them, their successors) to go into all the world unless He had foreseen in every part of the world believers and those who are predestined to the Kingdom of God. And so, that Kingdom of Christ's is called the Catholic Church, because what is catholic is universal.

[6] [Jesus] says: "*Preach the gospel* ...." "To preach" can also mean *to prophesy*. For a preacher proclaims the status of the future Kingdom, i.e., of the coming Kingdom. Elsewhere he is called a prophet, because he discloses secret and unknown matters. To preach the gospel is to evangelize. For preaching, evangelizing, and prophesying are the same thing. For to proclaim immortal life is an evangelization, or a good proclamation; for the fact that mortal men can—

rightly and by means of the teaching of the Savior, the Son of God—pass from death unto life is the best news.

[Jesus] says: "*... to every creature.*" This good news is to be preached to every creature capable of understanding the word. For no creature that is capable of understanding the word—whether he be barbarian, Scythian, Greek, or Latin—is excluded, wherever he is in the entire world.

[7] There follows [in the text]: "*He who believes and is baptized shall be saved.*"[13] This is the gospel: viz., believing in Christ as the Son of God. And he who puts on Christ in baptism will obtain that which he believes, viz., immortal life and salvation with Christ. He who believes in Jesus is made to be Jesus, i.e., to be saved. For Jesus is the Savior.[14] Matthew adds other things, viz., that [the Apostles] ought also to teach the doctrine of Christ.[15] But those who are now baptized or who amid obstacles[16] are presently coming to faith are saved. And so, properly speaking, the good news of salvation is *this*: viz., that faith furnishes immortality in the Kingdom of Christ.

[8] There follows [in the text]: "*... but he who does not believe shall be condemned.*"[17] [Jesus] does not say to be condemned both "he who does not believe *and* he who believes but is not baptized." For [only] faith is of necessity; baptism is a sacred sign of faith. Therefore, faith [by itself] suffices [for him] who has faith but who cannot obtain the sacrament [of baptism]—for example, the thief on the cross.[18] From this [passage] it is evident that one who does not believe in Christ, who promises to believers eternal life, is condemned, i.e., is damned with eternal death. For our spirit does not obtain that which it neither loves nor hopes-for. For love unites the spirit to the beloved. But he who-does-not-believe neither loves nor hopes-for. And so, he who does not believe that he can obtain eternal life remains in eternal death.

[9] [Jesus] says [in the text]: " *...shall be condemned.*" For after the gospel is preached and spurned, [the one who spurns it] will be justly condemned, because he has spurned the Son of God and has not believed in Him. By the word that speaks in the conscience of the unbeliever, [the unbeliever] will be condemned. Within himself he would be saying: "I was able to live but I assign to myself the death that I am undergoing." And so, he shall be condemned by his own judgment, and he shall be tormented eternally. For by assigning to himself death, he torments himself. And so, those to whom the gospel is

not preached are not thus eternally condemning and tormenting themselves. In comparison with unbelievers they are said to have no sin, if they otherwise have not acted against their tormenting conscience. As Christ said to the Jews: "If I had not come ...," etc., "they would not have sin."[19] [**10**] If you consider the worm-of-conscience, which does not die[20] but always gnaws, you will find that it is the judgment of God's word. For this word, which judges by means of reason, whose judgment is called the dictate of conscience, is nothing but that light—viz., the word of God—which illumines every man. And by means of that light [every man] reads within himself the judgment [of conscience].[21]

[**11**] There follows [in the text]: *"But these signs shall follow those who believe: [viz.,] they shall cast out devils in my name ...,"* etc.[22] Christ wanted these perceptible signs to be sacred signs of that Heavenly Spirit who is given to believers. For one and the same Spirit manifests itself by means of different powers in different believers—even as one human nature manifests itself to the senses in different ways in different men. Hence, that power of the nature-that-is-intellectual and that is of the essence of human nature, manifests itself in one man in one way—e.g., in the art of writing—[and in another man manifests itself] in another way in the art of speaking, in another way in the art of building, in another way in the art of governing. And so, in different ways the power of the intellectual nature shines forth. Likewise, in the different supernatural gifts of grace and of what is supernatural, the Divine Spirit, who is given to believers, manifests His power. [**12**] For when the soul receives this power from on high, then by means of signs that can be made only by that Spirit it manifests that it has received power. And for this reason Paul said that Christ—when He ascended on high, leading with Him captivity captive[23]—gave to men gifts, which [Paul] lists.[24] And these are divine gifts that signify the presence of the Spirit [and] that assure us that we are admitted into fellowship with Christ because we have His Spirit.

[**13**] And consider that by its presence the intellect brings it about that [our] animal nature is assumed into an association with [our] intellect's own nature—i.e., that the ignorance and darkness of the animal nature puts on the light of human wisdom. Similarly, the rational soul passes into an association with the Divinity through its union with the Spirit of God. But note [the following] difference: [viz.,] that the *intellectual* spirit is *created* in the animal nature by being breathed in

[by God]; for that which is animal precedes that which is spiritual, as says the Apostle.[25] However, when the *divine*[26] spirit is breathed-in, it is not created but is *communicated*. And so, there are different created [spirits] in different men; but [in men] the Uncreated Spirit is one and the same. [**14**] And so, in Christians, in whom there is one faith, there is also one Spirit, since faith is only a gift of the Spirit. For when the intellectual nature is elevated beyond itself, so that it sees truth that it does not understand—i.e., when in a very assured way [and] over and above its natural powers it apprehends truth, which it knows to be its life—then, of necessity, this [apprehending] occurs because of a higher Power. And this Power that is higher than the created intellectual power must be divine. For between the intellectual nature and the divine nature there can be no other intermediary nature.

[**15**] Now, of the signs that accompany believers, this [sign] is certain: [viz.,] that that spirit-of-faith removes devils (i.e., adversarial powers) and brings with it a new pronouncement, viz., the Heavenly and powerful pronouncement that is contained in our credal confession of faith. [This spirit-of-faith] removes serpents (i.e., futile promptings whereby the old man,[27] having been made futile, was infected). [This spirit-of-faith] also removes poisonous things (such as erroneous doctrines) that are at odds with its life. [Doctrines] imbibed and heard will not harm it, because once this Heavenly spirit is savored, it does not permit the soul to waver, with the result that the soul would be inclined toward another doctrine. For [this spirit-of-faith] contains the best [doctrine]. And by the hand of its power it cures the sicknesses-of-soul that have been contracted from the flesh. [It cures these] by bridling the lewd desires of the senses and by restraining the body so that the body obeys it. The spirit-[of-faith] works this [restraint] in all believers; and some believers, thus strengthened in the name of Jesus by faith, manifest by external signs these [workings of the spirit]—[manifest them] when they cast out demons, and so on. [**16**] Hence, take note of the fact that we find these deeds to have been done by believers who had this spirit. Therefore, we too who have this same spirit-of-faith do not doubt that in all of us the spirit works, in a spiritual way, those things that (in order to show its power through believers) it showed perceptibly in [believers] other than us. In this present world we can be led to things spiritual only by means of things perceptible.

[**17**] *"And the Lord Jesus, after having spoken to them, was taken up into Heaven, and He is seated at the right hand of God."*[28]

I understand that in Christ the human nature was taken up into Heaven, i.e., into incorruptibility and immortality. For Jesus said that no one would ascend into Heaven except Him who came down from Heaven—adding that He is the Son of man, who is in Heaven (John 3).[29] Thus, when the Son of man uttered these statements, He had not yet ascended, with respect to His human nature, into the Heaven of incorruptibility. For mortal nature had not yet laid aside the possibility-of-dying, which [Christ] proposed to lay aside by dying—as was fitting. But the *person* that spoke was in the Heaven [of incorruptibility], i.e., was in the divine nature, which is immortal. (Likewise, the Heavenly Father dwells in immortality, as Paul said.)[30] **[18]** But after the resurrection from the dead, Christ ascended unto the Heaven of the Father's habitation, i.e., unto immortality. To arise from the dead and from corruption is to indue a pre-existing material with an incorruptible and indestructible nature. Likewise, in the general resurrection the good and the evil [shall] arise. Thereupon certain of these [resurrected ones shall] ascend farther—unto happiness. And they [shall] ascend unto immortality, wherein dwells the Heavenly Father; and they shall enter into eternal life. The others will remain in the lower parts of the earth, i.e., in Hell. But in Christ the human nature arose from the dead [and] is no longer going to die. Thereafter, it ascended above all the heavens until it sat, or rested, at the right hand of the Father—i.e., [rested] in the might of His Immortal Power.[31]

[19] And consider why John the Evangelist and Matthew do not speak of the Ascension: [it is] because they saw that in the case of Christ the Resurrection is also the Ascension. For some men arise in whom [their] resurrection is not [their] ascension; and Christ the Judge determines whether they are to ascend or to descend. But in Christ-the-Judge resurrection and ascension occur together. And because this fact is [also] true only of those who are Christ-like: Christ, for our learning,[32] postponed for forty days[33] His showing evidence of the Ascension. [He did so] in order that in the meantime evidence of the Resurrection would be multiplied (though intermittently) so that [the evidence of the Resurrection] would be better apprehended. However, it is not the case that after forty days He decided *not* to show that He had arisen. For a little while after this [forty-day period] He showed to the Apostle Paul that He had arisen.[34] Therefore, it is evident that the Ascension occurred with perceptible signs in order that by means of these signs we might be persuaded of the truth of the Resurrection, which in Christ is also the Ascension.

[20] Perhaps someone might say: "Because resurrection is common to all, explain how and why this is the case." I answer that the manner [of resurrection] is not known. But according to some [writers] it can be said that there is in man a corporeal nature that is to a great degree celestial—just as in man there is a spirit that is to a great degree divine. And [it can be said] that this celestial nature, which is called a fifth essence [or fifth element][35] and which unites in itself an elemental [nature], remains after the elements [of the body] have been corrupted—even as, if gold had lead unitedly mixed with it, it would remain if the lead were dissolved. And [we can say] that man's spirit is inclined toward this [corporeal-celestial] nature and will be joined to it at the end of the world's motion. As a result, a judgment [will then] be made [by God] about the spirit that is united to such a celestial and incorruptible body. (A man consists of these both, [viz., spirit and body].) Furthermore, [we say that at the Judgment] a man receives either ascent because of his merits or descent because of his demerits.

[21] You might ask further: "Why does the text say that Christ was taken up [into Heaven], etc.?" I reply: Christ frequently refers to Himself as one sent by the Father, and He now is returning as a Victor; therefore, He is taken up in order to sit beside the Father. It is as if our Lord Pope Calixtus were to summon the returning Legate of the Holy Angel[36] to sit beside him (as we read that Peter summoned Linus),[37] so that [the Legate] would be in a position of equality, reigning with the Pope and with him judging all matters. [Let it be] posited that the Legate had manifested his faith and God's glory and that he had conquered the adversary (namely, the Turks) and had freed the Christians who were held captive under them and that he were returning with that victory [and] were leading captivity captive and were leading the redeemed behind the triumphal chariot.

[22] Therefore, understand [Christ's] ascension to be in the foregoing likeness of the Legate. Yet, [the likeness is] remote, because the Pope, who is the representative of God, received a relatively unimportant man to whom he entrusted his deputies so that [that man] would not be merely a private individual but would be a legate with the fullest power of the prince of the religion. And then [the Pope] made him—in accordance with the loftiness of the dignity and the merits of the faithfulness—ascend above all the heavens (i.e., the hierarchical gradations) of the Church (i.e., above all orders and dignities, all principalities [and] powers, etc.) unto an association with himself. [And the

Pope did so] by establishing him as a judge and by giving him all his own things—according as we read of Joseph,[38] who similarly ascended in Egypt, and as we read of Melchisedech,[39] who came to prominence, so that he was [both] king and priest. These men were types of Christ. Hence, because Christ took a human nature into a union with His divinity—[took it] all the way to immortality and to being situated at the right hand of God the Father's power—it is evident that the [human nature] was elevated above all the intellectual heavens, i.e., [above all] powers, thrones, and might.[40] [It was elevated] all the way to being seated with God the Father, of whose Ascension today is the feast-day—[a day] rightly joyous to all men.

NOTES TO *Assumptus Est in Caelum*

* Sermon CCLXXXIV.
1. Thursday, May 26, 1457 was the feast-day of Christ's assumption into Heaven.
2. Mark 16:19.
3. Peter Comestator, *Scholastica Historia*, Chap. 198 of the section *Historia Evangelica* (*PL* 198:1644 B-C).
4. Sermon LXXXV (preached in Erfurt on Thursday, June 3, 1451).
5. Mark 16:14.
6. Luke 24:41-43.
7. Mark 16:14.
8. Here (at **3**:2) I am reading "illum" with ms. *L* in place of "quem" with ms. V_2. The demonstrative "illum" refers to *interior homo*.
9. Mark 16:14.
10. Mark 16:15.
11. Acts 1:4-8. (Luke is regarded as the author of the Book of Acts.)
12. Luke 12:49.
13. Mark 16:16.
14. The name "Jesus" means *savior*. Matthew 1:21.
15. Matthew 28:19-20.
16. Note, below, the example of the thief on the cross.
17. Mark 16:16.
18. Luke 23:39-43.
19. John 5:22.
20. Mark 9:43.
21. Romans 1:18-32.
22. Mark 16:17.
23. Ephesians 4:8.
24. Galatians 5:22-23.
25. I Corinthians 15:46.
26. Here (at **13**:10) I am reading "spiritus divinus" with ms. *L*. Ms. V_2 omit "divinus".
27. Romans 6:6. Ephesians 4:22-24.
28. Mark 16:19.
29. John 3:13.
30. I Timothy 6:16.
31. "… in virtute immortalis potentiae." Cf. Ephesians 1:19.
32. Romans 15:4.
33. Acts 1:3.
34. Acts 9:3-5. I Corinthians 15:8.
35. The traditional four elements are earth, air, fire, water. Later a fifth element was added to the list. See Thomas Aquinas, *Quaestiones Quodlibetales*: Quodlibetum VI, Quaestio XI, Articulus XIX, ad 1.
36. The editors of the printed Latin text here refer to the entry, in the *Lexikon für Theologie und Kirche*, on Juan de Carvajal (1399-1469).

37. See *Le Liber Pontificalis: texte, introduction et commentaire* by L'Abbé L. Duchesne (Paris: Boccard, 1955). Vol. I, p. 118, lines 8-10. This is section 1, 3 on "Petrus". See also p. 6 of *The Book of the Popes (Liber Pontificalis): to the Pontificate of Gregory I*. Translated by Louise R. Loomis. New York: Octagon Books, 1979.

38. Genesis 41:37-45.

39. Hebrews 7:1-17. Genesis 14:17-20.

40. Ephesians 1:20-23.

Sufficit Tibi Gratia Mea*
("My Grace Is Sufficient for You.")[1]
[February 20, 1457; preached in Brixen]

[1] "My grace is sufficient for you" [is read] in [today's] epistle.

The Apostle, who asked to be freed from a "thorn," received the foregoing answer from the Lord. And he adds the reason for the answer: viz., that "power is made perfect in infirmity." The Apostle concludes: "Therefore, I shall gladly glory in my infirmities so that the power of Christ may dwell in me." By means of these [words] he instructs us that the power of Christ dwells in him who, in order to give to Christ the honor of power, glories that he is infirm.

Let us note, then, this epistle, in which the Apostle declares of the power of Christ that it dwells in him. He spoke of pseudo-apostles—ministers of Satan—who transfigure themselves into true apostles, even as Satan [transfigures himself] into an angel of light.[2] And he renders the Corinthians attentive to not being deceived by those whose end is according to their works.[3] And since many of them were glorying "according to the flesh" (as if [glory] ought to be duly accorded them because they were descendants of the prophets and the patriarchs): lest they be deceived because of this fact [of descendancy, the Apostle], like one who is foolish, lists about himself those things that are greater than are the things whereof *they* can glory.[4]

[2] Consider, then, that the apostles are ministers of justice. Therefore, Christ, whose apostles they are, is Justice. Some who feign being just—who under the guise of justice (i.e., by means of observing formalities and legalities) feign being apostles—aim at worldly gain and profit [and] seek their own advantage.[5] Accordingly, Christ is presented [by them] in the shape and outward appearance of sheep, but their disposition is that of wolf-like greediness. [3] Hence, in order to take away from the pseudo-apostles their pretext [for glorying], the Apostle abstained from a permissible receiving of things needful for living. Moreover, lest they would highly esteem themselves because of the fact that they prided themselves on being Jews and Israelites, he did some things (viz., he cited his condition and glory) that were commonly accustomed to be done not in accordance with God or with wisdom but rather in accordance with foolishness. For in Proverbs 24 praising oneself is forbidden.[6] For commonly it is not permitted; but [it

is] rightly [permitted] in the case of the Church's edification.[7] Therefore, [Paul] set aside that which is [commonly] permitted and did what is [commonly] forbidden—[did it] so as to take away from false apostles their rationale for believing [themselves to be superior] and so as to edify the Church. It is as if the Apostle were saying: "Set before your eyes the fact that I have walked in the plain view of the Church, and consider what kind of person I am in comparison to them and to all the things regarding which they vaunt themselves. Consider the story of my life, and you will find that I am indeed to be believed."

[4] But we ought to take cognizance of the Apostle's wondrous practical wisdom: no matter whether [what he said] would be reckoned to him for wisdom or for foolishness, no matter whether it would be construed as vanity or as glory, he did not for this reason remain silent, but he promoted the truth. Likewise, let us carefully consider what kind of man Paul was and consider that he suffered hardships patiently and underwent perils of body in order to preach Christ, with whom he was acquainted in the rapture unto the Third Heaven, or Paradise, at the time (as is believed) when he was blind for three days.[8] Christ introduced Paul to a vision of immortal riches, which He promised to give him as remuneration if he would serve as a servant faithful in preaching the gospel. And Paul believed the promise; and he bore witness to that which he saw; and he caused believers to hasten with him unto an apprehension of that treasure.[9]

[5] In this regard, note that the place of delights is the palace of God's glory, i.e., is that loftiness of ascent that is called the Third Heaven.[10] Kings have quite private places where they appear to their friends and show themselves to them in glory and majesty. Hence, in the less private places (e.g., the place of assembly where the domestics remain) they make an appearance augustly; and, secondly, they make an appearance more augustly in the Council, where the wisemen and the courtiers come together decorated with royal gifts. Nevertheless, [a king appears] still more [augustly] in his own private quarters, where he manifests himself to his friends in majesty and glory [and] with open treasures. To this third place of all royal delights there are admitted only the very trustworthy and very beloved, to whom it is granted to see the face of the king and to see him in majesty there where he manifests unbecloaked his most private and most hidden things—[manifests them] as to his only son. There [in the Third Heaven] Paul heard secret words that it is not granted to man to utter.[11]

[6] Earlier the Apostle said: "I will come [to telling of] visions and revelations."[12] Here he says that he heard secret words. It is necessary that seeing and hearing coincide. For example, he who reads a book hears the author of the book speaking. But he does not hear with his bodily ear; rather, he hears within, where he hears however much he sees. For he hears as much as he sees with an inner vision, i.e., with the intellect. Therefore, when he is caught up unto the word and conception of the writer—[caught up] by means of perceptible letters and human knowledge (i.e., by means of human reasoning and human logic and by means of a knowledge of [the meaning of] words)—he ascends unto the conception, or intent, of the author. And [the author's] conception, or word, is incorporated within the word, or conception, of the reader; and with this conception [the reader] descends to seeing, i.e., to understanding, the book; and by means of the book the reader ascends again unto the word and sees the author's wisdom. In an analogous way, the Word is the Father-Creator's Wisdom, which causes the intellectual nature that apprehends the Word to be conformed to itself.

[7] Let us say, then, that Paul was raptured and that in the rapture he saw, in the Paradise of delights for the spirit, the Word of God. And [let us say] that, by seeing, he heard secret words—viz., heard in what way Wisdom speaks secret words through which it infuses itself into the intellect, where it remains as the light of the intellect's life. For he who when thus rapt has received within himself the Word[13] through which the Creator described this book (viz., the book of the creation): he understands (by means of that Word, which is the Form of things) all the things contained in the book [of creation]; and within himself, where he has received[14] the Word, he comprehends all things. And whether he ascends or descends, whether he enters in or goes out: because he has the Word, or the Door,[15] or the Life,[16] he will find Paradise's pastures,[17] which are the food of immortal life.

[8] Augustine, in the sermon in which he expounds this epistle, says that Paul was raptured from corporeal things unto immaterial things that are likenesses of corporeal things (even as the imagination is related to the senses in the absence of what is perceivable).[18] And from something thus immaterial [Paul was raptured] unto an intellectual utterance, unto the Paradise-of-delights of all paradises-of-delights—i.e., unto a vision of the Trinity. [Augustine] says: "If a good soul has joy in the good things amid the whole creation, what is more excellent than the joy that is [obtainable] in God's Word, through

which all things were made?"[19]

And although Paul says that he does not know whether at that time [of rapture] he was in the body or out of the body,[20] nevertheless he thereby makes manifest to us great secrets. For our intellectual nature, which is called the inner man, is capable of light and of the intellectual word of God. For the Word of God is a Spirit and is heard only in the intellectual spirit and speaks within and from within. For it does not come from without as does a perceptible voice, which is formed from contracted air. And so, when the inner man is caught up unto the Word of God, it withdraws from the outer, perceptible world. And this separation is seen to be a [partial] withdrawing from the body and from every corporeal nature. But, nevertheless, since the soul does not on this account [altogether] depart from the body, which it animates, the withdrawing from the body is not observed. Accordingly, the rapture unto the vision of the Word of God does not appear to be a separation; for [the rapture] is [the place] where outside and inside coincide, because *there* 'to withdraw from' is 'to enter into'. [9] For the Word of God is the Logos, or the Absolute Form, which grants to every intellect intellectual-being. Thus, [the Word of God] is the Center of intellectual being. Hence, one's being raptured unto the Word is an *entering in* by *withdrawing from*, as in a case where one proceeds from the circumference to the center, [or] proceeds from the composite to the simple, [or] from the body to the spirit. Yet, this [proceeding] occurs in a coinciding, so that (1) withdrawing is entering-into or approaching and (2) outside is inside. But how it is that outside coincides with inside is known by God alone, who is outside of all things in such a way that He is within all things. And, hence, the Apostle [Paul] states that he does not know [how] this [coinciding occurs], but he declares that God knows it.

[10] Subsequently, we are taught here [in today's text] that the inner-man, which is immaterial, has a name as regards the outer-man. Paul was raptured unto the Third Heaven, although the same Paul was in Damascus. For in accordance with the carnal outer-man, with respect to which he was in time and place, he was a living and true man present in Damascus. But in accordance with the immaterial inner-man, with respect to which he was not in time and place, he was raptured unto the Word-of-God, which is not bound to space or time, both of which exist [ontologically] subsequent to Him and because of Him.

[11] Paul says that he heard secret words that it is not granted to

a man to utter.[21] He says "to a man" (viz., to one who is in time) because those corruptible ears could not grasp God's incorruptible secrets. Therefore, it is not granted to a carnal man to speak, and to unveil, the secrets of the Spirit of God. That Spirit who is the Word of God utters these secrets within the spirit of a man. In this [human] spirit the Word is received, and this speaking occurs in silence and in secret, because the words are secret [words].[22] What is secret is hidden. Speaking in hiddenness is a revealing in spirit. As we commonly say: "My conscience tells me this." That's when secret matters are revealed to conscience. For conscience says that God is to be loved because God is Goodness itself, which is loved in whatever things are loved. [12] The Word, or Logos, that is present in the desiring spirit reveals this basis for loving God. And this is the word that speaks in conscience. About this [word] the prophet said: "I will hear what the Lord will speak in me."[23] For it is reason that persuades [us] concerning [what things are] best—e.g., concerning justice, truth, graciousness, and the virtues. And so, to this Word, thus speaking in us, let us give a name that accords with our hearing it [speak]. For example, if [the Word] persuades us that justice is to be cherished, we call the Word *Justice*; if graciousness, *Graciousness*; if truth, *Truth*; and so on, with respect to all the excellences. Hence, we say that that Word is the Excellence of excellences, the Wisdom of holy wisemen, the Immortal Life of all who are living immortally—and whatever such things.

[13] [Let us note] next: this speaking-of-the-word that occurs in the hiddenness of our spirit—where conscience is the locus of hearing—is heard by seeing. When we wish to correct, in a brotherly manner, someone who errs: we commonly ask that he look to his conscience, which reproves him if he sins. This looking is his hearing the reproving [conscience]. Therefore, when the inner-man is caught up unto the Word of God (i.e., unto the locus of hearing, where the Word is heard to set forth hidden words in the secret-place, namely, of conscience: then the [inner-man], by seeing, hears those things of which it is not granted to speak. [14] The prophet said: "my secret to myself."[24] For to every rational faculty Absolute Reason speaks—secretly and in hiddenness—its own word, as it were, sent from the secrets of God to each rational spirit. And in this school of Christ, who is the Word of God, each one can apprehend and study the evangelical teaching that is vital and that is suitable to himself and that offers immortality.

As regards this topic, let the foregoing things be said in the foregoing way for the time-being.

[**15**] Next, let us reflect upon our theme that grace is a sufficiency. For to a faithful servant who has as his Master Him who is Graciousness itself, it is enough to have his Master's favor, [or grace]. For in that case, [the servant's] weakness does not diminish the favor but rather increases the Master's mercy toward the servant. For the Lord is very gracious to him because the very weak man is a very faithful [servant]. Such a faithful [servant] glories in his weakness because, [as a result of it], the power of the Lord's grace abounds in him. "Power is made perfect in weakness."[25] Accordingly, there follows [in the text]: "Gladly will I glory in my infirmities in order that the power of Christ may dwell in me." Elsewhere[26] [Paul] says: "When I am weak, then I am quite strong." Power is strength and stamina. Therefore, strength coincides with weakness. [**16**] When Paul thrice asked of Christ to be freed from that weakness-of-flesh, (viz., from the thorn [of the flesh]), he obtained not liberation but rather Christ's strength and power. This is the power that does not permit Satan to prevail with his temptings; but it does permit him to tempt. And when temptation reaches the point that because of the weakness of the flesh one despairs of his power to resist, then Christ, who has been invoked, is present and is the Victor over the Tempter. At His command Satan withdraws. Therefore, he who battles under Christ's [command] and who is in Christ's grace cannot be overcome; for, at the right moment, Christ's power is present. By "at the right moment" I mean the moment when human resources cease and no hope of further resisting remains. And so, Paul elsewhere states that he is not permitted to be tempted beyond that which he is able to bear but that [God] gives, together with temptation, a way of escape.[27]

[**17**] The Tempter is not overcome except by the power of Christ. Temptation is permitted for a time in order to show Christ's power— for the sake of progress on the part of the one who is tempted. But, at the right moment, our Helper is present. When He is asked, He delivers the one who is experiencing trials. And not only does He deliver him, but he also glorifies him, as if the one in and through whom the power of Christ wrought the victory had himself wrought the victory. [Christ] gives the reward of victory to him in and through whom He conquers. For the one in and through whom He conquers is His faithful [servant]. And so, [Christ] dwells in him through grace. The faithfulness of the servant is the abode of the Lord's grace. The Lord

ascribes to the faithfulness of the servant the triumph that He brings about by means of His own power and might. And so, faithfulness obtains the reward, because faithfulness is what attracts the strength-giving grace.

[18] Let us also reflect upon the phrase "is sufficient," where Christ said "My grace is sufficient for you." For nature does not suffice; only grace is sufficiency; it contains that which is lacking. To the servant of a king there is lacking nobility of birth, mighty strength, practical wisdom in deeds; and there are lacking to him many other things that are required in a royal minister. However, because of his faithfulness, he is in the king's favor, [or grace]. The king's favor suffices; it supplies all [that is lacking]. For it makes the servant noble, strong, and practically wise in the king's eyes. And his being—by grace—without defect in the eyes of the king is sufficient for him. [19] Grace makes a man worthy to be the adopted son of God, so that he is supremely happy as being an heir to the Kingdom of God. The grace of God is the form that perfects an infirm nature. Christ is the fullness of perfecting-grace, meant to be imparted to all. All [who receive grace] receive [it] from Christ's fullness, and from Christ's fullness they are perfected. Therefore, this grace is sufficient for all, even as [it was sufficient] for Paul. Christ is Absolute Grace, without which no one can be pleasing to God and through which all who are pleasing to God are made pleasing [to Him]—as in the case of the true Son of God, whose Sonship enfolds all grace.

[20] Let us, therefore, together with Paul, be faithful. And let us show faithfulness amid all hardship—[faithfulness] even unto death—just as did Paul. And [then] we will have a sufficient amount of Christ's grace, through which we will be like Him[28] in the glory of God the Father, who is forever blessed.

NOTES TO *Sufficit Tibi Gratia Mea*

* Sermon CCLXIX.
1. II Corinthians 12:9.
2. II Corinthians 11:13-14.
3. II Corinthians 11:15.
4. II Corinthians 11:18 - 12:18.
5. Re "seek their own advantage" (*"quae sua sunt quaerunt"*), note I Corinthians 13:5.
6. Proverbs 27:2 (not Proverbs 24, as Nicholas misremembers).
7. Thus, Paul is permitted to boast of his sufferings for Christ, inasmuch as these boastings edify the Church.
8. Acts 9:8-9.
9. Here (at **4**:16) I am reading, with ms. *L*, "secum" in place of "sensum".
10. II Corinthians 12:2.
11. II Corinthians 12:4.
12. II Corinthians 12:1.
13. John 1:12.
14. Here (at **7**:11) I am understanding *"concepit"* to have the same meaning as *"recepit"* at **7**:6.
15. John 10:9.
16. John 14:6.
17. John 10:9.
18. Augustine, *De Genesi ad Litteram*, XII, 34 (*PL* 34:483).
19. Colossians 1:16.
20. II Corinthians 12:3.
21. II Corinthians 12:4.
22. Throughout this sermon Nicholas uses *"verbum"* sometimes to refer to God the Son, who is the Word of God, and sometimes to refer to what Paul "heard" from the Son of God in the rapture. Moreover, the Word of God is eternally spoken, or begotten, by God the Father. Furthermore, the risen Christ is He who speaks, through the Holy Spirit, to believers. And so on. In developing his homiletical theme, Nicholas trades upon this manifold use of *"verbum"*. It is sometimes difficult to know whether or not to capitalize the English term that translates *"verbum"*.
23. Psalms 84:9 (85:8).
24. Isaias (Isaiah) 24:16.
25. II Corinthians 12:9.
26. II Corinthians 12:10. Nicholas is here alluding—not quoting exactly. (He seems not to remember that this passage is one that immediately succeeds his theme-verse.
27. I Corinthians 10:13.
28. I John 3:2.

Paraclitus autem*
("But the Paraclete ....")[1]
[May 31, 1444; preached in Koblenz][2]

[1] "But the Paraclete, the Holy Spirit, whom the Father will send in my name, will teach you all things and will bring to your mind whatever things I will have said unto you."[3] John 14.

Let the grace of the Holy Spirit be present with us; by means of a yearly feast-day we celebrate the descent of this grace unto the Church. God the Father created man; God the Son regenerated him; God the Paraclete instructs him. We have a certain natural being, in order in this world to be that which we are; and we have it from the Father. We have, over and above this mortal being, the capability of arriving at an eternal, spiritual being; and we have it through regeneration in and through the Son. In our spirit we attain this spiritual being through the Holy Spirit. Therefore, I am going to speak about this Holy Spirit, by whose guiding we proceed here below unto the promise and through whom we obtain happiness at the end of our journey. But because no one will be able to speak rightly about God the Spirit unless the Spirit speaks in and through him, and since the fleshly man does not perceive those things which are of the Spirit:[4] hence—in order that the Spirit may speak in and through me, and in order that your spirit may be aroused by the Spirit of the word-of-God that I am going to utter, and in order that in us the Spirit may increase the fire of divine love into a flame that ascends upwards—let us pray: "Come, Holy Spirit, fill the hearts of believers-in-You, and ignite in them a fire of love for You ...," etc.

PART ONE
Why the Sending of the Spirit of Christ Was Necessary

[2] When He preached in Capharnaum ..., Christ said (to those listeners who received His words in a sensory and fleshly way) that His words were spirit and life.[5] And since the bodily presence of Christ, together with His human and perceptible conduct, impressed on the sensing part of the Apostles' souls certain new and wondrous things, and since Christ, as He passed by and preached the Gospel, was the Sower of the word, and since the hearts of the Apostles were dry: those words, insofar as they were uttered and sown in the human soil of the

Apostles, remained in their literal becloaking and could not bear fruit unless they died with respect to their perceptibility.[6] And, thus, just as a man cannot—by means of his inner, imaginative power—envision [another] man as long as that other man is present perceptibly, so the Apostles could not apprehend Christ by means of their spirit unless Christ withdrew from their senses. For Christ said: "Unless I go away, the Paraclete will not come."[7] Hence, the Gospel says the following: "While still remaining with you, I have spoken. But the Paraclete ..., etc., will teach you...," etc.[8] The Apostles were able to have this doctrine of the Spirit only from the Spirit, so that they understood that the words of Christ are spirit and life.

[**3**] Now, Christ promised to send the Spirit of truth after He Himself was assumed [into Heaven]. This [promising] is to be construed as follows: Since Christ said that He Himself is Life and Truth,[9] He promised to the Apostles His own Spirit, viz., the Spirit of Truth, who proceeds from the Father.[10] For no one can say in truth that Jesus Christ is God and man [i.e., is Divine and human] except by means of that Spirit.[11] And no one can exclaim to the Father "Abba, Father" except by means of the Spirit of truth.[12] For only the Son knows the Father. And so, the Son calls Him whom He knows "Father"; and no one else [knows the Father] except him to whom the Son reveals [the Father].[13] But he to whom the Son reveals [the Father] is he who receives within his own spirit the Spirit of truth and of revelation. Now, Christ declared all things to the Apostles as to friends.[14] But in their spirits they could not receive—and thus did not apprehend—the things declared with spiritual vitality.

But in order that in their spirits they might taste of those things that He impressed on their ears, He commanded that they await expectantly the promise of the Father, etc.[15] [**4**] For the following is the way by means of which one comes from sensory apprehension unto spiritual [apprehension]: viz., [by] hearing of, and seeing, with wonderment the works-of-God that God worked in and through Christ and [by] waiting (and not wandering away but meditating on those works and expecting in highest faith a revealing of things hidden in the Spirit) and [by] praying without ceasing, as did the Apostles for ten days. Etc.[16] For after the Apostles, with greatest desire, persevered in prayer for ten days and awaited the Holy Spirit, the Holy Spirit descended on the eleventh day. Let us look at the [Biblical] story. Etc. But from [that] story we know in what way the Holy Spirit came in accordance with that expectation, and we know under what signs [He came]. But the

Gospel says that only he who observes the word of Christ can have the Father and the Son dwelling in [him] and that to him will be sent the Holy Spirit, who will teach all truth, etc.[17]

Let us consider the Gospel in its summary: "If anyone love me ...," etc.[18]

PART TWO
What the Spirit Is

[5] "But the Paraclete ...," etc.
Because here the Spirit who is the Paraclete is spoken of, we ought to take note of different spirits. For there is the Spirit-of-the-Lord, who is the Creator; [and] there is the spirit that is a creature. The Holy Spirit, who is the Creator, is the Union of the Father and the Son—i.e., [is the Union] of Oneness and of Equality [of Oneness]. From Oneness comes Equality; from Oneness and Equality [of Oneness] comes Union.[19] Etc. Here below, then, the Spirit is the Uniting Power of all creatures. And by the Platonists He is called the world-soul; by others He is called Fate; by still others He is called the divine disposition that inheres unchangeably in things.[20] For just as from oneness there derives otherness, or possibility, and just as from equality there derives the actuality of possibility, i.e., the form by means of which nothing is greater or lesser [than it is]: so from union there derives motion; for nothing can be brought from possibility into actuality except through motion. Similarly, in the case of artifacts we see that form is introduced through motion. Therefore, the motion of the universe descends from Infinite Union. Thus, God is omnipotent and is Absolute Necessity, through which there is the possibility of things. He is Infinite Wisdom, through which there is distinctness and formal disposition. He is Infinite Goodness, through which there is attraction. Accordingly, He creates, disposes, and attracts.

[6] And so, the motion of the universe derives from the Spirit of all things, and this motion is partaken of in various ways—in one way by the intellectual nature, in another way by the rational nature, in still another way by the sensory nature. For certain things partake of this uniting motion for the purpose of *existing*, certain for the purpose of *living*, certain for the purpose of *understanding*. "The Spirit of the Lord has filled the whole world ...," etc.[21] "Send forth Your Spirit, and they will be created ...," etc.[22] But we men partake of this universal motion not only in order to exist, not only in order to live, but also in order to exist

and to live and to taste—intellectually, in their Fount— (*a*) of the Being of omnipotence and (*b*) of the Life of eternal wisdom and (*c*) of Goodness itself.

[7] Therefore, the restfulness of the lowest creatures that partake of the Spirit of all things in a shadowy way consists in their being that which they are in this world. But the restfulness of animals consists in their living in a sensing way. The restfulness of things intellectual consists in their apprehension of life and of intellectual being, i.e., in their apprehension of the true; for the true is the object of the intellect.[23] Now, our spirit has an animal motion by which it moves the body so that the body lives in an animal way; and this motion is manifest only in children and simpletons. Insofar as [our spirit] is an image of God it has a motion by means of which it makes itself to be all things, for it is a likeness of things;[24] and this motion is manifest in men who have the use of reason. And our spirit has both of these motions because of its natural partaking—within its own order—of the Spirit of all things; for [our spirit] is a rational [spirit]. Yet, by means of these movements [our spirit] cannot attain unto rest. For (since its movement is toward the true) it does not attain the true by means of animal motion; rather, [by means of animal motion] it attains life that is corruptible. Moreover, by means of the rational movement by which it makes itself to be the likenesses of things, [it also does not attain the true], since a likeness is not the truth itself but falls infinitely short of it. Hence, in regard to the following, all human motion is rest: viz., in regard to the sensory life of this substance or in regard to an immortal, but sensory, life. But in this [motion] there was ignorance of all things, inasmuch as no one could go beyond the sensing of things or the likeness of the true. And, hence, all men posited this world as their goal.

[8] However, Christ, who is Truth, taught us about another, spiritual world and kingdom; and He made us capable of attaining it in and through Himself. Now, Christ has opened [this kingdom] for us. For that spirit which posits its goal outside of God [and] in [this] world is an evil spirit; it does not have rest, since its motion is not toward truth (where alone there is rest for the intellect) but is away from truth and toward the likenesses of the imagination. Hence, all these [thus-directed] spirits have a false and erroneous motion; their leader is the Prince of this world.[25] But this Prince of this world does not have any power over the truth or over the Spirit of Christ. Similarly, a shadow does not have power over the light; but when light approaches, it withdraws,

and its power is reduced to nothing, as says the Gospel.[26] There are, then, certain intellectual natures that have cloaked themselves with the shadows of ignorance, and they are moved away from the good, the true, and the just. But there are other spirits that move themselves toward the good, the true, and the just. And we apprehend this [fact] in the movement of our spirit. For although our spirit was created by God as good, nevertheless its motion—in order to be rational and to partake of Divine motion in a higher degree—is of free choice. Therefore, if [our spirit] turns away from the good by means of a movement toward what is false and evil, then it consents to this movement. Therefore, that motion to which it thus consents is prompted by some apparent good. Hence, we are said to be prompted to this movement by the seduction of an evil mover. Accordingly, we believe that an evil tempting spirit suggests these things to us. Hence, the doctors [of the Church] assert that each man has an evil spirit and also a good spirit. But this evil spirit induces in a general way to evil things and is subject to the orders of princes who concur in the seducing. Thus, when someone is inclined to the sin of licentiousness, the motion results from a spirit of fornication. And so on. For every motion of turning away from God by means of some particular transgression is done under ther influence of some prince of the world. Yet, all princes of the world are subordinate to one prince, about whom [we read] here in the Gospel.[27]

[**9**] Likewise, all intellectual spirits are powers. And there are powers that move and incline toward the virtues. And there are various spirits that partake of the good nature of the one Supreme Prince, i.e., of the Supreme Spirit; they have been turned to Him and they turn [others] to Him. For all spirits separated [from a body] work, insofar as they exist, either by turning [others] away from the power of the Most High (a power which is the Holy Spirit) because they are turned away or by turning [others to the Most High] because they are turned [thereto]. Now, Christ says that the angels of all those men always see the Face of the Father.[28] These angels have charge of us. (The Psalmist [says]: "He commanded His angels concerning you ...," etc.)[29] And they watch over us with marvelous diligence; and they take extreme care to present us to the Most High. For as Origen says, because of this [caretaking] they know that they serve God pleasingly.

[**10**] Therefore, with regard to every motion toward an end, ascend unto a certain contracted beginning of it, and understand there

the governing divine power, or angel. You see one motion in the leonine species, another in the wolverine species, still another in the ovine species—and so on as concerns all specific natures. Therefore, as regards this power which you see to exist variously in all things that are united in a species: affirm that it is the power of God, partaken of in this contracted way. Now, the power of God is sometimes called an angel—for example, by Christians. Philo, who was a Platonist, said that even demons are spoken of as learned animals. Hence, there are some spirits who are in charge of the movements of the elements, others who are in charge of the movements of the stars, others who are in charge of the movements of reason, others who are in charge of the movements of the senses, etc. Nonetheless, there is one Divine Spirit that in this way is variously and multiply partaken of. By comparison, in a music-organ one wind (*spiritus*) is received in the various ducts or pipes: in and of itself the wind is *one* but in its operation it is multiple, in accordance with the variety of the receiving pipes. Similarly, all kingdoms, with regard to their governing motion, are subject to certain spirits—as we read in [the Book of] Daniel regarding the kingdom of the Persians.[30] Moreover, the universal Church is subject to a rector, as is every church (as [we read] in the Apocalypse).[31] Likewise, the church in Trier [is subject to a rector]; so too is each gathering, whether of the religious or of citizens, etc.

[11] And we must note that just as the Divine Spirit is Love (*amor sive caritas*), or Union, so all such powers-of-union, or spirits-of-union are preservers also of peace. But there are evil spirits who turn away from peace and love and who are prompters of divisiveness. Therefore, consider what wars are waged among spirits and what evil occurs from the triumph of an evil spirit. Hence, since there are some spirits whose movement is from God [and] since there are other spirits whose movement is from the Prince of the world,[32] a man is often deceived because he does not know how to distinguish between spirits; for Satan fashions himself into an angel of light.[33] Therefore, we are commanded to take heed and to test the spirits as to whether they are from God.[34] But unless the Holy Spirit teaches us and brings to our minds words of truth, we shall not attain the distinguishing. And, as Paul says, the discerning between spirits is granted to us in and through the Holy Spirit.[35] Therefore, it is the Spirit-of-the-Lord through whom occurs the motion of all the things that are moved and in whom are all the things that are moved. For He is the Beginning, the Middle, and the End of all motion; He contains all things and fills all things.[36]

PART THREE
What the Holy Spirit Works in Those to Whom He is Sent, and How He is To Be Received; Five Questions

[12] As to the third [topic]—viz., to whom [the Holy Spirit] is sent—it must be said here that the Holy Spirit is sent to those who are intellectually and affectionally capable [of receiving Him], those whose spirit is moved toward the one, the true, and the good.

[13] **How ought we to prepare ourselves so that the Holy Spirit be sent unto us?** I answer: Since the Holy Spirit is the Power (*virtus*) of God, He will be sent only unto a virtuous [*virtuosus*] spirit. For there cannot be [divine] power in a spirit that is insincere and unvirtuous. Rather, a spirit ought to be virtuous, in conformity with its motion toward the one, the true, and the good. Indeed, the principal thing is that [a spirit] move itself (*a*) only toward the One, who is Being itself, i.e., toward the Father; (*b*) only toward the True, i.e., toward the Son; (*c*) only toward the Good, i.e., toward the Holy Spirit. For motion that is toward the one, the true, [and] the good is motion in which Father and Son and Holy Spirit can be present. He who prefers God to everything in the world moves away from the world (which is situated in much divisiveness and in evil) and toward the Father. He who prefers truth to all else moves away from the treacherous deceptiveness of this world unto the Son of God. He who chooses the good in its purity leaves behind all of this world's apparent good. He who habituates his spirit to these motions makes it virtuous. For the whole man will be virtuous if his spirit does not allow his sensual impulses to deviate from this pathway but rather controls his animal body with a bridle and with spurs. For [in this way] he adorns his house with practical wisdom, courage, justice, and moderation,[37] so that in him there can be the theological virtues of faith, hope, and love. It is necessary that our spirit take note of the fact that the words of Christ are spirit and life.[38] [Our spirit] must grasp these [words] and sit and meditate upon them[39] and be aware that unless sensual influence abates, [the Holy Spirit] will not be able to be present in our spirit. We must prayerfully ask Him, implore Him, etc.

[14] Let the house be carefully prepared! Let it be purified by a purging of the uncleanness of sins, for the Spirit is not like a swine, etc. And [this purging] is the getting rid of sensuality, because the sensual man does not perceive the things that are of the Spirit ....[40] (Bernard [says]: just as water and fire are not compatible, so carnal delights and

spiritual delights [are not compatible]). And this [getting rid of sensuality] is the expelling of unclean spirits. "Create in me a clean heart, O God ...," etc.[41] After the purifying, one must adorn [the house] with various pictures of holy meditations. Likewise, through importunate prayer [the Holy Spirit] must be invited; for He is not like a buffoon who goes to a wedding uninvited, etc. The Apostles prayed for themselves and for others (Acts 8). When invited, [the Holy Spirit] comes quickly: "I wished, and understanding was given to me; I called, and the spirit of wisdom came upon me ...."[42] And we ought to call upon Him every three days, not at the last moment. ([See] the end of Luke: "But remain, until you are indued with power from on high.")[43] And note what company the Apostles had when they called upon the Holy Spirit: viz., the company of Mary, the Mother ..., etc. Be serious in this [invoking]. Likewise, it is necessary that you serve Him rather than the world, that you serve the Spirit rather than your belly, etc. Isaias 42: "Lo, my servant; I will uphold him. [Lo] my elect; my soul has taken delight in him. I have given my spirit upon him."[44] As regards John the Baptist: "The child grew and was strengthened by the Holy Spirit ...," etc.[45] Moreover, one must prepare a bed for Him, because He is not like a miller who sleeps amid the commotion [of the water-mill], etc. Isaias 11: [the Spirit of the Lord] will rest upon him who is humble and quiet.[46] In addition, it is necessary that you receive His household also, for He is not a rustic lord ..., etc.

[15] How is the Holy Spirit in us? God is present in His creation in a twofold way: either (*a*) by means of His essence, presence, and power (and in this way He is present everywhere) or (*b*) spiritually and by grace when He gives gifts of grace—as occurs here [in the giving of the Paraclete]. Hence, [God the Holy Spirit] comes bearing a gift. (Romans 5: "The love of God is shed abroad in our hearts by means of the Holy Spirit, who is given to us.")[47] One is saved not through grace given freely but rather through grace that makes one pleasing [to God], i.e., through love; for without the Holy Spirit one is not saved ..., etc.: if I do not have love, I am nothing ....[48] This love pleasantly joins the soul, through love, to God; and it is called *a pleasant love*. And it enjoins all the powers of the soul and of the body to serve the Beloved in every place and at all times ..., etc. Also, it is called *an ardently desiring love*, because it ardently desires to serve; and it is called *an operative love* or *an active love*. There is another stage [of love], through which [the soul] urges that the Beloved be loved, praised, blessed, etc., by all. And then love-of-neighbor flows forth; and it is ascribed to the Holy Spirit (although the works of the Trinity are undivided) because it proceeds in the manner of a gift ..., etc. The Holy Spirit, because He is holy, comes by way of sanctifying.

[16] In what way is the sending of the Holy Spirit [to be] understood? I answer that the sending of the Holy Spirit is described as follows: it is the proceeding of love from the Father and the Son unto creatures for the sake of creatures' sanctification. Only a rational nature or an intellectual nature is sanctifiable, because only [such a nature] is capable of attaining God by way of understanding and by way of affection. And sanctity is nothing other than the grace that makes one pleasing [to God]; or rather, the love that the Holy Spirit infuses at His coming [is the grace that makes one pleasing to God]. Moreover, fear first arises from one's meditating on his sins, from severity of judgment and of punishment; and [this] is a servile fear, and it is the beginning of wisdom.[49] Next, [the fearing spirit] reflects on the goods of the Creator—[goods] which the Creator has bestowed; and [the spirit] is ashamed of its offense, etc. And this fear of the Lord is the initial fear through which the Holy Spirit first enters into the mind. But where the [fearful spirit] reflects not on his own [affairs] nor on punishment but on the things that have to do with honoring and reverencing God, then the fear will be filial fear; and [this *fear*] is the first gift [of the Spirit].[50] Next, the mind is made *devout*, i.e., is made generously benevolent. Hence, it strives (*a*) to recompense God for all that He has bestowed and (*b*) to recompense its neighbor for God's sake, giving the neighbor whatever compassion it can, etc. And [this] is the second gift [of the Holy Spirit]. But because discernment is necessary for this [devoutness of mind], there comes the gift of [that] *knowledge* which is a supernatural discerning among things doable. And because such hardships of temptation occur, there comes next the gift of *courage*; then comes the gift of *counsel* for the purpose of ardently accomplishing those things that the spirit is counselled. And the foregoing are the gifts that have to do with the active life. Next, comes the gift of *understanding* that is present in the contemplative life. Through this gift [our spirit] understands[51] the wondrous power of God and His marvelous works and [the requirements] of His law, etc.[52] Next, there is the gift of *wisdom*, [given] so that one may taste how sweet the Lord is, etc.[53] (Note: a visible sending is evident through signs; an invisible sending occurs without a sign.)

[17] In what way are we to regard the differences of the gifts? I answer that (1) there are certain gifts of the Spirit together with which there is *not conferred* the grace that makes one pleasing [to God]: for example, servile fear [of God] and faith that is not in-formed [by love]. (2) There are certain gifts of the Spirit together with which [the aforementioned grace] is *not always* [*conferred*]: for example, the gifts of tongues, of miracles, of prophecy. (3) There are other gifts by means of which holiness *is always conferred*; indeed, they are the sanctifying of a creature: for example, love, which makes a man acceptable and pleasing to God ([and] this [making acceptable] is [what is meant by] sanctifying). Accordingly, with the infusion of love the Holy Spirit is given. For [love] is the virtue of virtues and is their form, giving meritorious being—something which the other virtues cannot have apart from love, because without love a man is nothing ..., etc.[54] Augustine, *On the Trinity* XV: love by itself distinguishes the children of God from the children of perdition. Now, love cannot be a fixed disposition (*habitus*) that is acquired from frequent acts; for human exercisings cannot (however much they aim to do so) attain the ultimate end—attain it in the supernatural way in which love moves the mind both here below and in Heaven. Rather, love is a fixed disposition that is specially infused by God through the Holy Spirit. And among created gifts, [love] is the most excellent [gift]. Or rather, it is a certain partaking of the Uncreated Gift, viz., the Holy Spirit, from whom it flows directly into the rational spirit, flowing subjectively into the will, enlivening all the powers of the soul and directing [the soul] unto God.

[18] For just as the Holy Spirit is the Union and indissoluble Bond by whom the Father and the Son love themselves and us, so the power of love is a certain union by means of which we are united lovingly and formally to God and, in and through God, are bonded with our neighbor. And this [connectedness] is [what it means for] God to dwell in us and for us to dwell in God. [This connectedness] does not occur after the fashion of moral friendships, which—with a view to what is good, honorable, delightful, or useful—bind [the friends] together for the sake of political association; rather, this love is most lofty with respect to divine and beatific association. It has orderliness; for, first of all, [it directs us] above ourselves unto God on account of God. For he who acknowledges God [only] when it benefits him loves himself more than he loves God, and he is outside of love. Secondly, [through love] one is brought unto himself, so that he loves himself as a participant in God's glory. Thirdly, [he is brought] unto that which is on a horizontal plane with him; i.e., [he is brought unto] his neighbor as unto a fellow-seeker of happiness. But he who loves his neighbor not for God's sake but for his own sake is not [abiding] in love. Fourthly, [the one who has love is brought] unto that which is below himself, viz., unto his body, so that he nourishes it, rules over it, chastises it, so that it may be made a partaker of happiness. But love (*caritas*) is not a desire-filled loving of one's flesh (*diligere carnem in desideriis*) ..., etc.

[**19**] Therefore, since love is the life of the soul, every sin that is contrary to love is a mortal sin. For example, contempt makes a sin to be mortal, because contempt is opposed to love ..., etc. And so, in an extended sense, every sin is against the Holy Spirit; yet, there are some enumerated sins that are said to be *primarily* against the Holy Spirit. For some sins are against the Father: they are done out of weakness contrary to power, which is ascribed particularly to the Father. Some sins are against the Son: [they are done] out of ignorance contrary to truth or wisdom, which is ascribed particularly to the Son. Some sins are contrary to goodness, which is ascribed particularly to the Holy Spirit. Indeed, those things that are done from malice—e.g., malice such as despises and rejects those things through which sin could be avoided—are said to be against the Holy Spirit. And because the mercy and the justice of God prod us toward hope [in God] and toward fear [of God], then by means of despair and presumptive audacity one sins against the Holy Spirit.

Two things are considered to belong to the gifts of God: the knowledge of the truth and the aid of inner grace. Opposing these are a disputing of known truth (in order that one may sin more unrestrainedly) and jealousy with respect to a brother's grace (when one envies the fact that [one's brother's] grace increases in the world). Moreover, with regard to sin there are two things that ought to hold us back: viz., (*a*) the baseness, or disorderedness, of the act and (*b*) the smallness, or meagerness, of the good which is obtained by means of the sin. In the beginning, [the good] is rejected by means of unrepentance—i.e., by having the intent of not repenting. Thereafter, it is rejected through stubbornness, for [stubbornness] reinforces the mind's resolve to cling to the sin. These sins have no excuse and, hence, are not forgiven. But because God's mercy can assist some men to return to their heart and to receive contrition for certain sins, the remission of these sins does also occur, etc.

[20] **Why is the Holy Spirit commonly called Teacher, Liberator, Strengthener, Comforter ..., etc.?** I answer: [He is called] Teacher because He teaches about true life, in opposition to hypocrisy and fraud. Likewise, [He teaches] about true justice, as opposed to greed; about true well-reputedness, as opposed to licentiousness; about true justice, as opposed to pride, which does not allow a man to know himself. Moreover, [the Holy Spirit] frees man from servitude. The law of the Spirit of life-in-Christ set Paul free from the law of sin and of death (Romans 8).[55] (II Corinthians 3: Where the Spirit of the Lord is, there is liberty.)[56] [The Holy Spirit] strengthens in the good, as in the desert John [the Baptist] was strengthened by the Spirit ..., etc.[57] Likewise, [the Holy Spirit] aids and defends His host against His every adversary. (Job 26: The Spirit of the Lord has adorned the heavens.)[58] Similarly, He inflames His host's love for Him. (Romans 5: God's love is shed abroad ..., etc.)[59] Moreover, He receives His host into His own palace.[60] (Your good Spirit leads unto His land ..., etc. Henceforth, says the Spirit, ..., etc.)[61] Moreover, through the Holy Spirit we have forgiveness of sins, victory over our enemies, glorious gifts, grace-given rewards. As regards the first [of these, see] Ezechiel 36: "I will pour forth upon you clean water, and you shall be cleansed ...," etc.[62] "Create [in me] a clean heart ...," etc.[63] II Corinthians 7: "Let us cleanse ourselves ...," etc.[64] As regards the second-mentioned [role of the Holy Spirit]: "The Spirit of the Lord came mightily upon Sampson, and Sampson tore the lion apart."[65] The lion is the Devil: I Peter 5: "Your adversary, the Devil, ...," [etc.].[66] As regards the third [role of the Holy Spirit]: Isaias 11: "A virgin will go forth from the root [of Jesse] ..." (and the other words down to the words "upon Him the Spirit of the Lord"), etc.[67] Regarding the fourth [role]: "The Kingdom of God is not food and drink but is justice and peace and joy in the Holy Spirit" (Romans 14).[68]

[21] Furthermore, the Holy Spirit is Comforter because He illumines the intellect: He infuses the bright ray of knowledge, while inflaming the affections. He bestows the ardor-of-love, while purifying the affections. He reduces the pain-of-temptation, while delighting one's spiritual taste. He affords the sweetness-of-devotion. Take note of how it is that the Holy Spirit is water, fire, ointment, etc., and is all those things that cause growing, purifying, or cleansing. Note that a fervent fire increases with the wind of adversity; thus, one who has the Spirit ..., etc. ("By means of tribulation you have enlarged me ...," etc.)[69] The Apostles, rejoicing, departed from the presence of the council, for they were considered worthy ..., etc.[70]

NOTES TO *Paraclitus autem*

* Sermon XXXVII.
1. John 14:26. The Holy Spirit is called *the Paraclete*, a word deriving from the Greek παράκλητος, meaning *Comforter* or *Intercessor* or *Advocate*.
2. This was the day of Pentecost.
3. John 14:26.
4. I Corinthians 2:14.
5. John 6:64.
6. John 12:24-25.
7. Nicholas alludes to John 16:7. He does not aim to quote it exactly.
8. John 14:25-26.
9. John 14:6.
10. John 14:16-17.
11. I Corinthians 12:3.
12. Galatians 4:6. Romans 8:15.
13. Matthew 11:27.
14. Luke 12:4.
15. Acts 1:4.
16. Acts 2:1.
17. John 14:23 and 16:13.
18. "If anyone love me, he will keep my word." John 14:23.
19. *De Docta Ignorantia* I, 9 (26).
20. Cf. *De Docta Ignorantia* II, 9 (142).
21. Wisdom 1:7.
22. Psalms 103:30 (104:30).
23. Aquinas, *Summa Theologica*, Ia - IIae, 9, 8.
24. The allusion here is to the Aristotelian-Thomistic view that, in perceiving, the mind makes itself to be a likeness of the object perceived, so that perceptual images resemble the objects of which they are images.
25. The reference is to the Devil. John 12:31. John 14:30.
26. Cf. Matthew 4:16.
27. " ... here in the Gospel": i.e., in the Scriptural text for Pentecost, viz., John 14:23-31.
28. Matthew 18:10.
29. Psalms 90:11 (91:11).
30. Daniel 10:4-21.
31. In Apocalypse (Revelation) 2 each church is indicated to have an angel governing it, watching over it.
32. See n. 25 above.
33. II Corinthians 11:14.
34. I John 4:1.
35. I Corinthians 12:10.
36. Ephesians 1:23 and 4:10. Wisdom 1:7.
37. These are the so-called *cardinal virtues*, esteemed by the ancient Greek philosophers and incorporated into Medieval Christian philosophy.

38. John 6:64.
39. Cf. Deuteronomy 6:7.
40. I Corinthians 2:14.
41. Psalms 50:12 (51:10).
42. Wisdom 7:7.
43. Luke 24:49.
44. Isaiah 42:1.
45. Luke 1:80.
46. It is not clear to which passage of Scripture Nicholas is here referring. Cf. Canticle of Canticles (Song of Solomon) 3:1 and Isaias (Isaiah) 11:2 (not Isaias 65, as Nicholas writes and as the editors of the Latin text emend in their notes).
47. Romans 5:5.
48. I Corinthians 13:2.
49. Psalms 110:10 (111:10).
50. The seven gifts of the Holy Spirit are *timor Dei, pietas, scientia, fortitudo, consilium, intellectus, sapientia*. See Isaias (Isaiah) 11:2-3.
51. Here at 16:37 I am reading, with the Paris edition, "intelligat" in place of "intelligant".
52. In line 16:39 I disregard the editors' addition of the word "hic".
53. Psalms 33:9 (34:8).
54. I Corinthians 13:3. Throughout his discussion of love Nicholas uses the word "*caritas*".
55. Romans 8:2.
56. II Corinthians 3:17.
57. Matthew 3:1. Luke 1:80.
58. Job 26:13.
59. Romans 5:5.
60. Here (at **20**:20) I am reading "palatium" (with ms. U_2) in place of "pallatium".
61. See, respectively, Psalms 142:10 (143:10) and Apocalypse (Revelation) 14:13: "Blessed henceforth are the dead who die in the Lord, says the Spirit ...."
62. Ezechiel (Ezekiel) 36:25.
63. Psalms 50:12 (51:10).
64. II Corinthians 7:1.
65. Judges 14:6.
66. I Peter 5:8: "Your adversary, the Devil, goes about as a roaring lion, seeking whom he may devour."
67. Isaias (Isaiah) 11:1-2.
68. Romans 14:17.
69. Psalms 4:2 (4:1).
70. Acts 5:41: "... were considered worthy to suffer shame for [Christ's] name."

Spiritu Ambulate*
("Walk in the Spirit.")[1]
[September 7, 1455; preached in Brixen]

[**1**] "Walk in the spirit."

In this epistle Paul teaches us that man can walk in a twofold way: either according to the spirit or according to the flesh. Thus, the spirit and the flesh are parts of a man. Now, to walk is to move toward that which one desires. But the movement is because of the desire. Therefore, a man's movement is composed of mutually opposing factors, viz., of a twofold desire—[a desire] for things visible and [a desire] for things invisible. As the Apostle says elsewhere: "The things that are seen are temporal, [but] the things that are not seen are eternal."[2] [A man's] every movement is from the soul, which has a twofold spirit. [The soul has] one spirit that is corporeal. By means of it the soul proceeds unto this perceptible world. For example, by means of a bright spirit in the optic veins [the soul] moves toward visible things; and by means of another spirit it moves toward audible things; by means of another, toward things tasteable; by means of another, toward things tangible; etc. And all these things that are perceptible are called [by the Apostle] visible; and just as they are corruptible and temporal, so too this [corporeal] spirit is corruptible. By means of a second spirit a man moves toward things invisible, and [that] spirit is incorporeal and invisible and incorruptible, as are also those things toward which the man moves by means of that spirit. Now, the Apostle illustrates in his epistle both what the corruptible things are and what the incorruptible things are, toward which the soul moves.

[**2**] Certain philosophers stated beautifully that the soul is composed of *the same* and *the different*; and they likened the soul to number, which is both simple and composite.[3] For example, the number three is simple because it is not divisible (for it does not admit of either more or less); but, nonetheless, it is composed of the even and the odd. Yet, it is composed only of itself. (For prior to number nothing can be conceived.) For if you conceive of three units prior to the number three, they do not constitute the number three unless you conceive of them as united. But three units that are united are but the number three. Therefore, [the number three] is composed of itself. And because it is composed, it is from one thing and from another thing, i.e., from what

is odd and from what is even, or from what is indivisible and from what is divisible. And because number is composed of itself it is conceived of as self-moving.

Next, [these philosophers] likened the rational soul to number.[4] For the rational soul is simple and is composed, but is not composed of anything other than itself. Now, since it is from God, who is Simplicity itself, only immediately: it falls short of pure simplicity and is, as it were, a "composite simplicity." Just as in an eagle there is a certain light-weightedness (for this reason the eagle goes above the earth and flies unto the aether), so too the soul turns toward those things that are subject to change, or else it turns toward things eternal and unchangeable—things that always remain existing in one and the same way. Hence, the soul seems to be like a living number that is composed of the *even* (or divisible) and the *odd* (or indivisible). For a soul is a life that can be conceived of as a number that numbers.

[**3**] Indeed, [the soul] is a life that is composed of what is sensory, or divisible, and what is intellectual, or indivisible. And because [the soul] is like a living number, it sees within itself harmonies. For it measures external, perceptible harmony by means of an internal, incorruptible harmony. Moreover, the soul can be conceived of as a living number ten, which within itself has (1) the number that numbers all things and (2) all that which produces, in all things, proportion or harmony or beauty. For example, a [musical-]artist takes a monochord, and with it he produces from a proportion of numbers an octave; and from another relationship [of numbers he produces] a fourth; from another, a fifth. And from these [he produces] harmonies. And he approves of nothing in this art except what conforms to his own nature. For the only reason he knows that there is a harmony from one and two, or from two and three, or from three and four is that he finds in the sound a certain agreement with that which has its origin within himself. And he abhors dissonance because it does not conform to his own being. Hence, he has within himself that by means of which he *measures* and *numbers, compounds* and *divides*—as Boethius says that he unfolds to the external notes that which he harbors within himself.[5] By analogy, if the value of a golden denarius were alive, it could unfold itself and liken itself to many things and could enfold many things by likening [them] to itself. Similarly, the value of a ducat extends over many small coins from Verona; and it enfolds within itself the value of many such coins. For the intellect is, as it were, the value of the things that are understandable by it. These intelligible

things are under the intellect's jurisdiction, as are the forms of perceptible things. For the perfection of the intellectual nature enfolds all sensory perfection, even as intellectual knowledge excels all sensory knowledge and encompasses all such knowledge and extends itself in an unfolding way beyond all such knowledge and unites and collects all sensory knowledge within itself in an enfolding way.

[4] But because neither value nor proportion nor likeness nor unfolding nor enfolding can be understood unless number is first understood: the soul, which makes judgments about all these things, is rightly said to be like a living number, which of its own power can make judgments about all these things. But if someone were to say that number is quantity, I say that I do not mean that the soul is a living number in the likeness of a mathematical number or of a quantity but mean that it is a substantial number, from which the concept of mathematical [number] flows forth in a likeness. For a mathematical number presupposes a certain number that exists in and of itself and that makes a judgment about the mathematical [number].

Now, the soul is not either a number or a harmony or anything that is apprehended by the senses or imaged by the imagination. But because it is created in order that the glory of the Omnipotent Creator may be shown to it, it has an intellectual eye for seeing all the works of God and for discriminating and judging, so that [in this way] it can be elevated unto an admiring of the glory of the Omnipotent [Creator]. But all distinguishing, without which there is no judgment, presupposes number. For without *one* thing and *another* thing there is no distinguishing. But how is it possible that there be one thing and another thing without there being number? Therefore, if number makes possible distinguishing, then the soul can be called a certain living number that unfolds from itself numerical judgments and numerical distinctions.

[5] If, then, the soul is [created] by God in order to attain a vision of the glory of His majesty, then the soul has a body only in order to apprehend God's visible works, to the end [of obtaining a vision] of God's glory. And so, [the soul] ought not to be attached to the flesh or to visible things and ought not to give itself over to corruptible desires but ought in all respects to turn to magnifying the glory of the Great God. And thereby [it ought] to transfer itself by means of visible things unto the Invisible God, in order that God may be the intended End. God is Goodness itself, which is desired by all. Therefore, he who clings to the desires of the flesh posits his state-of-

rest there. His god is his belly.[6] But the spirit, whose essence is not flesh or blood, abhors these corruptible desires. However, the sensual man does not perceive those things that are of the Spirit [of God].[7] God is the Good Spirit, whom all good spirits desire.

So there are contrary desires: the desires of the corruptible nature are directed toward this perceptible world and are temporal; the desires of the incorruptible spirit are not directed toward this corruptible world but are desires to see the King of Peace's glory—a glory that is a peace that surpasses all understanding,[8] a peace than which nothing more joyous or more desirable can be thought of. Hence, Paul admonishes us to walk in the spirit.[9] And he adds the reason: because such ones do not fulfill the desires of the flesh. For the flesh has desires that are at odds with the spirit, and the spirit [has desires that are] at odds with the flesh. (For these [differing desires] are opposed to each other, so that you do those things which you do not wish to do.[10]) For example, if someone who is walking in the spirit sees a beautiful woman, he gives glory to God, and he turns to admiring Infinite Beauty, of whose light this [woman's beauty] is a certain very remote trace. He who thus walks in the spirit does not fulfill the desires of the flesh and does not commit adultery [in his heart][11] with that beautiful woman. For the beauty does not move him carnally but moves his spirit (by which he walks in the spirit) unto admiring the glory of the Creator. When such a man is moved to desire [carnal] union with the beautiful [woman], he thinks in the spirit: "if, even in corruptible material, that which is beautiful[12] is so attractive—if the beauty of the flesh is so appealing to the flesh—then how [greatly must] Absolute Beauty and Beauty *per se* attract the spirit to itself! And of what kind [must be] that delight of the spirit's union with Wisdom, which is Beauty itself!"

[6] Moreover, take note of the fact that the will cannot be compelled to give assent, although oftentimes, because of the resistance of the flesh, a man cannot do that which he wills [to do]. For in the members [of the body] the law [of the flesh] wars against the law of the mind.[13] And because every [act of] sin is voluntary and because the Law was put into place because of transgressors,[14] those who walk in the spirit are not under the Law. And so, [Paul] says that if you are led by the spirit, you are not under the Law.[15] For the spirit leads hearts upward unto God; but the flesh [leads] downwards. Christ said that He is from above because He was led by the spirit and said that the carnal Jews were from below because they were led not by the spirit but by

the flesh. Paul speaks of the works of the flesh as manifest, which are, namely, fornication, uncleanness, etc.[16] All these follow from fleshly desires and are temporal and corruptible. Indeed, they lead him-who-does-them to corruption and death. But because the Kingdom of God is eternal life, such [followers of the flesh] will not possess the Kingdom of God. The Law was set in place for men such [as these]; it is the law of death. Hence, by means of all these [fleshly movements the soul] turns to otherness and division. But the fruits of the movement by which [Paul] commands us to walk in the spirit are, as he says, love, joy, peace, etc.[17] For by means of this movement the soul turns to oneness and sameness. And so, the fruits of that movement are love, joy, peace, etc. All these [fruits] that [the Apostle] lists originate from, and exist from, oneness and sameness. Therefore, they are eternal and unchanging. For the soul proceeds toward union. Yet, strength that tends continually toward union becomes stronger. Against such individuals who are guided in such a way that they bear the fruit of life, no law is set in place. And the following is Paul's intention: [to say] that the Law does not justify; for the Law, set in place because of transgressors, forbids sin. However, the prohibition does not justify; rather, faith does. Faith makes us walk in the spirit; it justifies, (as we clearly apprehend from the fruits enumerated by Paul).

[7] Paul concludes: "Those who are Christ's have crucified their flesh together with its vices and lusts."[18] And such ones have put to death their earthly members, in which there [now] lives only the spirit of Christ. Note that [Paul] says that the flesh is crucified together with its vices and lusts. For the Christian, who is obliged to follow Christ, ought not to permit to his flesh the liberty of walking according to vices and lusts; rather, [he ought] to be fastened with nails to the Cross by way of his unceasing memory of [Christ's] death. For in regard to those whom the flesh (and its vices and lusts) controls: they are subject to the Prince of this world[19] and are not Christ's. For Christ's Kingdom is not of this world.[20] And no one can be of His Kingdom unless he overcomes the Evil One through crucifixion.[21]

[8] Because the conflict of which Paul [speaks] is the beginning and the root of every conflict and every dispute, a certain preacher[22] marvels at this conflict. For it is as if two friends who were raised together from childhood, [and] who had lived together on good terms, [and] whose way of life could not exist without each other's association, were to contend with each other. For there cannot be a greater

friendship in this world than that of the soul and the body. This fact is evident because "friendship" refers to union: it is characteristic of friends to will and not to will the same thing.[23] And such a union, [viz., a union of friends], varies. For example, [there is a union] of citizens who live together in one state and who like one another. A closer union [consists of] those who live together in one house and are of one and the same set of parents [and] who like one another even more. The union of a man and a woman is still closer. Lastly, the soul is united with the body so as to constitute a single human being; this is the closest [union], and [these two] love each other exceedingly.

[9] *Among the first* [group, viz., the citizens,] strife and disagreements arise, and one part [of the citizenry] endeavors to destroy the other. (But by nature the spirit does not wish to be separated from the body. Accordingly, Christ said: "Let this cup pass from me ...," etc.[24]) *The second [kind of] friends*, [viz., those living together,] divide things that are common to them; for example, brothers and sisters [divide] possessions. (However, the body and the soul never desire to divide-up; rather, they share all things with each other, and actions and being-acted-upon are connected. Aristotle in [Book] I of *On the Soul* [notes]: 'Someone's saying that the soul rejoices or sorrows is like his saying that the soul weaves or builds;[25] for no operation of the soul occurs without the body.') The *union of a husband and a wife* is a close union. "For for this reason a man leaves his father and his mother and will cling to his wife."[26] Nevertheless, if one of them dies, the surviving one marries someone else. However, *the body and the soul* are not related in that way; for the body never would will to have a different soul—and vice versa. Moreover, the soul has so great an inclination for the body that it cannot be happy unless it is joined to its body. Hence, just as [the two] were conjoined in regard to what was merited, so they shall be united with respect to their reward. And there is no soul that has had a body so unseemly that the soul would not rather be united to it than to the very beautiful world. For [the soul and the world] would not be congruent with each other; and a perfecting [power] ought [always] to correspond to what is capable of being perfected by it. Now, in this friendship [between the body and the soul] the soul is found to be the more faithful, since it is earnestly concerned over caring for the body. Hence, [the soul] devises whatever things are necessary for the body's preservation, loveliness, and pleasure. For example, reason devises crops for [the body's] nourishment, in order to preserve it. It devises ointment for [the body's] pleasure and also devises pow-

ders and medicines, pleasant colors and pleasant tastes. Likewise, [it devises] different arts-and-crafts that conduce to the comeliness of the head and of the entire body. Etc.

[**10**] Therefore, since the friendship [between body and soul] is so great, it is strange that Paul says, to wit, that [the body and the soul] are opposed to each other. Moreover, since the flesh is so weak that without the soul it cannot either exist or live, how does the weak flesh rebel against the very strong and very quick spirit? Then too, how will our flesh—naked by nature and lacking horns and claws—battle against the spirit, which is armed with knowledge and with skills? The preacher Aldorf[27] answers that the battle is conducted by means of motion: viz., the motion of obedience, of habit, and of corruption. [It occurs] by means of the motion of obedience because to obey its Creator is something innate to every creature; and only the sinner and the demon are exceptions; for a sinner's will resists the Creator. And so, it is proper that [the sinner], because of disobedience, is fought against by his own subordinate. And this is the point that Isidore[28] makes as regards an arrogant man: his body will not be subjected to his soul, nor will his soul be subjected to his reason—if his mind is not subjected to the Creator. But all the things that are subject to us are rightly subject to us when and if we subject ourselves to Him from whom they have been made subject to us. And so, although the body and the soul have a friendship, nevertheless (as the Wise man says)[29] on the part of two existing friends it is something sacred to honor truth [above friendship]—and [to honor] especially to that Truth which is the Fount of truth [and] which said "I am the Way, the Truth, and the Life."[30]

[**11**] Moreover, the reason that the flesh has desires contrary to the spirit is that each thing acts in accordance with its form. For example, choleric individuals are easily moved to anger; "sanguine" individuals are wanton; etc. But the flesh is like a heated cauldron that boils and bubbles, as says Jeremiah 1.[31] And the soul always supplies the firewood, viz., the vital nutrients, i.e., food and flavors. And from everywhere [the soul] draws that from which it feeds that flame: by way of the eyes [it draws in] beautiful colors; by way of the ears, melodious sounds; by way of the mouth, pleasant tastes; by way of the nostrils, pleasant scents. And it receives all these things in excess of the rightful norms. And so, from these things the heart is kindled and inflamed because, in addition, all flesh is corrupt and foul. From the

flesh goes forth a foul smell that causes infection more than does spoiled food. And so, since the soul is bent in the direction of the flesh, it receives the foul odor that the flesh gives off because of its licentiousness. Hence, it is not surprising if [the soul] is corrupted and made bestial. Chrysostom [notes]: through every carnal act a man is made like the animals—and especially through acts resulting from lust.

[**12**] The teacher Matthew of Cracow, in his book, raises questions as to God's having done all things well. And, among other [questions, he asks] why the soul was united to the lowly clay[32] of the flesh. He answers that [this creating] was done very reasonably in order to display the divine majesty, which could indeed join together such different things. For who would have believed that between such disparate and different things there could be a union such that one person could be made from them? Moreover, it was reasonable that after God willed to create substances, He would create [substances] of each kind: viz., an immaterial [substance], a bodily [substance], and [a substance] composed of both [the immaterial and the material]. Furthermore, [this creating was done] so that the immaterial creature, although noble, would avoid pride and would learn to be humble. [And it was done so that he would learn] not to despise even the lowest of creatures but to govern [them] and to care for [them]—[to do so] (1) in the light of the fact that he himself can be joined to them with very great union, with very great inclination, and with very great agreement and that he can incur poverty so great that he will need these [creatures] for many goods, and (2) in the light of the fact that they can be made so dignified and so influential with that spirit that they can render it inclined even to things lowly. And not only was that union [of body and soul] reasonable, but also, as it seems, it was so necessary that without it immaterial and corporeal creatures would have been without order and without agreement; and, thus, the order of the universe would have been less perfect.

Lastly, [Matthew of Cracow] says (using many words) that the whole corporeal nature would not by itself arrive at being able to assist the angels in praising God—(for that [angelic] nature was created for these acts-of-praising)—unless [the corporeal nature] were joined to the rational spirit.[33] Hence, man can help the angels in their praise of God. And [he can help] to repair angels' ruin and to elevate the corporeal nature.

[**13**] [Matthew of Cracow] asks why God created material things

to be so appealing. He answers:[34] Given that the conjoining of something suitable to the object-perceived causes pleasure, then after [God] created things that perceived and that were animated, [viz., ensouled bodies], He ought also to have created pleasurable things. And He did so in order that His infinite delight could be detected in creatures and because [these] delights could not be enjoyed unless they were present [both] in the spirit and the flesh. For if they were not present in the flesh but only in the spirit, the flesh would be altogether despised as base. For who would be concerned very much to obtain food, drink, and clothing, to beget offspring and to rear them—things that require concern, trouble, and effort—if it were not *pleasurable* to make use of such things and if to lack these things were not detrimental? (As a result men would be less concerned to preserve life both in the individual and in the species. Some men are already tired of this [preserving of life—tired] because of such worries and toils.)

Hence, reason demanded that there be great fleshly delight (1) in order that, at times, the delight would offset that weariness and [those] toils, (2) in order that, at times, an [otherwise] hesitant spirit's crown and victory and approbation be [due to its] great activity, [and] also (3) in order that, at times, from the greatness of our delight in the flesh we would be persuaded of the greatness of the delight in the spirit—a delight that is difficult to believe (since it is rarely and dimly perceived and since we are more readily persuaded from the baseness of the body's delight). For if there is such great delight in base, foul, and shameful (and, hence, detrimental) works of the flesh, how incomparably greater is believed to be the delight that comes from that most noble work—viz., the union of the spirit with God, who is supremely good and supremely delightful. Moreover, [God created the rational soul as united to a body] so that the spirit and the flesh would, like certain marital partners, be judged to be equals in the following respect: that since the spirit sometimes is so elevated from, so alien from, and so withdrawn from, the flesh that in a certain way it does not endow the flesh with sensation (or, at least, seems not to sense by means of the flesh), so too there would be a certain operation of the flesh that would withdraw from using reason.

After it was *suitable* that there be such great pleasure in the flesh, it was exceedingly *necessary* that [the great pleasure] be present only in a base work, lest, if the work were noble, men would be strongly attracted [to it in terms of pleasure] and would (since reason would be set aside) become bestial. And so, it was expedient that [men] be disposed in such a way that the more strongly pleasure would attract them, the more strongly a work's shamefulness, foulness, and baseness would hold them back. And also [it was expedient that] either the concern that is present in marriage or a sense of disgrace or the danger to honor and to the body and to the soul—which things are accustomed to follow fornicators—[would hold them back]. And [it was expedient that men] therefore not have grounds for complaining against God—as, nonetheless, they do complain (although unjustly) because they have to restrain themselves so greatly if they wish to turn [to God].

[**14**] The same man, [viz., Matthew of Cracow],[35] asks about the reason for which the body and the soul are united with such great discord. He answers, first, that in the state of innocence the soul was constituted with greater dignity than was the flesh. But because it misused its dignity for injuring God by inclining itself (against God's command) toward the flesh, it was deprived of the possession of dignity. But the fact that the *spirit* was inclinable to the flesh was due to the fact that also the *body* is conductible to better things than it naturally has an inclination for, so that it can obtain the delights of heavenly things and of spiritual joys. Moreover, it is evident that the immaterial creature and the material creature (which are so different that they scarcely fit together in the highest and ultimate genus) do not at all have the same natural inclinations, since [the two of them] are of disparate natures. Rather, [as is evident], the body is inclined toward material things; [but] the spirit, toward immaterial things. Therefore, if between them there was to be made a true union, it was necessary that they remain distinct, in some way, as regards their natural inclination. Otherwise, they would seem to be [numerically] *one* rather than to be *united*.

[**15**] But how would this distinction [between body and rational soul] be apparent, or what kind of distinction would it be, if the things united were in no way at variance [with each other]? Who would naturally believe that the spirit is in a *human* body rather than in a *brute* body if there were perceived only the corporeal operation and corporeal affection and [if there were perceived] no operation of the spirit (which operation is, as it were, extraneous to, and at odds with, the flesh)? For even now—not withstanding the obvious and clearly recognizable opposition and conflict [between body and spirit] many mindless people doubt or deny that there are in men souls or spirits. On the other hand, if [the two] were in every respect at variance [with each other] and if there were no interdependence between them or no mutu-

al adhering, then how would they be shown to be united? For things that are conjoined in such a way that they are not at all influenced by one another but rather [in such a way that] one [of them] easily turns (for one reason or another) wherever it will, without the other [of them], and is easily separated from the other: [such things] can be said to be *adjacent to* one another, not to be *united to* one another—as is evident in the case of stones that constitute a pile. And, thus, a good [finite] spirit or an evil [finite] spirit is not said to *unite* to itself a body but is said, rather, to *assume* a body. Nor was the Holy Spirit *united* to a dove, as the Word [of God] was *united* to [a] human nature.

Now, we fittingly say to be united those things that adhere to each other in such a way that because of a natural property (or otherwise indued property), or because of free and voluntary affection, the one is influenced by the other even to the point that what otherwise pleases or suits it, now pleases or suits it less with respect to it itself by itself.[36] And because such is [the relationship] between the body and the soul, the union between them is manifestly evident. And the fact that the one is influenceable by the other evidences their union. But the difference, and the opposition, of their inclinations shows their distinctness and their natural diversity. Furthermore, after man sinned with respect to his reason—in that he did not duly govern in accordance with reason and in that, in accordance with the flesh, he consented to the flesh's pleasure—he ought rightly to have been punished in both his parts [viz., body and soul] and by means of them both. And how could this be better done than that they thus influence each other and be at odds with each other and repel each other? Not only would the one struggle against the other but each would struggle with itself, since it did not keep the peace that was granted to it.

NOTES TO *Spiritu Ambulate*

* Sermon CCII.
1. Galatians 5:16.
2. II Corinthians 4:18.
3. See Nicholas's dialogue *De Mente* 6 & 7, as regards the mind and number.
4. *Loc. cit.*
5. Boethius, *De Consolatione Philosophiae*, Book V, Meter 4, 339 (*PL* 63:850).
6. Philippians 3:19.
7. I Corinthians 2:14.
8. Philippians 4:7.
9. Galatians 5:16.
10. Galatians 5:17. Romans 7:19.
11. Matthew 5:28.
12. Here (at **5**:40) I am reading (with the Paris edition) "quod pulchrum" in place of "pulchra".
13. Romans 7:23.
14. Galatians 3:19.
15. Galatians 5:18.
16. Galatians 5:19-21.
17. Galatians 5:22-23.
18. Galatians 5:24.
19. The Prince of this world is the Devil. John 12:31. Matthew 9:34.
20. John 18:36.
21. Galatians 2:19.
22. The editors of the printed Latin text here cite Aldobrandinus de Toscanella. And they refer to a passage in his sermon: viz., folio 185[va], lines 26-31 of Latin ms. R 1 at the Priester Seminar in Brixen, Italy.
23. Sallust, *De Coniuratione Catilinae* 20, 4.
24. Matthew 26:39.
25. Aristotle, *De Anima*, I, 4 ($408^{b}11$-13).
26. Mark 10:7.
27. Aldobrandinus de Toscanella, *op. cit.* (n. 23 above), folio 186[rb], lines 23-31.
28. Isidore of Seville, *Sententiae*, I,9,11 [*Corpus Christianorum Series Latina*, Vol. CXI, pp. 28-29]. *PL* 83:553.
29. The Wise man is the Lover of wisdom, i.e., "the Philosopher," viz., Aristotle. See his *Nicomachean Ethics*, I, 4 ($1096^{a}16$-17). See also *Auctoritates Aristotelis*, Ethica, Book I, Sententia 9 [p. 233 in Jacqueline Hamesse, editor, *Les auctoritates Aristotelis: un florilège médiéval* (Louvain: Publications Universitaires, 1974).
30. John 14:6.
31. Jeremias (Jeremiah) 1:13.
32. Matthaeus de Cracovia (Matthew of Cracow), *Rationale Operum Divinorum (Theodicea)*, Tractatus VI, Chap. 6 (at the beginning) [edited by Vitoldus Rubczyński and published in Cracow in 1930. See p. 137, lines 4-7]. See also

Genesis 2:7.

    33. Matthew of Cracow, *op. cit.*, Tractatus VI, Chapter 6 [p. 138].

    34. *Ibid.*, Tractatus VI, Chap. 3 [pp. 132-134].

    35. *Ibid.*, Tractatus VI, Chap. 7 [pp. 139-141].

    36. *Ibid.*, Tractatus VI, Chap. 7 [in particular, p. 141, lines 6 ff.]. At **15**:26 I am reading "de per se" (with the manuscripts) in place of "de [per] se" in the printed edition of the Latin texts. The former phrase is an expression sometimes used in Medieval Latin, so that the word "per" need not be excised.

Ex Ipso, per Ipsum, et in Ipso*
("Of Him, by Him, and in Him ....")
[June 12, 1446; preached in Mainz]

EXORDIUM

[1] "Of Him, by Him, and in Him are all things. To Him be honor and glory forever" (Romans 11 and in the epistle read at [today's] mass).[1]

As we are about to say a few things concerning the most holy Trinity—doing so by way of arousing-unto-wonderment rather than of disclosing the incomprehensible trine and one God, and doing so in order that we may be elevated unto honoring and glorifying Him—let us pray for God's grace.

PART ONE

Introduction of the Topic

From the Pauline Epistles It Is Shown That the Power and Wisdom of God Are in All Things and That in Man's Infirmities God's Power and Wisdom Are To Be Blessed.

[2] The Apostle Paul, inferring a certain very profound conclusion (viz., that God concluded all in unbelief, in order to have mercy upon all),[2] added: "O the depth of the riches!"[3] And he concluded: "To Him be honor and glory!"[4] Elsewhere the same apostle very wisely draws the following conclusion: that according to nature we are needy, sons of wrath, deficient, foolish, subject to the Prince of darkness. God—in order to show the riches of His grace in His goodness toward us in Christ Jesus[5]—willed that we obtain mercy in and through Him in whom God established all things that are in heaven and that are on earth[6] (as [we read] this in Ephesians 1 and 2), so that there not be anyone in the flesh who could glory over himself but that anyone who glories, glory in the Lord (as [we read] in I Corinthians 1).[7] [3] And to the end that the excellency be of God's power and not of us, we have this treasure in earthen vessels (II Corinthians 4).[8] [This statement] is as if to say: we who are in the flesh have a certain divine seed in an earthen vessel. For we are the offspring of God (Acts 17).[9] That is, we have a spirit formed in the image of God [and] formed as the seed-of-life, which can make life fertile—not [fertile] in accordance with the

flesh but in accordance with Him (viz., God) of whom [our spirit] is the image. But this seed cannot, of its own power, bring anything into actuality but [can do so only] by the loftiness of God's power. Similarly, there is in a grain of wheat a certain treasure of vegetative life—[life contained] in an earthen vessel, i.e., in that grain, which is composed of many elements from the earth. But this treasure cannot actually produce anything—in order that there actually be vegetative life—except with the help of a more sublime power, viz., the sun's power. And, thereupon, the sublimity of the sun's power works by bringing the seed of vegetative life into actuality when the grain hides itself in the earth and mortifies the earthen vessel, so that in this way that vessel does not prevent itself from being able to bear much fruit.[10] Likewise, in our case it is necessary—if the spirit is to bring the seed of life into actuality by means of the loftiness of God's power—that out of humility we hide this earthen vessel [of ours] in the earth (from whence it took its origin), reflecting on the fact that we are ashes from ashes, so that, subsequently, we not at all glory [in ourselves].

[4] And God will give prevenient grace, i.e., rain that moistens the earth of our sensibility, so that in this way the hardness of our bodily covering, which resists the motion of the spirit, may be softened. Next, [God] gives the grace that makes one pleasing—[gives it] through His sublime power, which moves the life of the spirit from potency into actuality, so that the spirit may bear fruit. And just as it is not the sun's fault that it does not effect in the grain-of-corn the power of the vegetative[11] life, but the responsibility rests with the farmer, who does not place the grain in the sun in suitable ways: so too it is not the fault of God's power that that power does not infuse into us all the things that are necessary for bringing the life of our spirit into actuality if we undertake the right activity. Now, the standard of right activity is Christ the Lord, in whom [God] determined to judge the world. For to follow in His footsteps is to come to perfection through Him without whom no one can obtain the glorious fruit of life. [5] Hence, we must take note of the fact that the excellence of [God's] power brings it about, in the case of your divine seed, which is of another world, that you mortify [yourself] in this world. For as the example of the seed of grain shows: in order to acquire a vegetative[12] life there ought to precede a mortification of the elemental power, which consists of a certain harmonious proportion-of-elements in the grain. And when in an animal the animal life is to be originated, the vegetative life must die. And if an intellectual life is to be originated, the animal life

must die. And, similarly, if something is to be brought from potency into actuality, the potency must die, so that it no longer is, if there is to be the actuality.

[6] Accordingly, if we intend to attain something of the next world in accordance with that which we possess in this world (in which that of the next world is present as a treasure in an earthen vessel), then that which is of this world must be mortified, in order that the treasure can be extracted. Hence, the Apostle Paul says elsewhere: If someone wishes to be wise after the fashion, namely, of the wisdom of the next world—[wisdom] that is hidden in the wisdom of this world as in an earthen vessel—let him become foolish, after the fashion, namely, of this world.[13] And this [becoming foolish is what it is] to mortify that earthen vessel of mundane wisdom, so that in this way [the earthly vessel of wisdom] is made wise through the loftiness of God's power. "For the wisdom of this world is foolishness with God" (I Corinthians 3).[14]

[7] And in this way we can understand how it is that the contrary [comes from] the contrary: from poverty (i.e., from the mortification of this world's riches) there arise spiritual riches; and from the mortification of this world's joy there arise joys of the next world—and similarly for other things, as is clearly inferred from the teaching of Christ in Luke 6 and other places.[15] And take note of the basic point: that this sensory world is a likeness and a befiguring of the eternal intellectual-world, which is the Kingdom of God; but the form of this world passes away (as says Paul),[16] because a likeness and an image are put aside when one reaches the real and perfect thing. [8] Therefore, the life of this world is not [true] life but is an image and a shadow of true life. [The case is] similar regarding wisdom and practical wisdom and joy and all other [such] things. Hence, one must mortify these likenesses, which harbor intellectually within themselves the seed of the real thing, so that (in a similar way) after the shadow and the image are put aside one comes to the exemplar. And note that just as the gladness of this world is an image and a shadow of the gladness of God's Kingdom, so too the sorrow of this world is an image of the sorrow of the Prince of darkness's kingdom. From these [considerations] you may surmise how much joy the saints who are in the Kingdom of God have and how much sorrow the damned have. And this latter consideration is very useful.

[9] Hence, turning [our thoughts] back to the Apostle [Paul], we say that in order to show the glory of the Great God, all things are that

which they are. Therefore, O man, receive with great marveling at God's goodness all the things that come to you or are given to you by God, and say: 'God gave being to me in order to show in me, who was nothing, the greatness of His goodness—so that by His omnipotent power I am that which I am. He made me to be a human being in order to show in me His great power when He will elevate me unto the company of the angels. He made me weak and infirm in order to show His power in me when He will work in me sublime things. He permits me to sin in order to show in me the power of His mercy and grace when I shall be converted to Him. He permits me to err in order to show in me the power-of-His-wisdom, by which He is able to elevate me unto the light of true knowledge. He permitted all men to sin in order that all would need grace, so that He could show in Christ Jesus, the Savior of all, the riches of His grace.[17]

[10] After countless such things: [say, O man], with Paul: 'He permits me to be weak in order that there may dwell in me the power-of-Christ, which is made perfect in weakness.[18] Although I am the chief of sinners, I obtained mercy in order that Christ Jesus could display His very great long-suffering in order to instruct those who are [so] going to believe Him [that they are brought] unto eternal life.'[19] And when you thus ascend, you will cry out with this same Paul: "Now to the King of the ages—the immortal, invisible, sole God—be honor and glory forever and ever. Amen" (I Timothy 1).[20] And let [the words] "O the depth of His riches ...," etc.,[21] be expounded (as is done elsewhere).

And this concludes the sermon's first part, which serves as an introduction of our topic.

PART TWO

Exposition of the Topic

(a) *On the Blessed Trinity, which is spoken of in the topic.*

[11] The second part [of the sermon] will concern the expounding of our topic insofar as the Blessed Trinity is spoken of to us in the topic. Now, as concerns this part, we must note that—as the same Paul says in the last chapter of I Timothy—God dwells in light inaccessible.[22] Hence, no one has seen Him or can see Him, because that light exceeds the power of intellectual sight. According, then, to this [passage] God cannot be seen, because He is invisible. And it is not the case that anything can be conceived to be like Him (Acts 17);[23] nor has [any such

concept] entered into the heart of man.[24] Therefore, He also cannot be named; rather, He is ineffable. Hence, in accordance with that habitation by which He dwells in light inaccessible, which is His own blessed divinity, He is unnameable by either "oneness" or "trinity".[25] Rather, His name is above every nameable name,[26] whether in Heaven or on earth, even though without Him nothing is nameable, since of Him and through Him and in Him whatever is nameable is named.[27] And so, God is unattainable Absolute Infinity.

[12] God is considered in another way insofar as He is our God and is the Creator-of-all-things, being in the world as a cause is present in what is caused. Because, then, all things are of Him and through Him and in Him as what is caused is present in its Cause, we ascend from the things caused unto the trineness of the Cause—[ascend] in such a way [as to infer] that without Him nothing was made but that all things are by Him[28] and that He is the Tricausal Beginning. Here Paul, who says that God is triune, speaks in such a way [as to indicate] that God's Essence is the Cause of all being. [13] But how are we able to attain unto seeing that God is trine and one? It is not at all possible for us to apprehend [this essence] by this way of ascent from things caused unto their Cause; nor is it possible for me to teach about [this essence], since essence, or quiddity, (even specific essence, i.e., essence contracted in accordance with a species,) cannot be attained, except with respect to the fact *that it is*. By comparison, we cannot see humanity by means of apprehending its quiddity; rather, [we can see] only *that it is*—[see this] *a posteriori* from human beings, who partake of humanity.

[14] Thus, we shall be able to be elevated a bit—in a certain loftiness of our enlightenment, with faith guiding us—unto the fact that the Divine Trinity *is*. Thus, being in the presence of the Seraphic and Evangelical spirits, we may exclaim in [our own] spirit: "Holy, holy, holy Lord, ...," etc. (Isaias 6 and Apocalypse 4).[29] But Isaias says that he saw the Lord sitting upon a throne high up, etc.[30] (See elsewhere [regarding this topic].)[31] Consider there [in Isaias] that since Isaias was in the spirit, he saw [the Lord sitting] on the throne high up, etc., and saw that the Seraphims covered the Lord's face and His feet with wings-of-power.[32] For the following must be noted, in particular: [viz.,] that with two wings they covered the feet of sensory movement, and with two wings they covered the facial movement (i.e., cognitive movement), for an acquaintance is made from [looking at] the face). And having been kept situated above His face by [two] other wings

(viz., by the motion of rapture), they flew unto Paradise (as we read also concerning Paul in II Corinthians 11 and Acts 22 and elsewhere, etc.[33]). And the following is, in truth, to be inferred [from the text]: [viz.,] that the Seraphic spirits revered the Trinity in oneness and the Oneness in trinity—as did also Moses (when he said *"beresit bara elohim"*)[34] and the other prophets. Hence, while the Seraphims were flying, they were exclaiming.[35] For in an intellectual soaring[36] one comes to that divine exclaiming, etc.

[15] But we who—having unclean lips, etc. (according to Isaias),[37]—are present in this world among sinners cannot *exclaim*, because we do not fly. But by faith we apprehend and see the Lord of hosts and the flying Seraphic spirits. But we come to the point of exclaiming when a Seraphic spirit ministers to us purification by means of a [live] coal from the altar of the Lord.[38] At that time, then, we exclaim; and we are sent to administer the Seraphic office in this present world, among the people. And take note of the fact that the Seraphic spirit approaches the preacher when the preacher comes to the self-knowledge that he is unclean and when he is purified in the loftiness of his intellect by a burning coal of zeal for, and fervor for, God. Consequently, after he is thus inflamed [and] is without fear and possesses purified lips: because of the fire of love he exclaims and proclaims …, etc. **[16]** Therefore, [a preacher] who wishes to stimulate his audience to exclaim as do the Seraphims must lead them at least to see by faith the Lord high up on His throne and to see that [the Lord's] house[39] is full of His majesty, etc.[40] Note that when by faith [a hearer] is led unto seeing God the Creator, then he sees that the heavens and the earth are full of God's glory.

[17] In the foregoing way I will lead you by faith, because you believe that God exists and that He is the Best of all things and is the Creator of all things. So, then, you see Him on high. For by ascending to the Seraphims *by way of all creatures*, you still do not see Him, because creatures are beneath Him, and He is on the highest throne above the Seraphims. But although He is above all things, He is nonetheless within all things. For, as Paul says in Acts 17: although He does not dwell in temples made with hands, because He is the Maker of all things, He is not far from any one [of us], because in Him we live and move.[41] And elsewhere Paul says that God is above all men and is present in all men.[42] And so, you see that of Him, by Him, and in Him are all things[43] **[18]** You see that He is none of those things which can be apprehended or named, even though in all things He is all things. Similarly, humanity is not any of the human beings; and, nevertheless, of it, by it, and in it all human beings are that which they are. And for this reason humanity cannot be far from any human being, because in it all human beings exist, live, and move in accordance with the fact that they are human beings—just as in God, the Creator, they exist, live, and move in accordance with the fact that they are creatures.

[19] Next, we see that from the gift of God all creatures have that which they have. But God gives nothing that He does not have. Therefore, God has all the things that are found in creatures. It is not the case that He has something other than Himself, since apart from Him there can be nothing. And so, His having is His being. Therefore, whatever is found in creatures is found in God—which is to say: it *is* God.[44] Now, plurality is only oneness that is partaken of in such and such ways. Accordingly, all the many things that are found in creatures are a participation in the one Infinite Power that is found to be received in such and such various ways. And the various modes of reception give rise to various names. Hence, God is the one and most simple Infinite Power, which fills the whole house of His creation. In accordance with one mode we give to this Power that is participated-in the name *being*; in accordance with another [mode we call it] *living*; in accordance with another [mode we call it] *understanding*; in accordance with another, *truth*; in accordance with another, *goodness*. And so, we call God Good, Life, Being, and so on. Hence, by means of all these names, which we ascribe in this way to God, we intend to say nothing other than that God is Infinite Power that is altogether simple, etc.

(b) *On the triad* fecundity, offspring, love *(or* union*)*.

[20] Now, we find with respect to man some three things that are very natural and without which this world could not exist; viz., fecundity, offspring, and love (or union). For since this world cannot partake of the Divine Power (viz., Absolute Eternity and Absolute Immortality) in which God alone dwells: falling short of Absolute Eternity, it partakes of Eternity in various modes. And this perceptible world partakes of Eternity in a temporal and motional way; and, hence, it falls into instability and corruption. Unless, then, this Divine Power, which is thus partaken of, were to have in its essence fecundity, offspring, and love in such a way that these three were the very simple Power that is partaken of by creatures in their own way: that Power could not be omnipotent and natural in such a way that this world could be filled

with its majesty, in order for this world to exist. Therefore, in the essence of the world, which partakes [of Divine Power], there is found fecundity, offspring, and union; the world has received this trinity through a flowing-forth. (Genesis 1: "Increase and multiply!")[45] And so, [the world] is present in the Creator as in its Fount. ([See] the end of Isaias, where Isaias proves by reference to the fact that God has given to others the power-of-begetting that He Himself also has this power.)[46]

[21] And here note carefully that this fecundity, offspring, and union are the simple essence of each thing and that these three things obtain different names in higher things and in lower things—in genera, in species, and in individuals, etc. For in the case of each thing that exists there is found (a) that by means of which it exists (and [this] is the fecundity), (b) that which [the thing] is ([and this is] the offspring), and (c) the union [of the fecundity and the offspring]. In the genus *animality* there is found fecundity, offspring (in accordance with the fecundity), and union. These are the simple essence of animality. The case is similar for the species. [22] Hence, in the specific essence of humanity: fecundity, offspring, and union *are* the humanity. And the fecundity of the entire essence begets the offspring; and the fecundity is in the offspring, and the offspring is in the fecundity. And the fecundity is in the union-of-love with the offspring, and the union is in the fecundity and in the offspring. And so, even though he who names human fecundity does not name either offspring or union, nevertheless he names the essence, since in fecundity are present offspring and union.

[23] And note that in the essence of a complete syllogism there are three propositions: a major [premise], a minor [premise], and a conclusion. But the three propositions are not anything other than the syllogism. Moreover, the minor [premise] and the conclusion are present in the power of the major [premise]; and the major [premise] is the fecundity of the syllogism. And the minor [premise] is the offspring of the fecundity because it is unfolded from the major [premise]. And the conclusion is the union of both [premises], etc. Hence, in the minor [premise] there is present the major [premise] and the conclusion: the major [premise is present] because [the minor premise] is the unfolding of the power of the major [premise]; and the conclusion [is present] because it is enfolded in the minor [premise]. The situation is similar in regard to the conclusion. Hence, if it could be conceived that the

major [premise] were the syllogism (and, similarly, [that] the minor [were the syllogism] and that the conclusion [were the syllogism]), then this [example of the syllogism] would be a certain likeness [to the Trinity], although a remote likeness.

[24] Similarly, there is the example with regard to perfect mastery [*perfectum magisterium*]. For in the essence of perfect mastery there is *activity, art,* and *delight*: from the activity comes the art; from the activity and the art comes the delight. And because we are craftsmen by virtue of crafting: the activity is the fecundity; the art is the offspring; the delight is the union. Moreover, there is a quite close likeness between temporal mastery and the eternal-mastery-that-has-to-do-with-creation. Likewise, in the essence of one's exercising [an ability] there is a *doer* (the fecundity), *that which is done* (the offspring), and *the doing* (the union) that proceeds from the doer and that which is done.

[25] Likewise, this consideration of fecundity and of offspring is found in the soul: memory is fecundity; intellect is offspring; will, or love, or delight, is union. Similarly, in the essence: *intellect* is fecundity of understanding, that which is *understandable* is the offspring, and that which is the *actual understanding* on the part of the fecund power-of-understanding and of the understandable offspring is the common bond. The case is similar with regard to love, or will, and with respect to all existing things, which cannot be otherwise except by participation in the triune Divine Essence. By virtue of this participation [these things] have a nature that is 'fecundity, offspring, and love—in a simplicity of essence.' Without these [three things] they could not have a nature or exist naturally and perfectly.

[26] Moreover, intellectual natures partake of this triune essence in their own way, so that fecundity, offspring, and love are the intellectual nature—even as in the human species they are the human nature and in plants they are the plant-nature and in elements they are the elemental nature. In the foregoing way [the labels "fecundity," "offspring," and "love"] are brought into harmony with Divine Scripture, which names fecundity *Father* and names offspring *Son* and names love *Holy Spirit*.

By means of my [present] treatment [of this topic] we are given closer assistance (as much as is granted to us) as we ascend in our investigation of the triune Divine Essence.

NOTES TO *SERMON Ex Ipso, per Ipsum, et in Ipso*

* Sermon LXI.
1. Romans 11:36. Cf. 16:27.
2. Romans 11:32.
3. Romans 11:33.
4. Romans 11:36 and 16:27.
5. Ephesians 2:7.
6. Ephesians 1:10.
7. I Corinthians 1:31.
8. II Corinthians 4:7.
9. Acts 17:28-29.
10. John 12:24.
11. Here at **4**:9 I am surmising "vegetabilis" in place of "sensibilis".
12. Here at **5**:6 I am surmising "vegetabilem" in place of "sensibilem".
13. I Corinthians 3:18-19.
14. I Corinthians 3:19.
15. Luke 6:20-25.
16. I Corinthians 7:31.
17. Ephesians 2:7.
18. II Corinthians 12:9.
19. I Timothy 1:15-16.
20. I Timothy 1:17.
21. Romans 11:33.
22. I Timothy 6:16.
23. Acts 17:29.
24. I Corinthians 2:9.
25. See J. Hopkins, "Verständnis und Bedeutung des dreieinen Gottes bei Nikolaus von Kues," *Mitteilungen und Forschungsbeiträge der Cusanus-Gesellschaft*, 28 (2003), 135-164. See also Cusa's *De Visione Dei* 17 (**78**).
26. Phillipians 2:9.
27. Romans 11:36.
28. John 1:3. Romans 11:36.
29. Isaias (Isaiah) 6:2-3. Apocalypse (Revelation) 4:8.
30. Isaias (Isaiah) 6:1.
31. Sermon XXXVIII (**4**).
32. Isaias (Isaiah) 6:2.
33. See II Corinthians 12:2-4. Acts 22:9-11.
34. Genesis 1:1.
35. They were exclaiming "Holy, holy, holy, Lord God of Hosts. All of the earth is full of His glory." Isaias (Isaiah) 6:3.
36. Nicholas regards the words of Isaias (Isaiah) 6:1-3 as having also a symbolic meaning, so that, for example, the angels-who-are-flying signify also an intellectual soaring.
37. Isaias (Isaiah) 6:5.
38. Isaias (Isaiah) 6:6.

39. Cf., below, **19**:14-16. God's creation is His house.
40. Cf. Psalms 71:19 (72:19).
41. Acts 17:24-28.
42. Ephesians 4:6.
43. Romans 11:36.
44. In God, all things are God, states Nicholas in many places: e.g., *De Docta Ignorantia* II, 5 (**119**).
45. Genesis 1:28.
46. Isaias (Isaiah) 66:9: "Shall not I that make others to bring forth children, myself bring forth, saith the Lord? Shall I, that give generation to others be barren, saith the Lord thy God?" (Douay-Rheims version).

Una Oblatione Consummavit*
in Sempiternum Sanctificatos
("By One Sacrifice He Has Perfected Forever
Those Who Are Sanctified.")
[April 2, 1455; preached in Brixen]

[1] "By one sacrifice He has perfected forever those who are sanctified."[1]

Christ is the one who by means of one sacrifice has perfected forever those who are sanctified. He is the King of kings and the Lord of lords.[2] John says in the first chapter of the Apocalypse that He who has washed us with His own blood is the Prince of the kings of the earth.[3] From the [Book of] Genesis's beginning we know that man was created in order to govern all the beasts.[4] Thereafter, in Genesis 4, we find that God said to Cain that sinful-desiring is subordinate to Cain.[5] I understand this [statement] as follows: that the inclination which results from the bestial, or animal, nature (i.e., from the sensory nature) and which is the inclination to sin is subordinate to man, i.e., to reason, and man will have control over it. Moreover, we find that men are set over men. These former are called kings; for such ones are rulers by nature, since in them the power-of-ruling that is from reason flourishes more strongly. For men who flourish in rational capability are, says Aristotle,[6] naturally rulers and lords over others. Accordingly, man is placed in charge of the beasts.

[2] Now, Christ, whose Kingdom is not of this world,[7] is the Prince of the kings of the earth. Just as there is a kingdom of a king who feeds men and a kingdom of him who feeds beasts, so there is also the Kingdom of Him who feeds the kings of men. For this Prince is He who has dominion over rulers' entire power of reasoning;[8] and so, He is the Wisdom of God.[9] For no faculty of reason that is devoid of wisdom is suited to rule. For only wisdom, which shines forth in reason, is obeyed. For when in his reason someone displays truth, which is wisdom, he is immediately obeyed; and one who hears, and who by means of hearing understands, complies with the biddings. Therefore, the Wisdom that is Truth is the Prince of kings, and His precepts are very palatable and pleasing precepts of life that enlivens; and they are full of love.

Therefore, just as man by nature is set over the beasts, so the inner man[10] is set over the outer man, which by Paul is called the sensual man.[11] And the Word of the Father is set over the inner man; and the Father is over the Word. Similarly, Paul said that the head of the woman is the man.[12] This [judgment] means only that reason has dominion over inclination.[13] Furthermore, Paul says that the head of man is Christ and that the head of Christ is God.[14] Now, just as the king-over-sensuality, [viz., reason,] is better than is the entire sensory nature (for the rational soul is better than all brute-animal desires), so the Prince-over-reason, [viz., Christ,] is better than all men. Accordingly, the humility of the Prince of kings is more virtuous than is all human humility, and His obedience is more virtuous than is all human obedience. And because obedience is better than is sacrifice,[15] obedience together with His sacrifice is the perfect sacrifice, for it enfolds within itself all the merit and all the pacifying-mediation that, through sacrifices, can possibly be made for the purpose of reconciliation.

[3] Furthermore, note that the text of Genesis states that God created man in His image and likeness, so that man is in charge of the beasts. It is as if [the text] said: True rulership is rulership on whose governance all things depend for their existence and for their being conserved. This is the rulership of God, the Creator. Man was created in the likeness of God, who is altogether sovereign; and man partakes of that divine power, [which he exercises] with respect to the beasts. Now, it is evident that rulership is not devoid of reason. Therefore, the rational power was created in the likeness of God. And we experience this fact because [our rational power] exercises control over our sensory, or sensual, nature. Therefore, since reason's governance extends over the sensory nature, it is evident that the outer man (which is the sensual man, since it does not perceive the things which are of God) ought to be subordinate to the inner man, which spiritually perceives the things which are of God. Hence, because [the inner man] perceives the things which are of God, it ought to rule over the outer man (in accordance with the fact that the Word, or Prince of Reason, speaks in it) and ought always to say: "I will hearken to what the Lord speaks in me."[16] And in this way [the inner man] preserves its likeness-of-God with respect to its rulership; and it increases this likeness the more it conforms its ruling to the divine precepts that it perceives.

[4] But if [the inner man] neglects its governing role, so that it does not rule over the dominating tendencies of the sensuality, then, as a result, the appetite rises up in disobedience, and the image of God is

darkened, and the power of the king is lost, and the role of a servant is assumed, and the likeness-of-God is darkened, so that, in the end, [the inner man] is subjected to the Prince of Darkness. But when the image of God does not remain in the inner man but rather the sensuality,[17] or the sensory appetite, subjugates[18] it, then that man cannot come to God, i.e., to its own [true] End. For the End and the Beginning of the image is God, who is the Truth of the image. And the image cannot arrive at its Truth[19] if the Truth does not shine forth in it—i.e., if it ceases to be an image. Therefore, Christ is the Restorer of the darkened image. He teaches us how it is that the image can be born anew from the bedarkenness. And He began to act and to teach, in order that by means of visible experience we might arrive at rebirth. And for us He was made the Way,[20] so that we might know how [in us] the image is to be restored in order for it to be the image of God. He was made the Exemplar-Truth, for He said "I have given you an example so that as I have done you too may do."[21] "Learn from me."[22] Etc. And we still have need that [in us] the image of the Living God be alive and have movement-of-life (so that as a living image which sees within itself Him of whom it is an image, it can within itself taste of God, in whom it finds rest and unto whom it is moved by continual desire). Therefore, Christ was made to be for us Enlivening Life. Therefore, with His own blood He washes away the uncleanness (coming from the clay of the earth) of the daughters of Zion. After the cleansing, He creates (i.e., restores) a new man that is in conformity with God,[23] and He breathes into his face the breath of life,[24] so that the image of God is reborn as a living spirit.

[5] And note that, necessarily, it pertains to Him who is to be the Renewer of the darkened image to have within Himself the exemplar and truth of him whose image He wills to renew. For otherwise [the renewal] cannot occur. And because only the Son [also] has within Himself the Father-Creator, and because only the Son knows the Father, whom no one has seen:[25] only the Son is the Savior, or Renewer, or Regenerator, of the new man. And no man, of himself, is able to renew his own image conformably to God, whom he has not seen. [He is] even less [able to renew] someone else's image. Hence, the Son of God is the only one [who can renew man's image]. He, without whom there is no [salvation], works salvation in all respects. And He says: "Behold, I make all things to be new."[26] The text says that only the Son knows the Father—[only the Son] and he to whom the Son wills to reveal [the Father].[27] Hence, God, who is hidden from

the eyes of all, can be revealed only by the Son; and the revelation is the renewal of the image, as is said above.

Note that the Restorer, or Renewer, of our image [of God] ought to have been possessed of our nature, in order that from His conduct we could be instructed about our infirmities and about the darkness of our image [of God]. And in Him the image [of God] ought not to have been darkened, or dimmed, by the darkness of sins. Otherwise—[i.e.,] if in His [image] there had not shined forth the Exemplar-Truth—there could not have been present in Him the mastery for restoring our image [of God]. Hence, if God the Father had not been present in the intellect of the Teacher, then how could the Teacher have restored [in us] the image of Him whom He would not have seen in and through His own image? Therefore, the Teacher of restoration could not have [been born] of the lust of the flesh, on account of which lust the image [of God] would have contracted a loathsome blemish (as occurred in the case of Adam's descendants, who exist as human beings as a result of lust and of blood relationships. Therefore, it was necessary that the Teacher of restoration be a human being and be born from a virgin-mother without a male seed. Accordingly, it was necessary that He be the Son of man.[28] And so, it was necessary that the Son of God, who alone knows the Father, be also the son of the Virgin. In order to be able perfectly to restore [our image of God], he was mortal, as are men. And he underwent, in succession, all the things that are contained in the Gospel. For thus, in the best way possible, the image of God in us was to be renewed by our Teacher and Lord. Therefore, nothing was done unnecessarily, nothing insufficiently; rather, [everything was done] according as our salvation required. And if together with this understanding you begin to understand [Christ's] deeds and if you inquire about our restoration, then you will find that by the most orderly providence of God all things serve this end perfectly.

[6] Consider the likeness of a grain of wheat. For Christ mentioned this likeness to the Gentiles, as John writes[29] and as on Monday we read in the Gospel. Christ wanted to disclose, with reference to Himself, that the Grain (which in John 6 is called the Living Bread that comes down from Heaven)[30] is not mortal unless it falls into the ground. For to the end that He become mortal, the Grain humbled Himself by falling into consecrated, virginal ground—[ground that was] not marred or barren but was good. And there He put on the form of a mortal man. And He descended into that earthenness in order, at length, to die. And [He did] this in order not to remain alone but to bear

much fruit. For the Wisdom, [viz., Christ,] of the Omnipotent Father would have remained without a human nature had He not put on flesh and in this way become subject to death. Now the power-of-the-vegetative-life that is hidden in a piece of grain does not die by virtue of the death of the grain of wheat but rather increases all the more, so that it is communicated to many things. Similarly, the divine[31] life's power that is hidden in mortal Jesus does not die by virtue of His death but rather increases and communicates itself, so that it bears much fruit. And when you consider (1) that the vegetative power in the grain is potentially so great that it is not in any way measurable and (2) that the divine power of the Word [of God] is likewise actually so great that it exceeds all understanding, then you see that [this] likeness is amazing.

[7] The likeness in regard to the true vine is perfect.[32] For Adam is like the vine which, though expected to bring forth grapes, produced wild grapes[33] because it was turned into bitterness, although it was created by God. Hence, all the branches that proceed from it, in accordance with its condition, bring forth wild grapes as fruit, and the branches are conformed to the nature of the corrupted grape-vine. But Christ is the new Adam;[34] and so, He is as a new true vine[35] that is healthy and fruitful. And the branches can be found to be fruitful only if they are germinating from the [True Vine]. Adam is the vine of corrupt [human] nature; Christ is the Vine of grace. Adam is the vine of the old man; Christ is the Vine of the new man.[36] Adam is the vine of illicit desire [*concuspiscentia*]; Christ is the Vine of ordinate love [*caritas*].

[8] Consider that the instituting of the sacrifice of the new law is in memory of a freeing from death, just as the instituting of the sacrifice of the pascal lamb was in memory of a freeing from death (as we read in Exodus 12). For the blood protected the house and saved the firstborn who were present in it so that they would not be slain by the Angel of Death, who, finding this protection, passed over that house. Therefore, [the passing-over] is called "*Phase.*"[37] Now, what are things firstborn except things consecrated to God? For the things firstborn pertained to God. Hence, Christ is the Firstborn of all[38] and is the Saint of saints.[39] By His blood he protects every firstborn so that he not be killed by the Spirit of Death but rather may live forever. This sacrifice was instituted in memory of this freeing from perpetual death. Note that memory is, as it were, a place or a container or a house, into which the soul gathers, and reposits, all the things that come to it from

this world by way of the senses. And memory has a door-of-entrance through which the perceptual forms of things enter into it. This door ought to be closed at night and marked—marked on the transom and the posts—with the blood of the Immaculate Lamb. And when the Death Angel, who is the Prince of this world[40] and of darkness and who goes about his business in darkness, sees that the door-of-memory is bedaubed with blood, he passes by and seeks elsewhere a soul whom he may slay. But when it is day, i.e., daylight, this door ought to be open.

We must take note of the fact that the children of Israel believed that Moses safeguarded his household by the blood of a lamb; and they experienced that they themselves, as they had believed [they would be], were saved. Faith, which comes by hearing[41] or by the word, saves by means of a perceptible sign that suitably signifies that which is believed. For he who is unbelieving obtains nothing from a visible sacrament. Hence, you know that the intellectual spirit, whose abode is the memory, is firstborn, because [this spirit] is breathed-out by God, who is its Life. And this spirit, the breath of life, is saved, so that the Evil Spirit (who is opposed to its life) cannot harm it if the door of memory is dedaubed with the blood of Him who conquers that Spirit by the shedding of [His own] blood. This bedaubing is done only in undoubted faith. If one spurns the perceptible sacrament of this faith, according as the sacrament was instituted by its Author: then, as is clearly evident, [the faith] is not true faith. Hence, this sacrifice is celebrated as a sign of the firmness of the covenant,[42] or agreement, (concluded through assured faith) between the Word of God and the acknowledgement of man.

[9] Moreover, you know [the following]: Christ is the Word who not only protects us, so that our Adversary the Devil[43] can do [us] no harm, but who also raises and enlivens the dead (and those conquered by the Adversary) and transfers them to being sons of God. Therefore, not only is He Medicine against malady, and not only is He the strengthening Food-of-life,[44] but He is also the One who conveys [us] unto Himself. Therefore, this faith is best signified by means of the visible form of bodily food, which expels weakness and furnishes strength—as do, basically, the wheaten bread and the wine. Hence, take cognizance of the fact that in the power of the bread and the wine—[a power] that expels the weakness of the flesh's ravenous hunger and that brings strength, or renews strength, (things which happen with respect to the outer man)—faith sees the power of the Word

working similar things in the inner man. And that which nature ministers to the outer man by means of visible food, faith by means of invisible Food (which is the Word of God) obtains in the inner man (which is invisible). Therefore, by means of [this] same food, [viz., bread and wine], that is ordained in this way by God through His Word, the body obtains desired nourishment; and, at the same time, so does the soul. The body [obtains it] by means of the digestive power and by means of the power of the union that occurs through a natural heat; the soul [obtains it] by means of the power of faith (which is the more digestive the stronger it is) and by means of the power of the union that occurs through supernatural heat—a heat which is *caritas*.

[10] Hence, you know that the perfect food for both men [viz., the inner man and the outer man] is found only in the Catholic Church, outside of which there is found food only for the outer man. Now, the Eucharist is the food for both men. Accordingly, insofar as it is bread digested in the stomach, it nourishes the body;[45] and it nourishes the rational spirit insofar as it is the Word-of-God-the-Son, received by faith. For the Word that is received by such faith that it is the Word of God the Son is a rich bread which furnishes complete satisfaction. But the nourishing power that is in the bread is principally from God, even as the power of the Word that nourishes the soul is from the Word of God, i.e., is from the divine substance. Hence, in the eucharist there is found a single substance from which these powers flow. It cannot be called the substance of the visible bread but [can be called] the substance of the Word. And Christ indicated this fact when, in the way in which Moses expressed this mystery, He said: "Man lives not by bread alone but by every word that proceeds from the mouth of God."[46] For the fact that the outer man can live from the substance of the bread does not exclude the fact that he can live from the substance of the Word that possesses the power of the bread. Hence, those who say that *both* the bread *and* the Body of Christ are present in the sacrament do not take note of the fact that the *substance* of bread is not necessary for nourishing if there is present a substance such that in it the power-of-nourishing is enfolded.[47] For the power of the lower substance is present in the power of the higher substance, as the Prophet says: "By the Word of the Lord the heavens were established and all their power."[48]

[11] But keep in mind that in the celebration of the sacrament the substance of the bread is supposed to be assumed into the more excellent substance of Christ. Otherwise, the sacrament would not be per-

fect—[a sacrament] in which transubstantiation ought to be present in every manner possible. This transubstantiation truly occurs when our nature passes over into gracious sonship with God;[49] I do not mean that our nature perishes but mean rather that our substance is assumed into the more excellent [substance of God]. Similarly, here [in the eucharist] the bread's nature, which is present in the eating, does not *perish*, but, rather, the substance is *transubstantiated*—i.e., is assumed into the more excellent substance. The divine prophet David expressed this fact for us when he said: "The law of the Lord is unspotted, converting souls and furnishing faithful testimony to little ones."[50] What is the unspotted law of the Lord except the word of God? This law, which is the word of God,[51] transforms souls—just as wisdom transforms our intellect, by making it wise. And [the word of God] furnishes to little ones faithful testimony to this transformation. That is to say, in regard to this sacrament [the word of God] furnishes exceedingly faithful testimony to this transformation, in which the substance of the bread is transformed into the substance of the Incarnate Word—[an occurrence] that is a very precise and very effective attesting to [the following fact: viz.,] that although our spiritual nature is seen to be human and ignorant, it can be transformed by the Word of God unto being a son of God and can be turned from the darkness of ignorance-of-God and ignorance-of-truth unto the vision [of God] and unto the light [of God].

[**12**] From the aforesaid it is evident that Christ is present in the sacrament—not spatially present but present together with the accidents of the substance of the bread. It is not the case that the accidents are present in the bread's substance. Rather, they are present in the power that flows from [that] substance which is more excellent than is the substance of the bread. Therefore, the substance of the bread, after having been turned into the substance of the Body of Christ, precedes [ontologically] every accident. So the accidents remain as they previously were; but the substance is transformed. By comparison, when an ignorant man is made wise, and when a layman is made a priest, and when a subject or a servant is made king, all [the accidents] remain what they happened to be; and only the ignorance is changed into wisdom, and the imperfect into the perfect. This is a close likeness; but it would be closer if the ignorance, and likewise the wisdom, were each a substance.

Nevertheless, suppose that someone were to understand the bread not to be *transubstantiated* but, à la Paul, to be *clothed upon*[52] with a more noble substance, as we expect to be clothed upon by the light of glory, with our substance preserved. (Certain ancient theologians are found to have understood [the Eucharist] accordingly. They said that *both* the bread and the Body of Christ are present in the sacrament.) One [who would make such a claim] would have to pay attention to the meaning of the expression ["clothed upon"]. For if he says that that light of glory is an *accidental* feature, nevertheless [that light] will be more noble than was the earlier substance (as Christ said of Judas that it would have been better had he not been born than that he be damned). And thus, in turn, the light of glory will be better than is the soul's substance. And so, [this viewpoint] is not much at odds with my point. However, I am giving the name "substance" to that than which nothing better is found in the bread. But if you call it an accident because it comes subsequently to the natural being of the thing, there is no difference [between us] except as regards the manner of speaking.

[13] Moreover, from the aforesaid you know that, necessarily, the Body of Christ is present in the sacrament without quantitative magnitude and, thus, is present indivisibly and completely in each part of the host. By analogy, if our memory recalls a mountain, the memory is not of greater magnitude than when it recalls a grain of millet. Moreover, the memory is present as a whole in whatever thing it remembers, and the thing that it remembers is present in the memory. For memory, which is not quantitative, takes on the things that it remembers; and this [taking-on] is for the thing to be found in memory. And if at one and the same time the memory were in many things (as one face is in many [on-looking] eyes and as one voice is in many ears, etc.), then the analogy would be more precise. [I will speak] of these matters elsewhere.[53]

NOTES TO *Una Oblatione Consummavit*

* Sermon CLXXXIII.
1. Hebrews 10:14.
2. I Timothy 6:15.
3. Apocalypse (Revelation) 1:5.
4. Genesis 1:26.
5. Genesis 4:7.
6. Aristotle, *De Politica*, I, 2 (1252^{ab}).
7. John 18:36.
8. Colossians 1:18.
9. I Corinthians 1:24.
10. II Corinthians 4:16.
11. I Corinthians 2:14.
12. I Corinthians 11:3.
13. Here one should note Nicholas's figurative interpretation of a passage that feminists regard as expressing an antiquated idea. Although Nicholas here gives a figurative interpretation, he does not regard it as precluding the traditional non-figurative interpretation. The two interpretations are equally valid, he would maintain.
14. I Corinthians 11:3.
15. I Kings (I Samuel) 15:22.
16. Not meant by Nicholas to be an exact quotation. See Psalms 84:9 (85:8).
17. Here (at **4**:8) I am reading, with the Paris edition, 'animalitas' in place of 'animalitatis'.
18. Here (at **4**:8-9) I am reading, with the Paris edition, 'subigit' in place of 'subegit'.
19. "… at its Truth": i.e., at its true Origin and true Goal, of which it is an image.
20. John 14:6.
21. John 13:15.
22. Matthew 11:29.
23. Ephesians 4:24.
24. Genesis 2:7.
25. Matthew 11:27. John 1·18
26. Apocalypse (Revelation) 21:5.
27. Luke 10:22.
28. John 1:51. Note, too, that "Son of man" is used in John as a Messianic title.
29. John 12:24-25.
30. John 6:51.
31. Here (at **6**:19) I am reading, with the Paris edition, 'divinae' in place of 'divina'.
32. John 15:1.
33. Isaias (Isaiah) 5:2. Wild grapes are sour.
34. I Corinthians 15:45-49.
35. John 15:1.
36. Ephesians 4:22-24.

37. Exodus 12:11.
38. Colossians 1:15.
39. Daniel 9:24
40. John 12:31.
41. Romans 10:17.
42. Here (at **8**:48-49) I am reading, with the Paris edition, 'compacti' in place of 'compactatorum'.
43. I Peter 5:8.
44. John 6:35.
45. Nicholas is not unaware of I Corinthians 11:34, which indicates that the eucharistic host is not intended to satisfy hunger and thereby to nourish the partaker's body. Rather, Nicholas is alluding to the fact that insofar as bread qua bread is nourishing, this nourishing power remains present subsequently to the transubstantiation.
46. Matthew 4:4. Deuteronomy 8:3.
47. Nicholas is here denying that there are *two* substances in the consecrated bread. Rather, there is but one: viz., the divine substance. See Sermon CCXXXV (**11**).
48. Psalms 32:6 (33:6).
49. John 1:12.
50. Not meant by Nicholas to be an exact quotation. See Psalms 18:8 (19:7).
51. Sometimes when Nicholas uses the expression "verbum Dei" ("word of God) he is referring to the Son of God (the Word of God); however, sometimes, as in the present case, he is referring to the Bible. Only the context can help us decide which referent is intended.
52. II Corinthians 5:2-4.
53. See Sermon CCXXXIII (**6**).

Una Oblatione*
("By One Offering ....")
[April 6, 1455 (Easter Sunday); preached in Brixen]

[1] "By one offering [He has perfected forever those who are sanctified.]"[1]

[2] Christ says that He is Life and is Enlivening Life.[2] The day before yesterday we heard about the tree that was placed in the middle of the inhabitable world, i.e., of the earth—a tree to which life was affixed.[3] We must consider that the inhabitable earth, established by God from the beginning, can be called Paradise. And on the earth there are the rivers Nile, Tigris, Euphrates, and Ganges.[4] And [we must consider that] the earth has, in the middle, a Land of Promise,[5] which occupies the center in relation to the whole of the inhabitable earth. And I will skip taking note of how much the Land of Promise is praised by Moses and the Scriptures. In this part of Paradise God took special delight, and He was present with men, with prophets, and with saints. And it is written (1) that He walked in the middle of Paradise at the time of the afternoon breeze[6] and (2) that Israel[7] (which means "man who sees God"), when resting there, set up a stone, which he anointed,[8] and (3) that Israel made an offering.

All of the foregoing things can be fittingly understood as regards the Incarnate Word of God. For He walked there in the afternoon, i.e., when the sun was beginning to start downwards, viz., after the midpoint of the course of time, from the sun's rising to its return unto the earth. And He looked for Adam—[i.e., for the human race]. For He came to seek and to save that which was lost from the house of Israel.[9] For He said that He was sent to those who were then dwelling in that central part of the world. And at God's voice, or God's word, sinners, [who descend] from Adam, hide themselves. For a thief hates the light, as do other sinners.[10] Moreover, [the Incarnate Word] is the Stone, or Anointed Rock—i.e., is Christ—and is the Offering and the Tree of life and the true Vine[11] and whatever else can be said along these lines.

[3] There [on earth] the first covenants between Israel and God were established: to wit, (1) that Israel would be God's and God would be Israel's God and (2) that Christ—who on the altar of sacrifice confirms the covenants—would be the Mediator. There [there was] the ladder, viz., the sacrifice, which ascended as a small cloud of smoke.

For the affections-of-holy-desires, on the part of a man who seeks God, ascend. This man is supported on that ladder, at its top; and the grace of God comes down [to him]. These ascendings and descendings can rightly be said to be angels who ascend and descend by means of the ladder;[12] for they are certain messages from Paradise, or certain spiritual declarations; and they are loving communications between God and the contemplating soul. Hence, it happens that there is there a temple to which the contemplatives ascend in order to pray.

Now, it is not strange if St. Ambrose[13] believed those who wrote (1) that Christ died where Adam died—both[14] of them [having died], that is, in the middle of that Paradise—and (2) that the Tree of death, viz., Adam, and the Tree of life, viz., Christ, meet in the middle of Paradise, viz., at Calvary. For in the life of Adam there is death. For although having a true knowledge of good and evil is something divine and makes a man closely like unto God, who is Life: nevertheless, eating of the fruit-of-knowledge—i.e., being puffed up because of knowledge—brings about death. But in the death of Christ there is life. For although He really died, nonetheless because [He died] innocently and out of obedience to the Father-of-life, then in accordance with the innocence and the humility and the obedience that He showed to the Father-of-life, He ought to have obtained merit and grace in the Father's eyes.

[4] But how would [Christ] obtain a reward from the Father of life if after the death that He underwent He would not have been capable of receiving a reward? Of itself, death is endless; therefore, the reward ought also to be such, viz., endless. Hence, the reward is the restoration of endless, or eternal, life; and this restoration is resurrection from death unto life. Note that when life is given to humans because of obedience to God, then there is assured hope that the Rewarder will give divine life. For unless God were to give divine life, how would He be just and good? Exaltation is the reward of humility; life is the reward of obedience and of [obedience unto] death. To Abraham, who obeyed even unto death[15] in the case of his son, God promised divine life when He said: "I am Your great Reward."[16] Hence, Paul says: "He who comes to [God] must believe that He is and that He is a Rewarder."[17] Now, the more humbly and out of love one undergoes death on account of obedience, the greater is the reward of divine life on account of merit. Therefore, God willed that the death of His beloved Son be a death than which no other death can be more innocent, more humble, and greater in love—[willed it] in order that

the Son would obtain exaltation above all others. Hence, this is the Tree of Life-that-enlivens. Therefore, the merit of Christ's death enfolds the complete reward of divine life. Accordingly, every spirit that dies in and through Christ's death obtains—because of participation in Christ's death—participation in the divine life in Christ, i.e., obtains Christ's reward. Therefore, Christ, who is the Firstfruits of the dead[18] [and] whom God raised up by way of reward, merited resurrection-unto-life for Himself as Head[19] and for all others who as members receive Him—[merited] for each [member resurrection] in his own order.[20]

[5] Pay careful attention as to why of all those who are able to die, the death of Christ was the consummate death. For because of His agony[21] we know that He was aware of the bitterness of death; and so, His soul was sorrowful unto death.[22] This knowledge of His death—[a knowledge] that was in His rational soul—made the bitterness of death incomparably more bitter than is any death of those who are ignorant of the bitterness of death and made [his death] a consummate death. And so, when He died He gave His soul over to death for our sakes. His is the consummate death; and in accordance with the magnitude of its bitterness, the reward was as great as would be merited by all the saints who can die because of obedience to God. Hence, since anyone who loses his soul (i.e., who dies) finds life, Christ's death is efficacious for enlivening all [souls].[23] Moreover, we must note that the soul that is fit for receiving a reward for death—viz., [the reward] of eternal enlivenment—is incorruptible, because [that soul] is the possessor of the reward of eternal life. Therefore, only man, who has a rational soul, can, by freely losing his soul, come to immortal life.

[6] On this day[24] Christ expounded Moses and all the Prophets to His two disciples who were going to Emmaus—[explaining] that it was necessary for Him to suffer and in that way to enter into glory.[25] Therefore, the puzzle is solved—[the puzzle] as to why God permitted our [fore]father Adam to sin and permitted us all to die as a result of that sin. (By comparison, Christ says that the man [in John 9] was born blind in order that God's glory might be made manifest by means of the restoration of his sight.)[26] For Adam's being permitted to fall into sin did not result from [a previous] sin that Adam [had] committed or that someone before him [had] committed, since no one preceded him. Rather, [he was allowed to fall into sin] in order that the glory of God might be manifested. For although sin, which God forbade to be done,

is displeasing to God, nevertheless God knows how to bring what is good from what is evil.[27] And this [same thing] can likewise be said of all those who are predestined unto glory [and] who are found to have been sinners; for example, [it can be said] of Paul. Wherefore after the many things which Paul says in Galatians 3 about our being justified by faith, or grace, he adds: "The Scripture has adjudged all things to be under sin, in order that the promise, [coming] by faith in Jesus, might be given to those who believe."[28] And later [Paul says]: "You are all sons of God by faith in Christ Jesus."[29] Paul says with regard to himself that God changed him from persecutor to apostle in order that God might manifest in him all long-suffering—[doing so] for the information of those who shall believe in God unto eternal life.[30]

[7] Hence, God willed to show this glory of His in His Son so that as by one man death came unto all, so by Jesus life would come unto all.[31] The Son glorifies the Father by manifesting the riches of the Father's glory and by conferring these riches [on us]. And the Father glorifies the Son, because through the Son He gives eternal life. Therefore, God wills that all men be in need of grace in order that He might manifest the riches of His grace in them all—[manifest these riches] through Jesus, upon whom (as upon a Fount) He conferred fullness of grace.[32] God permitted us all to be needy, in order that He might show Himself to be altogether perfect and to be the One who in Christ consummates and perfects all things. Consider Paul, [writing] to the Ephesians and the Colossians: [consider] how profoundly he preaches Jesus, in whom God willed that all things be restored.[33] And there is no other knowledge than this knowing [that restoration comes through Jesus].[34] And if you enter rightly into the Scriptures, you will find nothing except God, the world, and Christ; and you will find Christ to be the one in whom God reconciled the world unto Himself. Consider carefully: God the Father willed that even we human beings be partakers of His glory.[35] For what greater glory could there be for human nature than that there be found included in human nature the man who is God's Blessed Son, in and through whom all things in heaven and on earth are blessed? For without the word of God angels would be without life.[36] Divine reason, which is the word of God, is the wisdom that nourishes every rational creature. And by means of His word, which nourishes all rational spirits forever, God manifests, unto His[37] own glory, the riches of His wisdom.[38]

[8] Furthermore, in regard to those matters that are located in

another part [of Scripture]: note that the Prophet says: "I will freely sacrifice to You."[39] Herefrom [we see that] the will acquires the reward and distinguishes the works, since only someone who has free will can merit [anything]—i.e., [only someone] who is able to transgress but who has not transgressed ..., etc.[40] Without the will there is no reward. But the will has a certain freedom, which is its life. If the soul puts to death this freedom, then it reduces itself to bondage, for [in that case] the soul has surrendered its freedom. Therefore, if the surrendering that is the death of freedom, i.e., the death of the soul's own life, is done for God's sake, then he who thus offers himself to God in sacrifice, expects a reward. This reward is the bestowing of divine life. For he who dies for God's sake by renouncing his life, which consists in freedom, will obtain, in return, divine life. For God, as a generous Rewarder, gives divine life—i.e., gives participation in His own life—to that soul which has given to Him its own life. Now, he who professes Christ gives his life to God. (For Christ is the Teacher and Instructor and Head of this religion and is He who *did* that which He *taught*. Hence, He is the Way of obtaining divine life.) This profession consists in faith that is [in-]formed by love. Through this faith a man (1) renounces all that he possesses and (2) follows Christ. For as Christ, in all humility, becomes obedient to God up to the point of [undergoing] the most horrible of all horrors, [viz., death], so [the professing Christian] becomes subject to Christ, his Head.

Furthermore, be cognizant [of the following]: Those in a religious order are subject to their master, whom as a representative of Christ they prefer to themselves [and] through whom they serve under Christ. Moreover, those who are subject to the tribune of an army serve under the emperor of whom the tribune is the representative. In a similar way, a soul [of a man] in a religious order—[a soul] which has become mortified—serves in obedience to the superior who is set over it by Christ, who said with regard to the superiors: "He who hears you hears me; he who despises you despises me; and he who despises me despises Him who sent me."[41] Be aware that without true obedience, which mortifies our life, or our freedom,[42] we cannot expect from God the Father, who has sent us Christ, the reward of immortal and divine life.[43]

[9] Now, note that, properly speaking, freedom-of-soul is called *spirit*. Therefore, when there is present in a man not his own freedom but rather the commanding word-of-God, which he obeys, then the man's spirit is dead, and God's Spirit lives in him. And this is so

because [such a] soul is motivated only by arousal on the part of God's Spirit. However, "Spirit of God" can be construed in a different way: viz., insofar as [the Spirit of God] is concealed in governing precepts and governing laws. And in this sense we say that the spirit that observes the commandments is alive, because it is aroused by the Spirit of the word of God. But the Spirit of the word of God—the Spirit that is found in Christ— is the Spirit of salvation. For it is the Spirit of the spirits that have to do with the fulfilling of all laws. By means of this Spirit we are aroused to love not only our neighbor but also our enemies so as to benefit them. And this Spirit is, properly speaking, the Spirit-of-God, who makes His sun to rise upon good men and evil men.[44] Therefore, if we have in us the Spirit of Christ,[45] we must not doubt that we are member[s] of Christ and are enlivened by His Spirit and that we shall be there where our Head is. And we shall exist through that Spirit of the Son of God and shall be sons of God by participation.

[10] And note that the spirit-of-man that is properly called the freedom of the soul can be motivated by a good spirit; and [this] is [the spirit] that leads the soul to the right region, which is a paradise of delights for the soul. Or [the spirit of man can be motivated] by an evil spirit; and this [evil spirit] leads to a region, but not the right one. Therefore, when our freedom ceases and there commands within us the spirit that leads to things earthly (as is the case with the spirit of greed or of lasciviousness or of pride), then we are made servants of that evil spirit, by whose command we are motivated. Hence, such a soul is seen to be alive unto this world, because [that soul] is moved and stimulated by the things of this world.[46] And in this freedom-of-living there is servitude and death. But when the soul is moved away from this present world toward those things that are of the other [world], then we see that [the soul] is dead to this present world[47] and is a servant [in regard to that other world]. But, nevertheless, it is alive and free; for its serving is a reigning. For [a spirit] that is motivated by the Spirit of Jesus is seen to be separated [from this world] and dead [to this world] because of renunciation of [this] world. And, nevertheless, [such a spirit] rules over the world and the flesh. Hence, it is not a servant but is free, because the Spirit of Jesus adorns it with freedom.

NOTES TO *Una Oblatione*

* Sermon CLXXXV.
1. Hebrews 10:14.
2. John 14:6.
3. This is the Tree of life of which Genesis 2:9 speaks.
4. Genesis 2:10-14. The river Phison is deemed by Augustine to be the Ganges; the river Geon, to be the Nile. See Augustine's *De Genesi contra Manichaeos*, II, 10, 13 (*PL* 34:203).
5. Hebrews 11:9.
6. Genesis 3:8.
7. "Israel"—i.e., Jacob.
8. Genesis 28:18.
9. Luke 19:10.
10. John 3:20.
11. John 15:1.
12. Genesis 28:12.
13. Cf. St. Ambrose, *De Paradiso*, 5, 29 (*PL* 14:303).
14. Here (at **3**:19) I have corrected the printed edition of the Latin text by changing the editors' "utrique" to "uterque". See *Codex Latinus Vaticanus* 1245.
15. Here (at **4**:14) I am regarding "suam" as a word to be deleted.
16. Genesis 15:1.
17. Hebrew 11:6.
18. I Corinthians 15:20.
19. Ephesians 5:23 and 5:30.
20. I Corinthians 15:23.
21. "His agony": i.e., in Gethsemani. Matthew 26:36-42.
22. Mark 14:34.
23. Christ is the Firstfruits—whose Resurrection precedes, ontologically, the resurrection of all others unto life. "As in Adam all die, so also in Christ all shall be made alive." (See I Cor. 15:20-23 and 15:50-57.) In the present passage Nicholas is discussing the resurrection of believers—of those who have "died in Christ." Thus, he is echoing the emphasis of I Corinthians 15. He does not, however, anywhere deny that unbelievers shall also be resurrected—unto judgment and punishment and exclusion from God's presence.
24. "On this day": i.e., on the day that corresponds to Easter Sunday in the calendar of the Church—i.e., the day of Christ's resurrection.
25. Luke 24:26-27.
26. John 9:2-3.
27. Note Genesis 50:20.
28. Galatians 3:22.
29. Galatians 3:26.
30. I Timothy 1:16.
31. Romans 5:12.
32. Colossians 1:19 and 2:9.
33. Ephesians 1:10.

34. Philippians 3:10.
35. See Romans 9:23.
36. Psalms 103:4 (104:4).
37. Here (at **7**:29) I am reading "suam" (as does the Paris edition) in place of "eius".
38. Note Colossians 2:3.
39. Psalms 53:8 (54:6).
40. Ecclesiasticus 31:10.
41. Luke 10:16.
42. That is, we are to make ourselves servants of God. See Romans 6:22.
43. See Matthew 10:39.
44. Matthew 5:45.
45. Romans 8:9. Galatians 4:6.
46. According to St. Paul, the Christian's soul is supposed to be dead to this present world. See n. 47 below. See also Galatians 6:14.
47. Romans 6:11.

Iam autem Die Festo Mediante *[1]
("Now about the Middle of the Feast ....")[2]
[March 6, 1459; preached in Rome]

[1] Just as recently[3] when we held an assembly you heard the command given to me about making visitations, so now I am present and will begin [my visitation][4] with [some] prefacing remarks. Yet, nothing more effective can be taken [as a text] than can the Gospel—which was written for our learning.[5] [Today] in the office of the mass we read, from John 7, the Gospel-passage which goes as follows: *"Now about the middle of the feast Jesus went up into the temple and taught."*[6] [2] We [ourselves] are taught that in the midst of the feast-day we are to go up into the temple, surely a place of contemplation and of prayer. Therefore, feast-days are reminders that urge [us] to go up to the temple. And since very many people came together at that time, Jesus taught [them]. Note that Jesus teaches the word of God. And although [in the Gospel-passage] He does not indicate whom He taught, nonetheless it is sufficiently understood that He taught those who were going up into the temple—i.e., those who with an eagerness to approach unto things divine sought out the place dedicated to God. These are they who are teachable by God and who are eager to receive divine and heavenly teachings, which no one was better able to convey than was the Heavenly Teacher who is above all others. Jesus *taught*. What except salvation was He who is Jesus, or Savior,[7] able to teach? What except meekness [was He] who is meek, [able to teach]?[8] What except deep humility, He who is humble in heart?[9] What except an understanding of all the Scriptures, He who is Truth?[10] What except life, He who is Resurrection and Life?[11]

[3] *"And the Jews wondered, saying: 'How does this man know letters, when He has never learned?'"*[12] Surely it was wondrous and unheard-of that someone knew writings who had not learned letters. Here you have a text [that attests] that Christ naturally knew all the things that other men scarcely at all attain with [much] study. Christ was able to be known in and through this alone: viz., in and through the excellence of all men. For everything that all men who thrive mentally *can* know, Christ *was* actually. Men can know languages, and one man [knows] more of them than does another man; but Christ is the Living Word of God.[13] Men can be learned; Christ is Living Wisdom.[14] Men can live by rational life; Christ is Rational Life

itself.[15] Men can put on immortal life; Christ is Immortal Life.[16] Men can put on incorruption; Christ is Incorruption.[17] Men can arise from the dead; Christ is Resurrection.[18] The case is similar regarding every perfection acquirable by man, since, as is true, Christ is *actually* every perfection.[19] And you know that no one is so perfect that he could not be more perfect. And so, since the perfection of all men admits of more and less, it is not proportional to the perfection of Christ. For Christ's perfection is very lofty; no perfection can be greater or higher than it. Now, the maximum, than which there cannot be a greater, is in an actual way all things. For in its maximality it enfolds in an actual way whatever things can admit of more and less.[20] Hence, all possibility of perfection is derived from, and perfected from, that maximality and fullness.

[4] Moreover, consider the following: viz., that we have a concreated capability for perfection, in accordance with which we can dispose ourselves to be more perfect. Yet, we cannot bring ourselves from potency to actuality. For nothing that is in potency can bring itself into actuality, since potency is actualized by means of the actual. For example, that which is potentially hot is brought into actuality by that which is actually hot. In particular, by fire, which is actually hot, that which is capable of being made hot becomes actually hot. Now, the zenith of a student's perfection is that he be like his teacher. The zenith [of perfection] of the intellectual nature is that it be conformed to the Divine Word and Divine Intellect. Therefore, no teacher whatsoever except the Word of God can conduct our intellectual nature unto its own highest perfection. Therefore, no man can be happy except him who is Christ-like. No spirit [can be] happy unless it is conformed to the Spirit of Christ.

[5] Note that the text states that the Jews asked: "*How is it that He knows letters, when he has never learned?*"[21] Therefore, skill at letters is both from art and by nature. For if the art [of reading and writing] is absent, [letters] are not known; and if intelligence is absent, [letters] are not learned. Hence, in Christ—who is the Word[22] and who is the Omnipotent Art through which God made the world[23]—art and nature are seen to coincide. Hence, [Christ] knew all things because [in Him] art accorded with intelligence; He is Art itself and is the Understanding of all things knowable. The Jews would not have been amazed if they had believed that Christ was the Living Word of all formable words. By way of analogy: if someone were to conceive of a

certain piece of writing as alive with an intellectual life, he would not be amazed if the writing understood itself without a teacher, since he would notice that the writing's being was a living intellectual word.

[6] *"Jesus answered them and said: 'My doctrine is not mine but is His who sent me.'"*[24] [It is] as if He were to have said: 'You wonder from where I know letters and have a learning that can be had only from one who [already] has it and passes it along. But what if I have been sent to you? In that case, my doctrine would not be mine but would be the sender's.' And note that Christ said to the Apostles, "It is not you who speak but the Spirit of your Father."[25] Therefore, just as someone omniscient who is sent by him of whom he speaks does not need study in order to acquire an art—and, thus, he speaks on his own, [apart from having learned]— so [Christ] dissolved wonder. [It is] as if He were to have said: 'God, who sends me, speaks through me, His Emissary.' God, the Creator, who is Spirit, speaks through Understanding, or Wisdom.[26] Christ is said to be the Right Hand of the Father.[27] For just as the hand is the organ through which a man does all his works, so the intellect is related to the soul, because [the intellect] is like [the soul's] hand. For [the soul] does all its works by means of the intellect. Analogously, God [works all things] through His Wisdom, which is Christ.[28]

[7] And note that [Christ] says: *"My doctrine is not mine."* [It is] as if He were to say: 'My [doctrine] is mine in such a way that it is not mine, because I have been sent.' Similarly, the sending is of Himself[29] in such a way that it is not of Himself, since [the sending] is done not by Himself but by the Sender. Therefore, Christ wanted to show that He was sent by God, whom the Jews did not doubt to know all things. As the Jews were claiming, no one, apart from any studying on his own part, knows so much that he would be able to teach. And this [truth] has its sole exception in the case of an envoy, who teaches not his own doctrine but the doctrine of the sender, who speaks through the envoy. If so, then, [says Christ], I must have been sent and my doctrine must be the doctrine of the Sender. Similarly, the doctrine of the Son is His own and is not His own but is the Father's. For insofar as He is the Son, all that He has is of His Father. This fact is understood if the Son is conceived to be the Sonship. Assuredly, this revelation of the divinity is great— viz., [the revelation] that the begottenness by which God the Father begets the Son must be conceived as the Supreme Power's sending Himself. For in that case the Sender sends from His whole essence and

nature Him who is sent. And so, [the one sent] is called the Son because He has the rational being, and the co-essential being, of the Sender.

[**8**] Next, Christ shows that the Sender is God. And he shows this fact not in any other way than on the basis of experience, which is a teacher of things. And He says: "*If anyone wills to do His will, [i.e., the Father's will], he knows, on the basis of the doctrine [itself], whether it be from God or whether I speak [it] of myself.*"[30] Note both of these points. The Word very simply and very clearly indicates the fact that He is the Word of God. He says: 'If anyone [wills] to do the will of Him who sent me, and if he purposes to do so in every respect, then— these [antecedents] being presupposed—he knows on the basis of the doctrine [itself] whether it is from God. For the doctrine is of such great efficacy that within it is contained a light that is manifested to him who receives the doctrine. Therefore, he will know whether [the doctrine] is from God or whether I speak [it] of myself as a private individual and not as one sent from God.' For the Jews, who had already received God's precepts that were revealed to them by Moses, who was sent by God, were readily able to understand whether [or not] Christ's doctrine was from God, since Christ came [in order] to fulfill the Law.[31]

[**9**] Moreover, [Christ] adds how it is that this [distinguishing of doctrines] will be done: '*He who speaks of himself seeks his own glory.* He who seeks his own interests speaks unto his own advantage and makes himself the goal of his teaching. *But he who seeks the glory of him who sent him is truthful, and there is no injustice in him.*'[32] Now, since [Christ's] every teaching was only unto the glory and manifestation of God the Father and was the perfection of the teaching of Moses and of the prophets, [Christ] could be adjudged only as a true and just emissary. For a legate who gives all honor to his sender, and who sticks to his commission, is truthful and just. For even if the command of the sender were unjust, there would be no injustice in the legate, since he would not be arrogating anything to himself and would in no respect fail in doing his duty. All of the foregoing pertains to the fact that the Father, who sent Jesus, gave Him the commission to keep showing at all times works of mercy, even on the day of the Sabbath. And Christ, in curing a man on the Sabbath, wanted to show that He was not a violator of the Sabbath, because God commissioned [Him to act] in that way.

[**10**] There follows [in the Scriptural text]: "*Did not Moses give*

you the Law, and [yet] none of you keep the Law?"[33]—as is corroborated below. There follows: "*Why do you seek to kill me*—on the grounds, namely, that I have not kept the law concerning the Sabbath?" (For [in the Law of Moses] it was commanded that such a transgressor be stoned.) Now, Christ, who willed to die, first took care to remove all occasions [for dying. He did so] in order [later] to show that He willingly, but unjustly, died [i.e., was put to death] for the salvation of all men. "*The multitude answered and said: 'You have a devil. Who seeks to kill You?'* "[34]—as if [Christ] worked miracles not by means of a human art or by means of a divine art but rather by means of a thousand contrivances of a lying devil and as if, nonetheless, it were not the case that [the Jews] were for this reason seeking to kill Him. They denied this [intent] because of a fear of the people, on account of whom they did not at that time dare to admit that they sought His death.

[**11**] Jesus answered and said to them: "*I have done one work, and you all marvel.*"[35] He is speaking of the man whom He cured on the Sabbath at the pond [called] Probatica—about which [one reads] earlier, in Chapter 5.[36] "*Therefore, Moses gave you circumcision (not because it is from Moses [himself] but [because it is] from the fathers); and on the Sabbath you circumcise a man.*"[37] Originally, circumcision arose from the fathers, or patriarchs; later it was given by Moses, who also gave the law of the Sabbath. But the law of the Sabbath did not preclude circumcision, which was commanded to be done on the eighth day of birth, which was possible to be the Sabbath. [**12**] "*If a man receives circumcision on the Sabbath in order that the Law of Moses not be broken, are you angry at me, who have healed the whole man on the Sabbath?*"[38] God's law, as well as the law of nature (which preceded circumcision [and] which commands that we do to another what we would want done unto us), was not broken by the instigators of circumcision but was, instead, confirmed—just as circumcision [was confirmed] by Moses. Therefore, the law of the Sabbath does not infringe upon the law of God that is the eternal law. And no one ought to be angry about the fact that that law [of the Sabbath] is not obeyed [when one is circumcised on the Sabbath]. Now, in fulfilling the eternal law in regard to healing the whole man on the Sabbath, Christ acted in accordance with the command of Him who sent Him. Therefore, ..., etc.

[**13**] Moreover, consider [the following]: Not without very great

mystery is mention here [in the Gospel] made of the law of circumcision, of the law of the Sabbath, and of the healing of the whole man. For circumcision and the Sabbath rest upon covenants and agreements. But the healing of the whole man was mandated not by laws, etc., or by sacred signs of a covenant and of agreements, but by Christ, who alone healed the whole man. And [He did] this on the Sabbath because the Sabbath was instituted so that Christ, the Son of the Sabbath, would on His own day[39] heal the whole man. Note [the expression] "the whole man": [Jesus healed] not with respect only to the soul or only to the body but with respect to both.

[**14**] "*Do not judge according to the appearance, but make a just judgment.*"[40] He who looks at what appears and at the surface, or outer-covering, judges according to the appearance. But he makes a just judgment who looks not at the letter but at the intent; for the intent is the Law's meaning and quiddity. Here [in the passage above] we are taught that Christ revealed inward things and revealed the spirit of the letter; for He was the Message that was hidden in Scripture. Someone who according to the appearance judges that Christ is human, surely does not know Him. Rather, he must turn from [Christ's] teaching and works unto inner matters in order to see the essence from which this power derives; and in this way he apprehends the deity hidden beneath the humanity. The case is similar, then, concerning the Law's surface-statements and its hidden life-giving message.

[**15**] "*But certain ones from Jerusalem said: 'Is this not He whom the Jews seek to kill? And, lo, He speaks openly, and they say nothing to Him.'* "[41] Note [that] He speaks openly, because [He speaks] with the light of truth, which [the Jews] could not gainsay. "*Have the rulers truly known that this is the Christ?*"[42] Yet, how would they know? For if they knew, they also would not know. For Christ cannot be known. "*But we know this man, whence He is; but when the Christ comes, no one [will] know whence He is.*"[43] In the immediately succeeding chapter Christ answers, saying: "*I know whence I come and whither I go; but you do not know whence I come.*"[44] For although they knew according to the appearance, they nevertheless did not regarding this matter make a just judgment, in accordance with the invisible nature.

[**16**] "*Jesus therefore cried out in the temple, teaching and saying: 'You know me and know whence I am'* "[45]—[you know it], that is, in judging according to the flesh,[46] as is [indicated] in the immediate-

ly succeeding chapter. *"And I have not come on my own* but I was sent, as I showed earlier on the basis of your admission that I teach but have not learned letters. But one who is sent is not sent from himself and does not come on his own; rather, *He who sent me is true; Him you do not know."*[47] Behold, [Christ] shows that God alone is true and that He, from whom Christ comes originally, is unknown to the Jews. And so, [Christ] infers again that what is known according to the flesh is not opposed to the judgment that He is the Christ. **[17]** *"I know Him."*[48] The Son alone knows the Father.[49] *"And if I shall say that I know Him not, I shall be a liar like you."*[50] Note that the Jews who adhere to the outward letter [of the Law] are liars and that those who are like them are made liars. The father of the lie is the Devil.[51] Therefore, all liars pass over into a likeness of the Devil. One who is true can speak only the truth in and through the true one sent by him, since [the one sent] speaks the words of the sender. *"But I know Him, since I am from Him and since He sent me."* Note the conclusion that from Him who is true Jesus has, in an essential way, His being and His being sent. Likewise, Paul says that God sent His Son.[52]

[18] *"They sought, therefore, to apprehend Him; but no one laid hands on Him, because His hour had not yet come. But of the people many believed in Him."*[53] I understand "his hour" to mean the time when the consummation [of His mission] arrived. For Christ was first supposed to show two things: viz., (1) that He who was the Son of man was Son of God and (2) that He was going to undergo a voluntary death for the sake of our salvation. He showed the first thing by His words and by very true works that no people ascribed to anyone other than to God. He showed, secondly, that, being without sin, He was not justly worthy of condemnation but that [He underwent death] voluntarily on account of obedience[54] that redounded to our salvation. As long as these [two] things were not sufficiently shown, the time for undergoing death had not come.

[19] That He could be believed to be the Son of God had to be shown, because this belief renders certain His teaching and His promises concerning future things that are supernatural. Since these [future] things are such that they are not *seen* to be possible, it was necessary that Christ teach them on the basis of uquestionably reliable[55] authority. Now, no one doubts that God is truthful in His every word, no matter what He is speaking of. Yet, because of false apostles and prophets there can be doubt about whether or not someone is speaking God's words. But He who by His works shows that not only is He a truthful prophet of God but also is the Son with the full power of God the Father—assuredly, He provides a firm foundation for belief in His teaching. [20] To one who reflects, a second thing shows itself to be necessary: [viz.,] that since Christ, as God's Son and Messenger, taught that sonship with God can be obtained for those who are without sin[56] and who willingly obey God even to the point of [undergoing] a most shameful death, then the reward for that death can be only eternal life and a life than which none other is better—as is that life which *understands*[57] that it is alive. For how could it be that God (who is *just* according to the unreserved belief of all men) would as a reward give—to a believer-in-Him who dies for His sake—less than immortal life?

[21] It was necessary that Christ display in regard to Himself the following: viz., (1) that the Son of God is without sin and (2) that he willingly was going to obey the Father even to the point of death on the Cross and (3) that in this way He would obtain a glorious resurrection from the dead and would enter into glory and (4) that every believer would be made a partaker of His death and a partaker of His resurrection. But *that* believer who with consummate desire determines to will to be obedient (conformably to Christ) even to the point of death—[he] has already become a participant in Christ's death, even if it would not happen that he suffer physical martyrdom, as [such martyrdom] is true of St. Martin and of other holy professors. And I recall that elsewhere (with Christ teaching [through me]) I said something analogous (1) regarding consummate hatred (on account of which someone is a murderer)[58] and (2) regarding consummate concupiscence of heart (on account of which someone is an adulterer).[59]

[22] From the passage in the Gospel of John the Evangelist the foregoing points are clearly manifested, especially to one who is intent on finding them. Let these things—which have been said about the Gospel in the foregoing way very briefly and preliminarily—suffice.

NOTES TO *Iam autem Die Festo Mediante*

* Sermon CCXCII.
1. This title is supplied by the editors of the printed edition of the Latin text since the manuscripts have no title. The Paris edition uses the title "Sicut nuper dum", the first words of the text. In the Paris edition folio CXC is mislabeled as CLXXXVIII.
2. John 7:14.
3. "… recently": i.e., in February of this same year (1459).
4. Nicholas is making a pastoral visitation to Santa Maria Maior in Rome.
5. Romans 15:4.
6. John 7:14.
7. "Jesus" means *Savior*. Matthew 1:21.
8. Matthew 11:29.
9. Matthew 11:29.
10. John 14:6.
11. John 11:25.
12. John 7:15. "… know letters" : i.e., know how to read and to write and know certain texts and writings.
13. John 1:1.
14. I Corinthians 1:24.
15. Isaias (Isaiah) 1:18 (as applicable to Christ). I Corinthians 2:16.
16. I Timothy 6:16. Here (at **3**:16) I am reading "vita" with the Paris edition, in place of "virtus" with mss. V_2 and *L*.
17. I Corinthians 15:53.
18. John 11:25.
19. Matthew 5:48 as applicable also to the Son.
20. *De Docta Ignorantia* I, 5 and II, 1 (**96**).
21. John 7:15.
22. John 1:1.
23. Hebrews 1:2.
24. John 7:16.
25. Matthew 10:20.
26. I Corinthians 1:24.
27. Christ sits at the Right Hand of the Father. Matthew 22:44 and 26:64. From this belief arose the reference to Christ as the Right Hand of the Father.
28. I Corinthians 1:24.
29. "… is of Himself": i.e., He is the one who is sent.
30. John 7:17.
31. Matthew 5:17.
32. This is a paraphrase of John 7:18.
33. John 7:19.
34. John 7:20.
35. John 7:21.
36. John 5:1-18.
37. John 7:22.
38. John 7:23. The whole man (*totus homo*) is man qua both body and soul.

39. Matthew 12:8. Mark 2:28. Luke 6:5.
40. John 7:24.
41. John 7:25-26.
42. John 7:26.
43. John 7:27.
44. John 8:14.
45. John 7:28.
46. John 8:15.
47. John 7:28.
48. John 7:29.
49. Luke 10:22. John 8:55.
50. John 8:55.
51. John 8:44.
52. Galatians 4:4.
53. John 7:30-31.
54. Philippians 2:8.
55. Regarding Nicholas's use of "*infallibilis*" and its variants and cognates, see pp. 10-12 of my *Hugh of Balma on Mystical Theology: A Translation and an Overview of His De Theologia Mystica* (Minneapolis: Banning, 2002).
56. " ... without sin": i.e., without sin because it has been forgiven.
57. Cf. Sermon CCLXXXVII (**1–2**).
58. I John 3:15.
59. Matthew 5:27-28.

Respexit Humilitatem*
("He Has Regarded the Humility . . . ")
[July 2, 1446; preached in Mainz]¹

[1] "He has regarded the humility of His handmaiden" (Luke 1).²

Gospel-passage: "Mary, rising up . . .," etc.³

Because the angel had reported to the Glorious Virgin that her cousin Elizabeth had conceived in her old age: Mary, rising up, went out as soon as the angel departed from her. Etc.

PART ONE
The Things Which—according to the Gospel (Luke 1:39-45)—
Evoked Mary's Song (Luke 1:46-55) Are Considered
*under Various Aspects.*⁴

(a) *The manner in which God brought about the conception of Christ.*

[2] Now, we must consider the way in which the coming of St. John [the Baptist] was ordained in relation to Christ. For in order that Mary would believe that by the work of the Holy Spirit there could easily happen that which the usual law of nature denies to be possible: the angel mentions that [Mary's] cousin Elizabeth, who was sterile and elderly, had *conceived*—[had conceived] because no promise (*verbum*) of God's expresses an impossibility.⁵ Thus, when Mary heard of these things—viz., of the fact that her cousin had conceived (in transcendence of every mode of the law of nature), inasmuch as no promise of God's expresses an impossibility—she saw that her question was answered. [This was the question] about mode—the question that she put to the angel when she asked, "How will this [conceiving] be possible?" [The answer was], namely, that by the work of the Holy Spirit every word of God's would come true, because *possible* and *impossible* do not apply to God, since—beyond everything possible and impossible—He is pure Absolute Necessity itself. Hence, because His will *is* Absolute Necessity, that which He wills to be the case cannot fail to be the case. Rather, just as He is Absolute Necessity, so whatever He wills to be the case cannot escape from the necessity of being the case. Hence, the possible and the impossible are certain modes that have to do with the judgment of reason, so that one thing is said to be possible, another thing to be impossible. But God—who is beyond all

positing and negating, and beyond all that with which reason makes contact—is Absolute Necessity itself.

[3] Hence, with the question about mode answered—viz., [the answer] that God, who is not bound by mode, works all things by His word without this or that mode—Mary, by means of the example of Elizabeth, believed that the word announced to her was not impossible for God. And, hence, expressing her own faith, she said: "Behold, the handmaiden of the Lord; let it be done to me in accordance with Your word."[6]

[4] We must consider the following: that when Mary said to the angel "How shall this [conceiving] occur, seeing that I know no man?": then, having doubt about mode and expressing the reason for her doubt, she added mention of the mode-of-conception necessary according to the course of nature, viz., the union with a male. And the angel answers that the Holy Spirit ..., etc. Thus, he is replying: 'not in such a [human] manner, but the [Holy] Spirit will come upon [you] ...,' etc. And lest Mary have a further doubt about the manner in which the Holy Spirit is to come upon her, the angel said further: "and the power of the Most High will overshadow you."[7] [5] [It is] as if he were to say: 'Do not think that the Holy Spirit will come upon [you] in a way-of-coming by which one comes from place to place by a mode of descent by which either what is heavy descends or a dove comes down from a dove-cot to the waters or a ray of the sun descends to the earth—or in any other way. For the operations of God are free of all mode. Thus, God is the Absolute, and mode is a creature, so that whatever in order to exist requires a certain mode is a creature. Thus, for there to be a man, there is required that there be an animal in such a mode. And for there to be a lion, [there is required that there be an animal] in such a mode. And for a man to be begotten, there is required such a mode. And so on, as regards all [creatures]. Hence, all modes—which in order for something to be made have to come together—display deficiency. Accordingly, in God no mode is necessary in order that He exist or act or come or supervene, because His power is absolute and omnipotent—is unrestricted to, and uncontracted to, mode.

[6] Consequently, the angel said: "And the power of the Most High will overshadow you." [It is] as if he were to say: 'As for my having stated that the Holy Spirit is to come upon you: understand the Holy Spirit's coming upon you to be *this*: namely, the power of the

Most High's overshadowing you.' For God, who is not absent from any place, comes to the soul by means of grace when the soul is made pleasing to God by divine power. Just as He comes by means of sanctification when by divine power the soul is made holy, so [He comes] by means of justification when [by means of divine power the soul] is made just. And so on. Likewise, [He comes] by means of creation when by divine power a creature originates. Thus too, [He comes] by means of conception in the Glorious Virgin when the angel says: "Behold, you shall conceive," when by divine power the Son was conceived in the Virgin.

[7] Hence, because this conceiving occurred, apart from the mode of union with a male [and] by the power of the Most High overshadowing the Virgin, the angel says: 'He shall be called the Son of God.'[8] For just as a father's sons are called sons because of the fact that they have been conceived by means of the paternal power that is present in the father's seed, so Jesus will be called the Son of God in conformity with His having been conceived of the Virgin. For he was conceived apart from the mode of a father's seminal power; but He was not able to be conceived apart from a power. Accordingly, [having been conceived] by the power of the Most High, who is beyond all mode [and] who is the Blessed God, He who is conceived will be called the Son of God.

(b) *Spiritual rebirth, which occurs by the power of God.*

[8] The case is similar as regards the rebirth of our spirit. For apart from a power we cannot be born again, since without a power a spiritual birthing cannot take place in our soul. Nor can that power be according to some mode, because such a spirit cannot be born in us in the manner in which something physical is born, since from physical modes there comes only a physical birthing. Hence, in order that there take place in us a spiritual birthing, which may search out all things (even the deep matters of God)[9] and may live most happily, this [begetting] must occur by the power of the Most High's overshadowing our soul. This [overshadowing] is the Holy Spirit's supervening. To overshadow is to impart oneself protectingly and healingly—as Peter's shadow healed.[10] And the Psalmist prays: "Under the shadow of Thy wings protect me."[11] [9] Accordingly, that which is then born is called a son of God. For that birthing whereby we are thus reborn occurs by the power of God. Hence, [we are each] a son of God.[12] Thus, the virginal conception teaches us how it is that we are born again in spirit.

This rebirth is needful—as in John 3 Jesus said to Nicodemus.[13] St. Peter speaks of it in his canonical letter—[stating] that it occurs not by means of corruptible seed but by means of the Word of God, who lives and remains forever.[14]

[10] Therefore, as Christ gives an illustration: In the air there arises a blowing wind, which, nevertheless, cannot apart from a power arise there where it was not; however, that power cannot be attained, because we do not know whence that wind (*spiritus*) comes or whither it goes.[15] The case is similar when in the soul there arises a spirit which causes in the soul a movement of divine love. This is the spirit which enlivens the soul and which is born in the soul—just as the wind (*ventus*) moves the air and is begotten in the air. Now, wind is nothing other than living air, or moved air; and so, it is air that is born again. So too, a spirit is nothing other than a living soul and a soul born again through enlivenment. And since this is the case, we know that this [enlivening] proceeds from an enlivening power. But that [power], which is the beginning and the end of spirit, cannot be attained. Hence, it is a mode above every [other] mode; but it is attained by means of a likeness. Just as that which is begotten of flesh is flesh, so too spirit, since it is found to be born, is known to be born from spirit—not in the manner of flesh but in a manner [*modus*] that is beyond every [other] mode [*modus*].

[11] Hence, although Nicodemus did not doubt to be true that which was said about rebirth—[said] on the part of Christ, whom he confessed to be a teacher and to have come from God[16]—nevertheless, he had doubts about its mode. And he expressed the reason for his doubt: "How can a man be born when he is old? Can he re-enter his mother's womb and be born a second time?"[17] Jesus answered him [by saying] that he, Nicodemus, was speaking of a birth by which one enters into this world but [that] He, Christ, was thinking of him who is supposed to enter the Kingdom-of-God, which is not of this world[18] [and] which flesh and blood do not possess.[19] [12] Hence, in order for those who are born to enter into *this present* world, they were first in the womb, in which they were conceived and enlivened; and, thereafter, they were born. But after they are thus born once, they are present in this world, in which they must be *conceived anew* and enlivened anew—not in accordance with the flesh, as in the mother's womb, but in accordance with the spirit—in order that their birth be an entrance into the Kingdom of God. And this

conceiving occurs through faith that is [in-]formed by love. For the spirit conceives by faith; the spirit's sacrament is the water-of-baptism, which shows believers to be reborn as newborn babes.[20] But the Holy Spirit enlivens this *conceptus*; and the Holy Spirit is the Power-of-Love without which the soul cannot have life. For the soul is moved by love alone. For just as the spirit that is the wind moves the air, so love moves the soul.

[13] Accordingly, since Nicodemus still had doubts about mode and asked, "How shall this [rebirthing] come about?" Christ replied: "Are you a teacher in Israel and know not these things? Verily, verily I say unto you: We speak of that which we know, and we testify of that which we have seen. But you do not accept our testimony."[21] [This was] as if to say: 'Since you are a teacher in Israel and know not these things, you ought not to ask "how will this be done?" For if this were knowable with respect to mode, you, who are a teacher in Israel, would not fail to know it.' Thereafter [Jesus] adds: "We speak of that which we know"—as if to say: 'You ought not to have asked again how this [rebirthing] would be done; rather, you ought to have believed me. For earlier you avowed that I am a teacher and have come from God.' The teacher in Israel ought to have believed the Teacher come from God, because—like all teachers—He who is the Teacher come from God speaks of what He knows and testifies of what He has seen. But the teachers in Israel do not receive His testimony, because a knowledge of it does not fall within the scope of their mastery. Hence, they believe nothing except what they arrive at within their scope of mastery.

[14] Next, [Jesus] adds: "If I have spoken to you of earthly things and you do not believe, how will you believe if I shall speak to you of Heavenly things?"[22] [Thereby] He meant to indicate: 'I have now said to you earthly things about the wind-of-air [*spiritus aëris*]—[said] that wind (*spiritus*) blows where it will, and its sound is heard, but nevertheless we do not know from where it comes or whither it goes. And these [phenomena] are perceptual and are of this earthly world. But that of which I spoke in a likeness of this [wind] is similarly present to each one who is born of the Spirit. That is, in him is present a vital birthing and a Spirit of great power, whose voice is heard (as that voice of Christ was heard, which proceeded from the power of [His human] spirit), and, nevertheless, we do not know from where [this Spirit] comes or whither it goes.' For [the

people] ought to have supposed, on the basis of the earthly example, that they ought not to ask how there would be done that which does not occur in any knowable manner. Therefore, [Jesus] adds: "If I have spoken to you of Heavenly things, how will you believe ...?"[23] [It is] as if He were to say: 'Heavenly things—which have nothing in common with earthly things, since Heavenly things cannot be adequately illustrated by any analogy with earthly things—will never be understood by you who do not believe the Teacher whom you maintain to have come from God [and] who even now is guiding you by means of earthly examples.'

[**15**] [Jesus] adds: "And no one has ascended into Heaven except Him who has come down from Heaven, [viz.,] the Son of man, who is in Heaven."[24] [Thereby Jesus] gives the reason for the difficulty of belief in Heavenly things: 'Since you are unwilling to believe unless you understand the rationale, how then [do you expect to believe], given that no one by his own intellective power can ascend unto Heaven in order to see the things that are spoken of and attested to by Him who knows them and has seen them? For He alone who has come down from Heaven (viz., the Son of man, whom you, too, maintain has come from God, [maintain it] because of His works, which you have seen)—He has ascended unto Heaven and is in Heaven.[25] And for this reason you will not by any ascent of reason attain unto Heavenly things—you who are not of Heaven. Only the Son of man is seen to have come down from Heaven, when He assumed a humanity in accordance with the condition of this world, viz., in regard to flesh and blood—as even you maintain that He has come from God.'

[**16**] Hence, since the intellect of this Son of man was assumed by the Word of the Father (which Word is God), this intellect ascended unto the hidden things of God, which are called Heavenly things (because they are contrasted with things earthly), so that descending [and] ascending, as well as not-descending and not-ascending but being in Heaven, coincide in the Son of man. And so, He is one who is like the [brazen] serpent held up in the wilderness:[26] those who approached by faith and who looked upon the serpent—i.e., by turning toward it and seeking healing from their wounds—obtained through the serpent-that-was-set-up healing from the poisonous bites of the serpents of the wilderness. Accordingly, it is necessary that the Son of man be lifted up, so that whoever-believes-in-Him not perish

but have eternal life.[27] Hence, Christ concludes that rebirth with respect to the Kingdom of God is a liberation that does not allow a perishing; rather, that rebirth has eternal life. But since that rebirth is supposed to furnish an ascent unto Heavenly life, which is divine and eternal, and since no one can ascend except Him who descended, [viz.,] the Son of man: it is necessary that that rebirth be accomplished through faith in the exalted Son of man.

(c) *Christ's spiritual birth in us occurred exemplarily in the case of Mary.*

[17] We must take note of how it is that this [spiritual] birthing has its conception in faith, is conserved by hope, is enlivened by love. [This birthing] is spiritual, because faith is present in the intellect, which is spiritual, [i.e., immaterial]. Hence, this birthing is of an immaterial [*spiritualis*] nature. And there is begotten that which is conceived by faith, namely, Christ.[28] Hence, Christ is begotten in us spiritually by faith. Thus, we are reborn in spirit when Christ is born in us in spirit. And so, because Christ is in Heaven, we in this world are, by faith, like Christ-qua-conceived in the womb. And when we depart from this world, we are like Christ-qua-born. Therefore, belief in Christ's being conceived in us—a belief that works the initiation [*conceptio*] of regeneration—passes over into a completed birth and into a completed regeneration when we depart from the womb of this world.

[18] Hence, this Church of Christ's is like unto the womb of the Virgin, outside of which it is not possible that the *conceptus* of Christ exist. Now, by faith the Virgin Mary conceived; and, hence, all the things said to her by the Lord were accomplished in her, as is evident from the testimony of holy Elizabeth, who was full of the Holy Spirit.[29] Similarly, every spiritual conceiving of Christ arises from faith; and there will be accomplished all the things that are said by God to the one who believes in Him. Therefore, he who believes in the exalted Son of man as in Him in whom, he does not doubt, he will obtain justification, glorification, ascent into Heaven, and eternal life: in him will all things be perfected, because his soul will conceive and will bear a Son, who will be holy and great and who will be called the Son of the Most High. And this is the conceiving that is not of blood or of the will of the flesh or of a man but is of God.[30]

[19] Hence, we must consider that Christ was first conceived

in the soul of Mary so that she, reborn in spirit, would be such that in her the Word would be made flesh.[31] And the angel indicates to us this fact when he says that she was so full of grace that the Lord was with her. And fullness of grace is *this*: viz., that the Lord be present in the soul. From the Word, which Mary received, she had conceived in her soul, so that she passed into sonship with God,[32] since the Lord was with her. For she believed that she would obtain salvation in and through the Son of God,[33] who at a fitting time was to be seen in [earthly] association with men. And she sought to *become* that which she *found*. Now, she *found* the grace (1) to *become* the Virgin Mother and (2) that in her the Word would assume flesh. Therefore, she *desired* [*to become*] this [vehicle of grace]. Accordingly, she believed that [the Word is] the Word of all men's salvation and that the Word had to be incarnated. Thus, she conceived the Word by faith. And by means of this rebirth her spirit passed into sonship with God. And for that reason she found grace with Him who was with her, so that, as mother, she merited to minister flesh to Him who was with her. For she was the daughter of the King, and the King willed to be of her species. "For He has regarded the humility of His handmaiden."

[20] Hence, in the case of the Virgin the rebirth that preceded the conceiving of Christ was all the more necessary for Mary's salvation, inasmuch as without it she would not have been of the number of those who [will] reign in the [future] blessed life—even as no one at all can enter into the Kingdom of God apart from that rebirth.[34] Yet, with respect to salvation it is not necessary for each person to minister flesh to the Word-that-was-supposed-to-be-incarnated, although it *is* necessary for us that the Word assume flesh. Hence, since Mary qua mother, ministered flesh to the Word, she needed that which was necessary for us all for obtaining sonship with God. Therefore, she who begat the Son into the world imparted to us sonship with God. Only in and through the Son can we obtain sonship with God. Lo, how Mary is the mother of all! She begat us all as sons of God in and through the only Son of God.

[21] Moreover, it seems that our rebirth is exalted unto the Word by way of humility, even as by way of humility the Word descended into the flesh, so that the Heavenly and invisible Word is likewise said to have been born again when He, who was altogether imperceptible, assumed a perceptible humanity. So too, we who are in

this perceptible world are said to be born again when we assume the Word-of-life,[35] who is not of this visible and sensory world but is of the Kingdom of God. [**22**] And so, the Word is born again in the Virgin, so that He is the Son of man—[born again] to the end that *we* be born again as sons of God. Therefore, in order that He might be born to all men, He was born of the Virgin. And He who was born to all men does not have on earth a father whose son He is. Accordingly, Mary says: "[God] has for Israel begotten His Child."[36] For all people of God [are] as "Israel" (i.e., as "a man who sees God"). [God] begat His Child [for them]. And, hence, Christ calls Himself the Son of man and not the Son of this father or of that father, but the Son of *man*. Thus, just as there is present in a virgin a universality-of-conceiving that is indeterminate (so that she may conceive by this man or that man, as long as she is still unimpregnated by a man), so too the *conceptus* of the Virgin [Mary] is a universal *conceptus*—i.e., [is the *conceptus*] of *man* and not of *this man*. Accordingly, Jesus is the Son of God, who is the Father of all. And Ezechiel the prophet, who befigures Christ, was by God called by this name ["son of man"], because he was not provocative[37] but was humble, humane, and mild, so that he rightly preceded Christ in a befigurement.

PART TWO
Nicholas Expounds Mary's Song Verse by Verse

[**23**] Let us now examine, in consecutive fashion, the song of Mary.

After Elizabeth said to Mary 'Blessed are you who have believed, for whatever things were told to you by the Lord will be accomplished,' Mary declared: "My soul does magnify the Lord!"[38] [It was] as if to say: 'You, Elizabeth, my cousin, who bear in yourself the prophet of the Most High[39]—you exclaim that I am blessed and am blessed because I have believed the angel's words announced to me by God. And [you say] that because I have believed, then there are to be accomplished in and through me all the things that are so excellent that they excel all [other] great things. Because [of this prophetic exclamation] my soul rightly magnifies the Lord, who has willed that I conceive and give birth to Jesus the Savior, who will be great, seeing that He is the Son of the Most High. For my soul can do nothing but magnify the Lord, who has made it to be great and made it to be full of grace. [**24**] And my spirit, which is life and which is a most loving movement of my soul, can only rejoice in God my

Savior.[40] For how could my spirit rejoice in someone other than in God, who is my soul's Love, Salvation, and Life?'

[25] Therefore, when I see, O Lord, how it is that since You are the Most High you have regarded the humility of Your handmaiden and have deigned to indwell this humble, handmaidenly habitation, then there is immense rejoicing in my spirit. For, indeed, humility in the soul is regarded with so loving an eye of God that the *conceptus* of the soul, viz., the spirit, rejoices—as John [the Baptist], the *conceptus* of Elizabeth, leaped in the womb when Mary, who was pregnant with the Word of God, greeted Elizabeth in her home.[41] The spirit receives great joy when that which it loves is something great and when it experiences that its servantly and handmaidenly humility is not despised but is met with return-love. [26] Therefore, a rejoicing is said, unqualifiedly, to be present in the spirit when the Lord has regard for the humility of His handmaiden. For to a handmaiden nothing is greater or loftier than her lord. Therefore, rejoicing is greatest in the loving spirit of a handmaiden who is the handmaiden only of her lord, whom alone she loves when she experiences that her handmaidenly humility is pleasing to her lord and that it is met with return-love. Accordingly, how great was the rejoicing when the Lord loved His handmaiden so greatly that, having regard for her, He made her to be the mother of His only-begotten Son—[doing so], that is, by His Spirit, which *is* Love!

[27] 'For, indeed, because of this fertility all generations will call me blessed.[42] For since in and through the only-begotten Son-of-God, become human, all generations can obtain such a blessing that they are exalted unto sonship with God, they will rightly call me— the mother of this super-blessed Son—blessed. Indeed, they will call me blessed unqualifiedly and absolutely, in the sense of being altogether blessed. Indeed, they will extol me as unqualifiedly and absolutely blessed—as being one who is altogether blessed. [28] For just as every generation (whether it be past or be future) can have, in this unique only-begotten Son of God, the fullness-of-perfection of its goal and of its rest, and just as all the graces of the fertility of all women are ordered to this birthing—ordered as unto their own end-goal—[so too] all generations will call me blessed because [I am] the mother of mothers because of [my having] the fertility of all fertilities. For just as this perceptible world is a certain likeness of the other, intellectual, [world][43] and is, by means of truth, ordered to that

[other world] on which it depends for its likeness, so human propagation from generation unto generation depends on the only-begotten Son of God for its likeness and is ordered to Him through truth.

[**29**] 'Therefore, every propagated generation calls me the blessed propagator of the Only-Begotten One. For [the Only-Begotten] has done such great things for me! They cannot be greater. And they have been done for me by Him who alone is powerful,[44] whose every promise (*verbum*) is not impossible [for Him to keep][45] [**30**] And His name is holy—not as if it were made to become holy but [in the sense of being] absolutely holy. By participation in Him all holy things are holy. [**31**] And this powerful Lord whose name is holy is He who, since He is Absolute Power, is also the infinitely powerful Lord, whose mercy those who fear Him have experienced from generation to generation.[46] For, indeed, He has mercifully protected those who in humility fear Him; but by the power that He has exercised in the strength of His arm, He has scattered those who through deceit of heart are haughty.[47]

[**32**] He is the One who has put down the mighty from their seat.[48] For, indeed, all the mighty have been put down from their seat by the power of the Lord, whom they rejected. And He has exalted the humble.[49] For this [power of His] is the Power-of-power, which is mercy itself, so that it has regard for things lowly. And this having-regard-for is a viewing of the humble with an Eye of mercy. This viewing is an exalting.

[**33**] Indeed, the mercy of the Divine Power has filled the hungering with good things, for He fills all those things that receive Him.[50] And because the rich do not receive Him, who is the fulfillment of all perfection, He sends them away empty.[51] For although the rich are seen to be in ample possession of temporal goods, nevertheless when they set their heart on these their riches and do not receive God, they will be sent away empty. For without [the possession of] truth every rational soul is empty and void. [**34**] Hence, [Mary] adds: "[God], being mindful of mercy, has for Israel begotten His Child."[52] [It is] as if to say: 'Since this powerful and good Lord, who has regarded the humility of His handmaiden, is God (who is merciful and who is the filling up of every deficiency): He has brought about in and through me that He has begotten His Child for Israel. Thus, this Child, whom I conceived by the power of the Most High, is the Child who is the filling up of all deficiencies and in

whom Israel (i.e., the totality of men who see God) lives—as a father lives in his child. [**35**] And our merciful God, having been mindful of His mercy, has accomplished the foregoing, as He promised to our fathers—to Abraham and to his seed forever.[53] For in and through me [God], having now been mindful of His mercy, fulfilled for Israel this promise (made to the fathers) with regard to that super-blessed seed by means of which all nations would be blessed.'

Let the foregoing points have been thus briefly made, for the time being, as regards the song of Mary.

NOTES TO *Respexit Humilitatem*

* Sermon LXVIII.

1. Saturday, July 2, 1446 was the feast-day of the angel Gabriel's visiting of the Virgin Mary.
2. Luke 1:48.
3. Luke 1:39.
4. Here in the editor's heading I am reading "evangelium" in place of "evangelii". And I have changed "(*Luc. 1, 39-47*)" to "(*Luc. 1, 39-45*)" and changed "(*Luc. 1, 48-55*)" to "(*Luc. 1, 46-55*)". The heading here has verb endings that differ from those in the editor's Praenotanda (on p. 394). Within the Praenotanda "Canticum" is once capitalized, once not capitalized (without any apparent reason).
5. Luke 1:37.
6. Luke 1:38.
7. Luke 1:35.
8. Luke 1:32.
9. Cf. I Corinthians 2:10-12.
10. Acts 5:15.
11. Psalms 16:8 (17:8).
12. I John 3:2.
13. John 3:3-7.
14. I Peter 1:23.
15. John 3:8.
16. John 3:2.
17. John 3:4.
18. John 18:36.
19. I Corinthians 15:50.
20. I Peter 2:2.
21. John 3:10-11.
22. John 3:12.
23. John 3:12.
24. John 3:13.
25. John 3:13.
26. Numbers 21·9. John 3:14.
27. John 3:14-15.
28. Throughout this sermon Nicholas draws upon Meister Eckhart's theme of the birth of Christ in the soul of the believer. Cf. Nicholas's Sermon XVI.
29. Luke 1:41-42.
30. John 1:13.
31. John 1:14.
32. I John 3:2. See Nicholas's Sermon XXII (**41**). In that sermon see also (**37**). Note Nicholas's treatise *De Filiatione Dei*.
33. This is Anselm's theme. Mary's conception was pure because prior to her conceiving she was purified by faith in her son as Redeemer. See Anselm's *Cur Deus Homo*, Book II, Chap. 16.
34. John 3:3.

35. Cf. Romans 13:14. Philippians 2:16.

36. Luke 1:54. Nicholas seems to understands this New Testament passage in the above way, which differs from the usual understanding. Cf. Isaias (Isaiah) 9:6.

37. Cf. Ezechiel (Ezekiel) 2.

38. Luke 1:46.

39. " ... the prophet of the Most High": viz., John the Baptist. Luke 1:76.

40. Luke 1:47.

41. Luke 1:41 and 44.

42. Luke 1:48.

43. In *De Principio* (**35**:7-13) Nicholas writes: "Inmultiplicabile principium non est alterabile nec participabile, quia aeternitas. Nihil igitur in hoc mundo est eius similitudinem habens, cum non sit designabile nec imaginabile. Mundus est <mundi> infigurabilis figura et <mundi> indesignabilis designatio; mundus sensibilis est insensibilis mundi figura et temporalis mundus aeterni et intemporalis <mundi> figura; figuralis mundus est veri et infigurabilis mundi imago." *Nicolai de Cusa Opera Omnia*, Vol. X, Fascicle 2b, edited by Karl Bormann and Heide D. Riemann (Hamburg: Meiner, 1988), p. 50. The words in angular brackets have been supplie by me.

44. Luke 1:49.

45. Luke 1:37.

46. Luke 1:50.

47. Luke 1:51.

48. Luke 1:52.

49. Luke 1:52

50. Luke 1:53.

51. Luke 1:53.

52. Luke 1:54.

53. Genesis 22:18.

ABBREVIATIONS

MFCG *Mitteilungen und Forschungsbeiträge der Cusanus-Gesellschaft*

PG *Patrologia Graeca* (edited by J.-P. Migne)

PL *Patrologia Latina* (edited by J.-P. Migne)

PRAENOTANDA

1. References to Scriptural passages are given in accordance with the Douay-Rheims Version and, in parentheses, in accordance with the King James Version.

2. A reference such as "Sermon III (**4**)" indicates Sermon III, bold-faced division-number **4**, of the Latin texts in the series *Nicolai de Cusa Opera Omnia*.

3. Any italicized sub-headings within a sermon are translations of the sub-headings *added by the editors of the Latin text*.

4. Many of the source-references in the notes to the sermons are taken from the printed edition of the Latin texts. (Not all of these editorial references to sources are repeated in the present English notes; thus, some readers will want to consult the Latin editions directly.)

5. All translations (Latin, German, French) are mine.

6. In the translations brackets are used when English words are inserted to round out the meaning of a condensed Latin passage. Although these brackets detract from readability, they are essential for accuracy of translation. When Latin words are inserted into the translation for purposes of clarification, they are inserted in brackets if their case-endings have been changed to the nominative case; they are inserted in parentheses where the Latin text itself already has the nominative case.

CORRIGENDA FOR THE LATIN EDITIONS

Nota bene: An entry such as "p. 41 (**3**:1)" indicates page 41 of the respective volume and fascicle; margin-number **3** of the respective sermon on that page; line 1 within the section with that margin-number.

Vol. XVII, Fascicle 1

1. pp. 22, 24, 26, 28: correct running head to "XXVIII".
2. p. 41 (**3**:1): correct misprint to read: "de secundo et".
3. p. 74 (note for **2**:21-22): correct to read: "*Joh.* 14, 25-26".
4. p. 92 (**20**:20): use the spelling: "palatium".

Vol. XVII, Fascicle 2

1. p. 147 (**9**:17): correct to "optimum".

Vol. XVII, Fascicle 3

1. p. 217 (**5**:26): correct "humilin" to read: "humilitatem".
2. p. 237 (Praenotanda): correct "*aprilis*" to "*martii*".
3. p. 247 (line 4 of page): correct misprint to "*mortificationem*".
4. p. 247 (**14**:6-8): change punctuation to: "Considera—si non potuit Christus, propter te missus, ad Patrem reverti, nisi pateretur (ut Lucae ultimo)—quod merito et tu pati debes" ....
5. p. 263 (**26**:7-8): change "quaec - umque" to "quae - cumque".

Vol. XVII, Fascicle 5

1. p. 394 (Praenotanda): add my note 1 for Sermon LXVIII (my p. 464 above).
2. p. 397 (note for **8**:11-12): change to read: "*I Cor. 2, 10*".
3. p. 397 (note for **9**:8-10): correct to read: "*I Petr. 1, 23*".
4. p. 399 (**14**:6): delete question mark.
5. p. 429 (**14**:2): correct spelling to read: "rationalis".

Vol. XVIII, Fascicle 1

1. p. 45 (**6**:16): change to read: "quid < hoc > sit, quod". (surmise). (Cf. **6**:21-22.)
2. p. 46 (**6**:20): change "lumine" to "luminae".
3. p. 74 (note for **9**:15): add "*I Cor 1, 24*" and "*cf. Mt 23, 34*".
4. p. 77 (**17**:7-8): correct "integrae" to "integre".
5. p. 79 (add as note for **23**:4-5): "quae iudicium superexaltat: *Iac 2, 13*".

Vol. XVIII, Fascicle 4

1. p. 326 (**3**:19): correct "utrique" to "uterque".
2. p. 330 (**10**:16): delete comma after "servire"; put comma after "illud".
3. p. 333 (note for **6**:5-8): change "*Ex 19, 32 sqq.*" to "*Ex 19, 20-25*".
4. p. 334 (add as note for **8**:1): "autem: *om. p*".
5. p. 334 (**8**:14): add "< non >" after "suo" (as does *p*).
6. p. 337 (note for **13**:8): change to read: "superius: *v. supra n. 9*".
7. p. 340 (note for **19**:1-2): correct to "*Prv 16, 4*".
8. p. 344 (note for **6**:5): correct to read: "perditi filii: *v. Lc 15, 11-24*".
9. p. 345 (note for **8**:13-14): correct to read: "et - prophetam: *v. Is 45, 15*".
10. p. 358 (**2**:21): delete "< nec >".
11. p. 360 (note for **5**:15): change to read: "15-16) *Sap 7, 11-12*".
12. p. 361 (add as note for **7**:1): 'sacramenti: sacramentum *p*".
13. p. 370 (**2**:5): correct "Sapientia" to "supra".
14. p. 370 (note for **2**:19-20): correct to read: "*Mt 5, 28*".
15. p. 374 (note for **10**:5-6): change to read: "thesaurum in agro: *v. Mt 13, 44*".
16. p. 375 (add as note for **13**:18): "Dei formatum: deiformatum *p*".

Vol. XVIII, Fascicle 5

1. p. 409 (**4**:15): change punctuation to "salvatore. Ab".
2. p. 411 (add as note for **7**:32): "tribus annis: tres annos *p*".
3. p. 418 (**16**:52): change "maledicti" to "maledici".
4. p. 418 (**17**:7): put double-quotation marks around "Ecce enim". Put comma after "enim" and after "propheta". Delete colon after "propheta". Change "Veritatem" to "veritatem".
5. p. 452 (**15**:26): change "de [per] se" to "de per se"—an expression sometimes, though rarely, used in Medieval Philosophy.

Vol. XIX, Fascicle 1

1. p. 89 (note for **15**:9-10): correct to read "caeli – possunt: *cf. III Rg 8, 27*".
2. p. 90 (add as note for **18**:2): "quod: *om. p*".
3. p. 95 (note for **26**:12-13): correct to read: "*I Tim 6, 16*".
4. p. 95 (note for **27**:19-20): correct to read: "qui – habitabant:" ….

Vol. XIX, Fascicle 3

1. p. 193 (note for **1**:1): correct to read: "*Lc 22, 19; I Cor 11, 24*".
2. p. 193 (**1**:11): supply "non" before "localiter".
3. p. 198 (note for **10**:2-8): correct to read: … "AMBROSIUS *Epist. 76, 8*" ….
4. p. 266 (add as note for **9**:4): "Patre: generationis *add. p*".
5. p. 269 (add as note for **17**:14-17): "Cf. AUGUSTINUS, *Confessiones*, XII, 7 (*PL*

Corrigenda for the Latin Editions

    32:828-829)."
6. p. 269 (**18**:3): supply quotation mark before "corroborari".
7. p. 269 (**18**:7): supply quotation mark before "habitare".
8. p. 269 (**18**:1-8): emend the punctuation.
9. p. 271 (add as note for **25**:7): correct "derelinques" to "derelinquis", in accordance with the mss.

Vol. XIX, Fascicle 4

1. p. 300 (add as note for **6**:4): "Sicut: Sic *p* ".
2. p. 300 (note for **6**:5): delete this note.
3. p. 309 (add as note for **6**:6): "illi: corpori *p*".
4. p. 316 (**23**:14): delete comma after "nigredinem".
5. p. 317 (**30**:1): correct "quod" to "quoad".
6. p. 320 (**5**:5): supply question mark after "separabit".
7. p. 323 (**4**:9): correct "imcomprehensibiliter" to "incomprehensibiliter".
8. p. 347 (**13**:5): correct "desiderent" to "desideret".
9. p. 348 (**15**:7): correct "id" to "idem" (surmise: mss. here use "id" as an abbreviation for "idem".)
10. p. 353 (**36**:2): change "quodam modo" to "quod secundum".
11. p. 353 (**36**:2): change note to read: "quod secundum D_a".

Vol. XIX, Fascicle 5

1. p. 387 (**18**:12): change "verbum" to "Verbum".
2. p. 393 (note for **14**:5-7): revise part of sentence to read: "… AUGUSTINUS *In Io ev. tr.* 82, 4 (*Io 15, 8-10*)" ….
3. p. 393 (add to note for **14**:18): "*cf. Heb 1, 9* ".
4. p. 396 (Praenotanda, under "*Mss*"): change "U_1 *163^v (n. 26-28)*" to "U_1 *166^{rv} (n. 26-28)*".
5. p. 397: (note for **3**:16): change to read: "magni faceret: magnificaret *D L p*".
6. p. 399 (**8**:18): replace "Adeitas" with "Adaeitas" (surmise).
7. p. 400 (**12**:2): replace "Adeitas" with "Adaeitas" (surmise).
8. p. 404 (**24**:10): change "contracta" to "incontracta".
9. p. 404 (add as note for **24**:10): "contracta: incontracta *D* (in *supra lin.*) *L* ".

Vol. XIX, Fascicle 6

1. p. 482 (**4**:16): change "sensum" to "secum", in accordance with *L*.
2. p. 535 (Praenotanda, *Mss*): change "*L 265^v - 268^v*" to "*L 264^v - 267^v*".
3. p. 537 (**9**:10): change to read: "est promissio et verbum. Assequetur filiationem".
4. p. 538 (add as note for **13**:1): "patri: patre *L ex* patre *cor.* V_2 ".

Vol. XIX, Fascicle 7

1. p. 623 (add as note for **3**:1): interiori: interiore *L*.
2. p. 624 (note for **4**:12): change "*Lc 12, 11-12*" to "*Act 1, 4-8*".
3. p. 624 (add as note for **4**:20): "ardeat: adeat *L*". (End the sentence with a question mark.)
4. p. 625 (note for **7**:6-7): change "*Lc 2, 11*" to "*Mt 1, 21*".
5. p. 625 (note for **7**:7-8): change "*Mt 28, 19*" to "*Mt 28, 19-20*".
6. p. 625 (add as note for **9**:9-10): "non esset: non est esset *L*".
7. p. 625 (add as note for **9**:10-11): "sic se ipsos: se ipsos sic *L*".
8. p. 626 (note for **12**:6-7): change to read: "*cf. Gal 5, 22-23*".
9. p. 628 (note for **19**:15): change to read: "*cf. Act 9, 3-5. I Cor 15, 8*".
10. p. 628 (add as note for **20**:7): "quinta essentia: *cf.* THOMAS AQ, *Quaestiones Quodlibetales*, VI, 11, 19 ad 1".
11. p. 638 (**1**:11-13): change punctuation to read: "Nam est vas gratiae. Sicuti gomor mensura sufficiens manhu (nam cuilibet sufficiebat, Exodi 16°) sic hoc sacramentum" ....
12. p. 639 (note for **2**:16): change to read: "Christus – vinum: *cf. Io 2:1-9*".
13. p. 640 (add to note for **3**:12-13): " ... *et Io 18, 36*".
14. p. 644 (add as note for first line): "Qui me inveniet: *titulus in p*".
15. p. 666 (note for **20**:19): change to read: "20:19-20) Vos – audistis"....
16. p. 678 (**13**:5-6): change punctuation to read: "per leges, etc., neque sacramenta"....

BIBLIOGRAPHY

(Supplementary to the bibliography found in Jasper Hopkins, translator and introducer. *Nicholas of Cusa's Early Sermons: 1430-1441.* Loveland, Colorado: Banning, 2003)

Álvarez Gómez, Mariano. "Die Lehre vom menschlichen Geist (intellectus/Vernunft) in den Sermones des Nikolaus von Kues," *Mitteilungen und Forschungsbeiträge der Cusanus-Gesellschaft*, 31 (2006), 211-243 [includes report of discussion].

Aris, Marc-Aeilko. "Zur Soziologie der Sermones-Rezipienten," *Mitteilungen und Forschungsbeiträge der Cusanus-Gesellschaft*, 30 (2005), 93-115.

Beierwaltes, Werner and Hans G. Senger, editors. *Nicolai de Cusa Opera Omnia. Symposium zum Abschluß der Heidelberger Akademie-Ausgabe.* Heidelberg: Universitätsverlag Winter, 2006.

Bertin, Francis, translator and introducer. *Sermons eckhartiens et dionysiens.* Paris: Cerf, 1998 [a translation and study of five Cusan sermons].

Bredow, Gerda von, editor. *Cusanus-Texte. IV. Briefwechsel des Nikolaus von Kues: das Vermächtnis des Nikolaus von Kues. Der Brief an Nikolaus Albergati nebst der Predigt in Montoliveto (1463).* Heidelberg: Carl Winter, 1955 [Sitzungsberichte der Heidelberger Akademie der Wissenschaften. Philosophisch-historische Klasse].

Brient, Elizabeth. "Meister Eckhart and Nicholas of Cusa on the 'Where' of God," pp. 127-150 in Thomas M. Izbicki and Christopher M. Bellitto, editors, *Nicholas of Cusa and His Age: Intellect and Sprituality.* Boston: Brill, 2002.

Casarella, Peter. "Selbstgestaltung des Menschen nach Nikolaus von Kues und modernes Verständnis des Menschen: Aufgezeigt an Hans-Georg Gadamer," *Mitteilungen und Forschungsbeiträge der Cusanus-Gesellschaft*, 31 (2006), 29-52 [includes report of discussion].

Dahm, Albert. "Nikolaus von Kues zwischen Anselm und Luther. Das cusanische Verständnis unserer Erlösung durch Jesus Christus nach Sermo I (1430)," *Trierer Theologische Zeitschrift*, 107 (1998), 300-311.

——. "Vernunft und Glaube in den Sermones des Nikolaus von Kues. Gleichzeitig eine Begegnung mit den Büchern von K. Flasch (1998 und 2001) und U. Roth (2000)," *Mitteilungen und Forschungsbeiträge der Cusanus-Gesellschaft*, 31 (2006), 245-276 [includes report of discussion].

Dupré, Wilhelm. "Die Predigt als Ort der Reflexion. Einige Bemerkungen zur Philosophie in den Predigten," pp. 79-104 in Klaus Reinhardt and Harald Schwaetzer, editors, *Nikolaus von Kues als Prediger.* Regensburg: Roderer Verlag, 2004.

Edwards, Jr., O. C. "History of Preaching," pp. 184-227 in William H. Willimon and Richard Lischer, editors, *Concise Encyclopedia of Preaching.* Louisville: Westminster John Knox, 1995.

Euler, Walter A. "Entwicklungsgeschichtliche Etappen und schwerpunktmäßige Themenverschiebungen in den Sermones?" *Mitteilungen und Forschungsbeiträge der Cusanus-Gesellschaft*, 30 (2005), 71-91.

Gärtner, Kurt. "Die Vaterunserpredigt des Nikolaus von Kues," pp. 45-59 in Klaus Reinhardt and Harald Schwaetzer, editors, *Nikolaus von Kues als Prediger*. Regensburg: Roderer Verlag, 2004.

Herold, Norbert. " ... 'als ob im Gehorsam die Freiheit zugrunde ginge ...' Die 'Doctrina oboedientiae' in den Predigten des Nikolaus von Kues," *Mitteilungen und Forschungsbeiträge der Cusanus-Gesellschaft*, 31 (2006), 167-209 [includes report of discussion].

Hoenen, Maarten J. " 'Caput scholae rationis est Christus'. Verschränkung von Exegese und Philosophie in den Predigten des Cusanus," *Mitteilungen und Forschungsbeiträge der Cusanus-Gesellschaft*, 30 (2005), 43-69.

Hopkins, Jasper. Review of *Die Sermones des Nikolaus von Kues. Merkmale und ihre Stellung innerhalb der mittelalterlichen Predigtkultur* (Mitteilungen und Forschungsbeiträge der Cusanus-Gesellschaft, 30). Trier: Paulinus, 2005. Reviewed in *The Catholic Historical Review*, 92 (July, 2006), 311-312.

    Reviewed also in Mitteilungen und Forschungsbeiträge der Cusanus-Gesellschaft, 31 (2006), 292-299.

_____. "God's Sacrifice of Himself as a Man: Anselm of Canterbury's *Cur deus homo*," pp. 237-257 in Karin Finsterbusch *et al.*, editors, *Human Sacrifice in Jewish and Christian Tradition*. Leiden: Brill, 2007.

Hudson, Nancy and Frank Tobin. "Nicholas of Cusa's Sermon on the *Pater Noster*," pp. 1-25 in Peter J. Casarella, editor, *Cusanus: The Legacy of Learned Ignorance*. Washington, D.C.: The Catholic University of America Press, 2006.

Hundersmarck, Lawrence. "Preaching," pp. 232-269 in Christopher M. Bellitto, Thomas M. Izbicki, and Gerald Christianson, editors, *Introducing Nicholas of Cusa: A Guide to a Renaissance Man*. New York: Paulist Press, 2004.

Kandler, Karl-Hermann. "Bilder und Gleichnisse in den Sermones des Nikolaus von Kues," *Mitteilungen und Forschungsbeiträge der Cusanus-Gesellschaft*, 31 (2006), 9-27 [includes report of discussion].

Kijewska, Agnieszka. "Conception of Faith in Cusanus' *Sermon XXI*," *Acta Mediaevalia*, 18 (2005), 253-265.

Knoch, Wendelin. "Ekklesiologische Aspekte in den frühen Predigten des Nikolaus von Kues," pp. 29-44 in Klaus Reinhardt and Harald Schwaetzer, editors, *Nikolaus von Kues als Prediger*. Regensburg: Roderer Verlag, 2004. [This volume lacks a p. 28.]

Kremer, Klaus. "Einführung in die Gesamtthematik: Begründung des zweiteiligen Symposions und summarischer Überblick," [re symposium on Cusa's sermons], *Mitteilungen und Forschungsbeiträge der Cusanus-Gesellschaft*, 30 (2005), 11-41.

_____. "Wege und Art der Gotteserkenntnis in den Sermones des Nikolaus von Kues," *Mitteilungen und Forschungsbeiträge der Cusanus-Gesellschaft*, 31 (2006), 53-102 [includes report of discussion].

Lentzen-Deis, Wolfgang. "Der 'pastor bonus' und die kirchlichen 'pastores'. Gedanken des Nikolaus von Kues über die Hirtenaufgabe der Pfarrer in einer Homilie über Joh 10, 1-18," *Trierer Theologische Zeitschrift*, 100 (October-December, 1991), 276-288. [Deals with Sermon CCLXXX.]

Mertens, Volker. "Stimme und Schrift in der Predigt des Nikolaus von Kues," pp. 9-27 in Klaus Reinhardt and Harald Schwaetzer, editors, *Nikolaus von Kues als*

Prediger. Regensburg: Roderer Verlag, 2004.

————. "Die Predigt des Nikolaus von Kues im Kontext der volkssprachlichen Kanzelrede," *Mitteilungen und Forschungsbeiträge der Cusanus-Gesellschaft*, 30 (2005), 171-190.

[Nicholas of Cusa]. *Sermones I (1430-1441)* [Vol. XVI in the series *Nicolai de Cusa Opera Omnia*].

Fascicle 1: Sermones I–V. Edited by Rudolf Haubst, with the assistance of Martin Bodewig and Werner Krämer. Hamburg: Meiner, 1970.

Fascicle 2: Sermones V–X. Edited by Rudolf Haubst, with the assistance of Martin Bodewig and Werner Krämer. Hamburg: Meiner, 1973.

Fascicle 3: Sermones XI–XXI. Edited by Rudolf Haubst and Martin Bodewig. Hamburg: Meiner, 1977.

Fascicle 4: Sermones XXII–XXVI. Edited by Rudolf Haubst and Martin Bodewig. Hamburg: Meiner, 1984.

————. *Sermones II (1443-1452)* [Vol. XVII in the series *Nicolai de Cusa Opera Omnia*].

Fascicle 1: Sermones XXVII–XXXIX. Edited by Rudolf Haubst and Hermann Schnarr. Hamburg: Meiner, 1983.

Fascicle 2: Sermones XL–XLVIII. Edited by Rudolf Haubst and Hermann Schnarr. Hamburg: Meiner, 1991.

Fascicle 3: Sermones XLIX–LVI. Edited by Rudolf Haubst and Hermann Schnarr. Hamburg: Meiner, 1996.

Fascicle 4: Sermones LVII–LXI. Edited by Hermann Schnarr. Hamburg: Meiner, 2001.

Fascicle 5: Sermones LXII–LXXV. Edited by Marc-Aeilko Aris, Heidi Hein, and Hermann Schnarr. Hamburg: Meiner, 2006.

Fascicle 6: Sermones LXXVI–CXXI. Edited by Heidi Hein and Hermann Schnarr. Hamburg: Meiner, 2007.

————. *Sermones III (1452-1455)* [Vol. XVIII in the series *Nicolai de Cusa Opera Omnia*].

Fascicle 1: Sermones CXXII–CXL. Edited by Rudolf Haubst and Heinrich Pauli. Hamburg: Meiner, 1995.

Fascicle 2: Sermones CXLI–CLX. Edited by Heinrich Pauli. Hamburg: Meiner, 2001.

Fascicle 3: Sermones CLXI–CLXXV. Edited by Silvia Donati, Isabelle Mandrella, and Harald Schwaetzer. Hamburg: Meiner, 2003.

Fascicle 4: Sermones CLXXVI–CXCII. Edited by Silvia Donati, Harald Schwaetzer, and Franz-Bernhard Stammkötter. Hamburg: Meiner, 2004.

Fascicle 5: Sermones CXCIII–CCIII. Edited by Silvia Donati and Isabelle Mandrella. Hamburg: Meiner, 2005.

————. *Sermones IV (1455-1463)* [Vol. XIX in the series *Nicolai de Cusa Opera*

Omnia].

Fascicle 1: Sermones CCIV–CCXVI. Edited by Klaus Reinhardt and Walter A. Euler. Hamburg: Meiner, 1996.

Fascicle 2: Sermones CCXVII–CCXXXI. Edited by Marc-Aeilko Aris. Hamburg: Meiner, 2001.

Fascicle 3: Sermones CCXXXII–CCXLV. Edited by Walter A. Euler and Harald Schwaetzer. Hamburg: Meiner, 2001.

Fascicle 4: Sermones CCXLVI–CCLVII. Edited by Isabelle Mandrella and Heide D. Riemann. Hamburg: Meiner, 2004.

Fascicle 5: Sermones CCLVIII–CCLXVII. Edited by Heide D. Riemann, Harald Schwaetzer, and Franz-Bernhard Stamkötter. Hamburg: Meiner, 2005.

Fascicle 6: Sermones CCLXVIII–CCLXXXII. Edited by Heide D. Riemann. Hamburg: Meiner, 2005.

Fascicle 7: Sermones CCLXXXIII–CCXCIII. Edited by Silvia Donati and Heide D. Riemann. Hamburg: Meiner, 2005.

Reinhardt, Klaus. "Das Thema der Gottesgeburt und der Gotteskindschaft in den Predigten des Nikolaus von Kues," pp. 61-78 in Klaus Reinhardt and Harald Schwaetzer, editors, *Nikolaus von Kues als Prediger*. Regensburg: Roderer Verlag, 2004. [This volume lacks a p. 60.]

Schnarr, Hermann. "Die cusanische Hinführung des Menschen zu Jesus Christus in den Sermones. Wer den ganzen und wahren Menschen sucht, ist auf dem Weg zu Jesus Christus," *Mitteilungen und Forschungsbeiträge der Cusanus-Gesellschaft*, 31 (2006), 103-135 [includes report of discussion].

Stammkötter, Franz-Bernhard, translator. *Der Prediger auf der Porta. Drei Trierer Predigten des Nikolaus von Kues*. Münster: Aschendorff, 2005. [Introduced by Harald Schwaetzer, with a foreword by Klaus Reinhardt].

Steer, Georg. "Die Predigten des Cusanus im Vergleich mit dem Predigtwerk von Meister Eckhart," *Mitteilungen und Forschungsbeiträge der Cusanus-Gesellschaft*, 30 (2005), 145-169.

Thurner, Martin. "Das Kirchenbild in den Sermones des Nikolaus von Kues. Hilfe auch für heute?" *Mitteilungen und Forschungsbeiträge der Cusanus-Gesellschaft*, 31 (2006), 137-165.

Yamaki, Kazuhiko. "Buchmetaphorik als 'Apparitio Dei' in den Werken und Predigten des Nikolaus von Kues," *Mitteilungen und Forschungsbeiträge der Cusanus-Gesellschaft*, 30 (2005), 117-144.

Zani, Karl F. "Neues zu Predigten des Kardinals Cusanus 'ettlich zu teutsch'," *Der Schlern*, 59 (1985), 111-115.